Moscow Tram Stop

A Doctor's Experiences with the German Spearhead in Russia

Dr. Heinrich Haape

Foreword by Johannes Haape

Military History Editor Dr. Craig W. H. Luther

STACKPOLE
BOOKS

Guilford, Connecticut

Published by Stackpole Books
An imprint of The Rowman & Littlefield Publishing Group, Inc.
4501 Forbes Blvd., Ste. 200
Lanham, MD 20706
www.rowman.com

Distributed by NATIONAL BOOK NETWORK

British Library Cataloguing in Publication Information available

Library of Congress Cataloging-in-Publication Data

Names: Haape, Heinrich, author.
Title: Moscow tram stop : a doctor's experiences with the German spearhead
    in Russia / Heinrich Haape ; foreword by Johannes Haape ; with an
    introduction and historical commentary by Dr. Craig W. H. Luther
Description: Lanham : Rowman & Littlefield Publishing Group, 2020. |
    Original work published: London : Collins, 1957. | Includes
    bibliographical references and index. | Summary: "First published in
    1957, 'Moscow Tram Stop' is a classic of World War II on the Eastern
    Front. Heinrich Haape was a young doctor drafted into the German
    Wehrmacht just before the war began. He was with the spearhead of
    Operation Barbarossa when it invaded the Soviet Union. The drama and
    excitement never slacken as Haape recounts his experiences from the
    unique perspective of a doctor, who often had to join in the fighting
    himself and witnessed the physical and psychological toll of combat"—
    Provided by publisher.
Identifiers: LCCN 2019048495 (print) | LCCN 2019048496 (ebook) | ISBN
    9780811737906 (cloth) | ISBN 9780811767903 (epub)
Subjects: LCSH: World War, 1939–1945—Personal narratives, German. | World
    War, 1939–1945—Medical care. | Doctors—Germany—Biography.
Classification: LCC D807.G4 H3 2020 (print) | LCC D807.G4 (ebook) | DDC
    940.54/7543092 [B]—dc23
LC record available at https://lccn.loc.gov/2019048495
LC ebook record available at https://lccn.loc.gov/2019048496

∞™ The paper used in this publication meets the minimum requirements of American National Standard for Information Sciences—Permanence of Paper for Printed Library Materials, ANSI/NISO Z39.48-1992.

Contents

Foreword

THE DEEP GREEN HUES OF PINE TREES SHIMMERED THROUGH THE WINDOWS. My father stood in the light of the South African sunshine, putting on his tie. It was a very ordinary tie with horizontal and vertical stripes. Suddenly, he pointed to a spot where the stripes intersected and said, "Look, Hans, these are all little Iron Crosses for my fallen comrades in Russia." His voice was gentle, but I sensed the importance of his words. He still lived with the memory of his comrades who'd died in Russia thirty years before.

My father passed away not long after, aged sixty-six years. I was twenty-one years old at the time. I remember him as an energetic, positive person and a loving father. A man with a brilliant mind who returned home unbroken from war, determined to build a new life for himself and his family. Artistically gifted, he sometimes regretted the six years of productivity lost to war and captivity. However, he never railed against a past that could not be changed; instead, he was filled with deep gratitude that he was among the few who had returned home. He saw life as a blessing and a gift, a perspective that was nourished by unique personal experience.

I have often wondered whether my father ever suffered from symptoms of post-traumatic stress. I cannot recall that he did. Sitting at the fireplace in the large music salon of our home, he would sometimes relate to guests stories of his childhood in his father's parsonage in Germany, the collapse of the German Empire at the end of the First World War, the breakdown of Germany's monetary system in the inflation crisis of 1923 (when a loaf of bread cost one million *Reichsmark*!), his studies in medicine and psychology, and how he met my mother, a celebrated opera singer. They wanted to get married, but war broke out in September 1939. My father was conscripted to the *Wehrmacht* and only returned six and a half years later. My parents wrote several hundred letters to each other; my mother in particular wrote almost daily. Most of her letters close with the words *in Treue*—loyalty and faithfulness were the lifelong pillars of their relationship.

As the battalion doctor for 3rd Battalion, Infantry Regiment 18, my father experienced action firsthand from 22 June 1941, the very first day of the war between National

Socialist Germany and the Communist Soviet Union. With his comrades, he marched from East Prussia to the last stop of the tram line to Moscow. In just nine months, only twenty-eight of the original eight hundred men of his battalion remained. Most of them were killed; others lost to disease, sickness, and frostbite.

The war in the East was a war of unprecedented scale and unspeakable hardship. It was a war in which one battle that lasted just a matter of weeks could leave over half a million men dead, wounded, or captured. A war in which the Geneva Convention offered little or no protection and in which most did not dare to surrender.

As a doctor at the front, my father was caring for the severely wounded one minute and, in the next, risking his life defending his field dressing station against Russian attacks by mobilizing medical orderlies and the lightly wounded. Even during the most bitter retreats, coping with temperatures as low as -52° Centigrade, he never abandoned a wounded soldier. In the merciless war on the Eastern Front, death at the hands of the enemy was almost certain for any casualty left behind.

It is remarkable that my father always carried a sketching pad in his rucksack. In the midst of the carnage, he somehow found time to make portraits of the Russian people. He bandaged the wounds of Red Army soldiers, ministered to sick civilians, and never lost his ability to see the essential humanity of both friend and foe. When he later related his stories, he could highlight the many different ways people react in unusual situations. I am convinced that putting his memories to paper in the pages of this book helped him to cope with any lasting psychological effects.

My father spoke of encountering extreme life situations—those moments in which a person stares into the face of death, yet finds nothing within himself (or herself) with which to handle the crisis. He frequently quoted the philosopher Karl Jaspers who, in the aftermath of the First World War, wrote that in such moments the human mind is free to succumb to self-interest and fear or to rise above this and devote itself to the common good. The choice made in that instant will determine the arc of life. By overcoming self-interest and fear, one will find peace in the face of death and turn back strengthened and able to live a fuller life. All who face such extreme situations are free to *decide who they are* and who they want to be. I know that at the front my father was confronted repeatedly with such decisions, and I know that he unflinchingly chose to remain true to himself and, if necessary, to die for his comrades. Amid the apocalypse of the Eastern Front, facing each challenge anew made the difference: only then could one survive as a front-line soldier and as an integral part of one's community of comrades. Moreover, standing in for the common good not only enabled one to rise above self-interest and fear but also, by encapsulating the comradeship at the front, made it possible to endure the carnage of such a monstrous war.

Following confinement in several concentration camps, the Viennese psychiatrist and Holocaust survivor Viktor Frankl was one of the few to return home. In the camps, he was challenged by extreme life situations time and again. In his memoirs he writes, "Ultimately, man should not ask what the meaning of his life is, but rather it is *he* who is asked. In a word, each man is questioned by life; and he can only answer to life by *answering for* his own life."[1] The conclusion Frankl gleans from this is "After all [man] has suffered, there is nothing he need fear anymore—except his God."[2]

The fates of Heinrich Haape and Viktor Frankl could not have been more different. And yet both faced death a thousand times, withstood dreadful challenges, survived, and grew as individuals. Their actions show us what it signifies to be "truly human" and demonstrate to each of us in everyday life how to develop a true, mature, and humane character.

The young Germans who were sent to the Eastern Front had no choice. Most had been conscripted, and they upheld the oath they had taken to the bitter end. There is no doubt that the Red Army was taken by surprise by the *Wehrmacht* on 22 June 1941. The German soldiers and their allies were convinced the attack on the Soviet Union was preemptive and, perforce, unavoidable. After all, the Red Army possessed significantly more men and material, even in the immediate border regions. Stalin, so they were told, could strike at any moment to conquer Europe in the name of Bolshevism. Yet the German attack failed, foundering on the hubris and blindness of the political leadership, and became an unprecedented tragedy for our parents and our grandparents.

A staggering thirty to forty billion pieces of mail (letters, postcards, packages, telegrams) were sent during the Second World War on the German side alone. Mothers wrote to their sons; soldiers wrote to their wives and girlfriends, who sat at home consumed by fear, awaiting their return. Given the limits of communication technology, the simple letter was often the only source of news in the chaos and confusion of war. The mail meant everything to the war generation, igniting thousands of dreams and the longing to be able to see that beloved man or woman, family, and home once again. After the war had ended and the years of captivity were over, more than four million German soldiers failed to return home from the Eastern Front. The Red Army suffered more than three times as many fatal losses, and just as many civilian deaths. The western Soviet Union, central Europe, and Germany were largely in ruins.

This book describes the fate of eight hundred men and represents the experiences of more than ten million German soldiers who fought against the Soviet Union from 1941 to 1945. The events portrayed in my father's memoir may seem strange today, even unreal. Upon reflection, however, when we endeavor to understand the actions of our forebears, some of us may grasp the true meaning of the word *history*. It is not simply knowledge that is gathered and then shaped with the benefit of hindsight, often tinged with the ideologies of the day. Rather, history emerges with the movement of time from one moment to the next; it is a process that must always be experienced first. What the future holds cannot be foreseen: it remains pure speculation and hope for each individual.

For the person in the street in National Socialist Germany, it was unthinkable that their leaders were pursuing criminal policies the extent of which later came to light. During the war, most German soldiers could hardly perceive such a possibility; it was simply unimaginable. To the very end, they believed in the integrity of their actions, fought and died for their *Vaterland.* The tragedy of the war generation in contemporary Germany is that their children and grandchildren do not distinguish between the political leadership and their ideologically motivated cohorts, on the one hand, and, on the other hand, the common dutiful soldier. There is little analysis of, or impartial engagement with, individual fates as documented in this book. Out of ignorance all are tarred with the same brush, so that even the most upright and decent among the soldiers of the *Wehrmacht* are condemned collectively along with the Nazi leadership. It is indeed striking how many among the postwar generations have taken this approach in pursuit of their ideological interests.

Did the millions who lost their lives in the East die in vain? The question could drive one to despair. Putting ideology aside and focusing on the individual, one may concur with Viktor Frankl: "Life ultimately means taking [on] the responsibility . . . to fulfill the tasks which it constantly sets for each individual. . . . When a man finds that it is his destiny to suffer, he will have to accept his suffering as his task; his single and unique task."[3]

In the original manuscript of his memoir, my father summarized what, to him, was the significance of putting his experiences in words:

> *My testimony is a factual account about the life of upright and loyal soldiers, about the quiet heroism of my friends and comrades in desperate times, who fought for their Fatherland and lost their lives. May my sons be granted a more peaceful age.*

Johannes Haape
and my late brother Heinz
Caputh (near Berlin)
March 2019

NOTES

1. Viktor E. Frankl, *Man's Search for Meaning: An Introduction to Logotherapy,* trans. by Ilse Lasch and with a preface by Gordon W. Allport, 4th ed. (Boston: 1992), 113 (emphasis in original). Originally published in German in 1946 as . . . *trotzdem Ja zum Leben sagen: Ein Psycholog erlebt das Konzentrationslager.*
2. Frankl, *Man's Search for Meaning,* 100.
3. Frankl, *Man's Search for Meaning,* 85–86.

Acknowledgments

This new and expanded edition of Dr. Heinrich Haape's memoir of his participation in Operation Barbarossa, Adolf Hitler's surprise attack on the Soviet Union in 1941, is the first English-language edition of the book since 1959. The book (hardcover edition) was first published in Great Britain by William Collins, Sons and Co., Ltd., in 1957; this was followed by a paperback version in 1959 by Panther Books. A German translation appeared in 1980 and again in 1998 (both Motorbuch Verlag, Stuttgart).

In the original Collins edition—upon which this new edition is based—reference is made to a single individual in the acknowledgments: Major E. K. F. Rossler, for his wonderful translation of the text from German to English.

For this new release of Dr. Haape's war memoir, we would first like to acknowledge Stackpole Books; its senior history editor, Dave Reisch; and the entire staff at Stackpole for their encouragement and unflagging faith in the project.

We owe a deep debt of gratitude to Dr. Madeleine Brook, University of Stuttgart, for her excellent and lyrical translations of Dr. Haape's letters (Appendix 9) and several other documents. It was indeed a pleasure to collaborate with Dr. Brook.

Special thanks are also due Dr. David Stahel, military historian and instructor at the Australian Defense Force Academy and the author of several masterful studies on Operation Barbarossa, for patiently reading the text and offering useful suggestions and corrections.

We are indebted for the advice on technical details (e.g., transliteration of Russian place names) graciously furnished by Colonel David M. Glantz (U.S. Army, ret.). Praise is also due the terrific technicians at Henley's Photo, a decades-old institution in Bakersfield, California, for developing the stunning photographs and illustrations in this book.

Special recognition goes to Samuel J. Bertz and Christan Haape (the grandson of Dr. Heinrich Haape) for the many hours they spent diligently scanning and emailing us the voluminous correspondence between Dr. Haape and his fiancée/wife.

We would be terribly remiss if we did not, genuinely and from the heart, honor our lovely, dear wives—Therese Luther and Melanie Haape—for their patience and support during the preparation of this new edition of Dr. Heinrich Haape's memoir.

It is the sincere hope of all who have taken part in this important project, honoring a forgotten old warrior from a time long ago, that we have succeeded, even marginally, in reminding the world of an extraordinary and heroic man—the kind of man who, sadly it seems, comes along so rarely in our world today.

Dr. Craig W. H. Luther (Tehachapi, CA)   Johannes Haape (Caputh, Germany)

Introduction

I first became aware of Dr. Heinrich ("Heinz") Haape and his dramatic memoir of the Eastern Front more than a decade ago, when I began the many laborious years of research for my own book, *Barbarossa Unleashed*. I soon discovered, and acquired, the latest German-language edition of his book, *Endstation Moskau* (1998), only to learn that the book had first been released in English in the late 1950s under the title *Moscow Tram Stop*. Having found my German copy of the book a fascinating read—and, certainly, desiring to do "due diligence" as a researcher who left no stone unturned—I vowed to find the original English edition as well. Back in 2004, that took some doing, and it was only after many months of perusing the internet that I stumbled across the book at a "Used, Rare and Out-of-Print" antiquarian book store in Great Britain. About the copy being offered for sale, the seller duly noted, "Sound, but showing its age—dust wrapper a little tatty and grubby with creasing & chipping around the edges." No matter: I coveted this tattered old book and, I must admit, shelled out well over $200 to get it. The book—chipped edges and all—finally arrived at my home in October 2004.

About 2005, I think it was, during one of my many research trips to Germany, a dear friend and colleague put me in touch with Herr Johannes Haape, one of Dr. Heinrich Haape's two sons, who was living with his wife, Melanie, and two young children in a lovely little town outside Berlin. I was hoping that Johannes might help me bring to light more details on his father's harrowing experiences on the Russian front. Perhaps his family had maintained a family archive; perhaps they had preserved letters or photographs. I spoke with Johannes over the telephone for about an hour that day—somehow managing to convince him that I was a credible historian and researcher—and was told to my great delight that, yes indeed, he did possess a large collection of documents covering the lives of both of his parents. The family archive embraced, *inter alia*, hundreds of field post letters (*Feldpostbriefe*) sent by Dr. Haape from Russia during 1941–1942 to his fiancée (and future wife) Martha Arazym in Duisburg, Germany. Johannes Haape graciously offered to make these letters, and many other relevant documents, available to me for my research, and he even made a trip to Durban, South Africa, where he had been born in 1954, to retrieve some twenty-five cardboard boxes in which the documents had been packed away for many decades.

I made abundant use of Dr. Haape's letters and of his memoir in the preparation of *Barbarossa Unleashed*; in fact, the good doctor—and his incredible story—became a fixture in my book, whose cover is graced by one of his fine sketches. I also remained in close contact with his son, Johannes, and, after my book was published (2014), I was tasked by him with preparing an in-depth chronological history of the Haape family—back to its first recorded references in the early seventeenth century in the Westphalian town of Neuenrade, tucked in the verdant rolling hills of the Sauerland. To accomplish this goal, Johannes made available to me hundreds of additional letters that had passed between his parents, along with other vital documents and photographs; together, in 2014, we traveled to Buschhausen-Oberhausen, where his father had been born on 6 January 1910, the son of a Protestant minister; then on to Duisburg, where the lives of Heinz and Martha had fatefully intersected in 1938; and, finally, to the charming town of Neuenrade.

In the spring of 2015, we journeyed to South Africa, so I could unearth more about the Haape family and the final chapter of Dr. Haape's remarkable life. In 1952, he had emigrated from West Germany to South Africa with his wife and young son, Heinz Jr., because he greatly feared another war—the "Cold War" between America and the Soviet Union and their respective allies—was heating up, and Heinz was fully aware that, should it come to war, as a doctor, he would be among the first to be drafted. After nearly two years of bloody fighting in Russia (June 1941–May 1943), where—slowly, ineluctably— he had experienced the death of almost all of his close comrades and friends,[1] Dr. Haape had had his fill of war; besides, he intimated to Martha, he would never take up arms against his East German brothers.

I spent two years drilling down into the lives of Dr. Haape and his wife, examining hundreds of their letters in which they touched on every conceivable topic, from the most mundane details of everyday life to their most intimate hopes, dreams, and desires and, certainly, during the terrible years of World War II, their unvarnished fears for what the future held in store. During the course of my work, the essence of Dr. Haape the man—his character, his ambitions, his *Weltanschauung* (worldview)—was revealed to me one letter, one document at a time, and I came to "know" him, one might put it, "from the inside out."

Just who was Dr. Heinrich Haape, and why is his story of blood, death, and sacrifice on the Eastern Front, in the service of Adolf Hitler's monstrous and murderous regime, of relevance and worthy of our contemplation even today?

Let me begin by pointing out a salient fact: Dr. Haape was not a member of the National Socialist Party (NSDAP); he was not a Nazi sympathizer. His pastor father, Karl Haape, and his mother, Katharina ("Käthe"), were deeply devout Christians, and they passed on their faith to their five children, of whom Heinz was the third. His parents, both of whom died while Heinz was still quite young,[2] were also imbued with traditional conservative and patriotic values—*Kaisertreu* in the jargon of Wilhelmian Germany—and these values, later embracing an implacable anti-Communism, were instilled in Heinz at a young age. The young Haape, who nearly died of scarlet fever during the difficult trials of World War I, witnessed the collapse of Germany's war effort and the dramatic upheavals of 1918, which swept away the *ancien régime* and inaugurated the Weimar Period (1918–1933); in his poor and tiny mining town of Buschhausen, he observed pitched battles between radical revolutionaries and the *Reichswehr*. In subsequent years, Heinz, gifted intellectually and ever curious about the world around him, would have become acutely aware of the terrible atrocities committed against the Russian people by their fanatical Bolshevik overlords—crimes that only reinforced his bedrock belief in the Christianity of Germany and the West and his abhorrence of atheistic Communism.

Which leads us back to my original point—that Heinz Haape was no Nazi. About 1934, in his early twenties, he actually explored becoming a member of NSDAP. As Martha recalled in her memoirs, Heinz attended a meeting sponsored by the National Socialist Party and was so taken aback by the anti-Christian venom given expression to there that he simply got up and left. Never again did he apply to become a Nazi Party member. In the spring of 1943, after being recalled from Russia, he was asked to join the party. As he was now one of the most highly decorated doctors in the German military—the Iron Cross (First and Second Class), the Infantry Assault Badge, the Tank Close Combat Insignia, and the German Cross in Gold among his decorations for bravery before the enemy (see Appendix 2)—the Nazi Party, no doubt, saw an opportunity to exploit Dr. Haape for propaganda purposes, but Heinz saw through their designs and, as he recalls near the end of his memoir, rebuffed them brilliantly with Adolf Hitler's own words—that is, he vowed not to take off the field-gray uniform of the army until final victory had been achieved.

Perhaps there is no better illustration of the man Heinz Haape became, of the values he embodied, than a poem he published in the fall of 1933 in a commemorative booklet (*Festschrift*) honoring the thirty-five-year existence of the Protestant Man-Boy Association (*Evangelischer Männer- und Jünglingsverein*) in Buschhausen:

This life is hard, but man must meet it, whether arduous or untroubled [ob schwer oder leicht].

Be forthright in your actions.
Critical and unpitying of yourself.
Laugh, though you bleed within.
Trust only the few worthy to you.
Be guarded and question those unknown,
But be friendly to all.
Give to others that which nature gave to you.
Venture only what you can.

Be natural and open in your manner.
Be humble before God, faithful in prayer.
Pure be your thoughts, pure be your conduct.
Firm be your resolve and firm be your will.

—Medical student Heinz Haape, 1932

After completing his *Abitur* in 1932, Heinz pursued a course of study at several universities (Bonn, Düsseldorf, Kiel),[3] which, by 1938, culminated in a Doctor of Philosophy degree in psychology and a medical degree. Sometime in 1938, he accepted a position as a medical doctor at the *Kaiser Wilhelm Krankenhaus* in Duisburg. It was here, at one of the local "watering holes," in the fall of 1938 that Dr. Haape met a beautiful twenty-three-year-old woman from Vienna, *Fräulein* Martha Arazym, a highly regarded soprano and relatively new addition to the Duisburg Opera House; they quickly realized how much they had in common and fell irretrievably in love.

In July 1939, as the gathering winds of war whipped through the capitals of Europe, Dr. Haape was drafted into the military for three months' training as an artillery soldier (*Kanonier*). After his basic training, he was transferred to the *Wehrmacht* medical corps in October 1939. The details of his early military career need not concern us, as they are outlined in some detail in Appendix 2. Simply put, after several assignments in Germany, in the fall of 1940 he joined the elite 6th Infantry Division in Normandy, France; in the spring of 1941, his division, as part of the buildup for Operation Barbarossa (Nazi Germany's impending attack on Stalin's Russia), was sent to East Prussia and, eventually, to the Russo-German frontier.

At dawn on Sunday, 22 June 1941, the world held its breath as Adolf Hitler unleashed his seemingly invincible *Wehrmacht* in a surprise attack on the Soviet Union. Thus it was on this fateful day—a day that would forever change the world—that Dr. Haape, a second lieutenant (medical) (*Assistenzarzt*) assigned to 3rd Battalion, Infantry Regiment 18, 6th Infantry Division, got through his harrowing baptism of fire. Yet of the eight hundred men of his battalion who marched into Russia, only twenty-eight would remain after the first dreadful winter.

While it is beyond the scope of this brief introduction to "fight" Dr. Haape's war in Russia—after all, that is all laid out in magnificent detail in his memoir—some overarching observations are in order, for they illuminate certain themes:

a) From the first hours—not days, hours—of the war, Dr. Haape, his medical staff, and his fellow soldiers learned the hard way that the Red Army, unlike earlier adversaries, fought with an almost otherworldly ruthlessness and tenacity (some might say fanaticism) against the German invaders. As the opening chapter of *Moscow Tram Stop* reveals, the Russian way of war came as a shock to the *Landser*,[4] accustomed as they were to their easier—and more predictable—opponents in Western Europe. On the Eastern Front, German soldiers often met cruelty with cruelty, contributing to a brutal dialectical logic of atrocity and counteratrocity that characterized the conflict from start to finish. And yet it can still be stated with confidence—as my many years of research and study also reveal—that a large majority of *Landser* in the East fought honorably and within the laws of war, despite a National Socialist leadership that sought to wage a war of annihilation outside the canon of international law.

b) While the Russian campaign rapidly became more pitiless and cruel than could conceivably be imagined, neither Dr. Haape nor most of his comrades ever wavered in their belief that Soviet Bolshevism posed an existential threat that needed to be expunged, root and branch, whatever the cost in men and materiel, before it engulfed Germany and the West. This iron conviction runs like a *rote Faden* (literally, a "red thread," or recurring theme) through Haape's account and is manifest in his letters to Martha during his two years in Russia. Dr. Haape's entire upbringing—his unshakable religious beliefs, his patriotism, his recollections of the turbulent Weimar years, his understanding of the Russia of Lenin and Stalin—had prepared him psychologically for his role in Hitler's showdown with Soviet Russia. Perforce, like a majority of Germans, he supported the war as a necessary evil to spare the Christian West from godless Bolshevism. And yet, as a doctor, whose main business was saving lives, not taking them, he would never have supported Hitler's criminal policies in Operation Barbarossa, had he been privy to them. Indeed, his many sketches and drawings while in Russia, mostly sympathetic depictions of the Russian people, reveal a man with a gentle heart and a basic love of humanity.

c) Because the 6th Infantry Division's main battle line (*Hauptkampflinie*) in Russia was often so dangerously stretched and thinly occupied, Dr. Haape sometimes found himself in the thick of the fighting—defending his dressing station against a Russian breakthrough, leading a counterattack with a hastily assembled few, even personally attacking and immobilizing Soviet tanks bearing down on his dressing station. This was particularly so during the winter of 1941–1942, when his division—and, for that matter, all of Army Group Center—tottered for weeks on the edge of annihilation and during the tenacious fighting at Rzhev in the summer of 1942. In this sense, Haape's 6th Infantry Division resembled the German Eastern Front as a whole—too few men and too few weapons to meet the enormous challenges of Hitler's eastern adventure.

d) As the Barbarossa campaign of 1941 progressed, Dr. Haape's challenges as a military doctor expanded accordingly. If, aside from the wounded and dying (the lot of every doctor in wartime), the initial medical problems were largely benign—exhaustion, blistered feet, insects, dysentery, and more—by fall/winter of that year, serious and deadly concerns such as lice, spotted fever, frostbite, and hypothermia had taken their place. At times, the ruthless nature of his nearly impossible duties almost broke him, or at the very least took him to the brink of complete mental and physical collapse. (See, for example, Haape's awkward encounter with his regimental commander, Colonel Becker, at Christmastime 1941, as described in Chapter 20, "The Numbers Shrink"). The constant strain of service in Russia as a military doctor would, ultimately, permanently damage his health, contributing to two heart attacks much later in life. That he remained master of his personal destiny under such unimaginable conditions, while receiving a half-dozen major military decorations and the fulsome praise of his superiors, is ample testimony to the stalwart character of the man.

e) While perhaps peripheral to Dr. Haape's story, it is important to note that he was much more than a fine doctor and a brave and dutiful soldier. A man of towering intellect and ability, he was as comfortable quoting Goethe or Kant as he was removing a shell splinter from a grateful soldier's gut. Throughout his adult life he lectured—formally or informally—on topics ranging from history and psychology to literature and art. And he was himself a talented artist, as underscored by his many sketches and drawings in Russia, some created at -40° Centigrade. To the very end of his life, he also wrote plays and composed musical pieces, even operas, for which he received the critical acclaim of his peers.

In late November 1942, in a little village on the Volga, Dr. Haape married Martha Arazym by proxy,[5] a marriage they celebrated publicly and symbolically sealed in a church wedding in Krefeld, Germany, in April 1943. In May, he was permanently recalled from Russia and, after temporary assignments in Berlin and Duisburg, was posted at his request to Strasbourg in Alsace-Lorraine in September 1943, where he did duty initially as a battalion doctor to an artillery replacement and training unit. While his record is sketchy at this point, by the spring of 1944 he was working as a surgeon at a reserve military hospital there and, months later, became the chief medical officer (*Standortarzt*) for the entire Strasbourg area.[6]

In June 1944, he looked on helplessly as Anglo-American forces landed successfully in Normandy and his beloved 6th Infantry Division was cut to pieces near Bobruisk—their backs to the Berezina River, which they had crossed so confidently three years before—along with most of Army Group Center in the Soviet summer offensive of 1944. In a despairing letter to Martha on 14 July 1944, he wrote:

My dear, dear Martha,

The times are so terribly grave and I would like to be together with you as much as possible. Who knows what the future holds. In the East, things look bad, very bad and, barring a miracle, I will never again see my friends and comrades of my old division. . . . When will the Russians cross the German border? I am so sad and depressed. But we can do nothing but wait, fulfill what duty demands of us to the very end, and place fate, our fate, confidently in God's Hand, while staying true to ourselves.

This letter encapsulates virtually everything that Heinrich Haape stood for and fought for—the love of his wife, love of country, his solemn commitment to "duty," and, certainly, his deep and abiding religious faith. In late November 1944, he was taken prisoner in Strasbourg by French forces; yet somehow he ended up in American captivity. He was sent to an American military hospital for German POWs in Marseille, where he was employed at least part of the time as a surgeon. After some fifteen months in captivity, he was released in February 1946. (For the fascinating details of how he finagled his release, see Appendix 2.)

Dr. Haape returned to Stuttgart, where his wife had been singing at the city's opera house since the summer of 1943. (The Duisburg Opera House had been flattened in an RAF bombing raid on 20 December 1942.) While the immediate postwar years were difficult ones for most Germans, the Haapes were among the more fortunate—Martha was gainfully employed and Heinz had not been tainted by the stench of National Socialism, creating opportunities for him. From 1946 to 1952, he was editor-in-chief of a daily newspaper, an art journal, and a popular monthly magazine; he also lectured at a school of drama, wrote libretti for two operas, and painted.

He never again practiced medicine, however, in part at least because he did not want to make himself vulnerable to a military draft. The Berlin Blockade (1948–1949), the Soviet occupation of Czechoslovakia, the outbreak of the Korean War, and other flashpoints of East-West conflict had convinced him that the "German problem" (i.e., the partition of the country into East and West Germany) would not be resolved peacefully but would lead to war. As noted above, Heinz was convinced that, should war come, his skills as a doctor would make him among the first to be drafted, a fate he vowed to avoid.

While in captivity, Heinz and other German prisoners had occasionally mulled over the possibility of emigrating—to Spain, Canada, Australia, or other countries far from war and strife. Moreover, as a young man, he had often dreamed of adventure in faraway places, while his older brother Karl—a diabetic who passed away in December 1945—had plied him with tales set in that inscrutable yet intriguing continent of Africa. Around 1950–1951, Heinz made two exploratory trips to South Africa, searching for business opportunities and the best place for his family to settle. In a letter to Martha and his six-year-old son from South Africa in October 1951, he informed them, "I have laid the groundwork for our emigration to South Africa."

In the spring of 1952, Heinz made his move—he, Martha, and little Heinz Jr. permanently departed Germany for South Africa (he by plane, she and their son by steamer from Amsterdam). Leaving most of their possessions behind, the daring move was made on what can best be described as a logistical shoestring; in fact, at one point early on, the Haapes had little more than five pounds to their name, while Heinz's initial business ventures in South Africa turned sour—in part due to the actions of unscrupulous acquaintances or business partners. It was then, with failure staring him in the face, that he went so far as to give Martha—and their son—permission to return to Germany without him should they so choose—a chivalrous offer that Martha, as a devoted and loving wife, rejected out of hand.

Gradually, with the help of others (including the expatriate German community in the Durban area), Heinz began to build a good life for his family in South Africa. In May 1954, a second son, Johannes, was born, and the Haape family was complete. In the years that followed, Heinz began to have success as an entrepreneur, operating a plastic-ware factory (in collaboration with a German firm) and establishing the first of what would become a chain of successful bakeries that would continue to support Martha Haape long after her husband's passing. To bring opera to South Africa and, perhaps more important, to promote Martha's interrupted singing career, Dr. Haape and a small band of opera enthusiasts formed the Durban Opera Company; after eighteen months of rehearsals, the first production, in November 1959, was Mozart's *The Marriage of Figaro*, which Heinz directed himself.

Meanwhile, in 1955, with a 4,000–pound sterling loan, Heinz had purchased a two-and-one-half-acre plot in Gillitts (near Durban), a property that included a small cottage and a rondavel. Surrounded by rolling hills, tall grasses, and patches of eucalyptus forest, the Gillitts property would be the last stop for the Haapes in South Africa. The rondavel was soon outfitted as Martha's music room, and her grand piano (*Flügel*) was shipped over from Stuttgart. In the years ahead, as he became more successful, Heinz would slowly transform their Gillitts home into the image of a romantic European castle.

In 1956–1957, Heinz finally "put pen to paper" and wrote his war memoir, *Moscow Tram Stop*—or, rather, he dictated the narrative to Martha night after night after returning home from work. As Martha recalled years later, "I sat down at the typewriter and typed until my head dropped from fatigue onto the machine, then we would stop for the night."[7] The manuscript was typed with double spacing, so that Heinz could make alterations by hand, and it was given to Major Rossler, a man of German descent who had seen service in the British or South Africa army, for translation into English. Finally, Dr. Haape collaborated with Dennis Henshaw, a journalist from the *Natal Mercury*, to shorten and edit the text. The book was submitted to Collins in London, which snapped it up and published it in 1957. The first edition sold out quickly, and the reviews, particularly those written by British army veterans for various publications, were excellent. For reasons unknown, Collins never published a second English edition, although German-language editions, exquisitely translated by Fritz Bünger for *Motorbuch Verlag*, appeared in 1980 and 1998.

Heinz's *Moscow Tram Stop* was one of the very first accounts of the war with Russia by an ordinary German soldier to appear on the market.[8] In the ensuing years, Heinz sometimes told his family that he had written the book as a tribute to the memory of his lost comrades—for their memory, the pain of their loss, had never left him. Perhaps because of that pain, the indelible imprints left behind by what he had seen and experienced, Heinz's memory of the war remained razor sharp. Indeed, it is a tribute to his keen recollection of events that the book is so fundamentally accurate and contains few significant errors of fact, which is remarkable when one considers that, besides his memory, all he had to work with were his letters, some newspaper clippings, a brief diary, and a handful of official records of his division.

Following the publication of *Moscow Tram Stop*, Dr. Haape would live for almost twenty more years. In addition to his business ventures, he would continue to be a "mover and shaker" in the performing arts in the Durban area, building on what he had achieved in the 1950s. He staged operas with mostly local talent, while showcasing the remarkable talent of his wife. He also continued to paint and write poetry and libretti. His achievements in the arts were noticed by social and political elites in South Africa, among them high-ranking cabinet ministers.

In 1965, Heinz suffered a serious heart attack; it was followed by a second heart attack in 1968. Although he withdrew somewhat from public life in his final years, he remained active in business, the arts, and his various intellectual pursuits. In fact, it was in the late 1960s that he resolved to compose South Africa's first opera, although he had no formal training in musical composition. He composed the lyrics and spent days, months, and (eventually) years seated at his wife's grand piano working out notes by trial and error and jotting them down. Once a week, a friend, John Knuyt, who conducted the Pietermaritzburg Philharmonic Society Choir, visited Heinz and, together, they worked on the score. Finally, Stefans Grové, a professor of music at the University of Pretoria, was invited to Gillitts to revise and orchestrate the musical score.

On 18 May 1974, the music—the climax of Heinz's cultural work in Natal—had its world premiere in the Pietermaritzburg City Hall as an oratorio; it was titled *May the Land Worship the Lord, Praise and Exalt Him through All the Ages*—a passage Heinz had culled from the inscription on the bell in the tower of the Cape Town Castle, the oldest building in South Africa. The oratorio ends with the citizens of Cape Town celebrating New Year's Eve in 1699 and looking expectantly toward a new century. Martha sang the soprano lead of Melina. The state president, the honorable Jim Fouché, was the guest of honor.

It is my hope that this brief introduction has helped bring to life a man of extraordinary intellectual and artistic acumen, but most of all a man of dignity, honor, loyalty, and uncommon courage. The latter are attributes of character, and it is Dr. Haape's character that sets him so far apart from most men in contemporary Western civilization. As C. S. Lewis wrote so prophetically so long ago, "We make men without chests and expect from them virtue and enterprise. We laugh at honor and are shocked to find traitors in our midst." Today, we live in a collapsing and morally depleted world. Our enemies wage religious war against us, slay innocents by the thousands, overrun our lands, threaten our very way of life; yet our leaders—men (and women) without chests one and all—are too paralyzed by fear, disoriented by lack of faith, to even call out our tormenters by name, much less put them to the sword, because the Western culture that had produced extraordinary men like Heinrich Haape no longer exists. And with so few men like him to defend it, our once glorious civilization apathetically consigns itself to unremitting decline.

Heinrich ("Heinz") Haape passed away on 18 February 1976, following unsuccessful surgery for kidney cancer at a hospital in Germany. He was sixty-six years old. Martha would live for another thirty years, although she never remarried. After suffering a stroke in 2003, she passed away in South Africa in 2006. Both Heinz and Martha found their final resting place in the family burial plot in his hometown of Buschhausen/Oberhausen.

Dr. Craig W. H. Luther
Tehachapi, California
December 2015

CHAPTER I

Operation "Barbarossa"[9]

Five minutes to zero hour!

It is 22 June 1941, and I am standing with Battalion Commander Neuhoff and his adjutant, Hillemanns, on the crest of a small hill on the southeastern border of East Prussia, the wide plains of Lithuania stretching ahead of us but invisible in the pitch blackness before dawn. I glance at the luminous dial of my wrist-watch. It is exactly 3 a.m. I know that a million other Germans are looking at their watches at the same time. They have all been synchronized. Three tremendous Germany Army groups and the *Luftwaffe* are poised for the mighty onslaught.[10] Concentration upon concentration of companies, battalions, regiments and divisions lie ready; squadron upon squadron of the *Luftwaffe*—close and long-range reconnaissance aircraft, fighters, bombers and dive-bombers—are keyed to the highest pitch, awaiting zero hour.

Four minutes to go!

The whole of the German eastern front from the Gulf of Finland to the Black Sea has uncoiled for the strike against Russia. The strike will be made simultaneously from Finland, East Prussia, Poland, the Carpathians, Romania. The tremendous wall of fire along the 2000-mile front will destroy the enemy's defenses—of that we are certain.[11] The armies that will soon be pouring through the Russian lines have acquired the temper of steel and an invincible spirit on the battlefields of Europe. Every German soldier is fully conscious of the magnitude of this colossal undertaking. Whether he tries to peer through the darkness toward Leningrad, toward Moscow, toward Kiev, toward the Dnepr or toward the Caspian Sea, each man knows that a country of endless distances lies ahead of him.

Three minutes to go!

I think of my fellow army-doctors in Finland, where dawn has already broken. But deep night still enfolds us, a night without moon, the stars blanketed by low cloud. A warm

I

breeze blows from the Lithuanian plains and I realize that I am sweating slightly—but more from the awful suspense of these fateful minutes than from the sultriness of the night. In dead silence, our storm troops and pioneers are moving forward to the extreme boundaries of the frontier. It is happening on our sector and the same thing is happening along the whole front. There is an invisible comradeship in the all-enveloping mantle of the night. It brings a comradeship-in-arms with every one of the three million Germans who are standing ready to set ablaze the greatest military conflict in history: Operation "Barbarossa." A man lights a cigarette. There is a barked command and the glowing end drops earthward, sparks on the ground, and is stamped out. There is no conversation; the only sounds the occasional clink of metal, the pawing of a horse's hoofs, the snort of his breath. I imagine I can see a faint blush in the distant sky. I am eagerly searching for something on which to fix my eyes and divert my thoughts. Dawn is breaking. In the east the black cloud is graying. Will these last seconds never tick away? I look again at my watch.

Two minutes to go!

My thoughts turn to Martha,[12] linger with her. She will be asleep, as will the sweethearts—and the wives and mothers—of millions of other men along this vast front. They know nothing of what we are doing, of the dangers which the next few hours, the next months, perhaps the next years, will bring to their menfolk. To them this night is as a thousand others, and that is how we wish it to be. We will march. Places and names will change; some will cease to exist, others will be engraved on the memories of us all. Some will become a dim recollection, others will become history. We do not know which. Villages will be destroyed, towns will be desolated. Terrified human beings will stand lost by the roadside. Graves will mark the battlefields, will be scattered along the highways. And tomorrow night, where the horizon burns, there the war will be.

One minute to zero hour!

There is nothing of which we can think, except what will happen when the next second and the next have ticked by. The tense moment holds us breathless. We wait, our faces rigid, pulses racing. The whole world seems to be waiting. . . .

A mighty clap of thunder as thousands of guns roar forth at one stroke. Their flashes turn dawn into daylight. In a split second, more than two thousand miles of front is electrified into action. Hell is let loose and history is made. Guns of every caliber fire point-blank at the Russian lines. With a heavy, droning hum, mortar shells arc over our heads toward the enemy. Machine-guns and automatics rattle out their urgent salvoes. The Russians return the fire. We hear the whine as heavy shells rend the night above us. But the German fire intensifies into an overwhelming crescendo as our forward storm troops and infantry battalions pour into the enemy's frontier defenses. And the Panzers, we know, are crushing their way forward, spitting fire.

The east is aflame.

*   *   *

The 3rd Battalion, Infantry Regiment 18,[13] is still lying in prepared positions awaiting the order to advance. Our mission is to support the forward line methodically at any crucial point where enemy resistance stiffens. As the dawn tries to compete with manmade fire, we watch from our rising ground the rapid advance of our assault troops. Beyond us lie a thousand miles of Russian soil before Moscow,[14] which we know is our ultimate objective.

The 6th Infantry Division,[15] to which we belong, is part of Army Group Center under Field Marshal von Bock,[16] and it is to us, rather than to Army Group South, now advancing on the Ukraine, or to Army Group North driving toward Leningrad, that Germany will look for a sensational victory. We know that ours is to be the supreme objective.

The frontier customs post is already a blazing torch. The Russian frontier defenses have been pulverized by fire and taken by storm. Only a few concrete bunkers are fighting back bravely and desperately, but they will soon be surrounded and overrun. A Stuka formation rips eastward, then breaks off into attack, each plane plummeting earthward. The crump of their bombs mingles with the other sounds of battle. The Stukas re-form and go into the attack again, with guns blazing this time, then are lost in the distance. From our small prominence it is like a scene from a spectacular play. Motionlessly the tall figure of Battalion Commander Neuhoff stands beside me. He murmurs, as if to convince himself: "Now we are at war with Russia! War with Russia!"

The day has dawned, and with it the warm breeze has died away. More and more fires are lighting up the middle-distance and thick, dirty smoke-clouds roll lazily upward, spreading over the awakening hills and shadowy woods. The order comes to advance. Neuhoff dismisses the messenger with a curt order to our signalers. It is 3:45 a.m. It seems unbelievable that only 40 minutes have passed since the guns first spoke. We fall into position and move forward. It is a relief to be moving, but I sit astride my horse with a tense grip on the reins. Lump behaves restlessly and I try to relax. There is a baptism of fire ahead for man and horse. I wonder how I will acquit myself and I have a dreadful fear that nervousness will rob my hand of its precision. I feel behind me for my medical outfit, it is hanging from the saddle; everything is in order. Petermann, my groom, rides beside me, carrying two first aid outfits. The motor ambulance is a few hundred yards in the rear with my medical team—Dehorn, Müller, Wegener, and a driver.

We meet our first wounded soldier. He has a bullet wound in the arm. I remove the rubber tourniquet and emergency bandage which have been applied by a stretcher-bearer up front. There is little bleeding for the bullet has passed right through the arm, grazing the bone only slightly. I apply a pressure bandage and tie the arm in a sling. "How are things going ahead?" I ask him.

"*Unteroffizier* Schäfer has fallen and one officer—I don't know who he is. Otherwise no casualties as far as I know. But I am not sure what is happening—it was so quick, Herr *Assistenzarzt*."

"Go back along this road," I tell him, "until you meet the ambulance company, which is following us."

Smiling, he sets off. For him the war lasted only five minutes. I remount and give Lump the spurs, galloping to the head of the column. Petermann follows. I reach the battalion commander and his adjutant, Hillemanns.

"Everything in order?" asks Neuhoff.

"Yes, sir—only a minor case."

"What arrangements have you made to deal with the disposal of wounded?"

"Everything has been thoroughly planned, Herr Major."

"Yes, but what are your plans, Haape?" Neuhoff persists.

"This road which passes the customs house leads to the main highway to Kalvaria. *Oberstabsarzt* Schulze with his ambulance company will follow this road and take over the batches of wounded men that I have attended to. Serious cases will be carried to houses near the road and ambulance men or stretcher-bearers will be detailed to remain with them. The other battalion M.O.s[17] will do the same."

Neuhoff grunts: "Good!"

*　　*　　*

The dead officer was from our battalion—it was young *Leutnant* Stock, who had been killed by a Russian sniper's bullet. His body was lying in a trampled cornfield. Two men from Kramer's 11th Company, to which Stock had belonged, were digging a grave in the soft earth. Watching them were four Russian soldiers, blood seeping through their fresh bandages. My lively little orderly, Dehorn, was giving one of them a drink from his water-bottle. But two Russians had not received medical attention, although one of them had a gaping leg wound. My medical NCO Wegener was covering them with an automatic—evidently the one Stock had been carrying. My third medical orderly, *Gefreiter* Müller, was watching them closely; he wore a puzzled frown.

Wegener saluted, without lowering his automatic, and said: "We've treated these four men, Herr *Assistenzarzt*, but what shall we do with these two? They ambushed Herrn *Leutnant* Stock from behind this rye. Our men got them with a grenade. Do we have to give them first aid, too?"

"We're not the judges, Wegener," I said sharply. "Our job is to help the wounded— Germans and Russians alike, even if they have shot down one of our officers. Put that gun down." The two soldiers had dug the grave and were lowering Stock's body into the earth. Quickly, they shoveled the loose earth over it and knocked a rough birch cross into the ground with their trench-spades. That was all there was to it. The helmet and the identity disc hanging from the cross showed that *Leutnant* Stock, 21 years old, lay buried there. But there was nothing to say that this sensitive lad had been a brilliant pianist; that he had been able to make me forget everything when I listened to him play the "Moonlight Sonata" in the mess at Littry la Mine before we left Normandy. Now he had been jerked away from the fullness of life to the void of death in a split-second—the time it had taken for one small bullet to speed from the muzzle of a Russian gun into his heart. Hitherto I had always seen men lingering on the brink of death for a few minutes at least; never had I seen a life cut off so swiftly and cleanly. Stock's death had abruptly switched my thoughts from myself to my comrades. Introspection had vanished, and I was now looking at this new war through the eyes of the 3rd Battalion. Perhaps so much more would happen to the battalion that I should forget young *Leutnant* Stock and his sensitive fingers.

We passed the burning customs house, out of East Prussia into Lithuania.[18] The network of wire entanglements, spread over meadows and cornfields, was behind us and as we crossed the frontier, we entered a new world. The soil, the countryside, were the same on each side of the man-made barrier, but we stepped from the well-cultivated and cared-for land of East Prussia to stony fields, with ill-kept houses and poorly-clad peasants.

After one hour the war was over for these people. Civilians were already creeping out of hiding places; they looked helpless and confused. But we had no time to stop and give advice. Already the spearheads of our infantry were three miles inside enemy territory. And the Panzers, we knew, were at this moment driving deep into the Lithuanian plains, beginning the first of many encircling movements. Our *Luftwaffe* was not sitting idly by. From forward airfields behind our lines they put flight after flight into the air. The enemy was on the run; he had to be kept that way. All morning as we marched, our necks craned to see *Staffel* after *Staffel* pass overhead: the Heinkels and Dorniers with their persistent throb, the Messerschmitts with their ear-splitting whine—and the Stukas.[19] All flew over in perfect formation as if nothing in the world were easier than flying over contested enemy territory.

We heard a strange drone in the distance, getting louder. But even through our binoculars we could see nothing. Then through a break in the clouds they appeared—five, six, seven Russian bombers. Our columns halted, took what cover they could find along the roadside. Gunners jumped into the rye fields with their anti-aircraft guns. By now we could see they were not heavy bombers, but short and stumpy monoplanes and bi-planes, probably dive-bombers. They flew directly over our heads—we were not to be the target. The gunners on the ground opened up, and the Russian planes dived behind us and to our right. We heard the thud of bombs a mile in our rear and saw the clouds of dust rise. In less perfect formation, the aircraft set course for the east. We resumed our march.

The first prisoners! We gazed at them eagerly, anxious to make acquaintance with the new foe. They were about a platoon strong and wore shabby khaki-yellow uniforms, loosely-flapping, unmilitary-looking blouses and had clean-shaven heads. Their heavy faces were expressionless.

From a farmhouse came a shout for first-aid men. With Dehorn and Wegener, I stepped into the house and saw several civilians and wounded Russian soldiers. I gave first aid quickly and ordered Wegener to attend to the light cases, report to the ambulance company and follow up without delay.

I was finding that the horse was by far the best means of getting about. By galloping through the cornfields alongside the road I was soon able to pass the marching column and join up again with Neuhoff. Suddenly shots rang out not more than 50 feet ahead of us from a field of rye. Neuhoff pulled his horse back on to its hindlegs. We dismounted and in the confusion a volley of bullets went over our heads as Hillemanns, the adjutant, and a number of our men dashed into the cornfield, firing their rifles and automatics as they went. There was a mêlée in the tall corn, a confusion of revolver shots, upraised rifle butts and screams.

A tall infantryman from the H.Q. company brushed his way back through the rye. With his hands still gripping the barrel of his rifle, he shrugged and said: "Finished!" I noticed the butt of his rifle was splashed with blood.

Neuhoff and I strode into the corn. A commissar and four Russian soldiers were lying on the trampled earth, their skulls battered into the soil, which had been freshly dug and thrown up into a mound for their suicidal ambush. The commissar's hands were still grasping uprooted cornstalks. Our casualties were negligible—one man with a bayonet wound in the arm, another man with a grazed calf. A little iodine, gauze, and a couple of strips of adhesive plaster and they were ready to march on with the rest of us. Neuhoff, Hillemanns and I rode on together at the head of the column.

"I didn't expect that," said Neuhoff, rather shakily. "Sheer suicide, to attack a battalion at close quarters with five men."[20]

We were to learn that these small groups of Russians would constitute our greatest danger. The corn was high and made ideal cover for the small guerrilla bands, which stayed behind as the main body of the Russian forces were rolled back. As a rule they were fanatically led by Soviet commissars and we never knew when we should come under their fire.

As the sun climbed, the day grew hot; and as the men marched the dust rose, until we were all covered in a light yellow coating—battledress, rifles, faces, and hands. Men and vehicles assumed ghostly outlines in the dust-laden air. I wet my dry lips with a little water from my bottle and was glad when the order was given to halt. It was noon and we rested in a small wood. A flight of eight Russian bombers came toward us from the east. They circled to make sure of their target.

But this time they had to reckon with the Messerschmitts. The Bf 109's swooped like hawks into a flight of pigeons. They attacked from the sun, firing as they dived. Breaking off the attack, they zoomed to regain height for another attack and one by one the bombers were picked off. One Russian burst into flames, a second followed, and like two torches they sank toward the ground. It surprised me to see how slowly they fell. A wing broke off another bomber and the plane spun earthward. I noticed two parachutes drifting gently above it. Our fighters continued the attacks until every bomber had been shot down. The action had taken 10 minutes at most.

A dispatch rider roared up on a motor-cycle. One of the Russian bombers had crashed into an artillery column. Extra medical assistance was urgently needed. I galloped over and found 15 artillerymen already dead. Behind a hedge, nine more soldiers with serious burns were lying. Five of them were so badly burned that I held out no hope of their survival for more than a day or two. I sent a field-messenger for an ambulance—all nine men were stretcher cases. I filled in casualty cards for them: a schoolmaster from Duisburg, a locksmith from Essen, a miner from Hamborn, a tailor from Dinslaken, a forester from Lipperland, a tramwayman from Osnabrück and three students from Münster. It was two hours before I could leave them. I had lost touch with my battalion and nobody seemed able to give me directions. I worked out that if I headed southeast I would be bound to reach the road to Kalvaria, which was the immediate objective of the division.

With Petermann following me, I took a by-road, hoping it was a short-cut, but after a mile I heard shots and imagined that bullets were whipping past my ears. Being inexperienced, I could not gauge from what distance or direction they were being fired—or even if we were the targets, though we seemed to be the only moving objects in sight. We made for shelter behind some bushes and then I noticed a farmyard. It looked like good cover—unless it was occupied by Russians. But to my relief I saw German soldiers, and a *Hauptmann* appeared to whom I told my story.

"You're not exactly reporting anything unusual," he told me caustically. "We've been playing this game with them since early morning. My job's to comb these woods and corn-fields and get rid of these guerrillas.[21] I've already shot God knows how many and taken 120 prisoners, but I've lost some of my best men doing it. You've been lucky, Doctor."

"Lucky twice," I said. "Our battalion was ambushed this morning."

"That's happening all over the countryside," he told me. "These swines build up ammunition dumps in the cornfields and then wait until our main columns have passed before they start sniping. And what a mixture they are! I've got Mongolians, Tartars, and Kalmucks. It's a queer business fighting these slit-eyed bastards. Like being in China."

He directed me toward the Kalvaria road.

"I don't think you'll be bothered by any more of this rabble in the cornfields," he said. "I've cleared them all out in that direction."

This time I kept a sharp look-out. And then I realized that my feeling of irresolution had vanished. It had dawned on me that not every bullet finds its mark.

A broad stream of soldiers, vehicles and guns was moving east along the highway, among them a baggage unit from my own battalion. I galloped ahead, through the cornfields alongside the road. Larger and larger groups of Russian prisoners were passing us on their way to the rear. I came across our 10th Company's commander, bull-like, genial Stolze. He was hugely delighted at having successfully completed his mission of thrusting across country from a point some miles to the north and rejoining our battalion on the highway.

"Hey, Doktor!" he shouted. "Work for you. See that farmhouse?" His horse jostled mine as his huge hand pointed out the place, about half a mile away across the fields. "There are some wounded men there. . . ."

"Yours?"

"No, thank God. But they need a doctor—there's only a stretcher-bearer with them at the moment."

"Thanks, Stolze—I'll go over there."

"Oh, Doktor—better take a couple of my men with you for protection. But be sure I get them back. In one piece." He gave orders to an *Unteroffizier* and a soldier and with a wave of his hand rode off along the road at the head of his company to rejoin the rest of the battalion. I had heard nothing of my ambulance and medical team for several hours, so I sent back along the column to *Oberstabsarzt* Schulze for an ambulance. The marching men scattered to let it through as it hooted its way along the dusty road. I ordered the *Sankawagen*[22] driver to make for the farmhouse and rode after it with Petermann. A few bullets kicked up the dust behind us as we galloped into the farmyard.

In the big living room there were five soldiers lying on the floor; two of them were dead, their bodies still warm. The stretcher-bearer, a quietly-spoken middle-aged man, reported: "It is terrible. For the first time in my life I've really been desperate, Herr *Assistenzarzt*. The theory—I know that. But real wounds knock the theory out of your head." He looked at me with pleading eyes. "I hope it's not my fault the two men died. I tried—"

"Don't worry. They'd have died anyway." I glanced quickly at the three wounded men. "You seem to have made a good job of things in spite of forgetting your theory."

I attended to the stomach wound first. The bullet had entered below the stomach and had passed out to the left of the spine. The man's face was ashen and drawn with pain and cold beads of sweat were on his forehead. "You have a clean bullet wound through the abdomen," I told him distinctly. "It seems that only the small intestine has been damaged. You'll have to be operated on without delay, but the only immediate danger is internal hemorrhage—and as you were wounded a couple of hours ago and you're not dead yet, you'll survive." I gave him a smile. "The *Sankawagen* is outside; it will take you straight to the medical company where they'll operate on you. Don't worry—you're on your way home."

As his pain-racked face relaxed into a faint smile I closed both entry and exit holes of the wound with a plastic bandage, applied a covering of *Zellstoff*[23] and with my scissors removed bits of bloodstained clothing. The stretcher-bearer helped me to tie the man's knees up under his chin to ease the stomach. I gave him a sedative and an anti-tetanus injection, and had him wrapped warmly in a blanket and carried to the *Sankawagen*, where a casualty card was completed and hung around his neck. In the meantime, I turned to the second badly wounded man. Head wound. And unconscious. I cleaned and bandaged the wound and he joined the stomach case in the ambulance.

The third man had a clean bullet wound through his upper thigh. The rubber tourniquet had been well applied above the wound, but had been in position too long—the leg was completely numb. From my medical bag I took a container clip and told the stretcher-bearer to remove the tourniquet. Blood pumped out—the bullet had punctured an artery. Fortunately it was not the main artery, otherwise there would have been little hope of saving his leg.

I pressed a wad of absorbent cotton into the wound and with a single scissor cut opened the wound to the top and removed the wad. Quickly I applied the clip to the end of the artery. The bleeding stopped and the blood again coursed through the undamaged arteries of the leg which had been almost dead for the best part of two hours. The patient looked at me with questioning eyes.

"Now we must wait a while and see if the veins are damaged and whether the circulation will be strong enough to bring life back into that leg of yours. But your case is going well," I reassured him.

"Herr *Assistenzarzt*," the stretcher-bearer interrupted, "the peasant woman here has made you a big can of coffee."

Gratefully, I took the can of steaming coffee from the old woman, whom I had not noticed until now. I glanced at my watch—it was 3:15 p.m. We had been at war with Russia just 12 hours, but it was 18 hours since I had last eaten or drunk anything but water. I had no appetite, but a great thirst.

The woman handed me a big cup and said in fluent German: "I'm so happy our house has not been burnt. My mother was German, you know—a Baltic German. And as a young girl I was in Berlin for two years. Those were better days—the good, old days!"

"Here's to better days again!" I gave her a toast with my coffee and filled the cup again.

There was a crash of glass in the back room. "That has been going on all day," said the old woman. "Those Russians in the wood over there."

I ran outside and called the two men from Stolze's company. "It strikes me you didn't make a very thorough job of clearing all the Russians out," I said.

"We penetrated right up to the wood with *Oberleutnant* Stolze, and not a mouse stirred," said the *Unteroffizier.*

"Then who's that shooting?" I demanded.

"Perhaps our Herr *Oberleutnant* thought something should be left over for the back-line troops—so that they'd have something to put in their letters home."

"What's your name?" I demanded curtly.

"Schmidt, Herr *Assistenzarzt.*"

"And your profession?"

"Lawyer, with your permission, Herr *Assistenzarzt.*"

"I'm not surprised. Keen talker, eh? Well, you're handling my brief now, and you'll carry it out to my instructions. Is that clear?"

"Yes, Herr *Assistenzarzt*."

"See that you keep those Russians in the wood quiet."

"*Zu Befehl*," he replied and set up his light machine-gun facing the wood. Before he could fire, a bullet ripped through the roof of the ambulance. I ordered the driver to take it to a sheltered position behind the house and returned to my "leg" in the living room. It had turned pink and when I pinched the man's thigh and toes he could feel it. Now there was considerable venous bleeding. Time was precious. The clip was secure and I left it in the wound, but applied a pressure bandage. I gave him an anti-tetanus jab and had him carried to the ambulance on a stretcher. "Your leg will completely recover," I told him.

"Thank you, Herr *Assistenzarzt*," he said, with moist eyes, "and also you, Herr *Pfarrer*, for having prayed with me."

The stretcher-bearer tried to explain as he felt my questioning gaze on him. "We had plenty of time to think and were terrified to be stuck here unprotected with the Russians just across the pasture. But I believed the Lord God would help us. So I prayed. . . . You see, I used to be a padre. It seemed to comfort us and give us courage. . . ." He tailed off.

"You needn't excuse yourself." I was rather moved. "You did the right thing."

On the casualty card hanging around the neck of the stomach case I wrote in red pencil "To be operated on at once" with three exclamation marks, then shouted to the ambulance driver: "Now get to the medical company as quickly as possible. And report that two dead men are lying here for burial."

The ambulance sped off and ran into a hail of bullets as soon as it left the shelter of the building. I could only stand and watch with impotent rage—the prominent Red Cross was plainly visible in the bright afternoon sun. If a bullet found the engine and put the ambulance out of action, the stomach case would die—that was certain. Suddenly determined machine-gun fire rattled out from the front of the house. The lawyer had evidently pin-pointed the snipers, for the Russian fire stopped immediately.

"There are more than two dead men, Herr *Assistenzarzt*," the stretcher-bearer said uncertainly.

"What do you mean?"

"There are six more bodies lying in a hollow on the other side of the house."

"How many?"

"Six, Herr *Assistenzarzt*—and one of them is a doctor."

"Are you sure they're all dead?"

"The other men said so."

"We must make sure. Come with me, stretcher-bearer." I gave the lawyer orders: "*Jurist*, give immediate covering fire while the stretcher-bearer and I run along that ditch."

"*Jawohl*, Herr *Assistenzarzt!*" the lawyer grinned.

The hollow pointed out by the stretcher-bearer lay 100 yards away from the house. We made a dash for the ditch and plunged into it as snipers' bullets bit into the earth on either bank and showered us with dust. The machine-gun from the farmhouse chattered and I seized the opportunity to dash across the remaining 20 yards to the hollow.

Six bodies lay sprawled in the hollow. A stretcher-bearer lay on his back, arms flung wide, and four other soldiers lay close by just as they had fallen. And there was the doctor, lying face downward, Red Cross band on his sleeve, a bold red cross on the flag by his side. The contents of his medical pack were strewn around him.

As if afraid of being overheard, the *Pfarrer* whispered: "A hundred yards from here— see, there, behind those gorse bushes, the Russians were lying. The doctor had brought the wounded men into the hollow and was attending to them when the Russians started firing. I was watching from the farmhouse but could do nothing. The doctor stood up and waved his Red Cross flag, but they kept on firing at him. He fell, and they fired and fired until nothing more moved in the hollow. It was horrible . . . cold-blooded murder. . . ." His voice broke and tears were in his eyes.

We crawled over to the doctor and gently I rolled him over on to his back. The blond hair fell back from the brow and I looked down into the sightless eyes of Fritz!

For no reason, a picture of Fritz gaily boarding the train with me at Cologne station flashed into my mind—Fritz and I, two *Unterärzte* in new uniforms. And another picture of Fritz standing in the hotel room at Le Mans, in his pajamas, embarrassed because he could not persuade the charming young French girl to leave his bed. And I had furiously insisted on my right to occupy the other bed and had disgustedly turned the room into a *ménage à trois* for the night. But the next morning I had laughed. The French girl was delightful and Fritz's infectious gaiety defied censure. . . .

Silently I gazed down at my old friend as if by my own insistence I could will those tight lips to open and talk to me. Twelve hours' warfare, a few miles into Russian territory, and I had already lost one of my dearest friends. It was too much—too much for the first day of a war against a new foe, whose ways we had hardly begun to gauge. My overtaut consciousness half-refused to accept Fritz's death. The *Pfarrer* knelt beside me, waiting for my next move.

Without a word and without clearly realizing what I was doing I hoisted Fritz's body across my shoulders and trod heavily out of the hollow. There was silence now, both from the wood and from the house. The *Pfarrer* followed me.

I laid Fritz's body down in the orchard at the back of the farmhouse, and the two machine-gunners and Petermann joined us. I opened the tunic and shirt. Both were red with Fritz's blood and torn by the savage volley of bullets that had smacked into him at close range. I broke his identity disc, and then emptied his pockets of pay book, photographs, matches and cigarette case. I wrapped them all in his handkerchief and handed the bundle to Petermann. "We'll send that back," I told him as we walked back to the house.

In a corner of the kitchen were stacked the weapons of the dead and wounded who had passed through. I took an automatic with a full magazine and stuffed two extra magazines into my pockets. Into my top tunic pockets went two light grenades. I handed Petermann a rifle. Unasked, the *Pfarrer* also took a rifle and slung it over his shoulder.

"Let's keep those Russians quiet until we can get out of here," I said, "and at the same time we'll give them something to remember us by."

An amused smile played around the corners of the lawyer's mouth and I noticed he was looking at my Red Cross arm band, which was soaked with Fritz's blood.

"You're right." I answered his unspoken question. Deliberately I slipped it off my sleeve, folded it carefully and put it into my pocket. "That doesn't go with guns. And in any case it means nothing to the Russians. There's no Geneva Convention here.[24] I'm telling you, *Jurist*, I'm a soldier like the rest of you now."

We crept around to the front of the farmhouse and trained our sights on the point from which the Russians' main fire had come. I looked at the lawyer Schmidt. "Fire!" he commanded and the machine-gun, my automatic and two rifles poured their fire at head-height among the trees. "That will make the *Scheisskerle* keep their heads down for a while," Schmidt said. We set off back down the sandy farm road, using our horses as shields from a possible sharpshooter's bullet, and rejoined the main road along which the unbroken stream of men was still marching.

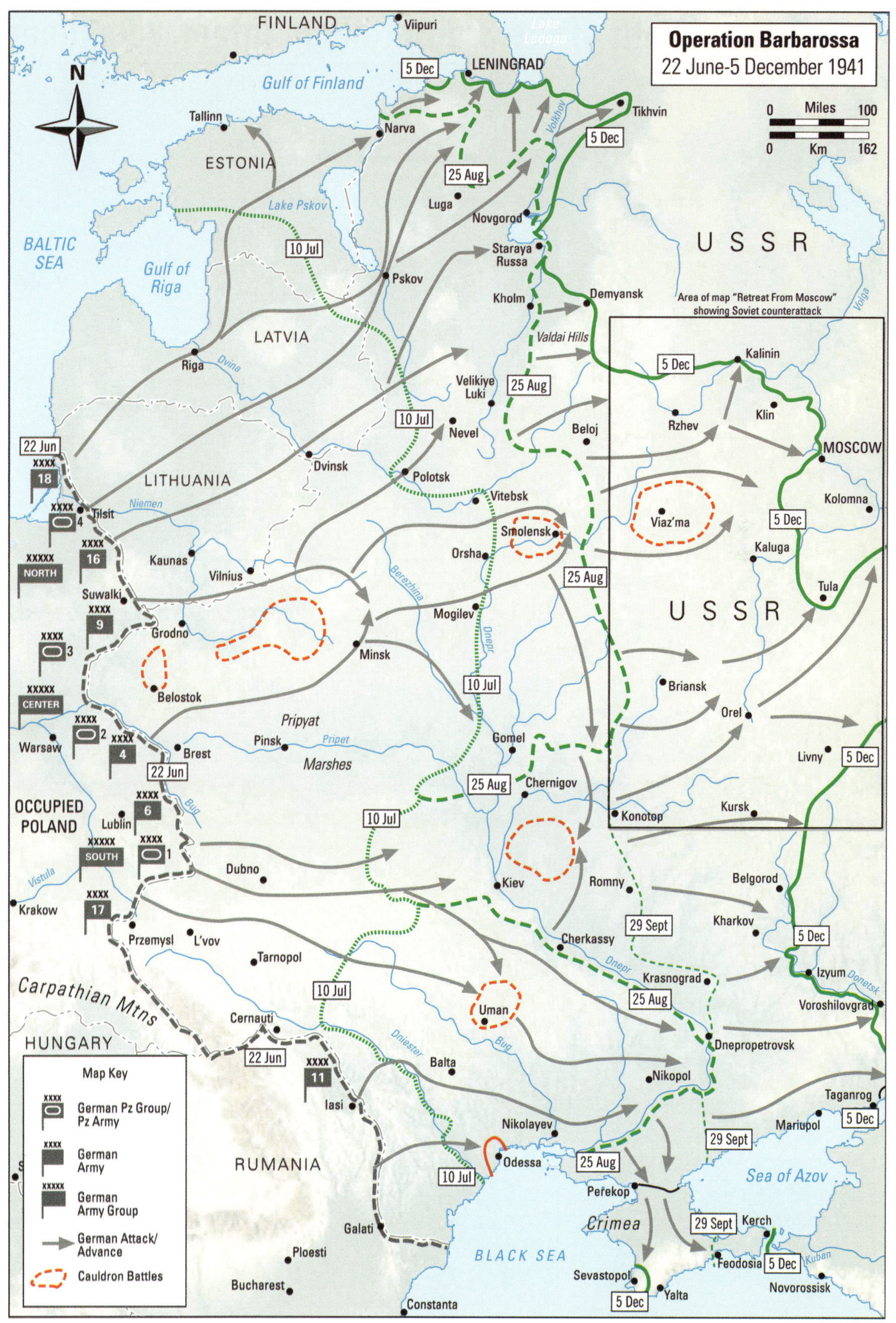

Operation Barbarossa: The Central Theater of Operations

Path of the 3rd Battalion, Infantry Regimen[t]

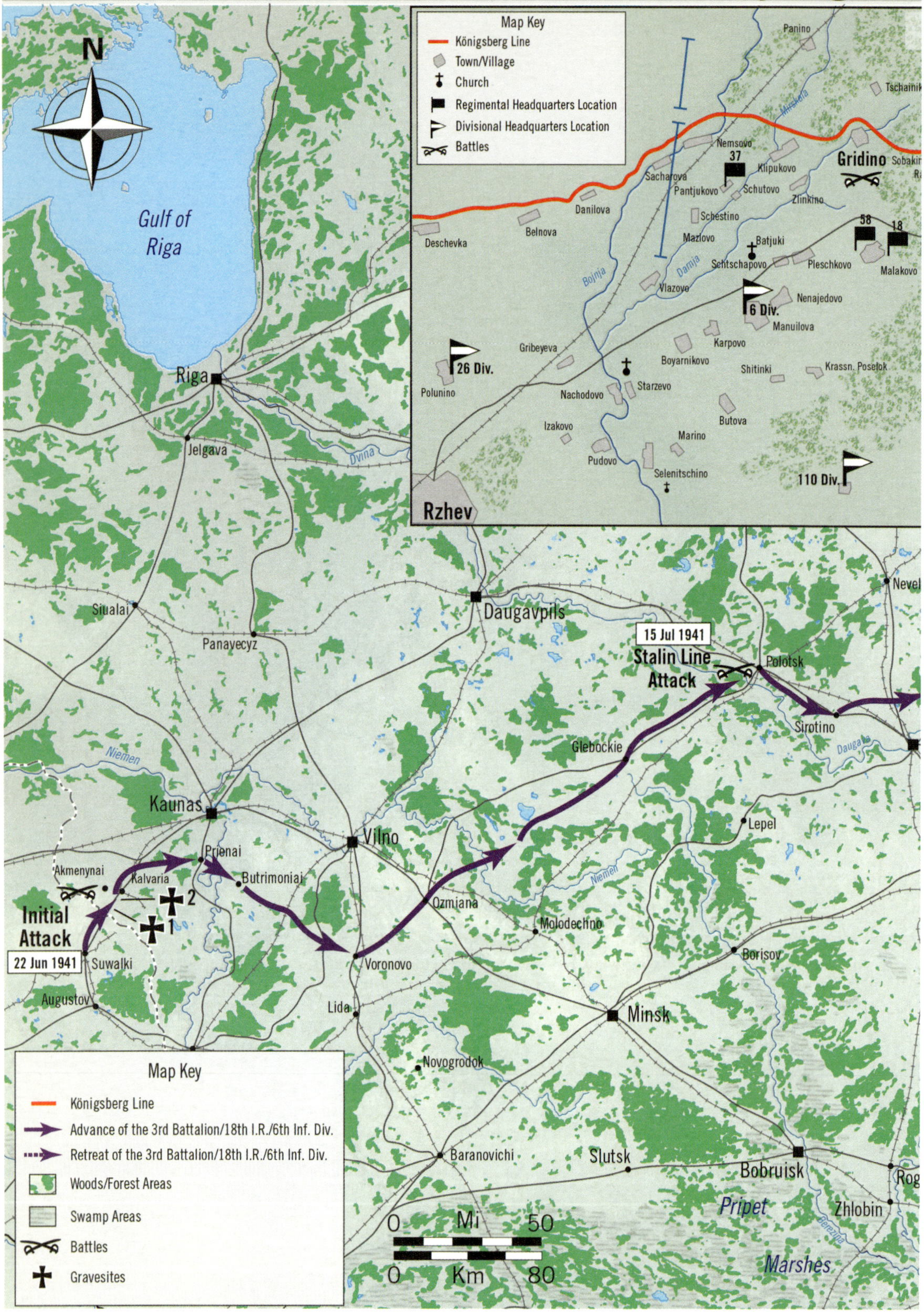

Path of the 3rd Battalion, Infantry Regiment 18

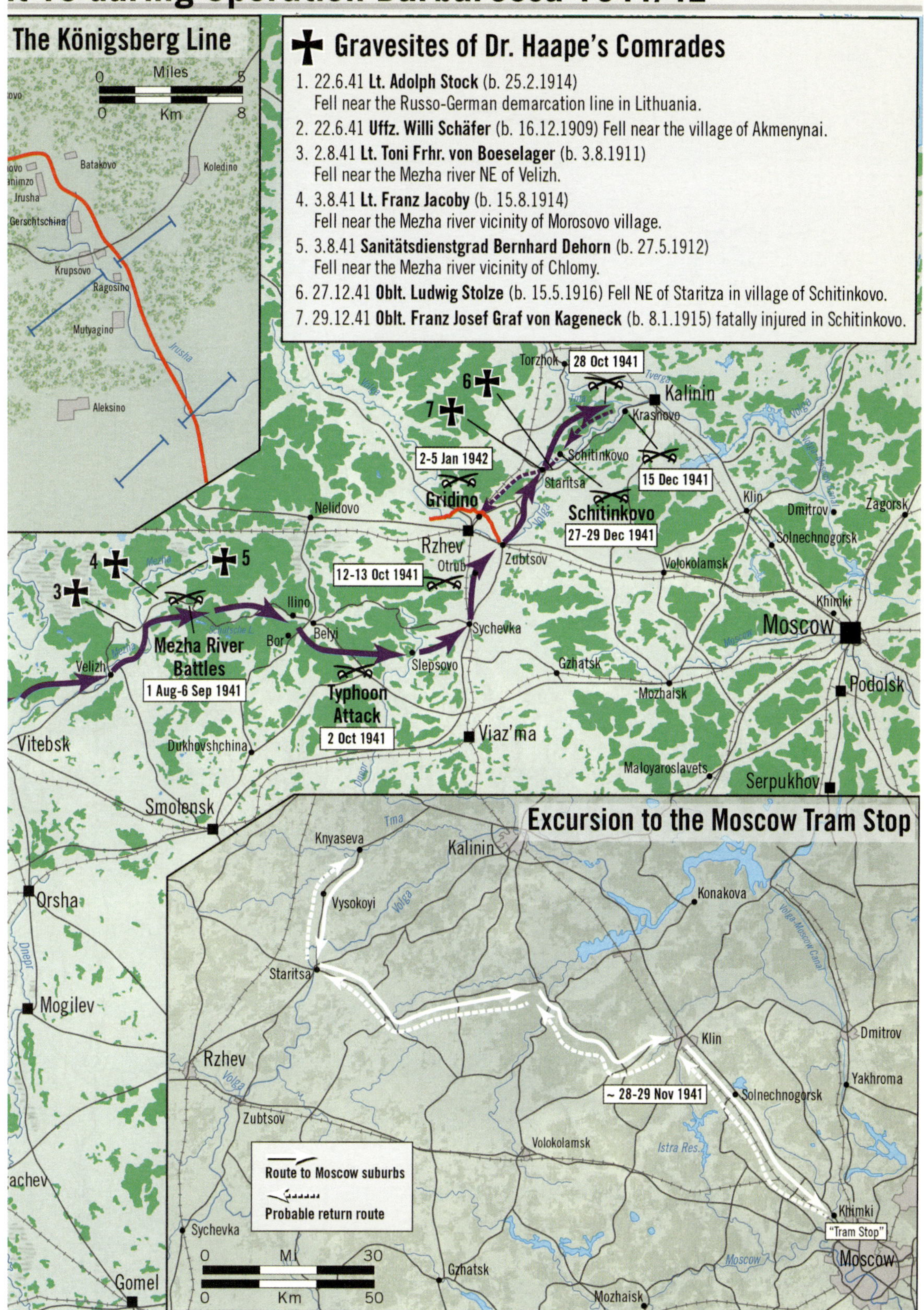

during Operation Barbarossa, 1941–1942

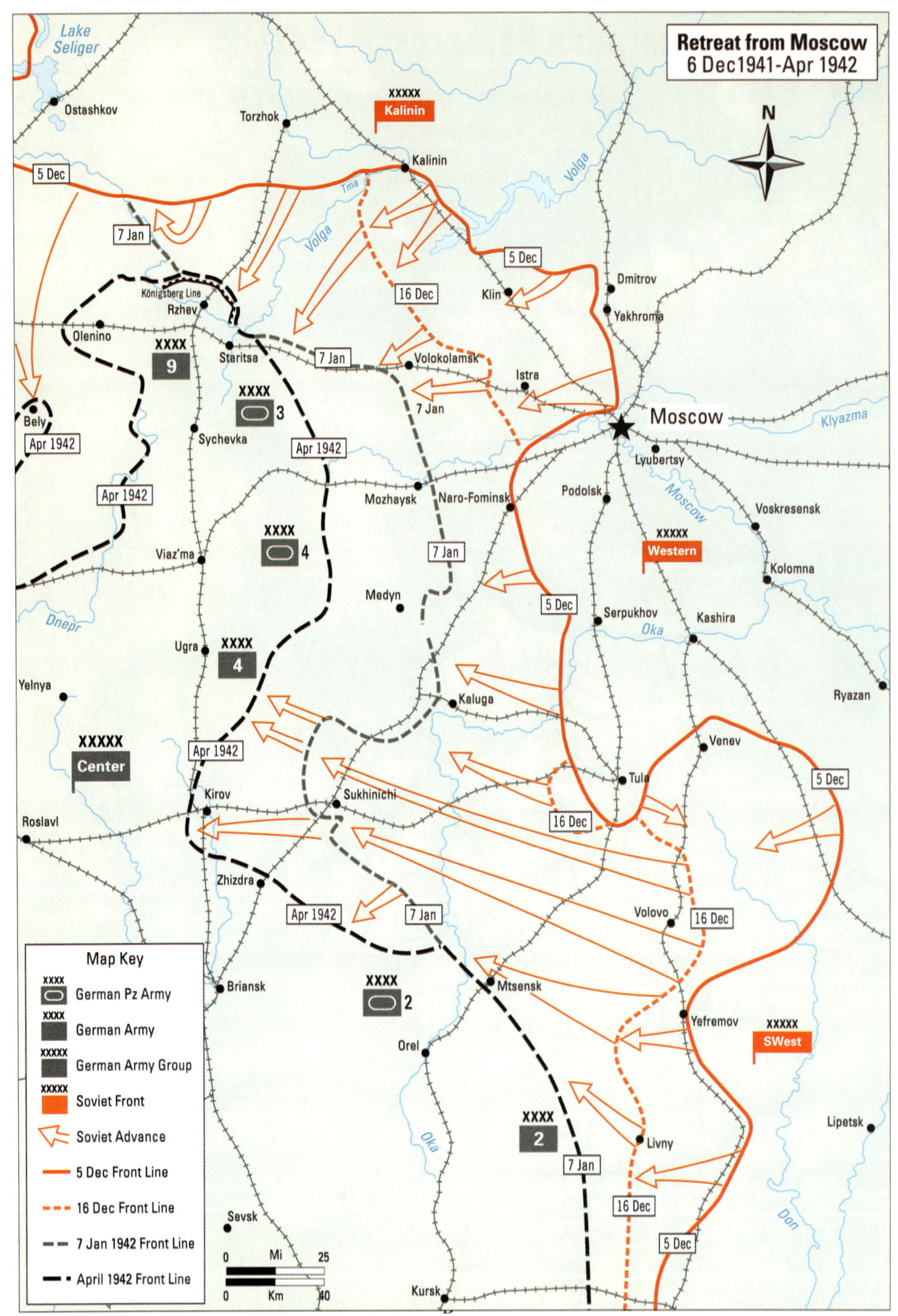

Retreat from Moscow, 6 December 1941–April 1942

CHAPTER 2

Medical Situation Unsatisfactory

OUR TROOPS WERE DRIVING INTO RUSSIAN-HELD TERRITORY FAST. APART FROM THOSE first few minutes after our dawn attack, there had been no organized resistance.[25] Whatever troops had been entrusted to guard the Soviet's western frontier had been shattered into fragments.[26] They were fragments which, as I had found out, could be dangerous to us as individuals, but to the German Army as a whole were at the moment but minor irritations under the skin. For the next few hours I toiled to apply balm to the injuries caused by these hostile fragments, these groups of fanatical Reds which harried our marching columns. Until late into the night I went from one casualty point to another. Most of the wounded had been given first aid by the stretcher-bearers, and it was only in the more serious cases that I gave assistance. That way I was able to make good progress.

The sun lingered for a long time above the western horizon, and cast long shadows ahead of the marching men on the Kalvaria road. It was past ten o'clock before the light faded to such an extent that I had to call for lights by which to tend the wounded. With nightfall, a chill breeze sprang up and blew across the plain.

I was leaving one of the casualty stations, my thoughts on catching up with my battalion for the night's halt, when *Assistenzarzt* Knust of the 2nd Battalion rode up and asked me to help him. Fourteen unattended cases lay at a casualty station on a by-road to the Memel.

We were lucky to find an ambulance and handed over our horses to Petermann with instructions to await our return at the crossroads. After half an hour's drive we found the wounded men in a pitiful state. They had received only the sketchiest first aid and had been waiting for a doctor since two o'clock. Through loss of blood, most of them were freezing cold, and, in the light of our hand-torches, many of their faces were drawn with long-endured pain. But the forsaken little group still had spirit. Four of the less badly-wounded had placed two machine-guns in position and had stacked hand grenades ready for any night attack, which was more than a possibility. We distributed a number of woolen blankets from the ambulance, which we put in such a position that we could work by the light of its headlamps. A stretcher-bearer, who had remained with the group, led us to the most serious cases, six of whom we quickly transferred to the ambulance. We attended to the rest and rigged an improvised tent to give some protection against the cold. They all kept their rifles and those who manned the machine-guns were each given an extra blanket.

"Another ambulance will be sent to collect the rest of you," we assured the stretcher-bearer. "At the latest, early in the morning. Good-bye and good luck!"

Knust and I climbed into the front seat alongside the driver. I carried my automatic[27] across my knees and could feel the two grenades in my pockets. Knust, who still wore his Red Cross arm band, fell asleep as the ambulance labored slowly forward into the night, headlights shining on the sandy road.

I wanted to fall asleep myself—my body cried out for rest, but my mind was too active; a thousand pictures of the day's events flashed before my eyes. Events that I had to try to sort out. The few miles of front on which I had been engaged during the last 20 hours were nothing compared with that long line of Germans advancing eastward from the Baltic to the Ukraine. In how many fields and woods and ditches were German soldiers dying, waiting for help that would not come—or that would be too late when it did arrive? Surely, I thought, the Army could have made better arrangements to deal with the hellish mix up of confusion, terror and despair that was left behind by the relentless forward march of our storm troops. The organization of the fighting troops and the paraphernalia of war seemed to have been worked out with amazing precision, but there appeared to have been a criminal disregard of the necessities behind the front-line troops. Surely it would even have been better to advance more slowly if it would have given us time to find and treat our wounded and bury our dead.

The regimental commander's field-car overtook Petermann and me as we rode along to catch up with the battalion again. *Oberst* Becker[28] sat in front alongside the driver, his adjutant in the back seat. I was determined to let Becker know what I felt about the disorganization behind the front-line troops and of the difficulties in attending the wounded. Usually the report to a commander was a stereotyped "Nothing special to report, sir." This time I had something to report. And I felt sure that *Oberst* Becker, strict disciplinarian that he was would be grateful to receive my report. His first concern was always for his soldiers, and I knew from Normandy that he held me in some regard—ever since the time he had noticed my habit of signing medical reports with an abbreviated "Hp." on the strength of which he had nicknamed me "*Haltepunkt*" (holding point). Nevertheless, I was pleased to hear him use my nickname when he stopped the car. "Hallo, *Haltepunkt*. How are things?" he asked, with a smile.

I saluted and reported: "Situation unsatisfactory in many instances, Herr *Oberst*. Information regarding locality of wounded men and their numbers is not always received. Officers and soldiers in the front-line show little interest in the wounded, and we get little or no cooperation from the fighting troops." Becker's eyebrows went up and his eyes steeled, but I was in full cry: "Wounded are spread over wide areas, therefore get little or no aid in many cases, Herr *Oberst*."

Becker glanced sharply at the automatic and at my sleeve. "Where is your Red Cross arm band?" he rapped out.

"I have removed it, Herr *Oberst*."

"Did you receive an order to that effect from higher authority?"

"No, Herr *Oberst*."

"Report to your divisional medical officer that you have discarded your arm band without authority." The *Oberst* cleared his throat, and continued: "Will you kindly refrain from criticizing the fighting troops and concentrate on carrying out your own duties? The care of the wounded is your responsibility; the fighting troops are no concern of yours. Kindly make a note of that." He barked an order to his driver and the car sped away.

I sat on my horse like a wet poodle, angry and completely deflated at the same time. Another rule of warfare had been added to my growing list—never to expect any help from the fighting troops. If, as in the case of the two men Stolze had lent me, any help was given, it must be accepted as an unexpected blessing. From that moment, I firmly resolved to build up my own system of care for the wounded and to become altogether independent. It was a good lesson, learned early, that was to serve me well.

Off the road to the right, an ambulance was standing beside a house. I went in, thinking my help might be needed, but found the doctor from the 1st Battalion already there and in control of the situation. He told me that three of our stretcher-bearers had been brutally shot down while attending to wounded during fighting around a concrete bunker near the frontier. My heart hardened further toward the enemy.

By now it was possible to ride for long stretches along the highway itself, which was emptying of troops as they prepared to snatch a short sleep. There were lights and a crowd of men around a shed, just off the road. Alongside the shed stood *Oberst* Becker's car. The sight of a goulash-cannon[29] drew me toward the group and the smell of soup made me realize how hungry I was.

"Well, *Haltepunkt*!" Becker hailed me. "Have you had anything to eat today?" He seemed to have forgotten completely the severe reprimand he had handed out an hour ago.

"No, Herr *Oberst*," I answered. My anger against the old warrior had evaporated.

"There's some excellent pea and beef soup. Come and try some. Real home cooking!" The thick soup from the huge iron pot was delicious and as I spooned it down I remembered what I had heard about the old *Oberst*. He always ate the same food as his men, but never collected his own food until he had first made sure that every man had been served. "Remember, *Haltepunkt*, a good meal keeps body and soul together," he was saying. "Never pass a goulash-cannon." He gave me time to finish my soup, then continued: "Do you know how far our division's reconnaissance troops have got today? To the Memel! The Memel has been reached, *Haltepunkt*! That means that on the first day we have penetrated 70 kilometers into enemy territory. Believe me, *Haltepunkt*, that is a wonderful achievement."

All the soldiers had been served and Becker's driver brought the old man a plate of soup and a big hunk of army bread. He broke off a piece and handed it to me. Between mouthfuls he carried on talking. "From your standpoint you think only of the wounded as being dispersed over wide areas—those were your words, weren't they?" His eyes twinkled as he glanced at me from under shaggy eyebrows. "Now from my standpoint, it's the fighting that really counts. Perhaps at the moment things aren't as nicely under control as we'd like them, but for the Russians it's catastrophic. Yes, I'm telling you, *Haltepunkt*, catastrophic!"

He bit off a piece of bread and wagged a finger at me. "Today's work will weaken the morale and will to fight of the enemy considerably. You'll see, tomorrow or the day after, the picture will be quite different. Then we shall be chasing on the Russians' heels as hard as we can go." He wiped his mouth with his handkerchief. "Yes, *Haltepunkt*, one's personal feelings are of little importance in war. That's a lesson that you young cubs must learn."

I swallowed a second cup of coffee, thanked and saluted the commander and rode off. It was two o'clock in the morning before I reached my battalion headquarters. Major Neuhoff called: "There you are at last! I couldn't have stood it any longer. For the last four hours *Unteroffizier* Meir has been following me about with a man who keeps his mouth wide open and can't shut it. For God's sake do something about him."

A man with his mouth wide agape was brought to me. Hillemanns and Lammerding, the Battalion *Ordonnanzoffizier*, stood by to watch what I would do. I was nonplussed; I had never come across a case like this before. The man's lower jaw had jumped forward out of its socket so that his mouth was a huge gaping hole in his agonized face. A moist and shivering tongue kept wagging, trying hopelessly to tell me something. I tried to work it out from anatomical first principles, and came to the conclusion that pressure would have to be applied against the stretched muscles of the underjaw to press forward and down and then snap the hinge-joint back into place. As it had come out, so it had to go back. I thought I knew what would happen theoretically, but whether it would work in practice remained to be seen. I wrapped two handkerchiefs around my thumbs.

"What's that for?" asked Neuhoff.

"Playing safe. I'd hate to have my thumbs between his teeth when his jaws snap shut."

I ordered the *Unteroffizier* to hold the man's head firmly against his stomach. He held him as if in a vice. The patient's eyes glanced at me suspiciously for a moment.

"Ready?" I asked him. He looked at me fearfully. I placed my thumb on the man's bottom teeth and pressed them as far backward as possible in order to get close to the hinge-joint. I took a deep breath and pressed forward and down with all my strength. The joint snapped back into its socket. The operation had been simpler than I expected. The patient opened and closed his mouth two or three times experimentally.

"Good," I said. "Now be careful in future not to open your mouth too wide. Soldiers should keep their mouths shut. Understand?"

"*Jawohl*, Herr *Assistenzarzt*," he said tentatively.

"How did things go back there?" Neuhoff asked me.

"Nothing special to report," I said. I had learned my lesson.

We joined the rest of the men in the shelter of a wood just as my ambulance with Wegener and Dehorn turned up. They had been working flat-out for 24 hours. It was now 3 a.m. I refilled my medical bag and crept into the small H.Q. tent with Neuhoff, Hillemanns and Lammerding. In a matter of seconds we all sank into a deep dreamless sleep for one and a half hours.[30]

Orders for Execution

ON THE WIDE, SANDY ROAD WE CONTINUED OUR STEADY MARCH TOWARD THE RIVER Memel.[31] The hour and a half's sleep had done more harm than good. It had not been easy to awaken the dog-tired men. Our bones were cold, muscles stiff and painful and our feet were swollen. We pulled on our field-boots only with great difficulty. A signal had arrived just before we broke camp. It came from German High Command and was in Hitler's name and it gave us something to discuss as the sun came up.

"All Russian commissars are to be shot on capture," said the order.[32] Neuhoff's face was serious and a little bewildered as he told us the news; he impressed on us that we were not to communicate the dispatch to the troops—it was secret information for officers only. The order went on to say that during the first day's fighting a large number of captured German soldiers had been cold-bloodedly shot in the neck on the orders of the Red commissars. Ambulance men and helplessly wounded soldiers had also been butchered. Conclusive proof of responsibility had been traced to the commissars.

Kageneck, Stolze and I discussed the order as we rode along. "To hell with shooting down a defenseless person, even if he is a criminal," declared Kageneck. "In any case, it's bad policy. You can't keep a thing like that secret, and what happens when the Russians get to know of it? The commissars will resist us to the bitter end, because they'll know they can't save their skins by surrendering. And look at the propaganda the Reds will get out of it!"

"Every man has a right to be tried as an individual," I put in. "What do you think, Stolze?"

Stolze frowned and considered carefully before answering. "As far as I'm concerned, I won't order anyone to be shot in cold blood. Anyway, I can't tell the difference between a commissar and a Red Army officer, and I'm not going to bother learning the difference. You can keep my opinion between the three of us."

There was no need for Stolze to worry about his opinion becoming known. Practically every officer in the battalion was of the same mind, and not a single captured commissar was shot on our orders. Most of them were found dead—either killed in battle or shot by their own hand to avoid capture. The few whom we took alive were sent back and soon lost their identity in the growing stream of prisoners. But we were to learn to our cost the power wielded by these fanatical Reds. Everywhere that we struck particularly bitter resistance we found a commissar. Every now and then our planes would drop illustrated pamphlets over the Russian lines calling on the soldiers to kill their commissars and surrender. And it often seemed that this propaganda was effective; time and again it was found that groups of Red soldiers had killed their commissars, who were usually hated men, before surrendering themselves.

The Memel bridge had fallen intact into our hands.[33] Under cover of a river mist, our pioneers had crossed the Memel in barges to thwart the enemy's attempt to blow up the bridge and von Boeselager's cavalry squadron had galloped across and secured the bridge-head on the opposite bank. Advance detachments of Höke's 2nd Battalion had reached the Memel and our artillery was at the moment sharply engaging a Russian battery.

We looked at our maps. The Memel made a large bend through densely-wooded country. "Not so bad," remarked Neuhoff with satisfaction. "In three hours we should be there ourselves."

But a special divisional order put an end to that line of thought! "3rd Battalion, Infantry Regiment 18, is to clear the wooded area south of the road to the Memel."[34]

We soon found the reason for the order. Two dispatch riders on the Kalvaria-Memel road had been shot down and a motor ambulance had been attacked by the Russians early that morning. Commands were shouted down the column and the battalion halted for a few minutes. With many curses the men of Stolze's 10th and Kramer's 11th Companies took up position in extended order along about four miles of the road. A distance of 15 paces separated each man in the human chain. They advanced through valley, hillside and thicket in open order so that every Russian would be flushed out of the sector.

The 9th Company under *Oberleutnant* Tietjen remained in reserve and every man lay down to snatch some sleep. I prepared my provisional first-aid post near Neuhoff's battle post and had everything ready in case there should be any fighting. Then I spread out a blanket in the morning sun and lay down to rest. Hillemanns was busy as usual with messages, dispatches and other correspondence. Major Neuhoff sat on a boulder, silently staring ahead. Turning toward us, but half-talking to himself, he said: "Major Höke's 2nd Battalion is already marching over the Memel bridge. And once again we're landed with the job of combing through 40 square miles of God-forsaken country, playing hide-and-seek with a handful of damned Russians. At the best it will be late afternoon before my lads get back. They'll be dog-tired, but we shall have to march till late at night catching up with the others. Two days of war, and two days we've had to sweep up enemy riff-raff."

"Yes," I consoled him, "but someone has to do these special jobs."

"Special jobs be damned!" exploded Neuhoff. "You mean clearing up the bloody mess left by the others."

The first four prisoners captured in the woods by our men were brought in. Three were dressed in civilian clothing,[35] but the closely-cropped hair gave them away as soldiers. Two of them were Mongolians and glared at us strangely through slit eyes. While Neuhoff was sitting on his boulder eyeing the Russians curiously, we learned that one of the dispatch riders shot down at dawn had been *Gefreiter* Belzer of our battalion. His pockets had been emptied and his dispatches taken. Neuhoff's mouth contracted to a thin line. "Murdered and robbed," he whispered, never for a moment removing his gaze from the Russian prisoners. "One of my men murdered and robbed. This man"—he jerked his head at the uniformed Russian—"send him back to the prisoners' assembly area." He turned his cold eyes on the three in civilian dress. "These three hedge-snipers, these damned street robbers, I'll have them executed at once." He called for an NCO and six men from the 9th Company. The firing squad came to attention in front of him.

Nobody else moved or uttered a word and Neuhoff turned to Hillemanns and asked: "What do you think about it?"

"As you ordered, Herr Major," replied Hillemanns, as always correctly dutiful.

I looked closely at the three prisoners, who had clearly not understood a word of the conversation and were unaware that their fate was in the balance. The prisoner nearest to me was a slight lad, about 18 years old. His civilian clothes hung on him loosely. He returned my look with frank and bewildered eyes. He did not look a *franc tireur*, I could not believe he was. He had almost certainly got into civilian clothes with the idea of losing himself among the Lithuanian population and avoiding capture.

Neuhoff was clearly needing more moral support than Hillemanns's obedient reply had given him. More bolstering than Hitler's recent orders had supplied. This was a new kind of warfare to the old soldier, who had hitherto played the game of war according to the rules. He wanted someone else to agree with his grave judgment. "Is it not so, Doktor, that we must make short work of these murderous thugs?" he inquired.

I could feel only pity for these ragged creatures standing in front of us, so helpless and forlorn. "I really don't know, Herr Major," I replied. "Are you quite sure that these men are snipers in civilian clothes? If Herr Major can find anything in the way of weapons or incriminating documents on them, then their death is warranted by military law. If not, I'd let the miserable devils go rather than burden my conscience."

Neuhoff looked at me challengingly. I looked him in the eyes and saw doubts appear. "Search them," he ordered.

Identity cards, a few pieces of dry bread and a handful of dry tobacco were all their pockets contained.

"Send the damned rabble back to the prisoners' assembly area," Neuhoff ordered harshly. He swung on his heel without another glance at me, but I knew that he was relieved, that he had shrunk from exercising the death sentence. He inspected the horses and made sure they had been properly fed and watered. He patted the neck of his own brown gelding and gave him a lump of sugar.

"Now I'll have to rewrite my report to the regiment," said Hillemanns angrily. He was being kept busy, while my hands were idle for a while. Dehorn was checking my medical bag, while Müller who could never be without work, was cleaning and oiling my automatic. I had sent Wegener back with my Mercedes to look for my medical wagon, which had not yet caught up with us.

The sun climbed in the sky and I lay down in the shade of an elm tree and gazed through its fretwork of branches at the white clouds.

*   *   *

My thoughts wandered and turned to Fritz; I wondered if he had been buried yet, buried like Stock, with the simple birch cross as his only memorial. Fritz, the young Nazi, enthusiastic, but not fanatical; Fritz, for whom a day was too small a compass to hold his energies, a lifetime a confining cell for his ambitions, the war a great and gay adventure. That was how he had been when I had first met him.

"*Köln Hauptbahnhof!*" The loudspeakers had flung the voice around the steaming vault of Cologne Main station on that afternoon in early November 1940. "*Köln Hauptbahnhof!*" The voice had echoed through the explosive hiss of steam from a locomotive, an unnecessary echo, for the soldiers who spilled out of the arriving train could see the name everywhere—on the walls, on the bridges, on the seats, on the electric lights. In England, we had heard, all station name-boards had been removed, even the roads were unsignposted now—it would confuse us, the English people thought, when we invaded their island. We had no need to resort to such subterfuges and invasion of the Fatherland was out of the question. France was finished, the Maginot Line breached with unimagined ease and the Englishmen thrown off the Continent—by many of these men and lads in field-gray uniform who had turned Cologne Station into a crossroads for the *Wehrmacht*. Our Army now stood poised on the northern coast of France, gazing across the narrow Channel toward its next objective, England. And it was to be the personal objective of the five *Unterärzte* who were claiming their kit from the luggage counter.

We had said good-bye to Germany in student fashion—with five bottles of Liebfraumilch on a terrace overlooking the Rhine—and now made for the train that would take us on the first stage of our journey to Granville, Normandy. Our inner *Schweinhund* were troubling us again. It was a pity, because several *Feldwebels* in the early part of our military training had gone to endless trouble to eliminate them. "Personality!" I remembered one *Feldwebel* shouting, "So you think you've all got personalities. You're wrong— you've each got an inner *Schweinhund*. And the *Wehrmacht* doesn't approve of men with inner *Schweinhund*. It's my job to get rid of them and make you good grenadiers." So we had learned to shoot rifles in July and August 1939.[36] The war with France and England had found us learning how to dig field latrines and throw a grenade. The fighting in

France began and we had learned how to apply a field-dressing, administer a bed pan and ride a horse. Then the *Wehrmacht* had remembered that somewhere back along the line we had also been fairly competent civilian doctors and we were handed back our stethoscopes and scalpels. But just to prevent that inner *Schweinhund* taking control again, the Army kept us in a state of suspended military animation as *Unterärzte*. And as "cadet-doctors" we ranked somewhere between a *Landser* and an officer, entitled to a salute from an ordinary soldier, but compelled on our part to salute everything from a general to a letter-box. . . .

* * *

We gave our inner *Schweinhund* a last royal fling in Paris. With fine disregard for our responsibilities, we stayed there for a day and a night before pursuing our cheerful way across Northern France, stopping for another night at Le Mans. The Divisional Medical Officer at Granville brought us down to earth and in a few well-chosen words left us in no doubt that we were now in an active theatre of war.

We were split up and posted to different battalions, and as the staff car took me through the leafless apple orchards of the Calvados region, I fell to wondering about the men with whom I should fight the real war. We should be a closely-knit group, which only mutual trust could weld together. I had a fair amount of confidence in myself as a doctor, rather less as a soldier; I hoped that my new comrades would make allowances for me.

But Major Neuhoff had been unimpressed by his new *Unterarzt*. He had looked me up and down and I had returned his gaze with a fair amount of interest. The late arrival of the new doctor for 3rd Battalion, Infantry Regiment 18, passed without comment from Neuhoff, but he had remarked on the lamentable fact that I had no front-line experience. Perhaps, he suggested, that could be remedied on the other side of the Channel. Did I, by any chance, play *Skat* or *Doppelkopf*? I did? Then I could at least do something; my presence at the card table would be appreciated after dinner that night. *Leutnant* Hillemanns, the battalion adjutant, would show me to my room.

Hillemanns's manner was as wintry as the November sunshine, and I reflected on the words of *Oberstabsarzt* Schulze, the officer commanding the 6th Infantry Division's Medical Company: "In case you are not aware of it, you have been appointed medical officer to one of the three battalions of General von Rundstedt's most élite regiment. Herr *Oberst* Becker will be your regimental commander—he is an outstanding officer with an exceptional combat record in the first war as well as in this war. Congratulations!" I hoped that my troublesome inner *Schweinhund* would attune itself to the demands of a crack regiment. There had seemed to be the slightest twinkle in Neuhoff's eye in spite of his gruff manner, and perhaps this Adjutant Hillemanns would prove to be human, although while he was showing me around the deserted mess his manner was very, very correct. The 3rd Battalion had commandeered part of the main hotel in the little town of Littry la Mine; our mess was on the ground floor and the bedroom to which Hillemanns showed me was in another wing of the hotel. He instructed an *Unteroffizier* to take me to the medical quarters. . . .

Three soldiers sprang stiffly to attention when I entered the old villa which was to be my first hospital. *Unteroffizier* Wegener talked a lot and obviously sought to impress by playing the part of the seasoned campaigner. *Gefreiter* Müller said nothing. He was a strapping and likeable young man, very blond, and I soon found that he did nearly all the real work. Dehorn, the third man, was a dark-eyed, wide-awake little man who had only recently arrived with a fresh draft from Germany. He was from my home town, Duisburg, and I at once made him my personal medical orderly and batman on the strength of it. Wegener was visibly pleased that I had not taken his willing horse Müller. Dehorn proved to be unusually handy and seemed to have the gift of discerning my wishes at a glance. After he had put all my possessions away, with a few of my favorite books lying handy and Martha's picture in a prominent place on the dressing-table, I dismissed him. A parcel of shoes and other oddments that I had bought for Martha in Le Mans was still in my bag. I had been unable to find anybody to take it back to Germany for me, although at this time many soldiers who had served through the French campaign were going on leave. Everyone had thought that the *Wehrmacht*'s sweep through France to the Channel coast would be followed almost immediately by invasion of England. The barges, the tugs, the motorboats and the fishing boats were congregated in the harbors of Northern France. Operation "Sealion" had been rehearsed until every German soldier was word-perfect in his part, but the curtain would not rise on the next act. . . .

*   *   *

I had turned up for mess punctually at 6:30 that evening and Hillemanns had introduced me to the battalion officers. *Oberleutnant* Graf von Kageneck, who commanded the battalion's 12th Company, bade me a friendly welcome.[37] He had chiseled aristocratic features and a faint smile hovered around his mouth. I took to him immediately. *Oberleutnant* Stolze was cast in an entirely different mold and greeted me boisterously. He was a great good-humored giant, with the physique and assurance of a bull and a hearty laugh that rang out loud and often in the mess. His guffaw would usually be accompanied by a friendly pat on the shoulder of his companion that would almost bring the poor man to his knees. Stolze commanded 10th Company; I gathered that his troops loved him to a man and would follow him through fire and flood. In direct contrast, the Battalion *Ordonnanzoffizier*, *Leutnant* Lammerding, relied on a quick wit and a ready tongue to hold his own in the battalion. Sarcasm and irony were his two weapons, and only Kageneck with his quick repartee seemed capable of countering them. But Lammerding's sarcastic tongue lashed only those who were in a position to defend themselves, he was never malicious, and his insouciance, as is often the case, masked ice-cold courage. The two other company commanders, *Hauptmann* Noack of 9th Company and *Oberleutnant* Kramer of 11th Company did not share the mess as they were stationed some distance from Littry.

It did not take me long to discover that an *Unterarzt* with no front-line experience counted for very little in the 3rd Battalion. Apart from Major Neuhoff, I was the only officer in the battalion entitled to a car and nominally I had a Mercedes at my disposal. However, I was never able to use it, for it had been commandeered by Hillemanns and Lammerding for headquarters' use. And I fared no better in the matter of a horse; Westwall came into my life. He was undoubtedly the worst nag in the battalion—Don Quixote's steed would have sniffed at him in disdain—and yet I had more traveling to do than any officer in the battalion. Occasionally, by working myself into a frenzy, I managed to induce this overgrown cart horse to break into a gallop and immediately I became the center of attraction. My success then depended on my ability to look as foolish as my horse—only then did we appear to be acting in unity. Neuhoff made it quite clear that he expected little from his *Unterarzt* except that he should make a fourth for *Doppelkopf*— and a long losing streak earned me little regard in that direction. At 31, I was the oldest officer in the battalion, with the exception of Neuhoff and *Oberleutnant* Kramer, but my nebulous rank made me the most junior member of the mess.

An inspection one day by the regimental commander, *Oberst* Becker, did nothing to bolster my morale. Becker was a soldierly figure, in spite of his 50 years and the first-war wound, which caused his left arm to hang stiffly at his side. And his eyes missed nothing. He took me to task for saluting with the battalion officers, when as an *Unterarzt* I was not entitled to salute. But at the mess dinner that evening he went out of his way to chat with me about my work and had jocularly nicknamed me "*Haltepunkt.*"

By degrees Neuhoff came to accept me, as a *Doppelkopf* player and as a doctor. From across the card table and from conversation with Lammerding I was able to form a picture of his character. He had risen from the ranks of the old *Reichswehr*[38] to his present rank and post, but had apparently reached the limit of his military capabilities. His mind ran in a groove that his army boots had worn with the years and he found himself out of his depth in some aspects of modern warfare. As a result of a light but chronic inflammation of the tear ducts, his eyes were inclined to be watery and Lammerding had nicknamed him "Major Teardrops."

Hillemanns, like his commander, had risen from the ranks, but he was very ambitious. He was 100 percent thorough, almost to the point of pedantry toward himself as well as toward his subordinates. His field boots always shone like glass—even five minutes after returning from a route march through muddy November fields. His hair was carefully parted and never cut in other than exact army-approved style. What he lacked in individuality and personal charm he made up with meticulous knowledge of rules and regulations and in soldierly bearing.

Leutnant Stock, one of the youngest officers in the battalion, had filled in a good many details for me. He was a likeable boy of 21, sensitive, and a brilliant pianist; he was almost pathetically grateful to find someone with whom he could discuss music, having been rather cold-shouldered in the mess on account of his youth. Lammerding, Stock told me, rarely joined in political discussions. He had gone straight from school to a military academy, but was said to have provoked something of a crisis in his home by refusing to join the Nazi Party, although his brother was a high-ranking SS leader. He showed little respect for anyone, even Neuhoff, but was a thoroughly efficient officer, upon whom the commander leaned heavily. *Oberleutnant Graf* von Kageneck took life equally light-heartedly. He belonged to an old aristocratic family, his father was a respected general from the First World War, and his four brothers were all officers of outstanding merit. One of his ancestors was Prince Metternich, and Kageneck was married to the Princess of Bavaria. Young Stock was a shrewd observer and I was sorry when he was attached to Kramer's 11th Company, stationed away from Littry. . . .

* * *

November gave way to December and still the invasion exercises continued along our stretch of coastline to the east of the Cherbourg Peninsula. Our troops were trained to the minute and, following their sweeping victories in France, were in great fighting heart. We were under no illusions that the brunt of the fighting would have to be borne by the infantry once a foothold was established on English soil. The transport of tanks and artillery across the Channel would present problems, and it was more than likely that we should be able to count on their help only when the fighting in England was well underway. Undoubtedly the *Wehrmacht's* greatest strength lay in the infantry and the way that every platoon of every company had been trained as an independent fighting unit, which would land on the English beaches absolutely self-sufficient. Supplies would have to be brought over later, but during the first few days we were sure that we could win the major victory—that of firmly establishing ourselves on enemy soil. And the knowledge that the Ninth and Sixteenth Armies, which lay superbly equipped along the French coast, would outnumber the defenders by 10 to one encouraged our belief that we could withstand substantial losses and still meet the remnants of the British Army on more than favorable terms. Even the news that the English were preparing to use burning oil on the sea against the invader did not discourage us, nor did the scattered bombing raids of the Royal Air Force (RAF), which sank some ships of our invasion fleet as they lay in harbors and inlets along the coastline. The bombing was confined to the ports within easier reach of England than was our sector, and the only aerial visitors we entertained were the flocks of seagulls which wheeled inland as the skies darkened and the winter seas flung themselves at the coast. It was now too late in the year for "Sealion" to be launched and we surmised that the assault on England would take place in January or February, depending on weather, wind and tide. . . .[39]

The German Army prepared for the first Christmas it would spend in France for 25 years. Men were sent on leave, and I arranged for Dehorn to spend Christmas with his wife. He set off happily, laden like a Christmas tree with presents for his own family, for Martha and for the families of Wegener and Müller.

Kageneck had taken it on himself to supply the mess with a Christmas roast, and to this end invited me to join him on a stag-hunt in the Forest of Balleroy. It served only as a spur to his devil-may-care nature that hunting in the forest was strictly reserved for the General Commanding and his personal guests. We encountered an artillery major on a similar poaching expedition in the forest, but Kageneck out-bluffed him, so that the major counted himself lucky to get away with a friendly warning. And, unwittingly, in blundering his way out through the thickets, he sprang a fine stag for us. We accepted the Christmas roast as the personal gift of our unapproachable superior, the General Commanding.[40]

Thick snow fell a couple of days before Christmas, and the battalion held a traditional Christmas Eve dinner in the mess, but I could not get into a party mood—there had been no letter from Martha. Kageneck, Stolze and the others went off after dinner to celebrate with their companies, and Lammerding and I found ourselves wandering through the snow-carpeted streets of Littry. Music drew us to a small café, where a party of townsfolk were at the height of their revelry, although it was past curfew time. Lammerding assured the anxious proprietor that he could have an extension of time and we settled back at our table with a bottle of wine to watch the dancing, which was becoming wilder and wilder. A dark-haired French woman snatched Lammerding's cap from the table as she danced past, and mockingly flaunted it as she danced her tango. But an explosive situation developed when the woman's husband roughly seized the cap, threw it back at Lammerding and then faced him challengingly. Tight-lipped and white-faced, Lammerding was on his feet immediately, his pistol in his hand. The music stopped and there was a tense silence as every eye watched Lammerding. Urgently, I whispered to him to take up the matter the following day, when the Frenchman was sober, and the innkeeper undertook to ensure that the man presented himself at our battalion headquarters in the morning. Next day the Frenchman apologized to Lammerding for his insult to the *Wehrmacht* uniform.[41]

On 31 December my Christmas mail arrived, and I decided to spend New Year's Eve alone with Martha's letters. Müller, who was acting as my orderly while Dehorn was away, made a fire of fragrant pine logs, and from my Christmas parcel, I put Martha's miniature Christmas tree with its tiny candles on the table and stacked her presents around it. The honey-scented Advent candle gave me enough light by which to read her letters and a few fresh twigs of pine on the fire gave off the scent I had loved as a child.

Another Christmas Eve spent with Martha, when she visited my family, came back to me, and I remembered her pure voice as she sang Christmas carols. It had been only a few months earlier that I had first seen her, singing the part of Margarethe in *Faust* on the stage of the Duisburg Opera House. The young doctor from the Kaiser Wilhelm Hospital had slipped into a seat in the stalls whenever he had a night off duty from the accident ward. And I had been enthralled by the delicacy of her Butterfly,[42] the poignancy of her Mimi and the fire of her Carmen. Her artistry compelled my admiration, and when I met her, her sincerity had confirmed my love. But soon I had gone into the Army, so we had not become engaged. Unwillingly, my thoughts came back into the room at Littry.

Outside it was wintry, cold and wet; thick snow still covered the rooftops, but it was turning to slush in the streets. A raw, damp wind blew in from the Channel and the long icicles hanging from the eaves started to thaw. The New Year, 1941, stole quietly in to the sound of small avalanches of snow slipping from the roof. . . .

Slowly the battalion came to accept the *Unterarzt* with no front-line service. Neuhoff left the running of the sick-bay entirely in my hands, and I even managed to get hold of a presentable horse, after I had issued an ultimatum to Hillemanns. Lump was given to me. His best years lay well behind him, he had a hard mouth and at a trot he was anything but comfortable, but he had spirit and preferred a rousing gallop to a walk. When accompanied by other horsemen he was difficult to hold, for he insisted on being in the lead. Lump was Major Höke's old charger and was accustomed to being ridden at the front; life at the rear under a mere *Unterarzt* did not agree with him. Westwall was now degraded to his true calling in life; he was put between the shafts of the ambulance wagon. The final nod of approval of my position in the battalion came from *Oberst* Becker, who told me that he had recommended me for promotion to *Assistenzarzt*. The *Oberst's* accolade came at the end of a "surprise" 7 a.m. inspection—about which, fortunately, Kageneck had tipped me off. I knew that the inspection was as a result of complaints by *Hauptmann* Noack, our 9th Company's commander, with whom I had disagreed on our first meeting. However, through the intercession of Kageneck and Stolze, Noack and I had reconciled our differences, and shortly after that he was transferred to the command of the regiment's 14th Anti-Tank Company.[43] His place as commander of 9th Company was taken by *Oberleutnant* Tietjen, an efficient little man who was determined to make good in military life. He kept his troops on their toes and asked me to lecture them on first aid and field hygiene. Tietjen was a friendly chap, but I always felt that he attended a mess function as another, though not unpleasant, duty to be performed, and excused himself as soon as was decently possible so that he could return to his company affairs.

Noack, too, I found out, was a good comrade and a fine soldier; I wrote off our first unpleasant meeting as part of my settling-in procedure with the battalion. But *Oberleutnant* Kramer, the commander of 11th Company, was a man with whom I could never have been friendly, and my dislike of him was shared by the other battalion officers. One sunny day in late January, Stolze and I were out riding and decided to pay Kramer a visit. He had quartered his company in a huge château about five miles from Littry, where he lived like a feudal lord. "Château Kramer," Stolze called it; the place was a monument to Kramer's inferiority complex, which stemmed from the fact that he had risen from the ranks.

It was a striking contrast to call on our way back at the house in which Stolze's company was quartered. In 10th Company there was willing discipline, engendered by boundless respect and affection for their genial commander. Stolze was lucky, too, in having as his senior NCO *Oberfeldwebel* Schnittger, the best NCO in the battalion. We found him supervising the cooking of a pot roast of pigeons, which he had bought in the market. Two healthy blond lads, identical twins, were the cooks. They apparently extracted the maximum amount of enjoyment from the confusion they caused among the belles of Littry. The market, Schnittger told us, had been swamped with pigeons following a *Wehrmacht* order to massacre every pigeon in Normandy. The French had been sending messages across the Channel by carrier-pigeon, but the townsfolk had been up in arms when the Army's executioners, overzealous or with too scanty a knowledge of ornithology, had also wrung the necks of every pouter pigeon and dove in the town. . . .

January and February had slipped by and spring had come to Normandy, but it had brought us no new weapons—which a persistent rumor said were being awaited before the invasion would take place. All it brought were further crops of rumors and a commando raid by the British. News of the raid leaked out, although the *Wehrmacht* had tried to keep it secret. A small group of Englishmen had landed near Grandcamp, where our division's invasion boats were waiting, had crept up to a radar station on the cliffs and, without firing a shot, had made the entire garrison prisoner. They had taken the radar set—which was on the highly secret list—to pieces and had taken all the pieces away with them. To rub salt in the wound, they had taken along with them, also undamaged, the radar unit's cook.

The commando raid was not without its psychological effect on us, particularly as our troops were keyed to a high pitch of impatience at the monotony of the daily routine exercises. At last we thought the order for "Sealion" had come. Neuhoff called all his officers together in the mess. Instead he dropped a bombshell. The invasion of England had been indefinitely postponed and we were to prepare for a long move. Our objective, even our theater of action, was at present unknown. We were under secret orders.

By night we left Littry, and for several weary days our train ground its way eastward across France and Germany, by-passing the big towns, often shunted into out-of-the-way sidings for two hours at a time.[44] We had sweated while packing our stores and equipment in Normandy's early spring, and we traveled into deep winter. At Allenstein thick snow still lay on the ground, the wind bit frostily and the East Prussian lakes were bound in ice. We left the train and marched eastward through the winter weather, every night without a break. In the daytime we slept in haystacks, barns and houses that the countryfolk placed at our disposal. We were being toughened up for what lay ahead.

A new word took the place of "Sealion" in our conversation—"Barbarossa." It fitted in well with this lonely frontier land of Germany, the land of Teutonic knights and guardians against the east. We marched to Filipovo in the Polish Suwalki region,[45] only 12 miles from the negotiated Russian frontier. And we trained for war against the east, a war that would be fought on a vast scale against spaces and masses. 170 divisions, it was rumored, were being marshalled against Russia—more than three million men.[46] As we marched to our frontier positions, the meaning of "Barbarossa" had come home to us. . . .

*   *   *

"May I bring Herrn *Assistenzarzt* something to eat?" Dehorn was standing beside me, looking down at me. I jerked out of my reverie and nodded. Müller, I noticed, had finished

29

cleaning my automatic and was now busily sorting bandages. Neuhoff and Hillemanns were chatting as they ate a meal, and Dehorn carefully picked his way over to me carrying a brimming plateful of goulash and peas.

One of our dispatch riders pedaled up on his bicycle. Our companies had reached the Memel on a full front and nine more prisoners had been taken; 200 or 300 Russians had got away by swimming across the river, but had abandoned their arms and equipment.

"A thankless job and not much to show for it," commented Neuhoff. "I imagine our men will rest for an hour and arrive back here between four and five o'clock. See to it, Hillemanns, that the food is good, plenty of it, and that coffee is waiting for them."

We waited for the troops to return. As far as the dispatch rider knew there would be no work for me. He was wrong. There was plenty.

There were no battle wounds, but nearly every man had bathed his burning feet in the river before marching back, and a great many of the men had blistered and swollen feet as a result. I had an instruction inserted in battalion orders: "All soldiers are strictly forbidden to wash or bathe their feet unless it is reasonably certain that there will be no marching within the next 24 hours. Instead of washing and bathing, it is recommended that the feet be rubbed with dripping or deer fat. Supplies are procurable from *Unteroffizier* Wegener and are to be drawn upon by all companies." It seemed to me that 800 men with stinking feet were preferable to 800 men with blisters for treatment.

CHAPTER 4

The Long March

THE MEMEL LAY 25 MILES BEHIND US AND THE MIDDAY SUN BEAT MERCILESSLY DOWN on the marching columns. With dry, cracked lips, red eyes and dust-covered faces, the men marched eastward with only one wish—to lie down for a few hours' sleep. But the march continued relentlessly over roads and tracks, through woods and open fields.[47]

Our shock troops—the cavalry squadrons and the bicycle detachments—were far ahead of us. They secured the road for us and clung tenaciously to the heels of the retreating enemy, who in our sector was fighting back with steady delaying tactics. But as we marched through roadside villages there was a new spirit abroad. We sensed the change from the first two days, when the streets were empty as we tramped through ghost villages. Today, big numbers of Lithuanians lined the road as we marched past. Here and there a green and yellow flag fluttered lazily in the mild breeze. The Lithuanians now believed in a German victory and their flags symbolized a new Lithuanian liberty. Some of the villagers threw cigarettes to the soldiers or handed them mugs of water and loaves of freshly baked bread.[48] One could see from the eager hope in their eyes that they gave of their meager possessions gladly, strong in the belief that the Russians would never return.

Shortly after noon we rested for a couple of hours in the shade of a wood. The men, using their gas masks, a boulder or an outstretched arm for a pillow, fell asleep instantly. My work started at every halt. Always, the queue at my dressing station brought another crop of sore and blistered feet. Today, there were also several cases of heat exhaustion and I gave injections against heat stroke. Polluted water was another hazard and until tea could be prepared by the field-kitchen I rationed out filtered water from the apparatus that we carried. The men had all been injected several times against typhus, para-typhus and dysentery, but I was taking no chances. It was a standing instruction that no man should drink water that had not been boiled or filtered.

But you cannot stop a thirsty soldier with a throatful of dust from drinking the first water he sees—not by merely issuing a battalion order, anyway. Müller solved the problem for me. One morning a number of capsules had been found near a well. I tested them and

31

found them to be harmless but the rumor got around that they were poison capsules with which the Russians were poisoning all the wells.[49] I did not bother to deny the rumor. At the evening halt Müller and Dehorn triumphantly escorted six crestfallen soldiers to me, who admitted having drunk from the "poisoned" well. One of them was Semmelmeyer, a great humorist who was also the assistant cook, and therefore had less excuse than the others.

"How did you catch them?" I asked Müller.

"Quite simple, Herr *Assistenzarzt*. I told all the men that by treatment we could save the lives of any men who had drunk from the well—otherwise they'd probably die."

"And what are we to do with them now? You're the doctor."

"Why not pump their stomachs and dose them with castor oil?" suggested Müller. Dehorn laughed.

"You're a hard doctor, Müller. I think they're too tired for stomach pumping, but we'll give them three spoonfuls of active animal charcoal and a good spoonful of castor oil. It won't do them any harm and it will teach them a lesson."

Next morning 18 more worried men reported to Müller and asked him for doses of charcoal and castor oil. After that, the only complaints came from the kitchen bulls, who were kept at full stretch every halt providing tea and coffee for the men.

Mile after mile we marched, by-passing Grodno and heading toward Lida. Russian aircraft flew overhead, probably making for the Memel bridge behind us. Flak dotted the sky with white puffs, but the marching men had no eyes for something which was not their war. Each man's war at this stage was circumscribed by the next few steps he would take, the hardness of the road, the soreness of his feet, the dryness of his tongue and the weight of his equipment. Beckoning him on was the thought of the next halt. Just to stop, to have no need to put one foot in front of the other for a few hours, was the dream of every man. There was no singing, no joking, no talking that was not strictly necessary. The column marched in silence. Occasionally, a foray into the surrounding fields was necessary. It was carried out punctiliously, but it was discipline, not enthusiasm, that now bore us along.

The red sun sank slowly through the dense clouds of dust that we left in our wake. And into the darkness our march continued. We wished that the Russians would make a stand—anything, a battle even, to relieve the painful monotony of this ceaseless, timeless tramping. It was 11 p.m. before a halt was called at a big farmhouse. We had covered close on 40 miles that day!

An hour later a regimental dispatch rider arrived with a message that the following day would be a rest day for the battalion. Many men were already asleep, but those who were awake greeted the news with cheers. The cheers failed to disturb their sleeping comrades.

*　　*　　*

The pretty milkmaid on her way to the cowshed was greeted with a chorus of shouts and whistles by the men who were bathing naked in the pond by the farmhouse. The men's thoughts were running along more normal channels again after a good night's sleep—and the milkmaid did not seem uninterested. Those who were not in the pond—I had relaxed my order about getting feet wet as there would be no marching today—were stripped to the waist and barefoot, washing their bodies, their socks and bandages, or mending their clothes. Everyone was in high spirits.

The distant rumble of gunfire still continued; it seemed no farther away than the previous night and I was uneasy. It was Kageneck who found out later in the day that two entire Russian armies were encircled at Belostok and for two days had been fighting desperately to break out of the steel ring. The firing came from the beleaguered fortress of Grodno.

A line of men with well-washed feet was awaiting examination and treatment. And at last I could give them the attention they needed; for once there was no hurry. I iodized the small blisters and applied protective plasters, disinfected and punctured large blisters, removed the skin of suppurating blisters and covered the wounds with thin bandages so that the patient could still wear boots. Never had I cut and removed so much skin in one day. Only a few cases had to be sent back to the Medical Company; there was a small number of other cases, including dysentery—I suspected they had been drinking contaminated water. One man had been thrown from his horse and two others were suffering from acute inflammation of the eyes, caused by hours of marching through the dust. On the whole, though, the men had stood up well to the first three grueling days of the campaign. I considered it my responsibility to present Neuhoff with a battalion of fit men when the fighting really started; we could not afford wastage at this stage.

Stolze, bare to the waist, was passing the afternoon sitting on a bundle of hay eating fried potatoes when a Lithuanian peasant ran through the farmyard gesticulating wildly. "Komm!" bellowed Stolze and beckoned the peasant over to us. We could not understand a word the Lithuanian was saying except his repeated "Russke." He kept pointing to the edge of a wood about 200 yards away.

"Russians in the wood," I said.

"Can't be many, anyhow," Stolze muttered through a mouthful of potato. He grabbed his automatic pistol, stuffed a few hand grenades into his trousers pockets, and, still stripped to the waist, gathered 10 of his men and walked toward the wood. After about 10 minutes he reappeared, waving cheerily and pushing in front of him three prisoners—a Russian officer and two soldiers.

The prisoners were interrogated in the living room with the large fireplace. Lammerding recorded the proceedings. An interpreter with a sketchy knowledge of Russian battled through somehow and managed to get from the three men the main information we wanted.

Our attack on the Russians on 22 June had caught the men sleeping in a concrete bunker at the frontier. They had no idea that we were at war with them, but when our Pak[50] shells started hammering the walls of their bunker they had determined to make a fight of it. But our troops gave them no opportunity to be heroes. Column after column of German troops simply by-passed them into Russian territory and they realized that further resistance at that point would be futile and that they would be lost if they stayed on. During the night, the small garrison had slipped out of the bunker with the intention of regaining the Russian lines and when Stolze had captured them they had been wandering about at random for four days. They were now exhausted and desperately hungry, had no idea of their whereabouts or of the situation, and their capture now seemed a matter of indifference to them. The main point of interest that had emerged from the interrogation was that the Red Army had been quite unprepared for our attack on 22 June.[51] In our section at any rate, we had attacked what was virtually a sleeping army.

Wegener returned in the Mercedes and brought with him a young *Leutnant* who had been posted to the battalion to replace the fallen Stock. His name was Bolski and inevitably, behind his back, he was referred to as "Polski," a nickname that infuriated him, because, although he originated from the Baltic, he hated the Russians and Poles like the plague. And his hatred extended to the English, although he had an English grandmother. He seemed to be driven by some inner compensatory urge to stress on every possible occasion that he was a German from East Prussia. Neuhoff posted him to 12th Company, under the wing of Kageneck. And with Kageneck, who was 100 percent blue-blooded German, he tried even harder to convince himself and anyone who was willing to listen that he was 150 percent German.

Shortly before sunset we heard the soft melody of a lute coming from the bower adjoining the house. Lammerding and I found an old Lithuanian seated near the house playing to a few soldiers. His long, snow-white beard made him look like an ancient bard. We asked him into the house to play for us. He sat by the fireplace, his hands quivering over his instrument. Officers and men stood about or leaned against the walls and door-way listening in silence.

As if out of distant depths that we could not at first comprehend came weird chords, first searching and appealing, then gradually developing into a coherent theme of exquisite melody, sad, almost melancholic, yet with no touch of morbidness. To me these plaintive melodies were the expression of the soul of a frontier nation, which had suffered subjection and bondage for many centuries. And then, gradually, the mood changed; turbulent and provocative tones grew into a throbbing and angry rhythm. The old man's face, which had been serene, as if no longer interested in worldly matters, was transformed. His eyes flashed with an inner fire and he started to sing in a foreign tongue. His voice was feeble with age, but true to every note. It seemed that he was conveying the thanks of a nation that had regained its freedom.

Those who followed the German Army and took over administration of Lithuania made a sad blunder when they failed to recognize this cry for freedom and did not call upon the help of these people in the fight against the Reds. There was a reservoir of goodwill waiting to be tapped. Instead it was dammed up by shortsighted oppression.

Some of the soldiers who had been listening to the old man took the opportunity to have a look at the inside of the farmhouse. The massive stone oven in the center of the living room amused them; it was about 20 feet square, had an open fireplace and a number of apertures in which stood primitive-looking pots. The thick walls of the oven divided the house into semi-enclosed rooms.

"Hey, Uncle!" called one of the soldiers. "You must have a big family. Why do you want an oven as big as this?"

The old man smiled. He knew enough German to understand what they were getting at. "Will you be in Russia this winter?" he asked in his thin voice.

"Perhaps."

"Then you will find out! And perhaps you won't laugh."

*　　*　　*

At 2:30 a.m. we were again marching eastward. The road was more atrocious than ever, and in the darkness became a nightmare succession of steep hills, pot-holes and ruts. The night was pierced by the shouts of drivers trying to coax their teams of horses through the sandholes and up the hills. There were short halts while the horses regained their breath, then harness would be pulled taut again while horses with heaving flanks took the strain. The wagons would creak and once again the heavy wheels would grind into the sand and sink down.

But the forced march had to continue, the wheels had to keep turning. Two or three sections of each company were detailed to accompany their wagons and act as push commandos.[52] As soon as a wagon slowed down, the men would spring forward, grab the spokes and throw their weight forward to keep the wheels moving. The sun rose and still the grim march continued, men and horses working in concert to drive the heavy wagons forward. The men stripped off their tunics and shirts. Sweat ran down their backs, the red dust settled on them and caked hard. One squad would be relieved from its push commando duties by another, and would find blessed relief in marching.

The *Wehrmacht*'s shock troops, motorized units and artillery batteries were given use of the best roads in the advance into Russia. The infantry with horse-drawn transport was allocated the by-roads in between. We cursed our roads of sand or lime, but on we labored and reached our next bivouac at 2:30 a.m., after 24 hours' marching with only two brief halts. A few hours later we were again marching, over hills, through woods, ever deeper and deeper into the endless spaces of Russian territory. Without realizing it, we ate up the miles.

Then on the ninth day of the war—30 June—we received the first official report of activity in other sectors. It came in the daily orders from General Strauss, Commander-in-Chief of the Ninth Army, of which we were a part. Neuhoff gave the report to Lammerding to read aloud while we rode along.

In cooperation with the Fourth Army and two Panzer groups, the encirclement and destruction of strong Russian forces has succeeded. The enemy has lost 100,000 prisoners; the killed and wounded greatly exceed this figure. 1400 tanks and 550 guns were left on the battlefields by the defeated armies. A vast amount of material, not yet estimated, was abandoned in the woods. This battle was only the preliminary to the mighty and progressive destruction of Red armies in the area between Belostok and Minsk.[53]

We gasped at this overwhelming tale of victory.

"Those figures will shake the world," said Neuhoff, exultantly.

*   *   *

For the next two days the march continued, over the same appalling roads, but with less need now for those sudden forays into the fields to guard against snipers. The Russians now seemed to be completely on the run and, from all reports, we were harrying them so closely that it was difficult to see how they could ever turn and make a stand before we were hammering on the gates of Moscow.

On 2 July Kageneck found a soldier's newspaper somewhere, dated three days earlier. It was called *The Breakthrough* and had been issued by a field propaganda company. It gave us a coordinated report of progress along the whole eastern front for the first time. At the next halt Kageneck read the crudely printed pamphlet, headlines first:

VICTORY MARCH ON EASTERN FRONT—LAST HOUR COUNTER-STROKE THRUST INTO MIDDLE OF RUSSIAN ATTACK—POWERFUL FRONTIER DEFENSES PIERCED ON FIRST DAY—GIGANTIC ENCIRCLEMENT OF RUSSIAN ARMIES—BREAKTHROUGH ATTEMPTS BY RUSSIAN TROOPS THWARTED—OVER 4100 ENEMY AIRCRAFT AND PANZERS DESTROYED—FORTRESS BREST-LITOVSK FALLEN—VILNA AND KOVNO IN OUR HANDS.

The eagerness with which the soldiers listened while Kageneck read the detailed news of the successes of the first eight days showed how cleverly the Propaganda Minister had chosen his words. The news came at just the right time when many men, weary of the never-ending forced march, were wondering whether the attack on Russia was justified or necessary. Their doubts were now blown away on the wind of Goebbels's words. It was clear now: Germany had been forced to attack by the concentrations of Red troops which were preparing to attack the Fatherland.[54]

Kageneck concluded: "Whole squadrons of Soviet aircraft were destroyed on the ground—on their own airfields—before they were able to take off on their deadly missions to bomb innocent German wives and children. The tremendous numbers of aircraft, Panzers, other war material and prisoners which have been destroyed or captured are due to the exemplary cooperation of the German armies. But at the same time they give a staggering picture of the mortal danger that had been concentrated on the eastern frontiers of the Reich. It is quite evident that only at the 11th hour were we able to frustrate the Russian-Mongolian plans to invade Central Europe, the consequences of which would have been tragic beyond belief. The entire German nation owes its deepest gratitude to its brave soldiers."[55]

When we were alone, free for a while of the sycophantic Bolski's company, who had been sticking to Kageneck's side as a sort of self-appointed aide, I sounded Kageneck.

"What do you think, Franz?"

"You mean who's the real attacker?"

"Yes."

Kageneck gave his views candidly: "Bolshevism and National Socialism can't in the long run tolerate each other. That's indisputable. And of course we were the attackers. The only question is: was it necessary? If we'd agreed to let the Russians help themselves as they wished—Constantinople, Persia, India and so on—then we wouldn't have been at war with Russia today. Then we could have come to an agreement with England and later perhaps have worked together with them against the Bolsheviks."

"Yes, but who started this war?"

"It doesn't really matter at all who started it. Totalitarian countries can attack whenever they feel the right moment's arrived, without reference to anyone. England and America first have to prepare their people before they go to war. By marching into Poland we spared England the moral problem involved in a declaration of war."

"God help us if we don't win!"

"Yes, God help us," agreed Kageneck fervently. "But even if we do win, we'll still have a mess to clear up at home."

Next day it was the same old story—march, march, march.

Stolze thought we should never see another Russian soldier. We had been lucky that the pincer movement at Belostok had been successful, because we had protected the northern flank of our encircling army and should have been in the thick of things had the Russians managed to break through the steel ring. Now our Panzers and Panzer Grenadiers were involved in heavy fighting at Minsk, and we heard that Army Group North driving hard toward Leningrad, had captured Riga, while Army Group South had taken the important Polish town of Lemberg.

Kageneck, Bolski and I were riding together when we learned from a field newsletter of the Red atrocities in Lemberg. Before they evacuated the city, the Russians had first held a carnival of murder. Their political opponents had been shot, particularly those with German connections or who were suspected of Nazi sympathies. Women, children and old men had been murdered or imprisoned.

"The bells of Westminster toll," Bolski intoned, "and the Archbishop of Canterbury and the English are praying that God will grant victory to their beloved, godless Bolshevik brethren." He spat on the ground to show his disgust at that accidental English grandmother.

We were still marching through what was once Poland, heading for Oszmiana.[56] For the first time we were using captured horses. My ambulance horses had been replaced;

old Westwall had dropped dead in harness and the other had reached total exhaustion.[57] Müller and I had improvised a small four-wheeled cart, which was ideal for field work. It was being pulled by two little Russian panje horses. The cart carried my medical outfit, bandaging materials and other equipment for which Müller was responsible. We christened our two little panje horses Max and Moritz. Max was black, Moritz was brown. They were wonderful little animals, perfect for the work and for the country through which we marched. They never stuck in sand or mud and could carry on for hour after hour, week after week, with their light, twinkling steps. They pulled the little cart over heavy country right to the heights overlooking Moscow, through the winter mud and snows, through the heavy fighting of the retreat to Rzhev, without the slightest distress. I came to rely heavily on Max and Moritz and, from that time on, my heavy ambulance was of secondary importance to me and frequently caught us up after a week or a fortnight when our forced march was halted. Otherwise we never saw it.

It had taken only 12 days of the campaign to show how completely unsuited was our transport to this type of country. The wagons were far too heavy for moving on these incredibly bad roads and tracks. Our beautiful, well-bred horses were altogether too food-conscious and were not acclimatized. This became particularly noticeable during the winter fighting. Whereas our German horses needed long rest periods, heavy meals—and food for them was rarely obtainable in quantity—the panje horses picked up their food at the roadside and in the woods. They kept fit and strong on winter rations of a handful of straw, bark from trees and lichen moss. They ate when food was available for them but never seemed to worry if they had to go without. They stood up to extremes of heat and cold equally well and if no water was available in the winter when wells were frozen solid, they would happily munch a mouthful of snow.[58]

Their instinct was amazing. During snowstorms they huddled together and protected each other from the wind, their shaggy, bearlike winter coats keeping the snow from their skins. Unerringly, they sensed the deep spots in the snow and never wandered from the hard tracks. They had the sure feet of mountain goats and trotted gaily eastward while our heavier horses floundered up to their bellies in snowdrifts. Many of our soldiers owed their lives to these great-hearted little companions, for if a man was lost in the woods or in the deserts of snow they could put their trust implicitly in the panje horses to find their way back. Often when we were cut off from all contact with the rest of the division they saved us from hunger and death. And in the end their carcasses provided us with meat. But it was like eating a friend.

In the drive toward the Russian-Polish frontier, the push commandos still sweated with our heavy wagons. They had been ideal for France, but were a hindrance for this campaign. They became a positive handicap during the fierce winter fighting. Neuhoff reported the transport difficulties under which we were laboring; no doubt the report was sent onward to higher authority. But nothing was done. It appeared that to the High Command the smashing victories overshadowed everything.

CHAPTER 5

In Napoleon's Footsteps

NAPOLEON'S ROAD WAS OUR ROAD. WE WERE NOW MARCHING TO MOSCOW LITERALLY IN the 129-year-old footsteps of Napoleon's army.[59] And it was much easier going then over the sandy roads that had brought us to Oszmiana.

Two-thirds of the wide road to the east was surfaced with old but strong cobblestones and the other third was firm sand. Our columns now marched easily, heavy traffic on the cobbled portion and light traffic—including our imperturbable panje horses—on the sand track. Flanking each side of the road were lines of centuries-old birch trees, which stood like some old, élite Napoleonic guard. The cobbles had been laid by the French Emperor's Corsicans in 1812 and it must have been a colorful stream of 600,000 men that Napoleon led into Russia—all along this route. Of his 600,000 men, only 90,000 ever reached the outskirts of Moscow in that dreadful winter, and of those only a few hundred ever managed to stagger back to their homeland.

As our troops, drably-uniformed shades of that earlier army, marched onward it was natural that every man's thoughts should be on the little Corsican whose burning torch of ambition was snuffed out in the snow and ice of the Russian winter. The ghosts of the Imperial French Army marched along the road with us and perhaps sent a small shiver down our spines as we remembered school-room pictures of the ghastly retreat of 1812.[60]

Kageneck was comparing Napoleon's progress with that of our army. "Napoleon had no contact with the enemy, except for a little Russian rearguard action," he said, "until he ran up against the Moscow defense line at Borodino."

"Then how do you account for his enormous losses on the march into Russia?" asked Jakobi, one of Kageneck's officers.

"The tremendous distances beat him," said Kageneck. "He couldn't maintain his supplies."

"Don't forget disease," I threw in. "Did you know that during the war in 1870, four times as many men died of disease as were killed in action? So what must Napoleon's

39

losses have been? Especially from dysentery, cholera, typhus in summertime, and spotted fever in winter—not to speak of frostbite. Spotted fever was Napoleon's biggest enemy; he had terrible casualties from it. Even today, 20-year-olds might pull through, but men of 40 or 50 who haven't been vaccinated are practically doomed."

"What causes it?" asked Jakobi.

"Lice. But only the infected lice carry the disease. And, believe me, we'll have to fight them too. Or we'll be slaughtered."

"What about inoculations?"

"Not enough serum. Perhaps we've enough to vaccinate 5 percent of our troops. Maybe just enough to protect those who are especially susceptible to the disease."

"Have you been inoculated, Heinz?" Kageneck asked me.

"No. And I don't think it's really necessary as long as I stay in your hygienic company. I wish Bolski would stop scratching his head, though." Bolski was not particularly amused.

"What do distances matter to us?" he demanded.

"A hell of a lot," Kageneck growled. "As much as they meant to Napoleon."

"Nonsense!" said Bolski scornfully. "This is the 20th Century and we have Adolf Hitler for a leader—not Napoleon."

"So what?" asked Jakobi.

"We have the greatest army and the greatest military leader of all time. Distance means nothing today." He was encouraged to greater heights of oratory: "Let us not forget: we are not a spear thrown haphazardly into space, which may or may not find the target. We are the sword of the new Germany, wielded by the best hands, and when called upon are always ready to cut and thrust until our enemies are completely destroyed."

"Well spoken! Very nice indeed—splendid, in fact," applauded Jakobi sarcastically. "Goebbels had better watch out or Bolski will have his job."

"My dear Bolski," said Kageneck courteously, "you have solved all our problems. Particularly a little personal problem of mine. I'd been meaning to pay a visit to auntie since morning, but now you've really given me the urge to do it at last. Thank you!" He galloped off toward a clump of trees.

*   *   *

Our pleasure in marching along Napoleon's cobbled road was short-lived. The order came for us to leave it and head northeast toward Polotsk. We had been forced-marching toward Minsk, but the battle there was over and we were no longer needed. Air reconnaissance reports said that the enemy was sending up strong reserves to the front through Smolensk and Vitebsk. Evidently his intention was to stop our advance on Moscow along the line Polotsk to Orsha. And by stopping us there, the Reds would also deny us the use of the main highway between the rivers Dvina and Dnepr, along which our Panzers could have raced toward Moscow.[61]

We are back to the old conditions of wretched roads, dust, heat and thirst, to insufficient drinking water and to the push-commandos. It is so today; it will be the same tomorrow—mile after weary mile of back-breaking monotony.

Marshlands take the place of dreary moorland and a line of trees marks the course of a small river. There is nothing out of the ordinary about the river, but to the exhausted men it might be a stream of Paradise, for the order to halt is given as we reach its banks. We look at our maps and then gaze across to the opposite bank, silently. The stream is the Berezina; the other bank is Russia. We stand at the edge of Poland and gaze across to where the forests rise in the distance.

And we remember that it was on the banks of this river that the last 10,000 of Napoleon's retreating soldiers were defeated. All but a few hundred were annihilated; a few hundred only reached the west bank, on which we now stand, and carried back to France the tidings of the greatest military catastrophe in centuries. On the Berezina the remnants of that 600,000-strong French Imperial Army fought the last battle on their own, deserted by their emperor, who was already in Paris.

Our Westphalian Grenadiers, the gallant 6th Division, is to remember the Berezina, too—a stretch of the Berezina 150 miles to the south, among the Pripet Marshes. But we know nothing of that as we linger on the river bank, and we treat it as a good omen when one of the men finds a bronze eagle of Napoleon's army, half-hidden by a road near the water's edge.

The insignia finds its way to one of our propaganda units, which makes capital out of it. The field newspaper says: "In the same way as Field Marshal and *Führer* Adolf Hitler succeeded in adapting and applying the Schlieffen Plan and leading the German divisions to a glorious victory in France, so will he now take up the symbol of the great Corsican and lead the *Wehrmacht* to a great and conclusive victory against the Russian colossus. We are at the dawn of a great era and a mighty, unified Europe. Napoleon failed to realize this great ideal, which will become fact under the guidance and leadership of the *Führer*."

For an hour or two we rest by the Berezina. We bathe our heads and dust-caked upper bodies in the river. The fresh water cools our burning eyes and refreshes our cracked lips. Then forward again—marching and marching, but into Russia itself now.

On the 21st day of the war, 12 July, we receive a few field newspapers and are momentarily cheered by seeing in print the news of the Battle of Minsk: "The Battle of Minsk is over. Four Russian armies opposed our Army Group Center. They have been defeated—either destroyed or routed; 300,000 prisoners have been counted, as well as 2,600 captured or destroyed tanks and 1,500 guns. The enemy has suffered enormous and bloody losses. . . ."[62]

As we march the enemy continues to withdraw eastward. It seems as if our battalion is never to catch up with him. As if our war is to be an uninterrupted marathon march—to the Urals, perhaps, or even farther.

With great relief we hear the news from Intelligence. The enemy is digging in on the line Polotsk-Orsha-Vitebsk. Rivers, lakes and dense forests form a natural defensive line, and concrete bunkers and Panzer-traps reinforce the weaker spots to make a strongly-fortified system—the Stalin Line, the first barrier in the Reds' defenses of Moscow.[63] There is no longer any doubt that the enemy intends to stand and fight. We are happy, we can laugh at the dust, the heat, the thirst—for only another 20 miles' marching lies ahead. Our vanguard and the Panzer units are already involved in heavy fighting. Enemy resistance on the east bank of the Dvina is becoming stiffer by the hour. News filters back that our Panzer units and mechanized troops have now received orders to cease their attacks and are to hold their positions until the divisions following have caught up with them.

At last the war is waiting for us!

The column swings cheerfully along the road. There is a point to the marching and the objective is only a few miles away.

The day after crossing the Berezina,[64] we are ordered to halt and pitch camp behind a bare hill. From its crest we see the little village of Gomely lying below us, at the junction of two lakes. Ahead, to our right, stretches a lake as far as we can see, and a narrow strip of water joins it to another lake on our left. Behind Gomely and the lakes lie the deeply-serried Panzer traps, bunkers and barbed wire defenses of the Stalin Line, which it will be our job to pierce. This time our battalion will not be in reserve. We are to be the first wave of assault troops to storm the narrows at Gomely.

*　　*　　*

Scouting patrols brought news next day that our task would not be too easy. Russian troops occupied Gomely and had destroyed the bridge over the narrows connecting the two lakes. Prisoners taken by the patrols gave us valuable information. Two concrete bunkers controlled the approaches to where the bridge had been, and the narrows at which we had hoped to ferry across would be under cross-fire from five bunkers. More bunkers lay to the rear. First we should have to clear the village of Reds; then cross the narrows; clear the bunkers near the village and finally overcome the rear-line bunkers and field positions that had not already been knocked out by artillery fire.

Through my medical staff I gave the order that the troops were not to eat anything during the six hours before the attack started. That way they would stand a better chance of survival in case of a stomach wound. Even one slice of bread, I emphasized, would cause extra blood to flow into the intestines, and in the event of a wound, internal hemorrhage would be much greater. *Oberst* Becker and his Regimental Adjutant, von Kalkreuth, arrived for a short conference with Neuhoff, Hillemanns and Kageneck. While it was in progress I distributed green camouflaged mosquito nets as protection against the swarms of mosquitoes that plagued these marshy districts in summer—and more particularly as protection against an over-sized variety of stinging gnat, which we had nicknamed "Stukas." Their attacks at night were vicious.

Neuhoff held a conference of the battalion officers at eight o'clock that evening. The heat had gone from the sun, which still lingered, anxious to make the most of its brief summer reign. A soldier was playing a popular German tune on a mouth-organ and a small group of men lazily joined in the choruses. The smell of the inevitable goulash wafted across on a faint breeze from the field kitchen. And a mile away the Russians were waiting for the next day's attack.

Hauptmann Noack of the 14th Anti-Tank Company, an *Oberleutnant* of a pioneer company, and *Oberfeldwebel* Scheiter of the 13th Infantry Gun Company, together with the other battalion officers, listened to Kageneck explain the sequence of our plan of attack.

After being softened up by artillery fire, the village of Gomely was to be stormed and cleared of Russian troops. Noack and Scheiter with their light armament were to take up suitable positions on the captured ground and engage the nearer enemy bunkers with point-blank fire. Assault troops from our rifle companies, supported by pioneers, commandos with explosives and flamethrower specialists were to take advantage of this engagement of the bunkers to cross either the narrows or the tip of the lake in rubber dinghies and then attack the bunkers and enemy defenses on the other side. All pioneers not used in this operation were to repair the broken bridge to enable reserve rifle companies to cross and widen the bridgehead on the other side. They were then to consolidate their positions. As soon as the bridge had been repaired, the rest of the battalion, with the heavy weapons, was to cross and establish itself on the other side. Without delay the attack would continue to the bridge at Dalezkye, three miles farther on. And from there a new thrust would be made into the wooded area of Sarotschka—to Point 62 on our map. This was the first day's objective.

In the light of our plan of action, I worked out the disposition of my own little medical force. Wegener was to remain with Neuhoff's staff during the attack. Müller had the job of following up with my medical panje wagon without taking any risks. He was also to direct ambulances to their proper destination and was to join the staff only when fighting had ceased. Petermann, with his horse and my Lump, was to stay close to the horses of the Neuhoff and Lammerding. Dehorn and I would accompany the attacking troops on foot so as to be on hand to attend any wounded without delay. *Oberstabsarzt* Schulze had placed an extra *Sankawagen* at my disposal, which was to stay in constant touch with Müller.

The commanders of the various attached units had gone back to their own troops and the officers of the 3rd Battalion sat and chatted for a while. Neuhoff was serious and thoughtful. Hillemanns, as always, was busy with his daily paper war. Kageneck, Stolze and Lammerding were chaffing each other in their usual way. And even the younger officers seemed to show no special concern for what the morrow would bring—in fact, most of them seemed anxious to get on with it. Hillemanns gathered together his papers and issued around the battalion Neuhoff's orders for attack, which ended: "We of the 3rd Battalion, officers, NCOs and men, go into the attack fully believing in our victory for *Führer*, *Volk* and *Vaterland*. Signed, Neuhoff, Major. In the field 14/7/41."

By the last hour of daylight I wrote a long letter to Martha, without dwelling on what lay ahead. I felt tired and was pleased that a few hours' sleep was possible before the first troops moved into their positions at 3 a.m.

*   *   *

It was the last hour before dawn and our companies lay in tall grass, bushes, or cornfields, camouflaged and hidden from enemy eyes. Behind us were ranged 38 batteries of artillery of varying caliber. As well as 21cm heavy howitzer batteries,[65] there was "Fat Lina," a huge 25cm gun, whose special assignment was to blast the strongest bunker dominating the river crossing. Close to me were several 88mm anti-aircraft guns,[66] which were to pour direct fire at the gun apertures of the bunkers.[67]

There was still half an hour to go until the guns opened up so I sought shelter from the clouds of stinging gnats in my Mercedes. Dehorn followed me. Wegener and my driver were already sitting inside, smoking. I lit a cigarette, partly for something to do and partly as protection against the gnats. Still the "Stukas" came at us so we closed the car windows.

There was a long silence.

More for something to say than because it was necessary, I asked Wegener: "Are you sure of your duties?"

"Yes, Herr *Assistenzarzt*."

"Good," I said. "You prepare the stationary casualty station while Dehorn and I move up with the attacking troops."

The sun came up deep red. North of us there was desultory firing by the Russians, interspersed every now and then by the heavy crack of one of the enemy's mobile railway guns. In our sector there was no movement. The outsize red ball in the east did not yet illuminate the countryside fully and the fir trees loomed blackly like dark sentinels on the edge of the lake. In front of us—before Gomely, and beyond on the other side of the lakes—marshland gave way to meadow and meadow to cornfield.

Behind a clump of bushes near our car, the NCOs in charge of the four 88mm guns were standing, smoking one cigarette after another.

Tension held us in its web.

Wegener took his medical case, saluted and set off. Neuhoff, Hillemanns and Lammerding passed.

"What's the time?" I called to Lammerding.

"Twenty-one minutes to four exactly—regimental time. Twenty minutes to go!"

"Thanks. Good luck! Try and keep out of my hands, Lammerding."

"Don't worry, I will." He grinned.

The sun rose higher above the eastern horizon. It would soon be light enough for the 88's to give direct fire.

The four gun-crew NCOs threw away their cigarettes and walked slowly toward their guns.

CHAPTER 6

Storming the Stalin Line

"It is time, Dehorn," I said, getting out of the car and slamming the door behind me. Dehorn slid out of the back seat and slung his medical rucksack over his back. We stood by the nearest 88. Its muzzle was trained on the bunker to the left of the broken bridge—trained directly at the bunker's firing aperture. The gun detachment commander peered at his watch. "One minute to go . . . 30 seconds . . . five seconds." He raised his arm. "One second. . . . Fire!" He dropped his arm to his side.[68]

We gazed intently at the bunker. The first shell was nearly on target, but a little high, though it had swept away the camouflage over the firing aperture. But the blast from the 88 against which we stood was only one of dozens. The high ground was now alive with flashes and the earth trembled beneath our feet. The leaves on the bushes quivered and the blasts cut shimmering swathes in the long grass. The thunder of the guns seemed to rumble around the heavens and a steel avalanche of destruction hurtled down on the village of Gomely and the defenses on the other side of the narrows.

The anti-aircraft guns rained their deadly effective fire against the dark bunkers and above the din "Fat Lina" was thundering away with her deeper note—intent on pulverizing the large bunker to the left of the narrows. The other bunkers were under heavy fire from the 21cm howitzers, while the 10.5cm howitzers, the 15cm infantry guns (s.I.G.) and the long-range 10cm cannon hurled their shells into the enemy-occupied village.

Buildings burst into flame, disintegrated. Earth, bricks and beams were flung high into the air as, house by house, Gomely was systematically wiped off the map. We could see figures of Russian soldiers running out of burning buildings, collapsing in the streets. It was difficult to imagine that anyone could ever live through that devastating bombardment. And all the time the howitzers slung their loads of high explosive across the lake at the concrete and steel bunkers. That they should still stand was unthinkable. That the bombardment could maintain its level of destruction was unbelievable. For a long hour the artillery hammered away at the frontal defenses of the Stalin Line, while the infantry waited, hidden from view.

On the stroke of five o'clock, every gun raised its elevation and carried on blazing away—but now at the second line of defenses. The shells screamed over the heads of our assault troops as Tietjen's 9th Company and Stolze's 10th Company ran down the slope of the hill to the flat land bordering Gomely. In a few minutes they were in the burning village,[69] while hundreds of pairs of eyes followed their progress. The 11th Company we kept in reserve for the present.

"Come on, Dehorn," I said. "It's our turn for the village!" We walked down the slope, across the flats and reached the beginning of Gomely's main street. Machine-gun fire kicked up the dust around us and zipped over our heads. Evidently the enemy bunkers had somehow survived that merciless pounding, although from what we could see most of them were partly destroyed. We ducked and dived for a ditch. Heavy smoke drifted over the village, across the narrows, and hung over the lake and the tenaciously resisting bunkers. As the smoke lifted momentarily, I noticed that the battle seemed to be concentrating at the far end of the village, near the destroyed bridge.

Dehorn and I worked our way forward under cover of burning houses, keeping away from the streets, which every now and then would be raked by enemy machine-gun fire. Dead Russians lay in the streets and open spaces, many of the bodies horribly mutilated by our artillery shells. A wounded man from Tietjen's company met us. A grazed shoulder. We took him into a house that had been half blown away, but which was not burning. Machine-gun bullets ripped into the gables and wooden beams.

"Careful! Into the back room—it's safer," I warned. The half-house was empty. In a few minutes we had attended to the wound, which was clean. There were no damaged bones. I gave the man a morphia injection to kill the pain and he was soon cheerful again.

"This is a good place for a dressing station," I told Dehorn. I turned to the wounded man. "*Unteroffizier* Wegener will be along soon. Wait for him and tell him that he is to prepare the dressing station here."

Dehorn placed a white flag in front of the door and we weaved our way forward toward the fighting, sometimes crawling, making what use we could of cover and smoke, until we were near the ruins of the bridge. Only the wooden piles still stood out of the water, and lively cross-fire from the opposite bank raked the narrows. The bunker on the left—the big bunker, nearest to the bridge, that we had most feared—was silent and dead, a tribute to the work of "Fat Lina." But the bunker on the right was still firing away steadily and was supported by machine-guns from bunker number three a short distance farther along the shore of the lake.

A score of dead Russian soldiers were sprawled at the approaches to the bridge and two bodies lay across the wooden struts half-submerged in the water. They had been shot by their own men in the bunker garrisons while trying to escape across to the other bank.

Our own light guns had now edged closer to the bridge, and one of Noack's 37mm guns[70] opened up against the badly-damaged bunker to the right, which, miraculously, was still resisting strongly. The firing aperture was now a gaping hole and soon shell after shell was slapping into it. A dense cloud of smoke rolled along the street and covered the narrows and the bridge. Dim shapes were charging through it toward the bridge; I recognized Schnittger as one of them. It looked as if they were going to cross the narrows by leaping from pole to pole of the wrecked bridge. I strained my eyes to follow their movements, but the smoke that was hiding them from the Russians across the water hid them from my eyes, too.

Two or three tense, expectant minutes ticked away. Then the smoke gradually cleared. Schnittger and his men were clambering up the banks on the other side of the water—they had half-swum, half-swarmed across the wreckage of the bridge under cover of the smoke cloud. They charged toward the stubborn right-hand bunker, but more smoke drifted across and hid them from view once again. From out of the smoke we heard the rattle of German automatic weapons and the blast of hand grenades. Schnittger's men were in close combat with the Russians holding the trenches between the bunkers. The smoke cleared and more German soldiers were on the other bank. Noack's 37mm had stopped firing and flamethrowers were mercilessly searing into the bunker's apertures.

No further sound came from the bunker.

The remaining field defenses were being systematically rolled up, although the third bunker, farther over to the right, was still in action against us. In a matter of moments the pioneers secured running boards across the piles of the bridge, and group after group of assault troops ran across. Two men were hit by fire from the third bunker, dropped into the water and sank, but the stream of men continued across.

From the other side I heard repeated cries of "Doctor!" and with Dehorn at my heels I jumped for the bridge. We ran, balancing precariously on the narrow planks; bullets seemed to be whining in every direction around us. Pausing briefly to regain our breath when we reached the opposite bank, we panted uphill toward the bunker that had just been silenced. The nearest trench was now occupied by our own soldiers. Just behind it, a 21cm shell had gouged out a huge hole. "All wounded into here!" I yelled and jumped in. Dehorn planted a white flag on the edge.

Three lightly wounded men crept into the hole and one seriously hurt man was dragged in on a stretcher. He had a clean shot through the lungs, but the bullet had not damaged any large artery. I injected him to calm his nerves and told him to lie on his other side. "Don't move your body at all," I told him. "Only complete rest will stop the bleeding."

Another stretcher was man-handled into the shell hole. The soldier on the stretcher was semi-conscious and had a terrible gash in the throat. He must have lost a lot of blood. His pulse was very faint, and it was doubtful if he would survive the shock much longer. Yet, I thought, if I gave him an immediate blood transfusion he might just make it. It was a chance worth taking, for without a transfusion he would certainly die.

Fortunately I had my small Braun-Melsungen transfusion apparatus with me and we were comparatively safe in our deep shell hole. Our guns were laying their sights point-blank at the next line of Russian field defenses, but the Russian artillery was still replying with spirit, though fortunately their shells were not exploding in our immediate area. But bursts from Russian automatics made us duck our heads involuntarily.

"Blood donor!" I shouted to a stretcher bearer of 10th Company. "Blood donor, Group O."

"How do you know that?" I heard Stolze's voice. The man with the torn throat was one of his men.

"Group O is always safe," I told him. "But what's that blood on your own arm?"

"Oh, it's nothing—just a scratch." It was only a superficial wound and I dressed it while I waited for a blood donor to be found. Fortunately, I had made all my preparations in East Prussia for blood transfusions. I had classified every man in the battalion according to blood groups and had decided to draw all my donors, for simplicity's sake, from Universal Group "O." These men I had tested for syphilis and had then made a list of their names—but Müller knew them all by heart. In spite of the fact that we completely ignored the Rhesus factor, we rarely had a complication following a transfusion at the front.

(SS troops had their blood group tattooed under the right arm, so that a doctor could tell at a glance what blood group was required. Later, this brand spelt death to many of these SS men as it was an infallible means of identification.)

"Damn that third bunker," said Stolze. "The bastards won't give in. We've by-passed it for the time being and we'll have to smoke them out later. But they keep picking off our men one by one." He went off.

The blood donor sat in front of me—a powerful Westphalian from Lipperland with arteries like a horse. He grinned at me: "Take as much as you like, Herr *Assistenzarzt*. I've got too much blood."

A tremendous explosion nearly caused the needle to jump out of the vein. "What was that?" I asked.

"Schnittger's just blown in the iron door of the bunker—that's all. It takes more than a bit of Russian iron to keep Schnittger out," said the blood donor.

After I had transferred 500 c.c., I noticed a slight color return to the patient's pale lips and the pulse beat more strongly. I let the burly Westphalian go and injected the patient with 500 c.c. of saline. His pulse returned nearly to normal; he was out of immediate danger. I carefully tested the pressure bandage to make sure there would be no more bleeding.

Of the brave Russian bunker crew, only one man survived and his burns were so ghastly that I held out little hope for him. However, I ordered two Russian prisoners, who seemed to know something about first aid, to bandage him and gave them more dressings with instructions to attend to other wounded Russians.

Several companies had now reached the east bank of the lake and were fanning out for the assault on the deeper defenses of the Stalin Line. But the most difficult objective had been won—the Gomely crossing had been successful at the first attempt and the strongest defenses of the Russian front lines were out of action. With the help of Russian prisoners, the pioneers had, in the space of 40 minutes, built a new structure over the remains of the old bridge and our first heavy infantry guns were rolling slowly across it.

Dehorn and I returned to our main dressing station in Gomely. Max and Moritz, with the little panje wagon were standing in front of the door. "That's fine," I said to Dehorn. "Müller is already here—everything's going according to plan." Going through to the back room I called Wegener. There was no reply. Müller met me at the door to the room. "Wegener's wounded—a head wound."

Wegener was lying with other wounded men on a bed of straw. He was fully conscious, but his blood-soaked bandage showed that he was badly hurt. I removed the bandage. A rifle bullet had entered the back of his neck, and had passed right through his head, coming out of his right eye. It relieved me to see no sign of paralysis.

"Where did this happen? How is such a wound possible?" I asked Wegener.

"Here, behind the building," he whispered hoarsely. His voice tailed off. Müller carried on: "Behind the house. Wegener went to fetch more straw and just as he bent down he was hit and pitched forward into the straw. I was standing next to him and carried him inside."

"What awful luck," I muttered. "A stray bullet when the fight in the village was over."

Wegener's right eye had been completely shot out. Only the upper eyelid and a few bloody strands of flesh covered the hole. The underlid and part of the cheekbone were missing altogether. The entry wound at the back of the neck was small and there was not much bleeding—only slightly oozing capillaries. I tied another bandage around Wegener's head, leaving the left eye free, gave him an injection to assist the flow of blood and another pain-killing injection.

"Your right eye is gone," I told him gently, "but a specialist will fix you up as good as new apart from that. There's no damage to the brain and you'll soon learn to see twice as well out of your left eye. Cheer up, my boy—it's the end of the war for you."

The *Sankawagen* arrived. The three other men were lighter cases and Müller soon made them comfortable. Wegener had, in the meantime, fallen asleep. His pulse was satisfactory. With Dehorn I jumped into the *Sankawagen* to fetch the wounded from the shell hole and to pick up Wegener on our way back. The lighter cases were to wait for a later ambulance.

We drove carefully over the bridge, but now there was no fire from the third bunker. Although Stolze had looked upon it as being his meat, Bolski had been the man to put it out of action. While Stolze was talking about smoking it out from the rear, Bolski had taken a squad of Stolze's troops and had made a frontal attack. It had been a rash action, but completely successful. So far as his courage was concerned, Bolski had won his spurs at Gomely.

Our artillery fire was now directed against the ford at Dalezkye, and we could hear the Russians steadily thundering back. But we had nothing to fear from them at the moment while we gathered our wounded. The man who had been given the transfusion was satisfactory, and more than anything else in the morning's closely-packed events this made my spirits soar, for I had not given much for his chances of survival when I first saw him. Carefully, the *Sankawagen* picked its way back to Gomely to collect Wegener and then proceed to the Medical Company in the rear. Dehorn's eyes were sad as he watched it go—the loss of Wegener had affected him strongly. The war had hit home.

We marched along the road toward Dalezkye, following the majority of our troops. By the roadside were five fresh graves on which the birch crosses had just been placed. Two were from Tietjen's 9th Company, which had done heroic work on the left flank, one was from Stolze's company and one was from Kageneck's 12th. The fifth dead man was a pioneer. I glanced at my watch. It was 8:45 a.m.—the action had taken less than four hours.

"Who are the dead?" I asked the soldier who had erected the crosses and was now placing the steel helmets on them. He told me.

Four of them I did not know by name, but the fifth man was one of Stolze's twins. My mind went back to Filipovo, where they had played hand ball against the 9th Company. They had been all over the place and one of them had scored the winning goal. Laughingly, each had said the other had scored the goal—and none of us knew which one told the truth. Now one was dead. The joke was over.

"Where's the other brother?" I asked the man.

"He's just left—after he'd buried his brother. There he goes." He pointed with his small infantry spade along the sandy road to the east. Yes, there he was, walking slowly, head down. I grieved for the loneliness he would carry to his grave.

"We'd better get along." I pulled myself together. "There will be more work for us ahead." Our machine-guns were chattering in the distance.

The steps of the man ahead of us slowed down and he turned off the road into a wood. "Surely he's not going to shoot himself," said Dehorn urgently.

We broke into a run. The twin had disappeared into the wood. The dry branches crunched under our feet as we ran, expecting to hear a shot at any moment. There he sat on the trunk of a tree that had been felled by lightning. His head was in his hands and huge sobs shook his broad shoulders. He did not see us. For him the world did not exist at that moment. Half his world had been left behind, beneath the birchwood cross.

"Let's leave him alone, Dehorn," I whispered. "A man who can shed tears doesn't shoot himself."

Along the road we met Tietjen who told us that most of the first-line bunkers had been put out of action. Nearly all the crews had defended them to the death. Few prisoners had been taken.

The main attack of the battalion was now directed against the bridge at Dalezkye. But a few hundred yards short of it the enemy was resisting strongly from a farmhouse. Our fire engulfed it in flames, which spread to the outbuildings. As we stormed the building we heard the pitiful bellows of cattle as they burned to death. A white flag fluttered from one of the windows and another sharp fight was at an end.

Across the river at Dalezkye stretched a table-flat meadow, into the distance, where it met the dark line of a wood. The meadow was pockmarked with shell holes, but standing menacingly across the bridge was yet another bunker, uncamouflaged this time. Its sinister eyes were fixed on the bridge that it had been built to guard. Noack's anti-tank gun flashed shot after shot into those apertures—but not a single shot was fired in return. Suspiciously, the Pak stabbed the bunker again with shells, trying to provoke it into life. The bunker was silent. We stormed the bridge and crossed to the east bank of the river. Still not a sound from the bunker. Cautiously, our spearheads advanced across the meadow, jumping from shell hole to shell hole. Then they advanced erect, with eyes glued on the gun apertures. Three men whipped open the heavy steel door and hurled inside a few hand grenades.

A dead commissar lay on his back on the floor of the bunker, a bullet hole in the back of his head. Nobody else. The crew must have killed him and fled.

The first phase of the battle was over. It was 12:15 p.m. The Stalin Line had been pierced.[71] Our battalion assembled and Neuhoff reviewed the position. Nine concrete bunkers had been put out of action and all the Russian field defensive positions cleared up. Near the bridge I attended to the last casualties and arranged for their removal. Fortunately, there were no serious cases. After the medical personnel had all reported to me I found that, unlike the first day of our campaign, no wounded had been left unattended for any length of time. If *Oberst* Becker were to come along and ask me how things had gone, I could truthfully say this time "Nothing special to report." It seemed that it had been a good policy for Dehorn and myself to work forward directly behind the forward assault troops. There was more risk, certainly, but we had been able to attend to the wounded immediately and by doing so had undoubtedly saved one man's life.

Two advance patrols reached the woods about a mile and a half away and signaled that they were free of the enemy. When we reached them, we found a number of dugouts and prepared field defenses, but the Russians had either abandoned them or had been prevented from occupying them by our rapid breakthrough. The battalion marched through the dense wood toward Sarotschka.

And we were puzzled. Every man instinctively listened for the sudden shot, searched for the enemy sniper, waited for the thump of an enemy shell. It was uncanny. We had expected prolonged and bitter fighting as soon as the Russians made a stand. The Stalin Line, we knew, had been prepared by the enemy in 1939 as Moscow's first formidable line of defense, and it had been manned by troops specially trained to hold it. Yet we had broken through it and penetrated more than five miles. But behind us we could still hear the noise of battle. We had an uncomfortable feeling that perhaps we were the only German troops on this side of the Russian line. We were equally ready to be attacked from the rear as from ahead. And as we advanced, we continued to come across strong but unmanned defenses.[72]

It started to rain and in the shadow of the woods darkness began to fall. We reached our official objective for the day, Point 62, but Neuhoff gave no order to halt.

For another hour we carried on marching through the woods. It was as dark as Egypt's night and there were no roads.

We came across a few houses and barns—the homes of poor Russian peasants. They could not tell us much. Only that the Russians had passed through the area during the early evening, moving in both easterly and westerly directions. The news did little to reassure us.

At midnight we pitched camp—for four hours' rest, Neuhoff told us. All of us in the command tent awoke when a dispatch rider delivered a report from regimental headquarters at 2 a.m. In the north, strong German Panzer units had broken through the Stalin Line and had penetrated deep into Russian territory.[73] South of us, the assault had not been so successful. The German attacks had been halted by the concrete bunkers and Panzer traps—the Stalin Line still held. Our battalion had paved the way for the rest of Regiment 18.[74]

Chapter 7

The Burning Steppes

Our fighting luck was in. For the whole of the two days following our breakthrough we marched in light but persistent rain and our advance guard had only slight skirmishes with the fast retreating enemy. The company acting as our flank guard took many prisoners, defeated remnants of the fleeing Russians. Many of them carried no weapons and were looking for an opportunity to surrender. We saw no more Russian field defenses, and only occasionally was a desultory effort made to delay our advance.

The sun came out at noon of the second day and we soon forgot the two wet nights as it dried our uniforms and warmed our bodies. We were back to the old routine of marching eastward. The break through the Stalin Line was already a thing of the past, and we found it hard to believe that there had ever been an interruption in our relentless march to the east. On we went, without rest, without pause.

"I've talked Bolski into withdrawing his complaint against Stolze," Kageneck was saying.

The trouble had started at Gomely when Bolski had taken it on himself to borrow the group of men from Stolze's company to make that determined frontal attack against the stubborn third bunker. Stolze had intended to encircle the bunker and attack it from the rear, but Bolski had argued that the bunker was doing too much damage to troops crossing the makeshift bridge and had to be silenced immediately. He got in first—without Stolze's knowledge at the time. Bolski bravely stormed the bunker, carrying the concentrated explosive himself. They captured the strong point, but at the cost of two of Stolze's men. Stolze had been furious and had not been slow to let Bolski know—in public. It had been madness to make a frontal attack, he had said; Bolski had no right to meddle with his company, take his men and get them killed; Bolski had no idea of leadership and should have stayed in Poland where he belonged.

"I suppose that was Polski's real cause for complaint," I remarked to Kageneck.

53

Kageneck laughed. "Yes, that's what he was really sore about, and when he objected in a perfectly regimental manner that his name was 'Bolski' not 'Polski,' Stolze made matters worse by saying 'As far as I'm concerned, you can call yourself "Deutschski" if it's going to bolster your dignity, but keep your meddling Polish fingers out of my company!' Anyway, on my advice Bolski's withdrawn his complaint."

"Seems that Bolski has guts, after all."

"As a matter of fact, I've recommended him for the Iron Cross Second Class," Kageneck said.[75]

*　　*　　*

We halted in the early evening and I made my around of the companies, leaving Kageneck's 12th Company to the last so that, as usual, I could spend the evening with him. But Kageneck had gone to visit his friend von Kalkreuth, the regimental adjutant. By these unofficial courtesy visits, Kageneck maintained an excellent liaison with the regiment.

Oberfeldwebel Becker told me that Kageneck was expected to be away for most of the evening. He was a wide-awake man, this Becker, and was a candidate for officer's rank; his promotion to *Leutnant* was expected to come through shortly. His home was in the lovely forest-clad hills of the Sauerland and he reminded me very much of my dead friend Fritz. His belief in Hitler and Germany's future was the same, his reasoning followed the same line, and he was equally disinclined to ram his opinions down people's throats. Becker was a much smaller man than Fritz, and had been nicknamed "little Becker" to distinguish him from our tall, imposing regimental commander.

Leutnant Jakobi came up.

"Hallo, Doktor. I'm afraid I'll have to take over as host for Kageneck. I've got something very special to offer you this evening—a drop of heavy water."

"What the devil's that?" I asked.

"Genuine Russian vodka—at least 70 to 80 percent pure alcohol."

"But that's nothing, Jakobi. I've got 100 percent pure alcohol in my medicine chest; I drink a bottle every night!"

"Ah, yes, but it hasn't the bouquet of my heavy water." He produced a bottle and placed two glasses on a packing-case. Jakobi poured. They were liberal tots. "Little Becker" had unobtrusively withdrawn. "Well, here's to the liberation of Russia and Christmas in the Kremlin!"

"*Prosit!*" I replied.

We each took a good mouthful and swallowed. The stuff seared its way down like fire. For a moment neither of us could draw breath. Then we cleared our throats and Jakobi coughed.

"Why the cough?" I teased him.

"Why are your eyes watering?" he countered.

"Because I couldn't help feeling sad at the thought of the 12th Company drinking this weak stuff while we medical men have our 100 percent alcohol."

"Then have some more, Doktor." Jakobi thrust the bottle in the direction of my glass.

I dodged it. "You know, Jakobi, I think the French cognac suited us better than Russian vodka."

"You're right. But we'll just damn well have to get used to this bloody Russia. You never know what you're going to find from one minute to the next. Look at Polotsk—that was a hard nut. Those peasants fought like bastards. See this pistol . . ." He laid a huge pistol on the packing-case. "This is a Red Army pistol with which the commissar of bunker five shot himself."

"I don't give a damn if I never see another Russian bunker," I said.

"Then why the hell did you go so close to them?" Jakobi asked. "It's up to you how you carry out your job, but I'd say a doctor is too valuable a man to risk his life as you did. You were even across the straits before Stolze."

Vanity let me hear him out. It was pleasant to be told that I was a valuable asset to the battalion. I wondered idly if the trainee doctors at Düsseldorf were still being taught how to build field latrines. "You can't make hard and fast rules, Jakobi. Especially—as you say yourself—in Russia. I don't want to be a soldier. I'd go home and marry Martha tomorrow. But it seems that everyone has to be a soldier here."

Jakobi poured out two more drinks. "Then if you've got to play soldiers with us, for God's sake have a gun that will do you some good. That damn thing of yours would fit into your waistcoat pocket. It's just a toy."

"It's good enough for my needs," I protested.

"I insist. You must take this Russian pistol. In memory of our first drink of Russian heavy water." The vodka was beginning to affect us both slightly by this time and Jakobi ceremoniously buckled the belt with the pistol around my waist. I felt like an American cowboy.

*　　*　　*

Next morning the sun was hardly showing above the horizon when we were again on the march. We had by-passed the town of Polotsk and were heading due eastward toward Godorok, which lay astride the railway line from Leningrad to Vitebsk and Orsha. We marched in orderly battle formation and everyone was in happy mood. Our advance was quick and Moscow seemed just over the horizon. We had a good number of captured horses and were able to change the teams frequently. The sprightly little panje horses with their small wagons considerably lightened the march for the infantry. There were fewer skirmishes with the enemy, who was being chased in the direction of Vitebsk-Smolensk.

Steadily we drove toward Moscow. Every day brought us another 20 or 25 miles nearer our objective. I now had few cases of sore feet to doctor. Feet as well as minds had become attuned to hard, relentless marching. Everything now seemed easier and we felt we could march to the Urals if necessary. Pictures appeared on our march and were left behind us like passing ships on a long sea voyage. . . .

Black smoke clouds roll toward us. The town of Godorok is burning on the horizon— fired by the fleeing Russians. A few suicidal Red snipers[76] are winkled out of burning buildings and the town is taken. A deserted town. . . .

We swing south for 50 miles to clear up a few pockets of enemy resistance between Godorok and Vitebsk. We surround the enemy formations, send more prisoners back. . . .

Vitebsk, our biggest town, is taken. Again the Reds have put it to the torch. Scorched earth. . . .

Northeast again toward Velizh. The disorganized Reds fight here and there, but without a coordinated plan. We suffer few casualties. Neuhoff is exulting at the progress we are making along the road to the glittering prize: the capital of all the Soviets. . . .

Velizh is captured and is soon behind us. The number of prisoners and captured weapons increases rapidly. . . .

Twenty miles one day, 25 miles the next, then 30 miles. The troops are eating up the distance greedily, cheerfully. Only my old faithful Lump begins to feel the strain. I save him as much as I can and march on foot or ride in my Mercedes. Since Wegener was wounded I have acquired a new driver, *Gefreiter* Krüger. He drives cleverly on the crowded roads and looks after the car conscientiously. Müller has taken Wegener's place. He has strict instructions to keep the medical wagon where no fighting is likely. I cannot afford to lose Müller; he would be impossible to replace.

It is 25 July. Ten days since we stormed the narrows at Gomely and breached the Stalin Line. We have marched 200 miles deep into Russia itself. More than two-thirds of the road to Moscow is behind us. . . .

"By the end of August we shall be there," said Jakobi.

"Let's play safe and make it September," replied Kageneck.

Lammerding joined us. We were lying under a tree during our brief midday rest. "Here you are," said Lammerding. "Just come in—the official report on the battle of Smolensk."

Jakobi read the report:

In the middle of the eastern front, General von Bock's army group has brought the great battle of Smolensk to a glorious conclusion . . . tremendous and bloody losses inflicted on the enemy . . . 310,000 prisoners . . . 3205 Panzers captured . . . 3120 guns and vast quantities of other war material. . . . Luftwaffe under Kesselring[77] destroyed 1089 Russian aircraft . . . onslaught on the strongly defended Stalin Line. . . . Vitebsk taken . . . motorized columns thrust eastward toward Orsha–Smolensk on a wide front . . . on 16 and 17 July, Smolensk taken in brilliant fighting by a motorized infantry division[78] and held in the face of fierce counterattacks . . . tremendous battle developed to a depth of 250 kilometers, with the fiercest fighting near Smolensk and in the areas Vitebsk, Polotsk, Nevel and Mogilev . . . fate of the surrounded enemy forces was sealed. It was positive proof of the superiority of the German generals, the initiative of the subordinate commanders, as well as the extraordinary courage and stamina of the fighting troops. . . . This success is of the greatest importance for the continuation of further operations and the fall of Moscow can be regarded as a certainty.

Jakobi's hand fell to his side, then he handed the battle report back to Lammerding. "Fantastic," he said. "It's almost unbelievable."

We were all deeply impressed by this record of *Wehrmacht* success. Here were we, as a battalion virtually intact,[79] more than two-thirds along the road to Moscow; a huge and vital battle had just ended with the rout of the enemy; he must surely retreat now to the gates of Moscow. It was a triumph for Adolf Hitler, there was no question of that. We had to acknowledge his genius, and at that moment he was being hailed as the conqueror of Communism along the entire length of the front.

"Have you changed your mind, Kageneck?" asked Jakobi. "How about it now? . . . Moscow next month?"

"You might be right, Jakobi," Kageneck replied. "The roads are improving daily and there's a fast motor road from Smolensk to Moscow. Yes, we could be in Moscow next month."

"And then?"

"Leave it at that for the moment. When we take Moscow, we'll have the heart of Russia in our hands." His eyes held a faraway expression. "It could mean the end of the war. . . ."

"*Haltepunkt!*" It was *Oberst* Becker's voice. The regimental commander stepped from his car. I walked across to him and stood to attention at the salute. What was it to be? A rebuke, a little matter of discipline or a compliment, I wondered.

Becker took a small case out of his pocket. "In the name of the *Führer* and Supreme Commander of the *Wehrmacht*, you are presented with the Iron Cross 2nd Class for exemplary courage in the fighting at Polotsk," he said in a formal, yet friendly, voice. He pinned the Iron Cross and ribbon on my right breast and, shaking my hand, added: "I congratulate you. You risked a great deal."[80]

His adjutant, von Kalkreuth, handed me the citation and also shook me warmly by the hand. Becker walked across to Dehorn and pinned the Iron Cross 2nd Class on his tunic while the orderly's merry eyes shone brightly. The citation was similar to mine. I was content. My award would have meant much less to me had not Dehorn, who had shared all my dangers in the Stalin Line breakthrough, been honored in the same way.

Bolski was next for the Iron Cross 2nd Class for his work in the frontal assault on the third bunker, and then it was the turn of *Oberfeldwebel* Schnittger to receive the Iron Cross 1st Class for his outstanding bravery in leading the first assault across the narrows and silencing the deadly second bunker. One or two other awards were also made. *Oberst*

Becker seemed to know details of the part every man had played in the Battle of Polotsk and had a friendly and encouraging word for them all.

It had been a simple enough little ceremony under the trees, with the officers and men of the battalion standing around in informal groups. They now came up to shake our hands. Dehorn and I wandered across to Müller, who was with the ambulance and had not seen what was going on. He had been too busy cleaning out the inside of the wagon.

"Now, Dehorn," I said. "What are you thinking about at this moment?"

"I'm thinking of the end of the war, Herr *Assistenzarzt*, when it is all over and we're back at home. Then the others, the homefronters, will at least be able to see that I was there where the fighting was, and that I wasn't one of those who amused themselves at home. My wife will be pleased, too." It was the longest and most coherent speech I had ever heard Dehorn make.

Müller's face beamed when he saw our decorations. It was a genuine pleasure for him that our team, the medical team, had been recognized. He could not have been more delighted had the two medals been pinned on his own breast. He was like a football player whose team has won, though he hasn't scored a goal himself.

*   *   *

Next morning, Lump was dead.

Petermann's face was pitiful when he gave me the news and as he tried to break it to me he stuttered more than usual. "Wh—when I—I—I w-woke th-is morning and I—I—looked at the horses Lump was d-d-dead." He pointed. Under a tree, a few paces away lay my good old horse. He lay on his side, legs stretched out, stiff and cold. The relentless forced marching had sapped his strength and killed him.

"It's no fault of yours, Petermann," I said. "You looked after him well. Lump was just too old for this sort of thing."

We removed the halter; Lump's head fell heavily to the ground. There was no time to bury him, so we covered his body with branches and left him. I had to get a new horse as soon as possible. Our regimental veterinary officer, Nickerl, was away at the moment on a visit to the Veterinary Company. Nickerl was Viennese, a gay chap with a civilian approach to the war. I got on with him very well, largely because Martha was from Vienna and he was glad to talk about Vienna to me. I scribbled a note on the back of a casualty card and handed it to Petermann. "Dear Nickerl, My horse is dead—need another urgently, but no broken-down old cart-horse. Would prefer a young East Prussian horse. Will see you personally as soon as I can get away."

"Here, Petermann, ride at once to the Veterinary Company, wherever it is at the moment, and give *Oberveterinar* Nickerl this note. Wait there until I arrive, and in the meantime study the horses and see if you can pick out a good one."

We passed two burnt-out armored cars and four fresh graves—those of an *Oberleutnant* and three soldiers. Caterpillar tracks crisscrossed the roads and fields, and in a small wood to the left of the road were about 60 Russian tanks, facing in all directions. Many were damaged, but others had been abandoned undamaged. It was a commonplace incident along the road to Moscow. A few graves, a few burnt-out vehicles and the silence in the woods were all that remained.

Our marching column had little interest in the scene of battle; their eyes had become satiated with destruction. They wanted to get to Moscow. It was their only objective. They had been told it would be taken soon and to each man it meant the end of the march, rest, an organized life again, excitement, civilization, women, relaxation of discipline perhaps. Maybe, who knew, the end of the war! Victory! Every man looked to Moscow and looked no farther. It was the end of the road.

On 28 July we reached the Schutsche Lake and camped for the evening 10 miles from the town of Belyi. We measured out on the map—180 miles across country to Moscow! We had marched 600 miles from East Prussia, 600 miles in a little over five weeks.[81] Three-quarters of the journey covered, a quarter still to do. We could do it in a fortnight at the most, even with resistance stiffening as we approached the capital. Kageneck had been wrong. I told Jakobi. We could not fail to be in Moscow by the end of August. Winter's icy hand had pushed Napoleon away from the prize. But we would have Moscow in our hands long before winter set in—we could laugh at it then.

But for the next day there were no marching orders. We were impatient, but the troops were pleased at the idea of a day's rest. I gave them special permission to bathe in the lake.

On 29 July mounted troops were sent out to reconnoiter the wooded area of the Mezha ahead of us.

They patrolled 10 miles to the north, to the east and to the southeast without sighting a single Russian.

On 30 July we received the incredible order to prepare defensive positions.

The Cossacks Charge

During the next few days the whole of Army Group Center ground to a halt. A million men heard the order: "Prepare defensive positions." From Velikiye Luki southward to Roslavl 400 miles of front line became static. Panzers, motorized units, pioneers, artillery, infantry froze in their tracks and waited.

The corporal's wand waved over Army Group Center and turned it to stone.[82]

We were not to find out the reason yet. We did not, in fact, know at the time that the order applied along the whole vast central front. Did not know that the order "Dig in. Defend" had been given to the whole of that steel ring that was tightening around the throat of Russia. And mercifully, we did not then know that the steel ring would never regain its grip, that it would lose its temper in the snows of winter and would be finally sundered and shattered.[83]

The 6th Infantry Division was given a sector 30 miles long to defend,[84] of which nearly three miles was allotted to our battalion. Unbelievingly, we went about our tasks. Neuhoff and Hillemanns were away at a regimental officers' conference, and every man in the battalion was convinced that Neuhoff would return with the news that the order to prepare a defensive line was a mistake. For five weeks the daily order had been "March! March! March! Stick to it! We must follow the fleeing enemy and destroy him wherever he stops. He must not have time to regain his breath. The faster we advance, the faster he will have to run. Moscow is just beyond the horizon. Full speed ahead to Moscow!"

And now, when patrols told us that there was not an enemy for 10 miles or more around us, the order was given to prepare defensive positions. It did not make sense, even to the youngest recruit.

Neuhoff and Hillemanns returned and all the officers assembled to learn the news, eagerly expecting to hear that someone had blundered. But Neuhoff offered no explanation. There had been no mistake. He went straight to a map and indicated the various sub-sectors of the defensive line that he was allocating to the individual company commanders. Two companies were each given one and a half miles and one company was kept in reserve for counterattacks. Detachments of Kageneck's 12th Company were to act as reinforcements with their machine-guns. Two miles ahead of the main defensive line, a field guard, consisting of 40 men, was to be posted with instructions to report all enemy movements by messenger or radio to battalion headquarters.

Kageneck could contain himself no longer. "But why are we preparing positions here and inviting static warfare when the enemy is fleeing and there are no signs of him in our sector?" he asked Neuhoff.

"For operative reasons," answered Neuhoff curtly.

"What does Herr Major understand by operative reasons?" pressed Stolze.

"That also I do not know, gentlemen. No explanation was given, but it will sooner or later be apparent. At present it is our duty, as ordered, to build up a defensive system, to be on the alert and not to be taken by surprise." Neuhoff was obviously as much in the dark as the rest of us—and as bewildered.

The 3rd Battalion formed the regiment's right flank, Bickmann's 1st Battalion was in the center and Höke's 2nd Battalion took the left flank. *Oberst* Becker's battle post was two miles behind us and Divisional Commander Auleb's battle post was in the small town of Schutsche, on the edge of the lake. To the right of the divisional battle post was von Boeselager's now famous cavalry squadron. Each battalion placed outposts two or three miles in front of the main defensive line and by the evening of 30 July the line was already manned and systematically built up.

Next morning I set off in search of the Veterinary Company. Krüger drove me in the Mercedes, which was now in a shocking state. "Too old and worn," Krüger said laconically. "1937 model. Germany, French campaign, East Prussia, and now Russia. Two much even for a Mercedes." The oldest nag and the oldest car in the battalion had been pushed off on me while I had been an *Unterarzt* in France. I vowed that I would not leave the Veterinary Company until I had been given a good horse, and I would raise hell to get hold of a reliable car. But at the division I was told bluntly that a new car was out of the question until Moscow had fallen.

However, by the end of the day I did have a good horse—an East Prussian Trakener mare which Petermann had sorted out for me by the time I reached the Veterinary Company. I took it in spite of the Viennese veterinary officer's humorous protestations that to the Army there was no such thing as a good horse or a bad horse—they were all just horses. I christened the mare Sigrid and Petermann proudly led her off toward the Schutsche Lake, while Krüger and I returned in the Mercedes.

On the way back to our positions we passed a steady stream of civilians who had been evacuated from the villages near our defensive line. They were allowed to take as many of their personal belongings as they could carry, either on their backs or on their panje wagons, to other villages 10 miles in the rear which were to receive them. A few stragglers remained in one of the villages and we stopped to watch the peasant lads removing honey from the beehives[85] while their parents loaded the small panje wagons to capacity. Suddenly we heard a baby crying pitifully and realized the sound was coming from a deserted house.

I went quickly inside and in a wooden box near the oven saw a sickly-looking baby, about two months old. I called down the street for an interpreter and asked one of the Russians to whom the baby belonged. He pointed to the end of the village where an old peasant was leading a heavily-loaded panje wagon. His slatternly wife was trying to control eight children, while the older children were driving a huge pig along with them.

The interpreter told me that the family had abandoned the baby—there was no room for it on the wagon, and, besides, it was a sickly child, the runt of the family. I ordered the old man to go back and fetch the child and we drove on toward our battalion sector, but something made me tell Krüger to turn around and go back to the village.

The family was on the road to the rear again—father, mother, panje wagon, eight children and the pig, but again no baby. I lost my temper with the father and pulled my pistol out of its holster. Then the pig gave me an idea. "Tell him," I said to the interpreter, "that if he does not take the baby I will shoot his pig and confiscate it. He can take the pig *and* the baby—but no baby, no pig!"

The man had no intention of losing his precious pig, so he took the baby along.

*　　*　　*

The first day of August was a beautiful day—a day that had a holiday air about it. After breakfast we swam in the lake. There were few cases on sick parade and it was the first day of real relaxation since we marched from Suwalki for the attack on Russia.

Our midday meal was special holiday food, too. For the first time we had not the one dish, churned around in the goulash-cannon, but three courses, served separately: goulash (we could hardly expect to miss that), potatoes and vegetables. It was a masterly performance on the part of the cook. Dehorn had another surprise for me after the meal. He had captured some eggs and had beaten them up with plenty of sugar. We had eaten nothing sweet for weeks and our systems craved sugar. While we greedily spooned the over-sweet egg flip into our mouths, I casually asked Dehorn: "Have you ever seen an opera?"

"Yes, once. I went with my wife."

"Which opera did you see?"

"*The Magic Flute.* When I was on leave from Normandy last Christmas we saw your fiancée as Pamina, Herr *Assistenzarzt.*"

"And you only tell me this now! Why?"

"Herr *Assistenzarzt* never asked me."

"And how did you like her?"

"My wife said she was like a princess in a fairy tale."

"But how did you like her?" I persisted.

"She was wonderful, and sang so beautifully of life and death." Dehorn excused himself and rummaged for a moment in his rucksack. He came back with a Duisburg Opera program. I read "Martha Arazym—Pamina," and many other familiar names among the cast. I was filled with nostalgia.

"You're really a peculiar fellow, Dehorn," I said. "Fancy not telling me about it."

"I'm sorry, Herr *Assistenzarzt*. I've often wanted to tell you and then I've thought it was of no importance. Herr *Assistenzarzt* has other things to do and think about than listen to my stories."

"Dehorn, we have been together, night and day, for more than nine months and I know you by now—or perhaps I don't know you at all. But you know me inside out. I have only to clear my throat and you know exactly what I want. Yet in all that time I've heard you speak out on only three occasions; the first, when you thought the 10th Company's twin might shoot himself; the second, after we were given the Iron Cross—and even then you only spoke after I asked you what you were thinking; and now after our egg flip. In the future I expect you to tell me more about yourself and your thoughts."

"*Jawohl*, Herr *Assistenzarzt*." He smiled his usual friendly smile. "But I know no more that would be likely to interest Herrn *Assistenzarzt*."

"Lili Marlene" came into our lives that evening. The battalion officers were sitting comfortably together listening to the radio. It was a new set and we had tuned in to Belgrade. Our conversation ceased as Lale Andersen sang her nostalgic soldiers' tune. It appealed to Neuhoff strongly. "We will listen to it every night," he announced. "Lammerding, I leave it to you to tune in to 'Lili Marlene' every evening."[86]

Lammerding called his batman. "Kurt, I make you responsible for tuning in to 'Lili Marlene' every night, regardless of everything, whether there is an officers' conference, whether we are under artillery fire, or whether the enemy is attacking. As long as the radio set is not captured, 'Lili Marlene' will be played. Understand? Is that correct, Herr Major?"

"I'm not interested," said Neuhoff. "As far as I'm concerned, you're responsible, Lammerding."

*　　*　　*

Next morning I accompanied the staff officers on an inspection of the defenses; I wanted to be in the picture in case of any fighting. Nobody raised any objection to my accompanying them. My position in the battalion had now become almost independent. I was allowed to wander wherever I wished, and it suited me admirably. In this respect I was fortunate in having Neuhoff as my battalion commander, for many other front-line M.O.s did not have the same freedom. Their battalion commanders laid down the part they would play in every action and selected the site for the dressing station, which in many cases was not the best from a medical aspect.

Neuhoff, however, from the first day left the medical side of things entirely to my discretion and I issued a general direction that, except in special circumstances, the dressing station would always be next to the battalion battle post, a precaution that proved itself time and again in future fighting. The wounded always knew where to find me and, during critical situations, the final phases of a battle were usually fought around the battle post, and the wounded always had the feeling that they were being protected to the last. This feeling of security was vital to a wounded man.[87]

I was fortunate, too, to fall under *Oberstabsarzt* Schulze as regards medical matters. Every division had two motor ambulance sections, whose job was to carry the wounded from the front-line dressing stations to the Medical Company and then, if necessary, still farther to the rear, to the field hospital. Naturally enough, the divisional M.O. wanted to preserve his precious ambulances at all cost, while the front-line doctor wanted them to come to his doorstep, even under enemy fire, to avoid intermediate transport. *Oberstabsarzt* Schulze's sympathies were always with the front-line soldier and doctor.

As Neuhoff gave me such free rein it was necessary that I should keep closely in touch with the battalion's plan of action. In order to do this I had to see for myself as, of their own accord, the battalion officers did not bother to keep me informed. And on this August morning I rode back uneasy at the length of the defensive line we were manning.

"Not only too long—too many woods. Difficult country to defend," grunted Hillemanns.

Considerable movement of enemy cavalry formations in the wooded area between Rzhev and the Mezha had been reported by our aerial reconnaissance and, on a hunch, I filled Petermann's canvas saddle-bag with extra first aid supplies before I sat down for the first game of *Doppelkopf* since we had left Filipovo.

We sat around a crude table that had been knocked together by Kurt, and Lammerding dealt. Neuhoff was of the opinion that from now on we should have plenty of time for *Doppelkopf* as we looked like staying put. We played round after round and I had a winning streak.

*   *   *

The Cossacks put an end to our game. A dispatch rider brought an urgent message from regimental headquarters, which was followed almost immediately by an identical message from divisional headquarters. Neuhoff read: "Russian cavalry formations have broken through 1st Battalion lines in great depth.[88] Situation nebulous and confused. Only auxiliary troops and two outpost detachments are to be kept back for manning of your main defensive line. The remainder of 3rd Battalion is to attack enemy immediately in order to restore main defensive line of 1st Battalion."

Neuhoff commandeered my Mercedes and sent Hillemanns ahead to report on the position. Out of curiosity Dehorn and I went along with him. We drove slowly along the sand road and had soon left the head of the battalion far behind. I was not too happy, but Krüger had instructions that if anything suspicious happened he was to reverse behind the nearest bush and head back. Nevertheless, we kept our automatics at the ready.

The sun was setting over a dark wood to our left. It was there that we expected the Cossacks to be. Suddenly we heard the furious fire of our 10.5cm field howitzers and enemy shells exploding behind us. It seemed that fighting was breaking out over the whole defensive line deep into our positions. We drove on carefully. Some distance ahead, at a bend in the road, we saw a parked vehicle. We closed with it and to our relief recognized a German PKW.[89] A German cavalry captain stepped out of the dark shadows of some trees and held up his hand. "You are not to continue," he warned.

Hillemanns jumped out of the car, saluted and reported: "3rd Battalion, Neuhoff, on the march to the breakthrough with instructions to attack enemy and restore main defensive line." The cavalry captain made a gesture, Hillemanns lowered his hand from his cap and continued: "I request Herr *Rittmeister* to give me information regarding the situation. We do not know where the Russians are nor how deeply they have penetrated."

For the first time I saw the legendary *Rittmeister Freiherr* von Boeselager at close quarters. The Knight's Cross which he had won for outstanding bravery in France glittered in the last rays of the sun. He was the most decorated man in the division, was a man of few words, but by the fighting troops was respected more than the divisional commander. He stood before us, sinewy and self-confident, and listened to Hillemanns.

"My squadron will be here in a few minutes. Report to your commander that I will reconnoiter and find out the position. In the meantime, assemble your battalion in that farmyard over there and I'll send you information and suggest the best plan of attack."

"With respectful thanks," Hillemanns saluted and withdrew. I was relieved that our uneasy drive into the unknown was at an end. Several mounted men were already galloping up to von Boeselager. They dismounted and stood talking to him.

"See the one standing on the left of Boeselager. That's his elder brother," said Hillemanns. "He's the head of the house."

Forty minutes later the battalion moved off from the farmyard with orders to attack the enemy's unprotected flank. Dehorn and I waited for 10 minutes and then followed with the staff. Müller remained at the farmhouse with the field kitchen, ammunition reserve and supply unit. From the commander of the artillery detachment, Major Krüger, we heard of the Cossack attack.

In the early morning the outposts of the 1st Battalion, lying about three miles ahead of the defensive line, were surprised and completely overrun by about a thousand Cossacks. Only two out of 50 German soldiers escaped and were able to get back to their own lines to give first-hand information of what had happened to their comrades. The horde of horsemen had appeared as if from nowhere, shouting strange battle cries. Mercilessly, they had cut down the German soldiers with their flashing sabers before most of them had time to use their guns. Many of our men had been split practically from crown to toe by the deadly swords; others had been decapitated.

But the men in the sparsely-manned defensive line had barely time to grasp the horror of their comrades' death when the Cossacks were on them, too. They heard a blood-curdling *"Urrah, Urrah, Urrah!"* from a thousand enemy throats and the Cossacks charged. A few German soldiers panicked and fled. Other small groups fought desperately and, to a man, died. The enemy broke through on a wide front. The reserve company of 1st Battalion was thrown in, but too late to close the breach and the Cossacks, taking advantage of the confusion their surprise attack had created, carried the fight right behind the German lines to the vicinity of Becker's H.Q. A pioneer company fought alongside the H.Q. Company and artillery units fought back furiously at point-blank range, but it was obvious that our hasty defensive fighting lacked both system and cooperation.

Kageneck returned to report that our battalion's attack had fared well and that the Russian was in danger of being rolled up from the flank as well as from the rear. We heard heavy rifle and machine-gun fire and by ten o'clock that night Stolze had reached and recaptured the 1st Battalion's main defense line. Our 9th Company had destroyed several Russian infantry groups and had taken a large number of prisoners. The Cossacks rode off into the dusk like ghosts—back into the limitless depths of Russia from whence they had come that morning. The majority of them lived to fight us another day. It was our first experience of the Cossacks; they had given us a grim christening.

Von Boeselager's cavalry squadron pursued them and thrust for miles into Russian territory, on one of their piratical sweeps that had made the Russians fear them. They did not return that night except for von Boeselager's brother, who was brought back with a serious abdominal wound. I could do nothing for him, but sent him back immediately to the Medical Company for an operation. He died soon after he arrived there.[90]

We had no time to pitch a tent that night, but lay behind a low hill, fairly safe from rifle and machine-gun fire. Krüger had my Mercedes there, ready to move instantly. Müller and Petermann were still at the farmhouse and Dehorn and I each rolled ourselves in a blanket and lay down on the ground near the car.

It was a perfect night. A big moon sailed peacefully overhead and the fir trees cast their shadows over us. The noise of battle had died away until there was only an occasional staccato crackling of a machine-gun. When the morning mist rose from the Schutsche Lake and the first birds began to twitter, we awoke from our doze, stiff and cold. Dehorn and I moved into the Mercedes for warmth and sat silent, not trying to sleep any more. We were wondering what the new day would bring when, at 6 a.m., the Russian artillery opened up.

At first the shells exploded far behind us. Then some dropped closer, but to the right. Suddenly there was a deafening crash. A shell had struck and split a huge tree not 20 yards to our left. Shrapnel showered among the sleeping soldiers. Many of them awoke screaming to a searing pain.

Dehorn and I jumped out of the car and started to dash toward the shouting men. But before we had gone three yards, there was another hideous crash as a second shell exploded about 12 yards from us. A mighty hand lifted me and flung me back to the ground with tremendous force.

Molotov Cocktails and a Major Operation

Dust and smoke still obscured everything when the mist cleared from in front of my eyes. Instinctively I moved first my arms, then my legs. Nothing seemed to be broken. I picked myself up slowly and unsteadily. Soldiers were screaming and shouting. Evidently I had been dazed for only a few seconds. As my brain came back into focus, I could hear what they were shouting: "Stretcher-bearer! Stretcher-bearer!"

"Dehorn," I called. There was no answer. "Dehorn!" I looked around. Five yards from me lay Dehorn, his chest ripped open. I knelt down beside him. His skull was smashed and his brains messily scattered on the grass near his head. I turned away.

Someone else was calling for Dehorn. It came from the direction of my car. I ran across. A big piece of shrapnel had shattered both of Krüger's knees. He was doubled up in agony over the steering-wheel. I retrieved the medical rucksack from beside Dehorn's body and grabbed my medical case. I gave Krüger a quick injection of morphia to ease his pain while I searched for other casualties.

Jakobi was lying with shrapnel splinters in his chest, a penetrated abdomen, and his right knee and left foot were smashed. There were four other severely wounded men, and one was slightly wounded.[91]

Blood was running over my hand from a severe cut on my left forefinger, but it did not hinder my work. Three of the H.Q. staff tried to assist me as best they could, but they were clumsy and so nervous at the sight of so much blood that they only hindered me. They did not even know how to lift and carry a wounded man. It was cruel work to have to leave men crying out in their agony while I attended to another, but there was nobody else who knew how to ease their pain. I worked feverishly, but with an underlying determination that I would see to it that in the future all members of the battalion were given rudimentary training in first aid.

It was a blessed relief when the *Sankawagen*, which had been ordered by Hillemanns, arrived nearly an hour later with trained stretcher-bearers. The wounded men had all been attended to by the time it arrived and were carried to the ambulance. Neuhoff, Lammerding and Hillemanns had fortunately not been touched by the shell burst.

"Thank you very much, Heinz," said Jakobi weakly. He even managed a feeble smile. "The pain's gone." He glanced at the pistol he had given me. "Don't be scared to use that," he whispered.

"Good-bye for the present," I lied to him. "You'll soon be on your way home." He was in no pain now. The morphia had done its work. For the time being he felt secure and comfortable and had no realization of the seriousness of his wounds. I closed the door of the ambulance and knew that tomorrow his birch cross would be standing next to many others by the Schutsche Lake. He died within an hour.

My car had been struck by eight pieces of shrapnel, but the engine started when I tested it. I sat down in the old Mercedes to rest for a few minutes, lit a cigarette and tried to reconstruct the picture. Two shells had caused the damage. The first one had burst against the tree and had wounded Jakobi and the others. The second had burst on the ground within a yard or two of the first and had ripped into Dehorn and peppered the car, wounding Krüger in the process. Both shells must have come from the same gun muzzle, I considered. But if the Russian gunner had only shifted his sights by as much as a milli-meter, Dehorn would still have been alive to take his wife to the opera on his next leave and Krüger would not have to go through the rest of his life without legs. It was accepted artillery practice for the gunner to shift his sights after each round had been fired so as to spread the shells effectively over a wide area. Perhaps he had paused to light a cigarette between the two shells and had neglected to lay off the slight deflection. Dehorn's fate might have rested on that cigarette.

Müller arrived with the panje wagon at about nine o'clock. With him was Petermann, leading Sigrid. Both had heard of Dehorn's death and the tears stood in Müller's eyes, while the news had brought on Petermann's stuttering. I took them with me to find a resting place for Dehorn and chose a quiet spot beneath three young birch trees near a crossroads. It was a spot in harmony with Dehorn's peace-loving nature and would be easy to locate later, when the bodies were taken back to Germany for reburial. Silently, Müller and Petermann dug the grave and at eleven o'clock a firing party came along to pay Germany's last tribute to the willing little medical orderly. The body was laid in the grave, the salvo cracked and I spoke a few words of farewell. The firing party moved off and I left my two men to fill in the grave and erect the birch cross.[92]

Back at the battalion battle post Hillemanns told me that we had received orders to attack again at 2 p.m. The Russians were to be thrown back over the Mezha and their artillery captured or destroyed.

"Nice! Ten miles into enemy country. Broken ground. Woods. The Cossacks probably still there. . . ."

"Yet I believe it's the right thing to do," Hillemanns interrupted me. "We must teach the bastards a lesson. Or else we'll have no peace—shelling every day. Better this way."

Three Panzers joined us for the counterattack. They had been "borrowed" by Divisional Commander Auleb and were commanded by a young *Leutnant*, Pander. With them ahead of us we felt we could conquer the world.[93]

Russian fire from a village on the edge of a forest halted us. Between us and the village stretched open meadow land. Neuhoff sent a message to Stolze to thrust forward with his company through the wood at the right, by-pass the village and reach the River Mezha in order to cut off the Russian retreat. When he reached a certain point, Tietjen was to make a frontal attack on the village, against which Kageneck's machine-guns and mortars went into action immediately. Within an hour the village was in our hands in spite of suicidal charges by a small group of Cossacks and determined use by the enemy troops of "Molotov cocktails"—our first experience of this crude but deadly weapon, which set Pander's tank on fire.

But it was only when Stolze and his men emerged from the forest with a crowd of prisoners that we realized how effective our counterblow had been. Apart from the many dead and wounded Russians in and around the village, Stolze's company had annihilated practically every Russian who had tried to flee. Without opposition he had reached the banks of the Mezha ahead of the withdrawing Reds. He had allowed them to reach the water's edge and had then systematically wiped them out. Confused and panic-stricken, more Russian groups—infantry, cavalry and transport—had tried to cross the river ahead of the two pursuing Panzers. They had retreated right across the rifle-sights of Stolze's men.

When the reckoning was made we had captured 140 prisoners as well as a large quantity of arms and provisions. And my report that evening was: "3 Bat. I.R. 18—five dead, 29 wounded."[94]

Divisional H.Q. sent back its congratulations that this brilliant success had been achieved at such little cost. After all, five dead and 29 wounded meant nothing in the division's scheme of things. At divisional headquarters the junior *Leutnant*, Jakobi, was scarcely known—he was just a name. Dehorn belonged to the nameless ones, as did the other dead. And the lad with straw-colored hair whose eyes were glazed with pain and shock would be just another stomach case to the surgeons of the Medical Company. Fifty-fifty chance—might pull through. Try our best. What's that? His twin brother was killed at Polotsk? Too bad. Might manage to save this one for his mother.

By wireless I summoned three *Sankawagens* and dispatched all the wounded; the twin was one of them.

Among the prisoners were a few who understood first aid. With them, I examined the wounded Russians and had them carried into an undamaged house. One of the prisoners addressed me in fluent German.

"Where did you learn German?" I asked him, surprised.

"My parents taught me."

"And where do your parents live?"

"Near Itursk in Siberia. That is my homeland. Everybody there speaks German. Our forebears all came from Germany." He told me the history. Catherine II with many promises had induced a large number of German peasants to settle on the lower Volga and in Siberia. To this day their villages in Siberia had retained their German character, German language, even German songs. But they had been forced to fight for the Bolsheviks against us. The German-Russian was an interesting chap and could be of use to me. He knew something about first aid and could speak both languages fluently. He told me his name was Kunzle. "I'm taking you with me," I said. He said nothing, merely nodded his head. We went along the street toward the battalion's assembly point.[95]

In a barn a horse stood with blood streaming down its neck, and on the ground beside it lay a dead Cossack, his hand still clutching his saber. A machine-gun bullet had pierced the horse's neck and a jagged piece of shrapnel had torn a big piece out of its belly. Yet the faithful horse still stood guard over its dead master. I drew my heavy Russian pistol, placed the muzzle against the horse's temple and fired. The animal sank down dead beside its master. It was the only help I could give.

Wearily we marched back toward our defensive positions in the gathering darkness. Tonight we should be able to sleep, with no Reds this side of the Mezha; we were even well out of range of their artillery. But the thought of the young tow-headed twin jolting back in the *Sankawagen* with his stomach wound plagued me. I had been able to do nothing for his brother, nothing for Dehorn, nothing for Jakobi. Perhaps this lad would have to wait for his turn on the operating table; every minute counted with a stomach wound; perhaps a mother would open two letters within a month—twin sons, both dead. I asked Neuhoff for permission to visit the Medical Company before returning to our defensive positions, and Petermann and I galloped off toward the rear.

*　　*　　*

"They had another stomach case on the table when we arrived, Herr *Assistenzarzt*," whispered the stretcher-bearer who had accompanied the twin in the *Sankawagen*. I glanced briefly at the lad who lay on the stretcher against the wall, felt his pulse. It was slow and his lips were bloodless. He had been waiting about half an hour while the surgeons operated on the other stomach case.

I pushed through the door of the casualty reception room into a smell of ether and carbolic and went along the schoolhouse corridor to the room where Schulze had his office. "Come in!" he called in answer to my knock.

"Ah, Haape, what brings you here?"

"Herr *Oberstabsarzt*, one of my cases—a serious stomach wound—is waiting for attention. Can you tell me, please—is he the next for the table?" Briefly I told him the reason for my concern, of the brother he had buried near Gomely.

"As a matter of fact, he's scheduled as the next for operation," Schulze said, turning over his papers. "We could have kept five operating tables going at full pace today," he added.

"Thank you, Herr *Oberstabsarzt*. And—"

"Yes, Doktor?"

"If I may assist in any way, I should like—"

"Of course, Doktor."

I went through and scrubbed up, was helped by a medical orderly into a sterile gown and mask, no rubber gloves. They were suturing the man on the operating table. The surgeon, *Stabsarzt* Doktor Bockschatz, came through, shrugged off his blood-stained gown, peeled off his gloves and plunged his hands into a bowl of alcohol. "What brings our *Truppenarzt* here?" he asked me, with a twinkle in his steady eyes.

"The next case—one of my own men," I answered.

"Not the first, nor the last, I imagine."

"No, Herr *Stabsarzt*. But this lad is the twin brother of a boy we buried back along the road."

"What is it?"

"Abdominal. The bullet entered just above the navel and came out to the left and below the kidneys."

"Why do men have stomachs? We wouldn't say that in peacetime, eh, Doktor? All right, come on, let's carve your twin." The orderly tied his mask for him, held the fresh gloves while the surgeon forced his hands into them.

"Iodine!" called Bockschatz as he walked through into the theater. The twin was already strapped to the operating table. The assistant surgeon, his second assistant—a trained theater orderly—and two other skilled orderlies were in position. An intern stood at the patient's head, he was the anesthesiologist.

Bockschatz nodded to him and the ether started to drip on to the pad over the twin's mouth and nose. The orderly in charge of the instrument table silently handed Bockschatz a sterile wad of gauze with forceps. The second man poured iodine over it, making sure that the neck of the bottle did not touch the wad. Bockschatz iodized the entire middle part of the abdomen from the breast bone to the pubic hair. A large white cloth was placed over the patient's body. It had a long slit which lay over the patient's abdomen. The anesthesiologist pinched the abdominal skin with a pair of forceps. The patient still reacted. The ether dripped on to the mask and we all waited. Another experimental pinch. No reaction.

More sterile cloths were placed on both sides of the slit in the sheet and were clamped to the skin. The overhead lamp burned down on the abdomen. Bockschatz made a firm half-inch incision with his scalpel, starting a hand's breadth below the breast bone, down the middle of the abdomen to the navel, around it, and in a straight line to a hand's breadth below the navel. Two or three more incisions and the whole of the abdominal covering was open. The peritoneum shimmered blue-white.

"Clamps! Swabs!" Quickly the bleeding vessels were sutured. With the surgical pincers Bockschatz gripped the peritoneum, opened it with a small incision, continued with the straight scissors in the direction of the abdominal incision, and clamped the peritoneum on both sides to a linen cloth. The abdominal cavity lay open. The assistant inserted blunt hooks and the skin was pulled apart, right and left, and held. Unclotted blood flowed into the cavity. With a swab Bockschatz mopped up the blood mixed with intestinal content and bent down to examine closely the condition of the wound inside.

Fortunately the large intestine was undamaged; there was no immediate danger of dirt infection through coli bacteria. On the other hand, the small intestine had been perforated in several places and the covering of the great omentum was also torn and bleeding. Four hands worked expertly to stop the bleeding while two other hands held open the cavity with the blunt hooks.

Half-spoken words; instruments tinkled; suddenly the anesthesiologist said: "The patient's condition is deteriorating!"

"Oxygen," said Bockschatz conversationally. "Transfusion—you, Doktor." He turned to me. "And Periston . . . with a stimulant." The anesthesiologist took the mask from the big cylinder that the orderly wheeled up to the head of the table. I drew 200 c.c. of Periston blood ersatz into the syringe, a little Cardiazol to assist circulation, and injected it into the vein of the left arm. The surgeons had to remain sterile. I prepared the transfusion and as it started, the pulse gained strength although the lips remained bloodless. But the patient's condition improved from minute to minute.

Without pause the operation went on. The perforated small intestine and the great omentum were carefully sewn up. By now the patient's condition had improved so much that more ether had to be given.

Gently, but with utmost confidence, Bockschatz lifted the small intestine out of the abdominal cavity and laid it on the sterile sheet over the patient's abdomen. He examined it minutely to make sure that all perforations had been closed. Then into the cavity to close the entry and exit wounds in the peritoneum and to swab the last vestiges of blood from the cavity while the intestinal bundle lay beside the gaping hole. The abdominal organs lay exposed and clean. It reminded me of a clay model at medical school. Bockschatz reexamined everything—the stomach, the glands, the large intestine. All sound. The small intestine was lowered back into position in the middle of the cavity. Bockschatz and his assistant started to sew up the peritoneum with soluble gut.

"Serum—20 c.c.," said Bockschatz. The injection of peritonitis serum was given as there was still a chance of infection from gas gangrene or coli bacteria. The last knot was tied in the stitches of the peritoneum and the gut snipped. In layers the abdomen was closed and sutured. The entry wound above the navel was closed with a couple of quick stitches, the patient was unstrapped and the exit wound in the back similarly treated.

When the dolly dressing was in position on the abdomen scarcely 40 minutes had passed. The stretcher-bearers placed the twin on a field hospital bed and he started to regain consciousness. Bockschatz removed his gloves and bloody gown without letting his hands touch anything and prepared for the next operation. A man with a shattered thigh already lay on the table.

*　　*　　*

It was toward midnight when I walked into the staff tent. Pander was chatting to Neuhoff, Hillemanns and Lammerding. He seemed to be well-informed on the progress of the war and was emphatic that the thrust on Moscow had been stopped along the whole of Army Group Center's front. The bulk of the Panzer formations and many *Luftwaffe* squadrons were being sent to reinforce Army Group South, marshaling for an attack on Kiev. "That is Hitler's personal decision," Pander said, running his fingers through his badly-singed hair. "The generals advised against it. They wanted Moscow."

"That makes sense," said Hillemanns slowly. "We could have been in Moscow in a month. What do you think, Herr Major?"

Neuhoff considered for a minute or two. It was not often he commented on the actions of his superiors, particularly when the orders came from Hitler's headquarters. "If what Pander says is true," he said at length, "it means that the march on Moscow has been called off for some time. Mind you," he said, wagging his finger at Pander, "the men at the top know the overall picture better than we do, but it seems strange that when an army is advancing without resistance it should be halted. That's against all the rules of warfare as I was taught them."[96]

For Neuhoff it was almost a mutinous speech.

Von Boeselager's cavalry squadron returned after hunting the Reds deep in their own territory, inflicting heavy losses and keeping the enemy on tenterhooks. He brought word, too, that there was a no-man's-land 10 to 15 miles in depth.

We strengthened our positions;[97] the Reds made occasional bombing raids, notable for their inaccuracy; daily we sent out scouting patrols, but our counterattack to the Mezha seemed to have done the trick. The Reds were keeping quiet for their own good.

Patrol work came to be sought after as a break from monotony, and the only cases I had to treat were stings after patrols had robbed bees' nests in the forest and upset digestions after wild boar had appeared on the menu. The twin recovered strength enough to be sent back to hospital in Germany. We played *Doppelkopf,* swam in the lake, listened to "Lili Marlene," and—like the rest of the 400-mile front—stagnated.[98]

Stagnation

While we stagnated, the Russians worked feverishly to bar the road to Moscow.[99]

The Cossacks had not been slow to capitalize on our sudden and inexplicable halt. And the Red Army turned to good account the breathing space that had been flung in its lap. East of the Mezha, the Russians prepared a strong defensive system of trenches, bunkers, tank-traps and barbed wire entanglements. They laid minefields, reinforced their front-line troops, brought up supplies and gathered their strength to stand against us once more.

We had to sit helplessly on the Schutsche Lake and listen to stories brought back by our patrols of the rapidly developing Russian defensive system, and to read reports from our *Luftwaffe* spotter aircraft which saw the movement toward the front of fresh troops, guns and supply trains. Every day that passed meant two days lost in the drive for Moscow—the day that slipped by in tedious and self-imposed tasks—plus the extra day the Red Army would be able to delay us by virtue of being better prepared to meet our thrust when it came.

I filled in the dead days by training my replacements for Wegener, Dehorn, Krüger and two stretcher-bearers, all of whom I had lost during the last three weeks. In Krüger's place as driver I acquired Fischer, an exceptionally competent man, in civilian life a motor mechanic from Hamborn. He battled to get the Mercedes into reasonable order, but finally had to admit, "It's no good, Herr *Assistenzarzt*. Why not give me a three-day pass and I'll bring back a new car for you?" Fischer drove away in the Mercedes and in three days was back with an Opel Olympia, which he had built up from two Opels abandoned in a scrapyard in the rear areas. I thought it unwise to ask him how he had managed it.

Unteroffizier Tulpin took Wegener's place. He had served through the French campaign before coming to Russia, was very efficient, and far more courageous and hard-working than Wegener. In appearance, too, they were totally unlike. Tulpin had a narrow face with thin, compressed lips and acquisitive, piercing eyes. He reminded me for all the world of a gaunt parrot. But he had endurance, was quite unsparing toward himself in his care of the wounded, and was to prove thoroughly reliable during the merciless fighting that came later.

I detailed Müller to look after my personal welfare. Kunzle, the Siberian-German, was rigged out with a German uniform without shoulder tabs or insignia of rank. His duties were to look after the two horses, Max and Moritz, to help Müller whenever he could and, during fighting, to give first aid to Russian wounded. He came in useful also as an interpreter, for twice a week I had to visit a small camp for Russian prisoners beside the lake. Indirectly, this duty saved my life later on. Army orders laid down that all medical personnel who came into contact with Russian prisoners had to be inoculated against spotted fever, and I was given three inoculations from the limited amount of serum that was available.

At the end of August we received our first mail. For me there were 14 letters from Martha—she had written every day[100]—and two from my brothers. The air raids on the Ruhr had become increasingly severe, Martha told me.[101] The Englishmen were hitting back and bombing the industrial areas. She had spent much of her time in air raid shelters, and the operas were now playing in the afternoons, as night raids brought too many interruptions. Tchaikovsky's operas had been banned by Hitler. Martha had been singing in one the night before our attack on Russia. At the beginning of July she was singing in *Marriage of Figaro*, *Carmen* and *Madame Butterfly*, but some opera lovers, she wrote, were sarcastically asking when the American national anthem would be banned from *Butterfly*.

Martha had paid a holiday visit to her home in Vienna at the end of July. There she had found peace, for no bombs had yet fallen on Austria. But in a few days, she said, she was due to return to Duisburg to start rehearsals for the new season, which was to commence in September, although she mentioned that an engagement had been offered her by the Vienna *Volksoper*. Perhaps she had decided to stay in Vienna with her people. I wondered when our next batch of mail would arrive to answer my questions.

Next day I got to know von Boeselager[102]—via a dose of bacillary dysentery. Kageneck, who was a great friend of the cavalry captain, had recommended me to him as a doctor. I rode over to the cavalry camp and found dysentery had reached epidemic proportions owing to poor sanitary conditions.[103] Drinking water was being consumed unboiled, latrines were almost non-existent and the whole area swarmed with flies. Fortunately all the men had been vaccinated against dysentery and in that way were far luckier than a regiment that had been urgently sent to the front without inoculation and had suffered a great many fatal cases.

Boeselager had lost a lot of weight, had rheumatic muscular pains and inflamed eyes, but it was not in his nature to report sick. However, he proved capable of disciplining himself even to inactivity. I ordered complete rest, a good laxative, then sulfonamide and animal charcoal to be taken with plenty of gruel and as much liquid as possible. But he looked at me in scorn when I told him to keep a hot-water bottle on his abdomen.

In eight days he had recovered and entertained Kageneck and me to dinner in his well-lit tent. Hitler was on the menu. "Swollen-headed upstart! A coffee house politician who thinks he's a military genius!" Boeselager exploded. "Why doesn't he keep his hands off the war and let the generals do the thinking for him?"

"Because only he has the inspirations," said Kageneck gently.

"Inspiration is merely a fart that goes upward by mistake and finds its way into the head. Immanuel Kant," I said.

"We can't afford to treat him and his inspirations as a joke much longer," growled Boeselager. He poured some more red wine and leaned forward. "The Nazis are eating the heart out of the real Germany. When this war's over it's people like us who'll have to do something about it."

"Who'll help you?" asked Kageneck.

"Most of the generals. Talk will crystallize into action one of these days—particularly if we have any defeats. . . ."

"But generals aren't armies," Kageneck interrupted. "You know as well as the rest of us that all these young officers we're getting in our regiments are red-hot Nazis."

"And what about the troops?" I asked. "*We're* fed up because our advance on Moscow has been held up. But do you think the troops care? Not a bit! As long as they've got a place to lay their heads and two meals a day they're happy. They groused for a couple of days when we halted, but now they'd stay at Schutsche until the war ends—quite happily. And most of them don't care whether it's Hitler's Germany or our Germany that they're fighting for. Hitler still has a big hold over them. They still think he's infallible."

"We're all fighting because there's nothing else to do," said Boeselager. "Hitler or no Hitler, Germany can't afford to lose. . . ."

Idly I wondered how many similar discussions were going on in officers' tents along the eastern front that night.[104]

*　　*　　*

Under cover of an early morning mist two regiments of Russians burst through the thinly-held lines of our neighboring Regiment 37 and penetrated as far as their regimental battle post. Höke's 2nd Battalion was thrown in to plug the gap and we were sent there in time to mop up the surrounded Reds. They fought it out to the last man and the slaughter was fantastic, but they had also taken a heavy toll: the 37th's regimental commander had fallen as well as 10 other officers; eight more officers were severely wounded and more than 200 NCOs and men had been killed.[105]

Two days later, we were all back in our old positions and everything was quiet again. We had endless time on our hands and it seemed a good opportunity to give the troops lectures in first aid. I had been appalled by their helplessness on the morning that Jakobi and Dehorn were killed and had made up my mind then that nobody in the battalion would die for lack of someone to attend to him.

The lectures under the shady trees were informal affairs. A spirit of comradeship had been forged during the long forced marches and the officers and men were bound together by stronger ties than mere discipline.

These lectures on first aid, practical hygiene and infectious diseases paid rich dividends in the months ahead, particularly during the bitter autumn and winter fighting that followed. No wounded man was ever left lying unattended, even during the great retreat. We formed a tight community of mutual help.

*   *   *

"Soon it will be autumn. The war has lasted for two years now and we have been fighting the Russians for 10 weeks," I wrote to Martha.

It was 2 September, a balmy day of Indian summer and not a breath of wind stirred the fir trees.

"We have been living a quiet life for a month now while we await the order to attack Moscow, but the possibility of surprise attacks prevents us from relaxing completely. Today I again visited Dehorn's grave. I am sure that by this time you will have visited Oberhausen and given his wife my message. Perhaps it will help in a small way to ease her loss. There are always fresh flowers on the grave; Müller puts them there. One of the most wonderful things about this life is the comradeship; it is of a far higher order than anything one finds in civilian life. And, with nothing much else to do half the time, I am discovering Nature.

"As I write this I can see a small field mouse happily eating a piece of cheese that I placed at the trunk of a fir tree. The mouse's nest is in the roots. Of course, in the depths of the forests there are the wolves, bears and the elks that one has always associated with Russia—a different world, a more ruthless and powerful world than the world of my small field mouse. . . .

"I long for you, dear Martha—I long for peace and quiet with you, without the shadow of sudden alarms."

*   *   *

He was waiting for me as I drove out of the prisoners' camp by the lake—a tall, old Russian with a white beard and a threadbare overcoat. There was a touch of imperiousness as he raised his hand for me to stop and an inborn dignity in his manner as he walked toward the car. He addressed me in perfect German.

"Please excuse me, dear sir, for stopping you, but I have been waiting by the gate for you for several hours."

"What can I do for you?"

"My daughter is very ill. As you know there are no longer any of our own doctors here. I thought perhaps—"

"Where do you live?"

"About three miles from here. I know my request is presumptuous, Herr Doktor. . . ."

I opened the door and he stepped into the car, carefully laid his walking stick on the floor and, in spite of his threadbare coat, sat back with the air of a gentleman. He gave precise instructions to Fischer. I asked him his name. He belonged to a well-known old Russian family. "But the soldiers all call me 'the old Pan,'" he said. "Pan" was the Polish and White Russian word for "master."

The old Pan was evidently that rare thing in Russia, an individualist, judging by his house, which was the usual log cottage,[106] but lay rather isolated from the rest of the village and had well-kept trees and a cultivated vegetable garden on either side. At the back, the inevitable sauna-house adjoined a meadow.

"There are only my three daughters and I. My wife died in childbirth 14 years ago," the old man said as we walked into the house, which departed again from the normal by having a bedroom as well as a living room. On a proper bed lay the sick girl, who must have been about 20 years old. Her two sisters, one about 14, the other 17, looked inquisitively at me, but greeted me politely and walked out of the room without being told to do so. I examined the sick girl and diagnosed a serious attack of influenza. She lay breathing heavily with a high temperature.

"Your daughter is very ill," I told the old man as we walked back into the kitchen. "In order to bring down her fever, apply cold compresses afternoons and evenings and give her two tablets of Pyramidon three times daily. Nowadays there is an excellent remedy—Eubasin, which you can give together with the Pyramidon. Then Cardiazol as a heart stimulant."

"Yes, Herr Doktor, but where am I going to get all these medicines? We can hardly buy salt these days."

"Don't worry. I'll leave you a supply and I'll come around in a week's time to see your daughter."

"I am very grateful." The old man inclined his head. "Will you please have some tea? Greta!" The elder of the two girls brought us tea from the samovar and we sat at the table in carved oak chairs which belonged to another regime.

The old Pan told me his story. He had studied in Paris and Vienna and had been to Berlin, London and Monte Carlo during Tsarist days.

"How did you manage to stay alive?" I asked him.

"My wife was Swedish and we withdrew into the country where we hid ourselves and held our tongues until the bloodshed was over. By that time the Bolsheviks were in need of men who knew languages, so for some years I lived in Moscow and translated French and German into Russian—mostly foreign press articles and scientific treatises." He smiled. "I think in those days I knew more of what was going on in the outside world than people in the European countries knew about Russia."

"And today? Do the Bolsheviks still leave you in peace?"

"I'm content to bring up my daughters here. We mind our business. But, Herr Doktor, if you want to understand Bolshevism you must forget all about the Western brand of Communism. In practice, the Communism of Germany and France has nothing in common with Stalin's regime. A man here has no human rights—he is a working unit, valuable only so long as he can produce. Remember, Russia's 200 million human beings were the only raw materials that Bolshevism had at its disposal, in the beginning. And they were a thousand years behind the other European nations. Stalin has had to bridge a thousand years in 20. No wonder he became God!"[107]

"Yet you still have your holy icon in the corner."

"Yes, we do—and so do many of the peasants. But in a Bolshevik household you would find a picture of Stalin in the corner where we have the holy picture. He and Lenin have taken the place of God, you see." I got up to leave.

"Don't mention my ideas to anyone," he begged me.

"Of course not. But perhaps Stalin will not be sitting in judgment on you for much longer."

"Russia is great and Stalin is a hard man. It will be a long time before victory over Bolshevism is won," were his parting words.

Four days later I was drawn to visit the old Pan again. We drove up to the house and found the two girls frolicking naked on the lawn. The old Pan came out of the house and greeted me effusively: "My daughter is free of fever! I don't know how to thank you, Herr Doktor." He noticed my glance at the two girls, who were still running around the lawn, completely unembarrassed.

"Oh, the children have been having a sauna bath," the old man said.

"Children? They no longer look altogether like children!"

"And yet they are. Physically they develop earlier than most other nations, but they don't really become women until they're 20. I'm sure there's no other land in Europe where girls are so innocent."

"Strange! And we've always been told that Bolshevism glorifies free love."

"That was so at first, but it was an idea that could never have taken root. The Russians are a moral people, Herr Doktor. That idea was foreign to their natures—even the Bolsheviks have discarded it. In Moscow perhaps it is a little different."

My patient was much better and I prescribed further Cardiazol to stimulate the heart but took her off all other drugs.

Greta, her face glowing from the sauna bath, made tea and the old Pan told me more about Russia. An untrained worker earned only £15 a month, an artisan £100; engineers earned between £50 and £300 and scientists as much as £1000 a month, depending on the man's contribution to the building up of the State. These heroes of work often became very rich, particularly as they could also win Stalin prizes varying from £1000 to £10,000 for outstanding contributions to Russian progress. But they were not considered to be capitalists—they had not wrung their fortunes from the small man, but had been rewarded with a percentage of the amount by which they had increased the value of the State, the old Pan explained.

Taxes were very low, between 3 and 15 percent, but most of the money found its way back into State coffers through the State-owned warehouses and shops. A simple frock cost £5, a woolen frock was a luxury and cost £80. A pair of shoes cost £30, but an educational book only 10 shillings. A loaf of bread cost three shillings, but a pound of meat or butter was 30 shillings.

The apparent high wages paid by industry had caused the rural population to stream to the cities, but workmen's houses were not built. Splendid palaces, hospitals, schools and universities were built in their place in an effort to bridge the great cleft that separated the Bolsheviks from West European civilization.[108]

"Everything belongs to us, yet we do not even have our personal liberty. The State protects us, yet we live in terror of it. We have become a mighty nation and a desperately poor land at the same time," the old man ended. "And I am so poor that this is all I have with which to say my thanks." He gave me an old icon.

*   *   *

The first three weeks of September slipped away in an unhurried monotony of summery days,[109] until on 22 September we received orders to abandon our defensive positions near the lake and take over prepared positions near Rekta 10 miles southwest of Belyi. This was to be our jumping-off point for the offensive against Moscow.[110] We marched only at night in order to hide our movements from the enemy and reached our new positions on 26 September. The trench system had been well prepared and there were many bunkers to keep us safe from artillery fire. The Russians soon let us know why the bunkers had been built. Their artillery let go at us in concentrated fury. But in three days we had got used to it and felt quite at home.

Now there was plenty of work to do. The attack was to be launched on 2 October, we were told—the attack that would end in Moscow, 200 miles away. As at Polotsk our 3rd Battalion was to constitute the first wave. We had to break through the Russian lines and pave the way for the 1st Panzer Division.[111]

Kageneck, Bolski and I sat in front of a bunker studying an aerial photograph of the Russian positions we were to attack early the next morning. They were well camouflaged, but we could make out barbed wire entanglements and a deep trench system. "And behind that," Kageneck explained, "about three and a half miles back, the Russians have built a wooden bridge about two miles long through the marshes that lie between us and Belyi. It seems they've pulled down blockhouses and even whole villages to get suitable wood for the bridge. Several villages, marked on the map, have disappeared from the face of the earth. And that's going to make it all the more difficult for us to orientate ourselves tomorrow. Anyway, when we've broken through the Russian lines, we shall have to go for

83

this long bridge. The Russians built it so that they could eliminate long detours when they were building up their defenses; now it must become a key point of our attack. They may set a trap for us, but we must take that wooden bridge intact. As I say, it's two miles long, and once we're on it, we've got to carry on—we can't turn off it because of the swamps. When those are behind us, our own main difficulties are over."

Stolze ran toward us waving a huge poster. "Here! A personal message from the *Führer*. We're not forgotten, after all."

"Let's have a look," said Kageneck.

Bolski's eyes were shining. "A personal message from the *Führer*—wonderful!" he exclaimed. He settled himself comfortably, spread out the huge poster, and started to read aloud. It was like listening to Hitler speaking.

"*Soldaten der Ostfront*," read Bolski.

Since I called on you on the 22nd of June to stop the terrible danger which threatened our homeland, you have marched against the greatest military power of all time. It was the intention of the Bolsheviks, as we know today, to destroy not only Germany, but the whole of Europe. Thanks to your courage, my comrades, we have, in less than three months, taken more than 2,400,000 prisoners, more than 17,500 Panzers of all types, and more than 21,600 guns have been destroyed or captured. In addition, 14,000 aircraft have been shot down or destroyed on the ground.[112]

In a few weeks, my comrades, the three most important industrial areas of Russia will be firmly in your hands. Your names, soldiers of the Wehrmacht, the names of your divisions, regiments and battalions, will for all time be associated with the greatest victories in history. The world has never seen anything like it. The territory which the Germans have already occupied is more than twice as large as the German Reich of 1933 and more than four times as large as England. . . .

We now start the last great decisive battle of the year—the battle for Moscow. . . .

The Last Battle of the Year[113]

Powder smoke mingled with the morning mists that blanketed the earth ahead—a dull, dirty-white shroud, ripped open in places by the sharp flashes of bursting Russian shells. The flat stretch of land looked ghostly and uninviting, a place of death and of the dead. I stood with Schepanski, my new medical orderly, in the empty, damp trench and listened to the dissonant music of war around us—a tortured melody from a thousand raw, iron throats.

There was nobody to give us orders. I stood alone in my responsibility and sweated. My collar was choking me and I unfastened the top button of my tunic. Now I wished I had given way to the cowardly feeling of last night when Neuhoff had asked me where I wished to establish my dressing station. "Height 215," I had said after a moment's hesitation. It was the battalion's objective, beyond the strongly-fortified Red lines. I knew that by following closely behind our assault troops and being on hand when the breakthrough was made I could serve the wounded better, but neither Neuhoff nor anyone else would have questioned my decision had I elected to stay with Neuhoff and the staff until after the breakthrough. Now I wished there was an honorable way out for me.

From the trench, Schepanski and I had watched our artillery open up at precisely 6:00 a.m. and had been unprepared for the fury with which the Russian guns matched our bombardment—unprepared, though expecting it. Fascinated, we had watched salvo after salvo of smokescreen rockets, our new weapon, flash over our heads toward the enemy lines.[114] We had seen our pioneers ghost back through our lines after clearing and flagging a 30-yard-wide passage through the Russian minefield. Little Becker, his new *Leutnant's* badges gleaming, and Ohlig had jumped out of the trenches with their men and headed for the lane through the minefield. They had left us alone in the trench, to follow up 10 minutes later.

Soberly, the day broke in the east, like a gray monster, spreading relentlessly and menacingly toward us, seeking to engulf us. We went out to meet it.

No sooner were we clear of the trench than I felt better. I doubled up and ran through the lane in the minefield. Schepanski followed. A salvo of shells howled in my ears and instinctively I flung myself against the wet earth and pressed myself hard into a small hollow. Deafeningly, the shells exploded 50 yards to our right, showering us with soil and shattered sods of grass.

Up and forward again—keep going forward before the next burst catches up. I heard Schepanski gasping behind me. With less caution we ran across the uneven grass into a long hollow. It was a graveyard. Hundreds of Russians were sprawled in every position of death. They were the unburied corpses that had been left in no-man's-land after the fierce Red attack a month previously. Hundreds of mummified corpses, in uniform. They looked dried out and leathery, and when I accidentally tripped over a body it sounded as hollow as a drum. There was no smell of death about the place.

We ran up a small rise and lay panting for breath in the shadow of some thick bushes. Schepanski threw himself down behind me. I crept forward to reconnoiter, glanced up and felt my spine tingle. In the lower branches of a tree sat a Russian soldier, upright and motionless in the half-light, looking at me. I grasped my pistol firmly and tried not to breathe. But the Russian seemed not to have seen me.

And then it struck me! The Russian was dead—as dead as all his comrades in the hollow of death. I crept closer to him. His eyes were now only holes. His teeth grinned, yellow-brown, from shrunken lips, shriveled by the summer heat. Mummified and sunken, his parchment face stared at us. We paused and saw that his skin had been honeycombed by maggots. His rifle lay at the foot of the tree and his uniform was riddled with countless bullet holes. He must have been a sniper, caught in his tree by a burst of machine-gun fire. Perhaps others, like myself, had been fooled by the menacing attitude of the corpse and had peppered his lifeless body with bullets.

From the top of the rise we could see the Russian positions, lying about 500 yards ahead behind a network of barbed wire. And there were our soldiers, inching forward, making use of the slightest bit of cover. They were not yet within range for infantry weapons, and the Russian artillery seemed to have quieted down. Their shells were bursting harmlessly 200 yards in our rear although our own guns were still blasting away at the Russian lines. We took advantage of the lull in the enemy fire, ran down the slope, joined up with our men and made about 250 yards' progress.

Suddenly the world was in torment. Machine-guns and rifles opened fire on both sides, our mortars thumped out and simultaneously the Russian artillery opened up with redoubled and terrifying fury. We threw ourselves down and hugged the earth. Hundreds of shells of all calibers burst around us. The earth shook and I shivered as I realized that we were lying in the middle of one of the Russians' prepared defensive sectors. Every Russian gun had its sights trained on our piece of ground. We had given the Reds two months in which to range their artillery on to these defensive sectors and we were now caught in the inferno. Earth, sods and tree branches whirled through the air and I pressed my face into the churned-up soil.

For a moment the fire seemed to subside and I lifted my head to see Schepanski lying about 15 yards from me and frantically trying to dig himself into the ground with his bare hands.

Then the fire intensified and I was lifted bodily and thrown back to the ground. Shrapnel beat into the earth. I pressed my hands against my aching ears, wiped my eyes clear of dirt and brushed back my hair from my wet forehead. Hazily, I saw a deep, dark shell hole to my left. But no Schepanski!

"Schepanski!" I shouted. And again, at the top of my lungs, I screamed, "Schepanski!" But my voice was drowned in a fresh holocaust of bursting shells.

Quickly I jumped into the shell hole. But it was empty. Schepanski had disappeared—disintegrated.

The instinct of self-preservation dominated me and I was grateful for the protection of Schepanski's grave. It crossed my mind—illogically—that no two shells would strike in exactly the same spot. And I wormed my body into the soft soil of the shell hole.

For another 20 minutes the rain of death continued. It seemed an eternity, but then the Russian defensive fire lifted and concentrated on another sector.

Loose earth fell heavily from my uniform as I picked myself up. My helmet had gone and I wiped my dirt-clogged hair and took my field cap from my pocket. Hopelessly, I looked for Schepanski while I tried to regain my wits. As if in a dream I picked up a piece of his medical rucksack and automatically stuffed the few bandages it contained into my pockets. There were a few shreds of uniform, but that was all that remained of the new orderly.

Still bewildered, I sat down for some minutes in the shell hole, not doing anything. The machine-gun and rifle fire had now become more intense, but dully I realized that it could not harm me while I stayed in the hole. For a while I wanted to be safe—only safe. How strange that Schepanski had vanished from the face of the earth, I thought. But with the thought was no grief, no regret even. The whole thing had been an unavoidable accident. It was a pity—bad luck on Schepanski—but that was all my numbed brain registered. Of course Schepanski had not been a close comrade like Dehorn or Jakobi. It was no personal loss. And mixed with my thoughts was a deep relief that it had been Schepanski and not I who had caught that direct hit from the Russian shell. I secured my medical case to my belt and glanced at my watch. Fifty minutes had passed since that first leap from our trenches. Now I should have to remember my infantry training if I wanted to catch up again with my battalion. If I was to be wounded or killed I didn't want to die alone.

I crawled, threw myself down, ran a few paces and crawled again, until I came up with the last line of attacking infantrymen on our right flank. It seemed that the enemy barrage had not been so vicious here and our troops had missed its full fury. The Russian artillery fire had been just too late to catch them with its full force.

Close ahead was a mass of barbed wire, which had been blasted by our artillery fire. The remaining obstacles had been blown up by our pioneers or cut with clippers. Kageneck's machine-guns and mortars were giving continuous covering fire for our infantrymen, who relentlessly pressed forward. We no longer needed to fear the enemy minefields as they had taken such a pounding from our shells and rockets. Some of the Russian machine-gun fire subsided. The first line of trenches was in our hands.

The chatter of automatics and the blasts of hand grenades told us that our men were rolling up the next trench system in hand-to-hand fighting. Everywhere German infantrymen bobbed up, ran a few paces and then threw themselves to the ground. It was done so expertly that the Russian sharpshooters had difficulty in picking out their elusive targets.

Alternately running and lying prone, I crossed the last 80 yards and jumped into a Russian trench. Safety again. But there was no time to waste, for in the trench were eight wounded men, some of them in a bad way. Two of the wounded were stretcher-bearers, but fortunately with them was an unwounded stretcher-bearer. With his help, I attended to them as best I could, and looked over the parapet to see if I could find any more wounded.

The last wave of our troops had now reached this first line of trenches and our forward assault troops had captured two further lines. But the Russian fire was still dangerous and forced us to keep our heads below the parapet. Kageneck crawled along the trench and sat beside me. "If only someone would locate those damned swine, I could smoke them out with my mortars and machine-guns," he said. He took a brief glance toward the Russian sharpshooters and ducked as they fired at the movement. "Those bloody Red brothers are making things too damned uncomfortable for us," he added.

He risked a longer look over the parapet and crouched down with his binoculars resting on the lip. "I've got them!" he shouted. "About 30 or 40 of them coming toward us. They're against the light. I can't see too well." He ducked back into the trench. "Ivan is learning something from us: counterattack!" Once more Kageneck looked over the parapet. The advancing men were about 400 yards away. "Listen to that firing!" shouted Kageneck incredulously. "German machine-guns. They're using our own guns, the bastards."

Then he pushed his head forward as if he wanted to get right into the binoculars. "Well, I'll be damned! Those are German soldiers—our own men! Looks like Schnittger. . . . It is Schnittger!"

Again *Oberfeldwebel* Schnittger had initiated the decisive action. At Polotsk he had stormed the narrows, and now he had worked his way into the enemy's rear. The sight of Schnittger's menacing platoon demoralized the defending Russians, who surrendered on the spot or turned and fled into the woods. Many of them fell in the withering German fire.

Then, like one man, the 3rd Battalion swarmed from their trenches and hiding-places and dashed unhindered toward the clump of trees that marked our objective on Height 215. Schnittger and his men were first to reach it and jubilantly shouted coarse jibes as their grinning comrades toiled up the slopes.

The breakthrough had been made and the deeply-serried enemy positions were in our hands.

Tulpin appeared, unhurt, as the many wounded men were brought up to us. At first there were about 20, but more and more were brought along. We were able to attend to them thoroughly—stomach, head, lung, lightly and heavily wounded. What was more important, we were able to attend to them at once, thanks to having established our first dressing station at our objective. Transfusions were given to several men who were bleeding severely; they would probably have bled to death if we had not been on the spot.

Unteroffizier Schmidt, the sarcastic lawyer from 10th Company, panted up to me. "Over there, Herr *Assistenzarzt*! *Oberleutnant* Stolze! He trod on a mine, but he is still alive." He pointed to the Russian positions to the left of a ruined house. At that moment, the Russian artillery started up again, but was directed at the captured trenches, not at my dressing station. Tulpin, who had listened to Schmidt's report, stepped forward and asked: "May I go and fetch *Oberleutnant* Stolze, Herr *Assistenzarzt*?"

"And may I accompany him?" Schmidt asked quickly.

I hesitated for a moment, then said: "Schmidt, you will accompany me. You, Tulpin, carry on attending to the light cases. I'll be back soon."

"We have to pass through a minefield," Schmidt warned.

"Then let's get going."

We walked quickly until Schmidt put out a hand to stop me. "The minefield must begin here somewhere," he said. It was now broad daylight and we picked our way cautiously, avoiding all spots where the grass and undergrowth had been tampered with. The mines could not have been laid for longer than four or five weeks. Then we came to the area where our rockets and shells had churned up the ground and were able to breathe and walk more freely. We passed the ruined farmhouse and came to the spot where Stolze had been left, wounded. But there was no sign of him.

"What's this, Schmidt?" I asked. "I thought you left the *Oberleutnant* here?"

"So I did, Herr *Assistenzarzt*. I carried him to this spot." We doubled back around the other side of the house and then we saw Stolze. He was struggling through the ruins of the farm buildings his arm around the shoulders of a soldier who looked only half his size.

"Hallo, Stolze—not so fast!" I shouted at the top of my voice.

He turned and even at a distance I could see the wan smile on his face. His face and hands were grimy and bleeding in places. One of his field boots had been ripped and his trousers and tunic on the right side hung in shreds. He smiled awkwardly and explained: "That's where it caught me, Doktor."

"Come on, Stolze. Let's have a look."

First I looked at his eyes, but they were undamaged. Exploding mines often threw up a shower of dirt and splinters which blinded the victim. Stolze had been lucky. There were minor cuts on his chin, cheek and right hand, some deep gashes and splinters in the right leg, but the shin bones and the knee joint were apparently undamaged. I could not yet tell if there was any severe injury to the right foot.

"Not as bad as I feared, Stolze. Let's go to the dressing station and I'll give you a thorough examination."

We made quick progress back through the minefield, Schmidt and I practically carrying Stolze between us. No new cases had come in while I had been away, and I was able to give Stolze a detailed examination. Jagged steel had torn through the flesh of his right foot but his huge bones had taken the shock of the mine burst without breaking. "You've been damned lucky," I told him. "You'll be ready for duty again in a few weeks."

Stolze grinned. I gave him an anti-tetanus injection and followed it up with an injection of morphia, because he must have been in great pain, although not by a twitch of a muscle did he show it. When the morphia began to take effect, Stolze tried to get up. "I'm fit enough to get back to my troops now," he said.

"Listen carefully to what I'm going to tell you," I said as I held him down. "Tomorrow your foot will be badly swollen and you'll scarcely be able to move once the effect of the morphia has worn off. If you feel like some exercise, you can walk with the help of one of your men to that roadway over there, where a *Sankawagen* will pick you up in about an hour's time."

Supported by a soldier, he set off. He turned around and called to his company: "Don't worry, I'll be back with you soon. *Auf Wiedersehn*, and behave yourselves!"

Before Neuhoff and his staff arrived, all 26 wounded at Height 215 had been attended to; the 13 dead lay in a row. Hillemanns had also been wounded. A shot through the arm had put him out of action, I learned. After first aid treatment by Müller, Fischer had taken him to the Medical Company in my Opel. There was an immediate reshuffle of the battalion's officers. Lammerding was appointed adjutant in Hillemanns's place and little *Leutnant* Becker became *Ordonnanzoffizier*.[115] Bolski took over Stolze's 10th Company.[116]

*   *   *

Tulpin rushed up to me. "Herr *Assistenzarzt*—that serious lung case. He is deteriorating rapidly—seems to be choking."

"*Verflucht!*" I swore. The battalion was assembling ready to push on. I did not want to be left behind. I hurried over to the lung case. He was lying on the ground, struggling for breath—in a pitiful state. I examined both lungs, by auscultation and percussion. The diagnosis was obvious: it was critical pneumothorax. Excessive pressure of air between the pleura and the damaged lung had practically collapsed the right lung. The percussions were overloud and the auscultations on the stethoscope indicated that normal breathing sounds had ceased completely. But the worst feature was that the excessive pressure from the right lung cavity was pressing strongly on the heart and the left lung and had displaced them.

The wounded man would not last much longer—the wound aperture had acted as a sort of valve and too much air had entered the pleural cavity. I had no pneumothorax apparatus and there was no time to extract air from the cavity with a small syringe. There was one other chance. I iodized the right chest surface to prevent germs entering the cavity, and thrust a long thick needle through the pleura into the chest cavity. The air escaped audibly and gave some relief to the wounded man. Quickly, I clamped a long rubber tube over the end of the needle, fastened my lips around the end of the tube, and sucked the air out of the cavity to form the necessary vacuum.

It was an unusual and dangerous method, for if any air or spittle entered the chest cavity it would inevitably cause pleurisy. With utmost care I sucked the last air from the man's chest and then stuck strips of plaster over entry and exit wound as well as over the hole left by the thick needle. I left instructions that the patient was to be evacuated in the first *Sankawagen* along with the stomach cases and hurried after the battalion.

*   *   *

The pioneers went ahead to clear the roads of heavy anti-tank mines, and the 1st Panzer Division swept through.[117] Within 12 days they had daringly thrust 200 miles northeast to Kalinin, a brilliant stroke that cut the Moscow-Leningrad railway and established the left claw of the pincer that was to squeeze the Soviet capital to death.[118]

Our progress was, of necessity, less spectacular. We were approaching, as Kageneck had warned us, the long bridge of logs across the marshes. Without fighting, we had captured a large number of artillery pieces, which the Russians had been forced to abandon in their headlong retreat. Many of them were the 76mm type, which we called *Ratsch-Bumm*, because we heard the shell burst before the gun fire.[119] The shell had a terrific velocity and an almost flat trajectory. The Reds were in full flight and many infantry groups threw away their rifles and surrendered without a fight.

By late afternoon we had pressed the retreating Russians right to the edge of the marshlands, across which the only passage was the bridge of logs. They fled across it, but our heavy machine-guns raked the bridge and picked them off at will. As we saw them being mown down, unable to jump either to right or left to escape the crossfire, we thought uneasily of our own fate when we reached the other end of the crossing, which was likely to be under equally murderous fire from the Reds. But there was no alternative. We had to take our chance on the log bridge.

At dusk, our assault troops and pioneers set off across the logs and the rest of the battalion followed them after a short interval. If we could only make the crossing safely during the darkness, we would be in an excellent position the following morning to press home our advantage against the fleeing Red Army. The bridge was only six yards wide.

On the more solid ground, the poles lay directly on the earth; in the swampier places, they were supported by wooden piles. Our marching column stretched like eerie shadows into the fast falling night. The logs slowly sank under our weight and marsh gases gurgled on either side of us. Random and apparently aimless bursts of tracer bullets arced playfully and fantastically over our heads. Farther and farther we marched. We heard the tramp of our own monotonously marching feet. Nobody spoke a word. Our ears strained to catch any sound coming across the treacherous marshes.

Then, to the right of the causeway, I heard a voice calling pitifully. It became more and more distinct as we got nearer. The ghostly cries were in a foreign tongue—the pleading cries for help of a Russian soldier, only a few yards from the bridge. He was being sucked into the swamp, deeper and deeper. Silently, the German troops marched by.[120]

"Surely we can help him," I found myself whispering to Neuhoff.

"How?" asked Neuhoff. "I don't like leaving any poor devil to a fate like that. But anybody who leaves these logs will get sucked in himself. These marshes are bottomless."

Again and again came the agonized cries. I dropped out of the column and let the marching troops pass me. With the help of a soldier, I removed a loose pole from the bridge. We heaved the heavy log as hard as we could into the direction of the sinking man. The cries ceased and for a few moments we could hear the man splashing and struggling to reach the pole. We could see nothing through the darkness, and there was something uncanny in hearing a human being fighting for his life with every bit of strength he had left. He again shouted. There was a gurgling sound and I felt every hair on my body crawl. Then all was quiet. Dead quiet.

For a few minutes we were delayed while the pioneers quickly repaired a section of the bridge that had been blown up by the retreating Russians, but the last part of the crossing was anticlimactic. Enemy resistance was only weak and was soon overcome; by midnight we were on solid ground. We found some large haystacks and bedded into them for the night.

*　　*　　*

By late afternoon of the next day we had bypassed Belyi and were to the east of it. Thick clouds of smoke and the noise of heavy battle came from the town. We were ordered to march on and reach the main road from Belyi to Rzhev.[121] By straddling it, we should have cut off the retreat of the Russians. But we were slowed down by barriers of felled trees in the densely wooded area. Huge trunks, three or four feet in diameter, were lying zigzag for long distances across the road. Our troops cleared a passage with axes and used strings of gun cotton to blow a path through the larger trunks.

While we were delayed, a large number of replacements caught up with the battalion. . . . The men were fresh from Germany and were posted to the different companies. I selected one to take the place of Schepanski—or rather Dehorn—as my orderly and rucksack carrier. He was a stocky little fellow, blond and with a friendly open manner. I

92

saw from his papers that he had lost the sight of one eye, but had volunteered for front line duty in spite of it. He had been well trained at home in first aid and stretcher-bearer work. His name was Heinrich Appelbaum and he came from the Lipperland.[122]

"So you're prepared to be my right-hand man?" I questioned him.

"Yes, Herr *Assistenzarzt*."

"You're the third," I told him. "Lucky number three, they say. And you have three duties from now on. Remember them. First, always make sure you have bandages, syringes and all necessary material in your rucksack at all times. Second, always have the rucksack there when I need it. How you do it is your business. Third, you are to see that I always have all I need for my own comfort. You understand, Heinrich?"

"Yes, Herr *Assistenzarzt*."

"Now go to Petermann and get him to give you the new rucksack that *Unteroffizier* Tulpin has made."

Petermann was much relieved to be able to hand over the rucksack, for as he had told me, he loved his horses far more than the rucksack.

A horse was killed and a couple of soldiers lightly wounded when about 20 Red aircraft let their bombs go on us. It was the usual clumsy air attack,[123] but Neuhoff was taking no chances and ordered the battalion now to march in extended order.

"According to the map," he said, "there's a small village not far ahead. The staff, the 9th and the 10th Companies will be quartered in the village. The 11th and 12th Companies will remain with the vehicles and follow up under the command of von Kageneck."

Heinrich and I stayed behind to have a look at the two injured men. One had a calf wound, the other a splinter in the hand. By the time we had dressed the wounds, we had lost contact with the advance detachments, but as Neuhoff had said the village was not far away, I decided to follow them and instructed Tulpin to stay behind with the rear companies under Kageneck. I handed Heinrich a rifle and we set off, clambering across the tree barriers. We followed the sand road, on which we could easily make out the tracks of the advance companies. It was impossible to lose our way.

Nevertheless, after we had been walking for about half an hour, I began to feel uneasy that we had not yet arrived at the edge of the forest, but not wanting to betray my uneasiness to Heinrich, I said to him, probably to bolster up my own courage: "What we are doing now, dispatch carriers do a dozen times a day." I neglected to tell him that frequently the dispatch carriers failed to return. The more I thought it over, the more I wished I had remained with Kageneck, who by now was probably enjoying a cup of hot coffee at the field kitchen. But I comforted myself with the thought that fleeing troops are rarely dangerous unless you cut off their line of retreat.

All was deadly quiet in the road, although we could still hear the sounds of battle at Belyi. We walked another 10 miles when I heard voices around a bend ahead. "Good! We're getting to the end of our journey," I said. We quickened our pace and rounded the bend. I stopped as if paralyzed. Russians!

About 60 yards ahead, 20 or 30 Russians ran across the road from the forest on the right and disappeared into the trees on the other side. They seemed to have spotted us. I heard shouts. Another 10 men dashed across the road and disappeared into cover. I jumped behind some thick bushes to the left of the road and Heinrich dived after me. I grabbed my automatic and fired in the direction of the Reds. Heinrich followed suit with his rifle. At once, another three, then eight more Russians leaped across the road and followed their comrades. We pumped away a few more shots in their direction and I lobbed a couple of grenades into the forest. We listened tensely for five minutes, but there was no sound.

Then past the spot where the Russians had dived across the road, two German soldiers walked whistling toward us. They were dispatch carriers from Neuhoff's H.Q. taking messages to Kageneck.

"Where is H.Q. located?" I inquired.

"About one and a half miles farther on, Herr *Assistenzarzt*."

"Be careful," I warned them. "These woods are not yet free of Russians." Both of them grinned, probably thinking I was joking or seeing ghosts. "Ten minutes ago, about 50 Russian soldiers crossed the road along which you've just been walking."

"Ah! That accounts for the rifle fire we heard," said one of them, looking at me quizzically.

Their blasé attitude irritated me. "Now get on and deliver your messages and don't talk twaddle and dream on the way. Understand?" I said sternly.

They saluted. "*Jawohl*, Herr *Assistenzarzt*."

As they marched off, I could guess they were grinning and passing sarcastic remarks about doctors who saw imaginary Russians in the woods. I worked off my annoyance by preaching a sermon to Heinrich as we carried on along the road. "Those two bright sparks will dream their way through this war until they stop a bullet. Then they'll call at the top of their lungs for a stretcher-bearer. They're probably still sniggering because they think we've been potting at shadows in the woods. Good job for us and them that the Russians were on the run!"

With exaggerated casualness I told Lammerding of our adventure as I sat beside him eating fried eggs, but he was more amused than concerned. And I was left to ruminate on the streak in human nature that can never see danger in another's experiences.

"The Doctor's 50 Russians" became something of a standing joke in the battalion.

The Woodcutter's Prophecy

Winter advanced across the steppes to meet us and compressed our days into a shorter compass. Since "Barbarossa" started, we had already lost two and a half hours of daylight in the morning and darkness now fell three and a half hours earlier.[124] The nights were uncomfortably cold and damp and—unless it was completely unavoidable—we no longer quartered under the open sky, but sought lodging for the night in Russian villages, even though the houses were invariably bug-infested. But the retreating Russians sold their warm night quarters dearly. Their only real resistance came when we tried to turn them out of a village at dusk. Then they would fight like tigers for the comfort of a night spent around a peasant's huge stove.

We hoped desperately that Moscow would fall before winter took our armies in its icy grasp.

The din of the battle from Belyi awakened us before reveille sounded and again we were marching on the heels of the retreating enemy. We had not been long on the way when a formation of Russian tanks hurriedly withdrew to the woods ahead of us. And the villagers told us that the Russians had passed through only an hour earlier. Two abandoned enemy tanks fell into our hands—they had run out of fuel. We reached the road to Rzhev and learned with satisfaction that the breakthrough had succeeded all along the line and that our entire division was pursuing the defeated Reds.

In the evening we had to drive the Russian troops out of the village, which we had earmarked for our night's quarters. We herded the civilians into one half of their village while we took over the rest of the buildings. The Russian troops had already nicely heated them for us.

At several villages on the following day, the Russians had hurriedly prepared defensive positions and threw fresh troops against us. But fierce frontal fire and a pincer movement by our assault troops were always successful and caused heavy losses to the enemy. Those who escaped infected the resisting Red soldiers with their panic. Our losses were negligible.

On 5 October, we took five villages in this way and pursued the enemy until late at night. In the process the battalion's companies became quite widely dispersed and I attached myself to Bolski's 10th Company, which was in reserve. It was already 11 p.m. and we were night marching in order to catch up with the rest of the battalion for something to eat. We had eaten nothing all day, for, in spite of the frequent fighting, we had covered 25 miles. The night was cold and, to keep warm, I had dismounted and was walking with Bolski. Suddenly, in the light of a burning village in the distance, a dark shape loomed up at the roadside. It looked like a cannon, only that there was a faint glow at the bottom.

I grabbed Bolski's arm. "What's that?"

"The devil knows—queer, isn't it?"

"Hallo! Pass word!" we called. There was no reply.

Cautiously, we went toward it, automatics and hand grenades at the ready. There was another flicker of light and we made out the outline of a couple of horses and a field kitchen—our own field kitchen. One of Bolski's men lifted the lid and a magnificent smell of beans, onions and meat drifted toward us. But where were the kitchen "bulls"? There were no bodies or signs of fighting. We yelled the name of the cook, there was a rustling in the bushes and the cook and his three assistants crept shame-facedly out. Even the irrepressible Semmelmeyer was subdued.

"What the hell have you been up to?" demanded Bolski. "We thought the Russians had got you. For God's sake say something. Why did you desert the goulash-cannon?"

The cook seemed to have recovered his power of speech. "We were on the road to battalion headquarters when in the dark about 30 soldiers approached us. We thought they were our own boys, but when they'd surrounded the field kitchen, we realized they were Russians. At the same time it dawned on them that we were Germans. They ran away and so did we."

"Without saying good-bye to each other?" asked Bolski, while we both roared with laughter. "But come on, now you've found yourselves again. I've got a terrific hunger. What about you, Doktor?"

"Up to both arms."

We all had a ladleful of the stew—it was delicious. We gave thanks that the Russians had been so jittery when they stumbled across our goulash. At midnight we reached the rest of the battalion, which had halted at a farm not far from a village. Food was distributed to the famished troops and practically the whole battalion squeezed into the barns, which were half-filled with hay and straw.

"Thank God we halted here," said little Becker as I crept into a pile of hay beside him. "That village is full of Ivans. If we'd tried to quarter overnight there, we'd have had a real fight on our hands. Their feet are just as cold as ours."

No word came from Neuhoff. He had fallen asleep at once. It had become noticeable that the strains and stresses of these days were beginning to affect him more than the rest of us, and his responsibilities seemed to weigh more heavily on him by the day.

Becker had been right. The Russians had prepared defenses on the perimeter of the village, but the bulk of the enemy had slept close to the exit roads of the town and marched out half an hour before dawn. Their last rear guards evacuated the town as we marched in from two directions. Clearly, the enemy was in a hurry to get back to the vicinity of Moscow, but he must have been in a state of permanent unease at the thought that our Panzer divisions and motorized infantry divisions were already behind him, thrusting relentlessly toward Zubtsov, Staritsa and Kalinin.

We took a few minutes off in mid-morning to make the most of a State-owned dairy that was in full production. We all drank as much milk as we could swallow, ate fresh cream cheese with our Army bread and stuffed pieces in our rucksacks.

"Help yourselves, children," said Bolski, his mouth full of cheese. "It costs nothing. Father Stalin is standing treat."

A number of Russian dairy workers stood around and smilingly watched our soldiers gorge themselves. Kramer said dryly: "See, everyone is happy here in Russia—even the civilians. After all, Bolshevism has something in its favor. Nobody owns anything, so nobody can lose anything."

"*Prosit*! Heil Moscow!" Bolski said, lifting his mug of milk.

Next day, we took the town of Bukovo with little resistance[125] and captured a large number of prisoners. Our afternoon and evening were free, and Bukovo looked friendly and picturesque in the late autumn sun. The trees were preparing to shed their golden-brown mantles and the violet-brown clouds floating sedately in the sky reminded us that summer and autumn were bidding us a simultaneous adieu. Kageneck, young *Leutnant* Geldermann and I sauntered through the streets. The townsfolk were friendly and obliging. It was evident that they did not regard us as enemies or conquerors.

"It wouldn't be difficult to win them over to our side," remarked Kageneck. "We ought to be giving them back what Stalin and Bolshevism have taken away from them. There's still time—but soon it may be too late."

An old peasant stood at the hedge surrounding his wooden cottage. He was a wood-cutter—that much we could tell from the timber and axes stacked around his house. He would have made a wonderful study for a sculptor, for the weather-beaten face looked as if it had been carved out of one of his gnarled old trees.

"Look at that old peasant," I said to Kageneck. "He must have some memories. He saw the Tsarist regime; in fact, he was a mature man when the Tsar was butchered. And now he's lived for the other half of his lifetime under the Bolsheviks. I wonder what he thinks of it all?"

"I bet he's merely submitted to the Reds, never loved them," answered Kageneck. "Otherwise he wouldn't be looking at us in such a friendly way."

"If you ask me he loves neither the Tsars nor the Bolsheviks," put in Geldermann. "His struggle for existence has never changed. He's had the same misery, ignorance and poverty under both regimes."

"There's one question I know he'd like to ask us," continued Kageneck dreamily. "He's seen many soldiers—the Tsarist Guard, the Red Army and now the German Army. And he looks at us questioningly and wonders: Are you the same, or will you be different?"

"And," I added, "will you give us back our old Mother Russia and our Church?"

"Yes," said Kageneck, "and believe me, if we do that, millions will hail us as their deliverers; with their help we could really conquer Russia." Kageneck spoke quietly and with emphasis. I had never seen him in this mood before. Geldermann was listening with surprised interest. "If I could feel that this or something similar would happen, I should be a happy man," continued Kageneck. "I'd be satisfied that our victory would be permanent. Look at that old man's eyes; it's as if they demand a reply from us. God help us if we disappoint millions of people. If we do, they, too, will become our active enemies."

When we got back to H.Q., I took from my trunk on the panje wagon a sheet of drawing paper and a piece of charcoal. I took Kunzle with me as interpreter and set off for the old man's cottage. He was still standing at his hedge watching the doings of the soldiers. Through Kunzle, I explained what I wanted and he agreed. Yet when I started to sketch him, a shadow of fear came into his eyes. It was an expression that was never far absent from the face of every Russian we had met. The old man had no animosity to the Germans, he told me. His life had been hard and he was now in its winter. It mattered little to him what happened now—for himself. We chatted of the Russian winter. "The grubs are deep in the ground this year," he said. "It will be an early winter, a hard winter, a winter to remember."

His words were to return to me whenever I looked at the sketch, which I packed carefully away in my trunk.

*　　*　　*

During sick-bay hour I found the battalion's first louse. It was a fat baby louse. And it disturbed me.

I had to find out whether it was an isolated instance—I discovered it while dressing a patient's wound—or whether the troops as a whole were lice-ridden. So that evening I made surprise inspections of several houses where our men were quartered. I found that most of the men were wearing two or three shirts and pairs of underpants as protection against the cold—practically all the clothing they possessed that would keep the cold out now that their uniforms had worn threadbare.

Nearly every man was carrying a few lice, but in several cases, hundreds were clinging to the men's bodies.[126] They had bitten into the soldiers' skin underneath the leather waistbelt. "It's a bastard that I can't trust you men to report these things to me," I said. "And your medical orderlies must be asleep. Don't you know that the louse is the carrier of the most terrible disease it's possible to contract? Whole armies have been wiped out in no time at all with spotted fever. You may think the Russians defeated Napoleon; well, I'm telling you now that spotted fever, more than the Russians, drove Napoleon back from Moscow. The same thing could happen to our army," I bellowed. "Every soldier from now on is held individually responsible that he keeps himself free from lice." I gave Tulpin instructions that vermicide was to be issued to all the men, who were thoroughly to powder their clothing.

It was not altogether the fault of the men. I realized that. While we had been sleeping in the open during the warmer weather, or in our own trenches, there had been no danger. And during the static periods the men had plenty of time to wash and change their clothing frequently. But now the poor fellows were constantly on the move and sleeping every night in louse and bug-infested houses. They had no time to wash their clothing, little time to change it. And in order to keep warm they put on all their spare clothes and slept, dog-tired, in full battledress.

"And now, Heinrich," I said, when we reach our quarters, "we'll have a look at ourselves and see if we have any lice."

"Surely not, Herr *Assistenzarzt*. We changed our shirts this morning."

"Just the same, we'll have a look."

We both removed our shirts and searched. It was not long before I discovered the first louse on myself. We were both genuinely surprised. The final tally, after we had minutely searched every article of clothing, was four on me and two on Heinrich. I squashed them between my thumb nails. We powdered ourselves thoroughly with "Russla powder" and got dressed.

Neuhoff, Lammerding, Becker and I sat together at the evening meal when suddenly Lammerding interrupted the conversation: "Where the hell is that stink coming from?"

"Yes," said Neuhoff, "I've been wondering, too."

Lammerding sniffed around, got closer to me and said: "*You* stink. What is it?"

By that time I had got used to the foul smell of the Russla powder. "I have a progressive, hygienic and up-to-date smell, Lammerding. That's all."

"What do you mean, progressive and hygienic? You smell like a hospital sewer."

"Not a bad description. It's Russla powder—for use against lice. And if I'm not mistaken you'll soon be using it yourselves."

"What do you mean, Doktor?" Neuhoff asked indignantly. "I have no lice."

"Don't be too sure of that, Herr Major."

"Don't be silly! I never had a louse in my life!"

"I'm afraid for your own protection I'm going to ask you to prove that," I said.

Quickly we finished the meal and the three staff officers stripped off their shirts. Neuhoff discovered six lice, Lammerding one. Only Becker was free. Triumphantly I distributed Russla powder, for I was particularly anxious for Lammerding to smell the same as me.

Lammerding turned up his nose. "Now we all smell like forest donkeys," he said.

"No," I reminded him gently, "you're inconsistent. You now smell exactly like a hospital sewer."[127]

22 June 1941: At a combat station: the artillery fire is under observation. In the background a combat patrol is advancing. NATIONAL ARCHIVES; HEREAFTER CITED AS NA

German infantry on the march through dust and heat (summer 1941). HAAPE FAMILY ARCHIVE; HEREAFTER CITED AS HFA

An abandoned Russian artillery piece early in the Russian campaign. GERMAN WAR GRAVES COMMISSION; HEREAFTER CITED AS GWGC

Red Army prisoners of war. Dr. Haape describes his first encounter with Soviet POWs in some detail in Chapter 1. GWGC

A typical Russian village (summer 1941). Note German tanks at far end of the village. NA

A shot-up Panzer IV tank of Heinz Guderian's 2 Panzer Group. Note the *G* for *Guderian* on the rear of the tank. D. GARDEN AND K. ANDREW

German tanks in the "fog of war" outside Minsk (late June 1941). NA

A field conference on 8 July 1941: Field Marshal Fedor von Bock (left), Panzer General Hermann Hoth (center), and Air General Wolfram von Richthofen (right). As Bock's Army Group Center continued its relentless drive to the East, the field commanders had no idea that Hitler planned to divert their attack away from their coveted objective: Moscow. BUNDESARCHIV, BILD 101I-265-0047A-34, FOTO: MOSSDORF

A German assault gun near the Dnepr River taking on ammunition (summer 1941). The assault gun was a highly effective infantry support weapon. NA

Three graves of soldiers belonging to 18th Panzer Division. In the background is a light Panzer II tank. GWGC

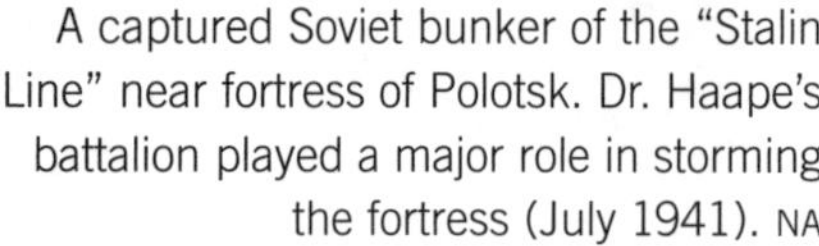

A German 21cm heavy howitzer (*Mörser*) firing on the "Stalin Line" (July 1941). NA

A captured Soviet bunker of the "Stalin Line" near fortress of Polotsk. Dr. Haape's battalion played a major role in storming the fortress (July 1941). NA

Russian children, barefoot and clad in rags—an image of the relentless poverty inside the Soviet Union. K.-H. HOYER

A German 15cm medium howitzer in action on 2 October 1941, as Army Group Center began its advance on Moscow. Dr. Haape's 6 ID would sustain some five hundred casualties on this day. H. SOHN

A Russian bunker position captured on 2 October 1941. NA

A captured Russian T-34 tank. These excellent tanks—perhaps the best produced by any combatant during World War II—first appeared at the front of Dr. Haape's 6th Infantry Division in October 1941, causing panic and confusion. GWGC

Elements of Dr. Haape's Infantry Regiment 18 advancing toward Sychevka, more than 50 kilometers south of Rzhev (October 1941). HFA

German motorized and horse-drawn supply columns advancing on the *Autobahn* toward Moscow (fall 1941). NA

Im Namen des Führers
und Obersten Befehlshabers
der Wehrmacht

verleihe ich

dem

Ams.-Arzt

Dr. Heinz Haape

III./Jnf.Regt. 18

das

Eiserne Kreuz 1. Klasse.

Im Felde ....,den 20.Oktober ....19..41..

Generalleutnant und
Kommandeur der 6. Division.

(Dienstgrad und Dienststellung)

Dr. Haape is awarded the Iron Cross, First Class. The award document is signed by the division commander, *Generalleutnant* Auleb. HFA

A Russian T-34 tank knocked out behind the lines of Infantry Regiment 18 in the fall of 1941. HFA

The German multipurpose 88mm antiaircraft gun in action on the Eastern Front. The "88" was one of the few German weapons capable of defeating the Red Army's T-34 in 1941.

The autumn rainy season, or *Rasputitsa* (literally, "time without roads"), transformed the Russian roadways into a miasma of mud and goo; the mud produced by just a few hours of rain was enough to transform a typical Russia road into a quagmire, significantly slowing all movement. PEN AND SWORD

A column of German infantry and vehicles (including a Stug III assault gun) advance on the central front (fall 1941).

The decimated remnants of Dr. Haape's 3rd Battalion abandon Schitinkovo (late December 1941). H. BRUENGER

Staritsa on the Volga River. At the end of December 1941, the remnants of Haape's infantry battalion hastily withdrew through the town toward the *Königsberg* Line. HFA

The main bridge over the Volga at Rzhev (mostly likely winter 1941/1942). The bridge was destroyed in October 1941 by the retreating Russians and repaired in rather unorthodox fashion by the German engineers. BRUCE SADLER

A knocked-out Russian BM-13 *Katyusha* ("Little Kate") multiple rocket launcher. The Germans dreaded the massed fire of the "Stalin Organ," as they christened it, with its infernal and distinctive scream. GWGC

The command post (CP) of 3rd Battalion (I.R. 18) at Malakovo, near Rzhev (winter 1942). HFA

A cemetery of 6th Infantry Division in Malakovo (winter 1942). HFA

The Army High Command (OKH) awarded Dr. Haape the highly prestigious German Cross in Gold in November 1942. HFA

CHAPTER 13

The Volga and the Mud

ORDERS CAME FOR US TO CHANGE THE DIRECTION OF OUR MARCH FROM NORTHEAST TO southeast. Aerial reconnaissance had shown strong enemy defenses on the Upper Dnepr; it was toward this area that we marched the next morning. It was raining—heavily.[128] The road soon became churned up and the heavy vehicles bogged down, moved forward for a few yards and stuck again. The panje horses and their wagons came into their own. Even the small 37mm anti-tank guns were hooked on to the panje horses and that way were able to keep up with the marching column.

The march on Moscow proceeded with gigantic strides in spite of the weather. We covered 25 to 30 miles daily in the pouring rain. We heard that 3rd Panzer Group,[129] for whom we had opened the way on 2 October, had broken all Russian resistance and without stopping had thrust far into the direction of Staritsa and Kalinin. The full might of von Bock's victorious Army Group Center was now converging on Moscow. Our pincer movements had caused one Russian bastion after another to fall. The steel ring that would tighten on Moscow was to be the greatest pincer movement of all time. We on the left flank were to be the claw of the pincers that would surround Moscow from the northwest, while the right flank of the Army Group was advancing on Kaluga and Tula and would squeeze the capital city from the southeast.

But the rain continued—rain such as this part of Russia had never in living memory experienced at this time of the year. So the Russian peasants told us. We marched on, but it got colder and colder and we were soaked through and depressed. The roads became quagmires and we thought bitterly of the winter clothing that had been promised us.

Two days after we had left Bukovo, late in the afternoon, the first snow fell in heavy flakes on the silently marching columns. Every man's thoughts turned in the same direction as he watched the flakes drop on the slushy roads. The first manifestations of winter! How cold and how long would the winter be? The black soil immediately dissolved the white flakes as if sucking them in, but as the late afternoon frost set in and snow fell more thickly, the countryside took on itself a white mantle. We watched it uneasily.

But by the evening we had reached the Upper Dnepr and were lying exactly 75 miles from Viaz'ma and 170 miles west of Moscow. Facing us across the river, which was narrow at this point, lay a strong line of Russian bunkers. Next morning we launched our assault across the river and by 6:30 a.m. the Russian defensive system was in our hands and the enemy was in full retreat. We thrust toward our next objective—the town of Sychevka.

The weather deteriorated. It became colder and snowed the whole day. But the snow did not remain for long. It was churned into the black earth, into which our vehicles sank deeper and deeper. The troops hauled and pushed the wheels of the transport; the gallant little panje horses sweated and strained; at times we had to take a brief 10-minute rest from sheer exhaustion; then back to the transport, our legs in black mud up to the knees. Anything to keep the wheels moving. To make up for lost time, and in a desperate race against the weather that we knew would worsen, we marched the night through and reached the area north of Sychevka on 11 October.[130]

Sychevka fell and towering pillars of black smoke from the burning town flattened and drifted over the fleeing Red Army and our formations which were combining to cut off the Russians' retreat to the northeast.[131] Company after company was thrown into the attack and by dusk many of the Red units had been wiped out. They had fought to the last man under the fanatical command of their commissars. Among them was one of the dreaded "punishment battalions" formed by Stalin from all those Red soldiers who had retreated without orders. Generals fought and died side by side with ordinary soldiers in these units.[132]

While hundreds of Russian dead and dying lay scattered in the fields, our battalion casualties amounted to only 21 dead and wounded. Among the dead was lighthearted young *Leutnant* Geldermann.

During the fighting I had instructed Müller and Kunzle to heat up a Russian room as my dressing station. I now had my hands full with the 14 wounded who were brought there. I sent Kunzle with bandaging material to have a look at the Russian wounded. He came back to say that large numbers of Russians were lying badly wounded on the battlefield. When I had finished attending to our own men, I went to have a look at them myself. Mounted on Sigrid, and with Petermann to accompany me, I rode into the uncertain dusk.

Cries for help came from a meadow dotted with haystacks, into the shelter of which many of the wounded had crept for warmth and protection. We rode toward one of them where there were two wounded soldiers. One was repeatedly making the sign of the cross and pleading with upraised hands.

"We must help him," I said to Petermann. But before I could reach the wounded man, his companion turned on him, swearing and threatening him. He whipped around to face us and spat out words that were full of hatred. Before I realized what was happening, he raised his pistol and fired at me. The shot missed me, Sigrid reared and I grabbed my pistol. But before I could draw it, the Russian had placed his pistol in his mouth and fired. He pitched over in the cold wet grass, dead.

Jumping off my horse, I walked toward the pleading Russian. He was still making the sign of the cross. I waved at him, replaced my pistol in its holster in order to reassure him and called out *"Karaho! Karaho!"* ("All right, all right!") He had been shot through the neck. As I bandaged him I looked at the soldier by his side. The dead man wore no ordinary uniform—he was a commissar.

It was madness to stay in this field of death. Quickly I completed the dressing and said to Petermann: "Let's get away from here. We'll have to think of some other solution."

The horses also seemed to sense the atmosphere of foreboding. No sooner had we our legs over their backs than they strained at the bit and galloped off toward the village.

Boeselager met us. "You got exactly what you asked for, Doktor," he said. "We must forget our civilized ideas here. A commissar doesn't expect our help."

I ordered Kunzle to commandeer 30 Russians from the village and take them along to help the wounded. Soon they were assembled before me. Young women and elderly men, one of whom was a partly-qualified doctor. I put him in charge of the group and through Kunzle instructed them to carry the wounded Reds to the big barn at the village Kolchose. I gave the Russian quack plenty of bandages and ordered him to write down the names of all the members of his group, so that none of them would shirk his job. I warned him that I would have anyone shot who failed to carry out my instructions. In future only Russian would help Russian.

*   *   *

For a couple of days the rain held off and on 14 October we crossed the Volga for the first time at Zubtsov. On 16 October we crossed it for the second time north of Staritsa. We were a day's march from Kalinin, which 3rd Panzer Group had taken by storm and which was to be the jumping-off point for the final thrust to Moscow. On the right wing of Army Group Center, General Maximilian *Freiherr* von Weichs's Second Army had captured Kaluga to the south of Moscow. The stranglehold on the capital had begun to tighten.

Another huge pincer movement had succeeded and the tremendous battle of Viaz'ma and Briansk—the southern bastions of Moscow—was developing. It was to be the greatest holocaust of the war.[133]

But the brief spell of fine weather was at an end. The rain again sheeted down, the temperature dropped, the rain gave way to hail, then snow. Then it rained again. The offensive faltered and bogged down. Marching troops and men on horseback squelched forward through the clinging mud, but vehicles sank three feet deep in the quagmire. Even the light panje wagons sank to their wheel hubs and we lashed runners like skis to the underside of the axles so that men and horses could drag them clear of the worst patches.

Motorized transport was left behind, tilted at crazy angles, blocking roads, embedded in the ooze. Then men and vehicles would take to the fields on either side of the blocked road, and the tracks would gradually widen until there was a churned-up, deeply-rutted swamp, 200 yards wide, along which nothing could pass. The mud seemed bottomless. Supply columns were unable to reach the front and petrol supplies were exhausted, so the Heinkels towed huge cargo-carrying gliders, which crash-landed near us and brought the Army's life-blood—petrol for the stranded Panzers and motor vehicles, which struggled on for a few miles, then bogged hopelessly down and were abandoned. We hitched our light guns and anti-tank cannons to the panje horses and transferred ammunition to panje wagons; somehow we dragged the field kitchen along with us, although hot meals occasionally happened—and usually did not.

The push had virtually come to a stop.[134] And still it rained—steel rods of rain that slashed us at every step we took and hammered on the wooden roofs whenever we found shelter for the night.

In these conditions Army Group Center brought the vast cauldron battle of Viaz'ma and Briansk to a victorious conclusion. The booty—tanks, guns and equipment—was never properly assessed. The number of prisoners could scarcely be counted, but it was said that more than 600,000 were taken.[135] The ever-growing stream passed us, heading west. A battalion, a regiment, a division was of small account on this vast battlefield. Yet each one, and each man in every unit, had to face and master the impossible conditions. The penultimate victory had been won. The Red Army had staked all on being able to hold us at Viaz'ma and Briansk. The last obstacle to Moscow had been overcome.

Now the Russians had one last ally, if only he would come to their assistance as he had done before. General Winter! Somehow we had struggled through the heaviest winter rains in living memory. Now I thought of the old woodcutter at Bukovo and his prophecy: "The grubs are deep in the ground this year. There will be an early winter." Perhaps the huge freeze would hold off long enough for us to capture Moscow.

On 21 October we stormed across the Volga between Staritsa and Kalinin and, breaking all resistance, thrust in the direction of Torzhok and shared quarters for the night with the artillery in a small village. We were on the alert, for strong Russian formations were marching parallel to us only five miles away.

The next morning was clear and bright; the rain and hail of the previous day had disappeared. We were preparing to continue our march to the northeast when a column of Russians was spotted by our observation post, marching unsuspectingly on the village. With Kageneck, I went to the observation post. A strong force of mounted Russians, followed by artillery, was emerging from the woods and heading for the village. On they came, rank after rank, gun upon gun, detachment after detachment. Our artillery and machine-guns were trained on the unprepared Russians. Then came the order to fire.

The first salvo from the field howitzers crashed on to the dense column from a range of 600 yards. It was slaughter. The Reds were thrown into helpless confusion; horses reared and fell; teams became unmanageable. The second salvo hit them from point-blank range and whoever still remained in the saddle galloped wildly toward the woods. Then our heavy machine-guns took over to continue the massacre while the Russians desperately threw themselves to the ground.

A number of the officers gathered in the observation post shouted with glee at the mass execution. I turned away, trying hard to remember the slaughter of our own troops on the Schutsche line by the Cossacks. Kageneck patted me on the shoulder and said: "Nothing can be done about it. Rather them than us. Kill or be killed."

The carnage was over, without a shot having been fired by the Russians. Before we marched off, I had the wounded Reds carried to a house, where I gave them what attention I could and left them in the hands of Russian civilians. Kageneck and I rode out of the village side by side. "I'm beginning to regard myself as a bit of a fool," I told him, "always wearily stitching together what others deliberately shoot to pieces. It's so damned illogical."

"It's war, Heinz. We must make the best of it," Kageneck shrugged his shoulders.

"What about all the prisoners we've taken?" I asked him. "What has happened to the half-million men we've captured during the last three weeks?"

"How can an advancing army handle numbers like that? It's an impossible position."

"So the best we can do is to herd them together in the open—in the freezing cold and the rain. Give them nothing to eat! Leave them to die! I believe they're actually turning cannibal."[136]

"Don't get too sympathetic," said Kageneck harshly. "What the hell can we do? Don't forget all our supply columns were bogged; and that the Russians burned their cornfields and destroyed all their granaries and other food supplies when they retreated.[137] They did that—not us. And they blew up the railway lines. It's on their own heads. You're just feeling depressed."

"You're absolutely right. I am," I said with feeling.

"Then think about our own difficulties and cheer yourself up," said Kageneck with a smile. "Do you realize we've had nothing but horse meat in our goulash for three days?"

There were two explosions ahead. "Stretcher-bearer and doctor to the front!" The familiar cry came back along the marching column. The tip of the battalion had walked straight into a freshly laid minefield on the road. I galloped to the front.

Three men lay in the minefield. Two had been killed instantly; the right leg of the third man had been torn out of the hip socket and portions of his entrails were hanging from his horribly gashed belly. He was screaming in agony.

The minefield was at the approaches to a small bridge spanning a stream. I stood about 30 yards from the horribly mutilated soldier, but it would have been madness to run to him across the road, even with the aid of a mine detector. The Reds were in the habit of using "wooden mines," which contained practically no metal parts and reacted weakly, if at all, to a detector. But I could not endure the screams of the wounded man.

The mines would not have been laid for more than a couple of days and, to the right of the road, grass and weeds were growing. Followed by Heinrich, I ran through the overgrown ground to the stream, waded through the water to the bridge, climbed on to it and reached the wounded man from the other side.

It was Max Steinbrink, a friendly lad, liked by everyone. He was twisting his body in agony and in his despair kept raising himself on his sound arm and staring horrified at his bloody entrails, which were dangling in the earth, and at the place where his right leg had been only a few moments before. Obviously he would be dead within half an hour, whatever I did for him. I had to make up my mind quickly, for the lad's agony was inconceivable.

His body jerked and he screamed: "Help me! Oh, Mother, Mother, Mother!" Then he seemed to realize for the first time that we were at his side and he entreated: "Help me, please."

The battalion had halted at the minefield and the men were gazing with horrified fascination as I whispered to Heinrich: "Morphia, Heinrich, morphia."

"I will help you," I told the lad.

Heinrich handed me the syringe and an ampule of morphia. I broke the ampule and drew up the morphia. "Another ampule, Heinrich." The wounded man groaned again and stared at us. "Oh, help me, please, Mother, Mother!" he screamed again. The one minute of preparation was to him a dreadful eternity of suffering. Heinrich stemmed the arm and I injected the morphia intravenously. Deliberately I sought the vein, because an intramuscular injection would have taken 10 minutes longer to work. It would have been brutal to prolong the misery of the doomed boy. The morphia ran through his veins. The twisted expression smoothed out and he looked at Heinrich and me with grateful eyes. He was no longer in pain. Heinrich knelt by him and supported his head.

"Now everything will be all right," I said to the dying lad as I took his hand. He no longer replied, but slowly closed his eyes. He pressed my hand tightly, as if saying farewell. I knew then that young Max Steinbrink had understood.

In a few minutes his grip relaxed, his head fell back and he died in Heinrich's arms.

"March!" came the order and the battalion skirted the minefield and crossed the stream while I stood on the bridge. I felt exhausted as if I had just completed a major operation.

Pioneers cleared the mines, others dug three graves near the bridge, three volleys rang out, three crosses were planted near the roadside and the battalion marched on in silence. We halted for the night at Vassilevskoye, a village at the tip of a wedge we had driven into enemy country. The villages on either side were still in Russian hands. I set up my dressing station and sick bay near the battalion battle post.[138]

"General Winter" and the T-34

That night the first case of spotted fever hit the battalion. Heinrich came to me and reported that a soldier had been brought in for treatment who appeared to be delirious. I went to examine him at once.

The man was running an exceptionally high temperature; he had a cough, the membranes of the eyes were slightly red and his face was swollen and distorted. Examination of the lungs revealed bronchitis but no pneumonia. His speech was incoherent and confused and he was restless and unable to concentrate. There was no longer any doubt in my mind; it was what I had feared would happen sooner or later—I had a case of spotted fever on my hands. In five days' time a number of large red patches would begin to show on the stomach and shoulders and would then spread over the whole body. This would be accompanied by a disordered brain and hallucinations and would probably end in death. I wrapped a clean blanket around the man and applied "Russla powder" liberally to prevent any possibility of infected lice spreading the disease. On the casualty card I thickly underlined in red the words "Spotted Fever." Then I sent him off in the ambulance and sat down to think.

The solitary case of spotted fever in the battalion was far more alarming than a score of battlefield casualties. I tried to think of the best method to attack the disease at its source—how to rid ourselves of the lice. It was clear that the Russla powder was ineffective, and I knew that the men loathed its smell and hated using it. I turned to Tulpin: "What do our men think of Russla powder?" I asked him.

"They joke about it and call it the lice feeder," he said bluntly.

I was under no delusions about the seriousness of the situation. Only small quantities of vaccine were available—next to nothing, in fact. And now our only protection, the Russla powder, seemed to be useless.

"We'll see just how effective this powder is," I said to my staff. I placed a glass of water on the table. "Now strip; we'll put every louse we find into that glass."

It was a strange scene—Tulpin's naked, wiry frame next to the sturdy muscular body of Heinrich. Müller sat on the first aid box and I sat on the only chair. Also, as a privilege of my rank, I retained my underpants. For some reason I thought it would look more dignified in front of my men.

One louse after another swam in the glass, and eventually our catch totaled 14. It was disconcerting; not one of us was free from the pests, and yet we had all religiously applied the powder. Müller's skin was red and inflamed, particularly where he had sweated and his clothing had rubbed the spot. It was eczema, clearly the effect of hypersensitivity to the Russla powder.

"Come here, Müller," I said to him. "Let me examine your rash more closely." As we moved under the lamp, the door of the room was thrown open and *Oberst* Becker and Major Neuhoff were framed in the doorway.

"*Achtung!*" I shouted. Everyone stood to attention. I was speechless, and so it seemed was Neuhoff. Becker broke the embarrassed silence by bursting into laughter. "Well," he said good-humoredly, "what's the matter, *Haltepunkt*? What on earth are you up to?"

I had recovered my wits and reported: "Three nude men and one man in underpants from Infantry Regiment 18 are hunting for lice in order to determine the effect of Russla powder, Herr *Oberst*."

"And what's the result of the investigation? I am interested to know."

"Not exactly reassuring, Herr *Oberst*."

"Why?"

"In the first place, the powder has an unpleasant smell and the troops use it only reluctantly. Secondly, the skin of some people is allergic to it. Notice this man, Herr *Oberst*"— I pointed to Müller—"he is hypersensitive to it."

"Is that all, *Haltepunkt*?"

"No, Herr *Oberst*. Worst of all—the Russla powder is not very effective as a vermicide. In spite of our using it regularly for the last 12 days, we have found 14 lice between us. There they are in the glass. And I have to report that the battalion has its first case of spotted fever. The patient was removed to the field hospital an hour ago."

Becker looked grave. "But that's a very serious business. What can we do about it?" he asked.

"Very little at present, sir. We will continue to use Russla powder, which helps a little, at least. I'll try to get as much vaccine as possible so that I can inoculate the most pressing cases, and our soldiers must be kept away from the Russian civilians as far as possible. . . ."

"Not so easy," Becker interrupted. "Anything else?"

"Yes, Herr *Oberst*." I was determined to take the opportunity of enlisting the aid of the regimental commander in fighting the threatened outbreak of spotted fever. "The troops must be closely watched and any suspicious cases isolated immediately, as well as the men who have been in contact with the patients. It will also be necessary to keep these areas under quarantine. Frequent washing of underclothing is essential." I paused and gave voice to the grouse that every man in the battalion had: "This will be easier when the winter clothing arrives, but at present the soldiers wear all their clothing in order to keep warm and have no change of underclothes. As soon as the marching stops and we occupy static winter positions, delousing stations must be built and systematic delousing of the troops carried out."

"That all adds up to a tall order," said Becker thoughtfully. "But you can count on me for all the support you need. Yes, yes—of that you may rest assured."

Becker glanced at Neuhoff, smiled and murmured enigmatically: "It will not be so simple under these conditions."

Neuhoff returned the smile and whispered to me: "Doktor, will you get dressed quickly, please."

"Certainly, Herr Major." I had been so absorbed in stating my case to Becker that I had forgotten that only my underpants saved me from nakedness. I grabbed my clothing and retired behind the stove. Neuhoff followed me and again whispered: "Doktor, get dressed properly and put on your belt and cap. You are being awarded the Iron Cross First Class."[139]

Fully and faultlessly dressed, I reported to *Oberst* Becker. He pinned the Iron Cross on my tunic, and said: "*Haltepunkt*, this is an acknowledgment of what you have done for your troops since 2 October. Will you particularly associate this award with proud memories of the storming of Height 215?" First Becker and then Neuhoff shook my hand and left.

"Clink!" I heard. Tulpin had upset the water and the lice all over the floor. My first duty as a holder of the Iron Cross First Class was to help the others to retrieve the lice and squash them with a pair of tweezers.

Then for a second I allowed myself to daydream. Rumor said that as soon as the advance came to an end, leave would be given—I knew I should be among the first to go. The Iron Cross would look well against my black evening dress. I'd be quite a hero back home.

Abruptly I came back to earth and the combined smell of Russla powder and the naked bodies of hard-working men. "Get dressed at once," I told them. "See to it that the sick bay is left looking respectable and we'll spend part of the evening celebrating this Iron Cross. My share will be the remnants of my coffee beans. The rest is up to you."

Heinrich whispered confidentially, "I've organized a few pounds of potatoes[140] and I'd give you fried potatoes, except that I have no fat."

"That's easily fixed," I said. "I'll prescribe for each of us two spoonfuls of castor oil. Will that be enough for your cooking?"

"Castor oil!" said Heinrich, horrified. "Surely we'll all get the bellyache."

"No," I replied. "I know this will surprise you, but it makes an excellent cooking oil. I haven't told you that before, otherwise you'd have taken it all for cooking. But this is an exception—we'll make another exception when any of you wins the Iron Cross. Just heat the oil in the pan for a couple of minutes and then put the potatoes into the fat."

Heinrich still looked doubtful. "Guaranteed no bellyaches," I said, with a grin.

*   *   *

Next morning the Russians attacked our flank. They were repulsed with bloody losses. We immediately counterattacked and pursued the enemy, who again abandoned many of his weapons and provisions. On 25 October, we captured several villages in succession along the road to Torzhok, after they had been softened by fierce Stuka raids. The next day, we struggled across a river[141] that was heavily in flood; by afternoon, we were only 14 miles from Torzhok and quartered outside a village called Mozhki, which was reported to be strongly occupied by the enemy, who had constructed a solid defensive system at this point.

A Fiesler Storch landed near us and out of it stepped *Luftwaffe* General von Richthofen[142] for discussions with General Auleb, *Oberst* Becker and other high-ranking officers of the division. Our regiment was to attack Mozhki the following morning; von Richthofen promised us Stuka support.

The weather worsened, with heavy rain and a light fall of snow. We were all wet through to the skin and our ammunition and provisions had not arrived. There was, of course, no sign of the winter uniforms, which had been promised two weeks before. A further inquiry by Becker brought the reassuring reply that they would reach us very shortly—they had only been held up by the rains. To add to my personal misery, I felt sick; I had probably caught a cold.

At one forty-five on the afternoon of 27 October, I lay with Heinrich in a hollow 300 yards from the Russian positions, while their machine-gun fire passed harmlessly overhead. Fourteen Stukas, in steady formation, approached the Russian lines and immediately over our heads peeled off into their attack. They dived vertically, screaming as they came. Everyone seemed to have chosen me as the target for its bombs. In spite of my confidence in our pilots, I pressed myself into the ground. But, miraculously it seemed, they pulled out of their dives and their bombs pounded accurately into the Russian positions. Beams, mud, sods of earth, machine-guns and men were flung high into the air; the earth trembled. Fascinated, we stood up to watch the spectacle. The enemy anti-aircraft fire now came only sporadically from one or two Russian guns. We launched our attack as the Stukas came in again, this time at ground level with machine-guns blazing. We stormed into the Russian defenses and whoever did not surrender was shot down at close quarters. By five o'clock Mozhki was in our hands. An hour later, all our wounded had been treated and the dead buried. At 7:30 p.m. we received a divisional order to clear Mozhki and return immediately to our original positions.

Rumors flew around the battalion. Why, after winning valuable ground, had we retired? Were we to dig in here for the winter? Had the attack of our 3rd Panzer Group on Torzhok bogged down in the mud? Was this to be the limit of our advance before swinging eastward to attack Moscow? Or had General Auleb got cold feet? All that we knew with any certainty was that our heavy formations and supplies were hopelessly bogged somewhere behind us and that it was still raining.

The T-34 was the main reason. Auleb had also decided that we had thrust too far forward and were exposing our flanks, but it was the T-34 that had caused our first withdrawal.[143] This new type of Russian tank had broken through our neighboring division's lines and we had nothing heavy enough to combat it.[144] A mighty juggernaut, the T-34 was said to be protected with impenetrable armor and early reports made it out to be invincible. Tales of the T-34's exploits raced along the front like wildfire. Our 37mm anti-tank guns were useless against it and were now nicknamed "the Panzer-tappers." A brave and determined detachment equipped with 37s had struck a T-34 more than 40 times, but the monstrosity had not even wavered in its course and had calmly lumbered up to our guns, driven over them and flattened them. Only our Panzer IV with its 75mm gun could successfully oppose the T-34s at this stage,[145] unless they came within range of our assault batteries or our 88mm anti-aircraft guns.

Our battalion officers acknowledged the fact that we were defenseless against this terrifying new weapon, but immediately set about trying to develop some new counter to it. Platoon commanders experimented with the preparation of concentrated explosives. The heavy T-mine was tied together with one or more hand grenades and covered in sacking in such a way that the fuse cap of the grenade was exposed. Anti-tank combat squads were formed, whose job was to rush toward the T-34 and hurl the home-made bomb in its path; the weight of the tank would touch off the explosive. It was a near-suicidal remedy and many of our men were to lose their lives applying it. Some were blown up together with their weapon and the enemy tank, but on the other hand, many T-34s were successfully destroyed. And what was more important, the battalion's infantrymen regained self-confidence when they saw the monster could be combated with a fair measure of success. The really effective 75mm anti-tank guns only came into service nine months later.

Mozhki was the most northeasterly point we reached and the northern flank of the main battle line was consolidated about 18 miles from Torzhok. By these means we secured the northern flank for the Second, Fourth and Ninth Armies, who threw themselves with all possible strength against Moscow. But this main thrust petered out after very little progress had been made. While in the far south Kharkov and Stalino had been captured by Army Group South, the Army outside Moscow was again halted by the mud. And still the heavy, gray clouds swept low across the dreary countryside. And the rain drummed down without ceasing.

*　　*　　*

The immaculately dressed major with the broad red stripes down his trousers stood in my doorway. He looked ludicrously out of place in the squalid Russian village. His heavy fur coat had drawn many an envious sigh since part of our battalion had returned to Vassilevskoye. The village was now occupied by portions of the Veterinary Company, supply and baggage units, artillerymen and an assortment of other second-line units and groups who were still trying to catch up with the front-line troops. The red-striped major evoked memories of Germany and more leisurely days; he—and his cozy fur coat—must have arrived very recently from the areas far to the rear of the front line. And now here he was walking into my crude dressing station. Instinctively, I jumped to attention and saluted like a young *Unterarzt* at training school.

"But, Doktor," he protested, "I have not come to inspect your station—only to make a personal and private call."

To what, I asked him, should I ascribe the high honor of his visit.

"Two matters, Doktor," he said with an exquisite wave of the hand to be seated. "Firstly, I wish to be acquainted with the true situation at the front. Secondly, I have a personal request as you are a doctor."

"I gladly place myself at your service, Herr Major."

"Do me a favor, Doktor, and give me the pleasure of your company at my quarters this evening."

"With pleasure, Herr Major," I replied, "a change of wallpaper will do me a world of good."

"Unfortunately, I cannot offer you that," the major said, with a smile, "but perhaps something which, as a front-line soldier, you may not have seen for some time."

He was right. The bottle of costly French cognac was a rare and glorious sight. The orderly brought it in from the major's luxurious motor car. He then returned for a fresh cheese, which the major ordered to be cut into small cubes. My mouth was watering while he unhurriedly chatted and opened the bottle of cognac. He seemed not particularly interested in the cheese while I found it increasingly difficult to pay attention to what he was saying. At last he toasted me. I lifted my glass and was about to rise when he said: "But, please, please, dear Doktor, remain seated. Let us dispense with all formalities."

The delicious cheese, washed down with cognac straight from France, prevented my contributing any but the briefest remarks to his flow of conversation. But I could not help thinking: "Can this be just sheer friendliness, treating a strange doctor with such extravagance? What lies behind it?"

A few glasses of cognac had induced a more relaxed mood on my part, before he came out with the reason for his hospitality. Very confidentially he told me—he had crabs. That was all; just ordinary crabs.

I told him not to worry; I would prepare a small bottle of a special solution, which would be sure to help him. "Use it three times in the way I tell you and I am sure it will banish your crabs, Herr Major, and these love butterflies—as the French so charmingly call them—will serve only to help you retain the memory of a pleasant romantic interlude."

"You are a poet as well as a doctor," he said with a laugh. He lifted his glass. We clinked and drained our drinks. The more we drank, the more uninhibited we became and the major spoke more freely about the way the war was going. He was far better informed on the overall situation than were any of the more high-ranking officers at the front. I could not have been more impressed had I been chatting to von Brauchitsch himself.[146]

"The picture I am going to give you of Moscow applied 10 days ago," he said. "You can take it as accurate. It is the official picture as we know it, built up from the interrogation of prisoners and reports from our own intelligence men." The Moscow newspaper *Pravda*, he told me, was writing openly that Moscow was in the greatest danger. The Communist leaders and the top generals no longer believed that the city could be held. Panic had broken out among the civilians and everybody who could get away was fleeing to the east. Families and relations of important people had already been evacuated by air. The State archives and the bullion of the State Bank, together with Stalin's secretariat and the staffs of nearly all important organizations had left the city. All key buildings, factories, even the Kremlin itself, had been mined and would be blown up when the Germans entered Moscow. Civilians were being armed with all manner of makeshift weapons. Women and university professors were being formed into fighting units, and in many parts of the city looting and plundering was rife.

But Stalin knew the importance of Moscow to himself, to the Russian population, and as a symbol to the world, and he was preparing to defend the city bitterly. He had ordered large numbers of Siberian troops and every available soldier in Russia to be thrown into the final battle for Moscow. But Eastern Russia was exposed and the Japanese might attack at any time without encountering the least resistance.[147] To add to the overall confusion and the mounting panic, railway lines were blocked by civilians fleeing from the city. From Moscow to the Urals, rail traffic was practically at a standstill and it was impossible to convey the troops.[148]

"Believe me, dear Doktor, when Moscow has fallen, the rest of Russia will be put out of action by revolution," the major finished.

I pondered on this heartening news for a moment. "According to what you've said, it's hardly possible for anything to go wrong for us," I commented.

"No, it can no longer go wrong. When the double battle of Viaz'ma and Briansk ended, about 80 percent of the total Russian forces for the defense of Moscow had been killed or captured. It's only unfortunate that the weather is against us and that our advance is now bogged down. But as soon as the rain stops, or the first frosts set in, take it from me, three armies will converge on the city—and then Moscow must be ours. It will be the end of Russia and it will make the world tremble."

It was very late, so I said: "Permit me, Herr Major, to get the medicine for you. I will go to the sick bay quickly."

"Would you not like me to fetch it myself tomorrow?"

"Better that you have it now, so that you can use it tonight and get rid of those little pests without delay."

The rain was still drumming down when I stepped into the street. I took a few quick steps, slipped and landed on all-fours in the mud. It didn't seem to matter at all and I set an irregular course for the sick bay. I told Müller to prepare a bottle of the solution immediately, while Heinrich tried to sponge the mud off my trousers. Müller returned with the bottle and a grin on his face.

"What's the joke?" I demanded.

"Herr *Assistenzarzt* smells very nice."

"You mean the cognac?"

"Herr *Assistenzarzt* smells of France."

"Perhaps we will soon be returning to France, my dear Müller," I said gaily, remembering the major's optimistic picture. "It's quite on the cards." And I weaved out into the street.

"It is only to be applied externally, Herr Major," I said as I handed him the bottle. "Just for safety's sake, I'd better write on the bottle." In big letters I printed on the label "Poison: For External Use Only!!"

The major took out his own fountain pen and went to the table. He crossed the room and handed me a large bottle of cognac on which he had printed in bold letters: "poison: internal consumption only!!!"

*　　*　　*

On 2 November, exactly a month after the battle for Moscow had commenced, our divisions went to ground.[149]

For several days we had been building bunkers and trenches in front of the stretched-out village of Knyaseva where our battalion had been allocated a defense sector of about two miles in length.[150] The earth was soft and it had been easy to dig in and prepare tank traps. We had catered for the T-34 by heavily mining both approaches to the village with T-mines that would detonate more than a ton of explosives at the touch of a button. In addition, every platoon had prepared concentrated explosives, combinations of T-mines and hand grenades, which would be available for immediate use against the T-34s. Outposts were stationed near the edge of the woods outside the village and our trench system was designed to link up with the neighboring battalion. My dressing station, next door to the battalion battle post, was protected by armor plating at the side from which danger might come and was even strong enough to protect us from the fire of tank guns.

Tactically, the minefields were cunningly placed, and our artillery carefully bracketed every conceivable target in front of us and could switch to any sector immediately. On 2 November, there was a discussion and it was planned to have a complete winter defensive line built up to maximum efficiency within four weeks, which would make us well-nigh impregnable as well as giving the troops sufficient protection against the cold. But we were still waiting impatiently for the promised winter clothing.

It was rumored that our defensive line was to be built up by reserve divisions, the Todt Organization and Russian volunteers while our active divisions continued to march on Moscow. If the worst came to pass we would then be able to retire to the defensive positions for the rest of the winter and gather our strength for a second assault on the metropolis in the spring. Everyone regarded this as a sensible plan.

These precautions had, in fact, been recommended by experienced combatant officers attached to the High Command, but they were rejected by Hitler as being strategically unsound. The *Führer* considered that the spirit of the troops would suffer if they knew there was a defensive line to which they could withdraw.

"Hitler is obsessed by the *Niebelungen* approach," Kageneck commented. "He would rather destroy all our bridges behind us."

But while we dug in, other divisions to the south were still plodding away in the direction of Moscow. They suffered heavy losses in men and material as the remnants of the defending Red Army struck at the mud-caked columns. We had been lucky enough to reach our objective—Kalinin and the Moscow-Leningrad railway—in good time. We were the northeastern cornerstone of Army Group Center, and when the Russians realized that the advance by our flank had halted, they strengthened the troops opposing us with additional tanks, artillery and infantry units. On 3 and 4 November there were light night frosts, which hardened the roads and eased our supply position, but at the same time made it easier for the Russians to bring up reinforcements.[151]

Neuhoff, Becker and I were busy inspecting the beards we had started growing when a messenger from 10th Company burst into the room and reported: "The Russians are attacking with strong forces and tanks in 10th Company sector and against the neighboring battalion."

In spite of rapid defensive fire from our artillery and anti-tank detachments, eight Russian T-34s had broken through where our defensive line joined that of the next battalion.[152] Fortunately, the following Red infantrymen had all been mown down by our machine-guns. The T-34s had overrun two of our 37mm Pak guns for us to learn at first hand that our defensive weapons against these monsters were really only "tank-tappers." Six of the eight juggernauts wheeled and made for the village on the right; the other two turned in a wide circle and came into our village street from the rear.

Not a soul could be seen as the two fearsome monsters trundled up the street. Every soldier was in hiding. I peeped through the closed window of my sick bay and watched apprehensively as the steel giants passed by at a distance of three yards from the window. I prayed that they would not fire a burst at my house, or it would come down about my ears. Suddenly a German soldier darted out from behind a house and flung a T-mine in front of the caterpillars of one of the tanks. There was an unholy explosion and the tank stopped with flames licking its underbelly. The crew jumped out one by one and tried to reach the undamaged T-34 but were picked off by our men. An attempt to blow up the other failed. The T-mine slid down the steel body of the T-34 and fell into the road, where it tore a huge crater. The T-34 fired a few times without doing much damage, then slowly turned and withdrew along the street to join the others in the neighboring village.

Soldiers swarmed into the street, from houses, slit trenches and hidden corners to examine the blazing T-34, which was the most up-to-date and powerful tank in the world. It was being mass-produced in the workshops of Stalingrad, Magnitogorsk and various factories in the Urals and Siberia. It was lower than anything produced up to then, had much heavier armor and the steel body was constructed at angles so that Panzer shells would ricochet off it. It had a heavily armored turret, a 76mm gun, machine-guns, and was considerably faster than any other tank we had encountered. Shells and machine-gun ammunition detonated inside the furiously burning T-34, but there was no danger, for nothing could penetrate the heavy armor.

The battle was still raging away to our right, where the neighboring battalion was beating off a fierce attack by the seven T-34s and masses of Red Infantry. But only six of our men were brought into my dressing station as casualties. One of them was Semmelmeyer, the assistant cook. He had been visiting a friend in 10th Company's trenches when a stray Russian bullet hit him in the neck. Now he lay pale and struggling for breath on the floor of the dressing station. He had evidently lost a great deal of blood and was suffering from severe shock; his pulse was weak and slow. The bullet had entered an inch below the left ear, but the wound itself seemed less serious than his general condition. It must have been an almost spent bullet, for, as I probed the wound, I felt the metal only two inches deep in the wound aperture. The bullet had lodged against the cervical vertebrae. The carotid artery, fortunately, was untouched, otherwise Semmelmeyer would probably have bled to death while being carried to the dressing station.

The condition of the wounded man suggested more shock to the nervous system than a collapse following loss of blood. Apparently the bullet had severed some vital vegetative nerve fibers, and perhaps was pressing against a blood vessel or nerve. Gently I inserted my blunt forceps into the wound, gripped the rear end of the metal firmly, and, without forcing, managed to withdraw the bullet. The flow of blood from the wound increased somewhat, but was purely venous. We lifted the patient a little in order to apply a light bandage, but his general condition immediately deteriorated. I ordered Müller to prepare a syringe with Cardiazol which would encourage the heart and circulation.

We secured the bandage and laid Semmelmeyer gently back on the straw, but he gasped weakly a few times and then stopped breathing altogether. Quickly I took the Cardiazol syringe, thrust the needle into the arm vein, and gave him the full injection. Müller automatically handed me the stethoscope and I listened carefully.

"The heart's stopped beating!" I exclaimed.

Müller and Heinrich stared at me with bewildered eyes. "Dead?" Heinrich whispered.

"Acute paralysis of the heart. We'll have to make an intracardiac injection." Müller gasped. "Yes, we'll inject directly into the heart. Quick, Müller—four-inch needle and one c.c. Suprarenin . . . Heinrich! Swab with iodine. Quickly, man!"

I iodized the heart region and as I dropped the swab Müller handed me the syringe with the long, thin needle. I plunged it into the fourth intercostal space, up against the sternum. The man's life depended on my ability to find the auricle at the first attempt. I directed the needle carefully down the rear surface of the breast bone and at a depth of one inch felt a light resistance. It was the heart muscle. I quickly thrust through it and took it as a good sign when, at the moment the needle penetrated the heart muscle, the heart itself contracted as the result of the mechanical stimulation. The needle still moved downward. It was now about two inches deep in the right auricle of the heart. I checked that the needle was correctly placed by drawing up dark venous blood into the syringe, which mixed with the Suprarenin. Then slowly I injected the Suprarenin and withdrew the needle. The stimulant was in the right place; now it was a question of whether it would be strong enough to overcome the paralysis.

"Artificial respiration, Heinrich!" I snapped, and as Heinrich set to work, I applied external massage to the heart. I paused a second to check with the stethoscope. And I heard what I had prayed for—an almost inaudible heart beat! The heart had started to function again.

"Hold that mirror to his mouth, Müller," I ordered. The glass was clear, but in less than a minute it misted slightly, then clouded over. Semmelmeyer had started to breathe again. Faintly at first, and then with more vigor, his chest quivered as Semmelmeyer took the first few breaths of his new medical life. I injected Lobolin into the vein of his arm as a stimulant and his breathing became appreciably deeper and more regular.

In about five minutes he opened his eyes and gradually focused them as if he was returning from far, far away. "Where am I?" he asked uncertainly, then his eyes traveled slowly around our three faces. "The pill merchants," he said. "Then I must have been wounded. Queer! That's damn funny, you know."

Müller and Heinrich laughed.

We attended to the other wounded after following up by giving Semmelmeyer an injection of 300 c.c. Periston blood ersatz to make good the loss of blood and bolster the heart. But by the time we had attended to the other casualties, Semmelmeyer was fit enough to accompany the four serious cases back to the Medical Company.

Fighting was still going on in the next village and ambulances would be at a premium, so I decided to send the five serious casualties to the rear in a convoy of five panje wagons. The men were warmly covered and laid on thick beds of straw for the journey.

Semmelmeyer had recovered sufficiently to call to the other kitchen bulls, who had gathered to see him on his way: "I've already salted the soup. Don't forget, now!"

Heinrich could not take his eyes off the giant from Cologne. "Back from the dead!" he kept muttering to himself in an awestricken whisper.

It began to snow. The earth was frosty and hard, the snow settled on the ground and the countryside began to assume a thick mantle of white. In one day we had faced for the first time the two major weapons which were to operate against us throughout the Russian campaign—the T-34 and "General Winter." The T-34 at the moment constituted the greater menace to our way of thinking; before many weeks passed we had revised our opinion.

My little column of five panje wagons, each with a Russian driver, one stretcher-bearer, Kunzle and *Unteroffizier* Tulpin set off resolutely through the snow. Müller's little horse, Moritz, tripped at the head and Max with his wagon brought up the rear. But it did not suit Max to be separated from his friend Moritz, with whom he had already trotted hundreds of miles across Russia, and Max's driver had continually to rein him back. I had given Tulpin instructions that after he had delivered the wounded to the Medical Company he was to proceed with the wagons to the rear of the neighboring village and offer to help with the transportation of the next battalion's casualties. I left it to Tulpin to act as the situation demanded and warned him not to expose the column to unnecessary danger. The assignment suited Tulpin's ambitious nature, and he acknowledged the order with a pleased "*Jawohl*, Herr *Assistenzarzt*." I calculated that the fight should be over in the next village by the time Tulpin arrived there and it would be then that the medical detachment of the battalion would be most in need of assistance with transport.

With a feeling of proud possessiveness, I watched the brave little column pass across a wooden bridge over a stream, which flowed like a long, dark artery through the white landscape. No other doctor in the division had at his disposal such a mobile, self-contained transport unit as my five panje wagons, I told myself. It made me independent of ambulances and the need to beg other means of transport when no *Sankawagen* was available. I returned to the dressing station, where Müller and Heinrich were washing the blood off the floor and making the place shipshape again. Müller was downcast.

"What's the matter?" I asked him.

"Everything here is in order, Herr *Assistenzarzt*."

"But there is something wrong," I insisted.

Heinrich spoke up: "Müller's worried about our column, particularly Max and Moritz. He's afraid, Herr *Assistenzarzt*, that *Unteroffizier* Tulpin may not take care of them—he risks too much and doesn't consider the horses like the rest of us do."

"They could easily break a leg on some of these rickety bridges—or they might be stolen," Müller burst out.

"But that might happen if any of us were with them," I said.

"Not if I were with them," replied Müller. "Besides, Herr *Assistenzarzt* knows that every unit is short of horses. Even the kitchen bulls are after them—they steal like crows. Anything's good enough for their pots."

"But surely, Müller, the wounded are the first consideration—and Tulpin is a competent NCO, isn't he?"

"*Jawohl*, Herr *Assistenzarzt*," Müller had to reply.

It did not seem the right moment to tell Müller that I had also ordered Tulpin to lend a hand to the neighboring battalion.

Late in the afternoon the telephone rang. Regimental H.Q. wanted information regarding our sector and told us that five T-34s had roared unharmed back through our defensive lines to rejoin the Red troops; two more had been put out of action. We were to be on the alert all night. I decided to fill in the waiting time by visiting Kageneck. I found him with some of his men at his company battle post. They were sitting around a huge Russian oven in which a fire blazed.

"The prosperous Russian citizen," I remarked as I stamped the snow off my boots.

"Come in! Have some tea!" Kageneck called jovially. "I can tell you this: I've found the only way to make tea—in a samovar. This must be a wonderful country in peacetime," he said as he poured me a mugful of tea. ". . . Sleigh bells, the samovar singing and a shot of vodka in your tea." He sighed dramatically.

"It's a pity that things aren't as romantic now," I said. "Soldiers sitting in the trenches out there without any winter clothing except a woolen cap to keep their ears warm—the wind biting through their threadbare uniforms."

"Anyway the frost has made it easier for the supply columns to reach us," said Kageneck. "And it's not so very cold—just below freezing point, that's all."[153]

"And how cold do you think it will get?" I asked him. Again, unbidden, the old woodcutter's prophecy leapt into my mind: "The grubs are deep in the ground—it will be a long and severe winter."

"Oh, I had news of Stolze today," Kageneck said. "He managed to get a letter through with the supply column. He avoided going back to Germany. He's in a field hospital in some Russian village—hopes he'll soon be back with us."

"That's Stolze! Others would have moved heaven and earth to get back to Germany."

"We shall probably need Stolze and a few more like him this winter," said Kageneck thoughtfully.

Darkness had set in by the time I left Kageneck's fireside and I was uneasy as there had been no news of my ambulance column. Outside, the moon was just lifting itself over the horizon, the snowstorm had died out and the countryside lay silvery-gray in the moonlight. Now and then a flare flew into the air from along our front line, as if to make it clear that the apparent peace was but a delusion. As I turned up my coat collar and walked through the powdery snow to the dressing station, I could scarcely hear the sound of my footsteps.

Müller was reading an Army magazine; Heinrich was sitting at the other side of the oil lamp, writing a letter.

"Heard nothing of Tulpin?" I inquired.

"Nothing at all," said Müller gloomily.

I sat down beside them. "Writing home, Heinrich?" I asked.

"Yes, to my wife, Herr *Assistenzarzt*."

"Where does she live?"

"At Hörste, not far from Detmold, near the Teutonburg Forest," he replied. "We have a small farm and she lives there with our little daughter and my father-in-law."

"So you're a warlike Teuton," I said to Heinrich, with a smile.

"So is Müller," Heinrich said. "In fact, so are most of the men in the battalion."

"That's fine! Then we've nothing to fear from the Russians. It's very kind of all you warlike Teutons to accept me in the battalion."[154] But although I was trying to take the men's minds off Tulpin and the ambulance column, anxiety was beginning to gnaw at me.

"I wonder why Tulpin's being delayed," said Müller after we had spent another half hour trying to hide our fears.

"Don't worry, Müller. It's a clear moonlit night."

I thought I heard a creak of harness and whipped open the door. One of my panje horses was padding along the road toward me. It was drawing a wagon, but there was no driver. On the wagon was a muffled form. The horse stopped in front of the open doorway. It was Moritz. And by the light of the moon I made out the figure of a wounded soldier on the wagon. He was well bandaged and wrapped in blankets.

"Tulpin!" I called. There was no reply. Heinrich and Müller joined me in the roadway with the oil lamp. Müller held the lamp over the wounded man. It was a *Feldwebel*; his pulse was sound and he seemed to be in fair condition. I asked him what had happened to the escort.

"I don't know," he answered. "We were ambushed by a Russian patrol as far as I could gather. There was shooting—I heard hand grenades and automatic weapons. Our column of wounded had just left the village. Not this one—I don't know how near or how far it all was—nor exactly what happened. I couldn't see a thing and couldn't move, because I've got a stomach wound. I only know that the wagon started moving and I could hear the horse galloping in front for a while. Then it fell into a steady trot. I didn't know where we were going. I called out for the stretcher-bearer, but he was no longer there. . . ."

"Moritz is wounded!" shouted Müller. "Here, look! He's wounded!" There was a gaping wound in Moritz's back, in the region of the kidneys.

"We'll see what we can do about that in a minute," I said and returned to the *Feldwebel*, who was from the neighboring battalion. "And how did you get here?" I questioned him.

"I honestly have no idea. We must have come a long way. Twice we went over a bridge. Apart from that I could see only the stars and the clouds—until the horse stopped and you spoke to me."

"Well, Moritz has delivered you to the right address," I said. "Let me have a look at your wounds."

Without removing him from the wagon I examined him quickly. It was mainly a bladder wound—an early operation would give him a good chance of survival. I ordered Müller to take Moritz out of harness and fetched a horse from the Headquarters Company stable, Müller harnessed it to the wagon, while Heinrich got ready to take the wounded man to the Medical Company. Reaction from his wound and his ordeal had set in with the *Feldwebel*. He broke into sobs and told me, "It is only by the grace and protection of God that I am here, Herr *Assistenzarzt*. I want to confide in you."

He told me that before he joined the Army he had been a theological student at the University of Bonn and had been troubled by doubts as to whether he had chosen the right career. "But on this ride in the panje wagon I pleaded with God to help me if it was His will," he continued. "I made a solemn vow that if He heard my prayer I would devote the rest of my life to Him. And, Herr *Assistenzarzt*, I'm really convinced that He heard my prayer and that a miracle happened. He guided the horse's steps to your door."

"But why are you telling me all this?" I asked.

"Because you're the first person I can talk to. After the war I shall go back to my studies. And I'll never again be ashamed of God's word. I'm not crazy, Herr *Assistenzarzt*, but my heart is very full."

Heinrich arrived wearing his warm overcoat and set off with the wagon. I saw the wounded *Feldwebel*'s hand lift in farewell and knew that he was still thanking God for his private miracle. Müller was still standing forlornly with Moritz, gently stroking the horse's muzzle. "Poor old fellow," he said. "He seems to be badly hurt. I wonder if there's any hope for him."

I examined the wound carefully and found that the stomach had been torn open and that serious inflammation would undoubtedly set in. There was only one thing for it—a merciful bullet. It was poor thanks for the gallant little Moritz's heroism.

"Give me the horse," I said to Müller, who looked at me with tear-filled eyes. He stroked Moritz's neck for the last time and the little horse tossed his head in a last salute. I walked down the road with my hand on his neck, as I had so often done in the past when we were getting to the end of a day's forced marching. I stopped in front of the building that housed the field kitchen and called for the kitchen NCO. "Here's a nice, young horse for you," I told him. "He's wounded, but otherwise perfectly healthy." The NCO looked surprised to see me leading the horse.

"There's only one thing. You must give the horse an instantaneous and painless death. I insist on that. Do you understand?"

The kitchen bull's face beamed. For him Moritz was no different from the dozens of other horses he had butchered recently. He nodded his head. "Herr *Assistenzarzt* may rest assured it will be done at once and efficiently."

I felt disgusted and nauseated by the deal, turned abruptly and left Moritz standing in front of the door with the kitchen bull—patiently waiting to be butchered. Behind me I heard a shot—a shot that meant the end of a long road through Poland, along Napoleon's road, through White Russia, across the bridge at Polotsk, past the Schutsche Lake, across the Volga to this small village, where the track led up to the door of a steaming field kitchen.

My thoughts were gloomy as I entered the dressing station and saw Müller sitting on the first aid box, staring into the flickering candlelight. There was no news of Tulpin. Perhaps Moritz had been the only survivor of the entire column. It seemed more than a possibility that he had bolted while the others were being butchered. The more I thought of it, the more certain I became that they had been attacked by a strong force of Russians and destroyed. I painted the picture of their destruction in the gloomiest colors. The minutes passed slowly while the candle guttered. We said nothing—just waited—and waited. I went over to the battle post, told Neuhoff of Moritz's return and asked if there was any news from Regimental H.Q. of the rest of the column.

"No—nothing," was the reply. The others prepared to go to bed. "What about you, Doktor?" asked Neuhoff. "After all, there's nothing you can do about it. Probably there'll be more *Schweinerei* tomorrow—you must look after yourself and get some sleep."

"At least I'll wait till Heinrich returns," I told him. "I've got some work to do at the sick bay, which will keep me occupied. Good night!"

Müller was still sitting silently on the first aid box. I asked him to hand me the battalion casualty list. There were 118 names. A total of 118 dead and wounded since 22 June. Was it much? No, not really—a little under 15 percent.

At the top of the list were the names of *Leutnant* Stock and *Unteroffizier* Schäfer. And near the head of the list were Dehorn and Jakobi. Then I read Krüger and Schepanski, Stolze and Hillemanns, and Max Steinbrink. To me the names seemed to stand out from the others on the list, as if they were more heavily inscribed. But I knew that many more names would be entered in the book and that many of them would be marked with the fatal cross. It was the Book of Death, Suffering and Pain. It was fortunate that I could not guess how long the list of destruction would become, how many more names—many of them dear to me—would have been written in the book when the balance sheet for the year was drawn up.

Voices outside! Müller and I rushed out. A group of panje wagons and men approached us. I counted—five wagons and four horses, Tulpin, Heinrich, Kunzle and four Russian volunteers.

Tulpin approached me and reported: "All wounded have been delivered to the Medical Company. The assistant stretcher-bearer has fallen out wounded; one volunteer is dead; one horse dead and one wounded; wagons and medical equipment complete."

So much for my gloomy picture! I welcomed them all back like a gift from the land of the dead. I was overjoyed. "Thanks, Tulpin," I said. "I'm glad you managed to get back." I examined the column closely. Little Max had drawn two wagons—the second one having been coupled to his own wagon when the other horse was killed. Müller had already examined his little horse from head to hoof and I asked him: "Everything in order, Müller?"

"Yes, Herr *Assistenzarzt*. He is unwounded."

The wagons were lined up outside the sick bay and medical equipment and blankets were carried in while Kunzle and the other volunteers led the horses into the stable. When we were all gathered in the room I called on Tulpin to give us his story.

He had delivered our own wounded to the Medical Company safely and then carried on to the neighboring village where they had to lie hidden until the Russian tanks withdrew. By the time the wagons had been loaded with wounded it was dark—they had a stomach wound, a lung case and three thigh wounds on the wagons. Just outside the village they were ambushed by Russians, but defended themselves as best they could, firing at the muzzle flashes in the darkness. Moritz had galloped away from his place at the head of the column after the Russian volunteer guiding him had been shot through the head. Another horse was shot and the stretcher-bearer was wounded in the arm.

Tulpin and his men beat off the attack and headed back to the village, where the neighboring battalion provided an escort for the journey back to the Medical Company. All the way, Tulpin had kept a sharp look out for Moritz and the stomach case, without result, he told me. When they reached the scene of the ambush, the dead horse's wagon had been attached to Max's wagon and the column reached the Medical Company without further incident. "Heinrich was already there, with our stomach case on the operating table. That's how it was Herr *Assistenzarzt*. That's all," Tulpin concluded.

When I arrived at Battalion Headquarters, everyone was asleep. But Neuhoff, who had for many weeks not been sleeping well, woke up. "Are they all back?" he whispered.

"All wounded have been delivered to the Medical Company. Tulpin was ambushed, but his whole conduct of the affair was highly commendable, Herr Major. He should be recommended for the Iron Cross Second Class," I whispered back.

"Let me have a detailed report in the morning, Doktor. I'll see to the rest." He turned over to his other side. In a couple of minutes I blew out the candle and fell asleep, hoping the Russians would leave us in peace for the night.

They remained quiet during the night and made no attack the following day, when a thaw set in again. Toward midday, Bolski appeared at the battle post, saluted and reported to Neuhoff: "Herr Major, I have ordered the arrest of *Unteroffizier* Schmidt on a charge of cowardice in the face of the enemy, as well as refusal to obey orders."

CHAPTER 15

Manic Depression, Fever and Frostbite

THERE WAS AN UNCOMFORTABLE SILENCE; NEUHOFF LOOKED ANNOYED AND UPSET. IT meant that a report would have to be made to Regimental H.Q. followed by a court-martial and the firing squad for Schmidt if Bolski were proved right.[155] Neuhoff read through the report while Bolski, grim and determined, stood to attention. Neuhoff dropped the report on his table and said nothing.

"Which Schmidt is it?" I asked. "Is it the lawyer Schmidt?"

"Yes—that's the one," Bolski replied abruptly.

"But he's a decent fellow," I protested.

"If you call him decent, then I don't know what a coward is," Bolski snapped.

"I can't understand it," Neuhoff said in puzzled tones. "He's always been a good soldier. Iron Cross First Class, Iron Cross Second Class." He paused, then turned to Bolski: "Won't you reinvestigate this matter carefully?" he asked him.

"If this cowardly conduct remains unpunished, Herr Major, it is bound to have a thoroughly bad effect on the discipline of the troops under my command. I regret that I must insist on proper action being taken on my report," Bolski replied stiffly.

"In that case I shall have to let things take their course. Thank you," said Neuhoff curtly.

Bolski saluted and marched out.

"Always trouble," Neuhoff said wearily when Bolski had gone. "I shall have to submit this to the Regiment. It will be the end of Schmidt. This report will mean the firing squad!" He threw the papers across the table to me.

The Russians had attacked the right flank of 10th Company; everyone had grabbed his weapon and had closed up to action stations. All except Schmidt, who remained sitting in a bunker doing nothing. Bolski walked along the trench and saw him. Schmidt looked wild and haggard and appeared to be terrified. Bolski ordered him at once to his post. Schmidt followed Bolski hesitantly to the machine-gun detachment in his charge, but remained there completely inactive, giving no orders whatever to his men. Once more—in the presence of Schmidt's men this time—Bolski ordered the terrified man to do his duty. But again there was no response. While he organized the defense against the Red attack, Bolski had to leave Schmidt, but he returned to the machine-gun later and discovered that Schmidt was no longer there. He found him cowering again in the bunker. After the attack had been repulsed, Bolski had Schmidt arrested and took detailed statements from witnesses, which were attached to the report.

On the face of it, it looked a clear case of cowardice and refusal to obey an order in the face of the enemy. But I found it impossible to believe, when I thought of Schmidt's spirited defense of the farmhouse on the first day of the war; when I recalled how full of spirits he had been at the Schutsche Lake; and when I remembered how unflinchingly he had done his duty on 2 October, the day he had won the Iron Cross First Class. Either Bolski's report was faulty or Schmidt was ill. There was no other possibility. I wanted to have a chat with Schmidt.

He was under close arrest in a room adjoining the orderly room; his weapons had been removed and he was guarded by two soldiers. He sat huddled in a chair, and when I entered the room he looked at me fearfully and helplessly. His appearance shocked me. He was quite unlike the boisterous man I knew. I ordered the escort to withdraw for a few minutes while I examined him.

It did not take me long to arrive at a diagnosis: acute depression, though I could not decide into what category the depressive state fell. But one thing was certain—the man was seriously ill, mentally.[156] "Don't worry at all, my friend. You are ill and I'll help you," I told Schmidt. He looked at me with terror-stricken eyes, but did not say a word. I recalled the escort and set off for the 10th Company trenches for a chat with some of his friends.

For eight days, they told me, he had been walking around in a melancholic state and had taken practically no interest in anything. There had been a sudden and complete change in his personality.

"And how was his appetite?" I asked them.

He had hardly eaten a thing, they said, but had spent his days sitting alone, staring listlessly into space.

Walking out of the trenches, I bumped into Bolski.

"To what do we owe the honor of this visit, Doktor?" asked Bolski banteringly. "We don't often see you in my trenches."

"I have examined Schmidt, and now I have just been making a few inquiries about him," I said.

Bolski flushed scarlet and his eyes narrowed. "Inquiries? . . . You don't mean to tell me you're trying to certify this man as not responsible. Or what are you up to, Doktor? I hope for your sake you're not up to any mischief." I made no reply and Bolski continued, getting more excited: "Every word in my report is correct and supported by witnesses. It's a case of downright disobedience and cowardice in face of the enemy. I'm insisting on this.

And it's my business and my business only, so, if you please, Herr *Assistenzarzt*, be good enough to keep your fingers out of my pie."

"Kindly leave it to me to decide what I must or must not do in this case, Herr *Leutnant*," I replied. "But I'll be frank with you—the man is ill and will *not* be court-martialed."

"That's the damned limit!" Bolski exploded. "Do you mean to tell me that you have the nerve to interfere with my authority and discipline with your queer notions? A man like that must be court-martialed."

"If your authority is dependent on court-martialing this man, then I feel sorry for you. As far as I'm concerned, I'll do my duty as a doctor—and I'm afraid your personal opinions don't come into the picture for me." I turned my back on him and went straight to Neuhoff to report.

Bolski had already telephoned him and complained of my interference in the matter. It made me all the more determined to have things my way. But Neuhoff had already sent off Bolski's report and the charge-sheet to Regimental H.Q. He did not seem sure what to do next when I told him of my diagnosis and the result of my investigations. The book of rules did not provide for this specific case and Neuhoff was at a loss.

"So you demand, Doktor, that *Unteroffizier* Schmidt be released from arrest and sent to your sick bay for treatment and supervision?"

"Yes, Herr Major."

"And are you aware of the responsibility you're taking on your shoulders? For my part, I can't do anything about it—the case is now in the hands of Regimental Headquarters."

"Herr Major, it's not a question of whether I'm prepared to take responsibility. It's a matter of doing my duty as a doctor, a matter of my own conscience."

"All right. You must know. It's something beyond my depth and I'm not able to judge."

"Herr Major, Schmidt has a serious mental illness, very much in the same way as one might have pneumonia or a heart attack. In those cases, the patient would be sent to hospital and given special food. There would be no question of whether he was fit to do his duty. He would be left to the care of the doctor."

"Do as you think fit, Doktor," said Neuhoff. He obviously felt relieved that somehow or other the responsibility had been taken out of his hands.

Ten minutes later Schmidt was my patient at the sick bay. I tried to comfort and soothe him and gave my staff instructions that under no circumstances was he to be allowed to leave the house or to be left alone. The danger of suicide was great. I gave him a sedative and encouraged him to sleep. Later I administered increasing doses of opium to counter his fear and perplexity. As a result his condition improved and next day he had periods of lucidity, which alternated, however, with moods of deep depression and fear. But I was able to piece together a picture.

Schmidt throughout his life had suffered at long intervals alternating manic and depressive states. And he revealed one of the abiding fears of his life when he said to me: "You know, of course, Herr *Assistenzarzt*, that by law my condition is classified under 'preventive measures against hereditary diseases?'" Schmidt paused wearily, then continued: "And of course you know that according to the law, I should be sterilized. But I'm a lawyer, I have my own business and a wife and two small children. Sterilization would disgrace and ruin me completely. Oh, if only my wife would stand loyally by me!" he finished hopelessly.

"Listen to me, Schmidt. I will arrange to send you home. Genuine depressive states can also come about as a reaction—as a psychopathological manifestation following intense and lengthy anxiety situations, especially in times of great stress and strain. In any case, that will be the diagnosis, with which I shall send you home, and it does not fall under the law about hereditary diseases."

He made no reply.

"Have you understood me, Schmidt?" I asked, slowly and emphatically.

"Yes," he replied at length, but there was no change in the weary tone of his voice, nor a glimmer of hope in his eyes.

My heart went out to Schmidt. He was in a desperate plight, even without the overwhelming depressive state which weighed him down. He was fully aware that he was to be court-martialed on charges that could mean only one sentence if he were found guilty. And the alternative was little better. He, the respected lawyer, would be found not responsible for his actions and would almost certainly be sterilized, his name would be made public and he would go through the rest of his life with the shadow of disgrace hanging over him. His business would be ruined, his family would probably leave him. In spite of any helpful diagnosis that I sent back to Germany with him, the doctors at home would undoubtedly condemn him to a living death. There was no way out.

When I returned to Battalion H.Q. the report had already been forwarded to *Oberst* Becker. Knowing the whole business was an embarrassment to Neuhoff, I asked his permission to visit Regimental H.Q. in order personally to present my medical report to Becker.

"Yes, I think that will be best, Doktor," Neuhoff replied.

Oberst Becker greeted me in friendly manner: "Well, *Haltepunkt*! How are you?"

"Fine as always, Herr *Oberst*. May I have your permission, Herr *Oberst*, to discuss a certain matter?"

"What is it? What is it, *Haltepunkt*? Come and take a seat."

"I would like to report, sir," I said, remaining at attention, "that *Unteroffizier* Schmidt has been released from close arrest because he is seriously ill mentally and cannot be held responsible for his actions."

"Now first of all, *Haltepunkt*, sit down and tell me exactly what is the trouble. You know very well an arrest is an arrest and can't be ignored for no rhyme or reason."

"*Unteroffizier* Schmidt is suffering from a state of manic depression—an enturbation of the psyche."

"What does all that mean, Doktor? It sounds like Greek to me."

"It is."

"I know that much, *Haltepunkt*. But talk like a sensible chap and leave out the soul business."

"We all have them, Herr *Oberst*."

"Yes, but they're elastic terms. Try and express yourself so that an ignorant layman can understand you. You mean that Schmidt is mad, I take it?"

"Yes, Herr *Oberst*, quite crazy—but he will revert to normal."

"Doktor, one question, please. You should know me by now, so let us deal with the essentials. If your diagnosis is acceptable as evidence before a court-martial, it will surely carry weight."

Without hesitation I replied: "My evidence will be absolutely sound, Herr *Oberst*, and is bound to weigh heavily."

"Very good then, *Haltepunkt*." Unexpectedly, he reached for Bolski's report and to my amazement tore it into two pieces; and, taking mine, without reading it, he did the same.

"The case is over as far as I'm concerned," he said.

"My sincerest thanks, Herr *Oberst*."

"It's now a matter for you, Doktor. For my part I'm glad this unpleasant business is over."

"I had prepared an argument, Herr *Oberst*, which I shan't have to use after all."

"What was it?"

"An interesting piece of case history—an earlier case of a manic depressive in our Army."

"Go on, then, tell me, *Haltepunkt*."

"One of Prussia's greatest soldiers, Marshal Blücher, sat in a farmhouse in 1809 in a state of deep depression. He was under a delusion that he was *enceint* with an elephant."

"You mean that he thought an elephant had put him in the family way? You're joking, Doktor."

"Not at all, Herr *Oberst*. It is an absolute fact. Like Schmidt at the moment, Marshal Blücher was going through a phase of acute depression. But in 1813, on the other hand, he was going through the manic phase, which had directly the opposite effect on his character. He went from victory to victory and, as you know, everybody marched too slowly for him. Before the battle of Leipzig he even wrote an uninhibited letter to the Crown Prince of Sweden, Bernadotte, calling him a damned gipsy scoundrel and telling him he should hurry. At that time, nothing was going fast enough for him—he was going through a hypermanic phase. The rest is history: the useless, terror-stricken Blücher of 1809 entered Paris in 1813 triumphantly, and was regarded by the rest of the world as a conquering hero."

"Very interesting, *Haltepunkt*. But see to it that *Unteroffizier* Schmidt doesn't give birth to any elephants. A litter of them would be a damned nuisance in this ice and snow. Remember Hannibal's elephants!"

Next day I provided Schmidt with carefully prepared documents and instructed Fischer to take him in my Opel direct to Staritsa for transport back to Germany. But poor Schmidt chose the third ending to his sad story. He hanged himself in a lavatory on his way back to Germany.

*   *   *

A couple of days later my appetite suddenly left me and by the afternoon I had a rigor, felt dizzy and my whole body trembled. I reported to Neuhoff that I was getting ill but could not yet diagnose the trouble. I said that I would lie down in the sick bay and keep observation on myself. I ordered Tulpin to take charge of the sick bay but to continue to report to me all puzzling or serious cases. Heinrich and Müller nursed me. In the late afternoon I developed piercing pains in my back and limbs, particularly in the shin bones.

A thousand assumptions and doubts shot through my brain, as is often the case when a doctor tries to diagnose his own ailments. But I narrowed it down to three possibilities— spotted fever, malaria or Volhynian fever, which was sometimes called "five-day fever." Spotted fever I ruled out, because my head was quite clear, in spite of slight dizziness. Also, there was no sign of the typical face swellings, conjunctivitis and low blood pressure. I excluded the possibility of malaria because the three usual types of malaria were practically non-existent in these regions. The increasing pains in my limbs and the continued rigor made me conclude that I was in for an attack of Volhynian fever. It was an unpleasant and very painful illness, but it usually ran its course in five days and was seldom fatal.[157] I was prepared to endure it now that I had made certain it was not spotted fever.

I called Heinrich and Müller to my straw bed and outlined the course that the fever could be expected to take. It was a lice-borne disease, I told them. In 20 hours my temperature would drop and for the next three days would be only a little above normal. Then the whole business would start again with attacks of fever and rigors, except that after the second attack, the lassitude would be more pronounced. Frequently, the illness had run its full course after two or three attacks. "Tomorrow I shall feel much better," I told them, "but at ten or eleven o'clock a fresh attack can be expected. At present there is no reliable remedy. I shall take Eubasin and large doses of Pyramidon in order to allay the pain and keep down the fever. I would also like to have my automatic and a few hand grenades beside my bed in case the Russians decide to pay us an unexpected visit—and that's about all. Let's hope that everything follows the course I've outlined."

I passed a miserable night, lying alone on my bed of straw. I could not sleep and tossed wearily, lighting one candle after another to keep the oppressive darkness at bay. The light also helped to discourage the thousands of bugs that crept out of the cracks in the timber of the old wooden house. I was hypersensitive to the noises of the night, imagining a Russian attack when I heard a few of our machine-guns nattering away. Snow was falling and I shivered as I thought of it and pulled up the blankets. Then I began to doubt my diagnosis. Perhaps it was spotted fever after all! Again and again I went over the symptoms and thought that perhaps I had not had sufficient experience of the disease to be able to diagnose correctly; Volhynian fever was unknown in Germany. Excruciating pains racked my limbs and I suffered a new attack of shivering. Müller noticed my restlessness and brought me a cup of tea. I drank a little, but there was a foul, furry taste in my mouth. I swallowed some more Pyramidon tablets. Outside the machine-guns rattled again. "Have a look, Müller. See if the Russians are attacking."

Müller looked outside and said: "There is nothing special, Herr *Assistenzarzt*."

Again I carefully examined my pistol and asked for extra ammunition. My tunic hung close by in readiness and my boots were near my bedside box. Müller lay down to sleep and I listened to my watch ticking and thought of Martha, of my home, of my brothers and sister and back again in circles. With an effort I made myself realize that if the fever subsided during the afternoon it would certainly be Volhynian fever and I tried to laugh at myself for all my senseless brooding. Early in the morning I fell asleep and in the afternoon my temperature had dropped and I felt much better.

Next day, a new 88mm anti-aircraft gun was delivered to us and Kageneck took over its tactical employment. It was a great relief to the entire battalion—at last we had something that could counter the T-34. We should now be able to engage the monster at a range of a thousand yards or more. And we knew that the "88" was a highly-accurate weapon, devastatingly effective even at long range. The new-born confidence of the battalion penetrated even to the sick bay. The men almost looked forward to the next clash with the T-34s.

We waited for them to come that day, but the enemy made no movement. As expected, I felt much better during the day, my temperature was nearly normal and I kept down the pain in my limbs with strong doses of Pyramidon. I was able to carry on with the more essential work in the sick bay, although I did not venture outside, where the temperature hovered around freezing point.

In anticipation, I dosed myself with sulfonamide on 10 November—four days after the first attack. And in the late afternoon the expected fever hit me with uncanny violence. It seemed much stronger than the first attack. Fortunately, the Russians left us in peace; there was only limited patrol activity on both sides. Again the night passed slowly and again I was overcome with an intense feeling of loneliness and homesickness. I was powerless to stop depressing thoughts that revolved in my mind. But even that night came to an end and by the afternoon the fever had subsided. It turned out to be the last attack; I recovered rapidly and by evening was feeling that it was good to be alive.

*　　*　　*

On 13 November we awoke and shivered.[158] An icy blast from the northeast knifed across the snowy countryside. The sky was cloudless and dark blue, but the sun seemed to have lost its strength and instead of becoming warmer toward noon as on previous days, the thermometer kept falling and by sundown had reached minus 12 degrees Centigrade.[159]

The soldiers, who up to now had not regarded the light frosts too seriously, began to take notice. One man who had been walking outside for only a short distance without his woolen *Kopfschützer* or "head-saver" came into the sick bay. Both ears were white and frozen stiff.

It was our first case of frostbite.

We gently massaged the man's ears, taking care not to break the skin, and they thawed out. We powdered them and covered them with cotton wool and made a suitable head-dressing. Perhaps we had managed to save the whole of the ears; we should have to wait and see.

This minor case of frostbite was a serious warning. The icy winds from Siberia—the breath of death—were blowing across the Steppes; winds from where all life froze, from the Arctic ice cap itself. Things would be serious if we could not house ourselves in prepared positions and buildings, and I stopped to think of the armies marching on Moscow across open country at this very moment. All that those men had received so far were their woolen *Kopfschützers*; the winter clothing had still not arrived. What was happening to the men's feet, for the ordinary Army boot retained very little warmth?

Then, too, the thermometer showed only 12 degrees below zero. Temperatures would drop to minus 24 degrees—minus 36 degrees—minus 48 degrees—perhaps even lower. It was beyond comprehension—a temperature four times colder than a deep freezer. To attempt any movement without warm clothing in those conditions would be sheer suicide. Surely the older generals had been right when, after the battle of Viaz'ma and Briansk, they had counseled "Dig in for the winter." Some of them were men with experience of Russia during the 1914-1918 war. At the most, they had said, continue the war through the winter only with a few thoroughly equipped and well-provisioned divisions. Make the big push in the spring.

If only the battle for Moscow had started 14 days earlier, the city would now have been in our hands. Or even if the rains had held off for 14 days. If—if—if. If Hitler had started "Barbarossa" six weeks earlier as originally planned; if he had left Mussolini on his own in the Balkans and had attacked Russia in May;[160] if we had continued our sweeping advance instead of stopping at the Schutsche Lake; if Hitler had sent us winter clothing.[161] Yes, if, if, if—but now it was too late.

Those Arctic blasts that had taken us by surprise in our protected positions had scythed through our attacking troops. In a couple of days there were thousands of casualties from frostbite alone; thousands of first-class, experienced soldiers fell out because the cold had surprised them.

Neuhoff and I conferred on the best ways of protecting our men against frostbite. They were ordered to wear their *Kopfschützer* and gloves, on cold days to wear as much underclothing as possible and always to wear dry woolen socks. They were also told never to wear excessively tight boots, but if necessary to have them stretched.

But newspaper was to be my major weapon against the Russian winter—at least until the winter clothing arrived. Newspaper in the boots took up little space and could often be changed. Two sheets of newspaper on a man's back, between vest and shirt, preserved the warmth of the body and were windproof. Newspaper around the belly; newspaper in the trousers; newspaper around the legs; newspaper everywhere that the body required extra warmth.

Now the great question: where to get all the newspaper? In my car I visited the rear, where the baggage and supply units were already preparing to settle in for the winter. These rear units had not yet dreamed of such desperate measures being necessary to keep the winter at bay. To them newspaper was just newspaper. We found old German papers, Russian newspapers, magazines and journals—and propaganda pamphlets by the thousand. Some of the leaflets were our own propaganda, others bore pictures of Lenin and Stalin. There was paper enough, and it amused us to think of Russian propaganda leaflets being used to keep German soldiers warm. I sent my panje wagons out to collect the paper, and the bearded doctor and his paper chase became a subject for jokes among the second-line units. Most of them wrote me off as bomb-happy.

We soon learned, too, to appreciate the Russian houses and acknowledged that even the poorest Russian knew how to build a protection against the winter. Each house was built around a huge oven, which had a massive fireplace at one side. Every activity in the house was centered on that oven. The outside walls of the houses were built of logs, made wind and weatherproof by tightly packed marsh-moss between the cracks. But the thick inside walls were built of stone and clay, which absorbed and retained the heat from the oven. Hours after the fire had died out a pleasant warmth radiated throughout the house. The ovens were never too hot for comfort, but were never cold. The poorer type of peasant family would sleep on top of the oven—the whole family climbing on to a special, wide sleeping ledge. Every house had wooden ceilings, a thatch roof and double windows that were never opened the whole winter through. In Knyaseva, nearly every house was single-storied, with only two rooms—a living-room-kitchen with a wooden partition and a second room in which occasionally there was the luxury of a couple of simple beds.

Adjoining the back of the house, and separated by only a partition, there were always sheds for cows and pigs. They were kept close to the peasants so that all could share the warmth.

During the winter the Russian villager seldom washed himself, if at all. A handful of water in the morning sufficed to wash the sleep out of his eyes. But in the summer they made up for their dirty but warm winter state tenfold. There was a *sauna* at the back of every house, about 50 feet away. The *sauna* was also built of logs, but had no windows. In the middle of the small, high room were some flat stones on which a fire was built, while ranging up one wall were wide wooden shelves. Against the opposite wall stood water barrels.

Sauna bathing is done communally—the whole family and perhaps one or two neighbors join in—and is an art. The fire is lighted until the stones are red hot; then water is ladled from the barrels on to the stones, which give off a cloud of steam that fills the entire room. The bathers sit on the shelves, the higher the hotter. When the pores are opened and perspiration is streaming out, the men and women beat one another's bodies with fresh birch faggots to increase the circulation of the blood still further. At the same time, the twigs fill the room with an aromatic spring-like smell. The steam bath and the flagellation go on for 15 or 20 minutes—as long as the individual can stand it, for it can impose a great strain on the heart. Then the whole body is washed down with cold water and vigorously rubbed with a rough towel. Usually the whole family follows the bath with an exhilarating run over the meadows and through the woods, stark naked.

Done judiciously, *sauna* bathing is a wonderful pick-me-up, although I enjoyed my first experience of it so much that I overindulged and had an alarming pulse rate of 120 a minute for two hours afterward.

Behind the *sauna* houses are the great communal barns where the corn and vegetables are stored. In the same way as the house contains only essentials, so is the whole of a Russian peasant's life ordered with only the practical end in view. Only essentials are grown in the fields—different kinds of turnip, cabbage, corn and sunflowers. Practically every villager has his own small holding and one or two cows—or only goats and a sheep if he is poor. Of course, every family has its indispensable little panje horse, which pulls the cart in summer and the sleigh in winter. Usually a few fowls run around the yard.

The breeding of thoroughbred stock and crop cultivation on a large scale was done only at the Kolchozes, the large communal farms. Everyone there, man, woman and child, had task work to do, there was little free time and the ownership of stock and size of land that could be individually cultivated was restricted to a well-defined minimum for each family. Only those who actively worked on the Kolchozes received a tiny percentage of the profits, depending on the size of the crops. This could be in grain or money and appeared to be about 200 lbs. to 300 lbs. of grain a year for each worker. These impressive Kolchozes, systematically established all over the country, were between 200,000 and 600,000 acres in extent; they dominated the entire Russian agricultural economy. Each one was run by a Communist Party member and his Bolshevik assistants.[162]

The scorched-earth policy laid down by Stalin had hit the Russian population hard. The retreating soldiers and organized groups of civilians stuck rigidly to Stalin's order: "Not a kilogram of corn, not a liter of fuel is to be left to the enemy. The communal peasants are to drive away all the stock. Everything which would be of use to the enemy is to be destroyed." The fact that millions of civilians were to be left behind in the denuded areas was ignored.

When the cold weather set in, individual Russian peasants came to us and asked what was to become of them during the winter—they had insufficient food to see them through. We could only reply that we ourselves did not have enough and stressed that it was Stalin who had ordered the scorched-earth policy. But we comforted them by promising that when Moscow had fallen, we should be able to provide for them. And huge grain elevators and stocks of provisions had fallen into our hands at Kalinin as a result of the terrific tempo of our advance, which had prevented Stalin's policy being carried out. Half of the houses in Knyaseva had been commandeered by us; the Russian population had been put into the other half. But we were already considering the desirability of evacuating the entire Russian population, so that we could have maximum protection against the winter.

The field telephone rang in the battalion battle post. Lammerding answered it and turned to us. "Post!" he said. The word ran like fire around the battalion. It was the first mail we had received since the end of September and only the third batch since the start of the campaign, nearly five months before.

In order to waste no time I sent Fischer in my Opel to the Divisional Post Office, and we prepared to celebrate in festive manner that evening. Extra-large fires were stoked up in the huge Russian fireplaces, special rations of tea were issued, and like children waiting for a party to start we hung around with unconcealed impatience while the post-carriers sorted out the mail for each company.

Chapter 16

Snow

Not every letter was welcome. While some men were showing around pictures of wives, sweethearts and babies, others were sitting and staring into nothing—for the world no longer held anything for them.

Like Seelbach, whose whole family—father, mother and three young sisters—had been wiped out in a bombing raid on Düsseldorf. They had been buried for two months and only now had he received the news. The long letter he had written to his mother the day before was now meaningless. He tore it up. The wooden horse, the ship and the jumping-jack which he had so painstakingly carved for his sisters he gave away. *Feldwebel* Stemmer of 10th Company, who had not heard from his wife for a long time, received a letter from a neighbor giving a detailed account of Frau Stemmer's behavior and disappearance. Stemmer was dazed and wanted only to get back to Germany, find his wife and kill the other man. But we were all beyond the Volga and could do nothing to change the course of happenings in Germany. Even a letter would take weeks to reach home. Many men were overcome by a feeling of their own impotence.

There were between 30 and 40 letters from Martha. She had numbered them all and only four were missing. She had refused the offer from the Vienna *Volksoper* and was back in Duisburg. She told me of her plans for our engagement party—it was to be an intimate family affair, a few friends invited, at my brother's house in Krefeld. They were all busy hoarding for the occasion; champagne, wines and liqueurs from France, the Rhine and the Moselle were already in the cellars, Martha said. And she had no doubts about the date of the engagement—January at the latest it was to be. Newspaper cuttings in her letters painted a rosy picture of the progress of the war. Press Chief Dietrich predicted a calm and hopeful Christmas; by then, the campaign in the east would be over—it was almost won, now, apparently.[163] All that would remain was "police action," for the Red Armies had been mortally defeated and would never rise again. Propaganda is an insidious weapon; its battle is won if the desire to believe it is present. So we half-believed Dietrich that the war would be won by Christmas, in spite of the evidence of our own eyes.

This was the time to use my bottle of cognac. Heinrich brought it to me and I interrupted the letter reading to call for a toast to Martha.

"Good God! Look at that!" exclaimed Neuhoff. "This chap lugs a bottle of cognac all the way from France to Moscow and only comes out with it now!"

"Martha's only just given him permission to open it, Herr Major," Lammerding put in.

"Where did you get it?" asked Becker. "And more important, where have you been hiding it?"

"Sorry, I can't tell you. I'm bound by my Hippocratic oath!"

The door was suddenly thrown open and a messenger from 9th Company reported: "*Unteroffizier* Biermann has been captured by the Russians, Herr Major."

"What happened?"

"He was on guard duty at the listening post, Herr Major, shortly before being relieved, when he was surprised by a Russian patrol, overpowered and dragged away."

"How do you know he was dragged away alive?"

"The troops in the trench behind him heard him call out," the messenger explained, "and the counter-patrol that was sent out found only his rifle and helmet. And the tracks in the snow showed that he was dragged away resisting. Not a shot was fired, Herr Major."

"Thank you," said Neuhoff. The messenger saluted and went out. "Well, there's nothing further we can do about it. The Russkies will try to squeeze everything they can out of him about our positions and then they'll probably shoot him. Damn! Damn! Damn!" He turned to Lammerding: "See to it that all company commanders are alerted. At the slightest sign of enemy activity, outposts are to get back to the trenches and give the alarm."

That was the end of the incident. Biermann—the first man in the battalion to be captured by the Reds—was wiped off the roll, a letter was sent by Tietjen to his next-of-kin, and 14 letters, unopened and unread, were returned to his young wife.

We never heard of him again.

*   *   *

A couple of days later our winter clothing arrived. There was just enough for each company to be issued with four heavy fur-lined greatcoats and four pairs of felt-lined boots. Four sets of winter clothing for each company! Sixteen greatcoats and 16 pairs of winter boots to be shared among a battalion of 800 men! And the meager issue coincided with a sudden drop in the temperature to minus 22 degrees.

Reports reached us that the issue of winter clothing to the troops actually advancing on Moscow had been on no more generous scale.[164] More and more reports were being sent to Corps and Army Headquarters recommending that the attack on Moscow by a summer-clad army be abandoned and that winter positions be prepared. Some of these reports were forwarded by Army Group Center to the *Führer's* Headquarters, but no reply or acknowledgment ever came. The order persisted: "Attack!" And our soldiers attacked.

In the extreme south Rostov fell into the *Wehrmacht's* hands and on our army front the ring of steel drew imperceptibly tighter around Moscow. But there was no doubt in the minds of our orderly room staff that the pathetic allotment of winter clothing meant one thing—we should be ordered to dig in for the winter.

"They're not fools at the *Führer's* Headquarters," I heard the orderly room NCO say. "If we weren't going to dig in, they'd have sent more winter clothing. That's logical."

Unteroffizier Stefanie, who was the brains of the orderly room, took a map of Russia from the wall and boldly ringed the important cities which would constitute the mainstays immediately behind our winter front line: Taganrog, Stalino, Kharkov, Orel, Viaz'ma, Rzhev, Kalinin, Staraya-Russa and Narva. These cities, he said, would maintain the supply line to the front during the winter months. With a bold red pencil he drew a thick line through the points he had mentioned and printed along it in clear letters: "Winter Lines—1941/42."

Unfortunately the battalion's orderly room staff proved to be no better prophets than the rest of us. They were right in one respect only—the 16 pairs of boots and 16 overcoats were the only winter clothing that ever reached us.

For a few days the weather was a little warmer, but to compensate it snowed heavily until a blanket of snow, three feet deep, covered the whole countryside. Nothing much happened on our front except daily, inaccurate artillery fire from the Reds, so our beautiful 88mm gun was withdrawn from us.

Far to the rear of our lines, however, things were happening. Daily, Russian parachutists were found—20, 50, even 100 miles behind us. And investigations and questioning of Russian civilians confirmed that the Reds were systematically dropping fanatical young Communist soldiers who recruited civilians, escaped prisoners and Russian soldiers in hiding and formed them into efficient and determined guerrilla bands. These groups were damning evidence of our failure to win over the civilian population. Had we merely broken up the Kolchozes and apportioned the land among the Russian population, the chances were that the peasants would at this moment have been handing over these guerrilla leaders to us. Instead, Rosenberg's[165] columns, the Brownshirts, had followed us into Russia to become the new political masters. They came not to give freedom, but to suppress and dominate. The Kolchoze system was retained, except that the Brown Ones now ran them instead of the Red Ones.

A divisional order lay on the orderly room table: "The 3rd Battalion, I.R. 18, is to detail a company immediately for the purposes of countering guerrilla activities in our rearward areas. The company is to be fully equipped and is to leave in battle order. It is expected that its operations will last from six to eight weeks."

Which company was to be detailed? That was the question facing Neuhoff, Lammerding, Becker and Kageneck as they sat around the table. Stolze had not yet returned to the 10th Company and Bolski did not seem sufficiently mature and reliable to be in command of a company that was to operate independently under unknown and hazardous conditions. *Oberleutnant* Kramer, who commanded 11th Company, had been in poor health and lacked the imagination for this type of work. There was no alternative but to detach Tietjen and his 9th Company. He was ordered to report to the Battalion H.Q., where his new duties were explained to him.

"*Jawohl*, Herr Major," he said without any show of surprise, but his eyes betrayed a mixture of pleasure at his lone assignment and regret at having to leave the rest of the battalion.

Next morning at nine o'clock, 9th Company paraded in full battle order for Neuhoff and *Oberst* Becker to inspect. It was a comparatively warm day—only a few degrees of frost—but snow was falling as the men of 9th Company marched away in their summer uniforms.

We never again saw *Oberleutnant* Tietjen and his 160 men. They did not return to the battalion, but until the end operated bravely and effectively against the guerrillas. They were completely independent and had to rely entirely on their own initiative in their dangerous mission. Gradually, an increasing number of Russian volunteers joined Tietjen and the company grew in strength and renown until it was known far and wide as "Tietjen's Group." The Russian volunteers were brave fighters and in the warfare that developed—very often in the thickly wooded areas—they lived like bandits. It was not long before we heard that the Russians had put a price on Tietjen's head. Many times he was nearly captured, but always reappeared like a will-o'-the-wisp, although many of his men met cruel deaths at the hands of the guerrillas.

*　　*　　*

Next day the Russians attacked our sector as if they were fully aware that we were one company weaker. Perhaps they had been told by their women spies, whom they were now systematically sending through our lines.

They were usually attractive girls, who could speak German well, and when questioned pretended they were fleeing from Bolshevism. It was extremely difficult for our soldiers to know whether they were telling the truth, for at this time many Russian civilians were escaping from the ruthless measures the Reds were applying, particularly in Moscow, in their efforts to save the city. The Bolsheviks had, for several weeks, been eliminating all citizens who had in the slightest degree shown themselves to be unenthusiastic Communists. A great purge was taking place and it ended for thousands upon thousands of simple Russians with a bullet in the nape of the neck. These political refugees drew grim pictures of life behind the Russian lines and confirmed what the major with the red stripes had told me: that the ceaseless rains alone had saved Moscow.[166]

But with these refugees came the good-looking and fanatical girl spies. With glowing hearts they were ready in the name of Communism to sacrifice their bodies to our sex-starved troops and their lives to the hangman's noose. Many a German soldier—and no doubt many an officer—unwittingly gave away information in the warmth of a bunk on top of a Russian oven. And like the commissars, these girls were prepared to die for their ideals.

Only the previous day two young Russian girl students had been hanged in Vassilev-skoye. Under cross-examination they had broken down and had been sentenced to death. Then, smiling and with shining eyes, they had proudly acknowledged that they belonged to the great Communist movement that would save the world. With the words "Long Live Russia!" they had placed nooses around their own necks and had jumped from the gallows. It was difficult not to admire such courage and their story spread through our troops, to whom they were known by their Christian names.

The Russian attacks on our lines petered out after two days of withering defensive fire. Our storm troops then counterattacked the retreating enemy and took a large number of prisoners. Among them was a huge Russian from Siberia, on whom I kept close watch. Through Kunzle I was able to determine that he was no great friend of Communism and he came out with a story that the commissars had stood behind them and had shot every Russian who wavered in the face of our counterattack. He and others had decided to allow themselves to be captured. In confirmation of his story, he pulled out of his pocket a care-fully folded pamphlet, one of thousands that the *Luftwaffe* had strewn over the Russian lines, offering safe conduct to any Red soldier who produced it.

"I think you have come to the right address," I told him, through Kunzle. "You will be given a German uniform without badges. You will no longer fight as a soldier, but will help to transport the wounded and will look after the horses. Kunzle will give you all the details. Will you remain with me and help?" I asked him slowly and deliberately.

"Yes," he answered readily.

I nicknamed him Hans. He told Kunzle that the Red Army had been warned that the Germans shot every Russian who fell into their hands, but when he had seen his best friend shot by one of the commissars, Hans had refused to believe this story. I looked through the pamphlet he had handed me. On one side were two pictures: the first showed a commissar, pistol in hand, driving the Russian soldiers against a German attack. He had already shot in the back three of them who had hesitated. The second picture showed the action the Red soldiers should take: two soldiers were attacking the commissar, who was lying on the ground, while the others were surrendering to the Germans. On the other side of the pamphlet the following instructions were printed in Russian and German: *"The producer of this permit does not desire to continue a useless bloodbath in the interests of the Jews and commissars. He is leaving the defeated Red Army and is going over to the side of the German Wehrmacht. German officers and soldiers will give him good treatment, will feed him and provide useful employment. This permit is applicable to an unlimited number of officers and soldiers of the Red Army."* As a reassurance to these deserters this note was added: *"Stalin's threat to victimize the families of soldiers coming over to the Germans is impracticable and will have no effect. The German High Command does not publish lists of the captured."*

In fact, the number of Russian deserters rose considerably during the next few days. It seemed that not only we, but also the Russian soldiers, were viewing the coming winter with some apprehension.

The Russians retaliated by a leaflet raid of their own. One morning we awoke to find the whole area littered with white pamphlets printed in Russian and German. We read the Bolshevik invitation: *"Instructions: The German soldier in possession of this permit has the right to pass through the front to Soviet Russia. This permit is to be handed to the first Russian citizen, commissar or soldier, who will thereby be duty bound to accompany the soldier to the nearest Russian Army staff."*

Everyone in the battalion was amused at this clumsy invitation to visit the promised land, but if the permits had given free passes back to France, many soldiers would undoubtedly have grabbed them and eagerly handed them to the citizens of Paris or to the Yvonnes and Yvettes of Littry.

On the same day some pamphlets of far more interest to me arrived at Battalion H.Q.—official leave forms. We were told that the first leave batches would soon be going home and that I was to be the first officer from our battalion to go, as I had not had leave for 14 months. There seemed little doubt that I would be going, for simultaneously with the arrival of the leave forms came two doctors—an *Oberstabsarzt* and his young assistant, *Unterarzt* Freese. They were attached to our battalion and were to work themselves into the routine and act in my place while I was away.

I was surprised that they had sent *Oberstabsarzt* Volpius—a man of 60, who had served through the First World War. Neuhoff was of the opinion that he had been sent to the front as punishment; and we learned later that that was the case, although we were never able to find out in what way he had transgressed. Their coming made no difference to my routine. The old doctor simply did nothing, but spent his whole day in the office, got in everyone's way and made himself thoroughly unpopular. When he tried to vary his diet of idleness by visiting Regimental H.Q. he was completely cold-shouldered. The *Unterarzt*, who was 24, helped me in the sick bay and watched all I did with great interest.

Tulpin suddenly started to act strangely. He was absent for a long period without permission one day, but when I questioned him, denied that anything was troubling him. I noticed that he was pale and restless and that the pupils of his eyes were abnormally small. I wondered if he was perhaps becoming addicted to morphia, but when Freese checked our stock of drugs, everything was in order. I had no real fault to find with Tulpin; he was a reliable worker and had proved his bravery, but I decided to keep a watch on him.

Oberleutnant Kramer sent me a message that he was far from well and would like me to visit him. He had scarcely eaten for several days and was suffering from bowel trouble. As soon as I set eyes on him I had no doubts as regards my diagnosis.

"Well, Kramer," I said, "it's caught up with you at last. The worst of it is that you're as thin as a ghost and you've got no strength left to fight it."

"I'm finished, Doktor, that's why I've called you."

"That's always the case with you clever bastards. When you're feeling well you treat doctors as a joke. You only call on us when you're hospital cases. You've got epidemic jaundice, Kramer."

"What's that, Doktor?"

"Virus infection of the liver. And it's attacked you because for weeks during the autumn you had those bouts of dysentery that you thought you could cure on your own." I examined him thoroughly; the further signs of the disease confirmed my diagnosis. The liver was enlarged, the pulse comparatively slow and the spleen slightly enlarged.

"Well, what's going to happen to me, Doktor?" Kramer asked.

"You're very sick Kramer, and in need of a long rest to build up your strength. You'll have absolute rest and treatment in my sick bay for a few days and then I'll try to get you flown back to Germany from Staritsa. With a little luck you'll be home the same day."

Kramer held his breath and gasped: "God! How is that possible, Doktor? That's too good to be true—home to Germany in one day! I can't believe it!"

Neuhoff reported to Regimental H.Q. and within a few hours, *Oberleutnant* Boehmer had been transferred from the 1st Battalion to take Kramer's place as commander of 11th Company.

Boehmer arrived, immaculately dressed, clean-shaven, tall and slender. He was barely 21, had been the youngest *Leutnant* in the division and was now the youngest *Oberleutnant*. He was a polished, though slightly conceited, youngster, the direct opposite to Kramer, who had risen from the ranks and had never been able to live it down in his own mind. Boehmer, too, had a slight inferiority complex, no doubt stemming from the fact that he had always been the youngest officer in the mess and for that reason had been nicknamed "Bubi," a name that had stuck. He tried to compensate for his youth and lack of experience by adopting a provocative and sometimes boastful manner.

He visited Kramer in the sick bay and the two men took an instant dislike to each other. Kramer was prepared to dislike anyone who took over his company and had been told by his *Oberfeldwebel* that Boehmer's first remark had been: "The company doesn't seem too bad; I think something can be made of it."

"Damned nerve!" exploded Kramer, after I had ushered Boehmer out. "First of all the company will have to make something out of him. Impudent damned puppy!"

I mentioned to Kageneck that I hoped to take Kramer to Staritsa in three days' time to catch a plane for the west. "I think I'll take him personally in my car," I added. "I can afford to give myself a little break with this sudden invasion of doctors."

"And I'm going with you," Kageneck announced. "Perhaps I can be of use to you; my brother's a fighter pilot in North Africa and he's sure to have some *Luftwaffe* friends at Staritsa."

* * *

I told *Unterarzt* Freese that he would be in charge of the sick bay in my absence and that he would have the old *Oberstabsarzt* in the background for support if necessary. To break him in, I allowed him to take charge from that moment and he worked with great interest and keenness. In the evening we would sit by the fire in the sick bay while I answered his questions. He had arrived fresh from training in Germany and was stuffed with theoretical knowledge imparted by people who had no idea of the real conditions of the Russian front. He was worried by the problem of asepsis—we had no sterilized instruments, washing of hands in alcohol, or germ-free bandages.

"Wounds are often dreadful and need immediate surgical treatment in the field," I told him. "It's amazing what a human body can endure, and in spite of the mud and dirt, results aren't bad at all. I think it's largely because we're dealing with healthy young people whose systems are strongly disease-resistant. No, forget about asepsis—that only starts back at the Medical Company."

"I hope my surgery won't let me down," said Freese.

"Forget about your surgery! Here it's bandages and plaster—the boys with the knives are also back at the Medical Company. Get your cases back to them alive. That's your job. Sometimes you need a bit of surgery to do it, not often. Speed, Freese, that's the thing! If there's a big attack and your dressing station's full, decide which ones need your help first. Head wounds aren't so serious—immediate and absolute rest. Stomach wounds—those are your danger cases. Get your stomachs back to the Medical Company as fast as you can. Use the sledges and the panje wagons rather than wait an hour for an ambulance. Your stomach case can live or die in that hour. Internal bleeding's the killer—that and internal dirt. Particularly if the colon's been damaged. Don't bother so much about closing the entry and exit wounds. Much better to spend a couple of minutes on the telephone to the Medical Company, telling them to ready up for a stomach case. Minutes count. Arterial bleeding: plenty of that, and you don't need me to tell you the treatment. Frostbite you've seen, and you'll probably know more about that than I by the time I get back from my leave. Remember, your first and last duty is to get the wounded back to the Medical Company alive and fit to be operated on."

"That all sounds quite simple," said Freese. I had to laugh at his boyish enthusiasm and refusal to accept life as a complicated business.

"Good! If you find wounds simple stuff, then let's have a look at some of the diseases you'll be up against. Take Kramer's hepatitis, for instance: I'd never met that at home, but here it's fairly common. Then there's spotted fever and Volhynian fever—all the filthy lice-borne diseases that are unknown at home. We've got Weil's disease—a spirochete, usually caused by water polluted by rats. There's Tularaemia, another infectious disease, spread by horse flies, but it can be caught by eating meat of infected animals, sometimes even from a rat bite. You know, Freese, there's no real protection here against all the best plague carriers—rats, mice, fleas, ticks and what not. One way and another you never know what's going to hit the men next. Great fun—good training—best of all it makes you appreciate your leave. Do you know how I'd spend it, if I weren't going to get engaged?"

"No, tell me."

"I'd present myself at a beautiful, white, antiseptic hospital, spend half my day scrubbing up under a running tap; spend the rest of the day playing with a gleaming set of surgical instruments, straight out of a completely sterile autoclave; and go to sleep every night in a highly polished hospital ward where the nurses had never even heard of spotted fever or a man with his guts lying in the dirt."

"That's what I've been dying to get away from," said Freese enthusiastically.

"Well, if this is what you wanted—you've got it!" I told him. "But you know, Freese, you can get awfully tired of lice as playmates."

Chapter 17

The Moscow Tram Stop

Staritsa lay before us, on the other side of Russia's stream, the Volga. It was an old city that even from a distance echoed the glories of Imperial Russia. The many orthodox churches towered above the humbler buildings of the city, their great cupolas thickly covered with snow, through which the circular windows gazed across the river like dark, staring eyes.

Fischer had driven the three of us—Kramer, Kageneck and me—back along the same road on which we had marched to Vassilevskoye. Through the villages we had taken by storm and past the graves of our comrades whom we had buried by the roadside. The 50-mile journey had taken less than two hours, for the snow on the road had been pressed into a smooth surface by the heavy traffic.

The Opel clattered on to the wooden bridge that our pioneers had thrown across the Volga before Staritsa. Masses of snow were overhanging the steep banks of the river and sluggish ice floes drifted downstream, jostling one another in the black waters. Soon they would drift no longer, but would cling together, first in the quiet backwaters, then on the surface of the river; they would thicken as winter's hand froze the countryside until they stretched from bank to bank. The Volga would continue to flow, but for months would be three, four, five feet below the ice. Then the snows would build up on the frozen river and the Volga would cease to exist as a feature of the landscape.

A feeble, wintry sun shone down on the snow, giving light but no warmth. But there was an air of peace over the whole scene before us that inspired even the inhibited Kramer to say: "It's peculiar—I feel as if already I'm at a colossal distance from the war. It's almost as if I hadn't been through all the experiences of the past few months. I feel like a deserter."

"And for the first time you're talking like a human being," I told him.

"What do you mean, Doktor?" he asked sharply. "Are you trying to tell me that I haven't been a human being?"

147

"Yes, just that," I replied quickly. Now was the time to let him have it. "Until now I've never known you as a person of flesh and blood—you've just been a military machine. Your mind has never deviated from the path along which it was drilled and trained. You've never understood or appreciated the meaning of fellowship. You've been so busy trying to be a success as an officer that you've never had time to be a man."

His eyes showed that the words had hit him like the blows of a hammer, but his iron self-discipline clamped down on the words he would have liked to say and all that came out was: "Thank you, Doktor. At least you have been frank. I know, at any rate, what *you* think of me now."

From the bridge we labored uphill, swung to the left of the city and headed across flat country to the airfield.

Kramer's transport for home materialized more quickly than we had expected. An old Junkers 52 was leaving for the west that morning.[167] Our luck was in; a seat was available. We bade a short farewell to Kramer, who was well wrapped in blankets for the long flight, and the old Junkers gathered speed over the snowy airfield, rose reluctantly into the air and hedge-hopped away toward Germany.

We never saw Kramer again. After his recovery, he was sent to a division on the southern sector of the Russian front and fell at Stalingrad a year later.

*   *   *

The world of the *Luftwaffe* might have been on another planet—it was a world of luxury compared with the modest world of the infantry, where comfort was governed by what the individual soldier could carry. We were considerably impressed.

All the *Luftwaffe* officers had the incredible luxury of real beds; they had French cognac and liqueurs; they even had chocolate dished out to them as a normal ration—chocolate containing kola to refresh and sustain them; and they each had a full kit of winter clothing.[168] No wonder they could laugh at life and make a joke of the war, these dashing cavaliers in soldier's uniform. They took it for granted that they should have preferential treatment over the other—and less distinguished—services. But as we lounged in their comfortable mess, we were won over by the light-hearted banter of this happy band of brothers, who seemed to know all the other *Luftwaffe* men on active service.

Kageneck's brother! Of course they knew him! Fine fellow. Still in North Africa, of course, fighting a gentleman's war. Doing very well, too—between France and Africa he'd shot down more than 70 enemy aircraft. So they told Kageneck, and another round of drinks was ordered to toast the desert pilot. And another drink to toast those poor devils, the infantry.

"Wouldn't have your job for all the gold in Russia, my dear fellow," the squadron medical officer told me. "Give me a front-line squadron every time. These boys live so well that they're never sick. And if they should get bounced by a Russki, they're dead and they don't come back. Either way they're no trouble to me. It's a gentleman's life."

I pointed out that life with the infantry had its compensations. Probably nowhere else was the comradeship and community of interests so close and binding.

"Rather have my life, my dear chap," said the doctor cheerfully, and I was inclined to agree with him.

Kageneck steered the conversation toward the position around Moscow. These men were the first to see any troop movements developing. They told us that in some places advance elements of our army were only 10 miles from the Kremlin—right at the gates of the city. Our final offensive, it was expected, would be launched within the week. This was startling news.

A reconnaissance pilot, a dark-eyed, lively Rhinelander, said: "It looks as if the big assault's building up—masses of ammunition and stores are being rushed toward the front and the armies to the south of Moscow are on the move all the time."

"And what are the Russians doing?" asked Kageneck.

"Sorry to tell you"—a little Frankfurt fighter pilot took up the story—"but one troop train after another is arriving in Moscow from the east. Of course, you can't tell how good these Red troops are. . . ."

Next morning in Staritsa we bumped into an *Oberfeldwebel* from 86th Infantry Division whom Kageneck knew. He had served near this division in France and knew many of its officers. The 86th was already beyond Klin, on the Kalinin-Moscow railway line, the *Oberfeldwebel* told us, and had pushed to within a short distance of Moscow.

"How is the road to Klin?" asked Kageneck.

"Good, Herr *Oberleutnant*."

"We should really take a run out that way," said Kageneck, turning to me. "I'd like to see some of my old friends."

After lunch in the *Luftwaffe* mess, Kageneck informed me that he had scrounged a tankful of petrol from the airmen. In a couple of hours we could be right on the Moscow front. "I think we should undertake this lightning tour," he added, with a grin.

"Oh, so we've got to the stage of lightning tours, have we? How do I know that you won't want to go to a cinema show in Moscow once you get there?"

"You must look at it this way, Heinz," Kageneck said with mock seriousness, "Klin lies about 50 miles from here; the distance from Klin to our battalion is far less than from Klin to Staritsa, so that if we drive to Klin we'll be nearer to our unit than by staying here."

"That's the same sort of logic that nearly landed you in the cart when you got your wife to pay that illegal visit to us in East Prussia. . . ."

"As a result of which she's expecting a baby any day now!"

"Congratulations, my dear chap! I'd no idea . . ." I pumped his hand, then laughed. "It seems to me that whenever you break the rules you land with your backside in the butter. We'd better pay that unofficial visit to Klin."

*   *   *

We arrived in Klin at 10 a.m., our small car loaded with farewell gifts from the *Luftwaffe* mess—a dozen bottles of cognac, 50 packets of kola chocolate, cigars, cigarettes and a variety of medical supplies. The airmen had appointed themselves as fairy godfathers to the poor, long-suffering infantrymen and, as there was no way for us to reciprocate, we had been more than a little embarrassed. The airmen had plied us with brandy to overcome it.

Optimism was running high in Klin. We were told that the great final attack on Moscow would begin within the next few days. Morale was at peak-level and everyone seemed confident that the city would fall before the year was out. Everywhere supply lines were being organized, and jumping-off points selected and captured from the Russians where necessary. Frostbite had taken heavy toll of many of the divisions, but the Panzer and infantry units were still battleworthy.[169]

The troops argued that rain, mud, snow and frost had failed to stop them; they had earned Moscow and now it must fall to them.

The 86th Infantry Division, whom we had really come to visit, were lying near to our own unit, we learned—back along the railway line, halfway to Kalinin. But we did come across detachments of the 1st Panzer Division, for whom we had paved the way on 2 October at the Schutsche Lake. And, we were told, other units of our Ninth Army—the 106th Infantry Division and the 5th and 11th Panzer Divisions of Reinhardt's Panzer Group—had already fought their way to within 10 miles of Moscow. They were the closest German troops to the capital. The 106th Division was in position across the main road from Klin to Moscow, so we decided to make the 40-mile journey to visit them.[170]

Snow was falling quite heavily as we set off. The sky was leaden and visibility through the whirling snowflakes was limited. Every noise seemed to be deadened as if all nature had been padded and plushed; even the hum of our engine seemed to be in a lower, more subdued key. It was as if the air was filled with an almost inaudible, but strange, music, a weird atmospheric droning, full of expectation. Both Kageneck and I were filled with strange forebodings of mighty events that would shake our little world, yet which were sealed and held secret by the heavens.

Everything in the landscape hinted the near approach of the city of Moscow, a city that had haunted our thoughts during the long, marching miles, and which now seemed to be approaching us like a city in a legend, screened from us by seven veils. Yet we had a strange feeling that the curtain of snow might lift at any moment—and there would be Moscow lying before us. We seemed to be getting very near to the great, pulsating heart of the Russian Bear.

Side streets appeared, turning off our road; the houses drew more closely together; huge hoardings appeared beside the road, the usual pictures of Stalin and Lenin; here and there a two-storied school building stood incongruously among the wooden shacks. But not a soul was in sight. Many of the buildings were burnt-out shells, a heap of rubble bearing mute evidence to a bombing raid or concentrated artillery fire. Not a building was occupied—every man, woman, child and beast had fled. The snow had drifted up against the doors of the wooden hovels and on the windowsills. An occasional *Wehrmacht* signboard, in code, showed us that we were still on the right road and Fischer was driving in the tracks left by two heavy German lorries, which must have been just ahead of us.

It was a sobering, almost frightening, thought that if we continued at this speed for only 15 minutes we should be in Moscow itself; and a further 15 minutes would bring us into the Red Square or to the walls of the Kremlin. We passed a number of vehicles parked on a vacant piece of land and then came to a regimental battle post. We drew up outside it.

Two officers appeared. We could not tell their ranks as they were wearing heavy leather coats over their uniforms. They looked at the Bielefeld divisional crest on our car, and, as Kageneck turned his window down, the little fat one with humorous eyes asked: "Well, where are you off to?"

"To Moscow," Kageneck answered without hesitation.

"That's where we're going, too. Perhaps you'd better wait for us," said the taller man, a gaunt fellow with a deep voice.

"Then it seems we're in the right place with the right people!" Kageneck said. "But would you tell us exactly where we are? We seem to have got off our track."

"Quite simple," said the small fat one. He pointed with his leather glove. "A little to the right of us and a little to the left of us are the Russians, and directly ahead of us—over there—is the tram station for Moscow. If the tram hadn't been put out of commission by the carelessness of our soldiers, you could have had a free ride into Moscow. It's only 10 miles away. But if I were you I wouldn't try to follow the tram lines in your car. In the first place, you won't see them because of the snow—in the second, you might meet more Russians than you bargained for. But if you care to come back in a week's time, you may be able to drive straight through to Red Square."

"Are you so certain?" asked Kageneck.

"More or less. Hitler seems to have made a pact with St. Peter. As you can see, it's getting warmer every day instead of colder. If it stays like this, conditions will be fine for the final push."

I pulled out a bottle of cognac from under the seat. "As we can't personally be present when you march into Moscow, allow us to give you this bottle. Then you can drink to our health when you arrive in Red Square."

The two officers were speechless. Then the tall one said in his deep voice: "My dear gentlemen, you can hardly expect us to accept that! We poor swines at the front haven't strong enough stomachs for cognac—we're not used to it."

"Neither are we," I answered, "but as we were offered it by the *Luftwaffe* we would hardly refuse. . . . Won't you sit in the car while we talk?"

Fischer got out and walked over to the orderly room and the two men got in.

We exchanged information; they knew as little about what was going on beyond their immediate area as we. Our solitary case of frostbite amazed them; their own casualties had been 25 percent—and their winter clothing had not yet arrived.

"It's a swine," said the tall man. "Our forward movement, our success or failure, can now be judged by the thermometer. Mind you, our troops are behaving magnificently. They're thinking of one thing—taking Moscow as soon as possible and having warm winter quarters. To them, as they feel at the moment, the fall of Moscow means the end of the war."

Their light-hearted attitude had disappeared; they were discussing with us what was uppermost in their thoughts. "And now," said the tall man, "we get this spell of warmer weather—why, the war might be over by Christmas. Just imagine," he suddenly said, in a tone that held something desperate; "there lies Moscow, only a stone's throw away. One more jump and we shall be there. It will be over. Surely we can't be denied it now!"

"Come on, Walter," said the fat man, "you're getting too dramatic. Moscow must be taken in cold blood."

"Just as long as it doesn't become too cold," Walter replied, "or else we could all get cold feet—forever." He turned to us. "You see, it comes back to what I said—the temperature, the winter. We can judge our success by the thermometer."

The fat man grasped the door handle and said: "Before we all burst into tears, it's time we went." He got out, not forgetting his bottle of cognac. "Don't forget to visit us in Moscow. It will be a great pleasure for us to show you the sights. We'll be expert guides by the time you arrive."

The two men walked toward the orderly room. Thick flakes of snow settled on their smooth leather overcoats and remained where they fell. Before they disappeared, the fat man proudly waved the bottle of cognac against the leaden-gray Russian sky.

The snow fell thickly and softly on their footprints, filled them and wiped them out.

There was a deathly silence all around. In front of us lay the tramway shelter and the telegraph poles silently pointed the way to the great city beyond the curtain of snow.

"Let's walk across and have a look at that tramway station," Kageneck said. "Then we can tell Neuhoff that we were only a tram ride from Moscow."

We walked silently down the road to the stone shed. There was not a movement around us as we stopped and stared at the wooden seats on which thousands of Muscovites had sat and waited for the tram to clang down the road from Moscow.

There was an old wooden bin attached to one wall. I felt inside and dragged out a handful of old tram tickets. We picked out the Cyrillic letters, which by now we knew spelled "Moskva."

Slowly we trudged back to the car. Kageneck broke the silence and spoke for both of us: "It must fall, yet . . . I wonder . . ."

Fischer turned the car around and we headed back along the white road.

The snow was falling a little more heavily now.[171]

CHAPTER 18

The Suicide Battalion and the Siberians

AS I STRODE DOWN THE SNOW-COVERED ROAD TO THE MESS I PULLED MY *KOPFSCHÜTZER*
around my ears and over my chin and nose until there was only a gap for my eyes. But the
icy wind from the northeast still stung my face and cut through my clothing.

Saint Nicholas' Eve—5 December 1941. It was to be the first organized mess night
since the start of "Barbarossa." And I had a special reason to celebrate. A few hours previously my leave permit had come through—I was to set off in three days' time.

It would take me 14 days to reach Duisburg and a further two weeks to return to my
unit—but I should have three whole weeks at home with my family and Martha. I was
lucky to have a car at my disposal, otherwise the first 12 miles to Vassilevskoye would
have been by sleigh. From that point, troop carriers would take us to Rzhev; from there
on it was by train through Viaz'ma, Smolensk, Orsha, Minsk, Brest-Litovsk and Warsaw
to Berlin. Joyfully, I had written to Martha telling her to arrange our engagement party
for 4 January. I hoped my letter would reach her before I arrived.

So it was that I paid little heed to the bitter wind as I walked to the mess on Saint
Nicholas' Eve. The thermometer stood at 30 below. It had fallen steadily since the day we
had stood at the end of the tram tracks leading to Moscow. There could be no final attack
on the city while this weather lasted.

But we were not allowing that to worry us for this one night. There was something to
celebrate, and we had the means of celebration.

I walked into the mess and stamped the snow off my boots. There was a huge fire
blazing in the open hearth and at one end of the room stood a banquet; Kageneck and I
had donated six of our bottles of *Luftwaffe* cognac and a cold buffet had been prepared—a
tray heaped with horse meat rissoles, cold roast horse meat, salt horse meat and Kommis
bread, cut into attractive snacks. A cold goulash sauce took the place of butter, and cigars
and cigarettes were plentiful.

Stolze was back with us after a spell in "those blasted field hospitals." He had refused home sick leave in order to rejoin the battalion and the welcome he was given by the men of the 10th Company must have made the decision worthwhile. Perhaps their joy at Stolze's return was tinged with relief at seeing the back of Bolski, who had been transferred to 11th Company under young Boehmer.

Neuhoff welcomed Stolze back to the fold and toasted the absent Tietjen. *Leutnant* Ohlig, as the youngest officer present, replied to Neuhoff's speech and ended with "Long live our Major!"

"Heil, Neuhoff!" we shouted enthusiastically; all except Bolski, who looked upon the salute as sacrilege.

Stolze, standing on the table like a huge rooster, led the singing. Again and again we sang:

> *Never, never shall we carry weapons,*
> *Never, never fight again.*
> *Let the other bastards shoot,*
> *We treat them with disdain.*

Stolze's huge hands beat time and his deep voice led the choruses.

Kageneck joined me at the buffet table. "Do you realize how cold it is tonight?" he asked me.

"Damn cold—that's all I know," I answered.

"It is minus 35 degrees. Do you know what that means? Even the *Wehrmacht* report no longer talks about the concentric attack on Moscow."

"On the thermometer you can read how the attack on Moscow is going. Is that what you mean, Franz?"

"Exactly."

Had we known it, at that very moment the decision was being taken to break off the great offensive against the capital.[172] The army commanders at last persuaded Hitler, against his personal wishes, to give the German armies the order to go over to the defensive.

General Winter had had the last say. The farthest point that our ring of steel had touched was that tramway station on the road in from Klin.

Nothing unusual happened in our sector, but I was advised by regimental headquarters that general leave had been postponed for a few days, but was certain to follow. It was inevitable that this should happen while our front line stabilized itself in its new defensive positions.

A bombshell burst on 8 December—Japan was at war with America! At war with America but not with Russia! We found it incomprehensible. Our dream of getting the Reds fighting on two fronts was shattered.

But the riddle was complicated further on 11 December—Adolf Hitler had declared war on America.[173] It seemed like an act of senseless bravado. Did we not already have enough enemies? Was not the position on the Russian front serious enough—an army without winter clothing facing an enemy with allies? Must we be at war with a hostile world?

Then came reports that fresh Siberian troops, equipped with superb winter clothing, were attacking our lines on both sides of Kalinin.[174] Stalin must have had a secret agreement with Japan for some time past, otherwise how dared he withdraw these divisions from the east.

Over the Volga the Siberian troops came and threw themselves against our 129th and 162nd Infantry Divisions. The Volga was no longer a barrier—it was completely frozen over; an army could have marched across it. Desperately, I prayed that the Russians would not break through and set the whole front aflame. It was a selfish prayer; at any moment I feared the instruction would be issued: "All leave canceled." I wanted to be away before the order was given.

Our battalion was asked to nominate its two bravest men for the award of a new decoration, the German Cross in Gold. It was a particularly high award that could be won only by front-line soldiers who had already won the Iron Cross, 1st and 2nd Class, and who had since distinguished themselves in action from seven to 12 times. The Cross was to be worn on the right breast. If the matter had been put to the vote in the battalion, the men would undoubtedly have chosen the same as Neuhoff: firstly, *Oberfeldwebel* Schnittger of the 10th Company for his outstanding bravery at all times in the face of the enemy; secondly, Kageneck for his superb qualities of leadership, his fearless conduct and his ability to make the right decisions at critical moments. The citations were prepared and forwarded to Divisional H.Q., for transmission to Berlin.

Still no word came that leave was canceled. The morning of 13 December was to be my new starting time, and on the 12th I received my leave papers and detailed traveling instructions. Only five men were going from the 3rd Battalion; I was the only officer.

Letters to be posted in Germany, money with which to send flowers to wives and sweethearts, messages by the dozen, were given to me. At the sick bay, *Unterarzt* Freese and the old *Oberstabsarzt* had officially taken over my duties and I had ordered Fischer to stand by in the morning with the car that would take me to join the troop transports.

But while we sat drinking a bottle of cognac at a little farewell party on the night of the 12th, the cold wind from Asia swept icily across the steppes, blowing the hard flakes of snow before it, and the thermometer refused to rise above the minus 35 mark.

"Good God, man, cheer up!" said Lammerding. "You're going home tomorrow. What the hell have you to look glum about?"

"I'm just afraid my good luck won't hold," I said gloomily.

"Now stop drawing the devil on the wall," commanded Neuhoff. "And don't forget to send those flowers to my wife."

Before I retired I presented one of my two remaining bottles of cognac to the mess for Christmas and New Year, handed out chocolate and cigarettes all around and sent over the remaining bottle of cognac to Kageneck's quarters.

*   *   *

The Russians nearly stopped me from getting away the next day. As I was shaving off my thick beard, the alarm sounded and Russian tanks and infantry swarmed toward our lines. But the attack petered out after two hours of fierce fighting. The wounded were brought into the dressing station—among them one of the men who was due to go on leave with me. He had about 30 pieces of shrapnel embedded in the back of his body—head, back and thighs. He would go back to Germany, but lying on his stomach with a casualty card around his neck.

For a while I helped Freese and the *Oberstabsarzt* with a few seriously wounded men and then was able to leave them to it. I said my farewells and punctually at one o'clock we drove off in the Opel. The three men in the back seat related in vivid terms how they had cold-bloodedly shot down the Ivans. But what had really made the impression on them was not so much the fighting as the way the Red soldiers were clothed.

"Did you see what Ivan was dressed in?" asked a man from 10th Company. "All that winter clothing."

"Everything," said the second man. "Fur caps with ear-flaps, jackets lined with cotton-wool, thick woolen gloves and trousers—and what about those felt boots?"

"What I wouldn't give for a pair of those boots!" said the third soldier. "My feet are just thawing out now—after only two hours outside."

"I reckon Ivan could burrow into the snow like a rabbit and have a damn good sleep in those clothes," the 10th Company man said.

"I doubt that. This bloody cold would strike through any clothing," the second man replied. "Never mind, we'll soon be sitting around the fire at home. I don't give a damn what happens then."

We slept in the supply units that night and Fischer returned in the Opel to the battalion. There were about 100 men going on leave from the 6th Division.

At seven o'clock next morning the troop carriers were due to take us to Rzhev. But by eight o'clock they still had not arrived. It was as cold as ever and every now and then we stepped inside the log huts to warm ourselves. An armored car drove up at eight-thirty; an officer from Divisional H.Q. got out and said: "Comrades, I'm sorry to have to bring you this news, but a short directive has just been received from the *Führer*'s headquarters canceling all leave. Every man is to return at once to his unit and report for duty." He paused as the men's voices muttered in protest.

"If you want to know the reason—the Russians have broken through at Kalinin.[175] The situation is confused and unpredictable. That is all."

There was silence among the men now. Nobody swore—the matter was too serious for swearing even.

It was not so easy to return to our units, but we made use of whatever transport was available. Toward midday, I came across some of our battalion supply transport. They were moving, lock, stock and barrel, toward Kalinin.

"Can you tell me what's happening?" I asked the *Feldwebel* in charge of the column.

"There's been a hell of a mix-up at Kalinin, Herr *Assistenzarzt*. Our entire battalion has been thrust into the counterattack and is at present on its way there."

"But who's holding our old position?"

"The neighboring units have taken over—relieved the 3rd Battalion last night."

"I can't understand it. Relieved in this weather and thrown into the fight!"

"But why is Herr *Assistenzarzt* worrying?" inquired the *Feldwebel*. "I thought you were going on leave, sir."

"All leave canceled," I snapped out.

The *Feldwebel*'s face dropped. "Then the situation must be serious."

"Surely Petermann and my horse must be with you somewhere," I said to him.

"Yes, he's with us. Back along the line, as far as I know."

"Then I think I'll wait for him, now that I've made contact with you."

It was not long before Petermann came along, riding his own horse and leading Sigrid, whose winter hibernation with the supply units had come to an abrupt end. Sigrid, at least, had her winter clothing. She had grown a thick coat and seemed to be in splendid condition. She nuzzled my pockets for the usual lump of sugar or piece of bread, but this time she was unlucky. Petermann stuttered in his excitement at seeing me after an absence of six weeks.

From him I learned the time that the 3rd Battalion had received orders to vacate their defensive positions and march to Kalinin—it was two hours after I had left for Vassilev-skoye and leave. Neuhoff and the rest must have commented on my good fortune.

By now it was so cold that I could not ride Sigrid for more than half an hour at a time. My feet particularly became so numb that I had to walk in order to keep my blood circulating. So for most of the time Petermann and I trudged along in the snow, leading our horses. At midday we made a short halt and stood around a field kitchen while we ate the inevitable goulash. But soon our march continued.

A severe snowstorm developed in the afternoon; it blew from the northeast, directly in our faces and we had to walk head-down into it. But although we screwed up our eyes as we peered through the blizzard, the fine particles of ice scourged our cheeks and the cold literally caused us pain.

Fortunately, I had gathered together an assortment of clothing that kept me reasonably warm. I thanked God for the roomy pair of field boots that I had secured for the long journey back to Germany. They were big enough for me to encase my feet in two pairs of woolen socks, then wrap them in flannelette and pad the soles with sheets of newspaper. I also wore two pairs of long woolen underpants, two warm shirts, a sleeveless pullover, my summer uniform and summer overcoat, and on top of it all, an important addition—a loose leather greatcoat, similar to those worn by the two officers we had met at the gates of Moscow. A pair of woolen gloves, a pair of leather gloves and two woolen caps completed my rig-out, and, in order to prevent the wind from blowing up my sleeves, I had tied string around my wrists.

It was a strange-looking assortment of men that was now advancing to repel the Russian attacks, for every man had tried to improvise winter clothing for himself: the troops had cut up and used every woolen blanket they could lay hands on, had put on every garment they possessed and were going into battle clad in armor of newspaper beneath their clothing.

Ceaselessly, mercilessly, the blizzard raged and as the afternoon wore on, the strength of the wind increased and hour after hour the ice-flakes were driven with savage fury into our faces. And we knew that this was but the beginning—we were marching toward uncertainty, toward the demands of a winter war that might be harsher than we could endure.

Many ambulances packed with wounded and frost-bitten soldiers passed us on their way to the rear. Then a lorry belonging to Schulze's Medical Company approached. I stopped the driver, whom I knew.

"What's happening in front?"

"*Alles kaputt*," he replied. "Two German divisions have been practically destroyed, it seems."

"And what about Regiment 18?"

"Neuhoff's battalion has orders to attack this afternoon. They're probably going into action now."[176]

"Where are they attacking?" I asked urgently.

"I don't know, Herr *Assistenzarzt*."

"And where are the Russians?"

"Everywhere—nobody seems to know precisely where."

The lorry moved off and once again Petermann and I faced into the wind. This time we mounted our horses, passed our supply vehicles and caught up with the *Feldwebel* who was leading the plodding snow-covered column. Silently we rode along. When we tried to converse, the wind seized our words and flung them away. I tried to imagine how our troops could possibly be attacking in this weather and how the wounded and frostbitten men could hope to survive. Unless we could stop the Red Army and reconstruct a main defensive front, losses would be enormous.

An ambulance came up on us from the rear, gradually overtaking the horse-drawn supply and baggage units. As it was about to pass, I asked the driver where he was going.

"To Gorki," he replied.

"And is Becker's regiment somewhere in that area?"

"Yes, to the right of it."

"Then I'm going along with you." I climbed in beside the driver and told Petermann to follow with the horses.

The driver hunched forward, nose practically touching the windscreen as he peered at the road. The windscreen wipers were inadequate to cope with the driving snow. We moved forward very slowly, the driver taking great care not to leave the road and get stuck in the snowdrifts on either side.

It was nearly four o'clock when we reached Gorki and stopped at the hastily organized casualty dressing station. There was no doctor, only an assortment of stretcher-bearers from various units, but not one attached to the 6th Division. There were scores of wounded and frostbite casualties. Evidently all the oddments from all the units fighting in the neighborhood had found their way here.

"Where are your field doctors?" I asked.

"Two have been killed," replied a medical *Feldwebel* with a huge scar on his forehead, "and we don't know what happened to four others—perhaps they've been captured by the Russians. But really we don't know anything—perhaps the Russians are just in front of us or even behind us, in which case we're all as good as dead."

"You're painting a rosy picture," I said sharply. "Now leave your imagination out of it and tell me what actually is the position ahead."

"This morning there was practically nothing left but the remnants of two divisions, so there can't be many of our men ahead of us. At about eleven o'clock a battalion marched through with orders to counterattack, and an hour later the headquarters of a regiment belonging to the 6th Division passed here, but that's all I know. Anyway, what can a mere battalion do against all these hordes of Russians?"

"Well, at last I have some sort of picture—even though it is a dismal picture. Are you senior NCO here?"

The *Feldwebel* hesitated and I suddenly realized that in my unofficial winter clothing he had no means of telling my rank or unit. Quickly I helped him: "I am an *Assistenzarzt* of the regiment that passed through here."

"*Jawohl*, Herr *Assistenzarzt!*" He came to the salute.

"In the circumstances I'm taking charge here for the time being, and you will act as next senior in rank. How many stretcher-bearers have we?"

"Seven or eight, I believe."

"Why do you believe? Don't you know how many there are?"

"Not exactly, Herr *Assistenzarzt*. Men have been passing in and out all the time. They make inquiries here and then go away. Everyone seems to have one idea—to get to the rear, to head west."

The ambulance that had brought me here had now been loaded with wounded and the driver was preparing to return to the Medical Company. Some of the casualties' wounds had been only partly dressed—some, not at all. Not one had been provided with a casualty card. I wrote a few lines to *Oberstabsarzt* Schulze, gave him the exact map reference of our position and asked him to send as many ambulances as possible to evacuate the innumerable wounded and frostbite cases in the building. With the message in his pocket, the driver pulled away.

We got on with the job of sorting out dead, severely wounded and lightly wounded. About 20 of the men were fit to fight if necessary; another 30 were in too serious condition, either from wounds or frostbite, to be of any assistance; the 15 dead we carried into the stable at the back of the house, where in a short while they were frozen stiff. I issued the less seriously wounded with arms, detailed the stretcher-bearers to collect wood for the fire, and from the uninjured men posted sentries, who were to be relieved half-hourly throughout the night. Many casualties kept arriving, but just before dark several ambulances came and evacuated the serious cases.

Prussian drill had asserted itself, on the surface anyway, the panic-stricken mood had been dispelled and the dressing station seemed quite a tight little fortress.

I went out into the road to have another look at our surroundings. The blizzard had blown itself out, and it seemed warmer, although that was probably only because the penetrating wind had dropped. Eastward and northward the battle continued and the night sky was brought alive by the vivid flashes of artillery. Two men approached me and I shone my torch in their faces. It was Freese and a stretcher-bearer of our battalion.

"Hallo, Freese. Where the hell have you come from?" I asked.

He was speechless.

"You couldn't have come at a better time, anyway," I continued. "For God's sake tell me what's happening at the front."

"But what the devil are you doing here?" he asked when he had found his tongue. "I thought you were on leave."

"All leave canceled," I told him. "Believe me, I'm just as surprised as you that I'm here."

"Then it's not only going badly with us," said Freese. "It must be bad all along the front."

"What's happening to the 3rd Battalion?" I repeated anxiously.

"As far as I can tell things aren't so good," he replied. "When I left there at five o'clock the battalion had just started the attack. We already had many casualties and cases of frostbite. But the worst of it was that our machine-guns were no longer firing. They'd frozen solid with the cold."

"And who sent you here?"

"Regimental H.Q. had heard that there was no medical officer in charge of this place."

"Well, now that you're here, Freese, you can take charge while I go to the front. But make sure that all the instructions I've given are followed."

"What instructions?"

"The *Oberfeldwebel* with the scar on his forehead will give you all the details. Come along with me and I'll hand over to you in front of all the men, or else the whole caboodle might fly apart. The men are ready to panic at a moment's notice."

The stretcher-bearer who had accompanied Freese took me back to Regimental Headquarters. We crossed the Volga, sliding down the steep, snow-covered banks, and trudging along the thick snow that covered the ice. Along the edge of a wood for 10 minutes and we reached the Regimental battle post in a nearby village.

Baron von Kalkreuth, the regimental adjutant, was there. He told me that right and left of Kalinin, the Russians had attacked with well-rested Siberian divisions, magnificently equipped for winter warfare. Numerically, they outnumbered us greatly. The Volga no longer counted as an obstacle in our defense line and the surprise nature of the Red Army's attack had succeeded perfectly. Kalinin was threatened with encirclement and the evacuation of the city had been ordered.[177] But our thousands of troops could only be got away if the lines of withdrawal could be kept free until the next afternoon. That was where the 3rd Battalion came in. Our men had been grimly thrown against the Russians in spite of the blizzard, the overwhelming superiority of the enemy and the deadly cold. One depleted battalion against units of four Siberian divisions!

"And was our attack successful?" I asked.

"Yes and no," von Kalkreuth replied. "The Russian attack was halted and as a result our lines of retreat from Kalinin are still open, which means a lot. But our counterattacks failed to reach their objective and petered out against the Russian defense. This appalling cold forced our spearheads to fall back on to the villages behind." He shrugged his shoulders. "Our fate tomorrow is quite unpredictable. And what will happen in the next weeks only God in Heaven knows."

"And our losses?" I demanded.

"Very heavy, especially as a result of frostbite. We don't know full details yet."

He paused and then went on quietly: "The 3rd Battalion can hope only to delay those masses of Russians for a few hours. Then, one by one, they'll be chopped down. It had to be done—one battalion had to be sacrificed. But it was like sending those men to their execution. I shall be surprised if more than half a dozen come out alive."

I decided to return to the battalion immediately. With a heavy heart, I took the stretcher-bearer and hurried on my way. The snow was still holding off, the heavy clouds had been torn apart, and the stars stood out crystal clear in the heavens. One star in particular—Mars, the planet named after the God of War. It seemed to be on fire and blazing a lone course across the heavens as it searched the battlefields around Kalinin. But suddenly, as if the star had seen enough, a heavy cloud sped across it and the wind from Siberia gathered strength. It became dark again and started to snow. The stretcher-bearer and I gathered our collars closer around our ears.

At the 3rd Battalion battle post a man sat alone in the small room, next to a smoky oil lamp. It was Major Neuhoff. Wearily, he glanced up as I entered. I saluted and stood to attention: "Reporting back for duty, Herr Major," I said.

"So you are back again," he said absentmindedly, turning back to the map that was spread on the table in front of him. His finger moved in a hopeless gesture across the map.

"We are finished, Doktor. We cannot get out of this." He looked up again. His eyes were moist and his fingers nervously tapped the edge of the table. "Finished, Doktor. That's the position. Now you know everything. My battalion is being sacrificed. Deliberately sacrificed to save our men in Kalinin."

"What are our casualties?" was all I could find to say.

"Don't know at present. Don't know at all. But the main dressing station is crowded with wounded men and men with frostbite. It's this damnable bloody cold that's murdering us," he burst out, then seemed to gather his senses again and went on: "Kageneck and Bolski haven't returned—probably both killed. Becker and Lammerding are trying to get in touch with Stolze and Boehmer. The 10th and 11th Companies, or whatever remains of them, are preparing to defend the two villages in front of us. And that's about all."

"Where is our dressing station, Herr Major?"

"Two houses away from here—down the road," Neuhoff said with hopeless resignation in his voice.

The dressing station was overcrowded and the air was thick with smoke; but it was pleasantly warm. The old *Oberstabsarzt* sat, as if exhausted, on a first-aid box, while Tulpin, Müller and Heinrich were working feverishly.

"*Himmel!* There is the Doktor," I heard Müller whisper to Tulpin.

"*Achtung!*" shouted Tulpin, automatically, forgetting that old Volpius was in the room.

"Don't be stupid, Tulpin," I said. "Well, that was a short leave, but I'm glad to be back where I belong." I turned toward the *Oberstabsarzt*, saluted, and said: "With your permission, Herr *Oberstabsarzt*, may I take over the dressing station?"

"Please don't worry about any formalities," said Volpius as he touched his cap without rising. "You can see, Doktor," he said, pointing to the overcrowded room, "in what a state we are. I always said we'd meet with disaster in Russia. Look what happened to Napoleon. Take it from me, not one of us will get out of this mess."

The old man's moaning irritated me. That sort of attitude from the senior officer would soon spread to the troops, particularly the wounded men.

"Whether we get home or not, Herr *Oberstabsarzt*, doesn't interest me much at the moment," I said sharply. "For the present it's up to us to evacuate the seriously wounded and the severe cases of frostbite. Without delay. Let's get on with it."

"Well, aren't we doing that, Herr *Assistenzarzt?*" he asked in a piqued tone, while he continued to sit on his box.

"I know that, Herr *Oberstabsarzt*," I said in a more conciliatory manner. I realized I had gone too far, particularly in front of the men. "But I would like to help with this difficult job. With your permission I will change into other clothes."

"Please forget all formalities," he said again, in a more friendly manner. "There's no need for them, since we've all landed in the muck together."

Heinrich opened my trunk, which I had left with him, and I pulled off my good uniform and changed into my battledress tunic and old pair of trousers. When I had hung my heavy commissar pistol on my belt, put on my steel helmet, and filled my coat pockets with hand grenades and ammunition, I felt much better. Within a few minutes I had organized my panje wagon column and sent off the first cases to Freese at Gorki. It was impossible for motor ambulances to reach us—they would never be able to negotiate the steep banks of the Volga.

It was a heartbreaking task trying to deal with the cases of frostbite. In many cases, toes and feet had frozen into a solid block inside the boots and we had to slit the boots from the top down to the toecaps. Systematically, we massaged the frozen toes with snow or icy water until they became soft and pliable again. But it was impossible to say how many of those feet would be saved, how many would become gangrenous. When we had dried and powdered the men's feet, we packed them in cottonwool and bandaged them heavily. Four Russian women, who were experienced in treating frozen feet, helped us throughout the night. In extreme cases, where the man could stand no more pain, we gave morphia injections, but we had to be very careful as morphia reduces the human body's resistance to cold.

In most cases the after-effects of frostbite were more serious than we expected,[178] for once the limbs had been thawed there was nothing that could be done by the medical company surgeons except wait. Wait and see to what extent the tissues were dead—wait and see how much of the limb would have to be amputated.

To add to our troubles, nearly every wounded man was also suffering from frostbite and exposure. Our work was bitter repetition, but at last we had attended to all the cases and I was able to visit the battle post to find out how things were progressing with the fighting troops.

Lammerding was there, calm and composed. He grinned when he saw me, and said: "Sorry your leave's gone to hell. Your luck seems to be right out. Probably if you picked your nose at the moment, you'd break your finger."

Little Becker came in, slammed the door and called out: "Hallo, Doktor. How was Germany? Hope you didn't forget to deliver my letter. Nice to see you back. Just in time for the fun."

He turned to Neuhoff and reported: "Kageneck is safe and sound. He'll be here in 10 minutes. At the moment he's having a discussion with *Oberleutnant* Boehmer."

Neuhoff jumped up violently. "What's happened? Where's he been all this time?"

"He tried to rescue Bolski before darkness fell."

"And did he succeed?"

"No, Herr Major. Bolski and 28 men were found dead in a hollow in front of the Russian-held village. All Kageneck was able to rescue were two men who pretended they were dead when the Russians killed everybody who showed signs of life."

"Good God!" exclaimed Neuhoff. "Where's all this going to end?" He sat at the table again and dropped his head.

I reported to him that I had evacuated all the serious cases to Gorki, where Freese was running the dressing station.

"How many casualties have we, Doktor?"

"I don't yet know, Herr Major. But they must be heavy."

Outside we heard voices, the door was thrown open and Kageneck and Ohlig walked in. We all sat around the table. The whole atmosphere seemed to have brightened with Kageneck's arrival. He radiated energy.

"We must apply the lessons we learnt today," Kageneck said. "The Russians, too, are faced with difficulties—it's important that we realize that. And I've found out from prisoners that they have also suffered heavy casualties as a result of frostbite."

"But those winter uniforms . . ." interjected Neuhoff.

"Not all the Russians are equipped as well as the Siberian troops. Many of them have no winter clothing to speak of. That's why they defended the village so desperately this evening—they didn't want to be driven out into the cold. But even so, I'm sure we'd have taken the village if the oil in our machine-guns hadn't frozen."

"And what can we do about that?" Neuhoff demanded. "Any suggestions?"

"I experimented this evening," Kageneck continued calmly. "I took one of our machine-guns into a house, thawed it in front of an oven, dismantled it and had all the parts polished so that not a drop of oil was left. When we reassembled the gun, we could fire it."

"But what about stoppages? A gun must be lubricated."

"There'll be more stoppages—bound to be—but the guns worked well without oil. That's the important point. We could use them."

It turned out that with a squad of 20 men and five of these unlubricated machine-guns Kageneck tried to rescue Bolski, who was lying in a hollow in front of the Russian-held village, his line of retreat cut off. Taking advantage of covering fire, Kageneck and a few of his men worked their way to the hollow, where they found 29 dead, including Bolski, and two wounded. The machine-guns had done their work well while Kageneck and his men withdrew with the two wounded soldiers who had shammed death. The lesson was there for us all to see: risk the extra wear on the guns and the extra stoppages rather than be without guns altogether when the temperature fell to minus 40 degrees Centigrade, as it had done this day.[179]

"And I'm of the opinion that we should let the Russians do the attacking," Kageneck continued. "That way we can keep in the protection of the villages and keep our guns warm in the ovens. When the enemy attacks we just remove them and set them up. They'll keep warm enough while they're firing. That way we could even keep them oiled. In any case, it's damned difficult for troops to attack over open snowfields in the face of an alert enemy."

"You speak as if you've solved all the problems of a winter war," said Neuhoff, a little testily.

"No, Herr Major," Kageneck replied, "certainly not. There are still plenty of problems to be solved—both for ourselves and the Russians."

"Then solve this problem, Kageneck. How do we fight without winter uniforms against these Siberians?"

"We must wear Siberian uniforms. If we haven't got them, then we must get them. Strip the Siberian dead and prisoners of their fur caps, their felt-lined boots, their cotton-wool clothing. The time will come when we can stand up to them on equal terms—and then we'll prove who are the better soldiers."

"You'd have a job convincing some of the troops I've met back along the road that they stand a chance against the Reds. They nearly all think we're done for already," I said.

"That's perhaps our biggest problem," Kageneck replied seriously, "this all-consuming panic. Without the utmost confidence in ourselves and our ability to beat the Russkies we can't hope to win through."

"Yes, we dare not lose our self-confidence," echoed Neuhoff, as if trying to convince himself. "We dare not, under any circumstances, lose our self-confidence."

"Just one last thing," Kageneck said. "In this frightful cold, our defense lines must be manned as thinly as possible, so that every man who can be spared can stay inside and keep warm. Pickets must be posted well in front of the village, they must be relieved often, and it's up to us officers to be vigilant ourselves and keep these outposts on the alert."

Neuhoff agreed. He was, I noticed, becoming more and more willing for Kageneck to take the decisions, while he rubber-stamped them. The situation had got beyond him and he was fast losing his grip.

"Aren't you chaps hungry?" asked little Becker.

"Hungry! Hunger's no longer the word for it. I'd have eaten my boots long ago if they didn't keep my feet so warm," Kageneck said.

Becker went out to organize the food and Neuhoff and Lammerding went to the next-door house, which had been turned into a temporary office, to prepare a report on the situation.

"What really happened to Bolski?" I asked Kageneck when we were alone.

"He was a fanatic and that's all there is to it," Kageneck replied. "An officer should act according to the situation that develops, not blindly follow a principle. Today his fanaticism led him into a hopeless situation from which there was no escape."

"And his platoon with him?"

"Yes. He led all those 28 men to their death. It was all so bloody unnecessary."

"What exactly happened, then?"

"His guns had stopped firing, he knew the enemy was much stronger, and at the beginning he had a good chance of extricating himself, because the Russians were concentrating on Stolze, who was still attacking from the left. But he saw clearly that Stolze was forced to break off his attack when his guns jammed, and he saw that Stolze had sense enough to withdraw."

"Stolze doesn't pull out for nothing."

"Of course not, and Bolski knew that. But according to the two wounded men Bolski wouldn't listen to the advice of his NCO. All he did was shout: 'For us there is no retreat—we are soldiers of the *Führer*!' Damned dramatic nonsense! And then when he realized that there was no longer any chance of retreat anyway, he was happy. In his small way he imitated Hitler by refusing to face facts. Hitler ordered the attack on Moscow when it was hopeless and sacrificed hundreds of thousands. Bolski sacrificed 28 and himself."

"But at least he sacrificed himself for an ideal. The man must have had courage, at any rate."

"Yes, I suppose so. You can't help respecting him for that."

Little Becker entered, followed by his orderly, who was carrying the food. Becker ordered a snowy-white cloth to be laid on the table and saw that the cutlery and plates were laid out immaculately. "Room service," he announced. The food was, of course, horse meat goulash.

"Splendid!" exclaimed Kageneck. "I need some food—my ribs were starting to rattle."

We sent for Neuhoff and Lammerding, but only Lammerding came in. He stamped the snow from his boots and sat at the table.

"Isn't Neuhoff coming?" I asked him.

"No, he said he wasn't hungry. He never is these days."

"What's happened to him?" I asked. "He looked shocking when I arrived this evening."

"He must have severe dysentery," Becker said. "He runs out every few minutes—I think it's wearing him down."

"I wonder whether it's an infection or nerves," I said. "I must see what I can do to help him."

Becker tried to slice the bread. The knife would scarcely cut through the loaf, although Becker used all his force. "This is the bloody limit," he exclaimed. "Even the bread is frozen."

"Smash it with an axe," suggested Lammerding.[180]

Back at the sick bay, the two survivors of Bolski's suicide squad had just been brought in by Kunzle and Hans on their panje wagons. One man was wounded in the lungs; the other had a shattered pelvis. But in both cases the frostbite caused by exposure until Kageneck had rescued them was as serious as their wounds. Neither of them guessed that they would probably have to have their legs amputated below the knees and would each lose several fingers. They were only thankful for being in safe hands.

Müller was talking to the man with the smashed pelvis. "Can I bring you anything to eat, Paul?"

"Do you know each other?" I asked Müller.

"Yes, very well, Herr *Assistenzarzt*. He is a postman in the next village to me. We used to sing together in the men's choir."

Postman! An idea came to me. With any luck he would be flown back to Germany within a day or two. "Listen, Paul," I asked him, "can you do me a favor when you get home—send a telegram for me to my fiancée?"

"Certainly, Herr *Assistenzarzt*. With pleasure."

On the back of a casualty card, I wrote: "*Fräulein* Martha Arazym, Duisburg, Börsenstr. 18.—Leave canceled. Postpone engagement celebrations. Am fit and well. Merry Christmas. Heinz."

*　　*　　*

The casualty register made depressing reading that night. There had never been so many names to enter. 14 December 1941 was a black day for the 3rd Battalion—182 casualties, dead, wounded or frostbitten;[181] in one afternoon we had lost about one-third of our remaining strength. But the "suicide battalion" had held out for many valuable hours against the Siberian hordes.

It was nearly midnight before I finished and was able to get back to the battle post. At last I had time to have a chat with Neuhoff about his health. He told me he was feeling very run down and depressed. He had lost his appetite and his resistance was rapidly being weakened by the repeated attacks of dysentery, which seemed to be getting worse. Neuhoff was obviously a very sick man, who was fending off a complete collapse only by a supreme effort of will power. He would not take the sleeping pills I offered him, saying that he had no time to sleep with things in their present serious condition, but he took a supply of Tanalbin as a palliative against his bowel trouble. There was no more I could do for him at the present.

The old *Oberstabsarzt* was still seated on the box when I returned to the sick bay. I suggested that he should take a rest at the battle post and with an effort he got up and went.

By 3 a.m. all seriously wounded men had been evacuated to the rear areas. The panje wagons had kept up a constant shuttle service and the drivers, particularly the Russian volunteers, Kunzle and Hans, had worked heroically through the unbearably cold night. Toward dawn I was awakened from a light sleep by Müller, who said: "There are cries from the wood in front of us. They sound like cries for help."

With an effort I roused myself and went outside with Müller. True enough, about 400 yards away someone was shouting for help. They were unearthly, agonized cries. I awoke Tulpin and Heinrich, sent Müller to Battalion H.Q. to alert a few soldiers and, accompanied by Heinrich and Tulpin, walked toward the shouts.

Cautiously, with guns at the ready, we crunched through the snow toward the wood. It might be a trap. The cries became louder and more pleading: "For God's sake help me, someone! Where is everyone? For God's sake come and help me."

At the fringe of the wood we saw a figure staggering toward us, his arms outstretched. He did not seem to see us. We called out to him: "What's the matter?"

"Aaah!" he screamed. "Come and help me. I can't see. They've gouged out my eyes."[182]

In a few strides we were at his side and shone a torch on his face. Where his eyes had been were only two bloody holes; bits of flesh hung on his cheekbones and the blood had streamed down his face and frozen there.

Tulpin grabbed his arm and quickly led him out of the wood, while Heinrich and I walked slowly backward after them, keeping the muzzles of our guns pointed toward the trees. The man spilled out his story. He was an artilleryman—one of four men who had gone out to lay telephone wires to an observation point beyond our positions.

"We weren't expecting to see any Russians," he said, "... then suddenly several shots and the other three dropped in the snow. I ran back the way we had come—straight into the arms of the Russians. They grabbed hold of me and dragged me along ... I shouted for help and one of them told me to keep quiet ... he spoke broken German ... but I kept on calling for help. Then they said something to each other and threw me to the ground. One of them came at me with a knife ... there was a terrific flash of light, a sharp pain and then the same with my other eye ... then total darkness. The man who had hissed at me in broken German grabbed my arm and whispered into my ear: 'There. Go straight forward, to your brothers, the other German dogs, and tell them we'll destroy them all. We'll cut out their eyes and send what's left to Siberia—that will be Stalin's revenge. Now get going.' And he gave me a push and I heard them run away through the snow." The man finished and broke into deep sobs.

At the sick bay we did our best for him, but it was a poor best. There was nothing anyone could really do for him. He would live, but in darkness for the rest of his life.

Then the Russians, determined to seize that vital escape road from Kalinin, attacked again just as dawn broke. Our soldiers grabbed their machine-guns from the warm ovens and fired into the waves of Red troops that poured out of the wood. The attack petered out in the snow in front of our hastily prepared positions. And as they retreated, our artillery and mortars let them have it.

No sooner had they disappeared than our men were out among the dead Russians, stripping them of their fur caps, fleece-lined jackets and those magnificent felt boots. There were about 60 pairs of boots for distribution and preference was given to men with light frostbite. In that way they could be kept battleworthy. We could count on no replacements, and even if any did arrive their fighting value would not amount to much. Every single man counted in the bitter struggle to preserve the front, for only by keeping our front line intact could we save the trapped divisions in Kalinin, and with luck perhaps save our own lives. The only soldiers sent back were those who were half-dead and totally unable to fire a rifle.

And as we managed to hang on to our small section of the front, so were the trapped units of the Ninth Army streaming out of Kalinin along the road to Staritsa. Men who would fight again. If the entire 3rd Battalion of Infantry Regiment 18 was wiped out it would be worthwhile in the overall strategy, provided the beleaguered army in Kalinin made good its escape. Even we could see that. We recognized the military necessity for what we were doing but it was heartbreaking to see the battalion being slowly hacked to death.

Nevertheless, there had been a tremendous upsurge of self-confidence in the battalion following the dawn attack. In addition to the 60 Red soldiers whom we had stripped of their warm clothing, fully twice as many again—not so warmly clad—were lying dead on the battlefield. Close on 200 frozen corpses lay in front of our positions, grim mementoes of the action.

But what pleased the sick-bay staff more than the pile of Russian corpses was that the sightless artilleryman had been avenged. Stolze had heard shooting in front of his sector and had sent Schnittger out with nine men to investigate. They had come across the patrol of 15 Russians who had just shot down the three artillerymen and blinded the fourth. Schnittger and his men had lain in ambush in the wood, and at close range had riddled the Red patrol with their bullets. Not a single Russian escaped.

Neuhoff called a conference to discuss the situation and while we were talking, Regimental H.Q. phoned to say that the main defensive line had been formed that afternoon to the rear of Gorki. Kalinin had been held long enough to enable the withdrawal of the Ninth Army to the new positions.

The Ninth Army had got out of the trap! We had managed to hold the road to Staritsa long enough for 100,000 men to get away to the south.

Neuhoff put down the field telephone and for the first time relaxed a little. He turned to us and said: "It seems our job is over. Thank you, gentlemen."

*   *   *

Sixty-four Iron Crosses had been won in the battalion's suicide stand and the German radio devoted a special program to the little battalion that had withstood the onslaught of four Siberian divisions so that half an army could escape.[183]

We toiled back across the frozen Volga. We did not hear the broadcast. Retreating armies jettison their radio sets.

CHAPTER 19

The Wind from the Steppes

THE RETREAT FROM MOSCOW HAD BEGUN.

It was a retreat that involved the entire German Army from before the capital. Three armies were falling back from the rich prize and were being hammered as they went by Marshal Zhukov and his hordes of warmly clad reinforcements.[184]

For our ill-equipped troops, retreat in many instances spelt death. Death with the thermometer standing at 50 degrees below zero. Fiercely, the wind from the far steppes of Asia continued to blow, driving the loose snow and ice before it. The highways could no longer be recognized except as lanes of hard packed snow. During the blizzards it was cold, bitterly cold, but when the clouds cleared and the sun hung low in the sky it was colder still. It was as if the sky itself had frozen into a crystal of cold lead. Death came with icy pinions and stood at our elbow. But our troops fought him just as, again and again, they formed up and fought the Russians. They retreated across the snow desert with their faces to the enemy.

Stolze's huge figure and powerful voice dominated during these days. He wore a Russian jacket with an enormous fur collar that all but covered his head. Every piece of clothing he possessed was on his body and accentuated his normal bulk until he seemed as broad as a cupboard. All of us seemed to have grown enormously in size and strength. All the officers in the battalion, except Kageneck, little Becker and myself, were over six feet tall, but even the tough and wiry Becker seemed to have grown to giant size.

I had closed down the dressing station at Gorki as we retreated through the village. Freese had done an excellent job and the *Feldwebel* with the scar had been a valuable assistant. Altogether, more than 300 wounded had been attended to at Gorki and sent back to the Medical Company. It was clear that the strain on *Oberstabsarzt* Schulze and *Stabsarzt* Lorenz must have been colossal, yet they had not only managed to attend to all the cases sent back to the Medical Company, but had also transported hundreds of casualties in safety through the bitter weather.

We retreated toward Staritsa and Rzhev, at the approaches to which we were to occupy the so-called *Königsberg* Line as our winter defensive positions.[185] Doubtfully, we asked ourselves if there were such a line in reality and, if not, who was to prepare the positions. "Retreat slowly but hold the enemy as you go," was the order. "Give your comrades behind you time to prepare the defensive positions." We hoped that we had comrades back there and that they were, in truth, preparing the positions.

We fulfilled our part of the contract. We retreated slowly and we held the enemy. Day after day, several times a day, we blunted each successive thrust of the Red Army as Zhukov threw division after division of Siberians against us, regardless of his losses. Our men fought and died. Not many at a time. But after every Russian attack there were fresh gaps in the ranks, a few more familiar faces missing at the field kitchen that evening. Young lads stood and fought next to the older men and breathed their last before they even started to live.

They were laid in hastily dug shallow graves in the snow. There was no time these days to fashion a birch cross. Death's solemnities seemed a mockery when it was impossible to consign a body to Mother Earth, when the corpse would be as stiff as a gun barrel within an hour and when the thaws of spring would disinter the body from its icy winter vault.

Every day we fought bitterly, threw back the Russians with bloody losses to themselves, and every evening disentangled ourselves from the grip of the enemy so that we could warm our frozen bodies in the shelter of some deserted hamlet.

In this unearthly cold, in which the breath froze and icicles hung from nostrils and eyelashes all day long, where thinking became an effort, the German soldiers fought—no longer for an ideal or an ideology, no longer for the Fatherland. They fought blindly without asking questions, without wanting to know what lay ahead of them. Habit and discipline kept them going; that and the flicker of an instinct to stay alive. And when the soldier's mind had become numb, when his strength, his discipline and his will had been used up, he sank into the snow. If he was noticed, he was kicked and slapped into a vague awareness that his business in the world was not finished and he staggered to his feet and groped on. But if he lay where he had collapsed until it was too late, as if forgotten he was left lying at the side of the road and the wind blew over him and everything was leveled indistinguishably.

Then there were the others, the small group of men who carried the responsibility. Those whose determination and self-control dared not give way in the bitterest snowstorm, or during the fiercest Russian attack. Again and again they gathered their remaining strength and refused to listen to the alluring music of Nature's invitation to die. But the tremendous strain made grossly unfair demands on their vital energy and played on their overtaut nerves to a point where something had to break. Many a man could stand it no longer and erupted into madness or slithered into childlike happiness.

The old *Oberstabsarzt* broke down. His nerves were completely overstrung and his nights became a torturing dream world inhabited by ghosts and Russians. He became a burden to us and was sent back.

Neuhoff, too, was approaching a complete nervous and physical collapse. Again and again he pulled himself together with an iron will, but the position of battalion commander had always been a little beyond his limited capabilities, and this, together with his crippling attacks of dysentery, worked on him to such an extent that he looked like a walking corpse. An ambulance picked him up and took him to the rear. *Oberleutnant Graf* von Kageneck took over command of the depleted 3rd Battalion.

We fought our way southward toward Staritsa and on 22 December found ourselves back in Vassilevskoye.[186] We had arrived there at the end of our sweeping march through Poland and Russia with practically a full battalion of 800 men. The fighting strength of the battalion was now 189 men, including officers and NCOs. It had shrunk pitifully, but was still battleworthy. Of the three battalions that composed Infantry Regiment 18, we had suffered the heaviest losses, but we had also inflicted very heavy losses on the Russians and could proudly boast that not once had we turned our backs on the enemy and that not once had the enemy succeeded in breaking through our line.

Doctors were becoming scarce, for many had fallen. Freese was sent back to Divisional Headquarters as a replacement and I was on my own again.

Every single man in the battalion was infested with lice,[187] but in face of the greater demands made on the medical unit by the constant fighting and the deadly cold, this was no longer of much consequence. The best I could do was to evacuate the spotted fever cases as quickly as possible and hope that there would be no epidemic.

Even diseases which normally would have given little trouble took on an extraordinary intensity under the conditions. Men suffering from dysentery were kept at the front as fighting troops as long as possible. It was becoming increasingly difficult, in any case, to send the wounded back to the Medical Company, which was overloaded with wounded and severe frostbite cases. So these poor fellows, weakened by the dysentery, tried to keep up with their fellows to the best of their remaining strength. If they exposed themselves more than three or four times a day to the demands of nature, they lost more body warmth than they could afford to lose in their weakened state, and death was lurking around the corner for them. Yet soiled clothing would also cause frostbite and death.

Without regard for the niceties, therefore, we cut a slit five or six inches long in the seats of their trousers and underpants so that they could relieve themselves without removing their garments.[188] Stretcher-bearers or their own comrades then tied up the slit for them with a string or thin wire until the operation had to be repeated. All the men had lost weight so the trousers were roomy enough to permit this solution. Many lives were saved by this crude remedy and many a soldier who would otherwise have been lost to us was kept in the firing line, more or less battleworthy.

If at all possible, the wounded were always treated in a warm room, and when a dressing had to be administered in the open, it was applied if possible without removing any garments. It was my principle never to abandon a wounded or exhausted man, and this with me amounted to an *idée fixe*; as far as it went it was good and gave me determination and an aim for which to strive. To have abandoned any man would have been murder, in any case, for we had heard some stories of the ruthless treatment meted out by the Russians to German wounded. Red prisoners we captured drew shocking pictures of the last hours of the evacuation of Kalinin.[189]

When the city was re-entered by the Red Army, our field hospital there still contained a large number of serious casualties. Piteously they had pleaded not to be left to the mercy of the Russians—they did not even have weapons with which to do away with themselves—but there were insufficient ambulances, so a few doctors were left behind to look after them. The Russians arrived, slaughtered the doctors and cleared the whole hospital in a matter of minutes by throwing every patient out of the window. Those who were not killed by falling on to the frozen ground were quickly dispatched by a shot in the back of the head and thrown into an open grave.

Stalin's instruction was: "The Germans are all criminals. Kill them all," the prisoners told us, and this story was told by many of them. There was no doubt that they were speaking the truth. Small wonder, therefore, that I determined to abandon nobody.

But this resolution nearly led to my undoing. With about 20 lightly wounded and sick men I had lagged behind our troops one afternoon. I was not very concerned, because we had thrown the Russians back in a counterattack shortly before. We were on the edge of a wood in the fading half-light of late afternoon when we saw a number of figures approaching from the direction of the Volga. We were dismayed when we recognized them as Russians. However, they had not seen us and we slipped into the wood with the idea of walking through it in the direction of our battalion until the Russians had bypassed us. But after we had walked through the snow-laden trees for a while, we came upon open countryside again. And in front of us lay two villages between us and the battalion. As we lay behind some bushes, spying out the land, several small units of Russians marched along the road, cutting off our retreat. It was obvious that the Russians intended to occupy the two villages for the night. We were completely cut off.

"We shall have to stay here until darkness falls and then try to sneak between the two villages under cover of night," I whispered to the men.

It was a clear, brilliantly cold, starlit night. We huddled together in a little hollow to keep warm and were tempted to make a dash for it before we all froze to death. But it would have been suicide to make our bid until the majority of the Red troops had bedded down for the night. Slowly the time passed until the hands of my watch crept together at the top of the luminous dial. Midnight.

By the one or two signal lights that hovered in the sky ahead, we judged that our defensive line for the night must lie close behind the two villages. With any luck, we could make it in less than an hour.

Polaris glittered in the heavens and gave us a constant bearing. We aimed to follow a route exactly between the villages, where there would be less chance of encountering the Russians, who would prefer to keep to the warmth of the houses on this bitter night.

We set off, our little band of sick and wounded. Four or five of the wounded men were being helped by their fellows. We struck the road along which the Russian troops had marched earlier in the evening, and the temptation to make faster time on the hard-packed snow instead of floundering across country through snowdrifts was irresistible.

"Form up into a squad," I whispered. "Walk boldly and for God's sake try to look like Russians!"

I swung along at their head and the little squad of cripples marched after me. Our hearts were pounding and our rifles and automatics were at the ready. From a low shed to the left of the road came a shout in Russian.

"Carry on marching—and don't fire," I said urgently to the men behind. The Russian outpost must have had no doubts that we were on his side, for why else would we be marching in that direction and in that area? But the road no longer seemed such a good idea and once we were out of earshot, we left it and plunged into the snow drifts to the right, struck a hedge, on the lee side of which the snow lay less thickly, and followed the line of it toward the gap between the villages.

Blood racing, we left a village on either side of us and were congratulating ourselves on having negotiated the most difficult part when we suddenly spotted four or five Russians crouched sround a machine-gun in a snow-filled hollow beside the hedge. They were directly in front of us, but with their backs to us, facing our lines, from which direction any danger must come. We held the advantage of surprise. Silently, I held up my right arm and the men gathered around me.

"Fire all together when I fire," I whispered. Tensely, we crept toward the machine-gun nest. Then in the starlight I saw one man turn toward us, but without alarm.

I gave him a burst from my automatic and he pitched back among his comrades. Simultaneously, one of my men lobbed a grenade into the hollow and fire spurted from every muzzle in our squad. The Russians had no chance.

We fled toward our lines and pitched flat into a hollow just as two other Red machine-guns opened up on us. But their aim was wild.

Our next problem was to avoid being fired on by our own troops. Carefully, we crept along toward our positions and when we were somewhere near them, I sent an NCO, who was suffering from only light frostbite, to establish contact. He was successful and 10 minutes later Stolze was pumping my arm and the men of the 10th Company were clustered around us listening to the details, somewhat exaggerated by a wounded *Unteroffizier* with a sense of the dramatic.

Of the 20 men who were with me, eight suffered severe frostbite as a result of their exposure that night.

Chapter 20

The Numbers Shrink

As Christmas drew near, the Russians attacked more fiercely.[190] The snow was already so deep that we sank into it above the knees, and this caused the frostbite cases to increase in numbers, even among men who wore felt-lined boots. As they floundered through the deep snow, it fell unnoticed down the top of the high boots. It thawed, gradually robbed their feet of their warmth and then froze around the feet in blocks of ice. Then the men fell helpless in the snow, unable to move, and had to be carried to the makeshift dressing station.

Many stretcher-bearers had been lost and I was unable to cope with the increasing numbers of frostbite cases, so I was forced to detail Heinrich, Müller and the others to bring them in.

It was while he was carrying a frostbite casualty that Müller was wounded; three fingers were shot off his left hand. As I dressed and bandaged the mangled hand I reflected that I would rather have lost anyone but Müller. He had been a tower of strength since the first day of the campaign.

"Fit for transport—seated." I wrote on his casualty card and handed it to him. Müller looked at it. To him the casualty card represented release from the front line, perhaps sick leave at home with his wife and children, a chance to stay alive instead of the odds-on chance of finding a grave in the Russian snows. He looked at the card, then looked up at me and said quietly, without a touch of dramatics: "Only three fingers of my left hand are damaged, Herr *Assistenzarzt*. I can still do my job here with my right hand. I should like to stay."

Tulpin, Heinrich and I looked at him and understood. It was a strange request, but perhaps we were all on the verge of madness.

"Good, Müller," I said, "but you will stay with us only until you have taught Heinrich to do your job and until things quiet down. Then I will send you back."

"Won't his hand get worse without proper treatment?" asked Tulpin. "I mean, mightn't he lose his whole hand as a result of staying here?"

177

"No, no, Tulpin," I replied. "I'll see to that. Tomorrow when I remove this pressure bandage and am sure that the bleeding has finished, I'll apply a special codliver oil bandage. I'll pack the damaged fingers in codliver oil ointment, the cells of the body will reassert themselves and throw off the tattered bits. The surgeon will then probably be able to judge better where to amputate."

"Don't you think he should at least go to the Medical Company, Herr *Assistenzarzt?*" Tulpin persisted. "I'll take him there and bring him back."

"No. The Medical Company is so overworked they'd have no time to look at finger wounds, let alone operate. Even the official reports[191] make no secret of it—the ambulances can't transport even one-tenth of the casualties that need to be evacuated. No, Tulpin, you needn't worry. Müller will be all right."

It suddenly dawned on me that Tulpin was showing signs of nervousness; the corners of his mouth trembled, his gaze was shifty and the pupils of his eyes dilated.

Stretcher-bearers brought in two seriously wounded men from 10th Company. The Russian attack was at its fiercest and more wounded could be expected, so I sent Tulpin and Heinrich to organize the removal of these casualties. Müller helped me to treat the two wounded men and I realized his worth as never before. Silently and calmly he got on with the job, anticipating my needs, never obtrusive. He helped reliably and humbly, without self-seeking, never expecting credit or praise. He was of the type seldom accepted at their true value, yet how different the world would be if there were more Müllers.

When the wounded men had been attended to we sat beside the oven. With his right hand, Müller placed a few more logs on the fire, without giving any sign that he was in pain.

"Let me give you an injection of morphia, my dear fellow," I said. "It will ease your pain."

Müller looked at me as if he wished to say something and then looked away into the fire, without replying.

"Whatever's the matter, Müller? Why do you look at me so strangely?"

"I'd prefer not to have morphia," he said. "I'm afraid of it."

Suddenly I knew why. A mystery in a corner of my brain had been solved. I wondered why I had not realized it before.

"Tulpin is a morphia addict, and you know it," I said quickly. "Isn't that it, Müller?"

"Yes, Herr *Assistenzarzt,*" Müller agreed, almost inaudibly.

"Then why the devil didn't you tell me when I asked you?" I demanded.

"I was afraid, Herr *Assistenzarzt.* Morphia is a dreadful thing. When a man starts to take it, it is worse than death."

"So you knew days ago, when *Unterarzt* Freese first joined us, that Tulpin was giving himself regular injections?"

"Yes, Herr *Assistenzarzt,* I knew then." There was a pause. Müller looked into the fire and then went on: "I didn't tell you because Tulpin had promised that he would cut down the injections and break himself of the habit. He promised me faithfully."

"But where did he get the morphia? Our check-up showed no deficiency."

"He brought supplies from France. He had them with him when he joined the battalion," Müller said. "But he promised me that when they were all used up he would stop taking it. And I believed him. After all, Herr *Assistenzarzt*, he is an educated man . . . he wants to continue his studies as a medical student after the war. He had everything to live for, and it would all be at an end if he carried on taking morphia."

Müller spoke as if it was a relief to unburden himself of the secret. It seemed that Tulpin had been wounded in France and had been given morphia injections. Perhaps they had been given injudiciously, but after that he had begun to inject himself and by the time he joined us in Russia he could not do without it. He had progressively increased the doses in order to gain the same effect, until he was a slave to the drug.

Then the real drama began. Müller had secretly treated an abscess which Tulpin had suffered as a result of an injection and from that moment Müller had shared the torment of failure, the emotional ups and downs of the drug addict's moods. He was the only one to share Tulpin's secret and in his good-hearted way had hoped he could help Tulpin to break the habit without anyone being the wiser. In his compassion, he had actually supplied morphia to Tulpin on two occasions, when Tulpin's supplies were exhausted and his body was crying out for the drug. Later, when he had refused it, Tulpin had helped himself from the drugs chest. Then suddenly he seemed to have a plentiful supply again and Müller had been unable to guess the source. Tulpin had actually returned my morphia, with the result that the check up by Freese had revealed no deficiency.

But Tulpin had thought he was found out, disappeared from the sick bay and left a farewell letter to Müller. Müller felt in his tunic pocket and produced a crumpled letter, which he handed to me. It was in a shaky, uncertain handwriting:

It is useless. You are the only one who knows how deeply I have suffered and I have decided I must make an end of it before I get more deeply in the mire—and you with me. I seem to have lost all my will-power, and by the time you find this letter I shall have done away with myself.

Please, Müller, I ask you as a friend never to reveal the truth to anyone. I am a slave to morphia and have been unable to keep the promises I made. When I am without morphia, I feel petered out, useless, and my whole body is filled with a dreadful longing for release—either morphia or death. It has become an obsession with me and I know it can only become worse. It is a problem which has no solution.

I know my efforts to break the habit have been deplorably feeble, but when I try to do without it I crave for the injection that will make me feel strong and happy. When I have taken the injection I feel the glow of it course through my body and it fills me with a thousand strange and beautiful fantasies; it is magic. It gives me power and courage to face life's problems. But without morphia I am lost. I know they suspect me, the others. They will cut off my supply and then I shall be lost. There is only one way out. I must take my own life.

I dropped the letter and looked at Müller. "And what then?" I asked.

"He didn't shoot himself, of course," said Müller. "He came back that night in utter despair. But he got over the mood—with more morphia. I feel much better now for having told you, Herr *Assistenzarzt*."

I handed the letter back to Müller, who threw it on the fire, then turned to me: "What are you going to do about it, Herr *Assistenzarzt*?"

"At present I'm going to do nothing, Müller. We're all fighting for our lives and we need every man. If Tulpin with morphia is as good as other men without morphia, then that's the way it will have to be for the moment."

"Can't you help him to break the habit?" asked Müller urgently.

"There's no time at present. If we survive this winter battle, then we may be able to help him," I replied.

I remembered Müller's wound and gave him three pain-killing tablets just as the door was thrown open and Tulpin walked in with a wounded man. We all got to work on his wounds. Tulpin was full of energy and confidence; now I knew why. Everything went on as if nothing had happened, but within I knew it was only a matter of time until I would lose two more faithful helpers, Müller and Tulpin.

The thought saddened me.

*　　*　　*

The wind outside howled its frosty tune and on the east side of the house the snow had banked right up the wall to the roof. Once again, the Russians' afternoon attack had been beaten off. Stolze had been a tower of strength during the fighting; he had led his men, as always, imperturbably. *Oberleutnant* Böhmen had won his spurs in the battalion; he had adapted himself well and had got over his initial lack of self-confidence. It was remarkable how quickly this war could turn a youngster into a mature man. *Leutnant* Ohlig commanded what was left of Kageneck's old 12th Company and the Staff— Kageneck, Lammerding and Becker—met every situation with calmness.

Two things were taken for granted these days—that the Russian would attack and that his attack would be repulsed.[192] The Red Army's losses were heavy, but an equal number of men seemed to swarm back to the attack in a few hours' time. Their reserves seemed to be inexhaustible. As well they might be—for Marshal Bulganin had given Zhukov an extra 20 divisions of Siberian troops with which to drive us from Moscow. But at the time we knew nothing of it.

The next night was Christmas Eve and we were determined to celebrate it. We had planned to put up a Christmas tree wherever we quartered for the night. In anticipation of the event, I was eager to evacuate as many casualties as possible, but only one ambulance arrived—sufficient to take the stretcher cases only. As usual I fell back on my Opel to evacuate the sitting patients. I told Fischer to clear them all that night.

He poured hot water into the empty radiator and heated the engine with a blow-lamp. Both operations had to be done practically simultaneously or the car would not start in the Arctic temperatures. But this time it caught, and Fischer drove off with his load. I warned him to drive slowly and avoid the snowdrifts at the side of the road.

"Don't worry, Herr *Assistenzarzt*," he replied confidently. "I know every snowdrift on the road." I watched the dimmed lights of the car fade away in the distance and hurried back into the warmth of the sick bay.

But Fischer did not return that night, nor was he back before the Russians made their usual attack at 11 a.m. on 24 December. It was thrown back with heavy losses and whatever wounded they could not drag with them were left on the battlefield. They sank in the snow and died. By the time we could get on to the battlefield in safety, all the Russian dead were so stiff and frozen that we could do nothing with their clothing, which had frozen to their bodies. We were even unable to strip their felt-lined boots off their legs.

Regimental H.Q. ordered us to withdraw that afternoon as they had broken through in the neighboring sector on the left and we were threatened with encirclement.

On my return to the sick bay to prepare for the withdrawal, I found an ambulance from the Medical Company waiting with the news that Fischer had been wounded and was being treated for a broken upper right arm and bomb splinters. A slow-flying Russian night bomber, which we referred to contemptuously as the "Tired Duck" or the "Old Sewing Machine" had dropped a bomb near the Opel.[193] Evidently it had seen the dimmed lights and a lucky hit had done the rest. It was the end of my car; it had been so badly damaged that it had been pushed into the snowdrifts at the side of the road and abandoned. Fischer was out of danger, but he would certainly be sent home and would be lost to us. This regular loss of men and materiel was beginning to affect me. . . . It seemed as if Fate was grimly determined to wear us down.

Blood-red, like a huge Chinese lantern and with as little warmth, the sun sank on the western horizon and reflected its dying colors on the wide expanses of snow. Icicles hanging from the snow-laden fir trees reflected its rays and in their translucent beauty served as an ironic reminder that it was Christmas Eve. In spite of everything the spirit of Christmas was in the air and we were illogically certain that the Russians would leave us in peace for the next 24 hours.

On one of the panje wagons was the small fir that was to be our Christmas tree in the village where we next halted. Heinrich had decorated the harness of Max and his new companion, rust-brown little Passel, with fir twigs. But the little horses were more practical than we and each tried to eat the green fir twigs off the other's harness. The panje horses ate anything—old dry grass off the roofs, bark, dry twigs and garbage, and when there was no water, they ate the snow. And although both had lost a considerable amount of weight, they seemed to thrive on their erratic diet.

Four panje horses and wagons were left behind with Tulpin, who was to withdraw with the bulk of the battalion, the wagons to carry weapons and ammunition if there were no wounded. Heinrich, Müller and six lightly wounded men, Petermann and the two riding horses made up my little company. I told Kageneck that I wanted to get a short start on the rest of the battalion to avoid any repetition of the previous business when we had got ourselves cut off by the Russians.

"Fine," said Kageneck. "See that you have the Christmas tree waiting for us when we arrive. What are we going to decorate it with, by the way?"

"Cottonwool," I told him.

We had hardly got clear of the village when machine-guns rattled on our left flank and in a matter of seconds the whole sector had sprung into life. Our own machine-gun hammered back and our artillery thundered away.

The Russians had prepared a special Christmas present for us—their first night attack!

They must have known exactly the sentimental thoughts that would be in every German soldier's heart on Christmas Eve. And I knew that Kageneck would remain in the village until the Russian attack had been beaten back and until the counterattack had been made. I had just made up my mind to turn back and rejoin the battalion with Heinrich, while the rest of the column carried on under Müller when a Russian anti-tank shell struck the snow ahead of us—fortunately without detonating. Shell after shell followed and it was obvious that two or three Russian anti-tank guns had spotted us and were taking us under direct fire.

Müller grabbed little Max with his sound hand and ran forward, the lightly wounded men followed him as fast as they could go. Petermann grabbed his horse and Sigrid and started to run and Heinrich and I brought up the rear. Suddenly there was a terrific explosion and Sigrid sank down, dead, her belly torn away. Petermann lay on the ground by her side but appeared to be unhurt. The other horse galloped away wildly. One of the wounded men had been hit—he was rolling on the ground with shrapnel in his hip. Heinrich and I darted forward and heaved him up, each taking an arm over our shoulders. We dragged him forward as best we could toward where Müller and the rest of the column had found some shelter in a bushy hollow. Reeling madly, Petermann followed.

The Russians could see they had drawn blood and continued firing for all they were worth. But in their eagerness the gunners became erratic. They were shooting low, over open sights, and the shells were skimming over the surface of the snow like flat pebbles thrown across a pond. They kicked up bursts of snow as they went but not one of the shells detonated. It was an unusual sight, but we had no time to watch it.

Heinrich and I were gasping for breath by the time we had lugged the wounded man into the shelter of the bushes. With his undamaged arm, Müller assisted him into the panje wagon. Gradually, I managed to breathe the icy air into my lungs without any pain and my brain cleared. Petermann came up to join us. He was unhurt; the shell burst had merely thrown him violently to the ground and winded him. "Sigrid has been killed and my own horse has bolted," he stuttered apologetically.

"It doesn't matter," I told him. "The panje wagons and horses are more important at the moment. After all, we rarely ride our horses these days and at present only essentials are of any importance."

What we lose today we cannot lose tomorrow—it is one worry less, I thought. And I began to feel really sorry for myself: I was tired to the point of collapse and felt I could no longer face the endless daily misery, the bitter cold, the snow, the daily contact with pain and blood, and the loss of friends. Above all, I was tired of pretending to be courageous and imperturbable, tired of the pretense that I could meet every demand made on me. It was a lie and I hated the lie. If only I could relax, lie down, sleep for one whole night, be afraid. It would be a relief. But I knew there was nothing left for us but to carry on—or die.

"Come on, boys," I said, pulling myself together, "we've rested long enough and we're cooling off too much."

Without further incident, we marched to the next village and in the first house bandaged the wounds of the man who had been hit in the thigh.

Pulling out my map, I pointed out Terpilovo to Müller. "That's where you'll find the Medical Company," I told him. "As soon as you and the rest have warmed yourselves, carry on there and report to *Oberstabsarzt* Schulze." Heinrich and I wearily walked down the road toward Regimental H.Q. We found the house and I marched in.

Oberst Becker and *Oberleutnant* von Kalkreuth were sitting by a Christmas tree near the fireplace. It was a peaceful little scene—the two men drinking coffee beside the tree with its dozen or so candles flickering. I gaped and then vaguely reported that I had sent the column of wounded on to Terpilovo. I intended to report back to the battalion, I tailed off.

"Well, *Haltepunkt*," said Becker. "Sit down and drink a cup of hot coffee. It will do you a world of good—you look all in."

All the thoughts that for days past I had been pushing to the back of my mind burst forth and overwhelmed me. It had taken only a small key—the lighted Christmas tree and the kindly words of Becker—to unlock the flood gates.

"Herr *Oberst*," I heard myself saying, "it is Christmas and I don't know what to say. . . . I am completely finished—no rest by day or night. . . . I don't know where it's all going to end." All self-control had vanished and the tears shot into my eyes. I felt an uncontrollable impulse to cry like a child. I took the cup of hot coffee, turned away and took a gulp; it scalded my mouth and throat. But it did me good and gave me an excuse for the unsoldierly tears. My sudden burst of emotion died away and I felt rather foolish.

Becker and von Kalkreuth turned a blind eye to my loss of composure and for half an hour we chatted together while I warmed myself before the fire. Then I collected Heinrich and we marched back through the icy night to rejoin the battalion. On the way we passed Sigrid, and stopped for a moment to pay our last respects to the beautiful animal, now frozen quite solid. It was difficult to imagine that she had ever breathed. The sky over our battalion line was alive with tracer, signal lights, flares and the glow of fires.

"Fireworks on Christmas Eve," remarked Kageneck, when I reported back to him. "Our first night attack in the snow—always some new experience!"

Tulpin was hard at work in the dressing station and as the casualties mounted every one of us was kept working at full stretch. By 2 a.m. the Russian attack had been repulsed; two hours later we had attended to all the wounded and had them ready for evacuation; I fell into a dead sleep on the table. When Kageneck sent his orderly to invite me to join the Christmas celebration at Battalion Headquarters, Tulpin let me sleep.

Four candles were still alight on the bare Christmas tree when I eventually walked into the H.Q. "You're too late with your cottonwool," said Kageneck, "though God knows why we want cottonwool—we've enough real snow outside."

I rubbed my burning eyes and laughed foolishly; I was still not properly awake.

"But if the Russkies think they can stop us celebrating a good old German Christmas Eve, then there's still nothing to prevent us from celebrating Christmas Day like the English," Kageneck said as he produced a bottle of cognac.

"*Prosit!*" he toasted briefly, and we drained our glasses.

A messenger from Regimental H.Q. walked into the room. In his improvised winter clothing he looked like an Eskimo.

"Hurry up and close that door," barked Lammerding. "All the flies are coming in."

"Let's have a look at the Christmas pudding you've brought us," said Kageneck as he stretched out his hand for the message.

"Christmas pudding, Herr *Oberleutnant*?" asked the messenger in bewilderment. "I only have a message from *Oberst* Becker."

"Then you shall go back to *Oberst* Becker with a cognac to warm you up." Becker poured the messenger a drink.

"To the left of us things have gone disastrously, gentlemen," Kageneck announced as he read the dispatch. "We are ordered to disengage from the enemy immediately, otherwise we shall be encircled. Infantry Regiment 37 on our left flank has been unable to hold the Reds. We've no time to lose."

Five minutes later messengers were on their way to warn all the company commanders. We took two candles off the Christmas tree; the other two had burnt out. We were leaving nothing for the Russians. Half an hour later the battalion was on the march; only the rearguards remained to cover the withdrawal.

Regiment 37 was also in retreat—a badly shattered unit. After two days and a night without a roof over their heads, the Germans had been savagely attacked by a big force of Russians, who had broken through the German lines. The men had been demoralized by the intense cold of the previous 36 hours and were completely unable to withstand the Red onslaught.[194]

In some cases the cold had produced extraordinary emotional reactions among the German soldiers. Some of them became completely indifferent to danger. They had stood in groups around a burning barn, while shell after shell exploded around them as the Russian gunners pin-pointed the blazing target. But the Germans were quite careless of the danger, even though some of them were hit by shrapnel. They just sang carols, shouted and cheered, without making a move to avoid the shells that were by now crashing in their midst. They were filled with a lunatic ecstasy, as if the cold, the strain, the constant exposure to danger had brought on a mass frantic longing for death. They sang and died without knowing what they were doing. At last an officer intervened and sanity was restored. Meekly they followed as if in a trance and picked up their weapons again.[195]

Most of us had walked perilously along this border line between sanity and madness during the last few days. Laughter was never far from tears; optimism rubbed shoulders with black despair; and Death marched side by side in our ranks with Life. Nothing normal remained. And experience was teaching us that prolonged exposure to the cold gave rise to illusions and delusions that could be overcome only by a strong will and clear reason. Officers and doctors realized that it was a problem—perhaps the gravest problem—that would have to be taken into account during the winter fighting that lay ahead.

* * *

On that dreary Christmas Day we marched toward Kosnakovo. Leaden clouds promised more snow. Many men stumbled from sheer exhaustion as we wound our way southward across the snow desert. We had been reinforced by a platoon of Pioneers and two infantry guns and their crews. With them included, our fighting strength was about two hundred men. These weary remnants of the 3rd Battalion split up into small gray groups, which were visible from a great distance against the white background. We could make no effort at camouflage; there were no white winter uniforms.

A jeep approached and *Oberst* Becker and von Kalkreuth picked up Kageneck and Lammerding and took them off to the nearest village for a conference.

Little Becker and I walked on together in silence; there was nothing to say. The wind blew up and drove the snow and flakes past us in almost horizontal lines. Fortunately the wind was at our backs. Kageneck and Lammerding came out of a house and rejoined us when, about an hour later, we came to a small hamlet. *Oberst* Becker and von Kalkreuth followed them, got into their jeep, covered themselves with blankets and drove off.

Stolze joined us and asked Kageneck: "What's happening?"

"A hell of a lot. It's a bastard," replied Kageneck bitterly. "The enemy has broken through at Vassilevskoye and nobody knows his head from his arse at the moment. The Russians might be anywhere—at our backs, on our flanks, or even in front of us. We'll have to send out flank patrols."

"Through those snowdrifts?" asked Stolze.

"It will have to be done," Kageneck replied.

"And what about the rest of the front?" Stolze asked. "Surely it can't be as bad as this everywhere?"

"We're retreating from Moscow along the whole of the Army Group Center front," said Kageneck. "Three German armies, all with their backs turned on Moscow."

Lammerding took up the tale: "The situation has deteriorated to an alarming extent."

"And the foulest part of it all," Kageneck burst out, "is that nearly all our generals have been relieved of their posts."

"Brauchitsch?" asked Stolze.

"Yes."

"Guderian?"[196]

"Yes."

"Von Bock?"

"Yes."

"Kluge?"

"Field Marshal von Kluge is practically the only one of the old brigade left. He's taken Army Group Center from von Bock. Strauss has been relieved of command of Ninth Army; Rundstedt's gone; even Auleb has had the 6th Division taken away from him."[197]

"Then who the hell is our commander now that all the generals have been sent into the desert?" demanded Stolze. He grabbed Kageneck by the arm and for a moment we all stopped while the blizzard swept around us.

"We have a Christmas present, gentlemen," said Kageneck. "A new commander."

"Who is it?" Stolze demanded urgently.

Kageneck pulled his *Kopfschützer* firmly around his ears and looked hard at Stolze: "*Gefreiter* Adolf Hitler has assumed complete command of the entire German *Wehrmacht*."[198]

Natasha Petrovna

There was silence for a minute, broken by Stolze. "Well, we'll have to make the best of it," he said. "What are our new commander's orders?"

"Our retreat is to stop, regardless of Russian attacks," said Kageneck unemotionally. "The 6th Division and one other division are to occupy a defensive line in front of Staritsa immediately. The Staritsa Line, it's to be called. From there we're not allowed to retreat one step."

"And where exactly is this Staritsa Line?" asked Stolze. "I've never heard of it. And, anyway, how are we to form a solid defense line in this confused situation? I'd say it can't be done."

"How observant you always are, Stolze," Lammerding remarked sarcastically.

"Shut up, you fool," retorted Stolze angrily, "the situation is bad enough without you being funny."

"The situation stinks like a sewer and we're all sitting prettily in the muck," said Lammerding. "Do you want it in plainer words, Stolze?"

Stolze mumbled something through his ice-covered *Kopfschützer* and strode back to his company like a huge Jack Frost.

Lammerding and Becker were walking along behind us. "What do you think of this Staritsa Line business?" I asked Kageneck.

"Not much. By what we can gather the Staritsa Line was drawn on a map in the *Führer*'s Headquarters back in East Prussia.[199] It was drawn through a line of villages that were only names on that map, and according to *Oberst* Becker it was drawn without regard to the terrain or the physical features of the country."

"How can anyone sitting in East Prussia possibly know the conditions here?" I demanded.

"And now Hitler is trying to ape Stalin," Kageneck continued. "He has given a strict order—for reasons of my own I haven't mentioned it yet—that we are to burn down every Russian village before we leave it."

"And the Russian civilians?"

"Nothing is said about them."

In my imagination I saw Russian women and girls energetically helping in my sick bay with the wounded. I saw them massaging the frostbitten feet of our soldiers and now I saw them standing pathetically in the snow while we burned down their houses. "And what are you going to do?" I asked Kageneck.

"I don't know yet, but an order is an order. I'll probably herd the civilians into a few houses, so that at least they have a roof over their heads, and then burn the rest of the village. One thing I will not do is leave women and children without protection from this appalling cold."

Late that afternoon we occupied Kosnakovo. In 10 days we had fought a retreat of 30 miles, every mile bitterly pursued and attacked by the enemy. We had no contact with him that night. And the following day, 26 December, we were ordered to occupy Schitinkovo,[200] a large village in the so-called Staritsa Line, which, according to Hitler's orders, was to be defended to the last man.

*   *   *

Schitinkovo was a village of about 100 houses, ranged, as with practically every Russian village, on each side of the road. From one end of the village to the other was a mile and the road through it ran due east-west. At the back of nearly all the houses, which were about 20 yards apart, was a *sauna* house. The Russians would attack from the north—that seemed certain, so we had a long front to cover. To the south of the village, about a mile and a half along a road leading at right angles from the village street, lay Terpilovo, where Schulze's Medical Company was quartered. The Volga lay behind them. *Oberst* Becker's Regimental H.Q. was located in a hamlet near Terpilovo. From there he also controlled the 1st Battalion, which occupied a village on the right flank.

A reconnaissance group under little Becker determined that Schitinkovo was free from the enemy and was occupied by weak detachments—about 40 men—of the 2nd Battalion of Infantry Regiment 37. Our weakened battalion, now down to less than one-quarter strength,[201] was reinforced by a platoon from the 13th Company with two infantry guns, and a platoon of anti-tank guns from the 14th Company. These, together with the 40 men from I.R. 37, which included a heavy machine-gun detachment, brought our forces up to about 300 in all. Kageneck was in command of the entire defense.

He had few enough men at his disposal, for the village would have to be defended along its entire mile length and in the direction from which the Russian attacks would come there was plenty of cover to conceal the enemy's intentions until the last minute.

We were facing a broad belt of forest, which at one point, to the east of the village, encroached almost to our lines.

Reports came in that the Russians had broken through in large numbers at Vassilevskoye and had taken Taschadovo, Gorki and Uschakovo, three villages within easy striking distance of Schitinkovo. There was no question that a desperate battle was brewing.

By 7:30 a.m. we had garrisoned ourselves in the houses of Schitinkovo and Kageneck had organized listening posts at the edge of the forest fronting our positions. A regular patrol was to be made along this line of outposts and the men were to be relieved regularly. Another difficulty that confronted Kageneck was that with the small numbers at his disposal he could not organize effective fields of fire from our strong points.

The Pioneers were, therefore, sent to clear firing lanes through the trees and lay mines at vital approach points. A wooden blockhouse was built and two machine-gun posts established to the east of the village. The artillery officer worked out map coordinates and ranges of key points in his firing zones and by the evening of 26 December we were as well prepared to meet the coming assault as the position would allow.

At five o'clock the next morning the Russians attacked both ends of the village with a full battalion on either flank. Our listening posts alerted us in time and we were able to bring effective fire to bear and throw the Reds back. An immediate counterattack sent them pell-mell back to Uschakovo. Eight prisoners were taken, 73 dead Russians were counted and a considerable number of weapons were captured. The battalion suffered not a single casualty.

And in the midst of all this, Kageneck, by some extraordinary means, heard that his wife, the Princess of Bavaria, had presented him with a pair of healthy sons.

Now we had an opportunity to equip our men with more winter clothing. Kageneck ordered that the 73 dead Russians be carried to the village and stripped of their felt-lined boots and warm clothing.

But the bodies were frozen stiff. And those invaluable boots were frozen to the Russians' legs.

"Saw their legs off," ordered Kageneck.

The men hacked off the dead men's legs below the knee and put legs, with boots still attached, into the ovens.[202] Within 10 or 15 minutes the legs were sufficiently thawed for the soldiers to strip off the vital boots.

Stolze had captured his own little personal booty. In hand-to-hand combat he had killed a Russian commissar and he came up to me, his face beaming beneath a wonderful fox-fur cap that he had taken from the dead commissar. I was lavish in my admiration of the prize. Stolze turned to his orderly: "If ever anything happens to me, see to it that the doctor gets this cap. Understand?"

"*Jawohl*, Herr *Oberleutnant*," said the orderly with a grin.

There was no further enemy activity that day—he was evidently licking his wounds and regrouping his forces. I took advantage of the lull to visit Terpilovo, behind our lines, to collect my medical panje wagon and Petermann. Müller, too, was there, but *Oberstabsarzt* Schulze had withdrawn across the Volga after establishing a casualty assembly area at Terpilovo.

Here I said good-bye to my faithful Müller. "It's time those fingers were treated," I told him. "You will go back with the next ambulance and with any luck you might be in Germany within a week."

"But, Herr *Assistenzarzt* . . ." he started.

"Now, my boy, on your way," I cut in. "We can win this war without you. I'll be seeing you back in Bielefeld." It was with a heavy heart that I shook Müller's hand.

For my dressing station at Schitinkovo I had commandeered the house next door to the battalion battle post and I was comforted by the sight of the massive stable behind my dressing station on the side from which the Russians would attack. It would be an excellent protection against their fire.

Everything was arranged in the sick bay ready for the expected attack and we were having our meal at six in the evening when *Stabsarzt* Lierow of the neighboring Infantry Regiment 37 called. He was a tall, wiry man of middle age and had come to ascertain our arrangements, as his regiment was occupying the defense line to our left, a mile or so to the west. We invited him to stay to dinner. The lackluster expression in his eyes gave way to a twinkle as he listened to our lighthearted banter. Before he left, Lierow and I made a mutual-aid pact. When the situation permitted we would render assistance to each other.

Every officer and soldier were ready for action at his post. We waited for the Russians to attack. We knew they would attack. And we wanted them to come. Anything to get things started.

Our intelligence had learned from prisoners that Stalin had ordered Zhukov in future to attack only at night as "the Germans do not care for night fighting and close combat." He was right, of course. No soldier likes hand-to-hand fighting and we hated fighting at night in the crippling cold when we would rather have been sleeping near some huge Russian oven. But it did not alter the fact that just as we had inflicted far heavier losses than we had sustained in the daytime battles, so in the night engagements we more than held our own.

But we were lucky this night; the temperature was appreciably higher than it had been for some time. We hoped we would have no trouble with our guns. Nevertheless, we kept them warm in the ovens until the listening posts should give the alarm.

And we waited for the Russians.

The patrols circulated between the listening posts. And 200 yards beyond the east end of the village, along the snowy road to the 1st Battalion's positions, our machine-gunners waited in their wooden blockhouse and in their two holes in the snow. Their job was to rake the wood with fire where it curved close to the east end of the village. Trees had been felled to provide firing lanes through the wood and any Russian who crossed these lanes would be taking his life in his hands.

The full moon swung up into the heavens; it was a cloudless sky. At 8:30 p.m., in bright moonlight, the Russians attacked in battalion strength from the north against the eastern end of the village—just where we had expected them. We were warned in time by our listening posts in the wood and the majority of our troops were rushed to the eastern end of the village. Only small groups were left to defend the middle of the village, and the 40 men from the 2nd Battalion, Regiment 37, were left to look after the western end of Schitinkovo.

The Russians attacked with close on a thousand men; we met them with 200.

The machine-guns along the road raked the lanes through the wood with fire; many Russians fell, but more got through and flung themselves out of the wood right into the muzzles of our automatics and infantry rifles. In the bright moonlight, and with the help of flares, the German fire was deadly and the Russians wavered and retreated. Our advanced artillery observer directed the fire of our guns into the sector toward which the Russians were retreating and Stolze and a body of men from the 10th Company followed up with a counterattack.

The men returned with Stolze's body.

He had followed the Russians too enthusiastically and too deeply into the woods. A Red machine-gunner, posted behind a screen of bushes, had sprayed a burst into the huge figure. It was the last thing he did. One of Stolze's NCOs lobbed a grenade into the bushes which blew gunner and gun into kingdom-come. But when they lifted Stolze's body from the snow, it was too late. Stolze was dead with four machine-gun bullets through his chest.

For the rest of the night the 10th Company fought like men possessed of demons. They could hardly believe that their jovial, beloved commander was dead, but were determined that he would have plenty of Russian company on his journey to the hereafter. Again and again the Russians regrouped their forces and attacked, and each time they were halted by the deadly rifle and machine-gun fire of our men. And as each wave of Russians was thrown back, our light infantry guns and mortars took their toll.

For five and a half hours the slaughter continued until the Russians had had enough and withdrew, trying to carry back some of their wounded.

But they left more than 100 dead immediately in front of the houses we had defended. Our casualties amounted to four dead and six wounded.[203]

Next morning we found groups of dead Russian soldiers in the woods. They were the wounded who had been gathered together but abandoned when the Russians retreated. More than 100 of them had been unable, on account of their wounds, to drag themselves back to the Russian lines and had frozen to death.

The morning of 28 December remained calm and gave us time to clean up the battlefield. The 200 dead Russians represented winter clothing sufficient to equip every man in the battalion who was still without it.

The bodies were carried, frozen into grotesque shapes, to the *sauna* houses and there the "saw commandos" got to work. It was a filthy business, but there was no place for the niceties of human conduct when death was waiting to claim the man who lost his body heat.

New firing lanes were cut in the wood, patrols paced the outer ring of our defenses and reconnaissance patrols crept farther afield to ascertain the Russian intentions. Some of them had brief skirmishes and during the whole day desultory artillery fire took place on both sides. Big movements of enemy troops were reported between Vassilevskoye and Gorki. Men cleaned their weapons and checked the large quantity of enemy weapons and ammunition that had been left behind when the Russians withdrew. Every Russian body was stacked, still frozen, in the barns. We could not afford to leave them lying in the snow as they would provide false targets during the next battle.

Kageneck was everywhere, supervising operations. In particular, he concerned himself with the issue of winter clothing that had been stripped from the Russian corpses. By the afternoon every man was rigged out to withstand the cold. But there was a disadvantage in wearing this captured Russian clothing—our men could be mistaken for Russian soldiers in the confused mêlée of a night action. It was therefore ordered that the fleece-lined Russian steppe jackets be worn underneath the men's ordinary tunics and that each man must wear his gray-green *Kopfschützer*.

The icy cold now seemed to have got rid of the last of the men's lice, so spotted fever was one less thing to worry about.

At last it was possible to relax in the dressing station, where everyone had been working at top pitch throughout the night and day. My little band had shrunk considerably and I had been sent a dentist, named Baumeister, to help me; the dental units had ceased to function altogether these days. For the time being I kept him as my personal assistant, which allowed Heinrich to take over Müller's work. Beside Heinrich, Kunzle labored, looking after the medical supplies and doing his best to help the wounded Russians who fell into our hands. To Kunzle there was no such thing as nationality—every wounded man, Russian or German, received the same attention. And my other Russian volunteer, Hans, in the midst of all the din and confusion of battle, continued calmly to transport wounded men and ammunition on his panje wagon or with a sledge. Not for a moment did it enter my mind that Hans might desert and run back to rejoin the Russians. I trusted the loyalty of this sturdy man from the Siberian steppes as implicitly as I trusted the rest.

And Tulpin? He was above criticism. Never once did he shirk his duty or betray the slightest sign of fear. But I noticed his dilated pupils, his trembling lips and the moistness of his hands. I watched him closely and pitied him for the tragedy he was playing out within himself; he was pursued by demons, which now had his will entirely at their mercy, which had him strapped to a pendulum that swung ceaselessly between heaven and hell. It would have been impossible to send him home for treatment and we could not afford to lose his valuable services. But if and when the Russian offensive collapsed I was determined to make him my personal patient and help him by every means in my power.

Stolze's body lay in a barn at the eastern end of the village—among the 10th Company men he had loved so well, men, who, after his death, had shown how close had been the bond between them. They had not dug a grave in the snow for him. They did not trust the Staritsa Line and wanted to inter his body in a proper German war cemetery behind the lines. They laid out his body on a long narrow sledge, rested his head on a pillow and folded his hands across his chest. This improvised bier was placed in the open barn in such a way that if we had to evacuate our positions in a hurry they could take him along at a moment's notice, either by hitching a horse to the sledge or pulling it themselves. They had gone to all this trouble in spite of dead weariness, hunger and long hours of danger and strain. Stolze could have had no finer tribute.

The day rushed to its end. In a cold, steel-blue sky, a frosty sun shed not a single ray of warmth and tried to escape with indecent haste behind the lifeless, snow-covered woods and the low hills in the middle distance, which it color-washed for a few brief minutes with the palest pink. The wounded had all been evacuated; the day's work was done; another night and day of the winter had passed and perhaps we were one day and one night nearer to our own destruction. Everything had been prepared for the battle that would take place that night. And perhaps because Russian and German alike knew that a further night of violence and wholesale slaughter lay ahead, the artillery of both sides stopped firing as I walked along the hard-packed snow of the road toward the barn where Stolze's body lay.

Black rafters stuck out from the thick snow on the roof of the barn like badly decayed teeth. Inside it was still light enough to pick out details. Gently I pulled back the ground-sheet that covered Stolze's body and powdery grains of snow rolled to the ground. Like sculptured marble, Stolze lay on the sledge. His eyes were closed and there was a suspicion of a smile on his mouth. If winter lasted for ever, I thought, Stolze's body would lie embalmed like this until the end of time.

Stolze's orderly was waiting for me outside. He saluted and said: "Herr *Oberleutnant* Stolze ordered me to give Herrn *Assistenzarzt* this fox-fur cap."

"Thank you, my friend," I answered absently. "Yes, that is so—I had forgotten." For many days I could not bear to wear it, but it was to prove invaluable in the two Russian winters that lay ahead.

Meticulously, I checked all preparations at the sick bay, issued first aid supplies to the companies and ordered my men to lie down and get some rest before the attack started. I stepped outside into the moonlit night, brighter even than the previous night. There was more than 35 degrees of frost again—and the thermometer was still falling. We might have trouble with the guns again in this cold. At Battalion H.Q. Kageneck was studying a map; Lammerding was out, checking the communication system to Boehmer's company and to the detachment from Regiment 37; Becker was doing the same with the 10th Company and the eastern machine-gun posts.

"What time will the bastards come tonight, Heinz?" Kageneck asked me.

"I think they'll wait for the moon to go down," I replied. "They took too much of a hammering in last night's moonlight."

"I agree," said Kageneck. "In that case we've got a few hours until they come. How pleasant." He sighed and folded the map. "I've done everything I can possibly think of— but that wood at the east end of the village is too close to our positions. It's our soft spot and will remain our soft spot."

We seated ourselves in front of the open fire and stretched out our legs toward the blazing logs. Bruno, Kageneck's orderly, came in with two cups of steaming coffee. He looked at Kageneck anxiously and said: "Herr *Oberleutnant* must lie down now and get some sleep—every minute of sleep is important now."

"Don't worry about me, Bruno," said Kageneck. "A restful hour like this is more of a tonic than a sleep from which one doesn't want to waken."

An old pendulum clock ticked on the wall. It was an unusual piece of furniture to find in a Russian cottage. "A ticking clock," said Kageneck after a long silence, "always adds something peaceful and comforting to a room. We had an old clock like that one at home. In fact, it is one of my earliest memories. I suppose I was about six at the time. I was convalescing after an illness and my mother had spent more of her time with me during my illness than she had spent with my brothers." He paused as his thoughts went back to his childhood. "And this old clock ticked away the time while my mother sat at my bedside and told me fairy tales. I never wanted them to end, and I thought that if I stopped the clock they would go on forever. But the clock kept on ticking until it became a symbol of evil for me. The clock was robbing me of precious minutes, it was ticking my mother's life away."

"Yes, that is the first impact of the spirit in life," I said. "It marks the birth of the thinking ego and from that moment on the boy can no longer live in the present only."

"I suppose you're right," answered Kageneck dreamily. "But the last hour strikes in everybody's life on some clock, Heinz. It's now nine-thirty. Last night at this time the clock stopped on Stolze. Sometimes, you know, I can't believe we'll ever get out of this mess unless a miracle happens."

"For God's sake don't start thinking in that strain," I said.

"Don't misunderstand me, Heinz. I'm not despairing. I'm just trying hard to face facts. When I see how we're being slowly whittled away—a few men today, a few more tomorrow and no hope of replacements or reinforcements—I can't honestly see much hope.[204] If tonight we kill 500 Russians and lose only 20 men ourselves, the proportion is still far too great for us to bear. Work out for yourself how many of our little band are likely to survive if this goes on much longer."

"But the situation might change at any moment. The Russians might withdraw; we might be ordered to retreat; anything might happen. There's only one way to stay alive and that's to act as if you're going to live forever."[205]

"Don't worry, Heinz. It was only the old clock that set my thoughts ticking. Say it was the clock talking—or imagine I was lying on your psychiatrist's couch if you like," he added, with a wry smile. He clasped me on the shoulder. "I probably wouldn't have talked like this if it hadn't been for old Hippocrates, Doktor," he said cheerfully.

There was a knock on the door and two soldiers from 11th Company walked in. Between them stood a girl. She had been found wandering about in the fighting line, the soldiers reported, and Boehmer had sent her to Battalion H.Q. as a suspected spy.

She stood there, her dark eyes filled with fear. She was facing men who, in the chaos of war, held absolute power over her. She was fortunate that she had fallen into the hands of a man like Kageneck to whom power meant justice, not despotism. Kageneck ordered her to take off her heavy woolen overcoat. She took off the coat, removed a military steppe jacket that she was wearing underneath it and slowly unknotted her head scarf and shook out her long black hair. She was a lovely little creature. Her rough skirt was belted around a slim waist and her high-necked cotton blouse was tight enough to show off her well-developed figure. She had delicate features, quite unlike most of the peasant women who had helped me from time to time in my dressing stations. The creaminess of her complexion was relieved by the touches of color on her cheekbones, where the biting wind had stung her face. She seemed to realize that she was dealing with a humane man, for the fear had left her eyes and she now looked at us boldly.

Kageneck questioned her and we were astonished at her command of German, which she spoke with a pronounced Russian accent.

"What is your name?"

"Natasha Petrovna."

"How old?"

"Nineteen years."

"What is your occupation?"

"School teacher."

"Where and what subjects did you teach?"

"My school was in Kalinin. I taught German, geography and physical culture."

"And what brought you here?"

"I am fleeing from the Russians. They want to shoot me because I acted as an interpreter for the Germans."

"With which division?"

"I don't know which unit, but I helped the Germans in Kalinin."

"What was the commander's name of the unit you helped?"

"I can't remember. I interpreted for many German officers and I can't remember all their names."

"Name one of them."

"They were all strange names. How can I remember them? The Russians have been chasing me ever since they took Kalinin. It has driven things like names out of my head."

Relentlessly Kageneck cross-examined the girl, keeping her standing in front of him. Inconsistencies cropped up. Without altering the tone of his voice, Kageneck pointed them out. She nearly broke down completely, pleaded with him to stop the questioning, resorted to tears and then recovered her composure when Kageneck stopped asking his questions. Kageneck ordered the two soldiers to search her overcoat and steppe jacket. They found nothing.

He turned to me. "Now it's your turn, Heinz. You're a doctor, so you'll have to act in place of a woman searcher. See if she's hiding anything on her body."

I was startled by the order. Up to then I had been regarding her as a possible spy, but also as the first attractive woman I had seen at such close quarters for several months. Hastily I tried to induce a purely professional attitude toward her.

"Come over here," I told her, and she followed me around the wall of the huge oven. I was startled by my own awareness of the contrast between her soft young body and the hard, masculine soldiers' bodies with which I had been dealing every day.

"I am afraid I must now search you," I told her, intending to feel her clothes and make certain that she was concealing no arms or papers in them.

"Yes, Herr Doktor," she said calmly. I went back into the room to fetch an oil lamp from the table.

When I went back with my light around the oven wall into the smaller room, her skirt was on the floor and she was slipping the blouse off her shoulders. Beneath her blouse she wore nothing, as was the case with most Russian women, but her breasts were firm and beautifully formed.

"That will be quite sufficient," I told her as she prepared to reduce herself to complete nakedness. She stood in front of me entirely unconcerned while I examined her boots, which she still wore, her skirt and blouse. I turned back to her and she lifted her arms above her head, so that I could see she was concealing nothing.

"Get dressed," I told her curtly.

"Nothing suspicious found," I reported to Kageneck.

"Quite sure?" asked Kageneck, with a laugh. "Have you really found nothing suspicious? I'm disappointed in you, Heinz."

"Oh, yes, I found a great deal. But nothing that points to her as a spy."

Natasha walked back into the room and looked at me with grateful eyes. She sat on the edge of the fireplace and fastened her steppe jacket.

"Very well then," said Kageneck, as he turned to the two soldiers, who could not take their eyes off the girl. "Report to *Oberleutnant* Boehmer that it could not be established with certainty that this young woman is a Russian spy." They saluted and withdrew.

Kageneck turned to Natasha: "You are a very young girl and I would like to give you one more chance. I will have you sent back behind our lines under escort and we will let you go wherever you think you can escape from your fellow countrymen who you say want to shoot you. But I warn you never again to let yourself be found in the fighting lines. I'm going to send an exact description of you to the division and describe you as a suspect. Go far away where there are no German soldiers or Russian soldiers."

Natasha stood calmly and said nothing.

"She can't remain here," said Kageneck. "Can't you accommodate her safely at the sick bay?" he asked me.

I summoned Heinrich and ordered him to take the girl to the sick bay and keep her under guard.

"We can't afford to let her go until after tonight's fighting," Kageneck said after she had gone. "We'll get rid of her tomorrow."

Lammerding entered, pulled off his gloves, and said: "Everything is in order at 11th Company. But what have you done with the little raven? She was certainly muffled up when I saw her, but even through all those clothes she seemed to have everything."

"That I can't judge," said Kageneck. "You'll have to ask the Doktor."

"Take it easy, Lammerding," I said, with a smile. "She's in my safe hands now. But I can tell you that everything she had was perfectly genuine. Nothing false about her."

Becker came in and Lammerding gave him a glowing description of Natasha. "This interesting creature is under guard at the sick bay tonight," he added.

"You'll have to excuse me," said Becker, "but I've no intention of visiting your interesting creature tonight. I'm dead tired."

"It's time we all had a rest," said Kageneck. "We can't do any more now. All our preparations are made. After midnight the moon will set and then, believe me, the Russians will attack." He turned to little Becker: "Are you certain that everyone is at his post?"

"I'll guarantee it," replied Becker.

"Good, then we'll go to bed," said Kageneck. "*Gute Nacht, meine Herren.*"

Back at the sick bay, Heinrich was taking his orders seriously, Natasha was sitting near the fire and Heinrich sat opposite her with his rifle across his knees. I stretched out my tired limbs on my straw bed and sank into a dreamless sleep.

Oberst Carl ("Corle") Becker, commander of Infantry Regiment 18, was awarded the coveted Knight's Cross on 1 November 1942. In early 1943, he was given command of 253rd Infantry Division, a position he held through the war's end, when he became a Russian prisoner of war. He would not be released from Soviet captivity until October 1955.
ALL PHOTOS FROM HAAPE FAMILY ARCHIVES.

Dr. Haape (center) with fellow officers in Malakovo at the beginning of 1942.

The commander of 3rd Battalion, Infantry Regiment 18, *Hauptmann* Noack (right) with Dr. Haape.

Stabsarzt Dr. Haape pictured with the German Cross in Gold with a colleague of a neighboring battalion.

Officers' conference at regimental HQ. Center front: *Stabsarzt* Dr. Haape; *Oberst* Becker to his right (wearing pale breeches).

Dr. Haape signing medical reports in his bunker.

Dr. Haape (right) and *Leutnant* Deppe. During the savage summer fighting for Rzhev in 1942, Haape was transferred to 3rd Battalion, Infantry Regiment 58. Among all the doctors of 6th Infantry Division who had been in the field since 22 June 1941, he was the only one who remained.

The long march through the summer of 1941 in sweltering heat and choking dust. By the end of July 1941, the division had marched 1,000 kilometers.

Cutting through barbed wire defenses on 2 October 1941—the first day of Operation "Typhoon," the drive of Army Group Center toward Moscow.

Stalin and Lenin poster and peasants at the marketplace.

Old Lithuanian playing guitar in front of a huge stone oven, on top of which (or beside) an entire peasant family slept in winter.

Natasha Petrovna, a young teacher (of German)
from Kalinin who worked as a spy for the Russians.
She would be hanged by the Germans.

Nina Barbarovna, a Russian medical student who
cared for civilian sick with medicines supplied by
Dr. Haape. She would be executed by the Red
Army in 1942 for fraternizing with the Germans.

Ruins of the cathedral of Rzhev at -52° Centigrade.

Two Russian helpers in heavy winter clothing who
assisted the Germans. With them a hardy panje horse.

Red Army soldier from Mongolia.

Weather-beaten face of an elderly, hard-working farmer's wife.

Twelve-year-old boy who believed firmly in the future
of Bolshevism.

Old Russian wood cutter from the headwater area of the
Volga.

ALL SKETCHES BY DR. HEINRICH HAAPE.

The celebrated Viennese opera singer Martha Arazym, who waited 2,000 kilometers away for Dr. Heinrich Haape's safe return. In December 1942, the two were married by proxy: Martha was at home on the Rhine; Heinrich was in Russia on the Volga.

CHAPTER 22

The Battle of Schitinkovo

WE HAD GAUGED THE RUSSIANS' PLANS ACCURATELY. THEY WAITED UNTIL THE MOON had set and then attacked. But we were ready for them; our men grabbed the machine-guns from the ovens and the fight was on. Without ornamentation, the official battalion report described the course of the battle for Schitinkovo:[206]

During the night of 28/29 December, at 0230 hours, after the moon had set, the Russians attacked under cover of darkness, with a strength of about two battalions and with unprecedented ferocity.

Favored by the darkness and the weight of their mass attack, the enemy advanced from the northeast and east and, in spite of maximum defensive fire, soon reached the fringes of the village. The attack was surprisingly strong and was carried out at great speed.

Our patrols withdrew, fighting, and gave the alarm. The machine-gun posts to the east of the village were overrun and put out of action, our machine-gunners being all killed or badly wounded.

As on the previous evening, Oberleutnant Graf von Kageneck succeeded, in spite of the fury of the attack and great difficulties which developed in the situation, methodically to concentrate his main defensive forces in the eastern end of the village.

Owing to the exceptional cold, machine-guns were less reliable and there were many stoppages. The telephone cable leading to the artillery was almost immediately put out of action by the heavy Russian mortar fire, which caused an unfortunate weakening of our defensive artillery fire.

As a result of the determined attack, the Russians gained possession of three houses on the northeastern perimeter of Schitinkovo. Immediate counter measures by the Battalion Commander halted the momentum of the attack and caused heavy losses to the enemy from rifle fire and hand grenades. The attack was brought to a complete stand-still. The artillery began to operate effectively again by means of wireless transmission.

But while our main forces (outnumbered nearly 10 to one) were occupied in resisting the enemy attack from the northeast, a second sharp attack, in strength approximately two full companies, suddenly developed from the northwest against the western end of the village. Portions of the 2nd Battalion and other attached troops from Regiment 37 were immediately thrown into the defense.

It was possible to stop the breakthrough by the second attack only by the most desperate and fierce defense by every available man in house-to-house and hand-to-hand fighting with grenades and automatics.

Meanwhile, during a counterattack in the eastern sector, Oberleutnant Boehmer was wounded and took no further part in the action. At the same time, a small group detoured and made a determined counterattack to throw back the Russians in the western end of the village.[207]

A counter-assault from the south by a company formed from the remnants of Infantry Regiment 329, led by Leutnant Scheel, met with determined resistance by the enemy, who had to be cleared individually from the houses at the eastern end of the village. In this action, the group from Regiment 329 sustained a 50 percent loss of men, including Leutnant Scheel, and his two platoon leaders, who were wounded.

With great fury, the enemy now launched a new attack from the north (at 0330 hours) as well as a frontal attack on the center of the village. At the same time, the Russian forces at the eastern end of the village broke across the street and pushed toward the road from Schitinkovo to Terpilovo. They captured the road junction and managed to encircle and seal off our troops fighting in the center of the village.

The center of the village being held by weak forces only, the enemy succeeded in capturing a number of houses not far from the battalion battle post and the dressing station. At the same time most of the houses in the eastern sector fell into his hands.

In little more than an hour since the moon had set, the Russians, deploying about 2500 men, had overwhelmed our small garrison of 300 and had captured most of Schitinkovo. The first attack, as we guessed, came from the dangerously close forest at the eastern end of the village, and our numbers had been too small to withstand that heavy assault and to repel the thrust which was made 15 minutes later against the western end of the village, a mile away. The final attack against the center of the village had been the last straw.

Little Becker and Schnittger with the remnants of Stolze's old company and the infantry-gun detachment had formed themselves into a small pocket of savage resistance at the junction of the Terpilovo road. They were grossly outnumbered by the encircling Reds but refused to yield an inch of ground. In the western sector, another small group, mainly Regiment 37's men, were trying to halt the Russian penetration from that end, and in the center of the village Lammerding with a small number of men was desperately defending the dressing station and Battalion H.Q.

The dressing station was packed with wounded and we were far too busy to pay any heed to what was going on outside—until a soldier with a gaping hip wound staggered unassisted into the overcrowded room. His face was a study in blind terror as he shouted: "The Russians are here! They're coming!"

His terror spread rapidly among the casualties. With terror-stricken expressions, badly wounded men tried to lift themselves but fell back helplessly on to their straw bedding. Not one of them had any doubt what his end would be at the hands of the Reds if the dressing station were captured. I shot a glance at the young girl standing at the corner of the oven and she returned my look, mockingly. There was no trace of the fear or gratitude she had shown when captured. At that moment I could cheerfully have put a bullet through her.

We were in no doubt as to the danger: the noise of fighting came nearer, and the rifle fire, the grenade explosions and the furious rattle of automatics sounded only 50 yards away—on the other side of the barn at the back of the dressing station.

A dead quiet descended on the room. I was conscious of Natasha's beautiful but cold eyes resting on me, and as I looked around the room every one of the wounded men was looking at me.

A hand grenade burst just outside the building and several windowpanes fell shattered to the floor. The Russians were on our doorstep.

Suddenly I realized that everything depended on me. The wounded men were all looking to me to take action—as the only officer present and as one of the few able-bodied men in the room. For some reason the realization gave me courage and the ability to act quickly and think clearly. There was nothing to do but play the soldier.

"Let's see what is really happening," I said, putting on my field helmet and grabbing my automatic. I had enough hand grenades in my pockets. "Heinrich, go to the stable and keep a watch on what is happening at the back of the house. Report any suspicious movements. Only Baumeister is to carry on with the wounded for the time being. Tulpin, you will immediately see that every man who can carry a rifle is armed—they will defend the house. At all costs we must prevent the enemy from hurling grenades through the windows—or it will be slaughter."

Everyone who could move was galvanized into action. I stepped from the room into the passage, released the safety catch of my gun and went down the three wooden steps into the street. It was icy cold and pitch-black. For some moments, until my eyes accustomed themselves to the darkness, I could distinguish nothing, in spite of the flares which were spurting up at each end of the village. Then a flare went up not far from the dressing station and its brilliant white light lit up the headquarters and my own building.

There! On the other side of the street, about 30 yards away! A Russian! He saw me first and his bullet plugged into the wall behind me. Before he could aim a second time—"Keep quite calm!" flew through my mind—I gave him a burst and he sank in a heap just as he was sighting his rifle for a second shot. In a few strides I leapt to cover behind a sledge standing around the corner next to the side wall of the house. To the rear of the house I spotted our little ambulance wagon with the two panje horses. The Russian, Hans, was lying on the ground hanging on to the team with his strong hands.

The Russian I had shot down—the first man I had indisputably killed—had been approaching us from the other side of the street. So we were partly encircled, and it was almost certain that he had not been the only Russian there. From behind my cover I peered into the darkness and by the light of distant flares was able to determine that the next house to us, about 20 yards to the east, was still in our hands. The next house to that was Battalion H.Q., which presumably we also still held. It was comforting.

Along the village street to the west most of the houses appeared to be deserted; at least there was no sign of fighting around them, except at the extreme western end of the village where the 37th were still holding out. At present the main danger appeared to be coming from the east, where the Russians were apparently "rolling up" the village. But between my dressing station and the advancing Russians were Lammerding and his men. A flare danced into the sky, there was a fusillade from German and Russian arms, and a confused shouting of German and Russian voices. I recognized Lammerding's voice calling to his men: "All ready!" Every time a flare was fired it was a signal for another brief duel of life and death. It comforted me to know that Lammerding was still in action; I knew nothing would shake him out of his imperturbable calm.

"Russians over there!" I heard Hans shout from behind me, and at the same time I spotted another Red soldier on the opposite side of the street. In the glare of the flare he was plainly visible and made as easy a target as the first Russian. Evidently he and his comrades had been trying to take Lammerding's men from the rear. As the Russian fell to the burst from my automatic, shots rang out from the dressing station. Tulpin and his light casualties were now in the fight. Then everything was dark again.

Flares were going up along the whole length of the road to the east of me and told of pockets of Germans resisting for their lives. The heaviest exchange of fire was coming from the Terpilovo road junction, where Becker and the heroic men of 10th Company were still holding out. German voices approached from the west and by the dying light of a flare I picked out Kageneck with a dozen men on his heels.

"Hallo, Franz!" I called. "Be careful. . . . Come here." In a second he was crouching at my side and asked: "What's the matter here? A new breakthrough?" In a few words I told him of the new attack from the north.

"So that's it! A frontal attack on the center of the village—well, that's the bloody limit."

"Lammerding is over there," I explained. "He's trying to seal off the village from the Russians in the east. But across the road there are some Russians trying to take him from the rear."

"If we don't stop that we'll be losing the battle post and the dressing station. Lammerding must hold out while we mop them up."

"How are things going at the other end?" I asked him as he was preparing to gather his men.

"The Russian attack's more or less petered out. The 37th boys have cleared all the houses and now they're picking off any Russians who try to attack across the snowfields," Kageneck answered, then placed a machine-gun in position by the wall and shouted: "All ready!"

Accurately he fired a flare toward the other side of the road. Its dazzling light picked out about 15 Russian soldiers. The machine-gun chattered a prolonged burst and the infantrymen fired at anything they thought was a Russian. Some of the Russians fired back, but several of them lay still. The flare died out and only distant flares gave a sickly, uncertain light.

Kageneck jumped across the street, followed by his men. Hand grenades exploded, automatics and rifles rattled and cracked, and I knew that from that direction I would have nothing to fear for the present. I also knew that Lammerding would let nothing through; it was not in his nature to budge an inch to any Russian.

Under cover of darkness, I ran into the dressing station and assured the wounded men—in as matter-of-fact a tone as I could muster—that the Russians had been thrown out of the western end of the village; that they were being held to the east and that a counterattack would soon be launched to drive them out of the village. The men visibly relaxed their tautened nerves, for when a man is unable to defend himself he becomes prey to unbearable fear. Again I was aware of two cold, dark eyes watching me as I spoke. For Natasha, at any rate, it made little difference who was the victor. She would live. I had oversimplified the situation in my efforts to cheer the men up; the fighting, actually, had been by no means decisive.

A few wounded men were brought in from the western end, which was a good sign. But from the east no wounded had reached us, which was a sure indication that the battle was still raging fiercely and that Becker's group was still isolated.

Without talking much we carried on dressing the wounded. Then I heard shooting from the direction of the stable at the back of the house, where I had left Heinrich to report anything unusual. I handed the man I was treating over to Baumeister and strode through to the stable. From behind the half-open stable door, Heinrich was taking aim across the snow. I ran across to him. "What's the matter, Heinrich?" I asked.

"Russians!"

"Why didn't you tell me?"

"I thought I could deal with them on my own, Herr *Assistenzarzt.*"

Eight bodies lay in the snow at the back of the stable. Heinrich had calmly shot them down, one by one. They had to approach across open ground and by the light of flares

Heinrich had done the rest. He was as cool as the snow itself and obviously quite prepared to take on a whole Russian company single-handed from the shelter of his stable. However, I reprimanded him for not having told me the moment he had sighted danger, and sent six of the lightly wounded cases to reinforce him.

The door of the dressing station was flung open and Bruno, Kageneck's orderly, rushed in. "Quick, give me a rifle and helmet!" he demanded. "Those Red swines took mine and wanted to take me along, too."

Tulpin handed him a rifle and steel helmet.

"Why, what happened, Bruno?" I asked him.

"We were throwing out the Ivans on the other side of the street. . . . I jumped behind a *sauna* house right into a bunch of them. I shouted as loudly as I could, and in a few seconds the Herr *Oberleutnant* and our men were there and rescued me. But one of them got away with my rifle and helmet."

We filled Bruno's pockets with ammunition and he ran out to rejoin Kageneck, who was outside the dressing station with the artillery officer.

He was talking rapidly. "If you're not sure of your targets, then fire into the village— anywhere you think the Russians might be."

"But what about the danger to our own men?"

"That's a risk we'll have to take. We're all in danger, so shoot and shoot for all you're worth. We'll have to risk hitting our own men," Kageneck replied, and stepped into the doorway as a Russian machine-gun fired a burst up the street.

Kageneck sent a messenger to the 37th troops, ordering them to keep a few men to defend the western end of the village and to send every other man they could spare to assemble at the dressing station. In the meantime, the artillery officer had established an observation post in the loft of the battle post.

"How many wounded?" Kageneck asked me.

"More than 40. The dressing station is filled to bursting point."

We could hear *Oberfeldwebel* Scheiter's infantry gun methodically firing shot after shot at point-blank range into the Russians. So Becker and his handful were still in the fight.

"Let's hope we're in time to reach Becker's group," Kageneck said to me. "As soon as we get those reinforcements from the 37th we'll attack with all we've got and dislodge the Reds house-by-house until we reach them. Once we've got those 10th Company men with us again we'll have a sporting chance of clearing the whole village."

Then came the thunder of our artillery from five miles away across the Volga, beyond Terpilovo. The first shells dropped near the edge of the wood at the back of the village, the second salvo was nearer the houses on the north side of the street, then salvo after salvo roared through the night and burst in the village, between ourselves and Becker's marooned detachment. It was pin-point accuracy and our men gave a cheer for the observation officer sitting in the loft.

About 40 men from the 37th had by now assembled at the dressing station and were split into two groups, 20 being detailed to join Lammerding on the north side of the street, the rest joining Kageneck's group, which was to recapture the houses on the south side of the street until they reached little Becker.

Ten minutes later our counterattack was launched and Kageneck and Lammerding were battling their way eastward down the street, house by house. At the same time, I heard lively rifle fire from Heinrich and his half-dozen crippled defenders of the dressing station. By the light of Lammerding's flares we could pick out 30 or 40 Russians working their way across the snowfield from the woods toward us. It was up to us to protect ourselves now; we could expect no help from Lammerding or Kageneck.

The wounded men fired as best they could. One man's left arm hung uselessly at his side; he lifted the rifle and aimed with his right hand only and reloaded by gripping the rifle between his knees. Another man with a shattered right knee leaned against the doorpost for support and ignored the terrible pain he must have been suffering.

Although we had the better positions, firing from cover against the unprotected Russians, we were not bringing sufficient weight of fire against them, we had no flare pistol of our own, and in the periods of darkness between Lammerding's flares the Russians were gaining ground.

Bullets were now thudding into the log walls of the stable, so I sorted out a further eight lightly wounded men from the dressing station and threw them into the fight. I placed them behind the huge piles of wood that had been stacked by the peasants between our house and the next. They had good cover and were able to rest their rifles while aiming.

I seized a rifle myself and with every flare that went up from Lammerding's group on our right, 16 rifles cracked out their well-aimed fire. The extra eight defenders tipped the scales and it was now obvious that the Reds could not hope to reach our dressing station before they were picked off. If any of them did manage to get through we should be able to wipe them out in hand-to-hand fighting; I had every confidence in my men, because they were fighting for their lives and knew it.

A sudden wave of exultation surged through me. I felt my dressing station had proved itself to be a really tight little fortress. In another two and a half hours the new day would dawn and by that time we should be masters of the situation.

A fresh batch of wounded men were carried into the room and this time they were from our men counterattacking to the east. They brought encouraging news of the progress being made. We packed more and more wounded into the corners and tried to leave a little space in the center of the room in which to operate.

And Natasha's dark eyes never left my face.

Bruno burst into the room. "My *Oberleutnant* has been wounded—in the head."

"Is he dead?" I asked urgently.

"No, he's lying on the ground, but he's still breathing."

"Tulpin!" I called. He followed me with the medical bag and bandaging material and we leapt across the street, heedless of the enemy fire. Two men had carried Kageneck behind a house, where he lay, conscious, but with blood spurting from his temple.

"It doesn't seem too bad," Kageneck muttered.

At a quick glance it seemed that the temple was only grazed, but I wanted to get him to a healthier spot for a proper examination, for the Russians were only a few yards away. I quickly applied a pressure bandage, and Tulpin and I half-dragged, half-carried him back to the dressing station, hugging the walls of houses as far as possible.

Back inside, I removed the bandage and fresh blood spurted out. I probed the skull with a cannula but found that it was smooth and undamaged. There was nothing serious.

"It's only a graze, Franz," I told Kageneck. "You've been severely stunned and the heavy bleeding is caused by the temporalis being grazed. You'll be quite recovered in a few days, I'm happy to say."

Kageneck smiled his relief. "I can tell you, it felt as if I'd been kicked by a horse," he said. "It bowled me clean over, I felt the blood streaming down my face and at first I thought my time had come."

The bandaging was completed and Kageneck felt his head with his hands. "That's fine," he said, "the bandage is quite firm. You know, there's really nothing wrong with me except for a few noises in my head—and those aren't too bad."

He was silent for a while and then said thoughtfully, "It's not as difficult as I'd imagined it would be to drive the Russians out of the houses."

"Why?"

"They're making one big mistake," he said, with a chuckle. "They're too anxious to get warm. As you may have noticed, it's a damnably cold night—a real bone freezer—and the Russians have been out in it for several hours. When they capture a house, they can't resist the temptation to go inside for a warm instead of getting on with the fighting. The commissars seem to have lost control in all the confusion. So all we have to do is charge the house, throw a few grenades through the windows and then pick them off as they rush out."

My eyes went to Natasha. She was listening intently.

"She understands German, Franz," I reminded him.

"Doesn't matter," Kageneck replied. "We won't often get this chance and after all," he continued with a cynical smile at her, "she should be grateful to know that we dispose of her persecutors in this elegant manner."

"Your dressing station's getting too crowded," Kageneck remarked, looking around. "It's dangerous to have so many men in one heap. Say a few hand grenades were lobbed through the windows. . . . What's that firing?" he asked suddenly as Heinrich and the men in the stable let go a volley.

"No need to worry. That's our own little private war. A few Russians tried to get us from the rear, but the situation is well in hand." I tried to sound very military and succeeded only in sounding rather pompous. "I intend to start evacuating the wounded as soon as that shooting behind the house ends. The seriously wounded I shall send by the two panje wagons to *Stabsarzt* Lierow in that village to the west. Those who can still walk or even crawl I'll take across the fields to Terpilovo as soon as our rear is free of the enemy."

"That's a long way," Kageneck remarked.

"Yes, it's all of two miles, but they'll be better at the Medical Company than here, and they have to go there sooner or later. It will be a good thing if you go with them for a few days' rest, Franz."

"What the devil are you thinking about?" Kageneck demanded angrily. "It's quite out of the question. I must keep the men together and we must break through and make contact with Becker's group."

"But you're—"

"I'm feeling a hundred percent fit again now, thank you, Heinz. Just stick to the men who are really wounded and stop trying to wet nurse me."

He got up and put on his field cap, as he could no longer wear his steel helmet over the bandage. "Must go and see to that artillery fire," he said. "It's high time it was directed more to the east, or our own counterattack will be running into it."

I accompanied him to the door and watched his white bandage disappear down the road toward the battle post.

The fighting had now been going on for more than two hours, and we had regained a great deal of ground. But the din was unabated—a wild confusion of sound from artillery, mortars, infantry guns, machine-guns, automatic rifles, pistols and hand grenades, interspersed with shouted orders in Russian and German. It was a good thing that not every bullet found its mark. Ducking across the street and past the bodies of several Russians, including the two I had killed, I saw the ghostly snow desert between us and Terpilovo lit up spasmodically by flares. I walked off the road and tested the depth of the snow. I sank into it above the knees. But if my column of walking wounded followed in single file, only the first three or four men would be really troubled by the deep snow.

The battle behind the dressing station was over. The few Russians who had not been shot down had pulled out. We had only one casualty—one of the men behind the wood piles had been killed by a bullet through the chest. Heinrich grinned cheerfully at the success of his little platoon. He was later decorated with the Iron Cross 2nd Class for the part he played.

Tulpin and Hans were to evacuate the seriously wounded in the two panje wagons to *Stabsarzt* Lierow when they were sure that the mile of road was clear of the enemy. Baumeister and Heinrich were to take charge of the dressing station in the meantime and treat any new casualties. With about 20 wounded who were prepared to risk the march through the trackless snowfields to Terpilovo I started. I went first, Natasha walked behind me. Slowly and silently, the column wound its way through the deep snow. We all carried weapons, except Natasha, for we were not certain that the country between us and Terpilovo was free of Russians. Some of the men, I knew, would barely be able to keep going until we reached the Medical Company, so I prayed that we would meet no resistance.

From half a mile away the fighting at Schitinkovo looked like a scene from a film. It was unreal to watch the drama being played out. Two houses in the village were burning fiercely and a faint shimmer of light in the east foretold the coming dawn. Judging by the flares that shot up from the village, our counterattack was making good progress and I estimated that not more than 50 yards now separated Kageneck from Becker's beleaguered group.

Half an hour later we reached the hard-packed ice of the road between Schitinkovo and Terpilovo and met two horse-drawn sledges on their way from the Medical Company to fetch the wounded from the badly mauled group led by *Leutnant* Scheel. I would dearly have liked to commandeer these two sledges for some of the worst cases in my party, but Scheel's men were probably in more urgent need of them. Some of my wounded men were now near the point of collapse, but it was touching to see how they helped each other on; men with sound legs helped to take the weight of others who were barely able to walk. One man was suffering dreadful pain at every step, in spite of morphia injections I had given him. His upper thigh muscles were in tatters, so I ordered Natasha to help me to support him. It was a slow and agonizing procession that hobbled along the icy road into Terpilovo. Just as we were nearing the village, I looked back again at Schitinkovo and it appeared that there was now fighting only at the east end of the village. Kageneck and Becker must have joined forces. The artillery had switched its fire to the edge of the wood, so that evidently the Russians were being cleared out of the village back the way they had come.

We staggered into the wounded assembly area and I accommodated all the wounded in a warm room, from which they would soon be on their way back by ambulance. The wounded men dropped on to the straw, and most of them now that the tension was over fell into a deep sleep of exhaustion.

"And what am I to do with you now?" I asked Natasha, who still stood by my side.

"I don't know," she answered, with a smile that I would have thought rather charming in other circumstances.

We walked out into the street. In the east dawn was breaking.

"Do the Russians treat German spies as well as we have treated you?" I asked her curiously.

"I've told you. I am fleeing from the Bolsheviks," she replied. "Why don't you believe me?" She turned her face up toward me and came a step closer.

I took her by the shoulders and held her at arms' length. Looking into her eyes, I said: "I'm glad, my girl, that it's not my job to pass judgment on you. But take a little advice. Go back—far behind the lines—and keep away from the front for your own good. But if you should return to the Bolsheviks, then you can tell them if you like—and if you have the courage—how well we have treated you."

Natasha remained silent.

"Now get moving, Natasha, and don't forget what the *Oberleutnant* told you."

She walked down the road toward the Volga and I forgot her in the urgency of organizing a second dressing station to accommodate all the wounded who would be arriving from Scheel's group.

Four days later, Natasha was caught with a group of Russian soldiers and under the eyes of the captured Reds proudly admitted that she was a spy. She was hanged from a tree.

The din of battle had died away and the somber, gray light of dawn spread across the snow as I tramped slowly and alone back toward Schitinkovo. A pall of smoke still hung over the village as I approached it and the melancholy picture of utter hopelessness weighed my spirits down to zero. In the distance, a lone sledge, drawn by a horse and with one man accompanying it, came along the road from Schitinkovo toward me. The sledge was carrying a wounded man. As the man and his sledge were about to pass me I stopped him. I recognized him as a horse attendant from Regiment 37.

"How are things at Schitinkovo?" I asked him.

"There are no more Russians. Everything is in order."

"And where are you coming from?"

"*Stabsarzt* Lierow sent me to transport this wounded man straight to the Medical Company."

"So *Stabsarzt* Lierow is in Schitinkovo to help?"

"*Jawohl*, Herr *Assistenzarzt*. He took an ambulance sledge to give a hand there."

"And who is your wounded man?" I asked.

"I don't know. He isn't from our regiment."

I bent down to the sledge and drew back slightly the woolen blanket, which was pulled over the man's head.

And looked down into the face of Kageneck.

*   *   *

"Franz!" I called out, shocked. "Franz!" I said, louder and more urgently. But his breathing was heavy and labored and he could no longer hear my voice.

I knelt by the sledge and examined the dressing on his head. He had another head wound. The bullet had struck him on the left temple and had come out of the right temple; it was a clean shot through the head. And it dawned on me, painfully and terribly, that the white bandage I had wrapped around his head had provided an excellent target for some Russian in the hand-to-hand fighting that had followed his first wound. My bandage had killed him. I examined the wound carefully, and my hopes faded. Kageneck was mortally wounded. Yet still I clung to a faint hope that a miracle might happen.

"We must take him to the Medical Company quickly," I said desperately to the soldier, "very quickly, but carefully . . . jolting is not good for him."

My hand was shaking uncontrollably as I replaced the blanket over Kageneck's head. My senses were incapable of fully comprehending what had happened. I was hoping like a child, deceiving myself, when it was obvious that nothing more could be done for my friend.

Again I repeated: "We must get him to the Medical Company quickly."

"Yes, Herr *Assistenzarzt*, that's where I was taking him," the soldier said, staring at me curiously. "Since when do doctors act as sledge drivers?" was his unspoken but obvious question.

"Then let's hurry!"

The soldier smiled, and said: "But I can take him on my own, Herr *Assistenzarzt*."

"Don't argue. Come on," I said and grabbed the horse's halter. We went rapidly, bypassing Terpilovo, where there was no doctor, heading for Schulze's station somewhere on the other side of the Volga. I spoke not a single word to the soldier as we went, but all sorts of fanciful notions of how Kageneck might be saved were dancing through my head—brain operations, specialists, a special plane from Staritsa.

We came to the Volga and carefully I steadied the sledge as we slipped down the steep banks. We crossed the river and panted up the bank on the other side. And suddenly I realized how hopeless it all was. I took a casualty card and wrote a few lines for *Oberstabsarzt* Schulze, asking him to do his very best for my best friend. It was irrational, I realized as I was doing it, for Schulze would do his best in any case, and he had also known Kageneck. But I tied the card on to Kageneck's top tunic button and stood there for a moment looking down at him for the last time. His breathing was deep and steady, yet for him, Russia, the 3rd Battalion and his comrades were gone forever.

The horse moved off and there, on the Volga, I remained for a while gazing at the sledge as it disappeared into the distance before I turned and slowly trudged back to Schitinkovo.

Little of that return journey stayed in my mind. Vaguely, I saw people, yet they did not interest me. Someone told me that Petermann had fallen, yet it made only a fleeting impression. If anyone had told me that the whole lot of us, down to the last man, would soon be killed it would have left me completely indifferent.

Many dead Russians and Germans were lying scattered all over the icy street, next to houses, bodies were hanging out of windows, and lying, half-covered with snow, in the fields, but there was only one among them I really noticed—Bruno. He was lying on his back, staring upward with glassy eyes. He had fallen by Kageneck's side, when the bulk of the fighting was over and the Russians were being driven out of the village. Half an hour after Kageneck had fallen, the village was in our hands again.[208]

In a daze, I visited my dressing station and found that all the casualties had been evacuated. Lierow was there. He had kept his word and given all the help he could.

"What is the matter with you?" he asked me. "Are you ill?"

"No, not ill, Herr *Stabsarzt*, only a little tired. This butchering has been a little too much and has got on my nerves."

"Yes, a lot has happened since I paid you that visit a couple of days ago."

"Yes, that was once upon a time, Herr *Stabsarzt*."

Lammerding had taken over command of the battalion. I found him with Becker at the battle post. They were full of energy in spite of the terrific strain they had just been through and were busy trying in the light of our casualties to reorganize our defenses for the next attack. Our battalion strength was now four officers, 31 NCOs and 106 men— a total of 141 men left of our original 800.

In the main battle for Schitinkovo the 3rd Battalion, together with the units from Regiment 37 and *Leutnant* Scheel's detachment, had lost 52 killed and 40 wounded. But the Russians left 300 dead in the village and woods—probably more, but with our shrunken force we had been unable to penetrate deeply into the woods for fear of ambush. At least a further 200 wounded had been taken back by the Reds and we had taken 28 prisoners, including a Russian officer. The character of the fighting had changed; prisoners were a rarity now.[209]

Lammerding and Becker were eager to hear if there was news of Kageneck. I did not tell them of my meeting with him on the road to Terpilovo and of my certain knowledge that he would never regain consciousness—they had enough gloomy things to think over. But I promised to visit the Medical Company to find out what had happened to him, and at the same time to find out the condition of Boehmer, who was not seriously wounded.

Our soldiers were busy piling the dead into heaps and preparing for the next attack by the Reds as I set off again along the road to Terpilovo. This time the road seemed longer; my limbs were lead-heavy and I found it difficult to keep going. Long and continual exposure to the cold had caused my body to lose too much heat; my *Kopfschützer*, pulled high over my head, was frozen stiff; and as I wearily dragged myself along the road I realized it was urgently necessary for me to warm myself before carrying on to the Medical Company.

A great silence lay over the countryside and the gray three-quarter light of the new day provided a somber background to my thoughts. The last two days had wrought a deep change in my outlook. Until Schitinkovo, the hardship and cruelty of war had been tempered for me by the close comradeship I had found in the battalion. Hardships had been eased by sharing them with my friends; the cruelty had been softened in association with men like Kageneck and Stolze who were naturally kindly. Now they and so many others whom I had come to regard as my friends were gone; the gaps could not be filled. I resolved never again to permit myself such close emotional relationships while this war lasted. It was a self-protective measure.

A medical *Unteroffizier*, who happened to be in Terpilovo with an ambulance, told me that Kageneck was no longer at the Medical Company—he had been sent straight back to Staritsa. My walk had been in vain. I went into a house in search of warmth. A few soldiers whom I did not know were there and made room for me near the oven. I sat down, but in a few moments slumped over into a heap, sound asleep. The soldiers covered me with a blanket.

It must have been about noon when an *Unteroffizier* shook me. "What's happening?" I asked him, with a start.

"Terpilovo is being evacuated, Herr *Assistenzarzt.*"

"What! Are you mad? Terpilovo being evacuated?"

"It has already been evacuated, Herr *Assistenzarzt.* We are the last."

"How long have I been asleep?"

"About three hours, sir. The evacuation was ordered an hour and a half ago. We are all on the way back." The *Unteroffizier* grinned and left the room.

It took me some minutes before I could gather my senses. I realized I was nicely warm, had regained my strength from the three hours' sleep and was ravenously hungry. I strode along the village street, trying to find a field kitchen. But there was nothing. Terpilovo was empty. Regimental H.Q. was about a mile and a half away to the northeast; it would be best for me to pay *Oberst* Becker a visit to find out what was happening to the 3rd Battalion.

Becker was talking to von Kalkreuth when I entered the regimental battle post. He sympathized with me for the loss of Kageneck, but his composure irritated me; it was obvious that to Becker, Kageneck had been only one of the several capable officers in Regiment 18 whom the fate of war had overtaken. Von Kalkreuth was more genuinely concerned, however; he had been a close friend of Kageneck. "Don't you think he might possibly survive his head wound?" he asked me straight away.

"No, Herr *Oberleutnant,*" I replied, "as far as I can see there is no hope."

"Now, listen to me for a moment," *Oberst* Becker interrupted, "during the last war I felt very much as you do, *Haltepunkt.* But a soldier must learn that Death is always by his side. And if we don't want Death to have complete power over us we must take it for granted that he may strike at any moment—either at us or our comrades. And we must take it as a matter of course. It's up to every soldier to develop that attitude, or he's not worth calling a soldier," he ended roughly.

I resented his cold-blooded approach, but later on had to acknowledge that this leathery veteran had been right.

Becker confirmed that the general order to withdraw had been received. Hitler had given his gracious permission for the impossible and imaginary Staritsa Line to be evacuated and had ordered that we fall back on the *Königsberg* Line at the approaches to Rzhev. Although the new *Königsberg* Line had not yet been systematically built up and prepared, it had been selected by experienced front-line commanders—Boeselager had been one of them—in accordance with tactical and strategical demands. It would, at least, be defensible.

There was little point in returning to Schitinkovo, which I felt I never wanted to see again, so I watched for the remnants of the battalion and rejoined them when they came marching along the road to Terpilovo that evening. In the meantime, I had a meal.

It was ironical that we had fought ourselves to death to defend Schitinkovo, as if Germany's fate depended on it, yet we evacuated it without any pressure from the enemy.[210] There seemed less point than ever now in the loss of Stolze, Kageneck and all the other brave men of the battalion.

By nightfall we had crossed the Volga and had set our faces toward Staritsa, some 10 miles to the southwest. A further 30 miles beyond Staritsa lay the *Königsberg* Line, which was to become indelibly engraved on the memories of the few of us who managed to survive the two bitter winters and the parched summer we were to spend there.

Again, throughout Germany a special broadcast was made, paying tribute to the courage of the German soldier during the fighting retreat from Kalinin. Much of the broadcast was devoted to the 3rd Battalion's rearguard fight and the culminating battle at Schitinkovo. And again we did not hear the program.[211]

CHAPTER 23

Scorched Earth and Panic

THE RETREATING ARMY MARCHED AGAINST A BACKDROP OF FLAME. SPECIAL "SCORCHED-earth commandos" were organized to carry out Hitler's adaptation of Stalin's earlier policy. But our men carried it out more thoroughly than ever the Russians had done.[212] The night shone red as buildings, whole villages, broken-down vehicles, everything of any conceivable value to the enemy, went up in flames. Nothing was to be left to the Red Army—and nothing was left. We marched with the flames licking our footsteps, marched day and night, with only short halts, for we well knew that we were the rearguard of the army that had fallen back from Kalinin; there were no troops between us and the pursuing Russians.

On the evening of 29 December we had crossed the Volga at Terpilovo; we marched the whole of that night, right through the next day and the next night, with the Russians on our heels. But if our spur was the enemy, the whip that flayed us as we marched was the unholy cold. Like mummies we padded along, only our eyes visible, but the cold relentlessly crept into our bodies, our blood, our brains. Even the sun seemed to radiate a steely cold and at night the blood-red skies above the burning villages merely hinted a mockery of warmth.

For long periods at a stretch each man was conscious only of the man who walked in front of him as the shrunken gray column marched ceaselessly toward Staritsa.

And silently with our column went the sledge carrying Stolze's body. The 10th Company men had captured a horse from the Reds for the sole purpose of pulling the sledge. But on the afternoon of 30 December a flight of six Heinkel 111s[213] flew over us from the south, turned, and came at us in a shallow dive. We threw ourselves off the road, into snowdrifts or into the ditch. Some men stood up and shouted, "We're Germans!" others swore as they dived for cover. But the Heinkels came in and dropped their bombs. In our winter clothing and in our rearguard position, the airmen's mistake was understandable.[214] The bombs exploded, throwing up showers of snow and frozen earth, but nobody was hit. But a near-miss had killed the horse and shattered the sledge carrying Stolze's body. The half-smile was still on the big fellow's face when the 10th Company men went to retrieve the corpse, which was as stiff as a gun barrel and unharmed. With shovels, Stolze's men set to work to enlarge a bomb crater which would act as a grave for their dead leader, for there was no other sledge they could commandeer.

Then the Heinkels regrouped and came in for another attack. The six men in the burial party threw themselves into the grave on top of Stolze. Another cluster of bomb craters appeared in the snow and the Heinkels set course southward. From fragments of the smashed sledge the men fashioned a cross for Stolze's grave and the gallant warrior was left to his rest beside the road of retreat from Moscow.

Dawn had not long broken behind us when a lorry came upon us from the rear. We split our column and walked by the sides of the road to let it through, hardly turning around because of the blizzard that was sweeping out of the east across the flat countryside. A quarter of a mile farther on, the lorry stopped and half a dozen men jumped out of it and raced across the fields to the shelter of a small wood. They were Russians.

We were not in the least interested in giving chase to the Reds, but the lorry represented a journey to Staritsa in comfort for the more exhausted men. We quickened our steps and gathered around it. But it would not start. One of the Russians, before he ran into the woods, had immobilized it. We had to leave it for we had no time to waste; it was now obvious that the Reds must be hard on our heels. It gave our men great pleasure to lob a few hand grenades into the truck and we left it satisfactorily ablaze.

Shortly before sundown on 31 December we reached Staritsa. Parts of the old city were in flames, a sign that our "scorched-earth squads" were already at work and that the city was in the process of being evacuated.

Staritsa wore a different look from the day that Kageneck and I had wandered around it. All the army formations that had been quartered there, the *Luftwaffe* squadrons, army staff and the multitude of rear-line units had already left the city.

But *Oberstabsarzt* Schulze and his Medical Company were still there: I found them in the old casualty assembly area near the Volga. Schulze was a desperate man when I arrived. Without warning, more than 500 wounded and sick had been dumped on his small unit as the rear-line units pulled out—and Schulze already had 500 of his own men on his hands. He was bitterly cursing the units which had abandoned their wounded without making any effort to evacuate them when they had time to spare. But to cap their cowardice they had ordered Schulze—if he could not manage to evacuate their wounded from Staritsa—to surrender them in terms of the Geneva Convention to the Russians when they walked into the city. Two medical officers, Schulze had been told, would stay behind with the wounded to hand them over to the Red Army.

It was an insane order. The Geneva Convention meant nothing and we had proof from Kalinin of the Russians' attitude to German hospital cases—and the doctors in whose care they were left!

"How can I order any doctor to stay behind, knowing he and his wounded will be butchered?" demanded Schulze. "Either we must evacuate, by God knows what means, all these wounded, or I must remain behind myself to wait for the Russians."

"How much time do you think we have left, Herr *Oberstabsarzt*?" I asked.

"Not long. The Russians are nearly here. But I have begged *Oberst* Becker to stay in the city as long as possible and try to delay the Russians. Most of the other units have already fled," he added bitterly.

Becker had reacted immediately to Schulze's request. Although he had at his command only a ghost of a regiment, together with a few odd remnants, he immediately deployed his men to guard the approaches to Staritsa. He sent our battalion to occupy positions two miles north of the city, to cover the withdrawal of the German left flank, which had been left exposed. I arranged with Lammerding to join him later as Schulze was desperately in need of help.

By the light of the blazing buildings of Staritsa, we commandeered every vehicle that could be found in the doomed city. When some of the few remaining units refused to hand over their vehicles, we took them at pistol-point. Panic was abroad that night as these rear units felt the breath of the Red Army on their backs for the first time and took to flight. Every lorry, sledge, even artillery and infantry gun carriages, were packed with wounded. Cases that we would normally have been afraid to touch were quite prepared to allow themselves to be wrapped in blankets and placed on jolting artillery limber wagons. Wounded with broken bones sat on panje wagons or rode on the backs of the unsaddled draft horses. We shot morphia into the worst of the cases, improvised seats and stretchers, but the wounded men were only too happy to take their chance—anything to avoid falling into the hands of the Reds. By eleven o'clock that night only 200 light casualties still remained at the casualty assembly area; all the others were on their way to Rzhev. The 200 who were left could, if the Russians made a surprise attack, be taken along with us and if necessary many of them could be made to march. Not a single man need be abandoned to the Russians.

Meanwhile *Oberst* Becker's calmness had put a stop to the panic in the city and the remaining rear-line units carried on with the evacuation of Staritsa secure in the knowledge that a thin line of German troops stood between them and the advancing Russians. Had they known how thin was the line their panic would probably have returned ten-fold.

It was confirmed that Kageneck had died at Staritsa of his wounds. I walked to the makeshift military cemetery near the Volga and found his undecorated grave—a grave in the middle of many more.[215] In front of me lay the frozen Volga, which I had crossed so lightheartedly with him only a month previously. At that time, Staritsa had been an adventure for us, but now the city was in flames and the old churches stood dumb and majestic among them. This was to be Kageneck's resting place—far away from his Princess of Baveria and the twin sons he had never seen. I said a brief farewell and went off to rejoin Lammerding and the battalion.

Lammerding had a surprise for me when at 15 minutes to midnight I arrived at the little log house, which he had made our battle post. He reached into his valise. "Believe it or not," he said, "I've been lugging this thing about with me ever since we left Littry." And he flourished a bottle of champagne.

"Now that only three of us are left it will go around nicely to toast the New Year," he added.

Becker walked in at five minutes to midnight and Lammerding popped the cork. "Sorry I couldn't keep the bottle on ice," he said, with a grin.

We drank a toast to 1942 and said nothing.[216] Our efforts to be festive were not very successful. We were sadly mindful of the missing faces and 1942 did not strike us as having entered on a particularly well-omened note.

*　*　*

"Alarm!" awoke us. It was 5 a.m. and as usual the shout hit me right in the guts. But this time we were lucky; the Reds rubbed only the fringe of our sector, and the attack petered out in the snow.

By nine o'clock that morning our formation had completed the evacuation of the old city on the Volga and the Russians marched in, hard on its heels. It was time for us to be leaving.

But no orders came for us to disengage that morning and by the afternoon Divisional Headquarters still remained silent. To make it worse, we did not even know where they or Regimental H.Q. were located. And the road along which we had intended to withdraw had been in Russian hands since 11 a.m. The neighboring regiment, belonging to the 26th (Cologne) Infantry Division had already informed us that they would be disengaging themselves that afternoon and would march toward Rzhev.

Little Becker managed to get through to Hirsch, the officer commanding the division's bicycle-assault unit, but he knew no more than we did. It was a critical position.

"What are you going to do?" I asked Lammerding.

"Nothing," he replied tersely. "Just wait. And leave it to Hirsch to get us out of this bloody hole."

Our radio section kept sending signals, but no reply came. Both Lammerding and I were depressed and nervous, so I decided to visit my medical unit. Tulpin, Heinrich and our dentist were in good spirits; they did not even guess how dangerous was the situation. To them it had improved for in three days we had had no casualties and no frostbite cases, in spite of the inhuman cold. Our winter clothing now seemed to be adequate and the terrific strain and hard marching of the last few days had had a narcotic effect—it had produced a lethargy which drove away the wish to think too deeply. This false optimism was as bad as Lammerding's gloom; both played on my tautly strung nerves. There was nothing I could do but wait, yet I could not wait in idleness. I had to do something.

Then I spotted a horse—a big German draft horse—standing in the snow. It had a gaping wound in the foreleg and the wound was frostbitten. Suddenly it occurred to me that we should probably be spending the winter in the *Königsberg* Line and that meat would become scarce. Nature had provided an excellent deep-freezer; it would be a good idea for the medical unit to have its own reserves of horse meat. The horse was doomed in any case. I would butcher it.[217] Then, at the same time, we would have our meat supplies and I would kill by action that cold fear in my stomach. Heinrich was a farmer, I was a surgeon; our combined talents should enable us to slaughter and cut up the horse in professional style.

But Heinrich was dubious and pointed out that once we had killed the horse it would freeze up immediately and be impossible to cut up.

"Then we'll take it inside and kill it," I replied.

The horse was reluctant to cooperate; the last place he wanted to enter was a warm Russian living room. But we dragged and pushed him in and firmly closed the doors on the three of us. In the small room the horse seemed to be twice its usual size—a veritable horse of Troy. And our courage seeped away as the horse made determined efforts to find an exit. Then, too, the enormity of what we were about to do hit us; it was all right for the veterinary officers, even the cooks, to butcher a horse, but Heinrich and I . . .

"Herr *Assistenzarzt*, shall—" started Heinrich.

"No! Stand firm, Heinrich. We must go through with this."

I took my knife in my left hand, pistol in my right, and taking careful aim, fired a bullet into the side of the horse's head. As it crashed to the floor, the powerful hoofs of this mammoth animal, which seemed to fill the room, shattered the table and bench.

Heinrich jumped on to the oven to avoid the horse's death struggle and I cowered into a corner for a minute before I screwed up courage enough to cut its throat. A great stream of blood started to pool the floor. I felt as if I had committed bloody murder.

Heinrich suggested we should take only the hindquarters, which weighed about 200 lbs. each. I overcame my squeamishness by reminding myself that to have or not to have 400 lbs. of meat can be a matter of great importance.

We skinned the rear end of the horse and severed the quarters. With a pole through the sinews we carried each quarter to one of the panje wagons outside and Nature's freezer started to work.

Orders to withdraw came through at 6 p.m., by which time the Russians had already started to place us under mortar fire. Schnittger and 20 men were detailed to act as a rearguard and it was with deep relief that we eventually reached the road along which the units of the 26th Infantry Division had retreated.

Every now and then we passed German vehicles, many blown up or burnt out. But some were still intact and loaded with supplies, although they had been immobilized. We helped ourselves to anything which would be of use to us, but it was obvious that these vehicles had been abandoned under enemy fire and we now had to reckon with the possibility of having to fight our way through to the *Königsberg* Line.

We marched as quickly as we could, but our column was spreading out more and more as the weaker men lagged behind. We stopped once or twice to close the ranks and I repeatedly warned Lammerding at the head of the column to reduce his pace. The thermometer stood at minus 45 degrees and every time we inhaled the frozen air our bodies lost heat and the cold seemed to penetrate the marrow of our bones until walking became a stiff and awkward business. Few of us were really aware of what was happening.

Because of the long detour we had been forced to make, the march from Staritsa to the *Königsberg* Line was nearly 30 miles. It was a desperate struggle for exhausted and frozen troops. Twice Lammerding fell down without knowing why. Each time he picked himself up with a laugh and shook his head with a puzzled expression.

"Must be drunk," he muttered the second time.

"It's the cold," I told him, forcing the words through my *Kopfschützer.* "Your sense of balance is partly numbed by the cold."

"Balls!" replied Lammerding.

"Look, for God's sake don't try and run all the way to the *Königsberg* Line," I implored him, "otherwise we shall arrive there minus our men; they're dropping farther and farther behind at the rear."

Lammerding and I let the column pass by us. At the tail end it was a sad picture. The men who were most weakened had gathered there and were trying to grope onward behind their comrades. I ordered the weakest to ride in turns on the panje wagons for a while. And interminably the night dragged through. Soldiers lay down in the snow and flatly refused to move; the Lorelei of the snow-wastes were singing to them. We slapped their faces, hauled them to their feet, kicked them as they lay on the ground, cursed them—anything to get them on the move again. When everything else failed we wrapped the hopelessly exhausted men in blankets and placed them on the panje wagons.

But the long night came to an end and at dawn we passed eight Russian soldiers, lying frozen stiff on the road. It must have been a Russian patrol that had been shot down by the men of the 26th Infantry Division. After 12 hours on the march, during which we had covered nearly 25 miles, we reached Panino. According to the map, we were now only four miles from our sector of the *Königsberg* Line.

A hundred serious casualties lay groaning on Panino railway station. They were lying on straw in the waiting room, inadequately covered with blankets. A train standing by the platform held several hundred more wounded men. It was the last train to leave for the south. Schnittger closed up and warned us that the Russians were on our heels, and the remaining casualties were hurried into the train. It steamed off, our battalion resumed the march and half an hour later the Russians marched into the station.

Von Boeselager met us two miles along the road and gave Lammerding instructions regarding the sector of the line at Gridino that the remnants of the 3rd Battalion were to defend. While Lammerding and the rest of the battalion carried on for the remaining two and a half miles to Gridino, Heinrich and I stayed behind at von Boeselager's battle post. With typical thoroughness he had built up the place into a fortress.

He looked at me with his steely blue eyes, noted that I was at the point of complete exhaustion and said: "Now sit down, Doktor—and you, Heinrich—and I'll give you some hot bouillon."

Heinrich got up to serve the soup, but von Boeselager pushed him down, saying: "I'll play the kitchen boy this time."

While we warmed ourselves at the fire and drank the scalding soup, von Boeselager told us what to expect from the *Königsberg* Line.[218]

"It's not the best of defensive lines," he said, "but at least it's been selected by tacticians and something can be made out of it."

"How long do you think we shall stay here?" I asked him.

"A long time, I hope. We can't withdraw any farther without making things worse. We're now at the stage where we must halt the Reds or perish. Every man who still has two legs has been sent to a fighting group. This is the line we have got to hold," von Boeselager concluded with deadly seriousness.

"Well, thank God the marching's over. Our men would rather fight 50 Russians each than march another 50 yards. But from what you've told me, Herr *Rittmeister*, I don't know whether the situation is serious or hopeful."

"We'll damn soon know," von Boeselager replied.[219]

CHAPTER 24

A Veteran's Tears

Von Boeselager was right. We damn soon knew. But first the Russians allowed us a day's peace at Gridino,[220] and we found *Oberleutnant* Boehmer and *Leutnant* Kiso waiting to rejoin the battalion. Boehmer had recovered from the light wounds he had received at Schitinkovo, and Kiso from the wounds which had put him out of action during the fall.

Boehmer as the senior officer now took command of the battalion, Lammerding reverted to adjutant, Becker took over the 12th Heavy Machine-Gun Company, *Leutnant* Ohlig 11th Company and Kiso was given the remains of 10th Company. Our battalion strength was now six officers and 137 NCOs and men.

In spite of the urgency of completing defensive preparations, the entire battalion was given six hours' rest period—a small enough concession, which seemed like six unreal, stolen hours. For the first time in 18 days our men were able to lie down to sleep, instead of stealing a few minutes' cat-nap between Red attacks and patrol duties. It was only then that I realized that a human being can stand far more exposure and strain than an animal; at critical moments he can muster his willpower and is able to conserve much energy by intelligent thinking.

The men awoke refreshed and with their fighting morale restored. It cheered us to see that Gridino would be easier to defend than Schitinkovo. Here the woods were nearly half a mile away from the village, the only unfavorable feature from a defensive point of view being a depression, covered with undergrowth and bushes, which led to a large Kolchoze barn near the village. The dressing station, as usual, was established next door to the battalion battle post and had its stable-end facing the direction from which the enemy would attack. In view of Heinrich's success at Schitinkovo, I left him to organize the rear defense of the dressing station from the stables which formed the back part of the house. Tulpin prepared the operating room.

We had roughly one mile of front to defend and the village was open to attack from three directions. The battalion had neither anti-tank guns nor infantry guns, but we had been promised detachments of artillery for the following day. It seemed we should have to hold them off until then by close fighting; 143 men to defend a mile-long line against attack from three directions!

The night passed peacefully. But at 5 a.m. the alarm was given.[221] Unseen, a platoon of about 25 Reds crept through the bushes on the heels of our withdrawing listening patrols and surrounded some of the houses. Boehmer and Becker counterattacked, the Russians threw more men into the fight, but after bitter hand-to-hand fighting the houses were recaptured and the Russians withdrew to the Kolchoze barn. Further counterattacks were launched, then the artillery came on the scene and the Russians were sent running. They left behind 65 dead; eight prisoners were taken, and two machine-guns and four mortars were captured.

Scarcely had the battalion re-formed and replenished ammunition than the Russians attacked again from the north. But the short pause had been long enough for most of our machine-guns to freeze up in the bitter cold. They were hastily thawed out in the ovens. One or two squads poured petrol over their guns and set fire to it. It heated the metal sufficiently for them to bring the guns into action again. The second attack was beaten back and this time 30 Russian corpses lay in front of our guns.

Boehmer knew that the next attack would come with nightfall. A few houses and barns were burnt down in order to shorten our defensive line, ammunition was prepared as machine-guns thawed out again.

Half an hour after darkness set in at 4 p.m., the first Russian machine-gun bursts swept the village, and cheering and shouting madly, the Russians attacked. Flares showed that there must have been 400 of them. German mortars and automatic weapons fired into the dense mass and the first wave of the enemy lay in the snow. The Russian attack wheeled to the extreme northern end of the village, where Kiso had prepared the first house as a defensive strong point. With repeated suicide attacks, the Russians tried to overrun the house. But even though Kiso and two of his machine-gun detachment were wounded and four of his men killed, they failed to break through into the village.

A further attack by about 100 Russians succeeded in taking several houses and in the counterattacks to dislodge them, first *Leutnant* Ohlig was killed by a burst of automatic fire from close range and then Lammerding fell, seriously wounded.

Reinforcements from Regiment 37 arrived to plug the gaps and after hours of fierce close-quarter fighting the enemy withdrew, leaving about 40 Reds surrounded in a group of houses. By 11 p.m. we were able to turn our attention to these Russian-occupied houses, which were burned down around the enemy's ears.

The Russians left about 150 dead in front of Gridino. The 3rd Battalion lost one officer and 11 men killed and two officers and 22 NCOs and men wounded; eight soldiers were also in the sick bay, so weakened by exposure, dysentery and strain that they were totally unfit for any further fighting. The dressing station was the all too familiar scene—crowded with helpless men lying on straw beds, groaning with pain, filthy, and smeared in blood. The atmosphere was a blend of stinking human bodies—for few of the men had removed a single garment during the past month—antiseptic and smoke from the oil lamps.

Breathing heavily, Lammerding moved restlessly on his bed of straw. His left arm hung useless at his side—a bullet from a Russian rifle had entered between his shoulder and neck, had severed several nerves in the arm and had pierced the left upper lung.

"I can't send you back until the bleeding in your lungs has stopped," I told him. "You need rest, so I'm going to give you an injection of S.E.E., which will take away the pain and allow you to sleep."

"A very elegant suggestion," he said, with a ghost of his usual ironical smile. "It's a pity I can't oblige you, Doktor, but with the best will in the world I can't sleep."

"I'll help you," I replied and gave an intravenous injection.

Thirty seconds later, Lammerding said in wonderment: "Queer! I have no more pain. What's happened? That's wonderful stuff you pumped into me." He paused for a few moments to make a further note of his reactions and then went on: "Feels very much as though I've had a few little drinks—very superior little drinks, of course. I must say I feel most pleasantly drunk, Doktor," he whispered with mock seriousness. "Where have you been keeping that stuff all this time?"

"It's a combination of Scopolamin, Enkadol and Ephetonin," I told him, "and in medical terms, it's used to stupefy the psyche."

Lammerding closed his eyes as little Becker walked in to have a look at him.

"He'll get some sleep now," I told Becker. "It will give his lungs a chance to stop bleeding. But I don't like the look of that arm—I doubt if he'll ever have full use of it again."

"Don't whisper like a couple of schoolgirls," came from Lammerding unexpectedly. "I'm greatly interested to know how I'm getting on. At the moment I'm not quite responsible for my own opinions, Becker. You see, the doctor's stupefied my psyche. Isn't that right, Doktor? But he doesn't really know what he's talking about because I feel as healthy as a sow."

"It's good to find you so cheerful," Becker said. He turned to me: "How is it he's still got so much bounce?"

"It's the effect of this drug. He's feeling in an elated mood and has no earthly worries," I answered.

"You mean you've made me drunk, Doktor. But tell me, how's the stock market outside?"

"Nothing to worry about," Becker replied. "You'll get a good night's sleep. The Russkies won't be back tonight."

We walked into the street and paused beside the row of dead Germans. They were to be taken to the military cemetery at Malakovo. Ohlig lay in the middle of the line. He had been a reserved youngster, a little afraid of Lammerding's sarcasm, hero-worshipping Kageneck, overawed by Stolze's brute strength. Now he had joined the others—Kageneck, Stolze, Bolski, Stock, Jakobi, Dehorn, Petermann . . . the line of dead men seemed to stretch endlessly down the snowbound road, into the faint redness of the distance where the houses were still smoldering. All comrades, all men of the Rhineland or Westphalia, all men of the original 800 of the 3rd Battalion—800 now reduced by tonight's fighting to 99.[222]

Next morning a small column of wagons was organized to transport the wounded to Malakovo.[223] The big wagon drawn by the two draft horses, was to carry Lammerding, Kiso and four others. Lammerding was drowsily awake and barely responded to our farewell handshakes. We should miss his irony, his ready tongue and his utter imperturbability.

We watched the small column move across the snow toward Malakovo. Half a mile away lay a wood, through which the road passed, and when the slowly moving column had got halfway toward the wood, Russian rifle fire cracked out from a direction which had seemed quite safe. Fortunately the Reds were firing from extreme range, but bullets were whipping into the helpless column. Instantly, two of our machine-guns poured their fire into the wood which hid the unseen enemy. The draft horse pulling the near side of Lammerding's wagon fell in his tracks. The whole column was jammed behind the first wagon. Feverishly, the drivers worked to remove the dead horse from its harness and drag it off the road. I could clearly see my Siberian, Hans, making herculean efforts to drag the still kicking horse out of the way. Our machine-gun fire had its effect, for the Russians were now firing wildly and sporadically as they ducked for cover and the column of wounded safely gained the shelter of some trees.

I hoped desperately that Lammerding would survive the terrible journey back to Germany and the safety of a hospital bed. These days there were insufficient ambulance trains running to the west.[224] Our wounded were being packed into cattle cars without protection from the deadly cold and with inadequate numbers of medical personnel to attend to them as they jolted through the snow deserts of Russia. Large numbers of German wounded died a cruel death on these trains.

Very often they were on the road for three weeks and proper medical attention could be given only at the railway stations of the large towns. At every station, fresh dead were carried out and placed in rows on the snow-covered platforms. And many a man whose initial wound had not been overly serious died of frostbite or gangrene before he reached Germany.

*　　*　　*

A messenger from Divisional H.Q. passed the column of wounded on his way through the wood and reported that only one man had been injured—a slight graze only—by the Russian fire. But the messenger brought us even greater news.

The 3rd Battalion, Infantry Regiment 18, was to be relieved by 2nd Battalion, Infantry Regiment 37.[225]

At 9 a.m. the first files of our relieving troops emerged from the wood. We watched the marching men approach us with surprise—this battalion was a good deal stronger and more battleworthy than ours. It still had its original commanding officer, Major Klostermann, and more than half of its original officers. I did my part by handing over my dressing station to my opposite number, *Assistenzarzt* Schüssler. He was a good man and an experienced front-line doctor.

The 37th soon learned that Gridino was not a healthy place. Two of their men were shot down by Russian snipers during handing-over operations.

"A grand place to defend!" grunted Major Klostermann. "You must be going without any regrets." He covered our withdrawal along the road to the wood with several machine-guns and an infantry gun.

It was just as well he did, for the Russians tried to ambush us in exactly the same place as they had fired on the column of wounded. Only one man was hit, through the thigh, and he was thrown on to a vehicle as we bolted for the shelter of the wood. Klostermann's covering fire hammered into the Russian hiding place. Some of the men could hardly run and at frequent intervals we all had to throw ourselves into the snow to regain our breath. To a man the battalion was at the point of complete exhaustion. The rapid breathing in of cold air pained my chest and I had a taste of blood on my tongue. But at last we reached the wood and staggered along the road through the trees.

Utterly weary and dejected, we emerged from the wood to find the village of Malakovo lying in front of us, but we were past caring what it looked like. It was a little larger than Gridino and had two streets in the form of a right angle. Depth as well as length—more difficult to defend, my mind automatically registered.

Silently, the 3rd Battalion straggled past the 21cm howitzer emplacements at the outskirts of the village, a slouching, ragged band, icicles hanging from *Kopfschützer*, felt boots shuffling along the icy road. There was nothing soldierly in the marching of these poor devils, yet they were a band of heroes, who had unflinchingly fought the Russians with every ounce of energy in their bodies—fought them to a standstill. And as they straggled along, out of line, out of step, bodies bent under the load of weapons and ammunition, it seemed that the last half-mile of retreat from Moscow would surely beat them.

Then from somewhere at the front of the column came a whisper: "The commander!" It was passed back along the line of exhausted men, passed on from man to man—"The commander."

We looked up and saw the indomitable figure of *Oberst* Becker, standing at the door of his battle post. At his side was von Kalkreuth. They were waiting to greet our arrival.

There was a movement down the straggling column. Not a single word of command was given, but the men instinctively formed up into proper marching order. They took up the step. Rifles were placed on their shoulders at the correct angle. They lifted their heads and looked straight to the front.

Suddenly Schnittger's powerful voice started singing. Then every man joined in. And the old song of a soldier's dream rang out. The men sang it as if they were on their way back to barracks, at the end of a peacetime maneuver.

> *From the mountains flows a stream*
> *Of sparkling wine so cool. . . .*

And Becker removed the *Kopfschützer* which had covered his head like a visor, and standing to attention, with his hand at the salute, he acknowledged the defiant song. The men marched past and came to the end of the song:

> *Lucky is he who can forget*
> *The woe and sorrow he has met.*

A few hard-wrung tears ran down the old commander's weather-beaten face.

Boehmer's voice rang out: "Halt! Left turn!" and the remnants of the 3rd Battalion stood at attention in front of its commander. Boehmer saluted smartly and reported: "3rd Battalion I.R. 18, reports as ordered for further duty."[226]

Hell Is Gridino

EIGHT HOUSES WERE ENOUGH TO ACCOMMODATE THE SHRUNKEN 3RD BATTALION. THEY were all in a row along the street of Malakovo; to the right of us was a detachment of paratroopers, newly arrived from Crete.[227] They were to bolster our numbers and act as a counterthrust unit whenever the line became shaky.

Our new quarters at the south end of the village had been heated and prepared for us. In a matter of minutes the doors of the eight houses were tightly shut; every man in the battalion took off his boots, lay down and slept right through a whole night free of alarms.

The world looked an altogether different place when we awoke 12 hours later. We could look at it through clear eyes again. We washed ourselves and breakfasted at leisure for the first time in three weeks. The bread was unfrozen and soft, and although the coffee was the usual *Negerschweiss* ("nigger sweat"), we drank it with relish, reveling in the novelty of being able to savor every mouthful.

Becker was cutting himself a slice of *Kommis* bread when he was handed an order which transferred him to *Oberst* Becker's staff as Regimental *Ordonnanzoffizier*. Shortly afterward the alarm sounded and we gathered with the paratroopers at the schoolhouse. We were staggered at their equipment. They had complete winter clothing, were spruce, superbly fit and equipped with the latest weapons.[228] By comparison we were a bedraggled set of tramps, no two men wearing the same sort of clothing, most of the men with scraggy beards. But we were happy to see the paratroopers, because they were given the job of clearing a wood where the Russians had infiltrated through the defensive line held by Höke's 1st Battalion. They made a thorough job of it, and returned in the afternoon carrying their dead comrades.

We were to learn much more of the Red Army's new infiltration tactics. Because of the icy cold we could only hope to garrison the villages, which often lay two or three miles apart. In the areas between there was usually nothing but an occasional patrol post, and through these gaps the Russians ghosted under cover of night and then appeared behind our lines.

That evening—it was my birthday—I was *Oberst* Becker's guest,[229] and found little Becker in good spirits after his first day's work in the rear villages among the baggage and supply units. He had even found a beautiful Russian girl, a medical student from Moscow, called Nina Barbarovna. I remembered Natasha and grunted sourly. As I walked back to my quarters I could hear the noise of night fighting at Gridino and thanked God that we were out of it.

*   *   *

Next morning I prepared an underground shelter beneath the house I had chosen for my dressing station, and welcomed another new commander for the 3rd Battalion—*Hauptmann* Graminski from the 1st Battalion. He was an earnest, serious man, calm and meticulous in his work, a commander who immediately gained the respect of the men. We discussed the position and decided that although we were fortunate to be stationed three miles behind the main defensive line, when we were thrown into the battle it would be because the situation was dangerous, and we should catch all the savage fighting.

Our Intelligence had intercepted a Russian radio message and we gathered that the Reds were preparing for a major attack against Gridino, which was the northeastern pivot of the *Königsberg* Line and stuck out like a sore thumb. The din of battle carried to us in the afternoon and it seemed that the Russians were putting out a preliminary feeler before the big attack. But when I wrote to Martha I mentioned little of the fighting, for the people at home had not yet been conditioned to realize what a serious change had come over the situation on the eastern front.

Casualties from Gridino were evacuated through Malakovo and late in the afternoon I saw *Assistenzarzt* Schüssler lying on one of them. The cheerful young doctor who had relieved me at Gridino had a load of shrapnel lodged in his stomach and evidently strong internal hemorrhage. He was well aware that his life hung by a thread, but managed to smile his thanks when I told him that I would telephone the Medical Company and ensure that everything was ready for an emergency operation.

"I think it will be too late," he whispered. And he was right. He died that night, shortly after the operation.

Stabsarzt Lierow took over Schüssler's job in Gridino.

We had another quiet night, but in the morning it sounded as though hell was let loose at Gridino. Heinrich was sitting next to me, ready for action at a moment's notice, when at 10 a.m., the telephone rang and a dispatch was read out: "*Stabsarzt* Lierow killed by shrapnel in head and lungs. Infantry Regiment 37 without medical officer. *Assistenzarzt* Haape to report at Gridino without delay."

"Now we're in for it!" I remarked to Heinrich. "They no longer look upon our battalion as a complete unit and we have the honor of being pushed wherever a man's needed. Damnation! It makes me sick. Are we the only battalion in the division! Why the hell can't the bastards send someone else for a change—one of those doctors from a division that's sitting in front of a warm oven—and leave us in peace for a while?"

Five minutes later we had reported off at the battle post and were on the road to Gridino. I did not risk going by sledge—I remembered the ambushes along that road too clearly. As we walked along I swore like an old miner—not so much at the danger we were heading for as at the lack of consideration shown by Divisional Headquarters in parting us from our battalion. Rebelliously, I walked along the icy road and Heinrich trudged silently by my side.

We passed through the wood without incident but on the open road approaching Gridino the Russians started to pump at us with their mortars. They soon got our range, and although the shell bursts were deadened somewhat by the snow, we weren't too happy about things. Erratically, we ran toward Gridino, dashing forward for a short stretch and then throwing ourselves flat in the snow. The Reds seemed to be expending an inordinate amount of ammunition on two such unimportant targets, and I could only suppose that they were indulging in a bit of sport. Perhaps a bottle of vodka was at stake on the result of the game.

Suddenly, I felt a blow and a sharp stab of pain in my left leg. "They've hit me!" I shouted rather dramatically to Heinrich, who was close on my heels, and I jumped sideways into a slight hollow in the soft snow, hoping to find some protection. Heinrich crouched by my side as I examined myself quickly without removing any clothes. Judging by the marks on my felt boot, and the pain, it appeared that two splinters had hit me—one in the heel, the other in the left shin. I felt the blood running into my boot, but I was sure that no bones were damaged. The thought struck me—and I hugged it with considerable pleasure—that this injury might mean I could get home at last. But the Russian mortar crews were trying to blast that newborn hope now that they had sitting targets. Their shells were bursting uncomfortably close.

"Come on, Heinrich. Let's get out of here," I said.

Heinrich ran ahead; I limped after him. Every 20 yards or so we flung ourselves flat in the snow. And that is how we arrived at Gridino—it must have looked like a comic obstacle race. We reached the shelter of the first house in the village and sat down on the steps. For some reason I started to laugh, long and wildly. Of a sudden it seemed immensely funny that after a mere two days of comparative ease we had now been dumped right back in the muck-heap, and to cap it all, not even with our own comrades but with a strange unit, whose members did not interest me very much at the moment.

Heinrich looked at me with wide and questioning eyes: "Are you all right, Herr *Assistenzarzt?*" he asked.

"It's all right, Heinrich, I haven't gone off my head. But how can one regard all this misery seriously? It's planned by rational people and the funny part of it is we all do exactly as we're told even though we know it's lunacy. Isn't that funny?"

"No, Herr *Assistenzarzt*," Heinrich replied stolidly, not understanding a word.

"Look, Heinrich, it's so idiotic that one can only laugh or cry about it. One can't take it seriously. And I prefer to laugh."

We made for the battalion battle post and I limped in to report to Major Klostermann.

"That would be the last straw if you had to fall out," he said when I told him of my shrapnel wound. "The dressing station is already filled to overflowing with unattended wounded."

"In that case, there's no alternative but to have a look at them, Herr Major."

All the wounded had been transferred to the building I had used as a dressing station. Dr. Schüssler had preferred a larger house, but one which was not so safe from the Russian fire. He had paid the penalty, as had many of his wounded, when artillery shells had exploded outside the building, peppering himself and the wounded with shrapnel. Now the building was little but ashes. The Russians had set it on fire and *Stabsarzt* Lierow's body was evidently somewhere in the debris.

The old dressing station was jammed with groaning men. It was not a large room and more than 20 men lay on the floor, few of whom had received any medical attention.[230] One stretcher-bearer was trying to administer to the needs of them all. I knew that the wounded would have to wait until nightfall before they could be evacuated along the dangerous road to Malakovo.

"Where are the instruments and medical supplies?" I asked the stretcher-bearer.

"There are none, Herr *Assistenzarzt*. They were all destroyed when the other dressing station was burnt down."

So we were dependent on my doctor's bag, whatever was in Heinrich's old rucksack, and the small bandage rolls carried by every soldier. The wounded men set up a pitiful clamor for attention, but I had to base my decisions on realities and ignore those seriously wounded men for whom I could do little. Two stomach cases and a critical head wound were wrapped in blankets and placed on heaps of straw, the head wound with his head propped up and the two stomach cases with legs drawn up. One of the stomach cases would obviously be unable to stand the strain of being transported. The prognosis regarding the head wound could not at present be reliable, but he also looked bad, and it was really a question of whether he had the reserves of energy to withstand the shock. The second stomach case looked more encouraging; the internal bleeding did not seem to be so strong. Next to him lay four lung cases, who, like the head case, had to be kept absolutely quiet.

It would have served no useful purpose to give these critically wounded men more time. The men with tourniquets around a limb were more urgently in need of attention. Experience had shown that in this cold it was inadvisable to transport any wounded men with rubber tourniquets in position—it usually ended up with the limb being amputated at the place where it had been tied. There were five men with tourniquets on either arms or legs. As prescribed, the stretcher-bearer had loosened the tourniquets every hour or so for a few minutes, but every time this was done the wounded men had lost more blood, which they needed more than ever just then. Four of the men I was able to help by applying pressure dressings, which stopped the bleeding sufficiently for the tourniquets to be removed. But the fifth man had an evil-looking wound in the lower left leg—a gaping hole in which bits of bone, pulped flesh and clotted blood were mingled. The wound was so close to the knee that the stretcher-bearer had been forced to apply the tourniquet to the thigh. I sweated to apply a suitable pressure bandage, but the blood still gushed out when the tourniquet was loosened. The man would undoubtedly lose his whole leg if he had to wait until nightfall for transport to the Medical Company. I had to operate with whatever instruments I had in my bag.

The patient was lifted on to the long kitchen table, which I had moved close to the window. His head was pillowed by a rolled-up blanket and the smashed leg lay on sterile gauze on top of another blanket.

"Have you the gut in your rucksack?" I asked Heinrich.

"No, Herr *Assistenzarzt*. Neither gut nor anesthetics." It was not Heinrich's fault. He was not to know when we left Malakovo that the entire medical supplies of this battalion had been burnt.

"Never mind," I said. In my medical bag was some ordinary string, with which I tied the casualty cards to the wounded. I cut four pieces, each about a foot long, and threw them into a pot of water that was boiling on the fire, ready for coffee-making. It would sterilize them. I took my scalpel and surgical forceps and dipped them in iodine.

Heinrich looked at me in amazement. "No anesthetic, Herr *Assistenzarzt*?" he whispered.

"Not necessary in this case. The tourniquet has already completely anesthetized the lower leg. He won't feel a thing." I carefully examined the gaping wound. Both the tibia and the fibula had been shattered and the muscles, nerves and blood vessels were badly torn. Blood was gushing from the anterior tibial artery and I could now see that the posterior tibial artery was also punctured. There was no hope of saving the leg, but by operating now I could save the knee joint.

I iodized the region surrounding the ghastly wound and with my scalpel removed the entire lower part of the leg. I did not have to go through bone—that had already been done for me by the shrapnel. The patient gave a sharp cry of pain and bit his lip to keep back further cries. But the pain was not at the point of amputation; it was in the region of the tourniquet around the thigh. I left the amputated limb at the bottom of the table.

Now it was possible to work. I cut away all the torn ends of flesh and muscle and clamped the main arteries. Heinrich removed the tourniquet so that the blood could flow freely again. Only a few minor vessels continued to bleed. Heinrich handed me the string and forceps from the boiling water, I dipped them in the iodine bath, tied every vessel carefully and then stitched up the two main arteries. Heinrich removed the clamps as I worked. The bleeding stopped and once again I iodized the whole wound. The iodine stung the man—he was already regaining sensation at the point of amputation.

Systematically, I now attended to all the lighter cases: nose shot away, removal of splinters, bullet-hole through the hand, grazes, and so on. The stretcher-bearer called across that one of the lung cases had taken a serious turn.

The wounded man looked badly shocked and his breathing was heavy and labored. The respiratory sounds in the right lung had ceased; the beat was hollow and loud. It was another pneumothorax, similar to the one that I had treated at Height 215 on 2 October. This time, owing to the amount of air in the pleural cavity, the mediastinum and heart had been pushed over to the left and greatly burdened.

As luck would have it, I had a large needle in my bag. I sterilized it in the iodine and plunged it into the intercostal cartilage, through the pleura and into the lung cavity. Soon the pressure started to equalize. This time I had no rubber tube, so I attached a 20-c.c. syringe to the needle and by sucking out the air from the cavity with this, was able to reduce the pressure. I injected the man with a heart and circulation stimulant and he was out of danger for the present.

I returned to the other cases, gave injections of pain-killing drugs to those men who needed them, treated the lung cases and shocked patients with S.E.E., injected Cardiazol into the men with interrupted circulation and gave every wounded man in the room an anti-tetanus jab. By the time I had filled out and signed all the casualty cards, I had been busy for three and a half hours without a break. I walked over to the battle post and for the first time remembered my own leg wound. I decided to pursue that little subject with Klostermann that evening, and merely told him the number of ambulances I should require after nightfall and gave him a list of the medical supplies that were to be sent.

The man with the head wound was dead when I got back to the dressing station. I tried an intra-cardiac injection, but it was too late. As I had expected, the bad stomach case had also died. I had both their bodies carried outside into the snow to make more room on the floor. A light over-pressure had arisen in the right lung cavity of the pneumothorax case and I alleviated it in the same way as before. Then I pulled off my boot and examined my left leg.

My shin wound looked more serious than it really was, for it was bleeding strongly. The bone was lightly grazed but it was essentially only a superficial flesh wound. It was difficult to see the other wound, but a splinter had lodged in the Achilles tendon and the pain in my foot was becoming progressively more acute. For the time being I did nothing but give myself an anti-tetanus injection and allow Heinrich to dress and bandage my skin and ankle.

It is much easier to jab a needle into someone else's flesh than into one's own, but the large gallery of interested spectators spurred me to give a fine imitation of *sang-froid*.

*　　*　　*

That evening the front was comparatively quiet and I played *Doppelkopf* with Major Klostermann and two other officers. Concentration on the game was difficult, because I found my mind wandering to my leg wounds; I found it quite easy to think up more and more good reasons why the injury to my heel called for hospitalization. My thoughts were vagrantly far away from the *Doppelkopf,* which the others did not seem to mind as it took a steady stream of pfennigs and marks into their pockets.

"Play up, Doktor! Your turn," said Klostermann.

I drew a card and slapped it on the table with a flourish as if I really meant business: "There you are!"

Klostermann with a smirk played his card and helped himself to some more of my money, while I laughed outright and thought to myself: "You go ahead and amuse your-selves playing *Doppelkopf* as long as you like—I'm going home."

It was my intention, after the game, to advise Klostermann gradually to scout around for another doctor. But before I could say anything he patted me on the shoulder and said: "I'm indeed very pleased to have an experienced doctor with us. I'm sure that in a short time you'll be very happy with us."

Nothing of the sort, was the rebellious thought that flew into my mind, but I said: "The splinter in my heel, Herr Major, causes me a certain amount of concern."

"Try if you can," suggested Klostermann amiably, "to get it healed while you are with us. I'll give you a specially roomy pair of felt boots so that your foot has the necessary comfort."

His practical approach to the matter was disturbing, and took the wind out of my sails. Then he continued: "But, Doktor, please understand me—I don't wish to influence you in any way. You as a doctor will know what is best for your injury."

"A splinter in the Achilles tendon is an uncomfortable nuisance, Herr Major," I per-sisted obstinately. "And I shan't be able to tell until tomorrow how the wound is likely to develop, and . . ."—I decided to pile on the agony—"it is also quite likely that inflamma-tion will set in. Perhaps even blood poisoning."

To hammer the point home I left the battle post with rather more of a limp than was strictly necessary. And as I hobbled back to the dressing station my memory spitefully reminded me of Müller, who had pleaded to be allowed to stay with us at the front after his fingers had been shot away. But of course things had been different then—he was still with the old crowd, not inconsiderately mixed up with a mob of strangers. Oh, well, I had until the next day to come to grips with my conscience.

Heinrich, in the meantime, had automatically started to prepare our defense from the rear stables. He had built wooden barricades at places which offered the best field of fire. *Stabsarzt* Lierow's orderly was in the dressing station and a wave of hot anger surged through me when I learned he had made no effort to retrieve his officer's body in order to give it a decent burial.

"Get out!" I told him. "Search the old dressing station until you find the Herr *Stabs-arzt's* body. If you can find only his ashes bring them. Even one finger of his body, so long as we can give him the burial he deserves," I ordered, thinking of his lovely wife and children, whose photograph he had so proudly shown me only a couple of weeks ago.

The orderly returned after a few minutes. "I can find nothing," he reported sullenly.

"Then come with me." Supported by Heinrich and accompanied by the orderly I limped along to the burnt-out house. Under a pile of blackened timber was Lierow's body.

"Carry it," ordered Heinrich, giving the batman a hard kick on the backside.

In the early hours of the morning, the enemy launched a sharp attack, which brought him within 30 yards of the dressing station. He was beaten back after fierce hand-to-hand fighting. At a critical stage of the fighting, an *Unteroffizier* who was suffering from severe frostbite of both feet asked to be lifted bodily up to his machine-gun post in the loft of one of the houses, where he raked the enemy with deadly fire in spite of his personal agony. When I learned that he had a wife and three children at home, my shame was complete.

Gridino was free of the enemy by the time dawn broke. And with the dawn my dreams of returning home had vanished. With Heinrich's help, I administered a local anesthetic to my left foot and without much difficulty removed the splinter from my heel. My fate was now bound up with the 3rd Battalion of 37th Regiment.

*   *   *

The next 10 days were concentrated hell as the Russians hammered ceaselessly at Gridino in an effort to break our defensive line and clear the way to Rzhev and Smolensk.[231] The whole of Army Group Center's front was called upon to repel the Red steamroller offensive, but the Gridino corner of the defensive bulge around Rzhev was the nearest point to Moscow of the whole front and took a tremendous pounding. Major Klostermann's outlook was bounded by the shrinking, disintegrating village. And my field of vision extended only from the dressing station to the big Kolchoze barn, 40 yards behind the house. That Kolchoze barn became our main concern.

On 8 January, the Russians captured it again and every man able to hold a weapon—stretcher-bearers, wounded men, Heinrich and myself—ran out into the bitter cold to engage them in fierce hand-to-hand fighting. The small infantry gun was used at point-blank range against the massive barn. We were inevitably being overwhelmed by weight of numbers when Klostermann staged a counterattack with some of his men and the Reds were thrown out. A renewed Russian attack during the night petered out in the face of concentrated fire from small arms and our heavy 21cm *Mörsers*. Toward morning, the Reds retaliated from a safe distance by plastering us with artillery fire.

The Russian artillery fire stopped at about 5 a.m. and we heard a screaming mob coming toward us from the east again. Their high-pitched "*Urrah! Urrah!*" came across the snow to us. On they came toward the barn, yelling and screaming at the top of their voices. A flare picked them out—a close-packed body of charging men. From our holes in the snow and our wooden barricades behind the dressing station we fired our automatics and rifles into the advancing mass. They went down by the dozen, but the men behind trod the bodies into the snow. They took the Kolchoze barn again, but this time we fired grenades into the barn, where the Russians were still kicking up an infernal din. Some of the Reds charged out of the barn right into the muzzles of our guns. Confused hand-to-hand fighting developed, but suddenly the mass of Russians in the barn took to their heels and fled into the darkness.[232]

Cautiously some of our men entered the barn. There were dead and wounded Russians littering the floor, victims of the grenades. But in a corner were two Russians singing raucously, quite oblivious of what was going on around them. Then it dawned on us—the Russians were blind drunk![233] From the less seriously wounded we gathered that the commissars, becoming desperate at the Red Army's inability to break through our lines in night attacks, had issued their troops with generous rations of alcohol, and when all the men were thoroughly drunk, had launched the attack.

And then something even more grotesque came to our notice. Two old women were cowering against the wall—in their muffled state we had taken them for men. They and about 50 more old men and women, civilians from the Russian-held villages, had been forced to run in front of the Red troops when they charged our positions. All but the two old women of this human shield had been shot down by us and trampled underfoot by the troops behind. But they had served the diabolical Russian purpose—50 useless civilians had perished instead of 50 soldiers. We went outside and, lying in the snow, was the evidence: defenseless, unarmed civilians bore testimony in death. Three were wounded but still alive. They were carried into the dressing station along with our own 30 wounded. Eight of our men were dead.

Our village was shrinking around us as house after house was burnt down or destroyed by artillery fire. Never-ending alarms kept us on edge day and night. Next day, 10 January, we were bombed by the *Luftwaffe* and nine of our men were killed. We cursed our own airmen for their stupidity and their accuracy. Then a patrol of 12 men was surprised by the Russians and practically annihilated; two badly wounded men staggered back. Two more Russian attacks were hurled back; in one of them, one of our own mortars was misdirected in the confusion and eight of our soldiers were severely wounded as a result. The Reds brought their terrifying "Stalin Organ" into the fight and plastered the village with mortar shells. While the "Stalin Organ" was playing its devilish tune, every man in the battalion lay flat wherever he was and prayed that none of the shells from that battery of destruction was inscribed with his name. Fortunately after Gridino had been plastered thoroughly the "organ" was moved to another sector to repeat its tune.[234]

I had a sore throat, was running a temperature and felt utterly weary and worn out.[235] But there was little chance to rest, for the next day the Reds started pumping "*Ratsch-Bumms*" and anti-tank shells into the village over open sights. The dressing station was hit—a shell burst in the stables. The Reds again attacked and captured the barn. This time they paid particular attention to the dressing station and rifle bullets whipped through the windows into the room. Our reserves counterattacked and again the Kolchoze barn was in our hands. We burnt it down during the night—it was too difficult to hold and was proving of more value to the Russians than to us. By the light of the blaze, and with the thermometer touching minus 50 degrees Centigrade, we hung our blankets outside for 10 minutes. For the lice, the cold meant massacre; hundreds dropped from the blankets into the snow, dead. There were no attacks that night.

It seemed that the impossible had happened, that we had turned the Russian attacks and forced another plan of action on the enemy. All the next day, 12 January, long columns of the Red Army marched westward past Gridino—but three miles away. We could easily pick them out against the white plain. There seemed to be no end to the columns. Our artillery kept going all day, blasting away at the marching Russians. Klostermann gave a satisfied grin and commented: "Whatever passes us we don't have to fight. This evening we shall be able to play *Doppelkopf* without interruption." But he knew, as did we all, that the new tactics of the Russians could spell even worse trouble for us later. They were obviously intending to outflank the western end of the *Königsberg* Line in an attempt to take Rzhev from the rear. However, we played our *Doppelkopf.*

Next day, 13 January, it became obvious that the Red Army had saved a few of their troops for our amusement. The attacks were resumed. The enemy left more than 300 dead in front of our positions, while our casualties were 41. But this disproportion of casualties, grossly in our favor though it seemed, was heavier than we could bear. The war of attrition was eating away at Klostermann's battalion just as it had sapped the strength of our own 3rd Battalion. It was inevitable that the Russian losses should be ten-fold our own, for we were firing from prepared positions, whereas the Russians were every time advancing against our guns across the open snow.

The lightly wounded men had again fought hand-to-hand battles around the dressing station, and once more I had been forced to forget my duties as a doctor and take my place with the fighting troops. Klostermann had come to rely on me—in the same way as Kageneck and Lammerding had done—to organize my own defense of the dressing station. And it was thanks to Heinrich's sound defensive positions and inspiring example to the medical personnel that we had come through.

On 14 January the Russians attacked twice, and a fresh batch of 30 wounded took over the heaps of straw on the dressing station floor from the previous day's casualties, all of whom had been evacuated. We removed about 250 Russian corpses from in front of our positions in order to clear the field of fire.

A dispatch came through from Malakovo. *"Russians have broken through 1st Battalion, Infantry Regiment 58, near Ranimza. Remnants of 3rd Battalion. I.R. 18, have been thrown into the counterattack. Russians were thrown back. Hauptmann Graminski, the Battalion Commander, fallen. Hauptman Noack to take over command of 3rd Battalion."*[236]

So the old mob was in the fight again! And now had Noack as the sixth commander of the battalion in the last four weeks: Neuhoff, Kageneck, Lammerding, Boehmer, Graminski, now Noack.

Simultaneously, there came a copy of the divisional dispatch from Rzhev: "*Russian breakthrough at Rzhev straightened out. But great Russian breakthrough at our backs, eight miles west of Rzhev. Dangerous.*" It was the last daylight message to come through to Gridino from Malakovo. Next day, 15 January, the Russians established support points in the wood—to the left, to the right and ahead of us—dominated the road to the rear, and plastered Gridino with shells. We had to wait until darkness for further communication with Malakovo. And even then nobody knew for certain whether on the next trip they would find the road blocked by the Russians. There was no field kitchen in Gridino and our food was brought from Malakovo after darkness fell. Wounded and dead were evacuated with the night temperature standing at minus 45 degrees.

During the night we at last received reinforcements—men from construction companies, from railway companies, members of the regimental band, all the odds and ends that could be found were sent for us to shovel into the furnace. These men were not battle-wise, and many of them were completely untrained in the use of arms. Specialists in various rear-line jobs, engineers, anyone who had two legs unfrostbitten and two arms capable of holding a gun was sent to us, for Gridino had to be held at all costs.

My wound was festering, it was impossible to get any proper rest, for the few remaining houses in the village allowed scarcely enough room to stretch one's legs, and there was always work to do, a new crop of wounded to attend to, the old ones to be evacuated.

The Russians attacked again, in the darkness of early morning, and the newly arrived cannon fodder was thrown into the fight against them. The engineers, the bricklayers, the surveyors, the specialists, highly qualified in their own jobs, had no chance. For they lacked the one qualification necessary for survival—battle training. Where we fired a burst at the Russians from the darkness and then quickly ducked to another position, the new men bravely stood their ground and fired from the one spot. A burst from a Russian automatic and the man was dead. We had too much work and were too utterly weary to clear the 400 Russian corpses from in front of our positions when dawn broke to herald 16 January. A roll-call of the reinforcements showed that of the 130 men who had joined us 12 hours before, 104 had fallen. Twenty of these were wounded, the rest dead.

Another brief twilight descended on Gridino, and we now had no more fuel for our oil lamps. We mixed benzine with cooking salt; it shed a miserable light, but it was better than nothing. And under the dim flickering of the lamps we performed minor operations, gave blood transfusions and dressed the wounded. With the resumption of our night ferry service, a young doctor arrived to assist me. He told me that *Oberst* Becker was seriously ill with fever. Next day, 17 January, I asked the youngster to carry on at Gridino while I went to visit Becker. The day was comparatively calm and I hoped that by taking a circuitous route to Malakovo I would get there without meeting any Russians.

Heinrich and I waited for nightfall and set off. Halfway along the narrow track we spotted a sledge and five soldiers approaching us. We were certain they could not be Russians coming from the direction of Malakovo. But evidently they were less convinced of our identity. They stopped and from a distance demanded: "Password!"

"Frankfurt!" I shouted, knowing it was the previous day's password and hoping we should be allowed near enough to explain that we had not been given the current password.

"Put up your hands!" shouted one of the five men. Heinrich and I slowly lifted our hands and became prisoners of the paratroopers. They ordered us on to the sledge and turned back toward Malakovo, keeping their rifles pointed straight at our bellies. But after I had used an extremely vulgar and typically German expression, they seemed to be more or less convinced that we were probably Germans after all. At any rate, the rifles were carried in a less threatening position. They deposited us in front of their commander at Malakovo, who recognized me and apologized for the mistake. I was able to thank him, with genuine appreciation, for the lift on the sledge. It had been much better than walking.

Immediately I went to examine *Oberst* Becker. He had pneumonia, with bad inflammation of the left lung. His condition was serious.[237] I promised to see him again in the morning.

My old friends were snoring deeply when I let myself into 3rd Battalion's battle post. But Noack and old *Oberstabsarzt* Volpius—who had somehow landed back with the battalion in my absence—gave me a hearty welcome. I refused a cup of coffee, drank a few mouthfuls of boiled snow and sank gratefully on to the friendly heap of straw. I needed to sleep Gridino out of my system.[238]

The Jaws of the Trap

But when I awoke from a dead sleep, Gridino was still with me. As I stretched my heavy limbs in the peace of the early morning, the harsh realization descended on me like a cold shroud that by nightfall I should again be back in that cesspool of horror and misery. There had been no time for thinking at Gridino and for a while as I lay on my straw bed I allowed myself the doubtful luxury of indulging in my imposing array of melancholy thoughts. They remained stubbornly centered in Gridino, that mile-long strip of front where, since 2 January, more than 3,000 men—Germans and Russians—had gasped their last breath.[239]

How different it was in Malakovo, a mere three miles behind the fighting line. It was another world, where the peace was shattered only by an occasional shell burst or a few bombs, erratically dropped by the odd Russian aircraft. Old *Oberstabsarzt* Volpius was able to lie down and sleep every night in the almost certain knowledge that his snoring would not be interrupted before morning. He was sleeping above me, on top of the oven, and his heavy snores continued loud and unbroken while I indulged my black-draped mood. Not for him the sudden "Alarm!"—the brutal cold of the night, the hand-to-hand combat, the silver light of flares, the white eyeballs of the enemy. And perhaps it was even worse for the Reds, I thought. Again and again they are thrown into the attack across the snowfields, to be wiped out by vicious crossfire . . . to face a band of determined men, now specialist dispensers of death. To meet the set faces and calculating eyes, to fight against grimly confident soldiers who use their automatics with trained artistry, who hold a burning grenade in their hands with cold deliberation to lob it at the enemy only when it will burst in the air above their heads. It is the artistry of death. Tonight I shall be part of it again. The groaning of wounded men will fill the suffocating, stinking room; their blood will spill on my hands. I shall struggle to stop pain and staunch the blood. And then I shall walk a few paces into the stables at the back, and my automatic will pump bullets into the bodies of the enemy. The same hand is forced to kill and to preserve life almost simultaneously. But the death of an enemy no longer burdens the soul, and the well-handled wound, the life of a comrade saved, restores one's sanity. The balance is somehow preserved in a world that is notoriously out of balance.

Old Volpius continued to snore, calmly and rhythmically. He had slept and snored beautifully for four weeks. His very inefficiency and general uselessness were his passport to safety. To him Gridino was of no interest, except that he liked to satisfy himself that the front still held and guaranteed him another night of sound sleep. The old *Oberstabsarzt* let go a prolonged crescendo snore, grunted a couple of times, and was awake. He reached for his thick-lensed spectacles.

"I have an itch," he announced irritably. "I hope you haven't carried too many lice, Doktor." His hand disappeared under the blanket and he scratched himself vigorously.

"Perhaps a few front lice, Herr *Oberstabsarzt*," I replied, "help to produce a sense of community and comradeship."

"You don't mean to suggest," he snapped, "that there is no front here. I can tell you we had a pretty hefty artillery bombardment yesterday, *and* that we were machine-gunned by enemy aircraft, *and* that several bombs were dropped on the village. But you were so sound asleep that you noticed nothing," he ended huffily.

By nine o'clock I was standing beside *Oberst* Becker's sick bed. He had had a fairly comfortable night, but a thorough examination confirmed my previous diagnosis—pneumonia.

He decided that he would remain at Malakovo, rather than be moved to Rzhev, and gave orders that Major Höke would take over command of the regiment until he recovered. I was to remain in Malakovo as his physician. Only when I went into the street and heard the distant din of battle did I realize that Heinrich and I did not have to return to Gridino! Not, at least, until *Oberst* Becker had recovered. I was now quite eager to play the front-line soldier from three miles behind the line and to share the dangers of life in Malakovo with old Volpius. With a beaming face, I hastened to Noack's H.Q. and reported myself to him.

Noack was overjoyed to have me back as 3rd Battalion's medical officer again, but Volpius's abject fear at the thought that he might be sent to Gridino in my place was pathetic. However, two M.O.s for 100 men was unheard of. Noack suggested that I try to make myself indispensable at Malakovo in other ways, and little Becker supplied the answer.

"It's absolute chaos in the rear villages," he said. "They're crowded with civilian refugees; they're crammed 25 and 30 in a house, not enough for them to eat, half of them sick, fever cases in the same rooms as everyone else. Bloody chaos! Why don't you make yourself responsible for them, Heinz? I'll even get a horse for you somehow."

But it was some days before Becker was able to put his plan into action. Bigger things were on the move; there was heavy fighting around Malakovo, and the fate of Rzhev and of every German soldier in this sector hung in the balance as the Red Army completed its great encircling movement from the west and all but cut our lifeline—the railway from Viaz'ma to Rzhev—at Sychevka.[240]

As the Russians drove to encircle us, the snow fell at Malakovo. Blizzard after blizzard raged down on us from the northeast blocking the roads and bringing everything to a standstill. Our horse-drawn snow ploughs could not cope with the heavy fall and from morning to night our troops were shoveling the roads clear to keep open our supply routes. On 22 January, when the front around Malakovo blazed into life again, the division reported that the situation in Rzhev was highly critical. General Grossmann was now in command of the division. He had taken over as successor to Auleb during the retreat from Moscow. He belied his name—he was a small man, but a bundle of energy.

Next day the news was worse. Seven Russian armies, under Marshal Zhukov, were smashing at our line in a mighty effort to complete the encirclement of the beleaguered German troops in the Rzhev area. With their last remaining strength and against fantastic odds, our 86th Infantry Division was defending the railway line from Viaz'ma to Rzhev, which had already been captured at various points by the Russians. Gridino was the northeasterly bastion of the German defensive line—a finger of defiance that seemed to incense the Red Army to one furious attack after another. But General Model, who had replaced Strauss in command of the Ninth Army, was a man of steely determination and resourcefulness.[241] He issued a general order that not a yard of ground was to be given and that every unit must fight to the last breath of the last man. He organized counterattacks and met the Russian steamroller with "provisional anti-Panzer sections"—makeshift units equipped with anti-tank guns, any anti-aircraft guns that came to hand, machine-gun detachments and riflemen. They were thrown against the enemy to free the railway line to Viaz'ma—our last remaining link with our homeland. Once that lifeline was destroyed, 600,000 German troops would be penned in a Russian ring of steel. We could fight until our ammunition and food ran out; and that would be the end.

But on 25 January a miracle happened. Gifts and comforts from the Bielefeld district arrived at Malakovo for the 6th Infantry Division.

They were "soft-soap" gifts sent by Reineking, the Nazi *Kreisleiter* for the district, who had formerly been attached to the 2nd Battalion of Regiment 18 as an ordinary soldier. He had been sent home to take over the Party job before the final push on Moscow. Now he sent us cigarettes, cigars, liquor and coffee beans.

"Condemned men always have one good meal just before they die," old Volpius remarked gloomily.

But we felt less ready to die now that we had liquor inside us and real coffee simmered in the fireplace. Even quantities of *Steinhäger*, the favorite drink of the Westphalians and Lipperlanders was included in the parcels.

"If coffee and alcohol can reach us, then ammunition will also be getting through," Noack commented, and we were all so pleasantly drunk that the situation around Rzhev began to look almost rosy.

To fill our cup of happiness to the brim, the front around Malakovo quietened down considerably.[242] Noack thought that the Russians had great Bacchanalian sympathies and for once were playing the game by leaving us alone to our revels. But, as before, the Red troops were merely being switched to the west, where they were making their best progress. And endless columns of Russians bypassed Gridino, heading for the rear of our positions at Rzhev.

The *Königsberg* Line had held. It had been held at great loss to ourselves, but 10 Russians had fallen for every one German and the enemy had not gained an inch of ground.[243]

Nina Barbarovna

Oberst Becker was making good progress and I felt it was time that I made myself indispensable in other directions to avoid being sent back to Gridino. Little Becker had brought me a gray mare, Vesta, and handed her over with a mock certificate of ownership which stated that Vesta was now my property, and that in recognition of my services I would be permitted to take her back to Germany with me after the conclusion of hostilities. The possibility that both the horse and I would survive struck me as somewhat remote.

Vesta was the best mare I had yet owned. She was a nimble-footed animal of medium height, well behaved and quick to sense danger. When her instinct told her that dangerous ground lay ahead, she would snort, stop dead, and then bypass the danger spot. Next morning I mounted Vesta and set off for the base villages, calling for a short while on *Oberfeldarzt* Greif, the Divisional Medical Officer, whom I had not seen since the withdrawal from Moscow started. I made a detailed report and he asked me, when I had time, to collate my experiences of winter fighting and summarize them in pamphlet form for use back in Germany, where doctors were undergoing special courses of training before being sent to Russia.

At the main base village I located the medical *Feldwebel* and asked him to accompany me to the houses which contained Russian civilians. The warm, stuffy rooms were packed with refugees, and after only a cursory examination I discovered two men suffering from spotted fever, lying among the healthy people, who, in their undernourished state, were particularly susceptible to infection. Protein deficiency showed in the many cases of foot edema, and many of the babies had rickets, a sign of vitamin deficiency. The mothers, on their unbalanced diet, could not produce the necessary quantity or quality of milk. From the medical point of view, conditions in all the houses occupied by civilians were deplorable. When I explained the dangers of the present state of disorganization to the *Feldwebel* he told me that a young Russian woman medical student, had, of her own accord, tried to help her people. Her name was Nina Barbarovna and he explained that for this assistance she was given a free meal once a day by the German field kitchen.

"Ah, I see! So this woman has managed to get you and the kitchen bulls working for her. From what I can see she's done very little here to justify her free meal."

"This girl is very good, Herr *Assistenzarzt*," said the *Feldwebel* earnestly.

"Take me to see her."

The *Feldwebel* led me to a house, which, like the others, was crowded to capacity. He pointed to a tall girl of about 20, who sat by the corner of the fireplace, sponging the face of an old peasant woman. She was dressed in a simple blouse and a rough skirt which accentuated the fineness of her body. She stood out in clear relief in the stinking, overheated room, and I noticed that she lacked nothing on the score of nourishment and health—thanks, no doubt, to the German field kitchen.

She arose as we approached, but stood motionless and composed, without any visible change of expression. Nothing exceptional in the way of good looks, I decided. High cheekbones, a clear skin and more delicate features than one usually encountered among Russian women. Her long corn-colored hair hung carelessly over one shoulder, her well-shaped breasts, innocent of any support, strained against the thin material of her cheap blouse, and she stood with a natural grace. She was not really beautiful, yet there was something magnetic about her. Her eyes! I suddenly realized. These were the slanting eyes of a cat . . . or a cat-like creature . . . yes, a panther. And for a moment I thought I saw a disdainful "touch-me-if-you-dare" look flash into them and the red lips tilted at an even more scornful angle. I involuntarily averted my eyes and turned to the *Feldwebel*. "She speaks German," he was saying.

She still stood motionless and self-possessed, but her whole body was alert.

"Do you speak German well?" I asked her—and an annoying little pulse-beat fluttered in my throat.

"Only a little," she replied in a slightly husky voice and with a pleasant accent.

"She speaks German very well. She understands everything," the *Feldwebel* put in.

"I see you are very well informed about her, *Feldwebel*," I remarked, with a knowing smile, and although her expression did not change I knew the light taunt had not escaped her.

"Have you really studied medicine?" I continued my questioning.

"For two years in Moscow," she replied. "My studies were interrupted when the Germans came near. Everything came to a standstill."

"And why are you here and not in Moscow?"

"I fled when the purge of traitors started at the end of October."

"Fled? Hmm! That's very interesting!"

"Why is it interesting?" she asked, and her eyes flashed a challenge.

"Because I am interested in everything that happens in Russia—interested, my girl, to know what is true and what is false."

"I am not your girl, Herr Doktor, and what I say is true."

The *Feldwebel* grinned, and I was taken aback by her ready reply, which put me instead of her on the defensive.

Rather lamely I replied: "I should also like it to be definitely understood that you are not my girl. You are only my medical assistant here—that is, if you know anything about the work. Whether you belong to us or the Reds will become apparent in due course. With these civilians in such an appalling condition there is much to do." I paused for a moment and then continued: "I should like you to get things in such order that very soon it will be necessary for me to come only once a week—to make sure that you are carrying out my instructions."

"I have no medical supplies, Herr Doktor."

"You will get everything you need to look after your patients."

For the rest of the afternoon I spoke to Nina and the *Feldwebel* in a strictly official capacity, outlining my program and giving them instructions. A complete house was to be cleared and used for spotted fever cases only. Nina was to live in a small house close by and attend to ambulance cases there. I ordered the *Feldwebel* to find out how many cows and goats were in the village and how much milk they produced. Half the quantity was to be delivered to Nina, who would be responsible for its fair distribution among the mothers with young babies. The following day, I told them, I would again visit them in the afternoon and expected to find that my instructions had been fully carried out.[244]

Rudi Becker visited the battle post that evening and I told him of the medical arrangements I had made in the rear areas.

"And what do you think of Nina?" he asked me, with a sly grin. "Wasn't I right?"

I avoided a direct reply. "To me she's merely a medical assistant—just like a sister in a hospital," I said.

"Yes, but sometimes hospital sisters can be very charming."

"Not so much to a doctor," I answered without a great deal of conviction. "My medical tutor always used to impress on us students not to get involved with the nursing staff. He was quite right," I continued pompously, while Becker grinned. "I shall treat this young woman fairly, but she'll have to work."

"Bravo! Well said, Doktor!" exclaimed Becker with a laugh.

"I'll tell you something, Rudi," I went on. "It's damned ridiculous the way this refugee from Moscow—if that's what she is—dominates the thoughts of our men. You won't find me queueing up for her favors behind the kitchen bulls and all those fools in the artillery who think she's their patron Saint Barbara."

Noack walked in with a bundle of German newspapers and press cuttings. Now we solved the mystery of the unexpected gifts from the *Kreisleiter* of Bielefeld. Reineking was back with us as a *Leutnant* and had personally seen to it that the gifts of cigars, coffee and liquor had got through the shakily held railway line to Rzhev. It was he who had brought the papers.

One of the papers told of the death of *Oberleutnant* Erbo *Graf* von Kageneck, who was credited with 67 victories in air combat. He was Kageneck's brother, the fighter squadron commander in North Africa, and had died on 12 January as a result of severe wounds received when he was shot down on 28 December. My mind flew back to the night before the Battle of Schitinkovo, when Kageneck had talked of death. That had been 28 December, the day his brother was shot down, and the day before he himself was killed.

Schitinkovo had really been the end of the 3rd Battalion. With Kageneck's death something else had died. Not the spirit of the men; even when they were being cut to ribbons there was never a case of cowardice. We had had our cowards in the earlier fighting, but they had all been weeded out, for it was better to be one man short than to have a man who might start a panic. I had no doubt that the garrisons at home were swarming with men who hadn't felt at home at the front. But cowardice in war is a strange thing. After a while a man finds it harder to face the scorn of his comrades than the guns of the enemy. At some time or another we had all been ready to run in blind fear, but the natural impulse was to stick it out with everyone else.

But we had been lucky in the 3rd Battalion; the spirit of comradeship had been something out of the ordinary. The spirit was still there, but the battalion as we had originally known it had virtually ceased to exist. Death had now become an impersonal affair. The lists of casualties that I compiled were now mere numbers, not an obituary of well-remembered friends. The dead were identity tags, the wounded were surgical statistics. If I happened to be still alive when the small remnant of the 3rd Battalion was wiped out, it would be the end of any desire for comradeship on my part.

The front was quiet and we stayed talking until late that night. And as the *Steinhäger* flowed—nightly drinking parties had become the rule—we became emotional, self-pitying, melancholic and maudlin in turn. Our conversation did not interest old Volpius who had retired to his bed after we had ignored a few attempts on his part to introduce his favorite theme—the 1914 war.

Probably as an aftermath of the night's drinking and conversation, the next morning I was again seized with an obsession to get home on leave, and I started casting around for excuses. I was able to think of a number of men who had been sent on leave with lesser claims than myself. My leave had been due to start in the middle of December; it was now the beginning of February and there was no word about it. I looked at my leg wound. It was still festering. The strain of winter fighting was beginning to tell on me. I gave myself a detailed self-examination and discovered a pronounced irregularity of the pulse, with an extra systolic murmur of the heart.[245] There! That was a warning sign that could not be ignored. Irregular pulse and a systolic murmur—they would get me home!

Things had been done according to my instructions when I rode over to the base village to inspect them that afternoon. Four dangerously ill patients were lying in the isolation house—all spotted fever cases. I explained to Nina and the medical *Feldwebel* that there was little we could do for them. Supplies of vaccine were still insufficient even for our own men. But the patients could be deloused and cleaned, as well as the places where they had been lying previously. I suggested that all the civilians hang out their clothing when the thermometer dropped to its lowest point and advised the use of Russla powder. But, I told Nina, no really effective cure for the disease was known. We could only try to strengthen the circulation, give Pyramidon tablets to reduce the fever and pain in the limbs, and sedatives to quiet the mental agitation. I handed out the medicines I had brought with me and went to have a look at the rickety babies and pregnant women. I made it clear to the civilians that Nina would have full authority to treat the sick and issue orders, and asked the *Feldwebel* to give her all the assistance she needed.

During all this I had scarcely glanced at Nina, except when I gave her an instruction. But I was conscious that I was getting active pleasure from merely being in her company. And I had noticed that she was wearing a bright red scarf around her head that framed her magnetic face as effectively as her long, blonde hair had done the previous day.

"It is for you to exercise full authority and do what you consider best," I told her. "You have my full support. We can help these people only if we have proper discipline among them. That is up to you."

She replied quietly, in her husky voice: "I have understood, Herr Doktor, and I will do as you say."

Her eyes held mine calmly, with none of the challenge with which they had first met me. She had serenity in her make up, too, and I found that her voice, with its pleasant foreign accent, had a soothing effect on me. I liked the serious manner in which she sought for the correct German words, and the unhurried yet confident way in which her graceful figure moved among the packed rooms of civilians. I suddenly found myself wanting to know more about her past life; I wanted to find out what thoughts, what memories and what hopes lay behind her compelling eyes.

I would have dearly liked to spend the evening talking to her beside a warm Russian oven, finding our points of common interest, and being for a few hours in the company of a beautiful and intelligent woman.

So I returned to Malakovo at a furious gallop.

CHAPTER 28

The Russian Steamroller

HEINRICH GREETED ME WITH THE NEWS THAT TULPIN WAS SERIOUSLY ILL. HE HAD A bad cough, a high temperature and was complaining of a headache and pains in the limbs. I went at once to the dressing station and found him delirious, but I could not determine whether it was caused by an overdose of morphia or whether it was a clear case of spotted fever. I visited him twice during the night and finally made my diagnosis.

Tulpin had spotted fever.

In order not to cause panic at the dressing station, I said nothing to anyone, but sent him back by sledge to the Medical Company with a sealed message for *Oberstabsarzt* Schulze, advising him of my diagnosis. Tulpin was out of the way before the tell-tale red spots appeared on his back, neck, forehead, hands and feet. For the time being I also kept silent about his addiction to morphia, deciding to visit him three or four days later at Rzhev, where I would discuss his case with the medical officer in charge there. I then had the dressing station thoroughly deloused and cleaned in order to minimize the chances of the disease spreading.

Back at Battalion H.Q., the divisional situation report of 5 February had just arrived. It explained the lull in fighting on our sector of the front. Our fate was being decided far behind our backs, where a critical battle was being fought. Powerful Russian forces, greatly reinforced by the thousands of Red troops who had marched westward in sight of the *Königsberg* Line, were making their heaviest attack so far against the Rzhev-Viaz'ma railway line in an all-out bid to capture it and then strike north to seal off the huge pocket of German troops in the Rzhev area.[246] Ironically, we could do nothing to influence the outcome; we had to sit on the *Königsberg* Line, which would become a mere name in history if we were encircled.

It was heartening that our north-facing front, stretching away to the east of us, had not given an inch of ground, but the Russian aim was to attack this line from the rear. Gorin's Russian Cavalry Group had thrust through from the northwest and had joined hands with the guerrillas behind us, 10 miles from Viaz'ma. Meanwhile, the 29th Russian Army was attacking Rzhev from the southwest and had reached the environs of that part of the city which lay beyond the Volga. A determined German pincer movement by our 86th Infantry Division, supported by SS units, and the 1st Panzer Division, had, however, succeeded in encircling this Russian Army, and in turn, the 39th Russian Army was desperately trying to free the encircled Reds.[247] The situation was hopelessly confused, but we knew that Tietjen's Group was fighting furiously and effectively in the deeply snow-laden woods between Rzhev and Belyi, where they were surrounded by Russian formations.

And at last we got the answer to a matter that had baffled us ever since the deep winter snows had blanketed the country—how the Russians managed to move their troops and equipment across country. While our final offensive on Moscow had bogged down in the heavy snow, and while in retreat we had been forced to stick to the roads, again and again the Russians had surprised us with their extreme mobility and their knack of springing up from unexpected directions. They had attacked from the snowbound plains and obviously had been independent of the recognized roads. Their secret was disclosed in the divisional report. They would form up their columns of men 20 or more abreast, pressing into service any civilians who happened to be in the area, and these columns would be sent out across the trackless snow. The first few files of men would flounder through the drifts, and fall to the rear exhausted. But the column would be driven onward, and by the time the human steamroller had done its work, a path would have been pressed hard in the snow. Marching feet of the following formations compacted the snow-ice further and then the light lorries and equipment were sent over the track, followed by the heavy vehicles and guns.

We had heard of the Russian steamroller. This was it! The trick of warfare was simplicity itself, was probably an integral part of Russian training,[248] but it was a vital piece of knowledge which had been missing from our textbooks. And in the aggregate, the lack of suitable light vehicles, the original lack of the correct type of horse, the lack of preparation for the bitter winter cold, the lack of warm clothing, the lack of medicines to treat the diseases we encountered, the missing information on how to keep a machine-gun firing in temperatures of minus 40 degrees, had added up to the retreat from Moscow—and now the danger of being encircled and cut to pieces at Rzhev.

*　*　*

The front was still ominously quiet, and Schnittger was detailed to take 20 men and relieve a section of paratroopers at a defensive point between Gridino and Krupsovo. He was issued with a good supply of canvas and blankets, for there were no houses at that point and our men would have to live like Eskimos, relying on the deep snow for shelter and warmth.

Day after day, I visited the base villages and had to admit that Nina Barbarovna, in her silent, calm way, was looking after the sick civilians extremely well. She carried out my orders meticulously and nursed the spotted fever cases as if dedicated to the task. One day the usual routine of my inspection was interrupted by the arrival of a sledge and several Russian civilians. A pregnant woman was lying on the sledge, which was being pulled by her husband. She had fallen from a stove on to a footstool and had broken several ribs. The accident had brought on her labor pains and she was in agony as we placed her on a heap of straw.

Immediately, I gave the woman an intravenous injection of S.E.E., similar to the one with which I had eased Lammerding's pain. Within 30 seconds her agonized face smoothed out and she relaxed, the pain numbed. The delivery took place without complications and soon the premature little son of the peasant was bawling lustily. The grandfather, a rugged old man in shabby clothes, entered, thanked us with wildly gesticulating arms and suddenly bent down and kissed my boots. I edged away and made Nina tell him that I had done only what any doctor would have done, regardless of nationality. Everybody then withdrew from the room, leaving Nina to make the woman and her child comfortable on their bed of straw. I listened to the lively conversation between the two women. Russian was a pretty language, and vocally very rich, particularly when spoken in Nina's husky tones. My instruments were packed and I was preparing to leave when Nina stood in front of me as if she wished to ask a question.

"Anything worrying you?" I asked her. "What is it?"

After a slight, nervous pause, she asked me in a low voice: "Herr Doktor, what is your first name?"

It was an unexpected question and I decided to pass it off lightheartedly. "It may be a Russian habit to exchange first names immediately after being introduced," I said. "In England, too, I believe it's customary to do so, but according to German ideas it's a bit early to call each other by first names."

Nina blushed scarlet and for several moments stood without saying a word. Then: "It is not I, Herr Doktor, who wishes to know, but the woman here wants to give her little son your name."

It was my turn to be embarrassed. "This is too much," I said. "The whiskery old grandfather wants to kiss my boots, the youngest citizen in the village is to have my name, and for the first time Nina Barbarovna blushes—all in one afternoon. It's too much."

Nina stood silently, as if unwilling to risk further embarrassment. "Well, Nina," I said. "Tell her to call her son 'Heinrich.' I only hope that in 20 or 30 years' time, this little Heinrich won't be fighting against my son Heinrich, if I have a son. If it's to end like that, I'd rather not go to all the trouble."

I was sorry that I could not do more for the wretched civilians in the area. It would have been better than all the medicines if they could have been supplied with the necessary and correct food. What they needed most were proteins—meat, milk and cheese. Hunger takes its toll quite systematically. In human beings, first the fat disappears, then the muscle substance is used up in order to be transmuted into energy. But at the same time, the body refuses to employ the slightest energy unnecessarily, so the sexual impulses sink to a minimum. The full breasts of young women shrink and disappear, eventually withering altogether; even the menstrual periods cease. Only at this stage does the substance of the organs themselves become affected. The vascular system degenerates, and fluids in the form of edema begin to appear—particularly in the feet, but also in the face. They frequently indicate a false gain in weight, whereas, in fact, a general deterioration of the whole system has taken place, very often with permanent after-effects.

Among the civilians in the village I had observed many grades of physical condition and I asked Nina if she could explain why some of the civilians were in various stages of hunger while others seemed to be in superb health, in many cases being fitter than our own soldiers.

"It is because many of them whose homes are in this area have hidden stocks of food," she replied, "whereas the evacuees from the front-line villages have nothing."

"Then why don't they share their food around? Or if they won't, then let us make them."

"That wouldn't be easy. The stocks of food are very well hidden. It is an automatic reaction of the peasant people to bury their valuable possessions in time of danger, and the owners aren't likely to give away their hiding places."

"Where *do* they hide the food, though?"

"In the snow," she replied, and went on with a ghost of a smile: "Food doesn't go bad in this climate."

"And how is it that you're in such good health?" I asked her curiously.

"In Moscow essential foods were fairly plentiful, and since I've been here, I've been assisting your soldiers at the field kitchen and I could always help myself to the leftovers."

Young Heinrich's yells interrupted us. He was wasting no time in proclaiming his hunger. Nina quickly helped the mother to feed the child, and the picture of peace and contentment made all the mad happenings outside seem remote and unreal.

"What do you think, Nina?" I asked, motioning to her to sit by the fireplace. "Is it right that there should be war; that people should die like this instead of living?"

She looked at me closely and seemed astonished that I should ask such a question. "Tell me, Nina," I insisted, "what do you think of it all?"

"People are born to do their duty to their country," she replied, as if she had learnt to say this automatically while at school.

"Then why do you flee from your own people and come to us?"

"I did not flee from my people," she answered deliberately. "I am in German-occupied territory because I had hoped you would bring freedom to the Russian nation."

"And are we doing?"

"No, I no longer believe it," she said. "The few reports we get from the occupied areas in the West show that it is merely the same tyranny in another form."

"But aren't we allowing *you* a great deal of freedom, Nina? Aren't you allowed to do as you wish? Don't we give you food when we've scarcely enough for ourselves and aren't I giving you medicines for your people even though I haven't a surplus?"

"I'm not talking about the German soldiers. I'm talking about those who follow you. The ones who come to rule this country—the Brownshirts. These people haven't freed us from the Bolsheviks; nothing is changed but the uniforms." Nina's eyes flashed and she straightened her body, but her voice never lost its calm tone. She went on: "They are now masters of the Kolchozes and took over what was left. We had hoped they would restore our land to us, but they kept the land and kept us to work for them. Even you soldiers have told us nothing of what we are to expect from you. You also are silent!"[249]

"You're too impatient, Nina," I suggested. "Rome wasn't built in a day, nor can a new Russian Reich be built in a year."

She did not reply, but continued to gaze at me impassively. Nina's clarity of thought surprised me, and I shared her disappointment and disillusionment.

"Do many Russians think as you do?" I could not help continuing with my questions.

"Yes, many indeed. But they will not speak. They fear the Reds and they fear the Germans."

"Then why do you speak so frankly to me?"

"I have nothing more to lose, for I have lost my homeland. The NKVD[250] will kill me as they killed my father and my brother, and I would not choose to live the life of an exile, like my uncle and aunt in Paris, who live with an eternal longing in their hearts for Russia."

The effect on our patient of the injection seemed to have worn off and every breath she took was agony for her. We applied a Leucoplast support bandage to keep the ribs in place and help to relieve the pain. "She can be taken back to her home this evening," I told Nina. "All patients who are not suffering from spotted fever are to remain in their homes and their own folk can do the nursing."

Wrapping myself up so that only my eyes showed, I went out into the severe snow-storm which had blown up, but I had every confidence in Vesta's ability to find her way back to Malakovo. In any case, by this time I had become quite Russianized myself and was wise to what was needed for survival. On the road back I did not meet a single person. Everyone had taken shelter in the warm log houses, which were almost buried by the deep snow. And again as I rode, my thoughts were almost exclusively of Nina. She was no spy[251]—of that I was now certain; and her fate as a fugitive from the Reds increasingly occupied my mind. If only Germany could offer some hope to these opponents of Bolshevism, and Nina in particular. But it looked as if we had left things too late. At our backs we now had not only the swarming Russian armies who had broken through in the rear, but also thousands and thousands of Russian guerrillas,[252] whose hopeful, half-welcoming attitude when we marched into Russia as liberators had now changed to hatred for our false politics, for our Brownshirt tyranny and for us. It was a hatred that had snowballed daily and was now surging like an avalanche behind us, waiting to destroy us.

CHAPTER 29

Rzhev

VOLPIUS LEFT US A FEW DAYS LATER, ON TRANSFER BACK TO GERMANY. NOACK HAD arranged the transfer; Heinrich and I drove him to Rzhev in the panje wagon. We set him down at the station, wished him soldier's luck, mouthed a few more meaningless phrases, and then set off in the sledge to have a good look at Rzhev.

In contrast to Staritsa, Rzhev was a modern city,[253] built to a rectangular pattern with its streets running parallel, north to south or east to west. It lay sprawled across the Volga and in a few short weeks had come to mean as much to our generation of Germans as Königsberg had meant to our forefathers. In 1942, East Prussia was not to be the bastion against the Siberian hordes; they had to be held at Rzhev. Although a thousand miles away from the Fatherland, Rzhev was Germany's fortress.

I had arranged for the paratroopers' medical officer to take over my duties at Malakovo, so we had time to spare. Persistently the thought returned to me that the road from Rzhev to Germany was still open and, with a bit of luck, would remain open for a return journey. My leave was overdue; it would be easy for me to be relieved at Malakovo by some young doctor from a base hospital and I could then find relief from Russia back home with Martha and my family. Nearly a year and a half had passed since the train with the five young *Unterärzte* had pulled out of Cologne station; it was more than two years since my last official leave. Nothing much was happening at Malakovo; I would not be missed for six weeks; in any case, nobody was indispensable—that had been proved a hundred times over in the 3rd Battalion. I worked myself up into quite a state of self-pity, and, perhaps as a result, I again felt the dull pain in the region of my heart. I quickly pulled off the three gloves on my right hand and felt the pulse of my left wrist. It was irregular and punctuated by a significant extra systole.

Heinrich glanced at me sideways through his ice-covered head-protector. "Aren't you well, Herr *Assistenzarzt*?" he asked.

"No, Heinrich. I don't feel too well. While we're in Rzhev I think I'll go to the field hospital and have myself examined."

The staff of the field hospital made me feel a ragamuffin—but it was not the first time that had happened. They had taken over the civilian hospital, a beautiful big building, where gentleman doctors, dressed in immaculate uniforms, ate their meals from tables covered with white linen. But there was more than one glance of envy at my medals from well-dressed young doctors who would undoubtedly have traded the security of a field hospital for the danger of the front. Among the doctors I knew was Professor Krause who had been a member of the medical faculty of Düsseldorf University when I had been a student there. We had met frequently in East Prussia, but that did not worry me for he was a highly efficient doctor, a former senior lecturer in heart diseases. After the meal, I visited him in his room and told him I had a special request to make.

"What can I do for you?" he asked me in a friendly manner, which encouraged me to lay my cards on the table.

"I have a very strenuous time behind me, Herr Professor," I began, "and after all the fighting since Kalinin my heart is not quite in order and—looking at the matter purely from a physician's point of view—I believe it is time I was granted some recuperative leave. I'd like to ask you, please, Herr Professor, to examine me with this end in view."

A barrier immediately seemed to come between us, but Krause answered in a matter-of-fact tone: "Good, then I will examine you tomorrow morning at ten o'clock."

Area H.Q. allocated me a house in Rosa Luxemburg Street which would also accommodate the two panje horses and we went off to find the spotted fever isolation hospital and Tulpin.

The place was a madhouse. Many of the men were delirious; some were unconscious. We entered Tulpin's ward, in which there were about 80 beds, all occupied. A man screamed at the top of his lungs, leaped out of bed and tried to hurl himself through the window. Another followed suit. Two medical orderlies ran down the ward, grabbed them before they could break the windows and dragged them back to their beds. Most of the men in the ward were doomed; only in a few cases would youthful elasticity and resistance enable the younger men to fight the disease during the next few weeks. Those over 30 were all virtually certain to die unless they had been inoculated, which very few of them had.

We were led to Tulpin's bed. His face was gaunt and sunken and he looked as if a leathery skin had been pulled over a skeleton. His eyes stared and saw nothing. Every now and then he muttered confused words; Müller's name kept recurring, a name which seemed to preoccupy him in his world of hallucinations. But he did not recognize us. There was no point in discussing his case with the doctor in charge or of mentioning his morphia addiction. It counted for nothing. In fact, everything in this place seemed meaningless. Tulpin was sinking toward death and eternal rest. Knowing what I did about him,

I realized that it would be a release from a life of torment, but Heinrich had been totally unprepared for the tragedy.

I placed my hand on Tulpin's hot, moist forehead, but he grabbed it and threw it off. "Get away!" he shouted, then raised himself up in bed, stared at me with wide-open insane eyes, and screamed: "Get away! Help! Away, away! Help me! . . . Aaah, Müller!"

The medical orderly came, placed a damp cloth against Tulpin's forehead and pushed him back on to the bed.

We were glad to get out of the house of death, where every corridor echoed with the screams of men driven mad by the infection carried by the Russian lice. Heinrich breathed a sigh of relief as we walked into the street, where several corpses, wrapped in canvas, were being loaded on to a lorry, which would take them to the military cemetery. They had survived the attacks of the enemy and they had dared the dreadful winter only for a tiny louse, burrowing into their unwashed clothing, to infect them all with the lymph of death.

By the hospital gate was a hand-drawn placard advertising a variety show with German and Russian artists, raconteurs, musical items, magicians and two Russian dancers; entrance was free and the show was to be held that night. It completed the palette of Rzhev: two miles away a Russian army was encircled in a great cauldron battle, five dead on a knacker's cart, a comrade mad and dying, and, to top it all, a variety show. We settled for the variety show and that evening took our seats in a huge dank cellar, with moisture dripping down the walls, in spite of the furnace which was roaring in one corner. We kept on our overcoats and gloves, and the cold was bearable, but the artists on the makeshift stage shivered, particularly the lightly clad Russian dancers, who performed in order to obtain a little extra food for themselves and their families. The audience laughed immoderately at the stale jokes of the raconteurs, roared their appreciation of the dancers and we streamed out into the night.

Bombs fell while we were in the cellar, but nobody paid any attention, for the place was completely bomb-proof. And for that reason we were unprepared for the sight of the field hospital, which had received several direct hits. Only half of the building was still standing; the rest was burning fiercely. Heinrich and I were in time to lend a hand in removing sick and wounded who were still alive beneath the rubble and it was well after midnight before we got back to our house on Rosa Luxemburg Street.

*　　*　　*

Professor Krause greeted me curtly the next morning when I presented myself for examination. He diagnosed arrhythmia and extra systoles and gave his verdict: "I do not consider any recuperative leave justified at present."

"But, Herr Professor, I feel utterly worn out—and there is an undoubted condition of the heart."

"You are mentally overstrained, Herr *Assistenzarzt*. That's your trouble—and that is all."

"In other words I'm hysterical!" I exclaimed heatedly.

"Call it what you will. As far as I'm concerned you're getting no recuperative leave. If you like I'll arrange for you to work at the field hospitals here in Rzhev for the next month. That will help you."

With scarcely another word I left the room, angry and bewildered.

The *Oberfeldwebel* of the hospital solved the riddle for me. He told me that Krause had recently been given strict instructions by General Model, the new commander of the Ninth Army, to keep back in Russia anyone who could still crawl. No cases could be sent back to Germany without Krause's personal approval. In my heart of hearts I had to agree that Krause's diagnosis was basically correct and that my systolic murmurs were merely the outward symptoms of an inner conflict, caused by prolonged efforts to control my emotions during all the bitter fighting, added to repeated disappointments about my leave. The final shock of being wounded had inevitably caused the physical body to react. But I had no intention of staying as a drudge in the field hospital for a month; if I could not go home on leave I preferred to sweat it out among my friends of the 3rd Battalion.

*   *   *

I looked at Noack questioningly: "It looks like the end," I said.

And as we studied the latest situation report by the companionable glow from the oven in the battle post on my return from Rzhev, the situation looked catastrophic. Briefly, two huge Red armies were now separated by a mere 20 miles. If they met, our lifeline back from Rzhev to Smolensk would be cut, and inside the trap would be 30 German infantry divisions, seven Panzer divisions, paratrooper units, SS formations and the staffs of our Fourth and Ninth Armies. That precarious 20-mile-wide corridor was dominated by the Russian artillery and around us there stood or moved 60 Russian infantry divisions, 17 tank brigades, 13 cavalry divisions and 20 ski battalions, most of them well equipped.[254]

"Yes, it looks like the end, admittedly," Noack replied, "but old Corle Becker says the Russian offensive is on its last legs, that they haven't the strength left to defeat us this winter."

"But the map isn't lying, and the winter isn't nearly ended."

"*Oberst* Becker isn't often wrong—he has the nose of an old war horse."[255]

"Then perhaps I'll still get my leave."

Noack laughed, and slapped me on the back. It was almost with a sense of relief that I sat in the battle post that evening—relief at being rid of the bastard town Rzhev and relief at having been prevented by Krause from deserting my comrades. For the one fine thing that had been born out of this destruction was the close bond of brotherhood that united officers and men. There were not many of the original 3rd Battalion left. Noack and I worked out the exact figures. Our battalion strength had been brought up to just over the hundred mark since General Model had sent to the front as replacements any man who could be spared from the base units. But of the original 800 men who had marched into Russian territory on 22 June, there remained only two officers—Rudi Becker and myself—five NCOs and 22 soldiers. The figures came as a shock to us, even when we remembered that a few men were on sick leave and might rejoin the battalion and that there were probably a few survivors in Tietjen's Group, of whose casualties we had no news.[256]

Yet it was extraordinary how the few survivors managed to keep up the spirit of the 3rd Battalion and imbue that spirit into our replacements. And more than any other man in the battalion, *Oberfeldwebel* Schnittger kept that spirit burning brightly. He and his morale seemed indestructible. The following afternoon I accompanied the small group which was taking provisions to Schnittger's outpost in the snow. We came upon a fortress of ice. In a hollow stood a large hut, its walls built completely of snow bricks, strengthened with branches and roofed with twigs and snow. It was floored with more twigs, canvas and blankets. Two paraffin lamps burned inside, day and night, giving an illusion of warmth. Blizzards had drifted the snow deeply against the hut on the weather side, so that now it was impregnable to the severest storm.

Schnittger ran his outpost like clockwork, posting his sentries and meeting every Russian attack imperturbably.

He gave me some bean soup, then boiled some snow over a paraffin lamp and made coffee from what was left of the gifts from Bielefeld.

I thought of my leave hysteria and looked hard at Schnittger, the best all-round soldier in the battalion. The forelock of his long, blond hair tumbled across one eye as he looked at me humorously. He was a seasoned veteran, experienced in hardship and slaughter, yet he looked more like the captain of a champion football team. The German Cross in Gold hung on his chest—the only one in the battalion now that Kageneck was dead. But his carefree manner belied the 40 times he had successfully led assault groups into the attack, the 120 patrols he had led into enemy territory. Schnittger would take it as an affront if it were suggested to him that he should take home leave.

The small supply column had left without me and as the sun hung cold and low on the horizon, he put on his furs and accompanied me for a good part of the way back along the snowy track to Malakovo.

Nina Here and Martha There

Christmas mail and a new radio set reached us simultaneously. The radio was much superior in size and tone to the one on which Neuhoff had been so fond of listening to "Lili Marlene." We could tune into every German station with ease, a wonderful thing after having been cut off from home for three months. We were also able to tune into the English programs and turned a blind eye to the orders prohibiting that harmless practice.

The mail had descended on us like an avalanche. It was the accumulation of several weeks and included hundreds upon hundreds of gift parcels. There were, of course, letters and parcels for 800 men—and very few of them remained. As we sorted the mail, almost every name brought back a vivid picture of the man to whom the letter or parcel had been sent, very often a picture, too, of the way he had died—this one before Christmas while the mail was on its way across Russia; that one after Christmas. We decided to stamp and return all letters that could no longer be claimed. But the parcels were opened, every man who took a dead comrade's parcel undertaking to return to the sender any article of material value, along with a personal letter. For the survivors of the 3rd Battalion it was Christmas in March. Nothing had gone bad in the Russian cold; everything was perfectly preserved. We had stacks of cake, biscuits, ham, every kind of sausage, chocolate, prunes, nuts, cocoa, cigars, cigarettes, tobacco, puddings, preserves, coffee, tea and dozens of other luxuries. Mothers, sisters, wives and girlfriends back in Germany had denied themselves these things or had traded other articles in exchange for them so as to bring some measure of comfort to their men in the Russian snows. In some of the parcels were pictures of women and of babies, and in one parcel of food was a tiny baby's shoe with a note: "He is now too big to wear this." The baby's father had died at Schitinkovo, his face completely blasted away by a Russian grenade.

Again I received a big pile of letters from Martha. My message canceling our engagement celebrations, as I had expected, did not reach her in time. Most of the guests turned up; but the fiancé was missing. She had sent me a miniature Christmas tree similar to the one she had sent me for the Christmas in Normandy. Noack had a similar gift, and with the glow of the fire, the flickering light from the candles and the deep snow outside it was not difficult for us to slip back ten weeks in time and imagine that it was Christmas. We were, in any case, never sure of the date, so 25 December was as good as any other to us. I found myself cheating with Martha's pile of letters and instead of opening them in date order, I started to read the one with the most recent postmark. By some freak it had taken only three weeks to reach us.

"Martha is to sing in *Romeo and Juliet*," I told Noack.

"But I thought you said that all enemy plays and operas were banned," said Noack.

"Yes, but the opera *Romeo and Juliet* is by Sutermeister, a Swiss composer."[257]

"Shakespeare was an Englishman."

"Ah, Noack, but even the English haven't yet decided who wrote his plays. Perhaps Goebbels has now discovered that Shakespeare was a German. But just a minute! ... Listen to this." I read from Martha's letter: "Dr. Ernst Fabry and I will be singing the duet from the balcony scene over the Frankfurt radio station on 3rd March at 8 p.m. Perhaps you will be able to hear it. . . ."

"Quick!" I said to Noack. "What's the date?"

"Haven't an idea. Perhaps it's 3 March today."

"Heinrich, do you know the date?"

"I think it's still February, Herr *Assistenzarzt*."

I picked up the field telephone and got through to Regimental H.Q. Von Kalkreuth's orderly told me that it was 2 March. I took a deep breath. Thank God! I fiddled with the radio switches and tried to get Frankfurt. At last I got it, but the reception was poor.

"Heinrich," I said, "where can we get wire? We must have a proper aerial—this aerial's a disgrace to the battalion. Let's go to the Signal Section. Even if the entire *Wehrmacht* collapses I must get hold of some wire." I pulled on my two overcoats, felt boots, and *Kopfschützer* and walked out with Heinrich.

Within an hour, a couple of hundred feet of wire crisscrossed through the stables and outside to the roof of the next building. Frankfurt came through as clear as a bell. I slept happily.

Next morning I left early for the rear villages to visit the civilian sick. I also wanted to examine and inoculate all the Russians who were working for us. Usually I left Malakovo at midday, but I wanted to make sure of being home early. No sound of fighting came from Gridino or Krupsovo; perhaps the front would remain calm for my big day. Even Vesta seemed to trot more exuberantly than usual.

Nina was not in her quarters and the door to the house was locked. An old woman from the neighboring house made me understand that she had gone to the next village to attend to the sick Russians there. I visited the medical *Feldwebel*, who confirmed that all the Russians in German service would assemble at two o'clock.

"Good. I'd like you to be there."

As we went into the street together, Nina Barbarovna walked toward us, her eyes opening in surprise at seeing me there so early. "Let us go to your quarters," I told her and handed my horse to the *Feldwebel* to lead, while I walked with Nina.

Her little house was pleasantly warm as she let me in with a slightly self-conscious air. On the table were German Christmas pastries and biscuits, evidently a present from some German soldier. For some reason it annoyed me to see the food on the table. Occasionally I had brought her some horse meat, but cakes and biscuits! No, that was going too far.

"Did you bake these cakes yourself—in this oven?" I asked.

"No, Herr Doktor," she answered like a young girl and blushed. "They were a gift from a soldier."

"I see. And what do you think of German cooking? Don't you think our women make good pastry?"

She averted her eyes, wrapped the cakes and biscuits in a kerchief and answered almost inaudibly: "Yes, very good."

"Perhaps you would have liked me to bring you some of the cakes I received from home?" I persisted, and then could have bitten my tongue out for making such an issue of the matter.

"No. I wouldn't want them," she burst out. "These cakes were given to me by someone who means nothing to me." She faced me challengingly and this time it was my turn to drop my eyes.

"Forget about the cakes," I grunted and called to the *Feldwebel* to come in and bring the list of Russians to be inoculated.

Shortly before two o'clock they started to straggle along—a few old men, some middle-aged women and quite a number of young girls who helped in the German kitchens. I intended to check them for T.B. and to inoculate them against typhus and paratyphus. I told the *Feldwebel* to admit the old men first, then the women, lastly the young girls. Nina had placed the vaccine and the instruments on a white cloth, which she had first sterilized by running a hot iron over it several times. The old men were examined and inoculated, but unfortunately one of them had advanced tuberculosis; I had to dismiss him from our service. Then it was the turn of the older women, who looked frail and under-nourished when they stripped to the waist. They all passed the examination, and the young girls— most of them between 14 and 17—came in. The *Feldwebel* began to look uncomfortable as they started to remove their clothes. His only medical service had been with the army, among men. This was new to him. He asked me if he could go and look after the horses.

"No, *Feldwebel*," I replied. "You can't leave me here all alone—and don't worry about Vesta. She's very well behaved."

The short-leggedness of these young Russian girls struck me. It was a feature I had noticed about most women from the Moscow district. They were well developed and sturdy, but not so long-legged or narrow-waisted as either Natasha or Nina, who obviously came from a different class. Soon the *Feldwebel* had got over his embarrassment and seemed to be actively enjoying his watching brief. I was sorry to have to discharge one sweet young girl from further service as she had clear symptoms of T.B., but when I looked at her downcast face, I instructed the *Feldwebel* that she and the old man should continue to be fed by our kitchens.

The inoculations were soon over and I was just about to pack my instruments away when the *Feldwebel* asked me if Nina was not also a Russian in German service. Should she not also be examined, he asked, in a highly correct tone but with a certain anticipatory gleam in his eye.

"Nina is my co-worker," I told him. "She's quite capable of judging if she is free of disease and of inoculating herself."

"I think it is advisable for you to examine me and give me the inoculations, Herr Doktor," Nina said in a matter-of-fact voice.

The *Feldwebel* smiled, but it did not suit me that he should be present when I examined Nina.

Before I could think of anything to say, she spoke up: "Herr Doktor, I would prefer you to carry out the examination alone." I ordered the *Feldwebel* to go outside and attend to the horses and with a glare at Nina he saluted and marched out of the room.

Nina started to undress, and in the way young interns are taught—against their natural instincts at that stage in their career—I busied myself in preparing the syringe and looking the other way. For the first time in my medical life I felt embarrassed. Many times I had examined good-looking women—better-looking women than Nina, I told myself—so it was ridiculous that I should be so afraid to turn around and look at her. Yet it still took a conscious effort to pick up my stethoscope and walk toward her. In spite of myself, I could not help taking in her breathtaking beauty of form. I felt the color rushing to my face and did not trust myself to speak to her. But Nina was completely unselfconscious and stood like a goddess beside the table, composedly watching my stethoscope sounding her healthy body. There was, of course, no sign of T.B., and I quickly gave her the inoculation.

"You are in splendid health and may continue to serve as my assistant," I told her.

"Thank you, Doktor," she said, with a smile and stood facing me with her back to the fire.

"Yes, you're in such good health, I don't think anything could touch you," I added unnecessarily. As she still made no move, I continued: "You may get dressed now," and walked toward the door. I was furious with myself as a doctor and as a man for my inward reactions to the thought and sight of Nina's body, and I hoped that nothing of the conflict had shown in my outward manner.

There was no longer time to visit the spotted fever cases if I wanted to make sure of getting back to Malakovo in good time for the evening broadcast. I mounted Vesta and said goodbye to Nina. When I glanced back along the white road she was still standing by the door of her house, her corn-colored hair blowing in the bitter, piping wind of early evening.

As I rode back I had a lurking feeling that in some way I had not been altogether fair to Martha. But what else could I have done? Nina had demanded an examination; demur on my part would have put me in a worse light, would have given rise to speculations in my mind, in Nina's mind perhaps, and most certainly in the *Feldwebel*'s mind. Nina had, after all, been just another female patient, another Russian to be inoculated. She happened to be blessed with a fine body, a fascinating pair of eyes, and an enigmatic twist to her mouth that made one want to find out what was going on in her mind, that was all. I had been in Russia too long; Nina had become part of my work; it was time I was sent home on leave. Then I would get engaged to Martha. In the meantime, I should be hearing Martha's voice, singing to me, in three hours' time; Nina would be forgotten, Nina with her corn-colored hair blowing in the wind, her calm restful manner, which was nevertheless a challenge—and her German pastries and gifts from every little love-struck *Gefreiter* in the rear villages. Thus my thoughts whirled as Vesta cantered back to Malakovo and darkness came down on the wintry scene.

*　　*　　*

By seven forty-five that evening we were gathered around the radio set—myself, Noack, Heinrich and Rudi Becker, whom I had invited around for the evening. The radio had been tuned in to Frankfurt for the past hour, I lit a big cigar that Martha had sent in her Christmas parcel and Heinrich had made some genuine tea. My watch was synchronized to the radio time; I had done that early in the morning. I kept glancing at it and counting the minutes and the seconds in a way I had done only three times before in Russia—when "Barbarossa" started on 22 June, on 15 July when the battle of Polotsk was fought, and on 2 October when the battle for Moscow began. Some music was being played on the radio, but I did not even hear it; my whole attention was riveted to that creeping minute hand. At last it was eight o'clock. The final chord of the music and then the announcer's voice: "You will now hear the overture to Heinrich Sutermeister's opera *Romeo and Juliet*, played by . . ."

I missed the name completely in my disappointment, for I had completely forgotten that Martha's duet was to be preceded by the overture. The music seemed to go on endlessly.

"Perhaps there won't be time for the duet," I remarked to Noack.

"Don't be impatient. It'll come," he said.

"I won't believe it until I hear Martha's voice."

At last the announcer's voice again: "And now the great love duet from the balcony scene, sung for you by Martha Arazym and Dr. Ernst Fabry."

There were a few introductory chords, followed by the exquisite harmony of the choir, the voice of Romeo and then Martha's reply. It came as a shock that every tone of her voice was exactly as I had remembered it—perhaps because the last year had changed me I had somehow expected that her voice would have changed too. But it was as if the last year had never happened. Martha was not in the room with me, I was sitting in my usual place in the Duisburg Opera House watching Martha and my friend Ernst Fabry playing the scene on the familiar stage. With exquisite restraint Fabry and Martha gave expression to the love scene and the perfect voices made mockery of the distance that lay between them and the little house near the icebound Volga.

The three other men were listening enraptured and I could see that they felt the same as I—that Martha was singing to us, for us, and I knew beyond all doubt that her emotions were not directed toward an imaginary Romeo, but toward me. A great happiness filled me as her voice began to fade away to the most delicate piano accompaniment and finally ended on her "My Romeo . . ." The duet was at an end. I switched off the radio and there was dead silence in the room.[258]

"Wonderful," said Noack at last. "Heinz, you must write to Martha and tell her how much we enjoyed it."

"I'd never liked opera until tonight, but that was magnificent," little Becker remarked. Heinrich looked at me with wondering eyes: until now the world of opera and the theater for him had always been peopled by remote beings—he was a little overawed at the almost personal contact that Martha had given him.

Long after everyone was asleep that night I lay awake and listened to the echoes of the beautiful melody I had heard. The tone of Martha's voice had bewitched me all over again. And for the first time for two or three hours—I realized it with some surprise—I thought of Nina, whose husky voice had bewitched me for the last few weeks. But now that Martha had sung to me, if Nina's was to be the voice of my siren, I should now be able, like Ulysses, to stop my ears with wax and resist it.

Furs and Fever

A RUMOR REACHED US FROM SO-CALLED RELIABLE QUARTERS THAT THE DIVISIONS which had borne the brunt of the war would be pulled out of the line in early spring and sent to France for recuperation. Unfortunately, it was revealed as a bit of wishful thinking almost the next day when General Model inspected a small, shrunken group of soldiers, exhausted from the hard winter fighting. Model had spoken his words of praise and the men waited expectantly for what was to follow: "Soon you will be sent to France for recuperation." But Model uttered no such words. "On, comrades, to new deeds," was his final injunction. Nevertheless, the rumors persisted, together with a fresh "parole" that replacements for the battle-weary battalions had already arrived in Rzhev.[259]

Instead of new troops to relieve us, however, all that happened was the withdrawal from Malakovo of the paratroopers. And with their going, the front near Malakovo erupted again; Russian formations attacked Gridino and Krupsovo, *Oberarzt* Knust, the M.O. of Höke's 2nd Battalion, was killed by a direct hit from an anti-tank shell, and I was sent as a replacement.[260]

Fortunately, a regular replacement came for Knust in three days' time and in that period I had only one casualty to attend to. It was that rigid disciplinarian, Höke himself! I sent him back to Malakovo with serious grenade wounds to his head and left knee. He would be out of the fight for two months and *Oberleutnant* Rhein, a parson's son and the only other holder of the Knight's Cross besides von Boeselager in the division, took over command of the 2nd Battalion. I detected a look of relief in the adjutant Kluge's face as we stood by the command post looking out across the snow. Höke had been a stern taskmaster. "Tell me something," I said to him. "Today is 9 March, as far as I know. There must be many dead soldiers lying beneath the snow. What happens when the spring thaw comes?"

"What do you mean?"

"The place will look like a knacker's yard once the snow has melted."

"Oh, we've already had a divisional order about that. When we're given the code word 'Spring Fever' the whole front will move back a mile into prepared positions."

"And when shall we know that spring is here?"

"The soldiers will tell you. There's a queer story going the rounds that they have a never-fail signal."

"What is it?"

Kluge handed me his field-glasses. "Over there in no-man's-land—see those trip-wires at about knee-height? If the enemy touches those it sets off land mines and hand grenades."

"What has that to do with Spring fever?"

"If you look carefully you'll see that the wire isn't strung on wooden posts the whole way along. Look to the left of those bushes."

I followed his outstretched arm and through the glasses saw a human arm sticking upright through the snow, the fist tightly clenched and the wire wrapped around the dead man's arm was acting as a stanchion. It looked like a menacing symbol; a threat from beyond the grave.

"The *Landser* reckon," Kluge was saying, "that when these arms thaw and drop we shall get the code word 'Spring Fever.'"

Later I heard that the 2nd Battalion withdrew to its prepared spring lines on the very day that the clenched fist dropped to the ground. It was probably mere coincidence.

*   *   *

Back with the 3rd Battalion again, my life slipped into its former routine. The morning after I returned—on 12 March—Noack accompanied me on my ride to the base villages, where I showed him my spotted fever station, my ambulance and the dressing station where Nina lived. Someone inside the house was singing a Russian song, but it was not Nina's voice. We knocked and entered. A young Russian girl of about 17 jumped up from her seat by the fireplace and put her lute on the table.

"Where's Nina?" I asked her.

"In the *sauna*," she replied.

Noack laughed. "Taking a *sauna* bath in winter?" he asked.

In broken German the girl answered: "Today not very cold; *sauna* very hot."

Noack grinned at me. "Your assistant must be a tough girl."

"Come—let us go to the *sauna*," I said.

"Prima! I've never seen a young girl taking a *sauna* bath."

We walked the 30 or 40 yards through the deep snow to the *sauna* house. "Hallo, Nina!" I called to give her warning.

The upper half of the *sauna* door opened and Nina appeared. She was wearing a light summer dress of some pale-blue material and her long hair was hanging loosely over her left shoulder. None of us said a word. Then Nina opened the bottom half of the *sauna* door, grabbed her felt boots, tucked them under her arm and ran barefoot through the deep snow to the house. Noack followed her with his eyes.

Nina was fully dressed when we got back to the house and introduced us to the young girl: "This is my friend Olga, who is keeping me company and helping me to nurse the spotted-fever cases. She has had the fever herself."

"Good!" I said. "We can always use help—particularly from people who are immune. But Olga was singing when we arrived. Tell her to carry on, Nina. The *Hauptmann* here would like to hear a few Russian songs. What about it, Edgar?"

"Perfect. Carry on singing while we warm ourselves."

Olga was not at all shy and sang her songs, which were permeated with homesickness, nostalgia and the painful renunciation of love. The Russians are great lovers of music and the melodies were haunting. When Olga had finished, Nina made tea in a samovar. Noack and I felt sorry that we had not brought with us some rum and Christmas cake so that we could have made a party.

*　　*　　*

"I beg to report that Nina Barbarovna is seriously ill with a high temperature," I read. The note was signed by the medical *Feldwebel* of the base area and had been brought to me by one of the men from the field kitchen back there.

As soon as I had finished my duties at the battalion dressing station I rode back to see Nina. She was in a restless sleep, with Olga sitting beside her bed. The symptoms pointed only too strongly to spotted fever; she was tossing on the straw bed, her face was flushed and sweat was rolling down her forehead. I took a cold wet towel and held it against Nina's brow and her tensed features relaxed slightly. In a few more minutes her eyes opened. They focused on me and she smiled faintly.

"I think I have spotted fever, Herr Doktor," she whispered.

"Perhaps. I'm not sure yet," I replied, bending toward her.

She smiled again. "I'm not afraid, Doktor. You will be able to cure me—just as you have cured some of those others." Her eyes looked up at me in complete trust.

I told Olga to stay at all times with Nina and on no account to leave her alone, and then ordered the *Feldwebel* to assign another of the civilians the task of nursing the other spotted fever cases. I tried to cheer myself up by remembering that the Russians had more resistance to the disease than the Germans, for it was so prevalent in this part of Russia. But I could not help realizing that first she had a grim battle with Death ahead of her.

Two days later my diagnosis was fully confirmed. Nina's body, particularly the stomach and shoulders, was covered with the typical red spots. As the disease progressed they would also break out on arms, legs, the palms of the hands and soles of the feet. Her spleen was greatly enlarged and her blood pressure had dropped considerably. Olga was nursing her with great devotion.

One of the other spotted fever cases in the village was near to death, but I tried to put the matter out of my mind while I talked to Nina and told her that I was going to fight with her and do everything I could to pull her through. I felt that I owed a double debt to this girl, who now lay humble and uncomplaining on the straw; she had been a loyal helper to me and had undoubtedly caught the disease herself through exposure to the other cases she had nursed. I had brought with me several woolen blankets and took her old ones from her for delousing. Then I gave her a couple of Pyramidon tablets and a sedative, and left further supplies with Olga together with drugs to quicken the circulation of her blood. Nina's eyes followed me as I left the room, but she was too weak to say goodbye.

*   *   *

Rudi Becker telephoned: Regimental H.Q. wanted a detailed inventory to be taken of all the material, ammunition, stores and animals at present held by the battalion.[261] It pointed to something in the wind and Noack asked Becker what it meant. Was it to be our withdrawal to France? Were we handing over to another regiment? Were we to retreat? Or to advance? It turned out to be none of these, but it was cheering news nevertheless. It seemed that old *Oberst* Becker had been right. The Russian offensive had finally petered out; the enemy was exhausted and our General Staff now knew that he would not be able seriously to trouble us again that winter. We could now sit back and take stock of our position.

The long, unexpressed weight of a hidden fear suddenly dropped from me and the war took on a different, less grim aspect. For every soldier instinctively knew that once the winter was over we should have more chance of matching the Reds. I walked to the window and looked out at the snow which had been the symbol of death during the last few terrible months. Until a minute ago it had seemed like a white blanket that would lie on the earth for eternity; now it seemed only transitory. In a few more weeks it would yield to the winds of spring, every day the sun would shine more warmly, the nightmare of winter warfare would be at an end and new life and hope would emerge out of this frozen world. My heart trouble, my systolic murmurs, vanished—I knew I would see my home and Martha again.

My first call was on Nina when I rode to the base villages the following day. The disease was at its critical point and she was fighting for her life. Little Olga sat by her side and held cold compresses to her forehead. I had provided them with plenty of meat and other food and took with me some bean coffee to assist the circulation of Nina's blood. Her pulse was still racing at the rate of 120 to the minute and the high temperature lashed the blood through the heated blood vessels. Her eyes were clouded and her thoughts confused in the consuming fires of delirium; the virulent poison of the disease was raging through her body. And yet she looked quite different from Tulpin. She had the abounding health and resistance of youth on her side, and it made me hopeful that she would pull through.

There was nothing further I could do for her; it was now purely a question of whether her body had the strength to overcome the disease. Helplessly, I dipped a cloth in snow-water and held it to her hot brow. It seemed that for a moment a flicker of recognition came into her eyes, but immediately it was gone and they assumed their vague, unseeing expression once more.

After visiting the other cases in the base area, I looked in on her again briefly and as I rode home was not ashamed to find myself praying for her recovery.

When I arrived back at the dressing station at Malakovo, Müller was waiting for me. He jumped to attention and I shook his hand warmly. Now I knew that my dressing station would stand up to all demands; there was no man I would rather have seen back on the battalion's strength. He told me that he had not been sent back to Germany with his injured hand—they had patched it up at a field hospital in Smolensk. But the uncomplaining Müller bore no grudge against the Army for denying him leave to visit his family. With him had arrived 14 replacements, including an *Oberleutnant* and a *Leutnant*, fresh from Bielefeld, who had heard such horrifying tales of the war in Russia that—they confided in me—they had made out their wills before leaving home. They were astounded, and mightily relieved to find things so quiet.

In fact, there was such a lull that at last we were able to bury the hundreds of men who had fallen in holding the main defensive line.[262] The military cemetery at Malakovo had grown tremendously in size and was now kept in order by a special unit which erected proper crosses inscribed with the names of the dead. The divisional priest, a Catholic, visited us and took charge of the burials, while the Evangelical pastor officiated at burials in other areas. Religious distinctions were forgotten and these men did their duty as true Christians, creeds forgotten.

We had time, too, to celebrate Heinrich's birthday on 22 March. Perhaps it was a pity, but Heinrich was such a masterchef with horse meat that he was deputed to prepare his own birthday banquet of roast horse meat and roast potatoes, cooked in castor oil.

Minor attacks which the enemy continued to launch against Gridino and Krupsovo were of great interest to the newcomers, but passed almost without notice by us. Reineking was piqued when Noack persistently lumped him with the inexperienced newcomers and continued to regard him as a mere novice. The difference between new and old hands at this game of making war in the snow was further accentuated on 25 March, when there was a three-hour thaw at midday. Then it became cold again and by evening a blizzard was raging across the wide snowfields. For the newcomers the brief thaw was of little consequence, but on us it made a great impression—it was the first sign of the approach of a new spring.

And the next day our winter clothing arrived! Huge quantities of fur coats, woolens, fur-lined boots, thick overcoats—all of it collected from the civilians in Germany after a moving appeal to the nation by Goebbels in December. He had told the people at home that we were equipped with warm clothing—we had plenty of it—but it was impossible to have too much in a Russian winter. So the good folk in Germany had sacrificed their fur coats, warm boots, jerseys, overcoats, anything that looked vaguely as if it would keep out the Russian cold, little knowing that we should all have frozen to death had we not been able to shoot the enemy down and pillage their dead bodies to warm our own. The patriotic pile of clothing looked rather ridiculous as it lay in the command post stable the day after the first thaw of spring.

At the same time came a shipment of skis,[263] sledges and white paint to camouflage our vehicles and guns—the very stuff which we had so desperately needed four months previously.

Christmas parcels, winter clothing, snow gear—we were now complete. The back log had now been made up. But only 28 of the 3rd Battalion's original 800 were still there to see it.

*　　*　　*

By now, with reinforcements, the battalion had grown to a strength of 160 men and, as we were relatively well rested, we were ordered to take over the front-line defenses at Kliponovo from the 3rd Battalion of Infantry Regiment 37. On 30 March we left Mal-akovo and occupied our new positions that evening. Our command post was the same house in which von Boeselager had given Heinrich and me hot bouillon when we had arrived there frozen to the marrow after the march from Staritsa. Nothing had changed; the command post was still a small fortress, but von Boeselager was no longer there. He had been withdrawn from the front and was now in Bucharest trying to impart some of the discipline and fighting methods of the *Wehrmacht* to the Romanian Army, to whom he was German military adviser.

Once again we were holding the front line. But what a difference! It was now a static war with patrols and raids, sharpshooters and artillery nuisance-fire part of the daily program, and daily claiming victims, but we had difficulty in making our soldiers take this type of warfare seriously and were continually having to urge them to keep wide awake. My dressing station was about 50 yards from the command post, which irritated me, but I did not bother to make any changes on this comparatively quiet sec-tor of front. Gridino, as usual, was the only place where there was regular activity and if our sector was disturbed it was always where it adjoined the Gridino sector on our right. Boehmer and his rested 11th Company held this part of the line while Schnittger and his men took a well-earned rest as reserve.

In three or four days we had bedded in and felt as if we had been in Kliponovo for ever. We built snow walls and straw hedges everywhere in order to interrupt the field of sight of enemy sharpshooters. At all hours of the day and night the Reds were liable to fire a few machine-gun bursts across the village street. It was a nuisance and meant we had to throw ourselves flat in the snow, but we now did that automatically. The newcomers from Germany, however, seemed to get quite a kick out of it.

Perhaps some of these men did not quite see the humor in a grim joke that was in progress when I called on Schnittger one day. He was sitting at the table in his house writing a letter to the family of a newcomer. A number of his tough veterans were lounging around the fire.

"What have you said, Schnittger—that he died a hero's death?" an *Unteroffizier* asked.

"In the line of duty to the Fatherland . . ." called another man.

"Better say he died facing the enemy," a third man said, and the rest bellowed with laughter.

The newcomer had gone to the field latrine at the back of the houses during the night. The latrine was nothing but a pole rigged across a hole in the ground. A Russian nuisance sniper had taken careful aim at the sitting target and the man had dropped dead into the pit.

"Nobody missed him until morning," Schnittger ended, and then added reprovingly: "There, you see, Herr *Assistenzarzt*—even you are smiling."

He carried on with his letter and I walked across the village toward Boehmer's positions. For a day I was in command of the battalion while Noack took advantage of a lull to visit Regimental H.Q. at Malakovo. Apart from Boehmer, whose company was holding the most dangerous sector, he had only five inexperienced officers, fresh from Germany, at his disposal. But I was fairly secure in the knowledge that nothing out of the ordinary was likely to happen.

Boehmer pulled my leg about my new responsibilities as we walked along the snow trenches toward the edge of a forest of firs, in which the individual trees stood out clearly in the bright moonlight. Suddenly a big hare bounded out of the wood, across the snow parallel to our trench. It was a sign, Boehmer said, that a Russian patrol was in the wood. These patrols had as little wish to fight as we and our orders were not to fire a shot unless absolutely necessary. But two more hares came hopping out of the wood toward us, and I thought of our monotonous horsemeat diet. Boehmer was looking at me quizzically. "What are the Battalion Commander's orders?" he asked me.

"Fire!" I said, making my first momentous decision as a battalion commander. Both our rifles cracked and the two hares dropped in their tracks.

"Now what happens to the Russian patrol?" I asked Boehmer.

"Oh, they'll go back and report that they had contact with the enemy in the wood and they'll be safe for the night."

By the time Noack returned late that night one of Boehmer's patrols had delivered the hares to me; one weighed 14 pounds, the other nine. As Noack stamped the snow off his boots I said: "Nothing special to report, Herr *Hauptmann*—only two Russian hares shot down without any losses on our side."

CHAPTER 32

The Journey Home

Silently and with an expressionless face, Noack handed me a sheet of paper when he came into the command post on the afternoon of 11 April. I took it mechanically and finished writing a line in my medical report before I looked at it.

A leave form! Already filled in and signed. Home leave—for me! And starting tomorrow. I was stupefied and sat looking at the slip of paper, my thoughts racing around the various things that could happen in the next 12 hours to stop it. The general situation could deteriorate—no, hardly in 12 hours. I might be killed—unlikely; besides I would take care that I wasn't. Some other battalion's doctor would be killed and I'd be sent as replacement. No, they would send another doctor. The Russians would cut the road to Rzhev or the railway line to Viaz'ma. No, their offensive had petered out. Then nothing could stop me! Tomorrow I'd be on my way, to Germany and to Martha.

Noack burst out laughing at the expression on my face, flung an arm around my shoulders and said: "You see, Heinz, even the Army has a memory." We laughed together like a couple of fools until I remembered that Noack, too, had good reasons for wanting home leave.

"Sorry you won't be coming along with me, Edgar," I said.

"Nonsense, my dear chap. Just make sure you give Martha a kiss for me—and call on my wife and tell her that I'll soon be home. Don't forget to do that, will you, Heinz," he ended seriously.

"Don't worry, Edgar. I'll tell her to prepare a bed of straw for you and to open all the doors and windows of your house so that it's cold enough for you to sleep at nights."

"And take back a few lice with you to make it really homey. . . ."

"And some horse meat. . . ."

"Tell her to bake some *Kommis* bread. . . ." We were laughing and back-slapping again when Heinrich came in.

277

"Heinrich, I've had enough of this bloody Russia. Pack my bags," I shouted to him. Heinrich looked at me as if I'd gone snow-happy.

"I've got my leave, Heinrich, you fool," I laughed. "Start packing my things."

A broad smile came over Heinrich's round face. "Congratulations, Herr *Assistenzarzt*. Yes, Herr *Assistenzarzt*, I'll pack at once," he said, beaming.

I planned to leave with Heinrich and Hans for Rzhev at four o'clock in the morning in the large sledge with two horses. It had always been my practice to visit the dressing station every night before retiring, but on this night I could not bring myself to do it. At the back of my mind was the fear that a stray bullet might end my leave before it began. Of the three men with whom I had traveled to Vassilevskoye on our way toward leave exactly four months before, not one remained alive—they had all been killed in the subsequent fighting. No, I was taking no chances with a signed leave pass in my pocket. Noack and I sat chatting about old times until late in the night. My possessions and my automatic were stacked against the wall, and when the last log of wood had burned out in the old Russian oven we lay down to sleep.

Within a few minutes, it seemed, Heinrich was shaking me. Anxiously I asked, "Alarm?"

"No, it's leave this time, Herr *Assistenzarzt*. It's nearly four o'clock and the Russian Hans is waiting outside with the sledge and horses."

Very quietly, while Noack and I were asleep, Heinrich had prepared a pot of strong coffee on the paraffin cooker behind the oven; he had also cut a large pile of sandwiches, which were waiting for me packed in newspaper. For the first time, it occurred to me that a long journey lay ahead. Heinrich poured me a cup of coffee and gave a cup to Noack, who crept out of the straw, rubbed his eyes and sat down beside me. We hardly spoke to each other—Noack was still half-asleep and I could think of nothing to talk about. I pulled on two overcoats and the rest of my winter clothing, shook Noack's hand and walked toward the door. He stood by the fireplace.

"*Auf Wiedersehn*, and good luck!" I called out helplessly. Sleepily he replied: "Good luck—and love to them all at home," and closed the door after me.

Heinrich and I seated ourselves in the back of the sledge and Hans took the front seat, reins in hand. It was a dark night with snow in the wind. We stopped at the sick bay for a moment. Müller was waiting at the door to say goodbye. I told him another doctor would be arriving to take my place some time that day, there was a brief "*Lebewohl!*" and the sledge glided out of the village.

A burst of enemy machine-gun fire cracked across the street behind us. It was always brutally unexpected and this time I ducked my head more quickly than usual. Enemy shells were bursting on Gridino, and over there where the flares were going up must be Krupsovo, I thought. Probably enemy patrol activity. Hans urged the horses into a trot. The "Tired Duck" droned and circled monotonously over the rear areas. It was the usual nightly symphony of the northeastern tip of the *Königsberg* Line, which I had come to know so well.

It stopped snowing and the moon came out from behind the ragged clouds, clothing the landscape in an eerie, gray wash. Hans allowed the horses to walk; we were now quite safe, beyond the range of the Russian artillery and a step nearer home. The only possible danger now was from one of the "Tired Duck's" erratic bombs—and if we got hit by one of those, I didn't deserve to go home on leave. Hans spoke to the horses in a coarse Siberian dialect, quite different from the gentle voice he used when talking to us, but it was with an almost artistic sensitiveness that this giant of a man—legally one of our enemies—guided us across the snowbound countryside in the last of the moonlight.

When we reached the base village I signaled him to turn left. He understood me at once and drove the sledge straight to Nina's house. A light was burning in the small cottage and Olga opened the door before I could knock.

Nina was lying in bed and gazed at me with large, clear eyes. They were no longer vague and troubled, but once again looked at me with that strange combination of penetration and mystery. I drew up a chair to her bedside and took her wrist. Her pulse was now regular and strong. The fever had left her. Before I could say anything she took my hand and pressed it. "I am very thankful, Herr Doktor, for all you have done for me. You are . . ." Tears came into her eyes and, for a moment, she turned her head away.

I let my hand rest in hers and said gently: "Soon you will be quite better, Nina. I knew you would pull through—you had the spirit."

Olga stood at the foot of the bed and beamed with pleasure. Outside I heard the voices of Heinrich and Hans—they brought me back to a realization that my duties to Nina as a doctor were over. Nina said something quickly in Russian to Olga and the girl went over to the samovar by the oven and poured a mug of tea, which she brought to me. She then filled two more mugs and took them outside, closing the door after her.

"I'm going on leave, Nina. I'm on my way to Rzhev now," I said suddenly.

"I know it," Nina replied.

"How did you know?" I was surprised.

"The *Feldwebel* told me yesterday." There was a short pause and then she went on: "And I knew that you would come here this morning."

She knew me better than I had imagined. I smiled and said: "I was not quite as certain as all that." But I knew I could never have left Russia without saying goodbye to her.

Apparently she knew that as well as I, and continued: "Olga and I have been waiting for you since five o'clock this morning."

I felt embarrassed and wanted to escape from the calm scrutiny of those disturbing eyes, so I got up and walked over to the fireplace. "Well, you may be right," I floundered, "but as a doctor it was also my duty to come and visit my patient. . . . And of course I wanted to say goodbye to you. . . ." I turned around and saw that Nina had got out of bed and was walking uncertainly toward me. She looked pathetically fragile; the fever had wasted her lovely body but the thought flashed across my mind that she looked more beautiful than ever. "Nina, my dear, you mustn't . . ." I protested and took a step toward her, just as she swayed forward and threw her arms around my neck to save herself.

I held her tightly to support her and she turned her face up to me. In her eyes there were now no secrets. Gently I lifted her and carried her across the room. She buried her face on my shoulder and her long hair hung across my arm. I laid her on the bed and arranged the blankets over her. "Why did you do that, Nina?" I asked her. "You're still too weak to leave your bed."

"But I didn't want you to remember me as a sick woman when you're back in Germany."

"You must stay in bed for at least another week, Nina, my dear. I shall give Olga orders that you are not to get up before then."

"Yes, Doktor, thank you. I will do as you say."

"And now I must be going. The men are waiting for me."

"You will be coming back to Rzhev, won't you, Doktor?"

"In about six weeks' time. I'm afraid my soldier's luck doesn't extend to being kept in Germany for the rest of the war."

"I shall still be here, Doktor."

Briefly, I clasped her hand and then walked out of the little cottage without glancing back. I did not look to right or left as we proceeded with our journey. Now I wanted only to get on the train at Rzhev and turn my eyes toward my home without another look at Russia and what lay behind me.

At ten o'clock we reached Rzhev railway station. It had been heavily bombed and the train stood at an open platform. Heinrich and Hans placed my luggage in a carriage and I sat by the far window. All the glass was out of the windows on the platform side of the train. More and more leave-men climbed into the train, although it was not due to leave for Viaz'ma for another four hours. Heinrich and Hans stood on the platform.

At eleven o'clock Russian aircraft droned overhead and bombs started falling. We jumped out of the train and took shelter, sprawling on our bellies in the snow between the rails. Several bombs fell on the station and two coaches of our train were so badly damaged that they had to be uncoupled. Fortunately there were no casualties and the locomotive escaped damage.

The train was rather unusual in its make-up. In front of the locomotive were three long freight cars—the two front cars filled with rocks and the one immediately in front of the engine with railway construction machinery and lengths of rails. It was part of the daily round of the Russian guerrillas—now organized to be an efficient thorn in our flesh by a new man on the scene, Nikita Khrushchev—to mine the railway line between Viaz'ma and Smolensk.[264] For that reason, every man going on leave was armed with rifle and ammunition, for the guerrillas often waited until their mines had stopped the train and then attacked it in force. Many a German soldier had died on the railway line between Rzhev and Smolensk with his thoughts on his family at home and his leave pass in his pocket. The railway carriages were in a shocking state as a result of air raids, land mines and sharp-shooting guerrillas. Many of the windows were smashed and attempts had been made to keep out the cold by covering them with blankets and cardboard. The heating systems on the trains rarely worked, or if they did provided just sufficient warmth to prevent ice forming in water bottles. But none of us cared very much about these refinements now. We were on our way home.

For no apparent reason the train started an hour late, at three o'clock. Heinrich and Hans waved to me until the train took a bend and I passed out of sight. The stretch of line between Rzhev and Viaz'ma was at this time completely in our hands and we had nothing to fear. By sunset we had reached Sychevka and before darkness fell I could pick out quite clearly the ground over which we had passed six months earlier. It was near here—and in the same kind of half-light—that the wounded commissar had fired at me when I went to the assistance of the wounded Russians. In those days the war had been a relatively pleasant business; we were still full of hope and marched as a full battalion. By eight o'clock we had reached Viaz'ma, where we stayed for the night on the station and were given *Kommis* bread, tinned sausages and warm "*Negerschweiss.*"

Next morning, with several extra coaches full of leave-men hitched on, we steamed out of the station toward Smolensk. There were now about 600 of us homeward bound.

At ten o'clock that night we struck the first mine, and now we realized why the train had crawled across the flat countryside—at never more than 15 to 20 miles an hour—all day. Thanks to the slow speed at which we were traveling, the engine managed to stop before it was derailed. The front freight car, loaded with stones, was off the rails and badly damaged. The leave-men swarmed out of the carriages and with a concerted heave rolled it off the line and down the embankment. Then, while most of the troops stood guard in case of an ambush, others set to work to repair the damaged track. In a couple of hours' time a new length of rail had been laid and we crawled forward toward Smolensk.

Suddenly, the pane of glass in the door next to me splintered and the train jerked to a stop. We were under fire from a wood that swept close to the line on our right. Many men jumped down on the blind side of the train and aimed their rifles from underneath the coaches; the rest of us fired at the wood from inside the train. The concerted fire from 600 rifles and automatics was evidently too hot for the guerrillas; the enemy fire fizzled out. One man had suffered the fate we all feared—he had been shot dead with his leave pass in his pocket. We laid him on the snow-covered platform at Smolensk railway station. From his papers we learned that his wife and four children were waiting to welcome him in Germany.

The train gathered speed across the safe countryside between Smolensk and Orsha, and for the first time in Russia we were able to look across the snowbound landscape and think of it as a friendly Christmas card scene instead of as our deadly enemy. But it was not until we reached Orsha that it really sank in that the war was behind us and leave lay ahead. The officer commanding the train gave the order—an order that sounded strange and unreal and conflicted sharply with our ingrained habits: "All rifles and automatics to be unloaded; magazines to be emptied."

Hundreds of bolts clattered in astonishment as the ammunition dropped out. It was carefully repacked in ammunition bags and the war was suddenly far away—shooting was strictly forbidden here!

At the newly built barracks near the station our eyes goggled again at the surprises this new world was offering us. Long rows of tables, covered with white tablecloths, were laden with a variety of food. Gaily colored candles burned, the room was comfortably heated and a military band was playing—as softly as a military band can—old German waltzes and folk songs. Red Cross nurses in white uniforms waited to serve us, but we hung back, uncertain how to act in the face of such civilization. We carefully placed our kit bags against the walls, took off our overcoats and some of the rags which had served to keep out the cold during the bitter winter fighting and placed them on top of the kit bags. Without a word we sat in our filthy uniforms at the spotless tables; quite a number of men carried their rifles to the table with them until the Red Cross nurses gently reminded them that they were no longer necessary—that there would be no "Alarm!" during the meal.

We ate in silence, quite overcome by the strangeness of it all; and the men who had sat down hard, brutalized soldiers of the winter war, left the table changed into decent peace-loving men by the human thought and kindness that had inspired that unexpected banquet.

At Brest-Litovsk the Army had prepared a different kind of welcome for us, but one which was the next stage and an equally necessary one in the process of making us once again fit to mix in polite society. We got out of the comfortable train, in which we had been able to sleep luxuriously for most of the journey from Orsha, through Minsk, to Brest-Litovsk, and walked straight into another special train which was equipped as a delousing station. We went in one end filthy and lice-ridden and emerged at the other end as clean as newborn babies. Everybody from *Oberst* to *Landser*, received the same treatment, and so did our uniforms. As we entered the train they were taken away from us, and at the other end they were given back after having been thoroughly deloused in an oven with a temperature high enough to kill even the louse eggs. We once again assumed our rank or lack of rank, boarded another comfortable German train and sped toward Warsaw, Posen and Berlin.

It was late afternoon when we at last crossed into Germany. There was no longer any trace of snow, the villages and towns looked beautifully clean and well kept, the wide fields were cultivated and the green winter corn was already shimmering in the ploughland. Four days before we had left a countryside still in the grip of icy death; now the earth was awake and the world was on the verge of another summer.

When the train glided into the station at Frankfurt-a.d.-Oder, well-dressed, friendly women of the town were waiting to serve us with coffee and sandwiches. They told us that ours was only the third leave train to come from the Russian front and we blessed our luck that we were among the first 2000 men to be given leave. A little hesitantly, the cultured women, members of a voluntary organization, inquired how things were in far-away Russia.

"The snow is still on the ground and the front is holding," some men said. But it was obvious from the polite interest and vague looks of the women that they had been told nothing of the realities of the winter war.

"Was it very cold in Russia?" an elderly, gray-haired woman asked me.

"Yes, very cold. Once winter came we were cold all the time," I replied.

"But we sent you all our warm clothing. I sent my best fur coat."

"They were a little late in arriving."

"But they will be in plenty of time for next winter," an *Oberleutnant* added humorously.

Darkness was falling when we reached Berlin. The homeward-bound troops spilled out of the train and were gone. I had to wait several hours for the night train to the Ruhr, but I had no wish to visit any of my friends in Berlin. They would be strangers to me and I would seem a stranger to them, I felt. So I wandered into the streets, which I had not expected to find so brightly lit. The city was teeming with soldiers—undoubtedly there were far more of them here than in Malakovo and Rzhev, and I felt out of place in my threadbare uniform. Every few yards I had to return salutes as the soldiers hurried past me. To get away from it I hurried down several steps into a little café, where gay music was being played. I ordered coffee and glanced around at the well-dressed civilians, who were gossiping and laughing animatedly at their tables. The waitress brought me corn-coffee, but it was scalding hot and was served not in a cracked mug but in porcelain. The thin feel of it brought the first realization that I was nearly home.

The food looked good on the other tables, and I remembered I had eaten nothing since the sandwiches on Frankfurt station. I called the waitress and gave her my order: soup, an omelette and veal.

"Ration tickets, Herr *Leutnant*," she said.

"I beg your pardon."

"Ration tickets. I must have them before I can serve you."

"I'm sorry, *mein Fräulein*, but I haven't any."

"Then I'm afraid I can't serve you. You know the regulations, Herr *Leutnant*. There is a war on."[265]

*   *   *

Martha and I left the Vienna Opera House with the brooding music of *Die Götter-dämmerung* still ringing in our ears and made for the roof restaurant of the Hoch-Haus for a late supper. My leave seemed to have been made up of Martha—and food. But no meal, not even our engagement feast, had quite equaled the sheer joy of our first breakfast together—an hour after the train from Berlin had dropped me in Duisburg. It was only coffee with rolls and honey but it wiped away all memories of horse meat goulash and *Negerschweiss*. While Martha was making the bean coffee—which she had bought on the black market and saved for my homecoming—I wandered around the familiar room and found that I could banish all thoughts of Russia by merely touching the things which were part of Martha's life—the Blüthner grand which stood in the bow window, the small table on which, next to a bowl of tulips, lay a letter addressed to me in Russia; my oil and watercolor paintings hanging on the walls; the writing desk on which stood the framed photograph of myself as a white-coated young doctor.

Martha came in with the coffee.

And almost everyone I visited seemed to have saved a little bean coffee, a long-cherished bottle of wine, a special kind of sausage. I was blatantly spoiled. Nobody seemed to realize that I would have been quite happy with a plate of plain pea soup. They all sensed that sacrifices had been made for them by the men in Russia; they vaguely suspected that around Christmas time there had been chaos. And as one of the first men to return on leave, I was repeatedly questioned about the conditions and asked to tell the truth about the eastern front. But whatever I said, they still kept on talking of the coming summer offensive and ultimate victory. The propaganda machine had done its work well. Martha showed great fortitude as she listened over and over again to the same gramophone-like replies to the same stock questions. It was always with relief that I heard them utter the usual platitudes: "Yes, the German soldier has done it again. It will all be over this summer." For then I knew that the talk would veer in another direction.

With Martha I visited Frau Dehorn. She was still in mourning and life had lost its meaning for her. But our visits to *Oberst* Becker's wife, to Frau Noack and to Heinrich's family were joyful affairs. We played with Heinrich's red-cheeked little daughter—she was two years old—and made Frau Appelbaum laugh until the tears rolled down her face at the thought of her Heinrich cooking horse meat in castor oil.

There were evenings of magic when I let Martha's voice carry me with her into another world as she sang Pamina, Butterfly and Juliet in the Opera House.

Martha and I celebrated our engagement. The house in Krefeld belonging to my elder brother, Hans, was crowded. Next day we took the train for Vienna—Martha had been given 12 days' leave from the Opera, which would take us up to the day I had to return to Russia.

In Vienna we lived only for the moment. We drove to Grinzing and the Prater and thrilled to the signs of spring in the Vienna woods. We saved *Die Götterdämmerung* and supper in the *Hoch-Haus* for our last evening in Vienna.

Martha suddenly looked at me with her dark eyes. "Tell me, Heinz," she said, "do you really think we shall win the war?"

"I hope so, but I don't know. It will be a colossal task."

Martha placed her hands on mine and silently we looked out over the old city. In the shadows of the night stood the ancient *Stefansturm*. The liquid Viennese piano music, washed over us and softly Martha started to sing to me. In a few moments the *maître d'hôtel* stood at our table, bowed to Martha, and said: "Will you not give us all pleasure by singing at the piano—a few Viennese songs, perhaps?"

"Yes, tonight I think I would like that," she said, and got up from the table. She whispered to me as she went: "But you know that tonight I shall not be singing for everybody. Tonight my songs are meant only for you."

*   *   *

The last day of my leave we spent at Bonn, on the way to Cologne, from where the special troop train would leave for Berlin and the east. Hand-in-hand we walked to the old Toll Gate. The Rhine flowed past below us and we sat on a bench and gazed at the Seven Mountains looming hazily in the distance.

"Heinz, why must you go back into the front line? Haven't you had your share?" Martha burst out.

"My leave's over, my dear. Nothing can alter that."

Three young boys came bouncing up the steps and climbed on to the old cannons from the wars of liberation. They played at war, giggled when they saw us on the bench, became self-conscious all of a sudden and ran off down the stone steps four at a time.

"There are so many young doctors at home who've never heard a shot fired," Martha persisted. "You have heart trouble, you need rest. Surely you can report sick so that they don't send you back to the front line."

I put my arm around her shoulders. "What about all those men who are holding the *Königsberg* Line around Rzhev? In many cases their war has been worse than mine. We need every man if we're to prevent the Russians breaking through and flooding into Germany. I think they need even me."

Martha remained silent for a long time and then got up and said: "In that case I can only pray that someday you'll come back safely."

Black and ominous, the old cannons were silhouetted against the evening sky; a fresh wind piped through the trees and the distant strains of music came to us from the Hotel *Königshof.* Slowly, we walked down the worn stone steps from the old Toll Gate. The dream was nearing its end.

*   *   *

Köln Hauptbahnhof. The scene was much the same as when five young *Unterärzte* had left for Normandy. Bombing raids had altered the appearance of Cologne somewhat, but the huge roof still arched across the station; steam and smoke still lingered among the steel girders.[266] The loudspeaker blared: "Special troop express for Maastricht, Liège, Paris is standing at Platform Four." The harsh, precise voice paused. "Special troop express for Hanover and Berlin, with connections to Warsaw, Brest-Litovsk, Smolensk will leave from Platform Three."

A train stood at each side of the broad platform, and around the doors and windows of each train stood the crowds of civilians who had come to see their menfolk off. But there could have been no greater contrast between the two sets of people. On one side there were loud farewells, laughter, joking, excited instructions regarding what the soldiers must bring home from Paris when next they came on leave. People said "Good luck!" and it was only words. On our side there was little talking, no laughter. It seemed that everything had already been said. Women wiped tear-filled eyes and the partings were sober and deliberate.

Martha put her arms around my neck and kissed me, the conductor's whistle sounded and the train glided slowly away. I looked long into Martha's dark eyes, which confidently believed in my return. I wanted that look to accompany me along the road that lay ahead. And I knew that at that moment I felt happy. I was privileged; fortune had blessed me profoundly.[267] The coaches behind me bulged around a curve and the white handkerchief in the distance was lost to sight. The warm wind of May blew on my face and ahead, 1000 miles of shining rails led back to Rzhev.[268]

Epilogue

The warm May breeze ruffled young Heinz's fair hair as he played with baby Johannes on the neatly mown lawn. The bent palms threw a little jagged shade from the hot South African sun; the tall azaleas leaned against the lighter green of the golden cypresses and the camellias were heavy with new buds, which were waiting to burst open with the coming of shorter days.

As if from a great distance, I watched the two blonde heads—Heinz, now 13 years old, born in a Stuttgart air-raid shelter in 1944, and Johannes, his name a tribute to the sunny land that had seen his birth and had given us peace. But my thoughts were not with my two sons in this small winter world of sunshine on the green heights above Durban—they were on the letter in my hand. Martha had just brought it to me from the postbox and it was written in the precise hand of Baron von Kalkreuth. A month earlier I had seen his signature, for the first time since the war, on a business letter from Germany. It had come as a complete surprise and I had written to him immediately. Now I had his reply. And my thoughts traveled back, 15 years back to that other May when I had said good-bye to Martha on Cologne station. . . .

*   *   *

May had brought spring to Rzhev and Malakovo. The snow had disappeared and in its place was mud, mile upon mile of deep, clinging mud.[269] Part of the journey from Rzhev to Malakovo I made by sledge—wheeled transport was hopelessly bogged. Noack had been transferred to 1st Battalion and Papa Neuhoff had resumed command of the remnants of the 3rd Battalion. Our reunion was a joyful one. The 3rd Battalion was not to be rebuilt, but was to function as a small unit. Our sector of the front was completely calm, the summer sun dried out the roads and fields, and the countryside took on a friendlier aspect. Spotted fever, even among the civilian population, disappeared with the warmth, and Nina, who had completely recovered her health, had little to do. She helped me when necessary and I came to appreciate her as a true friend.

In mid-July 1942 a Saxon division relieved us at Malakovo;[270] we entrained at Rzhev and went to a rest camp near Sychevka, where we were to be re-formed and sent to the Orel area. I was promoted to *Oberarzt*. But on 30 July the balloon went up . . . rumors spread like fire . . . great Red offensive on Rzhev . . . Malakovo already in Russian hands . . . powerful Red Army formations preparing for a triumphal entry into Rzhev. The entire 6th Infantry Division, equipped only with light weapons, was bundled into trains and a few hours later was thrown against the enemy. On the platform of Sychevka railway station I was handed an order to report to Infantry Regiment 58 of the 6th Division as Regimental M.O. I took Heinrich and the Russian, Hans, with me.

Rzhev had the atmosphere of a doomed city. Malakovo, Gridino, Krupsovo, Kliponovo had all fallen; the Russians were attacking in force on the other side of the Volga. The pillars of the bridge across the river were packed with explosives, ready to be blown. Regiment 58 occupied Polunino at the northern outskirts of Rzhev and during the same night Neuhoff with his remnants, Major Höke, and my other comrades were thrown into the fight on our flank. The morning of 31 July ushered in the fiercest fighting of the whole campaign, but after 10 days of hell it ended with the retreat of the Russians. Rzhev had been held.

Some of the Russian civilians had fled across the river into Rzhev from the villages around Malakovo. Among them was Olga. She sought me out among the chaos and burst into tears. Nina had stayed behind to look after the sick civilians, had been summarily tried by a Red Army court-martial for assisting and fraternizing with the Germans and had received a bullet in the back of the neck as a traitress. Olga had tried to save her but the trial had been a mockery and it was only through the help of a Russian soldier that she herself had escaped the executioner.

The Red Army renewed its attacks with tremendous force. Day after day they threw their thousands against our hundreds and tried to smash into the city with their tank formations. Their artillery, their "Stalin Organs" and their rocket missiles flattened every building in Rzhev. The German Army in the city lived underground. But General Gross-mann, commander of the 6th Infantry Division, kept his nerve, and not a man wavered in his duty. *Oberst* Becker and my new regimental commander, *Oberst* Furbach, were decorated with the Knight's Cross. So, too, was the incomparable *Oberfeldwebel* Schnittger. But Neuhoff was killed by a bullet through the head and Noack died from severe stomach wounds at the height of the battle. Von Kalkreuth and *Oberleutnant* Rhein of Höke's battalion were seriously wounded and evacuated.

And so for day after day we fought, the swiftly flowing Volga behind us, the Reds in front of us. We fought from trenches and holes in the ground. We threw back the enemy's shock troops and allowed the sheer weight of the Russian tanks to roll over us, so that we could then turn and destroy them in a hand-to-hand carnival of desperate fury. And every day my bunker dressing station would overflow with the wounded and dying. It was a macabre nightmare of repetition.

The *Wehrmacht* report told us that if we could hold the powerful Red forces in front of Rzhev, victory in the South was guaranteed. And our armies in the South kept their part of the bargain—they stormed victoriously forward into the Caucasus Mountains and on to Stalingrad.[271]

*   *   *

I was awarded the Panzer *Nahbekämpfungsabzeichen* for having put out of action two Russian T-34s in hand-to-hand combat. Heinrich had done the damage to the first T-34, which was stuck in a defensive ditch; I hoisted him up by the legs and he dropped a grenade down the monster's gun barrel. Emboldened by our success, a few days later I had put another T-34 out of action with a home-made T-mine and grenades as it was menacing my dressing station.

The German Cross in Gold was also pinned on my tunic at this time.[272] The second half of the citation read:

> *During the defensive battle north of Rzhev, Regimental M.O. Oberarzt Haape was in charge of the dressing station at Polunino. In the period 2-21 August, 1942, under the most primitive conditions, single-handed he attended to 521 wounded in the face of the heaviest artillery, Panzer, and infantry fire. Through intense sustained personal effort and excellent organization, he succeeded in attending to every wounded soldier, and in arranging for their evacuation to the rear areas. . . .*
>
> *During an enemy breakthrough at Polunino, Dr. Haape, with lightly wounded men, occupied a trench adjoining the dressing station, defended it and materially contributed to the success of the defense. When field telephones and wireless were out of action during the heavy fighting, Dr. Haape volunteered to take important reports on the situation to Regimental H.Q. at the same time that he was evacuating his own wounded. For several days Dr. Haape took over anti-tank defensive measures by laying mines and constructing other obstacles. During a Russian breakthrough on 18 August, Dr. Haape, as one of the two surviving officers, gathered together isolated remnants of the battalion and effectively organized new defensive positions, which contributed very materially toward sealing off the enemy's breakthrough to Rzhev.*

But for me it was a time when the hours, the days, the weeks were steeped in blood, inexpressible horror and suffering. But I found compensation in the fact that every wounded man who passed through my hands had been evacuated. Some died of their ghastly wounds; on many of them I had been forced to perform the crudest field surgery in order to give them a chance of survival; but all had received whatever attention it was possible to give them, and none had fallen into enemy hands. Losses on our side had been enormous, and because I had somehow lived through it all, I found myself to be, in 1942, one of the most decorated doctors in the *Wehrmacht*, and was granted special promotion to *Stabsarzt* with the position of Divisional Medical Adjutant to *Oberfeldarzt* Greif.

*   *   *

The last leaves had fallen and snow obliterated the scars of the great summer tank battles in front of Rzhev. Food had become scarce during the ceaseless fighting and many of the Russian civilians were starving.

We had held Rzhev in the summer dust and we held it against the Red Army's attack in the winter snows.[273] And on 24 November 1942, I forgot the war for a brief hour. In a blockhouse near the Volga, Martha and I were married—by proxy. Martha went through a similar ceremony at her home in Duisburg on the Rhine. Those who remained of my old friends were there. *Oberst* Becker officiated, little Rudi Becker was witness and *Oberleutnant* Boehmer also came along. *Oberleutnant* Kluge played the piano and conducted a small choir of soldiers and *Oberfeldwebel* Schnittger brought the good wishes of the handful of men that survived from the 3rd Battalion. "May you, my dear *Haltepunkt*, be as happy in your marriage as I am in mine," said *Oberst* Becker in a sincere and moving little speech. On the next two days we fought bitter defensive battles in the snow, but the enemy was thrown back. Boehmer was among our dead.

With the tremendous defeat at Stalingrad, more than a thousand miles down the Volga, our front was to be shortened. On 3 March 1943 "Operation Buffalo" began and we evacuated Rzhev without enemy pressure.[274] *Oberst* Corle Becker had been promoted to the rank of Major-General and had been given command of a new division. Höke, that intrepid and stolid soldier, was promoted to *Oberst* and assumed command of Infantry Regiment 18. Nine days after the retreat from Rzhev began, *Oberfeldwebel* Schnittger fell, leading yet another counterattack. The law of averages had caught up with him.

Back we went along the hard-won road and occupied our sector of the new defensive line at Dorogobuzh, east of Smolensk. It was spring again, and again I was handed a leave form. A high-ranking official of the Propaganda Ministry was in Smolensk. He offered me a lift back in his aircraft. We landed at Warsaw, then flew on to Berlin. Martha and I solemnized our marriage in church.

*   *   *

Farewell again, and back to Russia, where the German Army was being forced back and was preparing for the huge climactical battle of Orel. A wireless message saved me. I was recalled to Berlin to set down for the High Command the results of my experiences, and was offered a brown shirt on which to display my decorations. I declined to join the Party and in support of my stand quoted the *Führer*'s own words—that he would wear the field-gray *Wehrmacht* uniform until the war had been won. At my request I was sent instead to Strasbourg and attached to a reserve artillery group.

* * *

And while I worked in my white, aseptic Strasbourg hospital, the battle of Orel was fought. Success was claimed, but if success it was, then it was a hollow one, for this time our losses were enormous too. The tide was turning. The 6th Infantry Division received official recognition as one of the three best divisions in the fighting on the eastern front.

A third winter of hard fighting passed while I still stayed in Strasbourg. A new spring and a new summer swept across Europe into Russia and the Red Army launched a mighty offensive against the dogged Germany Army.[275] On 28 June 1944, the 6th Infantry Division was encircled near Bobruisk. At their backs flowed the river of Napoleon's final defeat—the Berezina. And on the other bank, between the 6th Division and their homeland, stood the Russians. The final order was given: "Redundant weapons to be destroyed; only iron rations and ammunition to be carried. Code word 'Napoleon'— every man for himself." The men of Infantry Regiment 18, every man of the proud 6th Division fought like devils. Little Becker fell, so did *Oberfeldarzt* Schulze. Major Höke fought and died at the head of his regiment; heavily wounded, he saved his last bullet for himself. A few crossed the river and slipped through the Russian trap; most died on the banks of the Berezina. A small remnant was captured and marched away into captivity. Perhaps 100 men, not many more, struggled through the Pripet Marshes and reached their homeland—100 from the 18,000 men who had marched into Russia under the Bielefeld crest. The 6th Infantry Division, the heroic Infantry Regiment 18, had ceased to exist.

* * *

The Americans, the Canadians, the British splashed ashore on exactly the same stretch of coastline where the 6th Infantry Division had kept watch in 1940. Trevières, Arromanches, Grandcamp, Balleroy—the names were written in the history books after all. Paris fell and I was made chief medical officer for the entire Strasbourg area. At one sweep in November 1944, General le Clerc's army was in the city. For two days our men fought back from a fort on the Rhine, but this time, in the West, I did not have to play the soldier. Then we capitulated. A French officer walked up to me. I handed him my revolver—the Russian commissar's pistol—and my war was at an end.

* * *

. . . I looked again at the letter from von Kalkreuth. He had tried to organize a regimental reunion at Bielefeld, he wrote, but only he, *Oberleutnant* Rhein of Höke's battalion and young *Leutnant* Austermann could be traced. But old *Oberst* Becker was now back. When the first chapters of this book were being written he was in Siberia, serving a long sentence as a "war criminal."[276] In late 1955, however, he was one of a batch of German prisoners released by the Reds. His wife had not known he was coming and she had joyfully welcomed back from the dead an old man; an old warrior who was willing to talk of the dark days at Rzhev, but who would say no word about Siberia.

Old Volpius finished his reluctant career as an army doctor at Stalingrad, where Kramer also fell. Lammerding was invalided out of the *Wehrmacht* after his severe wound at Gridino and studied law at Heidelberg. But when the Allied troops swept through France, he was recalled to the colors, and fell 14 days later—shot in the stomach while fighting at the head of his company in the Eifel. *Freiherr* von Boeselager was the last surviving cavalry commander of the war in the east and died while trying to hold up the final Russian push at Warsaw.

A letter to "Uncle Doctor" was delivered to me a few days before I received Kalkreuth's letter; it came from 17-year-old Malies Appelbaum, Heinrich's daughter, the little girl for whom I had drawn pictures when I visited Heinrich's farm on my first leave. "We still don't know for certain what has happened to my Daddy," she wrote. "We have heard nothing about him since 1944." Heinrich is dead. I know that, although I have no proof. Heinrich is dead, because he would never have allowed himself to be taken prisoner.

Müller? Perhaps he perished on the Berezina. I don't know. Or perhaps he is still in Siberia. Perhaps a score of men of the 6th Bielefeld Division are still in Siberia. They may never come back. Or they may set out on their long journey back to life tomorrow.

The author's son, Johannes Haape, and former U.S. Air Force historian and Eastern Front expert Dr. Craig Luther traveled by car 4,492 kilometers along the route of 3rd Battalion, Infantry Regiment 18, from the German-Soviet demarcation line to the Tma River, northwest of Moscow.

Sergej Stasikov (left), a retired lieutenant colonel of the Soviet army, with Dr. Craig Luther (back right) and Johannes Haape (front right) poring over maps, original war diaries of Infantry Regiment 18, and other documents.

The location of the original customs house described in the opening pages of *Moscow Tram Stop.*

The hill on which Dr. Haape stood with his battalion commander when the first shots of the war were fired just after 3:00 a.m. on Sunday, 22 June 1941. The customs house was at the foot of this hill and used to identify the site.

Stalin bust with garlands at the Stalin Line museum outside Minsk, the capital of Belarus.

A hearty meeting between Johannes Haape and a Soviet veteran of the Great Fatherland War.

Dr. Craig Luther at the entrance to
Uspenskii Cathedral in Smolensk.

Family members and girlfriends at the
graduation ceremony of young lieutenants
of the Smolensk Military Academy.

Graduation parade of the Smolensk Military Academy in the city square. Towering over the participants is an
imposing statue of Lenin.

3rd Battalion Battle Site #1: Storming the Stalin line (15 July 1941), across the river and up a steep slope to one of several bunker complexes.

3rd Battalion Battle Site #2: The Volga River at Borki. The battalion's suicide attack on 15 December 1941 took place here—across the frozen Volga to the village of Krasnovo.

3rd Battalion Battle Site #3: The central street in Schitinkovo, once lined by houses where desperate hand-to-hand combat took place on 29 December 1941 that took a heavy toll on the battalion.

Russian war memorial in the main street of Schitinkovo. Virtually every village and town visited by Johannes Haape and Dr. Luther had a war memorial of some sort.

Tablets with the names of Russian dead at the battle of Schitinkovo.

The eighty-five-year-old eyewitness to the savage fighting in Schitinkovo and her grandchildren in front of a house in Schitinkovo.

Relatives with picture of a fallen ancestor.

Pallbearers at Russian military cemetary in Rzhev carrying a coffin with the remains of ten Red Army soldiers.

All coffins are being carried into an open grave, watched by relatives of the fallen.

Red carnations and sand cast by mourners at open gravesite filled with coffins holding the remains of some 1,200 Red Army soldiers.

One of millions of German identification tags (*Erkennungsmarken*)—
this one with a bullet hole. This tag
belonged to a soldier in 5th Company,
Signal Replacement Battalion 16.

German War Grave Commission's stone commemo-
rating fallen German soldiers.

Dietrich Schöning, veteran of 6th Infantry Division, accompanied by Karl-Josef
Schafmeister, chairman of *Kuratorium Rzhew*, and Schöning's grandson Christian
laying a wreath. Herr Schöning, who survived years in Soviet captivity, passed away
just weeks after this photograph was taken.

The German military cemetery, part of the Peace Park at Rzhev, with long rows of
memorial stone columns, each bearing the names of approximately one hundred
soldiers buried there.

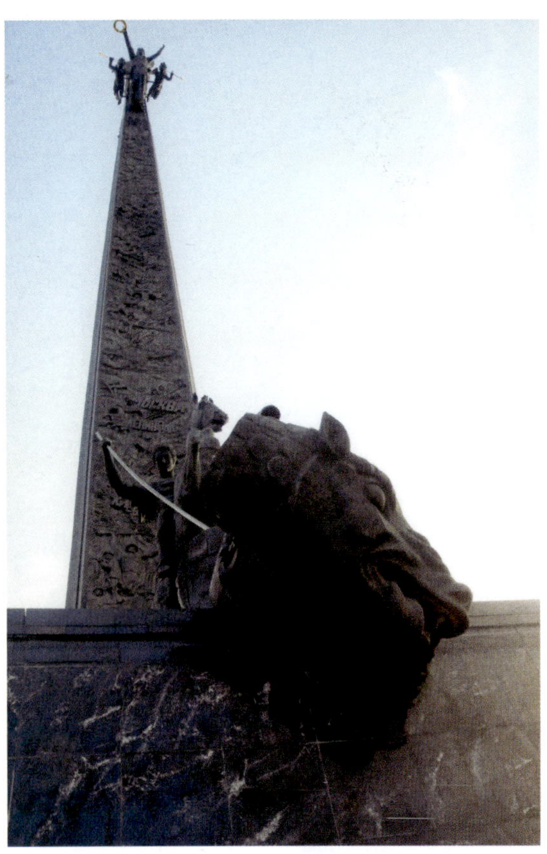

Russian war memorial at Victory Park in Moscow. St. George slays the German dragon.

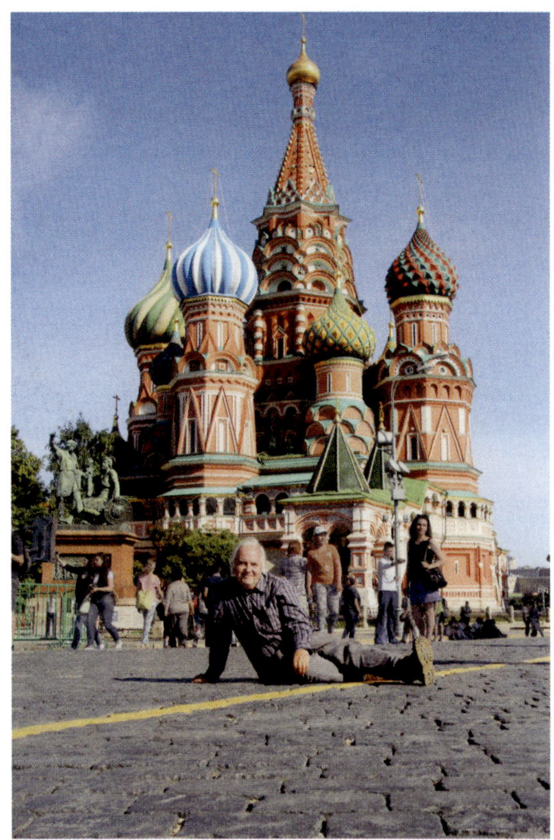

Basilius Cathedral on Red Square, Moscow.

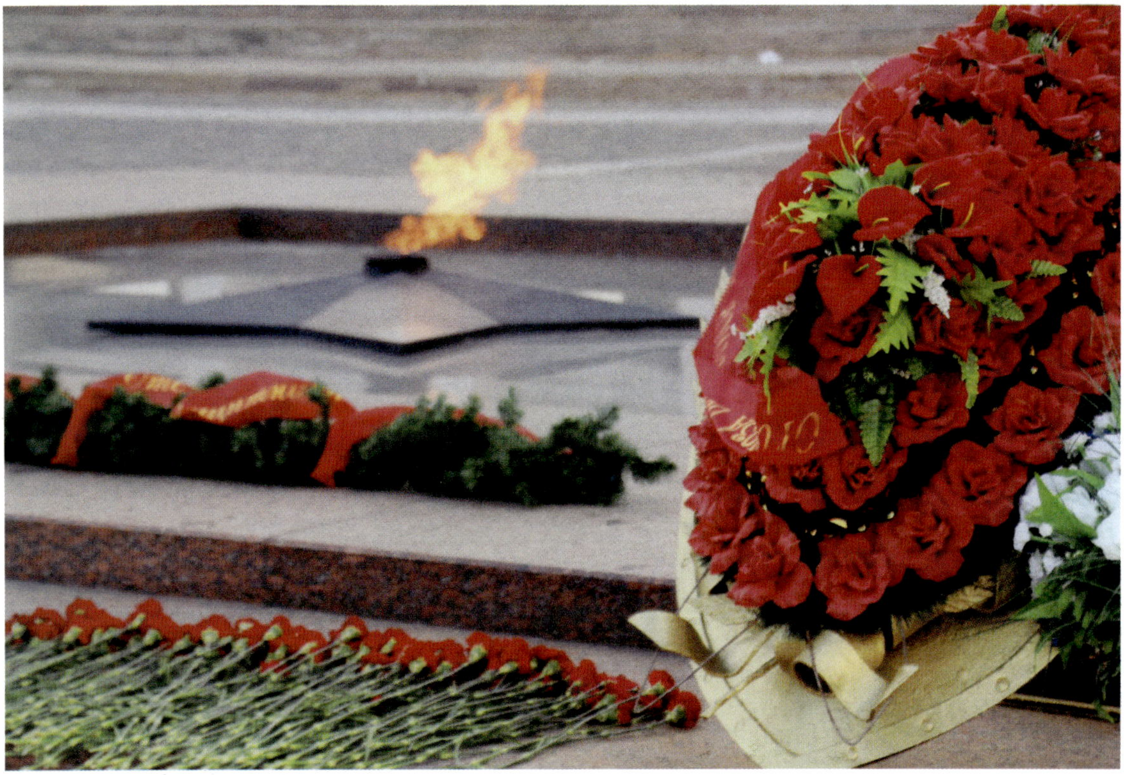

The Eternal Flame at Victory Park in Moscow.

ALL PHOTOGRAPHS IN THIS SECTION BY JOHANNES HAAPE.

Postscript

*In the Footsteps of Dr. Haape's 3rd Battalion,
Seventy-Five Years Later*

Johannes Haape

12 JUNE 2016

Spread out before us are the yellowed pages of the war diaries of Infantry Regiment 18, in whose 3rd Battalion my father—Heinrich Haape—had served as a medical doctor. The exquisitely detailed regimental war diaries—"Summer campaign 1941" and "Winter campaign 1941/42"—are written on two files. Alongside these is a list of the graves of fallen battalion members, with the coordinates of their locations. Around seventy military situation maps from the same period are also strewn across the table, showing the advance and battle plans of 6th Infantry Division, of which Infantry Regiment 18 was part.

Together with the American military historian Dr. Craig Luther and our Belorussian logistics expert Sergej Stasikov, a retired lieutenant-colonel of the Red Army, I sit in the dingy light of a room in an old hotel in the village of Suwalki, approximately 20 kilometers from the current border between Poland and Lithuania. Here by Suwalki the border runs along exactly the same lines that had been laid down in an amendment to the Molotov-Ribbentrop Pact, the nonaggression treaty between Germany and the Soviet Union, in August 1939. Almost seventy-five years to the day have passed since the first pages of the war diaries that lay before us had been written. We are overcome by an eerie feeling at the sight of these carefully collated documents. And yet their authors are not unknown to us. They, and the fate of the men of 3rd Battalion Infantry Regiment 18, are described in detail in the book by their comrade, *Assistenzarzt* (2nd Lt., med.) Haape. Over the next two and a half weeks, Craig, Sergej, and I—with the help of the original archive documents—will attempt to follow in the footsteps of 3rd Battalion in those historically portentous years of 1941 and 1942. We want to follow the road along which my father and his comrades marched; find the former battlefields on which they fought and where many of them died. Above all, we want to determine just how accurate the descriptions of these dramatic events in my father's book really are. Did it all really take place in the way that he describes? Are the accounts in his book historically accurate eyewitness accounts?

Our journey began by car from Berlin—first to Marienburg in former East Prussia, a mighty fortress in red sandstone that had been constructed by Teutonic knights in the fourteenth century as a bulwark against the heathen territories of the East. From there, we continued on to the *Wolfsschanze*, the Wolf's Lair, Hitler's command post during the Russian campaign. Construction of the command post—tucked deep inside a region of lakes, marshes, and dense forests of pine, spruce, beech, and oak—had begun in November 1940, eight months before the start of "Operation Barbarossa." It was here, on 20 July 1944, that the attempted bomb assassination of Hitler by Count Schenck von Stauffenberg took place.

Tomorrow we want to explore Filipów, a village some 20 kilometers west of Suwalki. This was where 3rd Battalion was stationed just a few weeks before the attack on the Soviet Union. The documents reveal that the battalion, along with Infantry Regiment 18, moved right up to the Vigra River, parallel to the Soviet border. We also know in which village the officers were ordered to meet for a final conference on 19 June 1941. The original war diaries and the situation maps lay out the exact sequence of the fighting on the first day of the campaign against the Soviet Union.

We are particularly interested in finding out how far we, seventy-five years later, will be able to trace the events recorded in the documents and described in such detail by my father.

13 JUNE 2016

The great German archaeologist Heinrich Schliemann once sent a telegram from Greece with electrifying news about his long search for the treasure of Mycenae: "I have seen the face of Agamemnon."

I felt something similar after finding the precise geographical location at which my father's book begins:

"It is 22nd June 1941, and I am standing with battalion commander Neuhoff and his adjutant, Hillemanns, on the crest of a small hill on the south-eastern border of East Prussia, the wide plains of Lithuania stretching ahead of us, but invisible in the pitch blackness before dawn."

There it was, that very hill on which my father had stood with his battalion commander. We recognized it thanks to the small border crossing directly at its foot, where once a customs house stood between German-occupied Poland and Soviet-occupied Lithuania. The customs house no longer exists, but—then as now—a sandy track still leads across the border in the direction of the town of Kalvaria.

We climbed up the hill and surveyed the view. It is still very rural; everywhere you look there are fields, meadows, and hills—most of the hills smaller than the one on which we were standing—woods, farmsteads, and here and there small clusters of houses. We returned to our car and drove along the sandy track and across the border. To the left, a narrow road led to two villages where, according to the regiment's war diary for 22 June 1941, fighting took place. Some buildings in the woods dated back to the war and were still partially in ruin. In his memoir, my father describes how the grave of *Oberleutnant* Stock was dug beside the sandy track, just a few hours after the attack had begun. We pulled out a list with the exact locations of the graves of some of the battalion's fallen soldiers. According to the list, *Oberleutnant* Stock's original grave should be in a farmstead near Galbanowka. We asked some farmers for the spot. We were directed to a small cluster of houses that stood under large trees, around 300 meters from the sandy track and approximately 4 kilometers from the border. We had found the original site of Stock's grave.

A little farther on, on the left of the road, we saw a broad, undulating field, where the ruins of the massive concrete bunkers of Akmenynai were visible in the distance. The 3rd Battalion had, for the most part, left these bunkers behind them on the very first day, keeping them to their left, and had continued marching late into the night until they had reached a point just outside Kalvaria. We visited Kalvaria, and, just as the 3rd Battalion had done, we crossed the broad Neman River near Prienai. Moving counter to the battalion's march route now, we drove about 60 kilometers northeast to Vilnius, the capital city of Lithuania, where we would spend the night. In the evening, we strolled through the beautiful baroque old town, past St. Stanislaus Cathedral and the reconstructed palace with its bell tower. A peaceful scene with friendly, cheerful people.

15 June 2016

We leave the territory of the EU behind us and cross the modern-day Schengen border to Belarus near Voranava.

Onward we go through what was then Soviet-occupied eastern Poland. The once striking cultural differences between Poland and Lithuania were largely homogenized during the Soviet era, but they soon reappeared after the collapse of the Soviet Union. We reach Minsk, then as now the Belarussian capital city. The city has evidently recovered from the war and stunningly displays its socialist heritage with grand buildings and generously proportioned roads.

On the way from Minsk to Polotsk, we make a stop to visit the huge, open-air Stalin Line Museum. Sergej is the expert here. He lives in Minsk, so he comes here frequently with his son and knows his way around. As at many other sites in the former Soviet Union, reconstructions of old defensive lines and bunkers, as well as dozens of tanks and artillery weapons of all calibers, are all displayed to the public in an area stretching over several hectares. The streams of visitors suggest the museum is enjoying brisk business.

We reached Polotsk's region of rivers and lakes in the afternoon. In 1941 this had been part of the feared Stalin Line. This defensive position, which had been developed by the Red Army since 1929, was intended in 1941 to halt the German advance. During the dawn attack against the Stalin Line on 15 July, 3rd Battalion was given the task of storming a strait in the river that was guarded by bunkers and to neutralize these with artillery support.

And suddenly, there it was—the scene described in the book. The narrow river, behind it the steep slopes, and at the top of the hill, along the crest of the rise, the bunker complex. With the book in hand, we stood on the riverbank and reconstructed the events of that dramatic morning. My father describes how he and his medical orderly, Dehorn, leaped across the river directly behind the first wave of the attack, following the stilts of a broken bridge and in the crossfire between two Russian bunkers, before scaling the steep embankment and establishing a makeshift dressing station in a shell crater at the top. Nobody had ordered him to move forward with the attacking soldiers. That was very unusual for a doctor. But because he risked his life to be at the forward edge of battle, he was able to save the lives of others. He provided life-saving treatment to casualties within minutes, without which many wounded comrades would certainly have perished.

We walked along to the bridge that crosses the river today and clambered up the slope to one of the bunker positions that my father describes. The heavy construction of reinforced concrete, behind which the Red Army soldiers were entrenched, still stands there, almost unaltered. The German artillery fire had torn gaping holes in the embrasures that were intended to watch over the strait. Someone had recently placed red plastic roses all along these apertures in the concrete. In the valley behind us lay the little village of Gomley, which had suffered badly in the fighting that day, and a few hundred meters behind the bunker complex stood a collection of memorials to the Red Army and partisan units.

16 June 2016

In the morning we visited the Great Fatherland War Museum in Polotsk. When the museum director heard my name, he pricked up his ears—he had read Heinrich Haape's book: in Russian! My jaw dropped! It turns out that my father's book had already been published in Russian in 2009 under the title *The Grimace of Death*. It's a translation of the English edition of *Moscow Tram Stop*. It was all done on the quiet by a Russian publisher without obtaining the rights for the book. The museum director fetched his copy from home because he wanted me to sign it. He was keen to emphasize how much he liked it because the author had seen the war with human eyes, rather than viewing it ideologically.

We departed Belarus and reached Smolensk in western Russia. From our starting point at Suwalki, the border defined by the Molotov-Ribbentrop Pact, we have already traveled 950 kilometers. We struggled to imagine what it must have been like in that summer of 1941, to have to cover such vast distances as an infantry foot soldier marching as many as 40 (or more) kilometers a day, carrying 25 kilograms of weapons, ammunition, and personal gear strapped to your back, across wretched roads in blazing heat and dust. The Infantry Regiment 18 reached the region north of Smolensk on 25 July, which means that they hadn't only marched 950 kilometers in just thirty-three days—they had also fought two large battles and many skirmishes with sharpshooters and partisans. The Red Army soldiers were experiencing similar conditions. Both sides demanded sacrifices from their soldiers that we can hardly fathom today.

We made a brief tour of Smolensk in our car. Its undisputed gem is the impressive turquoise and gold Cathedral of the Assumption (Uspenskii Cathedral), which towers high above the banks of the Dnepr River. A meeting with the director of the local office of the *Volksbund deutscher Kriegsgräberfürsorge* (German War Graves Commission) was on the schedule the following morning in order to plan a journey to the woods on the banks of the Mezha River, where 3rd Battalion had endured a grueling war of position from the end of July until mid-September 1941.

17 June 2016

In his tiny office, Uwe Lehmke gave us an introduction to the work of the commission. In Smolensk, sixteen people divided into three squads carry out exhumations and internments of the remains of former German soldiers. The soldiers' identification tags (*Erkennungsmarken*) play a decisive role in the task of identifying the remains. This is a small aluminum chip engraved with the number and unit of the deceased soldier. It would be hung around the neck of the deceased so that he could be identified at a later date. Uwe Lehmke showed us a small pile of these tags taken from the recently recovered remains of fallen soldiers.

Today's goal was to explore the area of deployment of Infantry Regiment 18 on the Mezha River and, if possible, to locate the grave of Dehorn, the medical orderly and highly esteemed comrade who had been the personal assistant to my father. After detailed discussion of the route, Yevgeni, an experienced member of the commission, was assigned to us. On the way, he told us about gravesites along the road between Smolensk and the Mezha that had not yet been investigated, but which were known to the commission. The first of these sites is thought to contain 910 graves and is situated close to a former German field hospital. Still on the road, he noted other sites with 50, 350, and 1,000 possible graves, one spot with 40 graves over which a new tarred road has been laid, 220 others that are about to be excavated, and yet another 350 graves that are located under four buildings that have recently been built. These gravesites were pointed out to us, all of them within an 80-kilometer stretch of our route, because we had a representative of the commission in the car with us. Without Yevgeni, we wouldn't have known a thing about these many graves. He also told us that there are many individual gravesites and smaller groupings of gravesites further away from Smolensk.

We finally reached wooded terrain and pushed on to the southeastern bank of Lake Schutsche. This was where 3rd Battalion was ordered to halt after Army Group Center, with over 1.3 million soldiers who had endured numerous forced marches, was unexpectedly brought to a complete standstill by an order from the *Führer*.

At first glance, this lake region seems idyllic. But even as we got out of the car the first mosquitoes and midges descended on us. We were told that great clouds of mosquitoes gather over the area of the lake at sunset. Even today, few people live in this region. In 1941, it didn't take long for the Red Army to notice that the advance of Army Group Center toward Moscow had come to a halt, and so they regrouped for a counteroffensive. And so, here, at the "end of the world," in the dense woods between Lake Schutsche and the Mezha River, a bitter war of position unfolded. I looked around me. This is where a highly modern army was pinned down in a war of attrition. This is where men risked their lives and died, full of faith in their *Vaterland*. I simply couldn't comprehend it!

Dehorn had been killed by a splinter in the head. My father writes that they buried him under three birch trees at a road crossing. Documents held by the *Deutsche Dienststelle* (WASt) in Berlin, which record the personal details of twenty million men in uniform, show that Dehorn's grave is located 800 meters west of the village of Chlomy, at the western fork of a road crossing.

Yevgeni brought out a map from around 1941. By combining this with a current map, we located the crossing from where Chlomy should lie to the right. But like so many others destroyed in the war, the village no longer exists. Then we discovered a path, set back from the road crossing, that led into the forest. This must be where Chlomy once stood. A comparison of the maps suggested that the road crossing had been moved slightly at some point in the last seventy-five years. I looked around for the three birch trees; they were no longer there. We must have got to within 200–300 meters of the grave, but the precise burial site of Medical Orderly Dehorn can no longer be found without expending a great deal of effort.

On our return journey to Smolensk, we stopped just outside the city at two large Russian cemeteries, each of which represented the final resting place for the remains of several thousand soldiers. Finally, we reached Dukhovshchina—the most recent of the large German military cemeteries established by the War Graves Commission in Europe and in which the exhumed remains from the region of Smolensk are laid to rest. In 2008, it was expanded to embrace seventy thousand gravesites. So far, the remains of around fifty thousand former *Wehrmacht* soldiers have been interred here. It has been estimated that roughly 140,000 Germans fell or went missing in action in the region around Smolensk. Much like Dehorn, the graves of many of them will most likely never be found.

18 JUNE 2016

While we were planning our route, many who had traveled in Russia warned us that the current crisis in Ukraine was likely to result in difficulties during the long journey from Berlin to Moscow, and that we would have to take that into account. Nothing of the kind occurred; we were given a friendly welcome wherever we went. And this morning was no different, as we observed the graduation ceremony of young lieutenants from Russia and other countries at the Smolensk Military Academy. The young men marched past us on the large parade ground in the middle of the city. Wives, girlfriends, and family members had come to see them, dressed in their best, beaming with joy and pride in their men. We spent an hour and a half in their midst. I made no secret of the fact that I come from Germany, and I was greeted warmly. Everyone was happy to be photographed. The retired director of the academy stood beaming and shaking my hand for the camera. And Craig's experience as an American was no different.

It was similar at the 777th anniversary celebrations of the city of Viaz'ma, where, in October 1941, one of the largest battles of the Second World War took place and several hundred thousand Soviets were taken prisoner. On Sunday morning we went to the church service there for the celebration of Trinity Sunday. A Russian war veteran, who was greeted by the provost and members of the congregation like a hero, shook me warmly by the hand. He claimed to have placed his own signature on the German Reichstag in May 1945. Now he was enthusing about his last visit to Germany, five years ago. He had been particularly impressed at how well the Soviet cemeteries in Germany are tended.

Always following the route of Infantry Regiment 18, our road led us around 250 kilometers farther. After two months at a standstill, on 2 October 1941, Army Group Center finally launched a major offensive toward Moscow. We found the spot at which, on that very day, Infantry Regiment 18 (or rather 3rd Battalion) succeeded in breaking through at Hill 215. After the death of Dehorn, my father was issued a new assistant to help him with his work as battalion doctor. Together with Acting Corporal (Med.) Schepanski, they joined in the attack so that casualties could be treated immediately. In doing so, Schepanski, who was just a few meters away from my father, suffered a direct hit by a shell and disappeared from the face of the earth.

During our journey we noticed that many areas, despite their natural beauty, appeared somewhat impoverished. The sparse villages that dotted our route were, for the most part, in poor condition. The countryside is green and fertile, and it rains enough. I wondered why there were not large numbers of smaller farmsteads.

Sergej explained that agriculture was still predominantly carried out by *kolkhozy*, collective farms. So while anybody could purchase land and plant whatever they liked, it was still the case that the old *kolkhozy* benefited from preferential prices for agricultural tools and fertilizers. A private enterprise had no chance in that sort of environment. This situation is apparently similar in other areas of business. For example, in one province a single family has the sole license to operate pharmacies. In other provinces there are monopolies on gas stations. After the collapse of the Soviet Union, rights and privileges reverted to old cliques and networks. The bulk of the economy remains in the hands of the few.

We finally arrived in Rzhev. Here we planned to spend the seventy-fifth anniversary of 22 June 1941 and to explore the area radially. First, we drove to the Peace Park, the military cemetery that was established by the German War Graves Commission on the initiative of the *Kuratorium Rshew*. The *Kuratorium*, which also supports hospitals, schools, and other civic institutions in Rzhev, was established in the 1990s by the veterans of 6th Infantry Division to promote reconciliation between Germans and Russians. Hence the name "Peace Park." This cemetery is unusual because it comprises two adjacent parts: one for Germans and one for Russians. This is where the remains of members of the *Wehrmacht* and the Red Army exhumed from the regions around Rzhev are interred. There are around thirty-four thousand graves on the German side so far. In front of the Peace Park stands a copy of the poignant sculpture by Käthe Kollwitz: *Grieving Parents*.

On the German side in particular, the whole complex radiates a comforting peacefulness. Many of the men of my father's 3rd Battalion lie in Russian soil in the countryside around Rzhev. Those who are successfully located and exhumed by the War Graves Commission will one day find their final resting place here.

It is 3,234 kilometers from Berlin to the Peace Park in Rzhev. Craig and I had the feeling that, in the cemeteries here, lay soldiers who had finally received the respect and acknowledgment due to them. This understanding helped us to make peace with the past.

20 June 2016

We are going to spend a week in Hotel Rzhev. The electricity supply is rather insecure in this old, nine-story building and is interrupted now and then. It's situated just above the steep slopes of the banks of the Volga, close to the historic bridge that was bombed during the war. The current flows slow and shallow at this point in the river, and a few kilometers downstream it reaches Staritsa and then Kalinin (now Tver): all fateful cities in which the most savage battles took place. We are staying long enough to try to get to grips with this part of history.

After the battles of Viaz'ma and Briansk, there was a gaping hole in the Russian defensive line outside Moscow; yet by mid-October 1941, Army Group Center was becoming bogged down in the seemingly bottomless mire of the fall rainy season, known locally as *Rasputitsa* or "the time with no roads," before ultimately freezing in the Russian winter. By early December, the spearheads of Army Group Center had come within 15 kilometers of the Russian capital and then ground to a halt.

While we have decided to set up base in Rzhev, in 1941 the 3rd Battalion marched on and crossed the Volga for the first time downriver at Ulitino, not far from Staritsa. On 26 October, 3rd Battalion crossed the Tma River and got as far as Eremkino, 100 kilometers northwest of Rzhev. It was the furthest point 3rd Battalion was to reach in the campaign.

We quickly found Eremkino. Outside the village stood a Russian monument with the names of 250 Red Army soldiers who had died in the area. With the exception of four names, all of them had died in November and December 1941. These men did not die in encounters with 3rd Battalion; the battalion had been redeployed to the east, in the direction of Kalinin. Here, the Red Army was on the verge of encircling the German units in the town. The 3rd Battalion received orders to halt the Soviet breach at Krasnovo on the Volga and to push it back. It was obvious that this undertaking couldn't succeed and that the assignment was a suicide mission aimed at giving the units stationed at Kalinin time to withdraw.

My father describes the progress of the battle. A field dressing station had been set up in Borki, on the western banks of the Volga, where the river formed a bend. A second had been set up in a small village on the opposite bank. The battalion began the counter-attack on 15 December 1941, moving from Borki out and over the frozen Volga River. We drove there and found the village by the river, at a point with steep embankments, just as it is described in the book. The target of the attack, Krasnovo, lies 3 kilometers east of the Volga. Now, in the summer, we had to drive a detour to get there. Today, the village is a prosperous place outside Kalinin/Tver, with villas among the most impressive we have seen on our journey.

Back in 1941, 3rd Battalion attacked with approximately six hundred men in temperatures of -40°C. Wading through snow 150 centimeters deep, they faced four thousand to six thousand Red Army soldiers who were trying to encircle Kalinin from the direction of Krasnovo. The attacking infantrymen had no winter uniforms, had no choice but to advance over open fields, and their automatic weapons were freezing up in the cold. Yet despite severe losses, the attack succeeded in checking the Soviet forces just long enough to ensure that the German troops escaped from Kalinin.

The *Wehrmacht*'s retreat from Moscow had begun.

Finally, the remnants of 3rd Battalion also fell back. It was a hellish march through snow and ice, repeatedly interrupted by fighting, and pursued by the Red Army, whose leadership could sense a change in fortunes. We drove parallel to the march route approximately 50 kilometers to the south, past the next battleground of Schitinkovo, and back to our hotel.

21 June 2016

Today, as it was back then, Schitinkovo is a hamlet surrounded by open fields and forests. We found an eyewitness to the events of 1941. The eighty-five-year-old woman was hosting her grandchildren, who capered around us. She spoke to us quite candidly about the time that the Germans had been there; they had stayed, so she said, for three months. In fact, their stay there must have been a little over two months. At first, six to eight soldiers lived in the village. Two were given accommodation with her mother: Siegfried and Jusop. Jusop came from Slovakia. The soldiers always had their own food with them, but sometimes food was bartered. When one of them received mail from home, he gave the children some of his chocolate. On one occasion, some soldiers came and requisitioned a cow from the family, which they then led away. After Christmas a new unit moved in. This was evidently the 3rd Battalion under the battalion commander *Oberleutnant* Count Franz von Kageneck. The woman said that he ordered the entire village population to sleep in two houses at night. During the day they could move freely and go about their normal business. This measure was a precaution against the severe battles that were taking place at night and kept the villagers out of the line of fire. Ultimately, it saved their lives.

The 3rd Battalion, reinforced by a number of smaller troop formations, remained there for three days. Contrary to their situation in Krasnovo, here the men had an advantage, because they could barricade themselves in the village. This was a relief for the soldiers, who, in temperatures of -40°C, were dressed only in summer uniforms. Their machine guns could also be warmed in the ovens so that they were functional during the attacks—and the Russians would attack at night. During a reconnaissance mission, *Oberleutnant* Stolze got caught in an ambush and was brought back to the village by his men: dead. During the third night, the Russians managed to break through into the village. There followed a dramatic battle from house to house. Everything hung in the balance. My father had to defend the field dressing station with the help of medical orderlies and the less serious casualties; it was a matter of life and death. A seriously wounded soldier, who had lost both his legs, had himself carried up into the roof timbering and from there he operated a machine gun. Finally, the men were able to once again eject the Russians from the village.

When the 3rd Battalion withdrew, only ninety-nine of the original eight hundred men were still with the battalion. Kageneck, a close friend of my father, was fatally wounded. My father describes how he accompanied the badly injured man past the village of Terpilovo to a point over the frozen Volga River. We followed the same route that he must have taken and found Terpilovo 3 kilometers away from Schitinkovo. Not far off, the Volga flows past.

In the rain, but in summer temperatures, we drove our comfortable SUV along the march route taken by the remnants of 3rd Battalion toward the historic city of Staritsa. The troops reached the city on 31 December. Panic hung in the air. The enemy was well equipped for winter fighting and numerically far superior. Only Prussian discipline and drill prevented the complete collapse of Army Group Center in front of Moscow.

We set about looking for the gravesite of Kageneck, who had died here in the field hospital. Thanks to information from his family, we soon found the spot. Today it is a peaceful patch of earth beneath a few trees not far from the Volga. My father writes of it in his book:

I walked to the makeshift military cemetery near the Volga and found his undecorated grave—a grave in the middle of many more. In front of me lay the frozen Volga.

From the German War Graves Commission we know that Kageneck was buried alongside thirty-seven comrades. My father's description is correct; he just did not want to say that his friend was lying in a mass grave.

Bit by bit, the remnants of the 3rd Battalion retreated further. Over and over again, certain sectors would be defended; again and again, the enemy would be beaten back before the battalion continued on its retreat. No withdrawal was permitted during an enemy attack. Finally, they reached the "Königsberg Line," approximately 15 kilometers outside Rzhev. Under no circumstances was this to be surrendered; "hold fast or die" was the watch word. Every man knew that there was no alternative.

When, in mid-January, 3rd Battalion was finally pulled back to Malakovo, 3 kilometers behind the main line of defense to act as a counterattack reserve, only twenty-eight of the original eight hundred men remained!

The survival strategy paid off. Even the massive Russian offensive was eventually spent—and thus ended the decisive winter battle of Moscow. By December 1941 the Germans and their allies had deployed 3.5 million men and several thousand tanks. Aside from the weather conditions, for which they were badly prepared, the reasons for the failure to take Moscow lay in the Germans' lack of reinforcements despite ever increasing losses. Fewer and fewer men had to accomplish ever greater tasks. Hitler had badly miscalculated. He had gambled everything on a quick and decisive Blitzkrieg. When this failed, the German High Command had no alternative strategy. Conversely, the Red Army was able to mobilize an ever increasing number of troops so that, by the end of 1941, it had deployed a total of 8.5 million men and tens of thousands of tanks and artillery pieces. In December 1941, the United States entered the war after Pearl Harbor. This development resulted in enormous supplies of weapons, trucks, and other war materials being delivered to the Soviet Union by America and England, and Germany having to fight not only in Russia but also against the Anglo-Americans in North Africa, Italy, and France. It had become a war against nations holding 75 percent of the world's resources that Germany could not win.

We saw the day out in our little inn by the Volga. Then it was off early to bed, because we intended to set off at dawn the following morning to join the commemoration for the seventy-fifth anniversary of the German invasion of the Soviet Union.

22 June 2016

At 4:00 a.m. Russian time, exactly seventy-five years after the beginning of the Great Fatherland War, we met in the center of town, on Lenin Square. About two thousand of Rzhev's inhabitants had come to pay tribute to their dead by candlelight, with songs and readings. Then they filed down to the Volga, where wreaths adorned with candles were laid on the river. Similar ceremonies were taking place at the same time all over the former Soviet Union.

Late in the morning we went across to the Russian section of the Peace Park. On this day the remains of 1,200 Red Army soldiers were to be interred. They had recently been located and exhumed in the area around Rzhev. Around 1,500 people attended the memorial here as well. Some carried photographs of their forebears—the family similarities were often striking. After a church service and a formal commemoration ceremony, approximately 120 caskets containing the remains were carried down into about four open graves the size of half a swimming pool. Before each grave was closed, mourners scattered a handful of soil and laid a red carnation at the side of the grave.

In contrast to the Germans, the soldiers of the Red Army had no official identity marker. Usually, a simple note on a piece of paper was left in an empty cartridge, but after seventy-five years these notes were illegible. It meant that at most 5 percent of the remains of Red Army soldiers could be identified, and they were generally buried in collective caskets. By contrast, the identified German soldiers were usually lowered into their graves in individual, 80-centimeter-long caskets.

All over western Russia, in Belarus, and in Ukraine, there stand monuments to commemorate the dead. Particularly in the area immediately before Moscow almost every village has such a reminder of the past. There are numerous museums, and you can find a small museum of the Great Fatherland War in almost every sizeable school. In Smolensk we saw a decorated tank. It is a common practice there for newly married couples to lay flowers on a tank. In the former Soviet Union the end of the war on 9 May (not, as in the West, on 8 May) is commemorated, as well as 22 June. The two celebrations each have a different emphasis: 9 May has a heroic note; 22 June resembles a requiem.

We discussed the memorial culture here. Who in Germany still marks the *Volkstrauertag*, the National Day of Remembrance? Have the millions of dead who fought on the German side less right, as people and individuals, to be remembered than Russians, Americans, Britons, French, or the dead of other nations? When the last living German soldier to have fought in the First World War died in 2008, not one of the better-known German politicians of the day made a public statement on his passing.

23 JUNE 2016

The delegation of thirty from the *Kuratorium Rshew* arrived on 23 June. They had flown to Moscow and traveled from there by bus. Of the original veterans of my father's 6th Infantry Division, who had founded the *Kuratorium* to promote reconciliation between Germans and Russians, only Dietrich Schöning had been able to make the journey. In a sign of respect for the *Kuratorium*, this year's delegation had been expressly invited to participate in the eight-hundred-year anniversary celebrations of the city. Craig and I were included as official guests of the delegation. Over the course of three days, we attended conferences of historians and visited schools and hospitals, all of which were supported by the *Kuratorium*. Also, the delegation were guests of honor at a reception hosted by the mayor of Rzhev. The highlight of the visit was the official wreath laying at the German and Russian cemeteries in the Peace Park, accompanied by Gütersloh, Rzhev's partner town in Germany.

Most of the delegation had come to remember their dead forebears. One lady from Melle, in Lower Saxony, was visiting for the third time to urge the German War Graves Commission to find the remains of her uncle. Now, finally, she could be reassured that his remains had been located and exhumed and would shortly be interred in the Peace

Park. The father of another delegate from Berlin had been interred in the original German military cemetery in Rzhev, which had later been razed by the Soviets. Garages had been built on the site. As a result, there was no place for this woman to lay a wreath for her father. So instead she brought a small brass plate, which she placed at the foot of the correct stone column bearing the names of fallen comrades in the Peace Park. A doctor from Gütersloh searched and found the name of his grandfather on one of the stone columns. Now, he said, he could make peace with the past.

My father's book ends with the winter battle of Moscow. He was deployed to Infantry Regiment 58, because 3rd Battalion, Infantry Regiment 18, had now shrunk to the size of a combat patrol and such a small unit could not justify having its own doctor. The battles around Rzhev raged for another summer and another winter. The Red Army tried desperately to break through the German positions in order to prevent the protruding bulge in the German front line at Rzhev from being used as a bridgehead for a renewed attack on Moscow. Around one million people lost their lives in this sector of the front line alone. As if by miracle, my father was redeployed to the west in mid-1943. It saved his life. The 6th Infantry Division, and his comrades of Infantry Regiments 18 and 58, were encircled and annihilated in the massive Soviet offensive in June 1944.

It is estimated that some thirty thousand soldiers served in the 6th Infantry Division throughout the war. After being encircled in 1944, only a few hundred managed to slip through enemy lines and make their way back to Germany. Some fought to the last bullet; others surrendered. Of those who survived the Russian prisoner of war camps, most returned home over a period of eleven years—between 1944 and 1955. In total, perhaps 10 percent of the men of the 6th Infantry Division survived the war and captivity in the East.

27 June 2016

We said our goodbyes to the delegation of *Kuratorium Rshew* and embarked on the final stage of our journey to Moscow. In his memoir, my father describes how, in late November 1941—that is, before the start of the Soviet counteroffensive—he drove with *Oberleutnant* Kageneck from their battalion positions to the town of Klin, and from there to the final stop of a tramline, which, in peacetime, serviced a route that ran all the way to the center of Moscow. We kept as closely as possible to the same route. Today, an asphalted highway with four lanes runs from Klin to Moscow. This road expands first to six and then to eight lanes. Somewhere along this route, around 60 to 65 kilometers from Klin and just a few kilometers from the old city limits of Moscow, the two men happened upon the tram stop.

In Moscow, we spent the day in the outdoor grounds of the Victory Park of the Great Fatherland War and visited the Russian headquarters of the German War Graves Commission and Red Square. We had driven 4,492 kilometers by car from Berlin to Moscow!

The city center is impressive. Broad roads and squares, high-rise blocks and ultramodern buildings, abound. The inhabitants, especially the younger generation, are fashionably dressed. It was striking that most Muscovites are slimmer than people in Germany. Jeans are not so common a sight; women frequently wear skirts and high heels. The shop windows in the city center seem similar to those at home. Limousines are evidently very popular. I had the impression that the city had experienced considerable developments since my last visit in 2001. Of course, there is also a side to Moscow that is neglected and unkempt, entire city quarters with dreary residential blocks dating from the Communist past.

An epic journey lies behind us. On the way from Berlin to Moscow, we drove through areas with many different cultures, encountered different peoples, and experienced a diversity of landscapes. We were confronted with the memories of the amazing bravery of soldiers on both sides, the atrocities and the magnitude of the war in the East from 1941 to 1945, indisputably the biggest clash of arms ever between nations. We explored the flashpoints of this epoch-making struggle and stood in the exact spots where my father once stood and endured his comrades dying one by one. Craig and I were able to confirm that his book is a precise and reliable eyewitness account, faithful to detail, and an authentic reflection of the experiences of the time.

Appendix 1

Comparative Military Ranks (German / American)[277]

OFFICER RANKS

German	American
Generalfeldmarschall	Field Marshal
Generaloberst	General
General (*der Infanterie*, etc.)	Lieutenant General
Generalleutnant	Major General
Generalmajor	Brigadier General
Oberst	Colonel
Oberstleutnant	Lieutenant Colonel
Major	Major
Hauptmann or *Rittmeister*	Captain
Oberleutnant	First Lieutenant
Leutnant	Second Lieutenant

NONCOMMISSIONED OFFICERS

German	American
Stabsfeldwebel	Sergeant Major
Oberfeldwebel	Master Sergeant
Feldwebel	Technical Sergeant
Unterfeldwebel	Staff Sergeant
Unteroffizier	Noncommissioned Officer

ENLISTED MEN

German	American
Stabsgefreiter	Administrative Corporal
Obergefreiter	Corporal
Gefreiter	Lance Corporal
Obersoldat	Private 1st Class
Soldat (*Schütze*)	Private (Rifleman)

Medical Ranks

Oberstarzt	Colonel (medical)
Oberfeldarzt	Lieutenant Colonel (medical)
Oberstabsarzt	Major (medical)
Stabsarzt	Captain (medical)
Oberarzt	First Lieutenant (medical)
Assistenzarzt	Second Lieutenant (medical)
Unterarzt	NCO (medical)

Appendix 2

Record of Dr. Heinrich Haape's Military Service (1939–1944)[278]

Jul 39: While working as a doctor at Kaiser Wilhelm hospital in Duisburg, Dr. Haape is drafted into the military for three months to be trained as an artilleryman (*Kanonier*). (Following basic training, he will join the *Wehrmacht* medical corps.)

Sep 39: Personnel records (*Deutsche Dienstelle*) indicate that Dr. Haape is assigned to Artillery Replacement Battalion 26 (*Artillerie-Ersatz-Abteilung 26*) in Düsseldorf.

Oct 39: Now a private in the medical corps (*Sanitätssoldat*), Dr. Haape is transferred to the 6th (Replacement) Medical Battalion in Amsberg.

Oct 39: Transferred to reserve military hospital in Paderborn (near the troop training grounds at Sennelager), where he works as a surgeon.

Nov 39: Promoted to *Unterarzt* (NCO, med.).

Jul 40: By beginning of month, transferred to reserve military hospital in Bad Driburg.

Aug 40: Transferred to reserve military hospital in Warburg; performs surgery on soldiers badly wounded in French campaign.

Nov 40: Receives orders to report to the 6th Infantry Division in Normandy, France; assigned as *Unterarzt* to 3rd Battalion, Infantry Regiment 18.

Mar–Apr 41: As part of buildup for Operation "Barbarossa," Adolf Hitler's impending surprise attack on the Soviet Union, 6th Infantry Division dispatched to East Prussia, then to Suwalki triangle, close to Russo-German frontier.

Jun 41: Begins Russian campaign with rank of *Assistenzarzt der Reserve* (2nd Lt. Medical), 3rd Battalion, Infantry Regiment 18, 6th Infantry Division.

Jun–Jul 41: Participates in battles along the Russo-German frontier; distinguishes himself during capture of Polotsk on the Stalin Line.

Jul 41: Awarded the Iron Cross, Second Class.

Aug–Sep 41: War of position (*Stellungskrieg*) along the Mezha River Line north of Smolensk.

Oct 41: Participates in Operation "Typhoon," Army Group Center's drive on Moscow; awarded the Iron Cross, First Class.

Dec 41–Mar 42: Participates in winter fighting and withdrawal to the *Königsberg* Line northeast of Rzhev; is lightly wounded by shell splinter.

Jan 42: Transferred to Infantry Regiment 37 at Gridino for ten days to provide medical support, following death of *Stabsarzt* Lierow.

Apr 42: Promoted by directive of the Army High Command (OKH) to *Oberarzt der Reserve* (1st Lieutenant, medical).

Jul 42: At end of month detailed from Infantry Regiment 18 to Infantry Regiment 58 (6th Infantry Division) as regimental medical officer and battalion doctor for 3rd Battalion (I.R. 58).

Aug 42: Involved in bitter fighting at Rzhev. Destroys Soviet T-34 in close combat and receives personal acknowledgment of General Bruno Bieler, Commander, 6th Army Corps.

Aug 42: Awarded along with all German soldiers on the Eastern Front who had taken part in the winter battles of 1941–1942 the so-called *Ost-Medaille*. Medal is mocked by the *Landser* as the "Frozen Flesh" (*Gefrierfleisch*) medal.

Aug 42: Evaluation of Dr. Haape by *Oberst* Becker, Commander, Infantry Regiment 18: "Continues to perform splendidly as medical officer at the front. Has a thoroughly decent and utterly steadfast character, mature personality. Has mastered the most difficult situations in the defensive battles and has proven himself in the face of the enemy."

Sep 42: Dr. Haape and his staff relieved from fighting at Rzhev and transferred to a quiet sector; awarded the Tank Close-Combat Insignia (*Panzernahbekämpfungs-Abzeichen*).

Oct 42: Evaluation of Dr. Haape by *Oberst* Furbach, Commander, Infantry Regiment 58: "As a medical officer, soldier, and a man equally outstanding [*gleich hervorragend*]. Rich in experience, practical in his thinking, independent, energetic and with his own ideas. Particularly dashing [*schneidig*] in the face of the enemy. . . . One could not wish for a better [military] doctor."

Oct 42: Late in month, Dr. Haape and his staff return to the front—to Rzhev.

Nov 42: *Oberarzt* Dr. Haape is detailed to 6th Infantry Division as divisional medical adjutant to *Oberfeldarzt* Greif, the 6 ID doctor.

Nov 42: Awarded the coveted German Cross in Gold (*Deutsche Kreuz in Gold*) by order of the "*Führer* and Commander-in-Chief of the *Wehrmacht*" for his role in the summer battle for Rzhev. Haape has become one of most highly decorated doctors in the *Wehrmacht*.

Dec 42: Evaluation of Dr. Haape by General Grossmann, Commander, 6th Infantry Division: "First-rate doctor, splendidly brave. Warmly support special consideration for promotion."

Dec 42: *Oberfeldarzt* Greif has been transferred to the Caucasus; Dr. Haape assumes responsibility for the medical care of 6th Infantry Division.

Jan 43: Receives preferential promotion to *Stabsarzt der Reserven* (Captain, med.) due to bravery in the face of the enemy; promotion is retroactive to 1 December 1942.

Feb 43: In a letter to a "Herr *Oberstabsarzt*" in Germany, Dr. Haape notes the following awards and decorations listed in his pay book (*Soldbuch*): E.K. II, E.K. I, Wound Badge, Infantry Assault Badge, Tank Close Combat Insignia, the Eastern Medal and the German Cross in Gold.

Mar 43: 6th Infantry Division takes part in Operation "Buffalo" (*Büffelbewegung*), the withdrawal of German Ninth and Fourth Armies from the Rzhev salient.[279]

May 43: Permanently recalled from Eastern Front; detailed to Berlin to prepare report on his experiences as a doctor in Russia.

May–Jun 43: Sent to Duisburg and assigned to Army Medical Echelon Duisburg (*Heeres-Sanitäts-Staffel Duisburg*); serves temporarily at a military hospital in Duisburg-Hamborn.

Aug 43: Participates in a three-week training course in Berlin.

Sep 43: Transferred to Strasbourg, where he initially serves as battalion doctor to an artillery replacement and training unit (*Art. Ers. u. Ausb. Abt. 215*).

Apr 44: By now (exact date unclear), he is assigned to Reserve Military Hospital II, Surgery Section 118, in Strasbourg.

Aug–Sep 44: Sometime after fall of Paris to the Allies, Dr. Haape becomes chief medical officer (*Standortarzt*) for all of Strasbourg.

Nov 44: Captured by Allied forces in Strasbourg and dispatched to an American prisoner-of-war (POW) facility in southern France (Marseille). Cares for sick and wounded German prisoners and performs numerous surgeries.[280]

Jan 46: Evacuated to American POW hospital in Göppingen, Germany.

Feb 46: Transferred to a mental hospital in Wiesloch near Heidelberg[281] (in an effort to gain release from captivity, Haape has simulated a serious mental illness).[282]

Feb 46: On 16 February 1946, Dr. Haape is released from American captivity; returns to Martha and their baby boy, Heinz Jr., in Stuttgart.[283]

Appendix 3

6th Infantry Division: Personnel and Weapons

	20 June 1941[284]	1 December 1941[285]	11 March 1942[286]
Combat Strength (*Gefechtsstärke*)[287]			
Officers	363	318	197
Civilian Officals[288]	13	16	25
NCOs[289]	2,080	1,877	1,390
Enlisted Personnel[290]	11,838	10,122	5,617
Horses	4,468	5,024	2,417
Ration Strength (*Verpflegungsstärke*)[291]			
Officers	460	396	273
Civilian Officals	85	87	83
NCOs	2,566	2,507	1,748
Enlisted Personnel	15,079	13,226	7,145
Horses	5,555	5,250	2,594
Total Available Weapons (*Verwendungsbereite Waffen*) (excluding small arms)			
light machine gun	455	371	307
heavy machine gun	142	89	55
light mortar 50mm	60	65	50
medium mortar 81mm	56	47	20
light infantry gun 75mm	17	19	6
medium infantry gun 150mm	6	4	5

	20 June 1941[284]	1 December 1941[285]	11 March 1942[286]
anti-tank guns	74	62	48
light anti-tank rifles (*Panzerbüchse*)	65	66	60
light field howitzer 105mm	36	33	24
medium field howitzer 150mm	12	9	5
anti-aircraft gun 20mm	12	10	6
light anti-aircraft gun	12	7	4
medium anti-aircraft gun[292]	3		
21cm heavy howitzer (*Mörser*)			3

Appendix 4

Dr. Haape's Fiancée Responds to Outbreak of War with Russia (from her unpublished memoirs)

(*Note:* The public reaction in Germany to the sudden outbreak of war with Soviet Russia was mixed. In Berlin, the official public response was stoical, demonstrating "complete trust in our *Wehrmacht*" and "facing the coming events with calmness and martial determination."[293] The reality was rather different. Many people, particularly those who had not seen it coming, reacted with a profound sense of shock. Yet there was also a great sense of liberation among many ordinary Germans, as the weeks fraught with speculation and rumor were finally over and "Germany could at last engage with what many of them regarded as their country's most dangerous opponent. Even the less ideologically committed would have absorbed the vehement anti-Soviet rhetoric of the early 1930s and adjusted only with difficulty to the tactical alliance with Moscow which had opened the war."[294] In the paragraphs below, Martha Arazym, Dr. Haape's future wife, recalls her response to the start of Operation Barbarossa.)

And now, as of this morning, we are at war with Russia. My mind was incapable of absorbing the idea, *least of all comprehending it. I was glued to the radio to find out more. The fanfares which almost caused me to tremble, introduced every bit of breaking news for the years to come. Then the announcement:* "The High Command of the German Wehrmacht announces . . ." *It is the 22nd of June 1941.*

A large photograph of Heinz looking very relaxed in a simple soldier's uniform hung in my living room. I looked at it for a long time, saw his clear eyes, his friendly expression, and the slight smile on his lips. I smiled back. Suddenly Heinz seemed close enough to touch. He was with me in the room. I whispered: "Dear God, protect him for me. Give him your blessing."

I lived in constant fear and trepidation, but was also filled with hope despite know-ing that my Heinz was in the gravest danger on the Russian front. I felt close to both God and to him. Daily I sat at my desk and wrote, *including him in all my day-to-day concerns. This way I always felt near to him. I also sensed how much interest in and engagement with my stories he showed. A strong, invisible bond united us, giving us both strength, hope, and faith in seeing each other again.*[295]

Appendix 5

"Pan Pankowski" (Account by Dr. Haape Omitted from Original Edition)

(*NOTE:* THIS ACCOUNT IS REVEALING IN WHAT IT EXEMPLIFIES ABOUT THE OFFICERS AND soldiers of the German 6th Infantry Division—that despite the criminal intentions of their political and military leadership, which, from the beginning, gave its soldiers on the Eastern Front free reign to operate outside the canon of international law, the great majority of the division's personnel fought a decent and honorable war under the most frightful conditions imaginable. Why this story was omitted from Dr. Haape's memoir is unclear.)

On the afternoon of the same day we reach Oszmiana.[296] We find few friendly houses there, only the same wretched-looking wood cottages we've seen everywhere. Perhaps because of that, it is the two churches which make the strongest impression in these miserable surroundings. A radiant white church with two spires seemed strongly influenced by western cultural circles and, in its construction, reminded us very much of the baroque—it seemed to embody both Polish and western influences. But it was the other church which aroused most of our interest. Behind its heavy walls and high gates the church's two mighty onion-domed towers gazed far off into the distance—a testimony to the Russian orthodox influence and making abundantly clear to us that we were now not far from the old Russian border.

In the town itself there is great unrest. The Russians have only just recently withdrawn and the locals report to us of atrocities, deportations and mass shootings, as had occurred in Lemberg. Our battalion staff establishes its quarters in a school. While both Lammerding and Hillemanns are busy making the arrangements, I stroll through the streets of the town—the first sizeable one we've come across. On a large meadow I saw hundreds of human beings who had been driven together and lined up in long rows.

What does this mean? We'd never witnessed anything like it before. And time and again I heard the plaintive cry of many: "Pan Pankowski, Pan Pankowski." I asked a soldier from the advance detachment, "Who is this Herr Pankowski?" "After the Russians pulled out, he and several others, or so it seems, claimed to have the authority in the town and they've driven all the suspicious people here. He wants to have them tried, in criminal court as he puts it."

I took a closer look at this Herr Pankowski. He didn't seem to me to inspire much confidence or trust, even if he fancied himself the new mayor of the town, or whatever he imagined himself to be. Most likely thinking I'm a German officer he approached me; in broken German with a Polish accent—the kind of accent I recognized all too well from my homeland in the Ruhr valley, with its many coal mines—he said, "I've gathered all the bad people here, they're all here: criminals, robbers, Jews, murderers, Bolsheviks."

He then simply tagged along after me, trying to convince me of what he'd just said. His shabby civilian guard, about 20 men, followed after him, awaiting his next orders. Everywhere we went I saw these people standing around, wringing their hands, whimpering; again and again I heard the pleading and plaintive cry, "Pan Pankowski." He, the new authority figure, mentioned the large number of people the Russians had killed before they left; yet he, the well-known Bolshevik hater, had managed to hide in a pit and avoid detection. But the bad people on this meadow, he assured me, had been the Russians' accomplices and henchmen. And he knew all of them! "They should all be shot immediately," he went on—"all bad people."

He reached into his breast pocket and pulled out a postcard with a picture of Hitler on it. He edged up so close to me that I got an unpleasant whiff of schnapps. He stuttered a bit and then, pointing excitedly at the postcard exclaimed: "That is my God—Hitler is my God, he will always be my God." As if an actor, he looked up suggestively at the sky and then, with some emphasis, stuck the postcard back into his breast pocket. He was enjoying his role.

I continued to hear the pathetic cry of "Pan Pankowski," beseeching and tormenting, like some melancholy musical accompaniment. "Who is your General?" he asked. "We need to have soldiers or guns in order to judge and punish these bad people." "Our Commander, Major Neuhoff, is the General," I replied.

I repeatedly spelled his name, while a civilian who stood behind Pankowski struggled to write it down on a dirty scrap of paper. "He is over there in the school," I explained. "But you will not do anything to these people here without having first spoken to my General, Major Neuhoff," I insisted. "Otherwise, bish bosh, and you're done for." He raised his hand in a greeting, a clear "Heil Hitler," and tried to assume a dignified bearing.

I found the entire affair dreadful. Suddenly, Kageneck and *Leutnant* Becker both showed up. I explained the unusual situation to them. "I've already heard about it," Kageneck replied, "and that's why we've come."

Pan Pankowski approached us and pulled out his "identification card," with the picture of Hitler on it; then the same antics as before. We'd soon had enough and made our way back to the school. "Just like in ancient Rome," I said to Kageneck. "Marius has barely been overthrown and Sulla's already seeking his terrible revenge. What do you think, Franz? How many personal feelings of revenge or of lust for murder due to their momentary feeling of power are behind their having mercilessly herded all these people here?" "It's always the same after a radical change in power," replied Kageneck. "The rabble rises up out of the dust and dirt and wants to play master. At the moment, they see the realization of all their dreams and wishes."

Kageneck immediately sought out Major Neuhoff and made a report. "We must direct an officer to straighten things out there urgently, otherwise there'll be atrocities, murders and rapes this very night."

At that very moment Pankowski again appeared, raised his right hand in the German "*Gruss*," and pulled his Hitler out of his pocket. "What a dreadful fellow," murmured Kageneck. "We should throw him out at once."

Pan Pankowski was given orders by Neuhoff to shepherd all the people he'd driven onto the meadow into the synagogue. There the German officer, selected by Neuhoff, would make his decisions based on his investigations. With a triumphant glow, Pankowski went off and met up with his "guard," who believed the "General" had confirmed their leader's intent.

A *Leutnant* was given the task of establishing order there, as well as the directive to set free as many people as possible, and indeed with an official permit (*Passierschein*). Only those persons who seemed genuinely suspicious were to be placed temporarily in German custody, in order to be fully investigated and, if necessary, brought before a proper court for punishment.

The *Leutnant* took two NCOs and six men with him and headed off for the synagogue. He was the son of a minister, a highly decent and just fellow, and so I knew that the matter was in good hands. In any case, we'd put a stop to the vindictive handiwork of that blowhard Pankowski. On the pass handed out to the many fortunate ones who were set free, the *Leutnant* wrote the date, "Oszmiana 4.7.1941."[297]

Appendix 6

Activity Report of the Divisional Medical Officer (Oberfeldarzt Greif) for 6th Infantry Division (December 1941)[298]

6th Infantry Division   Div. C.P., 2 Feb. 1942
Divisional Doctor

Activity Report for Month December 1941

The first half of the report period brought no changes or special events in comparison to the month of November. The medical units remained committed during the reporting period as follows:

Main Dressing Stations Ivanovskoye and Troitskoye, organized by Med. Comp. 1/6,

Local Hospital Negoshkino, organized by Med. Comp. 2/6,

Field Hospital Logunovo, organized by Field Hospital 6.

The Motor Ambulance Platoon 1/6 was subordinated to Med. Comp. 2/6, and the Motor Ambulance Platoon 2/6 to Field Hospital 6.

While the main dressing stations of Med. Comp. 1/6 received all sick and wounded from the front, provided them with medical care and sent them on to the appropriate rear medical services, the Local Hospital Negoshkino (Med. Comp. 2/6) and Field Hospital Logunovo (Field Hospital 6) were to accommodate those sick and wounded who in all probability would be fit for duty in four weeks' time. Both hospitals were equipped with internal medicine and surgical sections. Furthermore, the division had at its disposal the medical collecting station [*Krankensammelstelle*] in Rzhev.

Within the divisional sector there were continuously three and, for a time, four dental stations in operation; these were:

Dental Station Ivanovskoye at Main Dressing Station Ivanovskoye (Med. Comp. 1/6),

Dental Station Negoshkino at Local Hospital Negoshkino (Med. Comp. 2/6),

Dental Station Logunovo with a prosthesis section at Field Hospital Logunovo (F.H. 6).

The overall health of the troops was good in the first half of the reporting period. The general infestation with lice [*Verlausung*] had improved considerably in comparison to the previous month. The remaining de-lousing facilities, which were still under construction, were completed, so that every village had at its disposal at least one makeshift de-lousing facility.

In mid-month, the division took the first preparatory steps for an eventual withdrawal of the main battle line into the area northeast of Rzhev. Among other things, two railroad cars in Staritsa were loaded with medical supplies and equipment by the three medical units and dispatched to Rzhev. On 19 December, the division began the first deliberate pull back of the main battle line, and this went on in numerous stages toward an as yet undetermined line. On the night of 23/24 December, the Russians attacked on a broad front and, in the days and nights that followed, in an arctic cold reaching -40 Centigrade, they repeated their attacks countless times. In the face of the Russian pressure, the division withdrew according to plan in various stages by way of Staritsa into the area northeast of Rzhev, arriving there on 1 January 1942 and occupying a new defensive line.

These events challenged the medical services with special tasks. For the evacuation and care of the large numbers of new cases of sick and wounded, the retreat posed exceptional difficulties; they were due to the bitter cold, the utterly massive snowdrifts, the sudden onslaught of sick men, particularly frostbite cases, and of wounded, etc. During the withdrawal, the division was largely dependent on the horse-drawn medical company, as the motorized medical company—in view of the fact that most of the roads were not passable for motor vehicles, and due to the need to secure the vehicles—could not be employed in the forward most line and had to be withdrawn prematurely. A complete surgical group from the motorized medical company, with a large number of sledges for transport of the wounded, was allotted to Medical Company 1, which had also built numerous sledges for the wounded and had them at the ready.

The evacuation of the wounded from the forward most front, or from the field dressing stations to the main dressing stations could, for the most part, only be undertaken by means of the sledges. Further evacuations from the main dressing stations to Staritsa, by means of motor ambulances, only succeeded under the greatest of difficulties and through the relentless commitment of the ambulances. Because of enemy breakthroughs, the main dressing stations repeatedly had to be evacuated in a great rush, even under enemy fire—

resulting in the loss of all medical equipment—so that the wounded could be salvaged. But subsequently the equipment was always recovered.

At the end of the month, the difficulties of caring for and evacuating the sick and wounded reached boundless proportions when, on 29 December, Field Hospital 6 and Medical Collecting Station Staritsa were disbanded and, on 30 December, together with Med. Comp. 2/6, transferred into the area around Rzhev. On 29 December, a main dressing station of the division (Med. Comp. 1/6) was established in Staritsa and forced—despite the continued onslaught of sick and wounded—to accept 443 sick men from four different divisions left behind by the medical collecting station there.

Due to the rapid and aggressive pursuit of the Russians the question of providing medical care became secondary to the speedy evacuation of sick and wounded. With the help of vehicles of all type heading toward Rzhev, which were halted by officers and loaded with sick men; with the empty transport space of the division and the corps, the motor ambulances still available, and an ambulance train, by 30/31 December a total of 1,200 sick and wounded had been evacuated from the Main Dressing Station Staritsa and saved from impending capture by the Russians.

The health of the troops had badly worsened during the withdrawal and the infestation with lice had significantly increased. Measures to address the numerous cases of frostbite were not possible due to the lack of time and appropriate gear (felt boots). Well over half the cases of frostbite involved the lower limbs.

Losses during the reporting period amounted to:

195 dead

783 wounded

345 missing

1,521 sick (including 866 frostbite cases).

Appendix 7

Official 3rd Battalion (III./I.R. 18) Combat Report (Gridino, 3 January 1942)[299]

(*NOTE:* FOR DR. HAAPE'S GRAPHIC ACCOUNT OF THE BITTER FIGHTING FOR THE VILLAGE of Gridino on 3 January 1942, see Chapter 24.)

III./Inf.Regiment 18   Btl. C.P., 8 Jan. 1942
Operations Section [Abt. Ia]

Combat Report on the Defensive Battles
of III./I.R. 18 in Gridino

On 2 January 1942, III./I.R. 18, subordinated to I.R. 37, was assigned the sector of the "*K.-Stellung*" between Gridino and Klipukovo, with the mission of defending the position, improving its defenses and conducting tactical reconnaissance to the north.

In the days from 27–29 December 1941, the battalion had already parried three strong Russian attacks at Schitinkovo and dealt out heavy losses to the enemy in night combat, street battles, and local counterattacks. More than 350 Russian dead were left in front of and inside the battalion's positions, while 31 machine guns and numerous small arms were captured.

During these battles the battalion lost its proven leader, *Oberleutnant Graf* von Kageneck; the commander of the 10th Company, *Oberleutnant* Stolze; as well as six brave NCOs and enlisted personnel.

19 NCOs and enlisted personnel were wounded, while seven soldiers were incapacitated due to frostbite. The battalion, already badly depleted, possessed a combat strength after these battles of just four officers, 31 NCOs and 106 enlisted personnel, with six heavy M.G.s, five light M.G.s, one medium and one light mortar. Yet the awareness of the

victory over a numerically far superior opponent instilled in this little battalion a strength and self-confidence that became the foundation for the battles ahead.

The new sector of the battalion had a breadth of 1.5 kilometers, 800 meters of which was wooded terrain. *Oberleutnant* Boehmer, the new battalion chief, occupied the northern part of the village of Gridino—a cornerpost of the "*K.-Stellung*" vulnerable to attack from three sides—with light forces, and secured the open ground between Gridino and Klipukovo with regular patrolling by combat-capable patrols. The battalion received some Pak and infantry guns, while forward observers of the artillery were to arrive on 3 January.

The night of 2/3 January passed quietly. By means of tactical reconnaissance it was established that the enemy had occupied Tshainikovo and set up covering forces along the edges of the woods southeast of the village. As the enemy had approached Tshainikovo, the battalion's combat outposts there withdrew to the main battle line. As a result, covering forces on the eastern part of the position were reinforced by listening posts and a machine-gun.

Suddenly at 0500 hours—Alarm! The Russians attacked Gridino in company strength from the patch of woods northeast of the village. A platoon of about 25 men that worked its way unnoticed through the thick underbrush and, following on the heels of our listening posts, which gave the alarm, surrounded the first houses in the village. Several of the houses were immediately retaken by assault groups led by *Oberleutnant* Boehmer and *Leutnant* Becker, chief of 12th Company; they also kept those Russians who were firing out of the gardens so occupied, that the men of 10th Company who were still in the houses were able to emerge from them and join the battle.

Following short but intense close-up fighting, all of the houses were back in our hands, while the enemy who had made the original penetration was forced back into a group of barns set off to the side.

Now our main defensive action came into play from out of the houses and our positions in the gardens, whereby the Machine-Gun Company—which carried the main burden for the defense—inflicted heavy losses on the enemy. Following another counterstroke by riflemen of the 10th and 11th Companies, the enemy took to flight; while a forward observer, now in position, smashed the last retreating elements of the enemy with his battery. Our surprise attack cost the Russians 65 dead and eight prisoners.

Our own troops had barely formed up again, taken on ammunition, and destroyed enemy booty, when, around 1200 hours, the Russians, following close behind one of our patrols, attacked for the second time—this time from the north. But our tiny band was on the alert, their weapons readied with scrupulous care. Despite the icy cold, sheaves of fire from our machine-guns poured into the enemy, whose attack broke down in the snow 200 meters before Gridino. Leaving behind 30 dead, the remaining Russians, protected by a fold in the terrain, managed to withdraw, while by far the greatest part of the enemy force had yet to emerge from the woods.

After this second attack, it was apparent to the battalion that the Russians would try again in the coming night to capture the village. *Oberleutnant* Boehmer immediately strengthened his positions and distributed his forces in such a manner that, during any conceivable attack, they could be shifted to the vital point within the main battle line. Several houses and barns were also burned down and the main battle line thus shortened. Ammunition was placed at the ready, and measures taken to ensure that all machine-guns, which froze up again and again, were kept permanently thawed out. Further surveillance was carried out by covering parties and communications established with our neighbor. Barrage fire zones were discussed with the forward observers—three were now operating with the battalion—and dialed in through ranging fire, while detected enemy movements in Tshainikovo were taken under fire.

Dusk came at about 1600 hours. At 1630 hours the listening post reported strong noises and loud voices at the edge of the woods north of Gridino. 3rd Battalion Alarm!!! Everyone took up his assigned position. The main effort of our defense was toward the north. The first bursts of Russian machine-gun fire were already whistling into the village. The Russians attacked with *"Urrah!"* making quite a racket. Our artillery loosed its barrage fire and our heavy machine-guns expended belt after belt. But in the glow of the signal flares about 400 Russians were observed, who had managed to evade our fire and come precariously close to the edge of the village. *Oberleutnant* Boehmer directed that two additional heavy machine-guns be shifted to the endangered left flank. The forward observers directed the artillery fire . . . from the forward most line. The charging enemy forces were taken under mortar and rifle fire and, as a result of this sudden concentration of fire, the first Russian assault collapsed in the snow, leaving in its wake innumerable dead and wounded.

The battle's center of gravity now shifted to the northern tip of the village. *Leutnant* Kiso, who only hours ago had returned to the battalion, had transformed the first house there into a robust defensive position; which the Russians, with great tenacity and high losses, attempted in vain to storm. Although *Leutnant* Kiso and the machine-gunner were wounded, and several comrades from this brave garrison fell in battle, the Russians were unable to get close to the village.

Then, suddenly, robust machine-gun and mortar fire from the right—the Russians were attacking from the north with more than 100 men, as they had in the morning. Even our well-laid machine-gun and artillery fire was not able to stop them this time. The enemy reached the first houses and took the village street and our garden position under fire.

Again and again the enemy was thrown back by our counter thrusts, cut down by hand grenades, as we retook and held the houses. Our assaults were led by the last surviving officers of the battalion—*Oberleutnant* Boehmer, *Leutnant* Lammerding (the adjutant, who was also later wounded), *Leutnant* Becker and *Leutnant* Ohlig. The stubborn and tenacious nature of their assaults was reflected most conspicuously in the death of *Leutnant* Ohlig and several other comrades, as well as in the wounding of Lammerding and others.

In the end the Russians succeeded, but only due to their huge numbers, in forcing their way into the first four houses and bringing up 30 to 40 more men; however, on both flanks of the village, the enemy had already been neutralized by our machine-gun and artillery fire. An assault group of I./I.R. 37, which arrived as reinforcements, was committed to help seal off the enemy breach.

The struggle for the houses, bravely defended by a handful of men under the command of *Leutnant* Becker, surged on for hours. Yet the enemy opposite the other sector of the battalion (as well as his reinforcements) was beaten back and smashed through machine-gun and artillery fire, while his presumed assembly areas were taken under fire by our heavy howitzers (*Mörser*). Because the battalion C.P. was only tenuously linked to I.R. 37 by one of its patrols (*Spähtrupp*), the battalion contacted its own regiment [I.R. 18] by wireless to request urgently needed ammunition and reinforcements.

By 2300 hours the attack had been repulsed and the enemy breach—in which, according to the statements of a deserter, there were two *Politruks* and 40 men—sealed off. Our machine-guns were regularly thawed out and made ready for action. About half the enlisted personnel were relieved from their positions and able to warm themselves. When reinforcements finally arrived, covering parties (*Sicherungen*) were strengthened; houses occupied by the Russians burned down; and the main battle line recaptured in a counterstroke. The next morning, a large portion of the withdrawing enemy was put out of action through well-aimed machine-gun and rifle fire. More than 100 dead Russians were left in front of Gridino.

The 3rd Battalion losses at Gridino were: 1 officer and 11 NCOs and enlisted personnel killed in action; two officers and 22 NCOs and enlisted men wounded. On 4 January 1942, about 0900 hours, the battalion was relieved by II./I.R. 37.

Appendix 8

"The Doctor with the German Cross [in Gold]"
(War Reporter K. G. Schäfer)[300]

Obergefreiter K. G. Schäfer   19 February 1943
Prop. Comp. (mot.) 612
Field Post Number 14 156

Re: *Oberarzt* Dr. Heinz Haape
6th Infantry Division

THE DOCTOR WITH THE GERMAN CROSS [IN GOLD]
Judgment and Praise for the Medical Corps.

By War Reporter K. G. Schäfer

He keeps a portrait that shows him after the summer battle of Rzhev. His usually full, expressive features have become hard and haggard. His tired eyes lie in dark sockets. This is what a man coming from battle looks like, a fighter who has recovered his discarded existence in a terrible act of self-preservation. Yet he is a physician and has simply been fighting for the threatened lives of his Rhenish and Westphalian infantrymen.

In the winter battles last year, he, the last doctor, on a single day, attended to 160 men suffering from injuries and frostbite, even lending a helping hand to soldiers from other regiments. During the 20 days of the defensive battle at Rzhev, he cared for 521 wounded. An infantryman was carried into his narrow, low bunker, which was also the resting place for all those who had already been provided for and awaited that night's transport. An armor-piercing shell had shattered his lower leg. The infantryman would lose his leg at the height of the tourniquet on his upper thigh if he did not attempt the amputation, because setting the lower leg was impossible. An intravenous anesthetic failed as a result of the extreme shock from his wound. A direct hit from artillery fire had destroyed the medical equipment. With confidence in his skill and the duty of his office, he took action. He tied the leg off tightly in order to relieve the infantryman of his pain, amputated at the lacerated site, and bound off the blood vessels with iodized twine. It worked. This is one case of many. Yet while this was happening, shells rained down about the bunker and 50 meters away stood three enemy tanks that would only be destroyed later in close combat.

"The Army doctor has to be a master of improvisation in the field," commented the Oberhausen-Buschhausen-born *Oberarzt*. Theories all prove to be inadequate when faced with the uncertainties of war. The only thing he carried with him, for the sake of rapid mobility, was a doctor's bag. An orderly also accompanied him with a rucksack that contained the most important equipment. This was how he accompanied his infantry battalion, and later his regiment, behind and in the midst of the first wave through Russia right into the trenches of the defensive battles. He had to act like every other infantryman who carries his gun with him and owes his success to snap decisions. A recently stormed bunker, a depression, a dugout—all would be turned into a dressing station. And just as he would tie off blood vessels with twine if necessary, he would hoist the wounded onto his own shoulders if no orderly was there, carry him through targeted anti-tank and machine-gun fire, and would then procure horses, sleds, and transport. The improvisation doubles his work, but it's the only way. In 14 days he won't get a single hour's solid sleep. This energy springs from a forceful vitality and swells to medical passion. He does not retire when he, on the search for wounded, is himself injured and sustains slight frostbite. He organizes the resistance when the enemy is no longer prepared to spare even the wounded.

Improvisation requires mental agility. And improvisation in the midst of battle and danger requires nerve and courage. They demand of the doctor in action a soldierly heart, the knowledge of an infantryman, and a highly developed leadership personality. In contrast to the fighter who is fully fit for service, the wounded man needs calm, clear, lucid orders; where he might otherwise just need a slight nudge to pull himself together, he now lacks the self-confidence to do so. Even the wounded man can find himself in dangerous situations. Sometimes the doctor will require him to deploy his weapon. But the calm demeanor of the medical officer must be strong and tangible in order to be conveyed to others. The seriously injured will only draw hope from self-assured eyes. The doctor does not do it all alone, but his spirit is also that of his medical orderlies. He has gone through everything with them and faced the first difficult hurdles together with many a young recruit.

It has often been said that the doctor of whom we are speaking was frequently better informed of the situation than a company commander, who might be overwhelmed by the confusion of events. That requires of him the soldierly discipline of a battalion commander. If he is truly concerned for the security of his dressing station and wants to save the wounded, he must have a sure sense of orientation, which is often useful to more than just his role. At the very least, he is always the company commander of his area. He sets out covering parties, so that hand grenades do not fly unexpectedly into his bunker, and he also takes up his weapon, alongside his medical orderlies, the slightly wounded, and the stragglers, to secure the threatened area. To eliminate the imminent threat of the tank that has broken through, he seizes the Teller-mine from the hand of a soldier and destroys the steel colossus himself. That is why today he wears the German Cross in Gold beside his Infantry Assault Badge, the Wound Badge, and Tank Close Combat Insignia.

Doctors and medical orderlies, those who fight for life, pay the highest blood tax of all the units. He was not alone in his battalion or regiment, but he was the only doctor since crossing the Soviet-Russian border who remained at the front without interruption, despite himself being wounded. All the others were either temporarily or permanently out of action. As early as the fall of 1942, he had lost 100 percent of the medical staff who had set off with him through injury or death. Today this figure has already climbed to 160 percent. Such a degree of loss was his first shock. Right at the start of the Russia campaign, a shell ripped off the head of the medical orderly accompanying him. A few days later, his driver lost both his legs. Ever since then he has been accompanied by "Heinrich." "Heinrich," a Westphalian from the Bielefeld area, is blind in one eye and, although only fit for limited duty in the interior, he reported voluntarily for service at the front. Since October 1941 he has carried the medical kit bag of his doctor through the battles, aiding and fighting. In one day he cleared out the area of the dressing station by shooting down eight Soviet soldiers. The spirit of the Army Medical Corps shines brightest in this medical orderly, who has been awarded the Iron Cross (first class).

The persistence of danger is part of the improvisational challenge for successful medical activity in the field. But the combat is merely a complicating attending circumstance for the military doctor, a task that runs counter to his own office. It may only be marginal in determining the nature of his actions. "A military doctor must also be a physician of the soul. Every injured man is full of questions," says this *Oberarzt*. While tender emotions are banished from the martial armory, the doctor, as a psychologist and artist, may not forfeit them. "Throughout the war, I have retained a sense for all things beautiful," he says, showing icons and self-portraits beside impressive photographs of the Russian winter. This is part of his reflection in quiet hours. His technical background—he holds the title of Doctor of Philosophy and sees his research into medical and psychological frontiers as his life's work—benefits his work and his human, comradely appeal, and itself expands his limits and duties.

"When you get home, raise your first beer to my health," he says to a wounded man, whose thoughts immediately turn down paths of illusion and away from his pain. But he had already spoken plainly to the injured man about his wounds. "You're going to lose a leg," he says to him. But he tells him that he will still be capable of doing this and that. In the meantime, the thought of home has already half-lulled this painful revelation into the soldier's sub-consciousness. A *Leutnant* is brought to him who has lost the ability to speak or hear in the inferno of battle. After three days, during which he keeps the man close to him, the officer is once again fit for duty. He was able to restore this brave officer's self-confidence and belief, lost in his deaf-mute state. He does not use a commanding tone to dismiss a *Landser*, who is exaggerating a genuine complaint due to the conditions. He keeps him at the dressing station for a short time and has him tend to injured men. Faced with genuine suffering, he is ashamed of his minor ailment and recovers.

"Two things provide the infantryman with the greatest amount of self-assurance before the attack," a battalion commander stated recently: "Assault guns and a doctor." "Believe me, I didn't want any of this," our doctor remarks on his awards, and Heinrich concurs. But it is precisely this that is the decisive attribute of this doctor with the German Cross: the uncompromising, soldierly commitment to following his duty and his vocation.

War Reporter K. G. Schäfer

Appendix 9

Dr. Haape Records His War: Selection of Letters to His Fiancée Martha Arazym (May 1941–May 1942)

(*Note:* These letters have been edited to keep them focused on Dr. Haape's front experience during the first ten months of the Russian campaign; hence, intimate details of Dr. Haape's and Martha Arazym's personal lives have, for the most part, been redacted. All of the letters were written by Dr. Haape to Martha, with the exception of one fascinating and insightful letter from Martha to Dr. Haape, dated 10 August 1941, and one letter from Dr. Haape to his siblings, dated 12 September 1941.)

1941
20.5.1941
What should I write? I could tell of so much and yet so little of significance has happened. Everything is moving closer and closer to a particular goal.

We haven't been in East Prussia for some time; instead, we're 13 km from the Russian border! (In Filipów near Gołdap)

Nothing is certain in today's politics, because everything is possible, but I think we will soon be facing decisive events. It is the quiet before a storm which will roar to the east, into the boundless spaces of Russia. But we are in good spirits; we are the soldiers of the new Germany, with the confidence that there, beyond the difficult tasks that must be completed, lies the greatest victory. This is how the quiet dread of the boundless unknown, which dwells in a hidden corner of the heart, soon disappears and is overcome.

We are living here in the most primitive conditions, where lice, bedbugs, and scabies are no rarity, and against which I must wage my own battle, in addition to the illnesses. The weather is still bad here and there's a cold wind blowing. Still no little green leaves visible on the bare trees. It is bleak and unpleasant.

21.6.1941

In a few hours it will begin!

We Germans face an enemy with a three-fold [numerical] superiority; our regiment is in the very front line. The resistance must be broken, in spite of the bunkers, the human hordes, and all kinds of devilry. It's a war for Germany's greatness and future.

I have been completely calm so far. The world seems silent and untroubled to me, and just now I feel the peace of nature twice as deeply. Despite the fact that a lot, a very great lot of troops have marched up to the border, yet there's not a soldier to be seen! The weather is wonderful, the birds are singing and the trees are wearing a fresh green. A magnificent lake is just close by again and there's the same mood in the air that I described to you at Pentecost. A magical world of a truly living peace. Just before the storm that will make the earth tremble, with all its consequences!

22.6.1941

The first day in the campaign against Russia. We have a hard day behind us! The Russians fought like devils and never surrendered, so we engaged in close combat [*Nahkampf*] on several occasions; just now, half an hour ago, another four Russians were struck dead with the butts of our rifles. Our regiment's losses on this single day are greater than during the entire French campaign (21 dead and 48 severely wounded).[301] We were at the center of the attack [*Schwerpunkt des Angriffes*]. Of the regiment's 6 doctors, one is KIA (shot to the head) and another injured. And 4 medical orderlies are also KIA. We have pushed the Russian back along the whole line, except for a few bunkers that have not yet fallen. There is still hard fighting going on. I had a lot of work to do and frequently had to bandage comrades under heavy machine-gun fire. I have not yet had anything to eat today and only a very little to drink; we are cut off from our supply line!

23.6.1941

These two days were hard, really hard! Today we have had only a few casualties and no dead. But there is still no link to the supply train. In the last two days I have had only 2 slices of bread to eat and only little to drink. The dust mixes with sweat, settles in the skin and eats into it. My lips have swollen and in places they have split from the dryness. It's hot with a blue sky.

The war is even bloodier than I thought it would be, but we are setting a good pace and do not falter. Death is reaping a rich harvest. The battle was tougher yesterday than today. Yesterday we experienced several bombing attacks on our soldiers. We were low about the loss of our dear comrades and asking ourselves what is to become of all this if it goes on like this. There is shooting from every corn field, from every farmhouse. As I was bandaging up another Russian, the "pigs" shot at me constantly with machine-guns.

The Russians were carrying out another bombing attack, when suddenly German fighters arrived and shot 6 heavy bombers down. A magnificent air battle. . . . Germany's greatness and future is at stake and I can only say that at this moment I don't want to be anywhere else but here.

We will spend the few hours of nighttime rest sleeping in the forest. My gas mask, on which I lay my field cap, has been my pillow for days now. And how wonderfully I do sleep on it—better than in the nicest bed. That's the work of extreme, honest tiredness!

2.7.1941

I am superbly well! We don't have any contact with the enemy at all right now; we're marching on poor roads, following the motorized units that are hard on the heels of the fleeing enemy. The poor horses! They're emaciated and exhausted to the point of collapse. We go on relentlessly!

7.7.1941

We almost always have good weather at the moment and our path takes us further east in the direction of Moscow. Currently, the tanks are ahead of us and are not meeting any resistance from the enemy. We are taking prisoners daily from dispersed Russian groups who are mainly hold up in the forests. I think we will encounter the Russians again in the next few days; they are gathering for renewed defensive action. As you've also heard in the *Wehrmacht* Bulletin, 52,000 Russians defected when they realized the hopelessness of the fight. That was right in our sector.

So far, the two first days [22.-23.6.1941] have been the worst in every respect.

3.8.1941

I have never been so close to death as I was this morning at 0745. Except for a small shrapnel injury to my nose, which is so insignificant I didn't even need to bandage it, I was unhurt.[302] It has been awful in the last few days, so awful that I don't want to speak of it. What should I say? A few brief words.

On 2 [August], after bloody combat in the evening, we had beaten back the Russians, who had broken through with strong forces. The next morning we received heavy shell fire. I was with 10 people at the battalion command post. A shell struck 12 meters away from me; there were casualties. I called Dehorn, my orderly; we both got up, then a 2nd shell crashed into the ground 5 meters away from me. I was thrown to the ground by the immense air pressure. There were whimpering and screams all around me. After quickly regaining my composure, I immediately started to provide medical support for the soldiers and I found the following situation:

Dehorn's chest was torn open and his skull smashed, his brain lying next to his head. (Immediately dead.)

Leutnant Jakobi was lying with shrapnel lodged in his chest, shrapnel through the stomach, a shattered right knee, and his left foot was as good as shot off. He lived 1 hour longer and died.

Both the legs of my driver, who was lying next to me, were smashed.

Four others [were] severely wounded and one casualty with minor injuries.

We are in the midst of a struggle of the utmost severity; we must not allow ourselves to harbor any delusions about this, whatever the magnitude of our successes. The days are filled with martial events that can only be endured with healthy nerves and the utmost commitment of all physical and psychological energies. The theater of war is sober, dirty, prosaic, and the enemy facing us of an Asiatic brutality and tenacity; it is war in its most terrible, archetypal form.

Yet the way in which the German soldier will fight this war, in which the leadership will surmount the unprecedented breadth of this theater of war with world-historical, unique operations and drive the enemy to its final destruction, that is surely the most phenomenal heroic drama, of such great dimensions, that the history of the war has to show to date.

10.8.1941

(*Note:* Martha has just seen the latest showing of the *Wochenschau*—the official weekly newsreel—and found it deeply troubling.[303] Moreover, it is now apparent to her that the *Russlandkrieg* is not proceeding as planned.)

My best, dearest *Heinzlmann!*[304]

I can only say: Oh my God! Yesterday I saw another *Wochenschau*, it was simply nightmarish! Our poor soldiers seemed to me to be hollow-eyed from the immense strains. Their faces when they think they are unobserved, so very serious! My dearest, I can imagine only too well how you will also literally sacrifice yourself for your comrades! Hopefully you will also find your peace!

It's a Sunday again here; it is 7 weeks since the Russian war began. The Russian must be a truly terribly tough opponent and, what's more, using all possible illegitimate means. The assessment we made of this opponent really was false. We thought this enemy would be beaten in 4–6 weeks! But we are so grateful! We can imagine only too well, purely statistically, what <u>tremendous</u> things our German soldiers are achieving.

Your faithful

Martha

14.8.1941

I have just gone for a short ride past the front line, where our soldiers are in the middle of a defensive battle against the Russian divisions. We have been engaged in trench warfare for over 10 days now; we've built proper trenches and dugouts, and that's for operational reasons, so they say. It looks like another cauldron is being formed and then we will probably charge hard ahead toward the enemy to the east.

At one point the Russian broke through, but we beat him back over the Mezha in a tough counterattack. Unfortunately, we also had losses, but that's the way things are—

we're at war after all. Before every attack you think silently to yourself, who will be next? Never have so many bullets whistled about our ears as the last time; whistling and hissing in the air were the only things that could be heard. It was just our good luck that the Russians were too worked up and shot haphazardly. We captured a lot of weapons and ammunition. The Russian losses were heavy!

I also stood at the grave of my boy Dehorn again today. He was a good man; he died at my side in loyal fulfillment of his duties. It was like a stab through my heart to see him bleeding to death. He didn't speak a word; I had to take care of the other wounded. He was the dearest one to me of all those who die a soldier's death here.

At a fork in the road, in the forest, stands a simple birch cross with a steel helmet. A friendly fence, made of the same wood, embraces the tranquil spot of that final peace, decorated by simple means. The flowers, always fresh, bear witness to the love and remembrance of his comrades. Hanging inconspicuously on the cross is the Iron Cross Second Class [EK 2], which he received as an award for bravery and readiness for duty.

The sight of his grave evokes a long series of memories—he was at my side at my every step. Christmas in France, shopping, packing boxes, experiences and work on the coast, then East Prussia, and the crazy war against Russia. All these images are shared experiences. He was a good comrade, that little Dehorn!

But life goes on here; we don't have time to stand still for too long, for the demands of the present are stronger than the past. We will continue unwaveringly along our road, no one wishes to miss it—fortunate is the soldier who can experience the great final victory of our beloved fatherland, for which we will stake everything.

18.8.1941

Images from my memory waft unburdened through the bright day from the blue yonders of a happy time. It was a time when there was still peace, my heart was still young and saw life very differently; so I dream and forget the hardship of the present in this quiet hiatus.

The consequence of battle is terrible right up to the final destruction . . . yet another bombing attack from the Russians. To our left the artillery booms, our neighboring regiment is in battle. Two reconnaissance patrols are running!

This is what we have become! None of this disturbs me. The constant pitiless deployment, the many dead and wounded comrades, the struggles, the readiness to die make you dull and indifferent to the moment. Where your own safety is concerned, you become fatalistic; the possibility of death barely fazes you. Soldierly duty and faith in victory give us strength and purpose. We carry in our hearts unconditional hopes of victory and the certainty of a happy future for our nation. For you all at home, for our beloved Germany, no sacrifice is too great for us!

Nobody believes how tough and yet how tender the soldier is. A typical incident comes to mind: during a counterattack, when we were driving the Russians back into the Mezha, I was crouching flat against the ground together with an *Oberleutnant* (Iron

Cross First and Second Class, and Assault Badge). We couldn't go any further, because the enemy machine-gun fire was too heavy and the bullets were whistling around our heads in an overly perilous way—then he suddenly and without warning pulled a letter secretively from his pocket and said: "Hey, Heinz, what do you think—[my girlfriend] wrote to me!" And then he read to me, dreamily, the loveliest and most elegant words from a young girl from France. He had forgotten the war.

Hell was all around us. The tanks were blasting from all barrels; enemy anti-tank guns pumped shells with steely determination ahead into the balconies of a wooden house. Village houses burned brightly—a firework display. Our artillery thundered resolutely into the nearby piece of woodland, causing fragments to fly up; in brief—all barrels were blazing, a tough, dogged battle, where "everything is at stake."

Such is the soldier who has come to terms with it all, a few minutes' contemplation is enough for him to wander off into a world of yearning, desires, and fantasies.

I am happy to be able to be here in this interesting world! The soldier, where death is so close, you feel so very much what life is!

24.8.1941

Our division has to hold a line of 46 km against the constant attacks of the enemy, of which over 4 km have to be held by our battalion. A difficult task!

We have expanded our positions, proper field works with bunkers, trenches, etc.; let the Russian try his hand! He has been able to break through in two places—a stupid business, but after a few hours they were thrown out again with heavy losses. During our counterstroke, we found another 11 dead soldiers of our 1st Battalion, who, to a man, had stood firm with their machine-guns and rifles when the Cossacks suddenly stormed our line with a blood-curdling "*Urrah, Urrah!*" They were finally overrun by the superior forces and cut down at their weapons in close combat.

At the moment, it is all peace and quiet here in the forest, where I sit beneath old pine trees and write. I do not only see the terrible war. In quiet hours I tear myself away and look at the smallest things in the forest—how the wood mouse blithely nibbles a small piece of bread that I have put down. Here, there are bright beetles of a size and peculiarity that I have never seen at home—and so many interesting things—you just have to keep your eyes peeled and be able to listen carefully to nature.

It is all so very, very different here to home, a different world. Yet I find the old saying reaffirmed again and again: There is beauty in everything in the world! It's up to the individual to look for it and find it!

29.8.1941

Parts of our battalion have been detailed to our neighboring regiment to provide support and help sweep the enemy out, who has broken through over there with two divisions. In the meantime we are holding our sector with weak forces! We don't like this trench warfare much. I hope and trust that in about a week we'll return to the attack—that suits us better!

I have just heard the result of the counterattack: the enemy beaten back with bloody losses; reached and restored the old battle line. Over 200 non-commissioned officers and soldiers fallen on the German side, plus [many] officers dead and 8 wounded. The Russian losses incomparably higher as always! Time and again, he relentlessly throws reserves into battle, and our losses are not inconsiderable! Even the regimental commander has fallen; 4 days ago he had received the Knight's Cross [*Ritterkreuz*]. It is tragic.

However, I don't want always to be talking of the war, nor of the labors that the soldier has to undergo here, but instead say a few words about the poor possibilities for life in this Russian campaign: this is the land of vermin, headlice, crabs, insects, fleas and clothes lice. They are common and omnipresent here, making an overnight stay in a house impossible! That is why I have been sleeping either outside in the fresh air, in my tent, or in my vehicle since the start of the war—because of possible surprise attacks at night, so we are always ready, we remove at most our field shirts and boots, but otherwise remain fully dressed—and beside us our guns, primed and ready to fire.

And this is a monotonous, uncultural, enslaved country, this Russia! The only thing that is grown here is grain. No fruit, no vegetables—the people live in the most humble conditions.

Dysentery [*Ruhr*] is currently spreading widely among our soldiers, transmitted principally through the millions of flies, which do not give us a moment's peace. We can hardly get away from the flies. I've also recovered from a slight dysentery infection, but I've been able to continue my service in every way. The days are hot and the nights cold—bloody battle in a country with no borders or culture!

2.9.1941

You simply cannot imagine how we live here in such miserable conditions—in wet, damp, cold dugouts, foxholes, or temporarily in pitiful wooden lean-tos. No culture, not even the simplest contrivances of civilization can be found here. And we are constantly threatened by the enemy, by shell fire or attack. No variety, whether in life here or in the food. No vegetables, no fruit. Legumes for soup, potatoes with meat or canned food comprise, in the permanent, monotonous recurrence of the stew, our meals.

Please don't think that I'm moaning to you in writing this—if it came to it, I would gladly bear even more privations, but I want nothing more than sympathy for the wish list I'm going to write down now! There are no shops here, nothing to buy. Razor blades, comb, toothpaste, skin cream, soap, nail cleaner, writing paper, fountain pen, ink, *Frankfurter Zeitung*, *Koralle* [an illustrated magazine], card games, tobacco, all kinds of sweets, pocket handkerchiefs, etc.

11.9.1941

Today was another hot day with great successes for us; we even took over 100 prisoners when the Russians attacked, but we had fatalities and casualties, too.

This war is terrible, but we will triumph, even though the road is long and difficult! This is not to say that, what with the difficult things we have to experience, the thought arises: why are we at war with Russia? War with R. had to come, and the fact that it has now come—we should be grateful for that, because it is the only way to success! This dreadful war is the fate of our nation! [*das Schicksal unseres Volkes!*]

12.9.1941[305]

Dear Brothers and Sister!

You will have had news of me from Martha. I am sending this letter to you and ask you in turn to inform Martha of its contents! It is a short description of the Russian campaign as I have experienced it.

Since bounding over the border, when the Great War against Russia began, a lot has happened and provided death with a bountiful harvest. A terrible war—a battle using all means to the bitter end. In the first 5 weeks, our brave, active infantry division put over 1000 km from the tip of Suwalki in the direction of Moscow behind it under the most difficult conditions, on poor, broken roads. Since then, we have been in bloody defensive battles on a relatively thinly-held front. So for us the attack has now become a defensive action.

I could tell you a great deal of the toughness of the Russian resistance, the Bolshevists' fanatical commitment and will to destruction, who will even shoot their own wounded so that they do not fall into German hands.

So far, I have only been very slightly wounded on my nose. I'm very thankful that I have also been able to help my wounded comrades in the forwardmost lines, as I had imagined I would! So I, too, was awarded the Iron Cross Second Class after those first battles: "Due to commitment, courage, and cold-bloodedness before the enemy." I left the assistant doctor at the dressing station and accompanied the attacking forces myself; that way I was able to provide medical assistance to the wounded on the spot.

The horrors of mass death reach into the deepest recesses of the soul. Much vaunted words such as law of nations and the Geneva Convention are like laughter mocking humanity. Other laws of life hold sway here, the law of ruthless destruction.

We now know the necessity of the war and live in the proud joy of being able to be there right at the front. No sacrifice shall be too great for us, for Germany's greatness. Ahead of us lie the Red beasts, the boundless Russian space, and . . . winter. But so far the German soldier has broken all resistance! Victory is ours. How it will continue, we don't know! But too much analysis is not good for the soldier, so we say it short and simple: "*C'est la guerre.*" That is explanation enough for the martial demands and travails of battle.

15.9.1941

Brief word on the situation: the war with Russia will not come to an end this year. We are currently in the middle of the toughest defensive battle here, and the greatest demands are being made on efforts, commitment, and blood, so that the battles in the north can be ended all the more successfully and those in the Ukraine, the breadbasket of Europe, can be continued victoriously. So the war will not be brought to an end in this year. We are currently (in fact, since 28 July) standing, in a relatively thinly occupied line, against an enemy with far superior numbers. The broad countryside lies gray ahead of us, and the cold Russian winter!

27.9.1941

The war of position has reached its zenith! Some of our trenches are 80 meters away from the Russian positions. Everything has holed itself up in the ground. Provisions, ammunition, and other necessities are only brought up at night. We lead the life of a veritable military mole. The shells crash down all day around our little homemade dugouts. Next to my sleeping bunker a medical aid bunker has also been built, where I can shelter the wounded during the day and provide medical care; then they are taken back to the main dressing station at night. It is our justifiable hope that this boring and yet dangerous crap will soon come to an end.

I am well as always, our dear God has so far had his protecting hand over me in the most miraculous way, even in the most dangerous and difficult hours; and I hope that he will continue to bless my path!

The fact that I have come closer to God here on the battlefields of Russia is not due to fear and anxiety; I really do not feel those anymore and I am prepared to walk any path, even through the darkest gates of death if it must be! We look all dangers straight in the eye with clarity and calmness, just as we took an oath to do! No! Here reigns deep solemnity; here you are more directly confronted with all causal things; here God speaks to us at a close proximity, and I am not alone in hearing this speech!

1.10.1941

Things are finally moving onward; the war of position has come to an end for us. At dawn we will be assaulting the Russian positions. At the moment, we are making ready, just like the first day on 22.6.[1941]. Our advance is to head for Moscow through the wet and cold to break the Russians' spine. The long-awaited decisive battle is finally looming and however tough it will be, I am happy that the wretched war of position is over.

Even if I don't look it, I am always calm and detached, but the constant shell fire does get on your nerves over time. We were bombarded with the heaviest shells on a daily basis and you would wait for a direct hit on your dugout, which would tear you apart, as happened to many a soldier. Heavy shells also struck close to my dugout. We held our positions, sometimes under the toughest circumstances, repulsed attacks, made counter-attacks, endured bombing and attacks from low-flying aircraft. We held out and were master of our task, and so we were party to the successes in the south and the north. We are full of fighting courage and are storming ahead to the final battle. We all know that the road will be difficult, but an end is in sight!

5.10.1941

3 days ago saw the start of the great battle for Moscow and we are in the middle of it! You cannot imagine how hard this fight is. Since 3 [October] we have hardly slept a wink; the challenges are relentless. I have been able to help a lot and have looked death in the eye all too frequently. I have remained true to myself and our dear God has always miraculously protected me. On the first day we had 12 dead and 25 wounded in the attack on the well-prepared Russian positions. We broke through and are in action day and night. Today will be the first night in which I can stretch out on a straw bed in a barn. How I am looking forward to that—I am dog-tired! Tomorrow we will continue to pursue the enemy and however great the resistance, he will be beaten!

Deep sorrow runs through my heart. I am so sad for the bleeding and dying of my comrades. It is too dreadful! Such dear men have fallen and with such self-sacrifice. It is a holy war, for you all, for Germany. In quiet hours, it chills me how little fear I have when it comes down to it! I am very tired, good night!

21.10.1941

The weather has been very bad in recent days. We are marching through frost and snow-drifts. Today we will cross the Volga for the second time. The most severe demands are being made of man and horse. Hopefully the war will come to an end for us this year, which would mean that our division will not have to overwinter here in Russia.

I am convinced that the main Russian forces will most likely be destroyed, but that a war will still go on next year. The path that we Germans must go is tough, but we will prevail! We are ready to continue to endure everything that is necessary. I will tell you another time of the difficult battles we have had. . . . I haven't received any mail since 1 October.

23.10.1941

Tomorrow we attack! The objective: a larger town northwest of Kalinin. We now fight against the enemy pushing forward from the north.

Now I can tell you something very special: I was awarded the Iron Cross First Class today! At risk of my life I was able to save the lives of many comrades or considerably reduce their suffering! I have remained true to myself. I have taken part in every attack at the very front line. We are in God's hands. My hour has not yet come. Now I firmly believe that I will survive the Russian campaign. I have often thought when things were going crazy, that I would never see you again. I do believe the hardest has been achieved!

29.10.1941

The war has now taken on the kind of shape that means we are very nearly finished with it. Yesterday, Russian tanks broke through to our rear and occupied the division's only communication road. We have been living from the land for 14 days. We have had dead and wounded daily. At the moment, it is one German for every 10 dead Russians. We are taking a lot of prisoners. It's a desperate struggle of extraordinary severity that the Russians are carrying out. All that Russian bravery and courage will not help—they will be destroyed!

10.11.1941

Yesterday I wrote a postcard, which I sent with a severely ill *Oberleutnant* who was being transported by airplane. How much I would have liked to fly with him to be back at home, to have a few hours' peace. Since 22 June we have been nearly constantly at the enemy, constantly in battle, on the attack or on the defense. The holes in our lines torn by death or injury are deep!

Yes, it's possible to dream that you are in a happy, now almost strange atmosphere, in another world, but when the shells scream down or the Red tanks attack, then the music of our reality penetrates our ears. Then everyone silently does his duty. We are true to the oath that we gave to the *Führer*. We carry on.

How hard are the challenges of our time and how wonderful it would be to live in peace, but we do not want to think of that—the thought would make you go half crazy. Physically and mentally I am bearing up, in contrast to the many who are already physically and mentally coming apart from the strains.

There can be no thought of leave for the moment. The railways are so overburdened by the most varied requirements; for the moment every man is needed here. I will certainly be spending Christmas in the distant east!

13.11.1941

Yesterday was a great day! Something very special happened—I received mail for the first time in [1½] months and there was a letter from you dated 16 September.

27.11.1941

Something very special, happy, has suddenly entered into my soldier's life, which I would not have thought was even a possibility in recent times, what with the difficult enemy situation and the operations of our troops. Even though we are still in battle, I have been permitted, as the first medical officer of the regiment, to take leave, and I hope to be able to start my journey to Germany in roughly 8–14 days.

Could this be true? I can't believe it yet! Christmas at home! We will see each other at home!!

So if it comes true, if no particular unforeseen circumstances intervene—we will even celebrate our engagement then. I would like to set the celebrations for Sunday, 28 December 1941. Please make sure everything is in place for it. Cross your fingers that nothing else gets in the way at the last minute.

1942[306]

19.1.1942

A quick sign of life!

During the Christmas period we were in the middle of a tough battle. The New Year immediately provided us with new tasks, and they were all resolved. The toughest days of the Russian campaign. We have beaten back and halted the Russian assault, or so it appears at the moment. The most extensive killing that I have experienced. We are now only a small band and remember with pride the heroism and self-sacrifice, the good comrades who found death. We are defending with about 100 men against a far superior enemy. In night combat, man against man, the Russian lost 600 dead in 5 days. We also have bitter losses, but remained the victors!

I have had to bid farewell to my remaining friends. Our battalion was even named in the *Wehrmacht* Bulletin!

I am well as always. I've even survived the cold at down to -40 degrees[307] relatively well. My thoughts often turn to you all at home. How glad I am that the war is not in our country; that you all have it good. What we do here, we do for you, and we will not let up.

I was slightly injured by shrapnel on my left foot, but it is as good as healed now. I was still able to carry out my duties well. I am thankful and in good spirits!

25.1.1942

The mail is about to go out with the paratroopers, and I hope I can get this letter off with them.

I don't want to pretend to you and will write some honest lines: On 14 December 1941 a big Russian winter offensive began, with incredible volumes of men and materiel. We were pulled out of our old position and thrown against the superior enemy. Soon our division was also at the center of enemy assaults. A battle for life and death began and we remained true to our oath. I never thought I would see home again. The toughest battles of our battalion were on 15, 23, 24, 25, 28 and 31 December; on 1, 3, 4, 5, 16 and 17 January. Man-to-man combat, day and night, in ferocious cold between -25 and -41 degrees. Our battalion in particular has pinned immortal fame to its pennant, but it also bled more than the others.

Of the 13 officers of our battalion, 5 fell, 4 were severely wounded, 2 severely exhausted and ill, so that 2 officers and 25 men are left of the old battalion. All the others are dead, wounded, sick, or frostbitten. (The frostbite cases are particularly bad!)

I hope that we have made it and I am certain that I will see my beloved homeland again. It is rare that a unit has been so constantly in battle like we have, even in the World War.

27.1.1942

At the moment, after the last difficult weeks, I have had a little more peace without having to be behind the front. The Russian has been a bit quieter here where we are. He left thousands of dead in front of our division. It is harrowing. In some parts of our sector, there are dead bodies piled upon dead bodies. A good thing that it is so cold or else an awful smell of corpses would torment us too much.

I have not received any mail from you for weeks now. Not even Christmas greetings or a little package, except via the live messenger Albracht, who also brought me your loving greetings and thoughts! That was a happy hour for me!

I have discovered here what sort of indescribable things human beings can endure over a long period of time. The winter war demanded the utmost from us and it goes on still.

Yesterday it was even -46 degrees; so the days pass in frost and cold. The snow lies meters high—we are ready and hold the front!!

2.2.1942

My thoughts fly often to my German home. How might it all be going in this wonderful country!

How I would like to go to the opera again. Just imagine! You put on your good suit with clean underwear; you don't have any lice; you're freshly washed and not bitten by bugs. Then you walk along the beautifully tended streets and see well-dressed people! You don't see ragged, half-starved children and women begging for bread or hacking a piece of flesh from a dead horse that lies frozen on the path. You sit peacefully and comfortably on the cushioned seat; hear the expectant rustling of the programs; the tantalizing tuning of instruments. You are not troubled by Russian shell fire or pursued by the hidden thought you can never rid yourself of: *Alarm!* The Russians are attacking. There you peacefully sit. Then the doors are closed, the light goes out, and then it starts. You hear the wonderful melodies and are uplifted into the sublime atmosphere of art!

Here day and night skulk, drab and frosty, one after the other through the joyless Russian winter, interrupted by the all too familiar battle, wounds, and death of the best comrades.

Yet I often live my memories in an old, gloomy Russian room or a dugout.

16.2.1942

Our battalion, which suffered such heavy losses, is being rebuilt. Or rather: the 3rd Battalion, I.R. 18, is being slowly reconstructed from the remnants of other units and various replacements. The *Oberst* and Regiment Commander requested me. So I dutifully report that I am, once again, the battalion doctor with my old unit.

25.2.1942

My heart is so heavy when I think of the dirty swine [*Schweinehunde*] sitting just behind the front line, who are egocentric and have no experience of comradeship and no longer know what soldierly duty is: there are many such men. Only a few hold the line against the human onslaught of the bestial enemy; they fight and die in temperatures of -40 degrees and the rest stand despite this: an incredible, heroic drama!

Most people are not aware of what a strange relationship there is and what differences exist between the actual fighting troops and those units that lie further back. Just 10 km behind the line of battle there is no sign of war any more. Here victory is all hot air! You should hear those gassers talk, the great tales they tell of their few, occasional and minor war experiences. It makes me angry to have to listen to this hogwash. These rear area flunkies [*Trossknechte*] have forgotten how to fight and so have the bigwigs of the rear services.

I must speak it plainly: these men ran when the Russians broke through and . . . for many, many kilometers there was no stopping them, and they left a lot of materiel behind. We saw scenes reminiscent of the rout of Napolean in 1812. With our last reserves of strength, and much loss of blood, we just managed to make it. The Russian was thrown back. The scenes that I witnessed have shocked me deeply. At the moment, everything in our sector of the front is stabilized. The Russians who broke through have been encircled and destroyed!

10.3.1942

I have just removed my parka and returned to my dugout, my so-called dressing station. I write these lines by candlelight. Outside, shells are exploding and bursts of machine-gun fire sweep across the ground. I have just provided medical assistance to Major Höke, an excellent battalion commander with the 2nd Battalion, I.R. 18. He is severely wounded by shrapnel, but fortunately it is not life-threatening.

Well, you must be wondering why I'm with 2nd Battalion, I.R. 18. The battalion doctor, *Assistenzarzt* Dr. Knust fell; the Russian attacks are intense and they were in need of me here. And of course I also possess the necessary front experience in the forwardmost combat sectors and am not so easy to rattle.

And so I'm sitting right in the middle of this mess again! How long will things still go well for me? So I'm sitting here in this bunker and my thoughts fly away over the shell craters and corpses that lie in the deep snow, away over the sad expanses of the Russian territory to you at home. I do my duty in the northeastern corner of the fighting troops and am proud and thankful, despite the severe challenges.

I can no longer imagine that better days may yet come for me. The demands of war and of the future are so great that we can only go on sacrificing and can expect little of what remains. I also know that inside I cannot tear myself away from the fighting troops. It is simply my fate and I will bear it, come what may!

17.3.1942

First, a few words by Scharnhorst, which convey a profound truth about success in war: "Bravery, self-sacrifice, fortitude are the basic pillars of a nation's independence. If our hearts no longer beat for these, then we are lost, even in the midst of great victories."

Words that are easy to state with enthusiasm when one is far from the fighting troops. But when in the midst of it all, it is often hard, very hard, but we will succeed, nonetheless.

Outside, we are having the most severe snowstorms; drifts of snow lie up to 3 meters high. The storm has been going on for over 2 days now. At the moment, we are cut off from supplies. And the sleds aren't getting through the snowdrifts either. The bitter wind is cutting. It's minus 30 degrees, but it feels colder—we need spring!

I have sent you a combat report, too, which describes, in sober words, the battles of our battalion, which took place on my, on our engagement day.[308] A dreadful engagement day, but of incomparable heroic magnitude. A strange engagement day!

29.3.1942

I have just arrived back from a company evening, held by candlelight in a gloomy Russian parlor. The gathering was intended to allow the new recruits to get to know the old dogs of the front line a bit better. There was schnapps and roasted horsemeat as a special treat for the evening. And so all the boys sat together in the most primitive conditions and celebrated.

But none of us can be really cheerful anymore; death has raged through the ranks of our battalion too much. Everything is so awful.

The soldiers really did try to make everything as nice as possible. Stories were told, songs sung, and speeches held! The fighters at the front line are real champs! Always ready to go into battle with the Russian beasts and forces of nature without any rest or sleep. Ever ready!

And what will the morning bring? Our faces become serious, yet hard and steadfast! We know that we must bear the brunt of the decisive battle, and we want to be ready with pride, even if we should go under. Who else will do it and be master of fate, if we, who willingly volunteered for the front, do not hold fast as a matter of course.

We want to remain true to ourselves.

5.4.1942

The snow here is still a meter high, so still deep winter! Right now, I am sitting in the bunker. Yesterday we repelled a Russian assault and destroyed a tank in the process.

Today is Easter Day. I listened to the ringing of the bells and the organ music on the radio. I was in a celebratory mood and a deep yearning overcame me!!! For a short time I could be with the division and forget everything for a moment! You are my happiness and you are with me through danger and storms. It does me good!

7.5.1942

The train that will take us to the Russian interior will leave between 2 and 3 a.m. this night.[309] I have already broken off any direct connections with or ideas of home. I am now in the grip of visions of the grim winter and the challenges of the utterly uncertain future. It is hard for me after all! This unpredictable, cruel Russia. Uncertainty and doubt take the strongest hold of humans. I have just spoken with the Regiment Commander of the 186th [Infantry] Division (bearer of the Knight's Cross and veteran of the World War), who, among other things, told me: "It has never been so difficult for me to leave home as it is now and yet I have seen many a storm. Is it the same for you?" I answered: "It is the dreadful images of winter, which were suppressed by the happy days of leave and which now come back to the fore with all the greater force."

I am certain that I will return from this war, but the toughest days are certainly still right ahead of me. Do not think that I am afraid of what is to come—I will stand by my men unflinchingly, but I would be glad from the bottom of my heart if our unit was pulled from the line and received different orders. On the other hand, I am pleased to be back with my old comrades. I would make any sacrifice with them!

9.5.1942

Now we have just arrived in Smolensk.[310] It is typical Russia here—cold, icy. The snow is gone, but it is snowing disagreeably cold and damp on the wet ground, which soaks up the white flakes immediately, turning them blackish-gray. The railway station is completely destroyed and burnt out. The town is utterly in ruins. Our train stands and waits; it can't continue on yet, as the partisans have torn up the tracks again!

This is how we are slowly weaned off home and all peaceful experiences and prepared for the front. I have fully prepared myself for this and look forward to being back together with my old comrades soon!

Now I sit in the compartment and dream and am full of deep gratitude that I have you, my dear Martha. You are the dearest thing in the world to me. Your image is now more deeply ingrained in me. I am looking forward fervently to our future together.

12.5.1942

I arrived back at my unit on 11 May. To my great joy, no serious battles took place in my absence, so there have been no particularly heavy losses in dead and wounded. I was greeted with a huge "Hello" by my comrades, for whom I was able to be a messenger from home and tell them many dear and good things!

Well, now I am back here and am back as a soldier and looking into an indeterminable future and awaiting the things that are coming. Thus, I have to readjust myself entirely again and that is not easy!

When I look back, the winter lies behind me like a bad dream and an ineffable, happy dream of my leave. What different worlds they are!

During my leave, your image became more deeply ingrained in me, and I am so happy that it is you who is my bride. I love you so deeply and have truly learned to treasure you as a person.

Appendix 10

The Battle for the Rzhev Bridgehead (1942–1943) and Postwar German-Russian Reconciliation

Dr. Craig W. H. Luther

In his memoir, Dr. Haape provides a graphic account of the fighting outside Rzhev in the winter of 1942. Yet the battle for the Rzhev bridgehead—that northernmost corner-post (*Eckpfeiler*) of Army Group Center, which pointed ominously toward Moscow—would carry on into March 1943, when the Germans finally withdrew from the bridgehead of their own volition in a successful effort to shorten their lines and free up reserves.

The fighting for this vital strategic sector of the Eastern Front was grim, pitiless, and characterized by appalling losses of both German and Russian forces. From January to April 1942, the Red Army sustained more than 750,000 casualties (dead, wounded, sick, missing) during its Rzhev-Viaz'ma strategic offensive operation,[311] while Haape's 6th Infantry Division alone suffered just under 3,300 casualties over a three-week period in August 1942,[312] when it played a major role in repulsing the Red Army's summer offensive at Rzhev. Along with 6th Infantry Division, more than fifty German divisions were committed to the fighting about Rzhev—a clear indication of just how significant the bridgehead was to Hitler and his Army High Command.

All told, over a period of fifteen months, Russian combat losses on the Rzhev axis amounted to some half million dead and at least twice as many wounded (contemporary and postwar German accounts often recorded the poor training and tactics of the *Rotarmisten*, who time and again stormed the German defenses of the city only to be repulsed with horrendous losses in men and materiel). German losses, while much smaller in numbers, were no less devastating, given the *Ostheer's* chronic manpower shortages: several hundred thousand, including perhaps one hundred thousand dead.[313] To this day, the fields, forests, and swamps of the Rzhev region continue to disgorge the bones of German and Russian soldiers who perished in a blood bath that rivaled in intensity the fighting at Stalingrad (1942–1943) or at Verdun during World War I (1916).[314]

After the war, the dreadful meatgrinder that was the "Rzhev slaughterhouse"[315] was consigned to obscurity—the victim of Soviet censorship that sought to expunge from history the Red Army's epic failure to wrest the war-torn city[316] from its tenacious German defenders. As a result, this "forgotten battle" of the Russo-German War only began to come to light in the 1990s—following the collapse of the Soviet Union—due in part to the pioneering efforts of retired U.S. Army Colonel David M. Glantz.[317]

The dissolution of the Soviet Union and lifting of the "Iron Curtain" also created the opportunity for veterans of Dr. Haape's Infantry Regiment 18 to actively pursue reconciliation with the former Russian enemy. The initial contacts took place in 1992, with an exchange of letters between Erich Vornholt, director (*Vorstandsmitglied*) of the veterans' organization (*Traditionsgemeinschaft*) of I./I.R. 18, and Leonid Mylnikow, chairman of the Council of War Veterans in Rzhev. Vornholt's objective, as outlined in his letter, was "to secure the peace and to instruct the younger generation in such a manner, that war becomes a thing of the past." Mylnikow responded: "We want to live together as good neighbors, so that our grandchildren and great grandchildren will never resort to war. . . . You are welcome in Rzhev."[318]

The first visit of a German delegation to Rzhev since the end of the Second World War took place from 6–11 June 1993 (the delegation including veterans of I.R. 18, their families, journalists, and other interested parties). It led to a major breakthrough, as the German visitors made it clear that they had not simply come to honor their own war dead but those of their Russian hosts as well; moreover, both the Russian veterans' organization in Rzhev and the city administration (*Stadtverwaltung*) expressed their willingness to cooperate with their German counterparts in the future. During this initial visit, the German delegation also visited Russian schools, and the idea was born of an exchange of students between the two countries, along with an initiative to promote instruction in the German language for local Russian teachers. In the following year (1994), a Russian delegation from Rzhev—Russian veterans, teachers, students, journalists, and so on—traveled to Gütersloh, Germany, and the foundation was forged for regular (annual) visits between the two cities.[319]

The next step in the reconciliation process was the formal establishment of the *Kuratorium Rshew* in Verl, Germany, on 25 January 1995, and the selection of Ernst-Martin Rhein as its first chairman. Rhein had served with great distinction throughout the Second World War, garnering the Iron Cross First and Second Class during the French campaign of 1940 and, in December 1941, the coveted Knight's Cross as commander of an infantry company in Infantry Regiment 18 in Russia. In addition to being one of the regiment's most decorated and distinguished veterans, he was a strong proponent of reconciliation with the former Soviet enemy; simply put, a better man could not have been found to lead the *Kuratorium*.[320]

From its inception, the *Kuratorium* not only included veterans of Infantry Regiment 18 but also welcomed veterans of other units of 6th Infantry Division who had survived the prolonged and deadly combat in and about Rzhev. In the years that followed, comrades from an additional half-dozen divisions would join the *Kuratorium,* whose annual visits to Rzhev have not only enabled its members to engage with Russian veterans and local dignitaries but also provided generous humanitarian and financial assistance to the people of the city and its cultural and social institutions—assistance that over the years has included donations of clothing, shoes, books, and furniture; seeds for vegetables and flowers; equipment, medical instruments, and medicines for the hospitals of Rzhev; and financial support of schools and other institutions.[321] Vital to the organization's success has been the support of the *Evangelisch Stiftischen Gymnasium* (a Protestant secondary school) in Gütersloh, the Youth Exchange Program in the town of Verl (whose *Droste-Haus* embodies the "spiritual center"[322] of the *Kuratorium*), and the town of Gütersloh itself.

In the summer of 1997, efforts to promote student exchanges culminated in the first encounter of German and Russian youth, whose activities together included caring for grave sites in the Rzhev region; since that time, two-week summer youth camps (*Jugendlager*) in Russia, conducted in the German language, have become a regular event, while a small Russian student group journeys each year to Gütersloh. The year 1997 also witnessed an exhibition in Rzhev of sketches and paintings of the war-torn city produced in 1942–1943 by the now deceased artist Franz Josef Langer—at the time serving in Combat Engineer Battalion 6 (6th Infantry Division). The exhibition, which made a powerful impression on the inhabitants of Rzhev, was later shown successfully in both Verl and Gütersloh.[323]

By the late 1990s, in a collaborative effort on the part of the local Russian Duma, the German War Graves Commission (*Volksbund Deutsche Kriegsgräberfürsorge*),[324] and other interested parties, construction of a "Peace Park" (*Friedenspark*) was underway in Rzhev; embracing both a German and a Russian military cemetery, and, situated just beyond the city center, the *Friedenspark Rshew* was dedicated on 28 September 2002 in a solemn ceremony attended by some 2,000 persons, including 120 from Germany.[325] "Here in Rzhev," affirmed Ernst-Martin Rhein—observing that the two cemeteries shared adjacent spaces within the park—"something has succeeded that is utterly unique in the relations between our two nations."[326]

The realization of a German military cemetery within the Peace Park at Rzhev was heralded as a major victory by those on both sides committed to reconciliation between former enemies; however, it had been a hard-fought victory, as Herr Rhein—whose tireless and tenacious support of the project had contributed decisively to its successful outcome—recalled shortly before the dedication of the Peace Park:

From the promise of the mayor of Rzhev, Alexander W. Chartschenko, in 1993, to provide the Germans with a tract of land for a cemetery—as restitution [Wiedergutmachung] for the former German military cemetery with more than 2,000 graves that had been destroyed and covered with concrete[327]—to actual realization [of the promise], it has been a long and arduous path, paved with setbacks and bureaucratic obstacles. An aggressive, well organized minority of reactionary forces has sought to this day, by means of slanderous assertions, to prevent this peace project. But the city council and administration, Rzhev veterans, and the majority of the local citizens are willing to see the reconciliation process [Versöhnungsprozess] through to its end.[328]

In 2005, the work of the *Kuratorium*—its ongoing efforts to engender peace and understanding between the two nations and their peoples—caught the attention of then German chancellor Gerhard Schröder, who, on his trip to Moscow on the occasion of the sixtieth anniversary of the end of World War II, was accompanied by three young people from Gütersloh who had participated in the youth camps of the *Kuratorium*.[329] In December 2005, Erich Vornholt, who, as noted, had taken the first tentative steps in the long and sometimes difficult journey described above, was awarded the prestigious Medal of Merit of the Order of Merit (*Verdienstmedaille des Verdienstordens*) by the German government in acknowledgment of his many years of engagement for understanding and reconciliation; a member of the *Kuratorium* from its inception, by 2012 Vornholt had traveled thirteen times to the Russian Federation in pursuit of these noble objectives.[330]

In March 2009, the *Kuratorium Rshew*'s many years of dedicated work resulted in an official partnership (*Städtepartnerschaft*) between the cities of Rzhev and Gütersloh (the home base of the *Kuratorium*). As expressed on the *Kuratorium*'s website (December 2015), "Former enemies are becoming partners and friends."

Note: To honor the men and their achievements, the founding members (*Gründungsmitglieder*) of the *Kuratorium Rshew* are listed below:

Ernst-Martin Rhein (Infantry Regiment 18)

Erich Vornholt (Infantry Regiment 18)

Walter Stockmann (Infantry Regiment 18)

Friedrich Nebbe (Infantry Regiment 37)

Paul Ostheider (Infantry Regiment 37)

Wilhelm Wessler (Infantry Regiment 58)

Horst Paul (Son of Captain Paul, Infantry Regiment 18 and 58)

Dietrich Schöning (Artillery Regiment 6)

Hans Baumotte (Signal Battalion 6)

Herbert Rohde (*Traditionsgemeinschaft* Panzer Battalion 213 of the *Bundeswehr*)

Karl-Josef Schafmeister (*Drost-Haus* Verl)

Hans Becker (Guide for the Rzhev visits)

Rolf Furtwängler (Instructor at the *Evangelisch Stiftischen Gymnasium* in Gütersloh)[331]

Historical Commentary

Prepared by Dr. Craig W. H. Luther

1. All told, the Russo-German War (1941–1945) would claim the lives of more than four million German soldiers, including more than one million who perished in Soviet captivity. Soviet fatalities, both military and civilian, are currently estimated at twenty-seven million (or more), of whom more than fourteen million belonged to the Soviet armed forces, including more than three million who died in German captivity.

2. Dr. Haape's mother succumbed to cancer in 1928, at the age of forty-six; his father died in 1932 on the operating table during a routine operation at the age of sixty-seven.

3. While at the university in Kiel in the mid-1930s, during a local event, Heinz had watched as Hitler sped past in a speedboat, saluting with the *Deutscher Gruss*. It was the only occasion when he would ever see Hitler in person.

4. *Landser* was the German Army's World War II equivalent to the American "GI."

5. Marriage by proxy (*Ferntrauung*) had been introduced by the German government in 1939 to prevent the birth of illegitimate children during the war.

6. In 1944, Dr. Haape's university studies in Strasbourg culminated in the award of a postdoctoral degree in psychology.

7. Interview, Martha Haape with journalist Barbara Tauber, 459, n.d.

8. Some former German generals, such as Guderian and Manstein, had already published their memoirs by the mid-1950s. For example, Heinz Guderian's *Erinnerungen eines Soldaten* (Recollections of a Soldier) was first published in 1951 by Kurt Vowinckel *Verlag*; while Erich von Manstein's *Verlorene Siege* (Lost Victories) appeared in 1955.

9. The Barbarossa directive (Directive No. 21) was signed by Hitler on 18 December 1940. The operational plan envisaged destruction of the bulk of the Red Army west of the Dvina-Dnepr (Dnieper) river lines (to a depth of about 500 kilometers), followed by mopping-up operations deeper in the interior of the Soviet Union; however, if this plan failed, the Germans had no "Plan B." For the text of the directive, see H. R. Trevor-Roper, *Hitler's War Directives, 1939–1945* (London: 1964); for the original German text, see Walther Hubatsch, *Hitlers Weisungen für die Kriegsführung, 1939–45* (Frankfurt: 1962).

10. For Operation Barbarossa, the Germans amassed the largest invasion force the world had ever seen—more than three million men, 3,600 tanks and assault guns, 7,100 guns of all calibers, 600,000 vehicles, and 625,000 horses. These forces, organized into 148 divisions (including nineteen Panzer and fourteen motorized), were arranged in three army groups: North, Center, and South. The *Luftwaffe* forces in the East comprised some three thousand aircraft of all types, of which 2,250 were combat ready. In addition to this primary force structure, the German Army of Norway had, by 22 June 1941, deployed several divisions in northern Finland, where they would fight alongside their Finnish allies. The Soviet Union, in contrast, boasted a military establishment of about five million men arranged in 27 armies and 303 divisions; of this total force

structure, some 2.9 million men and 171 divisions—the Red Army's first strategic echelon—were stationed in the Western frontier zone, while assembling along the Dvina-Dnepr river lines was a second strategic echelon of five armies and fifty-seven divisions, about which the Germans had no intelligence.

11. Operation Barbarossa actually unfolded in several phases. The primary assault, along a frontage of more than 1,200 kilometers from Memel on the Baltic Sea, southward beyond Warsaw, to the Prut River, commenced on 22 June 1941. In the far north, the operations of German troops and their Finnish allies did not begin in earnest until late June and early July. Finally, on the far right (southern) wing, the joint German-Romanian attack from Romania began on 2 July 1941.

12. The reference is to Martha Arazym—a celebrated soprano at the Duisburg Opera House. Martha, twenty-six, had met Dr. Haape in the fall of 1938, and they had soon fallen in love; they would become engaged in December 1941, while Haape and his surviving comrades were fighting for their lives against furious Russian attacks in arctic temperatures.

13. Infantry Regiment 18 (I.R. 18), formed in January 1921 from former World War I veterans and *Freikorps* units, was, at the time, one of just twenty-one infantry regiments permitted the German Army under the terms of the Versailles Treaty. Gerd von Rundstedt, who as a field marshal would lead Army Group South into Russia in June 1941, had commanded the regiment in 1925–1926. As its fighting record in Russia soon revealed, I.R. 18 was one of the elite regiments of Hitler's *Wehrmacht*.

14. In the sector of Field Marshal von Bock's Army Group Center, the distance from the Russo-German frontier to the suburbs of Moscow was, as the crow flies, about 1,000 kilometers (ca. 620 miles); by the beginning of January 1942, Dr. Haape's regiment had marched over 1,600 kilometers. Horst Grossmann, *Die Geschichte der rheinisch-westfälischen 6. Infanterie-Division 1939–1945*, 112.

15. The 6th Infantry Division (6 ID) was mobilized in late August 1939 and transferred at once to the West Wall on the Franco-German border. The division did not participate in the Polish Campaign of September 1939, but played a role in the second phase of the French Campaign (June 1940). Thereafter, it was transferred to the demarcation line with Vichy France and, in September 1940, to the Normandy coast, where it trained for Operation Sealion, the planned (and later canceled) invasion of England. In March 1941, the division was sent to East Prussia as part of the buildup for Operation Barbarossa. Dr. Haape joined the division in November 1940. Commanded by *Generalleutnant* Helge Auleb since October 1940, 6th Infantry Division consisted of three infantry regiments (18, 37, 58), along with artillery, anti-tank, reconnaissance, signal, engineer, supply, medical, and administrative units. On 22 June 1941, the eighteen-thousand-strong division was assigned to 6th Army Corps of *Generaloberst* Adolf Strauss's Ninth Army. Although an infantry unit, 6 ID would soon acquire a reputation as one of the finest formations in the *Ostheer*.

16. *Feldmarschall* Fedor von Bock, the sixty-year-old commander of Army Group Center. He had commanded army groups in both the Polish and the French campaigns. Although his army group had played a secondary role in the defeat of France, von Bock was given the honor of reviewing the military parade in Paris on 14 June 1940 at the Arc de Triomphe. He was promoted to field marshal on 19 July 1940. After more than four decades of service for Imperial Germany, the Weimar Republic, and now the Third Reich, von Bock's spectacular military career had finally reached its zenith. As the commander-in-chief of Army Group Center, he controlled 50.5 divisions (including nine Panzer and six and a half motorized divisions) embracing 1.3 million men and more than 1,800 tanks—more tanks than the other two army groups combined.

17. M.O.s = Medical Officers. The divisional medical unit of 6th Infantry Division comprised two stretcher-bearer companies, one field hospital, an ambulance section, and the divisional M.O. with his adjutant and staff. Simply put, the work of a front-line battalion M.O. was to patch up the wounded men sufficiently for them to withstand the journey back to the divisional Medical Company, where the operations took place. In practice, however, the tasks of a German front-line doctor in Russia, such as Dr. Haape, would entail a great many unanticipated and daunting challenges.

18. Positioned on the far-left wing of Army Group Center, 6th Infantry Division began its advance out of an area known as the Suwalki triangle. The area was quite primitive with poor roads, and lay east of the Masurian Lakes and just beyond the historic boundaries of East Prussia. Haape's division had been transferred here—close to the frontier with Soviet Russia—in early April 1941. Haape mentions the transfer to Suwalki near the end of Chapter 3.

19. For technical and performance details on German armored fighting vehicles and aircraft taking part in the Russian campaign, see Craig W. H. Luther, *Barbarossa Unleashed: The German Blitzkrieg through Central Russia to the Gates of Moscow, June–December 1941*, Chapter 3. (Hereafter cited as Luther, *Barbarossa Unleashed*.) For similar data on Russian systems, see Chapter 4.

20. From the opening hours of the campaign, the German *Landser* (GIs) discovered that their Russian opponent was unlike any hitherto encountered. While mass surrenders in the opening phase of Operation Barbarossa were not uncommon (particularly of units formed by the Red Army from territories they had occupied in 1939–1940), most Red Army soldiers fought with an almost preternatural courage and tenacity. Field post letters sent by German soldiers from Russia in the first weeks of the campaign often contrast the tough fighting qualities of the Red Army with those of the French Army of 1940. Like Battalion Commander Neuhoff, German soldiers were sometimes shaken (even enraged) by the Russian way of war, which gave no quarter to the enemy and often resorted to what the Germans considered underhanded and treacherous methods. The outcome was a grim dialectic of violence, resulting in war crimes by both sides, such as the shooting of prisoners of war. And yet the Russian fighting man—begrudgingly, to be sure—quickly became an object of respect for the German soldier, who admired this adversary's toughness, resilience, and individual fighting qualities, if deploring his often brutal methods. Moreover, the *Landser* were often astonished by the excellent quality of much of the Soviet arsenal of weapons and equipment.

21. A common tactic of Red Army soldiers—overwhelmed by the *force majeure* of the German attack— was to withdraw into the ubiquitous forests and swamps of Belorussia and European Russia, which enabled them to resist their enemy's advance on more even terms. The *Wehrmacht*'s training and doctrine, as good as it was, had failed to prepare its charges for combat in such difficult terrain. Particularly in forest fighting, the Germans would have to learn the hard way, through trial and error, resulting in many needless casualties. See, for example, Luther, *Barbarossa Unleashed*, 97–98, 392–96.

22. *Sankawagen*, or simply *Sanka*—German military slang for a motor vehicle ambulance (*Sanitätskraftwagen*, also *Krankenkraftwagen*), as opposed to a horse-drawn ambulance.

23. *Zellstoff* = cellulose.

24. In July 1929, forty-three parties signed the "Third Geneva Convention," which was actually two conventions covering military personnel who fell into an adversary's hands; one of the conventions pertained to POWs and the other to the care of wounded soldiers. Signatories included the United States, Germany, Italy, France, and Great Britain (and its Dominions); Japan and Soviet Russia were not signatories. As Dr. Haape's account illustrates, from the opening hours of the war Red Army soldiers refused to honor Red Cross symbols, firing upon German field doctors, stretcher-bearers, ambulances, and Red Cross facilities.

25. Early on, 6th Infantry Division had encountered pockets of tenacious Soviet resistance on this first day of the campaign, particularly from well-defended enemy bunker positions. By early afternoon, however, 6th Army Corps headquarters considered the situation well enough in hand to order 6 ID to begin a general pursuit of the enemy. The division's infantry pushed forward along a sandy, dusty track under a glowing sun toward the Memel (Nemen) River, more than 70 kilometers beyond the frontier. A breakthrough had been achieved; yet losses had been heavy, as recorded in the divisional war diary: 54 dead (6 officers), 106 wounded, and 19 missing.

26. Facing Army Group Center along the Eastern frontier was the Soviet Western Front, commanded by General D. G. Pavlov; it comprised the 3, 4, and 10 Armies (and 13 Army HQ) made up of 671,000 men, 2,900 tanks, over 14,000 guns and mortars, and 1,500 combat aircraft. Of the tanks, less than 2,200 were operational, and most of these were obsolete models. Within days, Pavlov's front would be pounded into submission as a result of von Bock's relentless hammer blows. The rapid destruction of Soviet Western Front would reduce Stalin to fury. General Pavlov, along with several members of his staff, were tried for treason and executed.

27. Dr. Haape makes several references to his "automatic." He is referring to the MP 40 machine pistol, or submachine gun. This 9mm weapon weighed only nine pounds (without magazine), boasted a 32-round magazine, and had a practical rate of fire of 180 rounds per minute; it was carried by both NCOs and officers. By 1941, squad leaders (NCOs) in rifle companies, hitherto armed only with the Mauser 98K bolt-action rifle, had been equipped with the MP 40, providing a major boost in firepower. *Handbook on German Military*

Forces (Baton Rouge: 1990). Originally published by U.S. War Department as TM-E 30-451 (March 1945), 310-11 (hereafter cited as *Handbook on German Military Forces*).

28. *Oberstleutnant* Carl ("Corle") Becker—the forty-six-year-old commander of Haape's Infantry Regiment 18. Becker was an *Alte Hase*, who had fought with distinction in the First World War, being repeatedly wounded and earning high military honors. During the French campaign of 1940, he had distinguished himself as the commander of 6 ID's advance detachment (*Vorausabteilung*). In late 1940, he took command of I.R. 18 and, in August 1941, was promoted to full colonel (*Oberst*).

29. German field rations included staples such as *ersatz* coffee and black bread. Food and beverages were generally prepared in bulk in horse-drawn, rolling field kitchens—their iron pots affectionately called "goulash-cannons" (*Gulaschkanonen*) in the idiom of the always famished troops—and then brought forward for distribution in insulated containers. Dr. Haape makes repeated references to the ubiquitous "goulash-cannon," the huge iron pot with the stew, which he and his comrades consumed daily in wearisome repetition. For all men, regardless of rank, the food was the same—"adequate but monotonous." George Forty, *German Infantryman at War, 1939–1945*, 64. For fascinating details on (and photographs of) German field kitchens and their accoutrements, see *Handbook on German Military Forces*, 537–40.

30. For a unique and highly detailed depiction of the activities of both German and Russian doctors on the Eastern Front, see Karlheinz Schneider-Janessen, *Arzt im Krieg. Wie deutsche und russische Ärzte den Zweiten Weltkrieg erlebten* (Frankfurt: 1993, 2001). The book offers many graphic personal accounts of doctors on both sides and how they cared for their wounded.

31. The "River Memel," also commonly known as the "Nemen," is one of the largest in Europe, flowing from Belarus, through Lithuania and into the Baltic Sea. In German, the river has been called *die Memel* since the time of the Teutonic knights. In the color facsimiles of the German Army General Staff maps used in the preparation of this edition to track the advance of Army Group Center and 6th Infantry Division, the river is also designated as the Memel.

32. Beginning in mid-May 1941, the German High Command had ordered the promulgation of three notorious measures that were to shape German policy toward Soviet prisoners and civilians in the occupied territories. Most notorious among them was the Commissar Order of 6 June 1941, which, in crass violation of international law, authorized the summary extrajudicial execution of Soviet political officers. For a general discussion of the Commissar Order and other criminal decrees issued by the German High Command on the eve of Barbarossa, see Luther, *Barbarossa Unleashed*, 90, 190, 435–37, 443–46. For the most detailed history of the Commissar Order, the reader is directed to Felix Römer's masterful work, *Der Kommissarbefehl: Wehrmacht und NS-Verbrechen an der Ostfront 1941–1942* (Paderborn: 2008); see also Horst Boog et al., *Germany and the Second World War*, Vol. IV: *The Attack on the Soviet Union*, 481–521 (hereafter cited as *GSWW*, Vol. IV).

33. The velocity of the German advance enabled the 6th Infantry Division's advance detachment to seize a bridgehead over the Memel (Nemen), at the town of Prienai, on 23 June. The losses of the division for this day—recorded in the 6 ID war diary—reflected a major dropoff in the fighting: thirteen men killed in action, twenty-four wounded, and eight missing.

34. The 6th Infantry Division (and Army Group Center as a whole) was advancing across terrain that was monotonous and flat; it was also dissected by many rivers and streams, permeated by lakes, bogs, and marshes, and covered with immense tracks of dense primeval forest. Assignments to clear wooded areas of the enemy, however distasteful to the Germans who had to carry them out, were standard practice in the opening phase of the campaign.

35. In the opening phase of Operation Barbarossa, many thousands of Russian soldiers abandoned their uniforms for civilian clothing and fled in the forests and swamps behind German lines. Many, of course, would eventually be captured or killed, while others would make it back safely to Russian lines; some of these men, however, would help form the basis of a nascent partisan movement.

36. As discussed in the introduction, Dr. Haape, working as a doctor in a Duisburg hospital, had been drafted into the military in July 1939—for three months' training as a *Kanonier*. He was soon transferred to the *Wehrmacht* medical corps. However, it should be noted that every German soldier, regardless of his intended specialty, received a basic infantry training—a policy that paid dividends in the winter of 1941–1942, when rear area service troops were often pressed into combat to fill the gaps in the front lines.

37. A brilliant and honorable soldier, *Oberleutnant* Franz von Kageneck would become one of Dr. Haape's closest and most respected comrades. He had four brothers serving as officers in the *Wehrmacht*—one an ace *Luftwaffe* fighter pilot, while another commanded a tank company in Russia in 1941 in General Walter Model's 3rd Panzer Division.

38. The *Reichswehr* was the military organization of Germany from 1919 to 1935, when Adolf Hitler reorganized Germany's military forces under the new *Wehrmacht*. Traditional and conservative in outlook, the *Reichswehr* exercised a major influence on politics during the Weimar years.

39. On 17 September 1940, Hitler, unable to secure air superiority over the English Channel and British Isles, had postponed Operation Sealion. Several weeks later, the *Führer* canceled the operation outright, except as a deception campaign to deflect Russian attention from his impending buildup in the East.

40. From Dr. Haape's account, it is evident that his few months in idyllic Normandy, rich in cultural and historical traditions, with its lovely towns, ubiquitous orchards, forests, and charming coastline, was a peaceful and happy time for him, even as he tentatively—and quite successfully, as matters turned out—sought to win the approval and respect of his comrades. Yet Heinz was hardly alone in this respect: Dr. Luther has examined thousands of field post letters written by German soldiers on the Russian front, and among those men earlier stationed in France were many who recalled with longing and melancholy the halcyon days of late 1940 and early 1941 in that "civilized" country.

41. In a Christmas message to Martha, Dr. Haape described the incident at the café in fulsome detail, noting, *inter alia*, that as he and *Leutnant* Lammerding had observed the holiday revelry of the French patrons, they had quickly grown uneasy: "We watched as covert, hate-filled and ominous glances were sent our way. There was no love in their eyes, only deep, seething feelings of revenge—thoughts of retribution for a war that had been lost." Heinz's quick thinking during the incident helped to defuse a situation that otherwise might have turned deadly.

42. In Puccini's opera *Madame Butterfly*, Martha sang the part of "Ciocio-San," a naïve, young Japanese girl who, after being betrayed and losing her honor to a callous and cowardly American naval officer, commits suicide by cutting her throat with her father's hara-kiri knife. Over the years, Martha would sing the role many times and considered it her favorite. Many of Martha's admirers considered her the "natural Butterfly." Indeed, in a remarkable artistic achievement, she epitomized the lightness of the young girl developing into a mature woman.

43. In 1941, a typical German infantry regiment consisted of about three thousand men organized primarily into three infantry battalions, each with four companies—three rifle companies and one heavy machine-gun company. Each regiment was also outfitted with a company of light and medium infantry guns (13th Company) and an anti-tank (*Panzerjäger*) company (14th Company), furnishing regimental commanders with substantial organic firepower. See Luther, *Barbarossa Unleashed*, Chapter 3.

44. The pleasant period in Normandy ended abruptly for Dr. Haape and his comrades on 19 March 1941, when 6 ID began to entrain for transfer to the East. The loading was to take several days and required seventy-one trains in all. It should also be pointed out that, while in Normandy, despite the apparent lull in the war after the victory over France, the division had undergone tenacious and thorough training, which contributed in no small measure to the division's often brilliant achievements in Russia in 1941.

45. The transfer to the Suwalki triangle—and adjacent to the Russo-German frontier—took place over 6–9 April 1941. Because of the region's poor roads, the soldiers of 6 ID, accustomed to the fine, paved roads of France, struggled with "the greatest difficulties" as they marched into the triangle. The town of Suwalki itself—occupied by the division staff—with its houses of wood and straw, made a poor impression on the men compared to the clean, tidy homesteads of East Prussia. The hostility of local Poles in the region was a cause for concern and, on occasion, turned deadly. The German response to any Polish transgressions was often swift and brutal. Grossmann, *Geschichte der 6. Infanterie-Division*, 34–36.

46. In the spring of 1941, only officers with a "need to know" would have been privy to Hitler's impending invasion of Russia. This would not have included Dr. Haape; however, rumors were indeed flying fast and furious at this time, and, despite the *Wehrmacht*'s meticulous security measures, one obvious inference from the massive military buildup in the East was that Germany was preparing to attack the Soviet Union. That said, the overwhelming majority of German soldiers in the East only learned of Hitler's

actual intent on the evening of 21 June 1941, when the *Führer*'s proclamation to the *Soldaten der Ostfront!* was read out to them by their officers.

47. After three days of largely desultory combat, punctuated by brief periods of tenacious Red Army resistance (particularly on the first day of the war), 6 ID casualties dropped off dramatically and, from 28 to 30 June 1941, the division incurred no losses at all. The *Lageost* map of the German Army General Staff for 25 June shows 6 ID still in its bridgehead over the Memel at Prienai. The division then began to march southeast, its lead elements reaching Voronovo (ca. 60 kilometers south of Vilnius) on 28 June. On top of clouds of dust and unmercifully hot weather, the poor roads and blown bridges posed additional challenges to the men. A thundershower on 28 June brought temporary relief. As registered in the divisional war diary, from 22–26 June, 6 ID had taken 421 prisoners, killed 509 Red Army soldiers, and destroyed or captured weapons and equipments of all types. To chart the daily advance of the division, see Klaus-Jürgen Thies, *Der Zweite Weltkrieg im Kartenbild*, Bd. 5: Teil 1.1: *Der Ostfeldzug Heeresgruppe Mitte 21.6.1941–6.12.1941. Ein Lageatlas der Operationsabteilung des Generalstabes des Heeres* (Bissendorf, Germany: 2001).

48. As illustrated by numerous firsthand accounts, the German invaders were often greeted as liberators in the opening days of the campaign in the Baltic States, eastern Poland, and parts of the Ukraine. Yet Hitler's strategy of refusing to grant these people their liberty, and instead imposing another form of ruthless oppression, soon squandered the good will initially displayed by so many.

49. While Dr. Haape may have helped to spread a false rumor to deter his men from drinking unfiltered water, official German records reveal that retreating Red Army troops did in fact poison the wells of villages and towns. For example, 7th Panzer Division, which captured Vilnius on 24 June, ordered that the division's troops be alerted at once because the local wells had all been poisoned (*vergiftet*). How common a practice this was is not known.

50. "Pak" is the German abbreviation for *Panzerabwehrkanone*, or anti-tank gun.

51. Indeed, as General Franz Halder, chief of the German Army General Staff, recorded with satisfaction in his diary on 22 June, "The *overall picture* of the first day of the offensive is as follows: The enemy was surprised by the German attack. His forces were not in tactical disposition for defense. The troops in the border zone were widely scattered in their quarters. The frontier itself was for the most part weakly guarded. As a result of this tactical surprise, enemy resistance directly on the border was weak and disorganized, and we succeeded everywhere in seizing the bridges across the border rivers and in piercing the defense positions (field fortifications) near the frontier." Charles Burdick and Hans-Adolf Jacobsen (eds.), *The Halder Diary, 1939–1942*, 412–13.

52. Pushing details, or *Schiebekommandos*, as the Germans called them.

53. Minsk, the capital of Belorussia, several hundred kilometers beyond the Russo-German frontier, had fallen to the invaders on 28 June. In a vast pincer movement, the two *Panzergruppen* of Army Group Center—2nd Panzer Group (General Heinz Guderian) and 3rd Panzer Group (General Hermann Hoth)—washed around the flanks of Soviet Western Front in Belorussia; by 30 June their pincers had snapped shut, trapping large elements of Western Front's disorganized armies in a huge pocket that extended from Belostok (Bialystok) to Minsk. Clearing out the pocket would continue into early July.

54. Goebbels's propaganda and, indeed, Hitler himself attempted to justify the attack on the Soviet Union as a *preemptive* measure designed to thwart an imminent Soviet attack on Germany. Yet, as surviving German records show, there is no evidence to support such a claim. However, recent research into the Soviet archives by Polish-German historian Bogdan Musial (*Kampfplatz Deutschland. Stalins Kriegspläne gegen den Westen* [Berlin: 2008]) has revealed that Stalin was preparing an attack on Germany for 1942 or 1943. As a result, one can argue that Operation Barbarossa may have been justified as a *preventive* measure—that is, as an effort to prevent a threat from materializing that did not yet exist (but most likely would at some future date). For a detailed examination of this issue, see Luther, *Barbarossa Unleashed*, 191–97.

55. The line of reasoning expressed here by *Oberleutnant* Kageneck was quite common in the summer of 1941: The German invaders—generals and *Landser* alike—were often staggered by the enormous Red Army concentrations they encountered during the frontier battles and concluded that the German invasion had just managed to preempt a massive Soviet attack.

56. By the beginning of July 1941, 6 ID was advancing through the northeastern tip of Poland (territory occupied by the Red Army in September 1939) and making for the Dvina River. The division reached Oszmiana (50 kilometers southeast of Vilnius) on 3 July.

57. Similar to the marching infantry, great demands were placed on the German Army's horses during the *Vormarsch* (advance) through Russia, and they suffered accordingly. The horses, too, were adversely affected by the extreme heat and the poor sanding tracks over which they endlessly toiled. Horse losses began to mount early in the campaign; most severely affected were the heavy draft horses used to haul the light and medium artillery. Losses in 6th Infantry Division, however, were kept to a bare minimum, thanks to the solicitous concern of the division commander, General Auleb, who saw to it that the division's roughly six thousand horses were handled with special care. In fact, by September 1941, 6 ID had only lost a few more than fifty of its horses, the fewest of any of the thirteen divisions in Ninth Army. For the vital role played by horses in the German Army, see Richard L. DiNardo, *Mechanized Juggernaut or Military Anachronism? Horses and the German Army of World War II* (New York: 1991).

58. As Dr. Haape's observations illustrate, the panje horses—the small native breed of Eastern Europe— exhibited great endurance while being easy to feed, handle, and stable; thus, they were quickly drafted into service by the German Army. The hardy little horses were appreciated by rank-and-file soldiers and generals alike. In early 1942, Panzer General Joachim Lemelsen (47th Panzer Corps) jotted in his diary, "These panje horses are certainly tough animals. It is almost frightful [*ungeheuerlich*] what can be demanded of them, and they get by with just a little hay as feed and require no care" (BA-MA MSg 1/1148, *Tagebuch Lemelsen*, 14.2.42). Despite their renowned toughness, the panje horses were far too light and small for hauling artillery and, in many cases, horse-drawn vehicles.

59. The infantry of Army Group Center did two things in July 1941—they marched and they fought. After the initial frontier battles, however, they mostly marched, from dawn to dusk, as they sought to catch up with the tanks of Hoth and Guderian now ranging far to the east (fully laden, the German infantry soldier carried 25–30 kilograms of gear, to which might be added rations, ammunition—a crate of 300 MG shells weighted 8 kilograms—and components for machine guns and mortars). In early July, the infantry of Haape's 6 ID were temporarily assigned a decent road—the historic *Trakt Napoleonski* of the summer of 1812—but soon they were again tramping eastward across the miserable sandy tracks of Belorussia, through endless belts of forest and swamp, plagued by the unholy trinity of heat, dust, and thirst, desperately short of sleep, hungry, and tormented by the omnipresent mosquitoes. The division saw no major combat during the first two weeks of July 1941, aside from an occasional skirmish with Soviet stragglers who ambushed the marching columns from their hiding places in the woods. In forced marches of 30, 40, even 50 kilometers a day, which pushed the men to the limits of their endurance, 6 ID made for the Dvina River and the fortified city of Polotsk, part of the so-called Stalin Line, where the Red Army was determined to bring the advance of the left wing of Bock's army group to a final halt.

60. Prior to the start of Barbarossa, German generals and staff officers had carefully studied Napoleon's invasion of Russia and its catastrophic outcome (General de Caulaincourt's eyewitness account of the disastrous 1812 campaign drawing particular attention). They were, of course, fully aware of the historic challenges posed by time and space in the Russian theater of war. In their casually confident calculations, however, both problems, which had loomed so large in the defeat of the *Grande Armée*, had been dramatically diminished by what was perhaps the seminal invention of the modern era: the internal combustion engine. Powered by the modern, fossil fuel–driven engine—so their thinking went—the tanks, trucks, mobile artillery, and armored personnel carriers of the *Ostheer* would succeed where Napoleon had failed.

61. A key terrain feature along the historic invasion route into Russia was the strategically vital "Smolensk gate." Stretching between Orsha and Vitebsk, where the upper reaches of the Western Dvina and Dnepr rivers curl back sharply to the northeast, this landbridge formed a corridor 75 kilometers wide—enough space, according to Panzer General Hermann Hoth, for three armored divisions to maneuver. A German objective of paramount importance, the gate was protected along its western approaches by a broad belt of forests and swamps running north from the Pripet (Pripiat') Marshes. Hermann Hoth, *Panzer-Operationen. Die Panzergruppe 3 und der operative Gedanke der deutschen Führung Sommer 1941*, 45–47.

62. The reduction of the Belostok-Minsk pocket had come to an end by 9 July 1941. In his diary on 8 July, Field Marshal von Bock estimated that his army group had eliminated twenty-two rifle divisions, seven tank divisions, six motorized brigades, and three cavalry divisions; as of 7 July, Bock noted, 287,704 prisoners had been taken (among them several corps and division commanders)—a figure that, according to German estimates, was to rise to 324,000 over the next few days. The material booty was also staggering—more than 3,300 tanks and 1,800 guns destroyed or captured, along with the seizure of vast quantities of fuel, ammunition, and rations. While German figures for Soviet prisoners are most likely inflated (through inadvertent inclusion of civilians), Belostok-Minsk was, by any measure, an unprecedented victory. According to authoritative Russian figures published in the 1990s, Western Front suffered 417,729 casualties, including 341,012 "irrecoverable losses" (i.e., dead, captured, and missing), through 9 July 1941—out of a total force of almost 675,000 men. Western Front also lost 4,799 tanks (many having simply run out of fuel), 9,427 guns and mortars, and 1,777 combat planes (most of which were destroyed on the ground) during eighteen days of fighting in the Western frontier regions from 22 June to 9 July 1941. For Soviet losses in World War II, see Col.-Gen. G. F. Krivosheev (ed.), *Soviet Casualties and Combat Losses in the Twentieth Century* (London: 1997).

63. The Red Army had built strong defensive positions along and behind the Soviet Union's former (prewar 1939) frontier, fortifications the Germans christened the "Stalin Line." The Stalin Line was, for the most part, not really a line at all (like the French Maginot Line), but rather a system of fortified regions, each with bunkers, light artillery, machine-gun positions, and tank traps covering the primary axes of an enemy advance. One of the oldest fortified regions along the Stalin Line was Polotsk, which sat astride the Dvina River where the Soviet, Polish, and Lithuanian frontiers came together. Covering the approaches to the town were dozens of concrete bunkers, bristling with heavy weapons and machine guns; regular field positions, barbed wire obstacles, and difficult terrain features—including lakes and marshy ground, adeptly integrated into the defenses by the Soviets—added to the strength of the position.

64. The 6th Infantry Division crossed the historical Berezina River—literally, "River of Birches"—on 11 July 1941. It was here, in November 1812, on this right-bank tributary of the Dnepr River, that the remnants of Napoleon's retreating army were largely annihilated. Having covered 46 kilometers on this day, Haape's I.R. 18 was now beyond the prewar 1939 Soviet frontier. In the regimental war diary for 11 July, one reads, "The water situation is extremely bad. A large number of the local wells had been rendered unusable by the withdrawing Soviet troops." KTB I.R. 18: *"Der russische Sommerfeldzug mit dem I.R. 18."* Staats-und Personenstandsarchiv Detmold, D 107/56 No. 10 (hereafter cited as, KTB I.R. 18: *"Sommerfeldzug"*).

65. The 21cm *Mörser* 18 was the German Army's standard heavy howitzer. It had a muzzle velocity of 1,854 feet per second, a maximum range of 18,300 yards, and was quite accurate. Among the general headquarters (GHQ) artillery allotted to Army Group Center on 22 June 1941 were seventeen battalions (*Abteilungen*) of the heavy howitzers; General Strauss's Ninth Army, to which the 6th Infantry Division was assigned, had five of the battalions on *Barbarossatag*. For more on the weapon's technical details and photographs, see *Handbook on German Military Forces*, 336–37.

66. The multipurpose 88mm anti-aircraft gun was one of the most successful weapons of the war produced by any of the belligerents. Several versions of the weapon were built for use against air, ground, or sea targets. (Field Marshal Erwin Rommel's use of the "88" as an anti-tank gun in North Africa is legendary.) The gun possessed a rapid rate of fire (fifteen to twenty rounds/minute), long-range and high-muzzle velocity (2,690 feet/second). In the summer of 1941 (and beyond), it was often the only weapon that could reliably destroy the heavy Soviet KV and T-34 tanks, whose appearance administered a collective shock to the German invaders. See *Handbook on German Military Forces*, 349–50.

67. The war diary of Haape's I.R. 18 recorded that, on 14 July 1941, the following batteries were assigned to the regiment to support its attack on the Stalin Line: a battery of 21cm heavy howitzers (3./s.Artl.Abt. 860); a battery of 15cm rocket launchers (2./Nb.W.Abt. 3); and a battery of 88mm anti-aircraft guns (3./Flak-Rgt. 701). KTB I.R. 18: *"Sommerfeldzug."*

68. The German assault on Polotsk was conducted by elements of General Otto Förster's 6th Army Corps, attacking from due west and south of the Dvina, and General Albrecht Schubert's 23rd Army Corps—already operating on the river's northern bank—striking from the north. To supplement their organic light and medium howitzers, the divisions of 6th Army Corps (6 and 26 ID) were supported by general head-

quarters artillery (*Heeresartillerie*), including 21cm and 30cm heavy howitzers; 88mm flak batteries were also assigned to the attack. Stuka dive bombers of *Luftwaffe* General von Richthofen's 8th Air Corps provided air support. For accounts of the battle, see Luther, *Barbarossa Unleashed*, 499–501; Grossmann, *Geschichte der 6. Infanterie-Division*, 49–52; David M. Glantz, *Barbarossa Derailed: The Battle for Smolensk, 10 July–10 September 1941*, Vol. 1, 116–17.

69. The village of Gomely, situated around 25 kilometers due south of Polotsk, lay in the assault sector of Infantry Regiment 18. Several large lakes directly north and east of the village complicated the mission of the regiment, whose assault formations—some outfitted with flamethrowers—were personally led by *Oberst* Becker, the regimental commander.

70. The 37mm anti-tank guns of Noack's 14th Company (I.R. 18), essentially obsolete as of 1940, when they had proven ineffective against heavier Allied armor, continued to play a significant role as an infantry support weapon. Due to their serious shortcomings in the anti-tank role, a heavier 50mm anti-gun was introduced; however, by June 1941, these were only beginning to reach the forces in the field in small quantities. Both the 37mm and the 50mm guns proved ineffective against the heavier Soviet KV and T-34 tanks.

71. Despite the Russian snipers and difficulties due to inadequate maps, by 1100 hours, the lead elements of both Infantry Regiments 18 and 37 had broken through the Russian bunker lines and begun to roll up the remaining enemy positions from the flanks and rear.

72. As noted in the war diary of Haape's Infantry Regiment 18 (15 July 1941), "That the enemy had placed such weak forces in such a strongly fortified position was inexplicable. Due to the paucity of enemy artillery, the course of the attack, after our splendid heavy artillery and Flak had silenced the enemy bunkers, was characterized by the combat of our infantry assault groups, which with outstanding dash and reckless abandon [*mit hervorragendem Schneid und Draufgängertum*] set the morally inferior enemy to flight and took most of them prisoner. . . . During the attack the regiment seized more than 15 reinforced concrete bunkers." KTB I.R. 18: "*Sommerfeldzug.*"

73. As recorded on the *Lageost* map of the German Army General Staff for 15 July 1941, units of Hoth's 3rd Panzer Group were already ranging far beyond the Dvina River, as a second major cauldron battle began to take shape in the Smolensk region.

74. Infantry Regiment 18 had indeed played a major part in piercing the Stalin Line at Polotsk; that, however, was not the entire story: exploiting its initial success, IR 37, improvising a small, motorized assault team, raced through the wooded terrain and seized the portion of Polotsk below the Dvina River (the river ran directly through the town) in a coup-de-main. The stunning victory resulted in surprisingly few casualties for Auleb's 6 ID (eleven dead, thirty-six wounded)—a testimony to the impressive tactical skill of the German infantry, even when attacking a well-fortified (if poorly defended) position. *Oberstleutnant* Hennicke (Commander, IR 37) garnered the Knight's Cross for his special role in the operation. The fall of the fortified town helped to unhinge Soviet defenses along the Dvina River line.

75. Underpinning the *Wehrmacht*'s remarkable success in Russia in 1941—and throughout the period 1939–1942—were not superior weapons (for example, both the French and the Russians fielded better tanks, even if they didn't know how to use them!); rather, it was the application of key intangibles, such as the element of surprise, superior training, experience, and, perhaps most noteworthy, a military culture that pushed leadership and individual initiative down to the lowest levels of command. The doctrine was known as "mission tactics" (*Auftragstaktik*) and was a major force multiplier (even if, on occasion, it promoted outright insubordination!). German military tradition from the time of Frederick the Great had taught Prussian and German soldiers to resolve tactical and operational problems with originality, insight, and initiative. Hence, Bolski's impulsive, albeit successful, action was hardly unique. Even General Strauss (C-in-C Ninth Army), in electing to conduct a set-piece assault on Polotsk with several divisions, had ignored von Bock's explicit warning not to attack with a large force but to simply seal off the fortress and subdue it in deliberate fashion to avoid casualties. In this case, however, Strauss's instincts proved better than his superior's! For a detailed discussion of "mission tactics," see Luther, *Barbarossa Unleashed*, 182–85.

76. Red Army snipers were a feared and deadly presence from the very beginning of the Russian campaign. Often equipped with excellent automatic rifles, outfitted with telescopic sights, they struck often and without warning. On the second day of the war, units of Field Marshal von Kluge's Fourth Army complained

about the sudden appearance of enemy snipers, and the frustrations of Major Werner Heinemann (23 ID), expressed in a letter to his wife on 11 July, must have been universal among German troops in the summer of 1941: "Unfortunately snipers firing from concealed positions cause us endless problems. Two nights ago, a motor vehicle driver from my old 1st Company was murdered in the forest, as he tried to repair a flat tire. He was all alone." According to a statistical evaluation from 1944, 43 percent of German soldiers who died on the battlefield (i.e., those buried without ever making it to a field hospital for care) succumbed to shots to the head—a favorite target of snipers. See Schneider-Janessen, *Arzt im Krieg*, 423.

77. Field Marshal Albert Kesselring, whose 2nd Air Fleet was responsible for providing Army Group Center with air support.

78. By mid-July 1941, Panzer generals Hoth and Guderian had created the conditions for another extraordinary cauldron battle (*Kesselschlacht*), this time around the ancient city of Smolensk—the first major operational objective of Army Group Center. By the evening of 15 July 1941, the assault units of the 29th Motorized Division (2nd Panzer Group) reached the southern outskirts of Smolensk, where they would fight a ferocious three-day battle to clear the city. Meanwhile, also on 15 July, the northern pincer of Army Group Center's vast encirclement movement, Hoth's 3rd Panzer Group reached Iartsevo, 50 kilometers northeast of Smolensk, severing the main road and rail links with the city. Three Soviet armies, some three hundred thousand troops, most of whom were still engaged far to the west, were becoming trapped within the developing pocket, which extended from Smolensk westward toward Orsha on the Dnepr River.

79. The combat losses of Haape's 3rd Battalion, and of 6th Infantry Division as a whole, had hitherto been very light, a circumstance that would begin to change for the worse in August 1941.

80. "*Im Namen des Führers und Obersten Befehlshabers der Wehrmacht*," Dr. Haape was awarded the *Eisernes Kreuz 2. Klasse* on 24 July 1941. See Appendix 2 for the complete record of his military service from 1939 to 1944.

81. By 30 July 1941, 6 ID arrived at the Mezha River (some 60 kilometers northeast of Velizh) and the front of 3rd Panzer Group. In five and a half weeks, the division had fought and marched 1,000 kilometers from the Russo-German frontier.

82. On 30 July 1941, Hitler issued "Führer Directive" No. 34, ordering Army Group Center to temporarily halt its eastward drive and go over to the defensive along its entire 700-kilometer front. The order came in response to disturbing new developments, particularly the fierce and wide-ranging Soviet counterattacks against von Bock's army group, which had begun on 23 July; moreover, the two Panzer groups needed to be pulled from the line for rest and rehabilitation as soon as the situation allowed. (For the text of Directive No. 34, see H. R. Trevor-Roper (ed.), *Hitler's War Directives, 1939–1945*, 91–93.) Hitler's precipitous decision—inconceivable to the average *Landser*, as Haape's account illustrates—must also be seen in the context of the indecision and discord that now paralyzed the German High Command, as Hitler and his generals argued over the proper strategic approach for the next phase of the campaign. Simply put, Hitler's generals remained fixated on Moscow, whose capture, they averred, would prove decisive, while the *Führer*, arguing in broader economic terms, contemplated shifting the *Schwerpunkt* (center of gravity) of operations in the East from the center to the wings, with Leningrad and the Ukraine, at least temporarily, receiving a higher priority than Moscow—a strategy that, if implemented, would divert von Bock's armor away from the Soviet capital, now only 300 kilometers to the east. The dictator would not render his final decision until late August 1941.

83. In fact, Haape's metaphorical "steel ring" had already begun to lose its "grip": As early as mid-July 1941, the invading German forces were beginning to lose their momentum as they fanned out deeper into the endless depths of European Russia. Through mid-July, Army Group Center had averaged about 20 kilometers per day; thereafter, its forward progress plunged to just 4–5 kilometers/day. This precipitous decline, of course, was due in no small part to inexorably stiffening Soviet resistance. Another contributing factor was the German Army's growing logistical difficulties, as supply lines naturally grew more tenuous the farther its forces advanced to the East.

84. As noted in the divisional war diary, the front occupied by 6th Infantry Division along the Mezha River extended for 40 kilometers, a length considered virtually impossible at the time, at least according to prewar doctrine. (In Russia, however, in the years ahead, such vast defensive frontages would almost become commonplace.) The terrain posed an additional handicap—it was swampy and consisted almost

exclusively of heavily forested areas. As a result, the division could only mount a series of strong points anchored on local villages.

85. To the troops of Army Group Center, who found few fruits or vegetables along their routes of advance, honey from local beehives was considered a special delicacy. References in diaries and letters of German soldiers to the plundering of beehives are particularly common in the fall of 1941, when the men were often short of rations—due to breakdowns in the logistical system—and forced to forage for food and drink in the countryside and local villages. As one veteran of 6 ID recalled, "Beehives were doused with a pail of water and then plundered. Often we even ate the honeycombs."

86. German soldiers fortunate enough to have a radio set in the summer of 1941 might have been consoled by the mellifluous and melancholy tones of cabaret singer Lale Andersen's sentimental soldiers' song "Lili Marlene." As of August 1941, the song was beamed nightly at precisely 9:57 p.m. by *Soldatensender Belgrade* (Armed Forces Radio Belgrade) across the battlefields of Europe and North Africa, just before station sign-off. The Allies, of course, listened to the song, which became a favorite of both Axis and Allied troops. The staggering popularity of the original German version soon resulted in an Allied (English language) rendition of the tune. When Lale Andersen was asked in 1972 to explain the popularity of the song, she quipped, "Can the wind explain why it became a storm?"

87. Among Dr. Haape's personal papers is an intriguing document titled *Sanitätswesen* (medical service); in it, Haape lays out key details on his policies for organizing and performing his medical work in the field. Under "3. Medical Aid Stations," he writes, "The medical aid station is, if possible, to be located close to the battalion command post." The document is undated; yet since it also addresses frostbite and lice, Haape most likely prepared it in the fall or winter of 1941–1942.

88. The first major crisis for the 6th Infantry Division in its defensive battles along the Mezha River line came on 2 August 1941, when two Russian cavalry divisions—each composed of three Cossack regiments heavily armed with automatic weapons, artillery, and anti-tank guns—broke through the thin screen of Haape's Infantry Regiment 18.

89. PKW (*Personenkraftwagen*)—a passenger vehicle for personal use, such as Dr. Haape's old Mercedes. For the Russian campaign, a bewildering assortment of vehicles had been commandeered from throughout occupied Europe for this purpose. Many of these passenger cars were civilian vehicles, which tended to break down easily along the unforgiving Russian roadways.

90. The bitter fighting on this day had surged back and forth until early evening, when a 6 ID counterattack, led by Cavalry Captain (*Rittmeister*) and Knight's Cross holder Georg *Freiherr* von Boeselager, finally hurled back the attacking Cossacks, who left some three hundred dead before the German lines. As posted in its war diary, 6 ID sustained sixty-five casualties of its own, including twenty-five dead and missing.

91. In a letter to Martha on this day, 3 August 1941, Haape wrote, "I have never been so close to death as I was this morning at 0745." In the same letter he also observed, "We are in the midst of a struggle of the utmost severity; we must not allow ourselves to succumb to any illusions about this, whatever the magnitude of our successes. . . . it is war in its most terrible, archetypal form" (*Es ist der Krieg in seiner furchtbarsten Urform*). For Dr. Haape's complete letter, see Appendix 9.

92. Orderly Dehorn's makeshift grave offered an iconic image of the *Landser* in the *Russlandkrieg*: a simple birch cross with a steel helmet, and on the cross, hanging inconspicuously, the Iron Cross Second Class he had received as an award for bravery. Dr. Haape was profoundly affected by the sudden, tragic loss of Dehorn, his "lively little orderly." As he wrote to Martha several days later (14 August), "He was the dearest one to me of all those who die a soldier's death here. . . . He was a good comrade, that little Dehorn!" For more of the letter, see Appendix 9.

93. As noted in the divisional war diary, General Auleb had borrowed five tanks (Pz IIIs) from 19th Panzer Division of 57th Panzer Corps; three of the tanks were assigned to Infantry Regiment 18, two to Infantry Regiment 58. On the afternoon of 3 August, elements of both regiments, supported by artillery, combat engineers with flamethrowers, and the five tanks, set out to clear the forests of the enemy up to the banks of the Mezha.

94. The 6 ID's total losses on 3 August were sixteen dead, forty-seven wounded, and twenty-seven missing—many or most of the latter, no doubt, had also perished in the fighting.

95. To compensate for growing shortages of soldiers at the front, the Germans made ever-increasing use of Russian POWS, deserters, and women to perform certain tasks. For example, they built roads and trenches; worked as drivers, cooks, even typists and interpreters; and, as Haape's example indicates, also assisted German medical units. While many served their German masters faithfully, more than a few operated as spies for the Red Army.

96. Of course, Army Group Center was not advancing "without resistance" but had been facing furious Red Army counterattacks since late July. Neuhoff, however, a major and battalion commander, was understandably unaware of the "big picture."

97. 6th Infantry Division would remain in position along the Mezha River line for several weeks. The division's elongated front (by late August 1941, I.R. I8 alone was defending a 25-kilometer front with just seven combat-capable rifle companies) was soon braced with bunkers, trenches, mine fields, barbed wire entanglements, and infantry strong points, which meandered through the dense pine forests. The division's lines were often raked by Russian artillery fire, while the Soviet Air Force (VVS) became increasingly active; in fact, by the second week of August 1941, it had gained air superiority over the entire front of Ninth Army (to which *Generalleutnant* Auleb's 6 ID belonged). The Russians continued to strike at 6 ID outposts, often with numerically superior forces, while German assault parties (*Stosstrupps*) responded with vigorous actions of their own. Simply put, Haape's division, after marching more than two-thirds of the way to Moscow, was now engaged in a classic war of position (*Stellungskrieg*), similar to that experienced by their fathers in the Great War of 1914–1918. An additional challenge was the growing threat posed by Soviet partisans, spies, and espionage activities. See KTB I.R. 18: "*Sommerfeldzug*"; Hans-Adolf Jacobsen (ed.), *KTB des OKW*, Bd. I: 565; Luther, *Barbarossa Unleashed*, 559–69.

98. To the *Landser* of Haape's I.R. 18, the Mezha River sector must have resembled the end of the earth—uncomfortably hot, teeming with mosquitoes and other pesky insects, heavily forested, with a scattering of diminutive and largely dilapidated villages offering an almost imperceptible sign of civilization. In a letter to his young wife on 11 August 1941, *Oberleutnant* Juerg von Kalckreuth, adjutant I.R. 18, elaborated on this theme: "In the days ahead, I will, it seems, be able to write to you more often, as we are now stuck indefinitely in this place. It hardly seems right to us, but seems to be necessary in terms of the big picture. . . . It's a pity that, in our current spot, we are apparently in the most desolate part of this desolate country [*ödesten Teil dieses öden Landes*], where 10 decaying houses are marked on our map as a large village. You simply cannot imagine just <u>how</u> desolate this region is. Yesterday, in a letter, Frau Becker asked her husband [i.e., *Oberst* Becker, C-in-C I.R. 18] about a pair of Russian leather boots and furs. We had a good laugh about that, because the only things that one can actually purchase here (and then only if the locals are still around) are potatoes and perhaps some honey. . . Just now another insect dropped onto my table—that's No. 30 for the evening! The largest daily catch of insects among our staff to date is 170. (I have included a dead specimen in my letter to you.)" *Aus Briefen des Adjutanten Inf. Rgt. 18, Oblt. Juerg von Kalckreuth (26), im zweiten Halbjahr 1941 an seine mit ihm jungverheiratete Frau Gisela (21),* in Staats-u. Personenstandsarchiv Detmold, D 107/56 Nr. 4.

99. By August 1941, Adolf Hitler and his High Command were becoming increasingly nervous. The initial hammer blows of the *Ostheer* had failed to finish off the Red Army, much less topple the Soviet State, which was proving more resilient than the Germans had anticipated. The regenerative powers of the Red Army—its uncanny ability to constantly hurl new divisions, new armies, into the battle—astonished the German leadership. As Chief of the Army General Staff Franz Halder confessed to his secret diary on 11 August 1941, "The whole situation makes it increasingly plain that we have underestimated the Russian colossus. . . . At the outset of the war, we reckoned with about 200 enemy divisions. Now we have already counted 360. These divisions indeed are not armed and equipped according to our standards, and their tactical leadership is often poor. But they are there, and if we smash a dozen of them, the Russians simply put up another dozen." Burdick and Jacobsen (eds.), *The Halder Diary, 1939–1942*, 506.

100. Martha Arazym was indeed a prolific letter writer; in fact, over a two-year period from March 1941 to March 1943, she wrote well over 250 letters to Heinz.

101. During the winter of 1940–1941, the RAF continued to conduct small-scale night raids over Western Germany—raids that were largely ineffective at this stage of the war. The year 1941 would see forty

air raids on Duisburg—a primary RAF target due to its chemical, steel, and iron industries—causing eighty-seven deaths. Increasingly worried about the raids, Heinz, in his letters, repeatedly admonished Martha to retire at once to her air raid shelter when the sirens wailed. For the air war over Duisburg, see Michael A. Kanther and Marc Olejniczak, *Bomben auf Duisburg. Der Luftkrieg und die Stadt bis 1960* (Duisburg: 2004).

102. Georg von Boeselager, who was personally decorated for bravery by Hitler in January 1942, would, along with his brother Philipp, later join the anti-Hitler resistance; both would play a dramatic role in the abortive 20 July 1944 assassination plot, leading an unauthorized retreat of cavalry forces from the Eastern Front in a surreal night maneuver with the mission of using them to take control of Berlin and effect a coup d'etat. When the bomb failed to kill Hitler, the von Boeselager brothers barely succeeded in returning with their units to the front and avoiding detection. Georg was killed in action on the Eastern Front in August 1944, while his brother Philipp survived the war and died in 2008 at age ninety. For details, see Philipp *Freiherr* von Boeselager, *Valkyrie: The Story of the Plot to Kill Hitler, by Its Last Member* (New York: 2009).

103. During this period, cases of dysentery among the men of 6th Infantry Division increased alarmingly—the inevitable outcome of poor hygienic conditions, the exhaustion of the men from lack of sleep, extreme weather, lice and mosquitoes, and, of course, the many long marches and battles. As one soldier in 6 ID recalled his ordeal with the sometimes fatal affliction, "I also became sick one day. I had to do my business 25 times a day, yet nothing but blood came out." It was late August 1941 when Dr. Haape treated Captain Georg von Boeselager and his cavalry troop, which was suffering from nearly three dozen cases of dysentery. Von Boeselager, *Valkyrie: The Story of the Plot to Kill Hitler, by Its Last Member*, 62–63; see also August Freitag, *Aufzeichnungen aus Krieg und Gefangenschaft (1941–1949)*, 60.

104. It is telling that von Boeselager, who appears to be talking in conspiratorial tones against Hitler and his regime, did not shy away from sharing such dangerous thoughts with Dr. Haape. The conversation is cited by the later conspirator Philipp *Freiherr* von Boeselager as an example of growing dissatisfaction toward Hitler among members of the officer corps. See *Valkyrie: The Story of the Plot to Kill Hitler, by Its Last Member*, 63–65.

105. The costly battle noted here by Dr. Haape took place on 27 August 1941. It was a day Infantry Regiment 37 would never forget: strong Russian cavalry forces, attacking without artillery preparation—their approach hidden by thick sheets of ground fog—struck the regiment's overextended and sparsely held line at about 2:30 a.m. Exploiting their initial surprise, they rapidly broke through and got as far as the regimental CP. It was not until 1800 hours that desperate German counterattacks had restored the original main battle line. Some four hundred Russian dead blanketed the battlefield, while German losses were equally appalling, Infantry Regiment 37 alone sustaining 348 casualties: 10 officers and 162 NCOs and men killed; 13 officers and 127 NCOs and men wounded; 36 NCOs and men missing in action (as registered in the 6 ID war diary). Among the German dead was the commander of IR 37, *Oberstleutnant* Hennicke. When the Germans recovered their dead, many were found to have been diabolically mutilated—courtesy of an implacable foe who gave no quarter. The dead of IR 37 were buried on the periphery of a local village, where the Germans had set up another military cemetery; they were honored in a solemn Teutonic ceremony, a ritual that, by now, had become all too common. For a detailed account of this battle, see Luther, *Barbarossa Unleashed*, 567–69.

106. The primitive peasant dwellings, which had changed little, if at all, over the generations, were built of wood with thatched or sod roofs in "varying stages of decay," as one German officer recalled (Günther Blumentritt, "*Moscow*," in *The Fatal Decisions*, William Richardson and Seymour Freidin [eds.], 37). Unlike "the old Pan's," most peasant huts consisted of nothing more than a single simple room, dominated by a large brick oven for cooking and furnishing warmth, and on top of which (or next to) the family slept during the long, arctic winters. Adjoining the hut in the back were sheds for cows, pigs, and other animals. The huts thus tended to be filthy and were always overrun by insects. (As a rule, German soldiers, fearful of catching lice or contracting diseases, did not use peasant huts for quarters in the summer of 1941; this situation would change in the fall and winter, with the onset of freezing temperatures.) Furniture, made by the peasant himself, was "sparse and wretched," the huts having earthenware pots and wooden tubs, with a wooden box normally serving as a small cupboard. Cradles for young children were suspended from the ceiling on ropes, while newspaper was often used as wallpaper. Electric lighting was unheard of, with illumination, if available, provided by kerosene lamps or paraffin candles (in poorer areas the peasants spent the hours between sundown

and sunup in darkness). Toilets of any kind were unheard of—family members did their "business" outdoors, in outhouses or in the open, even in the depths of winter. The peasant homes, however, were often decorated with religious icons, reflecting the Christian faith of a deeply devout people.

107. To bridge those thousand years in twenty, Stalin had lashed his people ruthlessly. Through his war on the peasantry (e.g., forced collectivization of the farms), industrial Five-Year Plans, and civilian and military purges, he had, by the late 1930s, imposed his iron will on the Soviet people. From that point onward, no one dared to challenge his authority on any matters pertaining to war or peace. And while millions perished as a result of Stalin's policies, he managed to forge a backward nation into a modern industrial power that, by 1941, possessed the largest and most complex armed forces in the world, even if the Red Army was still in the throes of thorough and challenging reforms, including the reorganization and re-equipping of its mechanized forces. In the final analysis, it was Stalin's ruthless vision that contributed most significantly to the Red Army's ultimate victory over Hitler's Third Reich.

108. This "great cleft," as Dr. Haape described it, was strikingly evident to the German invaders from the opening days of the campaign. Passing through a depressing, monotonous landscape and impoverished villages, exposed to an alien "race" whose customs they far too often failed to comprehend, confronted by wretched scenes of poverty and human misery—the *Landser* were staggered by the overwhelming "otherness" of so much of what they observed and experienced. Whatever preconceptions they may have held, German soldiers were shocked by the destitution, deprivation, and human degradation they witnessed everywhere and attributed to the sinister and oppressive impact of Communist rule. Sarcastic references to the "Soviet paradise" abound in the soldiers' letters and diaries.

109. By late summer 1941, 6th Infantry Division, like many other formations of Army Group Center, at the end of a long and fragile supply line, had begun to experience nagging supply problems. Noted the war diary of Infantry Regiment 18 on 15 September 1941, "The insufficient deliveries of means for lighting have rendered the extensive staff work and other activities much more difficult; above all, the lighting for the medical dugouts [*San.-Unterstände*] is inadequate. The regiment's motor vehicle situation has worsened visibly. With the loss of the commander's personal vehicle, the last motor vehicle of the regimental staff is now also under repair. It is exceedingly difficult to acquire spare parts." Several days later, the war diary revealed that the health of the men of I.R. 18 had been adversely affected by several days of rain, resulting in numerous cases of influenza (*Grippeerkrankungen*). KTB I.R. 18: "*Sommerfeldzug.*"

110. According to the daily situation maps of the German Army General Staff, 6th Infantry Division was relieved from its positions along the Mezha River line on 6 September 1941; the division then marched a short distance to the southeast, occupying a line less than 50 kilometers west/southwest of the town of Belyi. Here it was to remain until 22 September, when, in preparation for Operation "Typhoon," the impending offensive of Army Group Center toward Moscow, it edged slightly southward (reaching a point below the village of Bor) and into its jump-off positions for "Typhoon." Ammunition and supplies were stockpiled and, on 29 September, the division's combat engineers began the treacherous task of clearing the German minefields before the main battle line, while heavy weapons were manhandled into position. The tension and excitement among the men was palpable as they prepared to cover the final 300 kilometers to their coveted objective—the Soviet capital of Moscow.

111. At the start of Operation "Typhoon," 6th Infantry Division was assigned to General Reinhardt's 41st Panzer Corps of 3rd Panzer Group. In the final days before the attack, 6 ID received about eight hundred replacement troops, but many had arrived too late to be of immediate use. With bad weather—rain, mud, and eventually, snow—just around the corner, the operations branch (*Führungsabteilung*) of the divisional HQ staff had traded its motor vehicles for horse-drawn transport (*Pferdezug*), while 6 ID medical units had replaced their motor vehicles with specially prepared *Panjewagen* for transport of the wounded. These measures would prove themselves time and again in the weeks ahead.

112. While Hitler's figures on Soviet losses may not have been precise, they were largely accurate; after all, the German successes all along the Eastern Front had been remarkable—even unprecedented—by the end of September 1941, so there was no need to exaggerate them. Indeed, Leningrad was now tightly encircled by Army Group North; in the Ukraine, Army Group South, cooperating with Guderian's 2nd Panzer Group from von Bock's army group, had smashed a half-dozen Soviet armies and captured 665,000 prisoners in the

greatest cauldron battle the world had ever seen. (Hitler, on 21 August 1941, had finally put a definitive end to the bickering with his generals, electing to seek decisions in both the north and the Ukraine before turning again to Moscow.) Yet the great victories concealed a troubling reality, which was that the *Ostheer* was slowly bleeding to death. By 30 September 1941, the *Wehrmacht* in the East had sustained well over half a million casualties, including 185,000 fatal losses, while losses in armor and aircraft were also enormous. The most grievous—and largely irreplaceable—losses had fallen on the combat infantry. On a positive note, the tank forces of Army Group Center had been significantly replenished in preparation for "Typhoon."

113. For Operation "Typhoon," Field Marshal von Bock had assembled an enormous strike force of about 1.75 million men arrayed in seventy-two-plus divisions, including forty-seven infantry, fourteen Panzer and eight motorized divisions. The army group's 1,400 tanks, arranged in three Panzer groups, made up the primary strike force, while the entire assault along von Bock's seven-hundred-plus kilometer front was supported by some four thousand guns (1,022 light and medium batteries) and the squadrons of Field Marshal Albert Kesselring's 2nd Air Fleet. The offensive actually commenced on Army Group Center's southern wing on 30 September—to enable Guderian and his 2nd Panzer Group to take full advantage of the prevailing good weather—while the main attack began at first light on 2 October 1941. For von Bock's complete order of battle, see BA-MA RH 19II/120, *KTB H.Gr.Mitte*, 2.10.1941; Ernst Klink, "*The Conduct of Operations*," in *GSWW*, Vol. IV: 668–69.

114. The reference to "smokescreen rockets" is to the German 15cm *Nebelwerfer 41* rocket projector. This six-barreled rocket launcher hurled a high-explosive shell more than seven thousand yards with devastating effect. Like Haape, many German soldiers were seeing it in operation for the first time on this day. For more on the weapon's technical details, see *Handbook on German Military Forces*, 395.

115. *Ordonnanzoffizier* = special-missions staff officer.

116. As Johannes Haape explained to Dr. Luther on a lovely spring day in South Africa in 2015—on the trail of Dr. Haape's postwar life there—his father had assured Stolze that, should he ever get himself into a "fix," he, Heinz, would get him out of it. On 2 October 1941, Dr. Haape made good on his word. Such a sacrificial commitment to his comrades was, Johannes explained, the key to his father's conception of *Kameradschaft*.

117. Despite furious enemy resistance, and the challenge of marshy, wooded terrain, 6th Infantry Division—with Dr. Haape's Infantry Regiment 18 spearheading its attack—had succeeded in tearing open a breach through which the tanks of 1st Panzer Division could begin their pursuit of the defeated enemy. Yet the cost had been prohibitive, the 6 ID war diary for this day (2 October 1941) recording 109 dead, 372 wounded, and 12 missing. Infantry Regiment 18 alone had sustained 43 dead (including three officers), 125 wounded, and 5 missing. KTB I.R. 18: "*Winterfeldzug.*"

118. The color battle maps of the German Army General Staff show the lead elements of 1st Panzer Division reaching the strategically significant town of Kalinin, more than 150 kilometers northwest of Moscow, by the evening of 13 October 1941.

119. The so-called *Ratsch-Bumm*, a 76.2mm divisional cannon, was one of the Soviet weapons that was most feared by the *Landser*. As one German veteran (30 ID) wrote to Dr. Luther, "We soldiers called it that ['*Ratsch-Bumm*'] because—in contrast to 105mm, 125mm and 150mm artillery—there wasn't a single moment between firing and impact, which is why you could hardly take cover" (Ltr., K. H. Mayer to Dr. C. Luther, 29 July 2014). A veteran of 6 ID recalled, "The '*Ratsch-Bumm*' was also a dangerous weapon. The discharge of the gun could only be heard after the impact of the shell. Hence the name '*Ratsch-Bumm*.'" Ltr., H. S. to Dr. C. Luther, n.d.

120. Not only Russian soldiers but also many Germans, wounded and unwounded alike, had the misfortune to fall from the frail plank causeways that led across the treacherous Ossotnja swamp and to drown; their bodies were not recovered until the following morning. See Grossmann, *Geschichte der 6. Infanterie-Division*, 68–70.

121. Dr. Haape's 6th Infantry Division was now pressing northeast toward the historic Volga River and the town of Rzhev, about 100 kilometers away. In contrast to the tenacious Red Army resistance on the first day of "Typhoon," 6 ID now found the going—at least for the moment—much easier, as noted in its war diary on 4 October 1941: "The night was peaceful. The advance goes forward, as the division is only encountering

enemy stragglers. . . . Resistance is minor." Losses for the day were a single fatality and five wounded. On the same day (4 October), Chief of the German Army General Staff, Franz Halder, observed with satisfaction that the general offensive of von Bock's Army Group Center was "developing on a truly classic pattern." Burdick and Jacobsen (eds.), *The Halder Diary*, 546.

122. The new orderly would soon become one Dr. Haape's most trusted and loyal comrades. In the months, and years, ahead, Appelbaum would often pen long letters to Martha, on Heinz's behalf, keeping her well informed of their activities at the front.

123. During the summer of 1941 the Soviet Air Force (VVS) exercised a relatively minor influence on the course of events on the battlefield. The tactics employed by both bomber and ground attack aircraft tended to be ineffective, with the result that Soviet air strikes were not always taken seriously by those Germans on the receiving end. As one German tank officer recalled, "It soon became clear that the Russian air force had only obsolete machines at its disposal, but above all that the pilots did not function nearly as well as our fighter and dive-bomber pilots, or the pilots of our Western opponents. This was naturally a great relief to us, and when Russian aircraft appeared, we hardly bothered to take cover. We often had to smile, in fact, when, for want of bombs, thousands of nails rained down on us from their bomb bays" (Hans von Luck, *Panzer Commander*, 66). Nevertheless, by late July 1941, the VVS had begun to register some success against the German armored spearheads; moreover, by fall/winter, a resurgent VVS would make its presence felt all along the front, at times gaining air superiority over an increasingly overstretched and attrited *Luftwaffe*.

124. As one German tank general complained to his diary, "the days are already becoming too short" (*Tagebuch Lemelsen*, 5.10.41). The war diary of Infantry Regiment 18 recorded on 3 October 1941 that darkness began to fall at 1800 hours. The shorter days had significant tactical implications for the advancing German troops, as they now had fewer hours of daylight in which to conduct operations. Although 6 ID still managed to make good progress, its movements in early October 1941 were also hampered by poor roadways and difficult terrain features, seriously reducing the mobility of motor vehicles and heavy weapons. On one occasion, elements of IR 18 captured a well-defended town but had to do so without the benefit of artillery support, for the utterly exhausted draft horses (*völlig erschöpften Pferden*) were unable to pull the guns forward in time. KTB I.R. 18: "*Der russische Winterfeldzug mit dem I.R. 18.*" Staats-und Personenstandsarchiv Detmold, D 107/56 No. 10 (hereafter cited as KTB I.R. 18: "*Winterfeldzug*").

125. As posted in the war diary of 6 ID, the lead elements of Haape's Infantry Regiment 18 reached the town of Bukovo on the morning of 6 October 1941.

126. As the temperatures began to plunge the problem with lice grew accordingly. As one historian observed, "Overcrowding in cold, wet and unsanitary conditions produced colds, influenza, disease and lice. . . . Lice were the scourge of the eastern front, an irritant contributing to ill-health and cumulative psychological depression. Painstakingly picked off the body, they could only be killed with certainty by cracking them between fingernail and thumb after they were gorged with blood" (Robert J. Kershaw, *War Without Garlands: Operation Barbarossa, 1941/42*, 189). A former German artillery officer recalled, "The lice were a torment that was to stay with us for months. . . . We scratched arms, legs, stomach, the small of the back, and it was a constant burning in the armpits. It was worst at night, and the men would thrash restlessly in their blankets." Siegfried Knappe, *Soldat: Reflections of a German Soldier, 1936–1949*, 218.

127. Unfortunately, the foul-smelling powder would prove virtually useless in eliminating the lice, as Dr. Haape soon discovered (to his displeasure).

128. The autumn rains began on 6 October 1941 along the southern wing of Army Group Center, and that night the first gentle snow fell, though it did "not lie for long" (Heinz Guderian, *Panzer Leader*, 233). Over the next two days, the rains spread across the army group's entire front, turning the unpaved roads to mud and slush and slowing the rate of advance. Because of the dangers posed by icing, poor visibility, and soggy runways, *Luftwaffe* sorties plunged precipitously, from 1400 on 6/7 October to just 139 on 9 October. The bad weather also disrupted the movement of supplies and the evacuation of wounded. For the moment, because the most devastating effects of the Russian rainy season (the "Rasputitsa," or "time without roads") had yet to be felt, the infantry units of Army Group Center—often leaving their heavier artillery behind—still managed to make notable progress, while the massive downpours often stopped the tank and motorized columns dead in their tracks.

129. On 5 October 1941, *General der Panzertruppen* Georg-Hans Reinhardt, hitherto commanding 41st Panzer Corps, took control of 3rd Panzer Group. Panzer General Hoth was transferred to Army Group South and given command of Seventeenth Army.

130. By 11 October, I.R. 18 had reached the town of Otrub, just 21 kilometers due south of Rzhev. The regiment's front—facing north and west—was now more than 15 kilometers in length and, thus, could only be defended by a scattering of weakly manned strong points (*schwache Stützpunkten*). (All told, the main battle line of 6 ID was over 50 kilometers in length!) Over the next couple of days, I.R. 18 would still manage to repulse furious Russian attempts to break through its lines in an effort to escape encirclement and destruction (on one occasion, the regiment beat back an attack by ten Red Army battalions!). A report filed by 1st Battalion (I.R. 18) noted that Red Army commissars brandished whips to spur their men on in the attack. KTB I.R. 18: "*Winterfeldzug*"; see also Grossmann, *Geschichte der 6. Infanterie-Division*, 74–75.

131. Supported by elements of 1st Panzer Division, infantry of 6th Infantry Division stormed into Sychevka on 10 October 1941; in two days of fighting (9/10 October), the division had sustained 32 dead and 130 wounded, as well as one man missing. Steady attrition was having its effect.

132. War Diary, I.R. 18 (10 October 1941): "Combat Morale of the Enemy: Despite his hopeless position, the enemy fights tenaciously and grimly [*zäh und verbissen*]. Some Russian soldiers have even blown themselves up with hand grenades to avoid being captured." KTB I.R. 18: "*Winterfeldzug*."

133. In the days after 2 October, the armored spearheads of Army Group Center had slashed deeper into the Soviet hinterland, rapidly enveloping the bulk of the Red Army's Western, Reserve, and Briansk (Bryansk) Fronts. By 8 October, Guderian's armor had linked up with infantry of Second Army northeast of Briansk, entrapping the shocked defenders of three Soviet armies. To the north, on the morning of 7 October, lead elements of 3rd and 4th Panzer Groups had joined hands at Viaz'ma (Vyazma), encircling another four Soviet armies and parts of a fifth. In less than a week, von Bock's infantry armies and mobile forces had ripped a 300-kilometer-wide breach in the Soviet central front. Elated by their success, the Army High Command ordered von Bock to begin a general pursuit of the beaten enemy toward Moscow; by mid-October, the main defensive line before the Soviet capital had been ruptured at several points. For an overview of Operation "Typhoon," see Luther, *Barbarossa Unleashed*, 639–47; for a highly detailed account, see David Stahel, *Operation Typhoon: Hitler's March on Moscow, October 1941* (Cambridge: 2013).

134. The dramatic challenges now posed by weather and terrain can be clearly followed in the war diary of Haape's Infantry Regiment 18. With supply lines breaking down, the regiment managed to sustain itself by living off the land (as did 6 ID as a whole). As noted on 19 October by the *Oberquartiermeister* of Ninth Army (to which 6 ID belonged) in his daily report to the Army High Command, "Resupply [of divisions] with rations and fuel extremely difficult; above it all looms the shortage of bread."

135. By 20 October 1941, the double encirclement battles of Viaz'ma and Briansk had largely flickered out. According to Colonel David M. Glantz, the three Soviet fronts lost seven of their fifteen armies, sixty-four of ninety-five divisions, eleven of fifteen tank brigades, and fifty of sixty-two attached artillery regiments; equipment losses amounted to 6,000 guns and mortars and 830 tanks. Most significantly, roughly one million Red Army soldiers were lost in these battles, of whom 688,000 were taken prisoner by the Germans. "By any measure, the results were truly catastrophic." Glantz, *Barbarossa: Hitler's Invasion of Russia 1941*, 153.

136. The German Army High Command (OKH)—indeed, Hitler himself—was stunned by the stupendous number of Red Army prisoners taken by the end of 1941—the figure of several million being generally accurate. The Germans were in no way prepared to feed, house, clothe, and provide proper medical care for such a teeming mass of humanity. As a result, disease, starvation, and death were rampant among Soviet POWs, while cases of cannibalism were not unknown. Despite the sublime indifference to such suffering at the highest levels of command, some German authorities did what little they could to improve the lot of the prisoners. Nevertheless, over the course of the war, as many as 3.3 million Russian soldiers would perish in German captivity. For a detailed discussion of German treatment of Soviet POWs, see Luther, *Barbarossa Unleashed*, 437–43.

137. As noted in Volume IV of the quasi-official German history of the Second World War, "Acting in accordance with the directive of the Communist Party Central Committee and the Council of People's Com-

missars of 29 June, as well as with Stalin's broadcast address of 3 July 1941, Red Army troops, along with the specially created destruction battalions, whenever there was an opportunity during their retreats, had applied the 'tactics of scorched earth' and destroyed 'all valuable chattels' on the greatest possible scale without regard for the needs of the population." "Scorched earth" tactics would be applied "just as unscrupulously" by the Germans during their retreat from Moscow in the winter of 1941–1942. Joachim Hoffmann, "The Conduct of the War through Soviet Eyes," in *GSWW*, Vol. IV: 906.

138. On 22 October 1941, control of 6th Infantry Division reverted back to General Förster's 6th Army Corps (the division had been assigned to 41st Panzer Corps—and for period of several days to 56th Panzer Corps—since the start of "Typhoon"). The 6 ID had performed its mission well—covering the flanks and rear of the Panzer forces as they advanced via Cholm–Belyi–Sychevka–Staritsa to Kalinin. In recognition of the division's accomplishments, Panzer General Reinhardt (C-in-C, 3rd Panzer Group) showered its soldiers with 400 E.K. 2 and 50 E.K. 1. Grossmann, *Geschichte der 6. Infanterie-Division*, 78.

139. For a picture of the official award document, see the first photospread in this book. For a complete listing (with award dates) of Dr. Haape's military decorations, see Appendix 2, "Record of Dr. Heinrich Haape's Military Service (1939–1944)."

140. By mid-October 1941, what the Germans called the *Schlammperiode* (the period of oozing mud and slime), the result of the incessant rains, had caused such catastrophic damage to even the few hard-surfaced roads that only a trickle of supplies (some of them brought in by aerial transport) was reaching the troops along the forward edge of battle. The men did their best to live off the land, but Soviet "scorched earth" practices, and the fact that many of the local areas had already been thoroughly picked over by marauding German troops, made this increasingly difficult to do. Many *Landser* saw their "rations" reduced to little more than tea and potatoes, which they "organized" from local villages and farms, while butchering their horses for meat became a necessity. All of this certainly held true for the men of Dr. Haape's 6th Infantry Division.

141. This was the Tma River, in the sector of 6 ID about 20 kilometers beyond—and parallel to—the much larger Volga. The 6 ID's bridgehead across the Tma would mark the farthest point of the division's advance into Russia in 1941.

142. *General der Flieger* Wolfram *Freiherr* von Richthofen—one of the outstanding tactical air commanders of the Second World War. He commanded the 8th Air Corps, the only *Luftwaffe* formation especially trained for the close air support (CAS) mission.

143. The sudden appearance of the Soviet T-34 tank in the opening days and weeks of the campaign had administered an adrenal shock to the collective German system. The 6th Infantry Division, however, did not experience its own "tank fright" until late October 1941. The T-34 was a medium tank that weighed about thirty tons, was operated by a crew of four, and was outfitted with a high-velocity 76mm main armament; the tank also boasted excellent armor protection and a top speed of 55 k/h. The T-34's 60 percent sloping armor was revolutionary, offering significantly enhanced protection against flat trajectory anti-tank shells, which often failed to penetrate and simply ricocheted away. The advantages of the T-34 over German tank and anti-tank models of 1941 (with exception of the multipurpose "88s") were enormous. For German veterans' impressions of the T-34, see Luther, *Barbarossa Unleashed*, Appendix 6, 680–85.

144. On 27/28 October 1941, strong Russian tank forces (elements of the Red Army's 8th Tank Brigade), among them T-34s, had also struck the deep right flank of I.R. 18 at Tredubje, eliciting serious alarm at 6 ID headquarters and evoking strong countermeasures. The division immediately bolstered its anti-tank defenses with a detachment of 88mm guns (*Flak-Kampftrupp*). Grossmann, *Geschichte der 6. Infanterie-Division*, 80–81; see also KTB I.R. 18: "*Winterfeldzug.*"

145. All Panzer IV tanks produced prior to June 1941 were equipped with a short-barreled 75mm L24 main armament. While the tank was originally conceived as a close support weapon and, thus, as a complement to the Panzer III main battle tank, its success in the Polish and French campaigns—and later against Allied and Soviet vehicles—soon led to its active use as an "anti-tank" tank as well. The Germans, however, began Operation Barbarossa with only 444 Panzer IVs allotted to the entire Eastern Front; moreover, the tank's main armament had no chance of penetrating the armor of a T-34 at ranges beyond 500 meters. Mass production of a longer-barreled Panzer IV (75mm L/43)—which could meet the T-34 on even terms—would

not begin until March 1942. Thomas L. Jentz (ed.), *Panzertruppen—The Complete Guide to the Creation & Combat Employment of Germany's Tank Force, 1933–1942*, 234.

146. The reference is to Field Marshal Walther von Brauchitsch, since February 1938 the commander-in-chief (*Oberbefehlshaber*) of the German Army.

147. While the thrust of the major's remarks was accurate, he was not abreast of developments regarding Japan: by August 1941, as the German advance slowed at Smolensk, the Japanese military had finally come to the decision to strike out into Southeast Asia and the Pacific and not to attack the vulnerable Soviet rear in Manchuria in support of Operation Barbarossa. This vital information was soon relayed to Stalin by Richard Sorge, a German journalist in Tokyo and Soviet spy, who had close contacts inside the German embassy. Japan's fateful decision enabled Stalin to withdraw desperately needed divisions from Central Asia and the Far East and to employ them against Hitler's *Wehrmacht*.

148. On 15 October 1941, panic and chaos had swept through Moscow as news of the German advance on the Soviet capital finally reached the city; the crisis reached its peak in the following days and was not brought under control until 19 October. The Soviet State Defense Committee (GKO), on 15 October, had decreed the immediate evacuation of most of the government to Kuibyshev, on the Volga River, some 400 miles to the southeast; factories, industrial installations, warehouses, and other facilities were prepared for demolition. By 31 October 1941, more than two million people had been officially evacuated from the city, and many others had simply fled. Stalin's dogged determination to remain in Moscow, and fight to the end, was a decision of historic magnitude, which helped to steady the shaky nerves and sagging morale of the Russian people. For a graphic, eyewitness account by a British war correspondent in Moscow, see Alexander Werth, *Russia at War, 1941–1945*, 232–42.

149. By the end of October 1941, growing Russian resistance, mounting supply problems, and brutal climatic conditions had brought the exhausted formations of Army Group Center to a virtual standstill. Since the start of "Typhoon," von Bock's divisions had come 230–260 kilometers closer to Moscow, while units of Fourth Army and 4th Panzer Group were little more than 50–75 kilometers from the Soviet capital. On 31 October, von Bock acknowledged that his army group's losses had become "quite considerable"; officer losses were such that more than twenty battalions were now commanded by lieutenants! As for 6th Infantry Division, it had expanded its bridgehead over the Volga and, from 23 to 31 October, pushed farther north to the Tma River, where it was finally stopped southeast of Torzhok by mounting Soviet pressure. Since 22 June 1941, 6 ID had sustained some three thousand casualties, and while these losses were comparatively light, as was always the case, they had been heaviest among the combat infantry.

150. On 3 November 1941, I.R. 18 issued new guidelines for the conduct of battle (*Kampfführung*): robust, permanently manned defensive positions were to be built, with the main battle line (*Hauptkampflinie*) embracing a string of strongpoints made up of foxholes for anti-tank protection (*Panzerdeckungslöcher*). (In mid-November a divisional order would expand these guidelines by calling for construction of a continuous trench system between strongpoints.) Active tactical reconnaissance was to report on any changes in enemy activity, while the regiment's relatively weak anti-tank defenses were to be buttressed by belts of mines (*Minensperren*) and a handful of self-propelled artillery pieces (*Panzerhaubitzen*). KTB I.R. 18: "*Winterfeldzug*."

151. War diary, I.R. 18, 4 November 1941: "Working tirelessly, day and night, the battalions continue to improve their positions, despite being seriously hampered by the paucity of building materials and equipment. The weather is becoming colder day by day, and the ground is soon frozen to a depth of up to one meter." KTB I.R. 18: "*Winterfeldzug*."

152. It was a common tactical practice of both German and Red Army forces to first locate via reconnaissance and then strike at the vulnerable seams between units of most any size—vulnerable because the reactions of the defenders, in situations when responsibilities were not always clear, tended to be slower. For an excellent account of German defense doctrine in the first years of the Russian campaign, see Major Timothy A. Wray, *Standing Fast: German Defensive Doctrine on the Russian Front during World War II. Prewar to March 1943* (Fort Leavenworth: 1986).

153. The average daily temperature in the Moscow region for November 1941 was 22.5° Fahrenheit. R. H. S. Stolfi, *Chance in History: The Russian Winter of 1941–1942*, 220.

154. In his letters to Martha, Heinz on more than one occasion uses the idiom *Mordskerle*—very loosely and ordinarily translated as "terrific guys," yet in the context of war and Russia also having a more literal meaning—to describe the soldiers of his battalion and 6 ID in general. He clearly admired his comrades as brave and noble warriors.

155. Discipline in the *Wehrmacht* during World War II was extremely harsh. As many as twenty-two thousand German soldiers were executed during the war, while the Imperial Army of 1914–1918 condemned less than fifty men to death. Opine Dr. S. Hart et al., "The German Army maintained order, discipline and combat effectiveness through a draconian system of military justice in which even minor offenses could meet with severe punishment." Dr. S. Hart et al., *The German Soldier in World War II*, 11. (Special thanks to Dr. David Stahel for the statistics in this note.)

156. Again Dr. S. Hart et al.: "One area where the German medical profession remained backward was in its recognition and treatment of mental and non-combat injuries. 'Battle fatigue' was not officially recognized in the German Army. Men displaying nervous symptoms were classified as either mentally or nervously ill. . . . Informally, many troop commanders did their utmost to help and protect troops suffering from battle fatigue by issuing them special leave, reassigning them from the front to other duties in the rear for rest and recuperation. . . . The Germans, however, retained a very macho—and rather unscientific—attitude toward battle fatigue. Many a soldier executed for cowardice had simply reached the end of his tether. . . . Psychological casualties really only began to emerge for the first time in significant numbers during the Eastern Campaign" (Dr. S. Hart et al., *The German Soldier in World War II*, 91–92). Sadly, Dr. Haape's courageous and compassionate intervention on behalf of the unfortunate *Unteroffizier* Schmidt would not have a happy outcome.

157. Although Volhynian fever was, as Dr. Haape observed, "seldom fatal," some cases would require a long convalescence.

158. By mid-November 1941, Haape's Infantry Regiment 18 had established a solid winter defensive line along the northern bank of the Tma River. The 6th Army Corps Commander, *Generalleutnant* Förster, paid a visit to the regiment on 14 November and expressed satisfaction with the good work it had done building up its front. The Red Army order of battle in its sector included several rifle regiments (e.g., 908, 914, 915). Moreover, the enemy enjoyed an advantage in artillery, in part at least due to ammunition shortages on the German side. KTB I.R. 18: "*Winterfeldzug.*"

159. Temperatures along the central front before Moscow had hovered above and below freezing during the week prior to about 11 November 1941, when permanent subzero readings finally set it. For daily temperature readings from mid-November through early December 1941, see Friedrich Hossbach, *Infanterie im Ostfeldzug, 1941/42*, 134.

160. It is a common misconception that Hitler's attack on Russia was fatally delayed for up to six weeks by the Balkan campaign in the spring of 1941. While the conquest of Greece and Yugoslavia temporarily removed several divisions from the original Barbarossa order of battle (e.g., the 2nd and 5th Panzer Divisions, both of which required major overhauls and partial re-equipping in Germany), the unusually heavy rains in central and eastern Europe in the spring of 1941, which severely flooded the banks of major rivers—such as the Bug in central Poland, the primary river barrier facing Army Group Center along the Russo-German frontier—meant that the offensive would in any case have been delayed. For a more detailed discussion, see Luther, *Barbarossa Unleashed*, 100–105.

161. Since Hitler and his High Command expected the Eastern campaign to be over by autumn at the latest, only the fifty-eight German divisions that were to remain in Russia as an occupational force were earmarked to receive the winter clothing and equipment. That even this modest (and clearly inadequate) supply of winter clothing and equipment didn't reach the front until early 1942 was due not to neglect but to the collapse of the German logistical system in the East in the fall/winter of 1941–1942, compelling German Army quartermasters to ruthlessly prioritize their supply shipments; indeed, it would have required 255 transport trains—which were urgently needed to supply the troops with ammunition, food, and fuel—to deliver winter clothing to these fifty-eight divisions alone. Thus the stocks of winter clothing and equipment languished in depots and railway sidings between Warsaw and Smolensk. Klaus Reinhardt, *Moscow—The Turning Point: The Failure of Hitler's Strategy in the Winter of 1941–42*, 170–71.

162. On 22 June 1941, Hitler's *Ostheer* had stormed into Russia with virtually no awareness of the country, its people, or their way of life. Moreover, whatever negative impressions the typical German soldier held, *a priori*, of the Soviet people were generally reinforced by his initial experiences inside the Soviet Union, where poverty and human misery abounded. While many German soldiers developed highly ambivalent, even contemptuous attitudes toward the civilian population—which could, and did, lead to brutal excesses against it—Dr. Haape, as is evident throughout his memoir (and reflected in his many sympathetic sketches of Russian peasants), always maintained a healthy respect and admiration for the Soviet people. For a detailed account of German soldiers' "cultural collisions" with what many of them derisively labeled the "Soviet paradise," see Luther, *Barbarossa Unleashed*, 420–33.

163. On 9 October 1941, in the euphoria of the German victories of the first days of Operation "Typhoon," Reich Press Chief Dr. Otto Dietrich—and, to be sure, not without Hitler's imprimatur—had proclaimed to the world that, with the "smashing" (*Zertrümmerung*) of the Red Army before Moscow, "the campaign in the east has been decided." Max Domarus, *Hitler. Reden und Proklamationen 1932–1945*, Bd. II: *Untergang (1939–1945)*, 1767.

164. Field Marshal von Bock had resumed Operation "Typhoon" on 15 November, after a permanent frost had set in and the roads again became traversable. His emaciated army group—since the start of "Typhoon" it had lost an additional 87,500 men and hundreds of precious Panzers—struck out in an effort to envelop Moscow from both north and south of the city. At first the remaining tanks—painted white to blend with the landscape, now blanketed by a light, dry snow—made surprisingly good progress, even if the shortened days, low-hanging clouds, and occasional snow flurries restricted their air cover. The new offensive, however, would soon peter out.

165. Alfred Rosenberg—an Estonian-born member of the NSDAP, whose anti-Semitic and anti-Christian theories made him a primary contributor to National Socialist ideology. In July 1941, Hitler appointed Rosenberg Reich Minister of Eastern Occupied Territories, where he competed unsuccessfully for influence against his more malevolent rivals: Goebbels, Himmler, and Göring. Rosenberg would be sentenced to death at the Nuremberg trials and executed in 1946.

166. Austrian military historian Heinz Magenheimer posits that, had "Typhoon" commenced just one week earlier (ca. 25 September 1941), the German armored spearheads would have succeeded in encircling Moscow before the advent of the Russian rainy season, which had brought their forward progress to a sudden halt; moreover, he characterizes the loss of this week as "fatal" to the outcome of the battle, while also implying that the seizure of the Soviet capital might very well have won the war for Germany (Heinz Magenheimer, *Moskau 1941. Entscheidungsschlacht im Osten*, 227–28). Yet while it is possible that, given an extra week of good weather, von Bock's tanks might have completed the encirclement of Moscow, such an operational triumph would not have altered the underlying conditions—among them America's impending entry into the war— that consigned Barbarossa to failure.

167. The Ju 52/3M was a trimotor transport that had first flown in 1931. Despite being obsolete, slow, and cumbersome, the Ju 52 was a "supremely reliable" aircraft, of rugged construction, simple to operate and maintain. To the *Landser* it was known affectionately as the *Tante Ju* ("Auntie Ju"). The Ju 52 served with distinction in all combat theaters of the Second World War—its many missions including airlifting supplies to surrounded troops, delivering ammunition and fuel to the armored spearheads or to forward airstrips, and evacuating wounded soldiers from the front. For a detailed assessment of the aircraft by an English test pilot who flew it, see Captain Eric Brown, *Wings of the Luftwaffe: Flying German Aircraft of the Second World War*, 132–39.

168. *Reichsmarschall* Hermann Göring had made sure his *Luftwaffe* units in the East were fully supplied with winter clothing and accoutrements. The small number of Waffen-SS formations on the Russian front also received their winter clothing.

169. Optimism may have been "running high" in Klin—so close to their fervently sought-after objective, Moscow. But reality was another matter. On 1 December, Field Marshal von Bock dispatched a gloomy teletype message to Army High Command; in it, he outlined the desperate state of his army group, insisting that the notion that the enemy had "collapsed" was a "fantasy" (*Traumbild*) and that continuing to attack was "without sense or purpose" (*ohne Sinn und Ziel*). He proposed that the attack be broken off and his forces

pulled back to a shorter, more defensible line. Klaus Gerbet (ed.), *GFM Fedor von Bock, The War Diary*, 375–76. For the German text of von Bock's teletype, see Rudolf Hofmann, *"Die Schlacht von Moskau 1941,"* in *Entscheidungsschlachten des zweiten Weltkrieges*, Hans-Adolf Jacobsen and Jürgen Rohwer (eds.), 163.

170. The German situation maps for late November and into the first days of December show the 106th and 35th Infantry Divisions straddling the road between Klin and Moscow, with elements of the 5th and 11th Panzer Divisions adjoining 35 ID on the right; the closest of these units were less than twenty kilometers from the outskirts of the city. In addition, by 30 November, the surviving tanks and Panzer grenadiers of 2nd Panzer Division had captured the town of Krasnaia Poliana, within artillery range of Moscow. Yet claims that German officers could make out the "golden towers of the Kremlin" through their field glasses—claims first made in German radio broadcasts during the war and perpetuated in postwar literature—are based on propaganda and clearly false.

171. While Dr. Haape provides no precise dates for the events described in this chapter, from a typed draft of his manuscript (preserved all these decades by the Haape family) it is apparent that the trip to Staritsa and, from there, to the regimental battle post and the solitary tram stop took place in the waning days of November 1941. The purpose of this extraordinary—and certainly hazardous!—journey had been to conduct a personal reconnaissance to the very tip of the German front before Moscow. *Oberleutnant* Kageneck in particular, it seems, had been disturbed by the paucity of accurate intelligence about the situation immediately outside the Soviet capital; as he told Dr. Haape before they began their excursion, "I'd like to know just exactly what's happening, because all the rumors are so staggeringly contradictory."

172. Since the resumption of Operation "Typhoon" on 15 November 1941, the depleted units of Army Group Center had advanced an additional 80–110 kilometers, reaching the very threshold of Moscow. Yet by the beginning of December, the operations of the army group had lapsed into little more than uncoordinated local engagements without strategic effect. By 30 November, personnel losses had climbed to 121,000 since the start of "Typhoon." Infantry companies, which had crossed the frontier with Russia on 22 June with complements of 175–200 men, had been reduced in many cases to just 20–30 combat soldiers (losses among experienced officers and NCOs were particularly devastating), while the Panzer divisions were burnt-out shells of the spectacular formations that had pushed nearly 1,000 kilometers to the periphery of the Soviet capital, several now possessing fewer than ten combat-capable tanks. With his army group reduced to tattered remnants, von Bock suspended his offensive on 5 December, his divisions going over to the defensive in the positions they had reached. Adding to the Germans' misfortune, the temperatures suddenly plunged to arctic depths on 4/5 December (-30° Centigrade and below), wreaking havoc with weapons and equipment and inflicting untold misery on the men. For more details on the final push of Army Group Center toward Moscow, see Luther, *Barbarossa Unleashed*, 644–47.

173. America's entry into the war would mean that some 75 percent of the world's resources were now arrayed against Hitler's Reich and the Axis powers. As early as October 1941, the United States and Great Britain had signed a Lend-Lease Agreement with the Soviet Union; by 31 December 1941, Lend-Lease had provided the Soviet Union with 669 tanks and 873 combat aircraft, helping to make up for shortfalls in Soviet production. In future years quantities delivered increased dramatically, with the United States alone supplying the Red Army with 7,537 tanks and 14,795 aircraft, more than 50,000 jeeps, 375,000 trucks, and almost 350,000 tons of high explosives (the latter filling the millions of shells that the formidable Soviet artillery used to pummel German defensive positions in 1943–1945). Without question, the Lend-Lease program contributed significantly to the ultimate Russian victory. Glantz, *Barbarossa: Hitler's Invasion of Russia 1941*, 228 (f.n. 2); Charles D. Winchester, *Hitler's War on Russia*, 137.

174. On 5/6 December 1941, the Red Army struck the dangerously exposed flanks of Army Group Center north and south of the Soviet capital. Stalin's carefully planned counteroffensive caught the Germans completely by surprise, as their intelligence had failed to detect the buildup of substantial Soviet reserves, including fresh troops from Siberia and other military districts beyond Moscow. Overwhelmed by the Red Army attacks, the Germans began to withdraw in a frantic effort to secure critical lines of communication and to avoid encirclement and certain annihilation. The overburdened logistical system now collapsed completely, meaning that little in the way of food, fuel, weapons, and ammunition reached the front. Frostbite began to cause more casualties than combat, while sicknesses associated with the terrible cold, exhaustion, and lack of

food took an increasing toll. Wounded German soldiers died from the shock of even minor wounds, while others froze to death on the way to rear area dressing stations or hospitals. (*Note:* Dr. Haape's 6th Infantry Division would not join the retreat until the third week of December.)

175. By the second week of December 1941, numerically superior Red Army forces had broken through the overextended German lines on both sides of the strategically significant city of Kalinin, threatening major elements of Ninth Army with encirclement and annihilation. At midday, 11 December, I.R. 18 received an urgent call from the chief of staff of 6th Army Corps. The perilous nature of the situation became clear when he queried the regimental commander: "Becker, how much time do you need to be ready to march with your regiment?" Infantry Regiment 18 was soon trudging through the snow and ice toward Kalinin. KTB I.R. 18: "*Winterfeldzug.*"

176. By 14 December, as temperatures plunged to -40° Centigrade, superior Russian forces had broken through the left flank of the neighboring 110th Infantry Division at the village of Krasnovo, on the southern bank of the Volga River. If the Russians succeeded in exploiting their breakthrough by cutting the only good road leading southwest from Kalinin to Staritsa, they would trap all German troops still located at and about Kalinin. To prevent such a catastrophic outcome, 6th Army Corps ordered 6 ID to commit Major Neuhoff's battalion (III./I.R. 18) to help restore the main battle line at Krasnovo and hurl the attackers back across the Volga. In discussions with 6th Army Corps prior to the start of the attack on Krasnovo, *Oberst* Becker lodged strong objections to the attack. In fact, he spoke in no uncertain terms of the "hopelessness" (*Aussichtslosigkeit*) of such an undertaking due to the wholly insufficient forces made available to him to carry it out—three depleted battalions (I./I.R. 254; I./I.R. 255; III./I.R. 18) that, collectively, did not amount in strength to that of a single full-up battalion. Despite Becker's objections, the attack went on the next day. See Grossmann, *Geschichte der 6. Infanterie-Division*, 90; Ernst-Martin Rhein, *Das Rheinisch-Westfälische Infanterie-/Grenadier-Regiment 18 1921–1945*, 116; KTB I.R. 18: "*Winterfeldzug.*"

177. To avoid encirclement and certain destruction, forces of General Strauss's Ninth Army would complete their evacuation of Kalinin on 16 December 1941.

178. Throughout the winter of 1941–1942, German doctors struggled with the problem of frostbite and how best to treat it. Frostbite affected both the upper and the lower extremities (e.g., scalp, face, nose, ears, hands, fingers, elbows, lower leg, feet, toes, even genitalia) and was typically divided into three degrees of severity; during the Russian campaign, however, German doctors encountered a condition of total freezing of the tissue, which they later (after the winter of 1941–1942) classified as a fourth degree of severity and which mostly ended with total loss of affected tissue or limb. That said, amputations tended to be a last resort, avoided whenever possible. Dr. Hans Killian, a surgeon with German Sixteenth Army in northern Russia, personally supervised the treatment of close to twenty thousand cases of frostbite during the winter of 1941–1942, resulting in just 393 amputations (only seventeen patients died, mostly due to septic complications). However, during that terrible first winter in Russia, the German infantry would experience 14,357 amputations due to frostbite (Dr. S. Hart et al., *The German Soldier in World War II*, 125), while tens of thousands of frostbitten soldiers were out of commission for periods of three to six months. Before the winter of 1941–1942 was over, the Germans would incur some two hundred thousand casualties from frostbite. For a detailed examination of the frostbite problem and its treatment in Russia in 1941–1942, see Hans Killian, *Cold and Frost Injuries: Rewarming Damages, Biological, Angiological and Clinical Aspects* (Berlin: 1981).

179. The impact of such arctic conditions on the finely tooled German weaponry was often catastrophic. Vehicles no longer started; transmissions froze up; engines froze while they ran; the breeches of artillery pieces froze shut; tank turrets froze solid; machine guns jammed (many German machine gunners resorted to carrying their bolt assemblies in their trouser pockets to keep them warm); artillery fire became irregular (the gunpowder seemed to burn differently); radios stopped functioning. One weapon that—for the most part—continued to perform reliably at any temperature was the Mauser 98K bolt-action rifle, the standard German infantry weapon throughout the Second World War. German infantry mortars were also largely immune to the cold. As one *Unteroffizier* with the elite Infantry Regiment "*Grossdeutschland*" (mot.) remarked in his diary on 20 December 1941, "Only we mortar men have virtually no problems with the cold.... We can always be relied upon!" Dr. Hans Heinz Rehfeldt, *Mit dem Eliteverband des Heeres "Grossdeutschland" tief in den Weiten Russlands. Erinnerungen eines Angehörigen des Granatwerferzuges 8./Infanterieregiment (mot.) "Grossdeutschland" 1941–1943*, 65.

180. The soldiers would often use a bayonet, axe, or other hand tool to chop off chunks of the frozen bread and then try to warm them, as eating frozen bread could result in stomach problems. Warming, or at least thawing out, the bread was not always possible, however, and more than one *Landser* became ill after consuming it cold to still his gnawing hunger.

181. The desperate counterattacks of Haape's 3rd Battalion described in this chapter actually took place a day later, on 15 December. While the losses of Haape's battalion were quite severe, Russian losses were also heavy, and the attacking Germans took one hundred prisoners. KTB I.R. 18: "*Winterfeldzug*"; Rhein, *Das Rheinisch-Westfälische Infanterie-/Grenadier-Regiment 18 1921–1945*, 117; Grossmann, *Geschichte der 6. Infanterie-Division*, 90–91.

182. As historian and expert in international law Alfred M. de Zayas has observed, "German aggression against the Soviet Union was met with vehement cruelty." Throughout the entire Russian campaign—in fact, from the very first day of the campaign—reports of the torture, mutilation and execution of captured German soldiers did not cease. These reports—thousands of them—were compiled and scrupulously investigated by the *Wehrmacht* War Crimes Bureau (established in September 1939). The bureau was no tool of Dr. Goebbels's propaganda machine, but rather a military investigative agency that performed its difficult mission honorably. Alfred M. de Zayas, *The Wehrmacht War Crimes Bureau, 1939–1945*, 167–68. For a sampling of the War Crimes Bureau's case investigations in the summer of 1941—gleaned from the official records of the bureau itself—see Luther, *Barbarossa Unleashed*, 467–68.

183. Despite making three desperate attempts against numerically superior enemy forces, Neuhoff's 3rd Battalion, supported by two weak battalions of 110 ID, and attacking through 70cm-deep snow at -40° Centigrade, was unable to recapture Krasnovo. Still, the battalion's sacrificial counterattacks had held off the enemy just long enough to enable Ninth Army's 27th Army Corps and the 110th Infantry Division to escape down the road from Kalinin. In recognition of the battalion's achievement—as recorded in the war diary of Infantry Regiment 18—58 E.K. 2 and 6 E.K. 1 were awarded, while two hundred bottles of champagne (*Sekt*) were distributed to the battalion along with a bar of chocolate for each man. As for Dr. Haape, working tirelessly, and at times under heavy shell fire, he personally provided medical assistance to more than 150 wounded and frostbitten men and ensured that they were transported to safety in the rear. Rhein, *Das Rheinisch-Westfälische Infanterie-/Grenadier-Regiment 18 1921–1945*, 117–18; KTB I.R. 18: "*Winterfeldzug*"; "*Besonders ausgezeichnet hat sich Oberarzt Dr. Haape*" (Haape Family Archives).

184. On 16 December 1941, Hitler issued his controversial "halt" order, enjoining that the front remain where it was and not another step back be taken. The order was aimed primarily at Field Marshal Hans von Kluge's Fourth Army, holding the front directly facing Moscow, and at Guderian in the south, who had responded to the Soviet counteroffensive with major retrograde movements—costly in men and materiel—despite von Bock's urgings to stand fast. On the army group's left wing, however, Strauss's Ninth Army, to which 6 ID was assigned, was allowed to continue its retreat. Eventually, as Dr. Haape indicates, the retreat would embrace all of Army Group Center.

185. On 18 December 1941, 6th Infantry Division finally began to withdraw from its positions in the Tma River sector (just above the Volga) to the southwest. The withdrawal would continue over the next two weeks in a series of small steps, in the face of an often vigorously pursuing foe, until reaching the so-called *Königsberg* Line (*K.-Stellung*) at a point directly northeast of Rzhev. On more than one occasion, the survivors of Haape's 3rd Battalion would fight desperately for their naked existence, their line of retreat marked by the lurid fires of burning Russian villages.

186. Vassilevskoye was a village about 20 kilometers northeast of Staritsa; by 2100 hours the next day, Dr. Haape's 3rd Battalion would be back in Ulitino, where it had crossed the Volga so confidently on 21 October 1941. KTB I.R. 18: "*Winterfeldzug*."

187. War diary I.R. 18, 26 December: "The increasing infestations of lice [*Verlausung*] have resulted in numerous skin diseases [among the men]." KTB I.R. 18: "*Winterfeldzug*."

188. On the Internet site "Axis History Forum" is this curious post from 15 October 2013: "I met Heinrich [Haape] in December 1971 at the [Ndumo] Game Reserve in Natal. I remember him telling my dad and myself—I was 12-years-old at the time—how he changed the toilet going manner of the German soldier by getting the soldiers a 'slit' at the back of their uniform so that they [did] not have to undress to go!" See http://forum.axishistory.com.

189. If the tattered remnants of the German Army during the retreat from Moscow managed to largely maintain discipline and unit cohesion—and they did—this was due in no small part to the paralyzing fear of being taken prisoner by the Red Army. Many letters sent from soldiers at the front, or diary entries, reveal the motivational role such fear played in the soldiers' ability to keep moving and keep fighting, despite the increasingly barbaric and pitiless conditions.

190. The 6th Infantry Division fell back methodically from position to position—to the "*A Linie*," to the "*Z Linie*," and so on. The retrograde movements normally began at dusk, which arrived early this time of year (about 1600 hours), and continued through the night until the new temporary line was reached, often only early the next morning. The Soviet pursuit was, at first, cautious, and the division suffered only a handful of casualties through 22 December. The next day, despite the deep snow and swirling drifts, the exhausted men and horses of 6 ID trudged back to a new intermediate line (*Zwischenstellung*) anchored on a group of villages about 15–20 kilometers northeast of Staritsa. The enemy pressure now intensified and the Russians attacked repeatedly, only to be beaten back each time by the German machine guns. Hundreds of Red Army soldiers lay dead before the German lines, but the bitter combat on 23 December had cost the 6th Infantry Division another 114 casualties (including twenty-six dead). The desperate and costly fighting would go on through the end of the year and well into January 1942.

191. For the activity report (*Tätigkeitsbericht*) of the 6th Infantry Division's divisional doctor (*Divisions-arzt*) for December 1941 see Appendix 6. The activity report concludes with the following observations: "The health of the troops had badly worsened during the withdrawal, and the infestation with lice [*Verlausung*] had significantly increased. Measures to address the numerous cases of frostbite were not possible due to the lack of time and appropriate gear (felt boots). Well over half the cases of frostbite involved the lower limbs. Losses during the reporting period amounted to: 195 dead, 783 wounded, 345 missing, 1521 sick (including 866 frostbite cases)."

192. The tactical proficiency of the Red Army during the winter of 1941–1942 still left much to be desired. On occasion the Russians attacked while inebriated and, in general, failed to adequately exploit what was for them—given the perilously weakened state of retreating German forces—an extremely favorable situation. In other words, the combat value of the typical Red Army unit was still well below that of the average German formation, even when badly weakened. At this point, it seems, Russian officers with the talents of a *Graf* von Kageneck were few and far between.

193. In the letters and diaries of many a *Landser* can be found references to these single-engine Russian biplanes, dubbed "Sewing Machines" (*Nähmaschinen*) by the Germans due to the strange noise emitted by their engines. Painfully slow, obsolete, and operating under largely primitive conditions, these ubiquitous little planes—officially designated "Po-2" or "U2"—conducted nuisance night raids on German positions. While they rarely caused any real damage to either men or materiel, "they had a psychological effect that should not be underestimated, depriving German soldiers and airmen of their badly needed sleep at night." Beginning late in 1941, the VVS (Soviet Air Force) had converted large numbers of the biplanes (hitherto relegated to the role of trainer aircraft) to light bombers and introduced them into front-line service. Christer Bergström and Andrey Mikhailov, *Black Cross Red Star: The Air War over the Eastern Front.* Vol. 2: *Resurgence: January–June 1942*, 33.

194. The night of 24/25 December witnessed savage fighting on the front of 6th Infantry Division. Particularly costly was the battle for Bukontovo, desperately defended by Infantry Regiment 37 against elite and marvelously equipped Siberian troops. Organizing the defense of the village was the regimental commander, who fought in the forward lines and, despite twice being shot in the head, remained at his post. Attack was followed by counterattack. The fighting was often at close quarters, with small arms and hand grenades, the German troops struggling to operate their rifles and machine guns with fingers so crippled by cold they barely seemed to function. Eventually overcome by superior enemy numbers, the regiment fell back from Bukontovo, having been forced to blow up two precious batteries of light artillery, whose horses had been shot dead during the fighting. For these two days the war diary of 6 ID recorded another four hundred casualties, among them 46 dead and 162 missing. The overall decline in the division's combat strength by late December 1941 had been frightful—the infantry battalions now reduced to little more than one hundred men apiece, with many of the losses the result of frostbite. See Grossmann, *Geschichte der 6. Infanterie-Division*, 94–98.

195. The bizarre and suicidal behavior described here by Dr. Haape is clearly an example of soldiers experiencing the effects of hypothermia. According to a major study published by the Office of the Surgeon General (U.S. Army), hypothermia is an ever-present "nemesis" in cold weather conditions that attacks the "weak and weary." Regardless of its origin, hypothermia is defined as a two-Centigrade-degree drop in the body's core temperature. Such a decrease in core temperature will affect every component of a physiological system. In military settings, the onset of hypothermia can be insidious, as it begins gradually and poses a major threat to the successful performance of military operations. As noted by the U.S. Army study, symptoms of hypothermia include hallucinations, amnesia, poor judgment, maladaptive behavior, slurring of speech, apathy, impairment of vigilance, and an overall decline in human performance. See Kent B. Pandolf and Robert E. Burr (eds.), *Medical Aspects of Harsh Environments*, Vol. 1, 352ff.

196. *Generaloberst* Heinz Guderian was relieved of command of Second Panzer Army (formally 2nd Panzer Group) by Field Marshal von Kluge on 26 December 1941. Although von Kluge and Guderian were bitter enemies, the decision to cashier the volatile, impetuous, and sometimes insubordinate Panzer general was the correct one: In late December 1941, Guderian had continued to withdraw in flagrant defiance of Hitler's orders to stand fast. As a result, von Kluge (the new commander-in-chief of Army Group Center) quickly came to the same conclusion that von Bock had reached earlier—that Guderian had lost his nerve and was no longer fit to command. For a brief but excellent discussion of the situation that led to Guderian's dismissal, see Russell A. Hart, *Guderian: Panzer Pioneer or Myth Maker?*, 78–81.

197. Worn out and sick, von Bock asked for, and was granted, a temporary leave of absence. He departed Army Group Center on the morning of 19 December and was replaced as army group commander by Field Marshal von Kluge; in January 1942, von Bock would assume command of Army Group South. *Generaloberst* Strauss, also exhausted and sick, was replaced as commander-in-chief of Ninth Army by *General der Panzertruppen* Walter Model, hitherto commander-in-chief of 41st Panzer Corps; however, this change of command did not take place until January 1942. On 31 December 1941, *Generalleutnant* Förster turned over 6th Army Corps to the provisional command of *General der Flieger Freiherr* von Richthofen (*General der Infanterie* Bruno Bieler would take permanent command of the army corps within forty-eight hours). *Generalleutnant* Helge Auleb relinquished command of 6th Infantry Division to *Oberst* Horst Grossmann on Christmas Day, 1941 (Grossmann was promoted to *Generalmajor* on 1 January 1942). See www.lexikon-der-wehrmacht.de; Marcel Stein, *Generalfeldmarschall Walter Model. Legende und Wirklichkeit*, 69; KTB I.R. 18: *"Winterfeldzug."*

198. On 19 December 1941, Adolf Hitler accepted the resignation of Field Marshal Walther von Brauchitsch, the sick, exhausted, and utterly demoralized commander-in-chief of the army, and personally assumed operational command of the army.

199. Prior to the start of Operation Barbarossa, Hitler had ordered construction of a field headquarters in East Prussia. Tucked deep inside a region of lakes, marshes, and dense forests of pine, spruce, beech, and oak, the "Wolf's Lair" (*Wolfsschanze*), as Hitler decided to call it, sat astride the Rastenburg-Angerburg railroad (eight kilometers east of the town of Rastenburg). Constructed by the Todt Organization, the austere and gloomy installation consisted of carefully camouflaged concrete buildings and bunkers and prefabricated barracks, sealed off from the outside world by layers of barbed wire, mines, steel fences, palisades, and earthworks. Hot, humid, and crawling with mosquitoes, a worse spot could hardly have been selected for the *Führer's* eastern headquarters! For historical details on the construction of the "Wolf's Lair," as well as several minutely detailed drawings, see Klaus-Jürgen Thies, *Der Zweite Weltkrieg im Kartenbild*, Bd. 5: Teil 1.1: *Der Ostfeldzug Heeresgruppe Mitte 21.6.1941–6.12.1941. Ein Lageatlas der Operationsabteilung des Generalstabes des Heeres*, vii–ix.

200. The village of Schitinkovo was located 15 kilometers northeast of Staritsa and directly above the Volga River.

201. On 27 December 1941, the rifle companies of Dr. Haape's 3rd Battalion possessed an average combat strength of just seven riflemen, five light machine guns with crews, and one light mortar with its crew. KTB I.R. 18: *"Winterfeldzug."*

202. *Oberleutnant* Kageneck's order was not unusual for German troops in the winter of 1941–1942. To get hold of the eagerly desired Russian boots—which would rapidly freeze to the feet and legs of the dead Red Army soldiers—German soldiers were known to use an axe or a saw to take off the legs of the unfor-

tunate victims, subsequently thawing out the legs and pulling off the bloody boots. In general, the Germans resorted to desperate expedients to protect their bodies from the arctic cold. They requisitioned, or pilfered, whatever articles of clothing they could from local inhabitants—even women's clothing—with the result that many men began to resemble gypsies instead of soldiers. In some cases, they made use of civilian workers to produce earmuffs, waistcoats, footcloths, mittens, and other clothing items. Most men managed to provide some protection to heads and ears by using rags and waistbands. Many *Landser* eventually acquired their "kit" of winter clothing from the bodies of Russian soldiers mowed down by the German machine guns. Erhard Raus, *Panzer Operations: The Eastern Front Memoir of General Raus, 1941–1945*, 90.

203. While the losses of Haape's 3rd Battalion may have been light on this day (27 December 1941), the 6 ID's total casualties—as documented in the divisional war diary—were prohibitive: 43 dead, 175 wounded, 119 missing.

204. By mid-December 1941, Hitler had seen the alarming reports on the front and been briefed by his chief Army adjutant, *Oberst* Rudolf Schmundt, who had accompanied Field Marshal von Brauchitsch (C-in-C of the Army) on a visit to von Bock's army group. Schmundt had assured the *Führer* that the situation was quite grave and that there was no time to lose. In response, Hitler took vigorous action to dispatch infantry reinforcements (initially via air transport) and new *Luftwaffe* units to the imploding front of Army Group Center. From the Replacement Army, some four and a half divisions—the so-called *Walküre* divisions—were to be prepared for transport. Hitler also ordered the transport of five divisions from the West and four more from the Balkans. From Germany itself, units that could "build, protect, and fight" in some manner were to be outfitted for winter warfare and dispatched posthaste to the East. Meanwhile, Göring's *Luftwaffe* was tasked with committing new bomber, twin-engine fighter, and transport units to the faltering front. The majority of these reinforcements were destined for Army Group Center. Ernst Klink, "The Conduct of Operations," in *GSWW*, Vol. IV: 713–14.

205. This was an attitude often expressed by Dr. Haape during his almost two years on the Eastern Front, and it helped him to withstand the terrible physical and psychological burdens of the war. Interview, Dr. C. Luther with Johannes Haape, 1 December 2017.

206. The official four-page Schitinkovo battle report, from which Dr. Haape has excerpted the key portions, bears the date 13 February 1942. The report was no doubt prepared by an officer in 3rd Battalion, Infantry Regiment 18. The title of the document is "Combat Report on the Operations of 3rd Battalion/I.R. 18 in Schitinkovo from 26–29 December 1941" ("*Gefechtsbericht über den Einsatz des III./I.R. 18 in Schitinkovo vom 26.–29.12.1941*").

207. German military doctrine assiduously promoted the concept of active defense that, in the winter of 1941–1942, meant that Russian attacks were to be met immediately with counterattacks before the enemy could solidify his position. The phrase *Gegenstoss im Gange* ("counterattack underway") appears repeatedly in German situation reports at this time. This active and flexible combat style, which often depended on the initiative of junior officers and NCOs, was at the heart of the German doctrinal concept of mission-oriented tactics. As historian Dennis E. Showalter has observed, "From platoon to army group, the Germans' superiority on the eastern front depended heavily on the flexibility of their command structure and the initiative of their front-line leaders." Historical commentary by Dennis E. Showalter in Fuchs Richardson, *Your Loyal and Loving Son: The Letters of Tank Gunner Karl Fuchs, 1937–41*, 138.

208. In his history of the 6 ID, General Horst Grossmann tautly summarizes the Battle of Schitinkovo: "On 29 December there was again bitter fighting for Schitinkovo. The enemy broke through. Under the determined and superior leadership of *Oberleutnant Graf* von Kageneck, house after house was cleared of the enemy in dogged close combat. The Russians attacked the village incessantly and the fighting for the houses went on and on. Every available man—battalion staff, messengers, signal personnel, lightly wounded men—was snatched up and hurled against the enemy. The Soviets were thrown back! But *Oberleutnant* Kageneck was mortally wounded. And so it went with him as it did with so many infantrymen—he died in combat before he could be recommended for the richly deserved Knight's Cross" (Grossmann, *Geschichte der 6. Infanterie-Division*, 98–99). Ten days earlier, however (19 December), a teletype message had arrived from Army High Command (OKH) awarding the highly prestigious German Cross in Gold to *Oberleutnant* Kageneck. KTB I.R. 18: "*Winterfeldzug.*"

209. According to the war diary of I.R. 18, in three days of fighting at Schitinkovo the Russians had sustained 355 dead. KTB I.R. 18: "*Winterfeldzug.*"

210. According to the 3rd Battalion's Schitinkovo battle report, the village was evacuated, as ordered, at 1645 hours, 29 December 1941. The enemy did not pursue. Despite abandoning the village, Haape's 3rd Battalion, along with supporting units, had thwarted the Red Army's main design—to effect an operational breakthrough to Staritsa and, thus, dangerously to the rear of the retreating formations of Ninth Army. Conversely, the loss of *Oberleutnant* Kageneck, a brave, brilliant, and experienced officer, who had been "the soul of the resistance," was a bitter blow. *Oberfeldwebel* Josef Scheiter, who had taken part in the fighting on this day, would later write about Kageneck, "Not only was he extremely brave, but he maintained an extraordinary overview of things even in the most critical situations. I actually saw how he, on the telephone, made a situation report to the regiment in which he laid out the course of the front line in precise detail, without even looking at the map." Cited in Rhein, *Das Rheinisch-Westfälische Infanterie-/Grenadier-Regiment 18 1921–1945*, 135–36.

211. On 28 December 1941, while her future husband was fighting for his life at Schitinkovo, Martha Arazym, at an intimate gathering in Krefeld with Dr. Haape's siblings and a few close friends, celebrated their engagement by slipping on her engagement ring. The next day, she finally received the telegram (see Chapter 18) stating that his leave had been canceled and asking her to postpone their official engagement party (which she had already done).

212. On 21 December 1941, 6th Infantry Division had ordered its men to lay waste to virtually everything in their path as they fell back on Staritsa. Specifically, a zone of destruction (*Wüstenzone*) was to leave nothing of any use to the persuing Red Army: All villages were to be burned to the ground, as well as isolated barns and peasant huts; all wells were to be blown up; all road signs removed; all stocks of grain and horse fodder demolished. KTB I.R. 18: "*Winterfeldzug.*"

213. The graceful Heinkel He 111 was one of the outstanding airplanes of the mid-1930s—which was the problem, for by the outbreak of war in 1939 it was already approaching obsolescence. The bomber was relatively slow and poorly maneuverable, and it carried a bomb load (4,000 pounds) too light for strategic bombing. Yet due to the German aircraft industry's inability to find a suitable replacement, the He 111 was to remain the backbone of the German horizontal bomber fleet throughout the war. During the crisis-ridden winter of 1941–1942, these planes transported troops and supplies to the crumbling front and, on occasion, functioned as "flying artillery" on low-level missions against Red Army forces. Attrition rates were frightful. See Luther, *Barbarossa Unleashed*, 131–32.

214. Such "friendly fire" incidents were quite common among all belligerents during the Second World War. According to the late U.S. Army Colonel David Hackworth, 15–20 percent of American fatal casualties during the Vietnam War resulted from "friendly fire" (Jonathan Shay, *Achilles in Vietnam: Combat Trauma and the Undoing of Character*, 125). The percentage of soldiers on both sides killed or wounded by their own forces during World War II was undoubtedly higher, in part because communications between friendly forces were much more primitive than during the 1960s–1970s (or than they are today). Dr. Haape and his comrades were fortunate to be spared on this occasion.

215. In a letter to Dr. Luther on 25 March 2014, Johannes Haape intimated, "My father did not want to mention that Kageneck was put in a mass grave. In *Moscow Tram Stop* he writes symbolically 'a grave in the middle of many more.' He did not want to reveal that his dear friend was put in a mass grave."

216. Dr. Haape kept a brief diary for most of January 1942, and much of his narrative of events for this month is gleaned from this diary. It begins as follows: "We brought in the new year at Bukrovo, four kilometers north of Staritsa, drinking champagne. Alarm at five o'clock!"

217. While thousands of horses were butchered during the winter of 1941–1942 to provide meat for the troops, many more died of exposure to the cold, exhaustion, or hunger. Observes historian Richard L. DiNardo, "The sufferings of the lightly clad German soldiers in the harsh Russian winter are well documented. Yet, the situation for horses was just as bad. The heavy Western European breeds especially suffered severely. Army Group Center's horse losses reached about 1000 per day during the winter. Many more horses were rendered weak or unfit by exposure. This severely affected the artillery of the infantry divisions." The artillery regiment of 6th Infantry Division alone lost eight hundred horses to starvation during this period.

DiNardo, *Mechanized Juggernaut or Military Anachronism? Horses and the German Army of World War II*, 48; Hans-Joachim Dismer, *Artillerie-Offizier im II. Weltkrieg. Vom Beobachter bis zur Kriegsakademie*, 100.

218. As recorded in the divisional war diary, the battalions of 6th Infantry Division—falling back in good order and without incident—had reached the *Königsberg* Line and occupied their assigned sectors by the afternoon of 2 January 1942. The positions of 6 ID extended for 17 kilometers from the village of Krupsovo to Nemsovo (right to left) and shielded the city of Rzhev—a regional railroad hub that was to become a major cornerstone of Army Group Center's defenses—to the northeast in a rough semicircle. The village of Gridino, in the sector assigned to Haape's 3rd Battalion, was 20 kilometers from Rzhev and in the center of the 6 ID line. The neighbors on the left and right were the 26th and 110th Infantry Divisions, respectively. According to General Grossmann, the "*K.-Stellung*" was a "bitter disappointment. Only in the handful of villages along the main battle line had modest defensive preparations been completed. Yet in the open spaces in between and particularly in the forest belts—from where the Russians were especially prone to attack—nothing had been done. Once again, the *Landser* were left to make do in the snow without adequate protection in bitterly cold temperatures down to -40 Centigrade." Grossmann, *Geschichte der 6. Infanterie-Division*, 103. (*Note:* In the ten days from 21 to 31 December, 6 ID incurred another 677 cases of frostbite.)

219. 1941 had become 1942 and, with the *Ostheer* facing a grave crisis, it was clear that Operation Barbarossa had failed. As of 31 December 1941, German forces in the East had sustained 302,000 fatal casualties, along with two to three times as many wounded—losses from which they would never fully recover. The wastage in armored fighting vehicles, artillery, and aircraft was equally acute. (For the most accurate accounting of German personnel losses, see Rüdiger Overmans, *Deutsche militärische Verluste im Zweiten Weltkrieg* [Munich: 2004].) Of course, the losses of the Red Army had been significantly more severe; by the end of 1941, dozens of Soviet armies—more than two hundred divisions!—had been destroyed, the Red Army sustaining a total of nearly 4.5 million casualties, including three million irrecoverable losses (dead, captured, or missing). And yet, by 31 December, the Red Army's line strength had risen to 592 division equivalents (compared to 401 division equivalents on 1 August 1941), while its total personnel strength had climbed from about 5.4 million on 22 June to an estimated 8 million at the end of 1941. This astounding increase was the result of the Soviet Union's admittedly cumbersome but extraordinarily prolific mobilization system that, from June to December 1941, generated more than 50 new field armies and a total of about 285 rifle divisions, 88 cavalry divisions, 12 reformed tank divisions, 174 rifle brigades, and 93 tank brigades. Indeed, as the late German historian Andreas Hillgruber observed nearly forty years ago, what was "decisive" (*entscheidend*) from a military perspective was the ability of the Soviet Union to make good its enormous losses by mobilizing and committing to battle millions of trained reservists in the final six months of 1941, enabling the Red Army to lose the rough equivalent of its entire peacetime army and yet effectively continue the struggle. Col.-Gen. G. F. Krivosheev (ed.), *Soviet Casualties and Combat Losses*, 101; Glantz, *Barbarossa: Hitler's Invasion of Russia 1941*, 68, 210; Andreas Hillgruber, *Der Zweite Weltkrieg, 1939–1945*, 69.

220. From 22 June 1941 to its arrival in the "*K.-Stellung*" on 2 January 1942, Infantry Regiment 18, in seventy-six days of marching punctuated by frequent combat, had covered 1,645 kilometers! Grossmann, *Geschichte der 6. Infanterie-Division*, 112.

221. The fierce Russian attacks described by Dr. Haape in the following paragraphs took place on 3 January 1942. For the official 3rd Battalion combat report, see Appendix 7.

222. According to the war diary of I.R. 18, the battalion's rifle companies now "boasted" an average strength of just one officer, four NCOs, and twenty men. Given the battalion's utterly attenuated combat strength, the regiment considered it "incomprehensible" (*unfasslich*) that the battalion had been able to hold on to Gridino—a village of "immense importance" to the entire position of 6 ID—in the face of furious assaults by a numerically vastly superior opponent.

223. The village of Malakovo (Malachowo)—several kilometers south of Gridino—was just inside the 6th Infantry Division's defensive perimeter; Infantry Regiment 18 had its headquarters in the village, while the headquarters of 6 ID was further back in Manuilova.

224. During the winter of 1941–1942, German rail operations almost completely collapsed. As early as December 1941, up to 70 percent of German trains had been put out of action by the effects of the arctic cold. (For example, the water pipes in German locomotives were not built inside the boilers, with the result that

70–80 percent of the water pipes froze and burst.) The result was a chronic shortage of wagons and locomotives, exacerbated by the destruction of railroads and bridges by Soviet partisans and the misdirection of supply trains; at times, rail deliveries broke down entirely. Throughout the winter, Army Group Center received just a third, and frequently less, of its daily quota of twenty-eight supply trains. Given such a deplorable state of affairs, it is hardly surprising that there was a serious shortfall of ambulance trains. Nor is it surprising that, during this first winter of the war, wounded men often froze to death because their trains were immobilized for hours at a time by the cold. See *Effects of Climate on Combat in European Russia*, CMH Publication 104-6, 21–23; Klaus Reinhardt, *Moscow—The Turning Point*, 245; Martin van Creveld, *Supplying War: Logistics from Wallenstein to Patton*, 173.

225. Despite being relieved and temporarily pulled from the main battle line, 3rd Battalion (I.R. 18)—as Haape jotted in his diary—was now down to just sixty-seven men, who staggered through the dense birch forest toward Malakovo. East of the village of Gridino, 6th Infantry Division saw major combat on this day—4 January 1942—and while the enemy suffered serious losses, casualties for 6 ID were just as dreadful: 78 dead, 219 wounded, 28 missing.

226. The war diary of I.R. 18 poignantly recorded the event: "The regimental commander personally greets the victorious 3rd Battalion upon its arrival in Malakovo with a brief inspection. The proud bearing [*Haltung*] of the brave little band is deeply moving [*erschütternd*]." KTB I.R. 18: "*Winterfeldzug*."

227. The *Luftwaffe* paratroopers arrived on 3/4 January 1942 (mostly by means of air transport) and were subordinated to 6 ID; they included two companies of a machine-gun battalion (*Fallschirmjäger-M.G.-Btl.*), a Flak company, and a company from an airborne assault regiment (*Sturm-Regiment*) attached to the M.G. battalion—a total of about six hundred troops. The stout veteran paratroopers would immediately make their presence felt. KTB I.R. 18: "*Winterfeldzug*"; BA-MA Nr. 598/4, *Tagebuch IV, General Grossmann*, 3.1.42, 74; Ltr., F. Strienitz to Dr. C. Luther, 18 March 2007.

228. The paratroopers were marvelously outfitted with a winter clothing kit and superb weaponry. Recalled former 6 ID Commander General Grossmann, "The paratrooper battalion belonged to the *Luftwaffe* and, as a result, was much better outfitted with clothing than was our infantry; naturally, they also received special rations, for example, chocolate—a monstrous injustice to our infantry." BA-MA Nr. 598/4, *Tagebuch IV, General Grossmann*, 3.1.42, 74.

229. In his diary on 5 January, Haape wrote, "That evening I was the guest of *Oberst* Becker. It was a marvelous evening. Punctually, at midnight, *Oberst* Becker stood up and ushered in my 32nd birthday with heartfelt and appreciative words. It was a birthday that had followed the toughest bloodiest battles at a critical moment in the winter fighting. The Russian assault was powerful and brutal, while our front was thinly held. Yet each and every man was utterly determined—here we will hold or we will die. I am thankful for the few peaceful hours of my birthday celebration. In this group the prevailing mood is one of comradeship until death" (*Hier herrscht Kameradschaft bis in den Tod*).

230. In his diary (7 January 1942), Dr. Haape noted that his "old dressing station" was filled to bursting with some three dozen mostly wounded men.

231. Despite his wounds—and a minor case of frostbite—Dr. Haape would remain in Gridino with 3rd Battalion, Infantry Regiment 37, until 17 January 1942, when the fierce fighting finally petered out. "*Besonders ausgezeichnet hat sich Oberarzt Dr. Haape*" (Haape Family Archives).

232. An entry in the war diary of 6th Infantry Division for 9 January graphically illustrates just how intense the fighting had been over the past few days: "All told, in the period from 3–9 January 1942, the division has successfully repulsed 34 attacks of battalion strength and greater, while inflicting substantial losses on the enemy."

233. In both primary and secondary literature pertaining to the Eastern Front, there are numerous accounts of Red Army soldiers inebriated during battle. In fact, this phenomenon sometimes even determined the outcome of tactical engagements—to the detriment of the drunken Russians, of course. Recalling the winter of 1941–1942, one former Dutch volunteer in the *Waffen SS* observed, "The Reds froze just like we did. But they thought that their vodka made them fit to fight, not only in winter. Modest in this habit they were not. Their craving was no 'happy hour' any more, but an uninhibited drunkenness. . . . When there was a shortage of vodka, the 'Ivans' knew how to compensate. They suctioned alcohol from the exhausts of

planes, and filtered it through the filter of their gas-masks, which cleansed the liquid to a good degree. Then they mixed the rest with a syrup, thus making it a more than acceptable liqueur, which they didn't sip, but just tipped down their throats." Hendrik C. Verton, *In the Fire of the Eastern Front: The Experiences of a Dutch Waffen-SS Volunteer on the Eastern Front, 1941–45*, 107.

234. In mid-July 1941—first at the important railroad junction at Orsha, southwest of Smolensk, and then near the town of Rudnia, between Vitebsk and Smolensk—the Red Army had introduced a new and highly secret weapon: the BM-13 *Katyusha* ("Little Kate") multiple rocket-launcher. Simply put, this rather crude device consisted (in its initial configuration) of rails mounted on the back of a truck and fired a salvo of sixteen solid-fuel rockets with 132mm caliber warheads. The Germans dreaded the massed fire of the *Stalinorgel* ("Stalin Organ"), as they christened it, with its infernal and distinctive scream. However, the *Landser* soon figured out that the rockets were largely inaccurate and the fragmentation effect poor—they were mainly effective against personnel caught in the open or against lightly skinned vehicles. Yet, as Dr. Haape's account makes clear, initial exposure to the weapon could make for a truly terrifying experience. For assessments of the "Stalin Organ" by German veterans of the Russian campaign, see Luther, *Barbarossa Unleashed*, Appendix 6, 680–85.

235. In his diary on 11 January, Haape wrote, *inter alia*, "It is not going well with me personally, and outside there are temperatures up to -48 Centigrade."

236. The village of Ranimza was located just a few kilometers southeast of Gridino. The 3rd Battalion sustained seven dead and more than a dozen men wounded in the attack; among the fallen was the battalion commander, *Hauptmann* Graminsky. As recorded in the war diary of I.R. 18, the fatal losses were the result of "friendly fire" from the supporting German artillery, whose shells fell short of their objectives and struck attacking friendly forces. Following its successful counterthrust, Dr. Haape's 3rd Battalion had been reduced to a combat strength of three officers, ten NCOs, and forty men. And more than a few of these men were suffering from first- and second-degree frostbite. KTB I.R. 18: "*Winterfeldzug.*"

237. *Oberst* Becker had already been ill for several days and, following examination by a doctor, had been consigned to bed rest. While Becker recuperated, command of the regiment fell temporarily to Major Höke (II./I.R. 18). *Oberst* Becker would not resume command of the regiment until 10 February 1942. KTB I.R. 18: "*Winterfeldzug.*"

238. Dr. Haape's diary on 18 January: "*Hauptmann* Noack, the battalion commander, has welcomed me back with great joy and friendliness . . . with deep inner satisfaction I fall into my bunk, after I've first put on new underclothing over my bitten up and scratched up body [*meinen zerbissenen und zerkratzten Körper*] and Heinrich has bandaged my foot, which is still lightly festering."

239. The increasingly depleted 6th Infantry Division, by tenaciously defending Rzhev against the enemy's furious and repeated assaults, was making a critical contribution to the desperate efforts of German Ninth Army to maintain its teetering front. A divisional order on 16 January praised "in no uncertain terms the accomplishments of the division since 2 January 1942, while also expressing the outlook that future operations will be even more intense. The divisional commander is certain that his division will continue to accomplish its tasks, which are of decisive importance for the war [*von kriegsentscheidender Bedeutung*]. The cornerstone Rzhev [*Eckpfeiler Rshew*], so vital to German operations, will stand or fall upon the ability of the division to <u>hold its ground</u>." KTB I.R. 18: "*Winterfeldzug.*"

240. At the time, of course, Dr. Haape—and his 3rd Battalion comrades—would only have possessed a general awareness of events unfolding along the hundreds of kilometers of Army Group Center's increasingly fragile front, and, by mid-January 1942, that front was buckling perilously under the inexorably expanding pressure of the Red Army's winter counteroffensive. The army group's crisis, in fact, reached its apex in mid and late January 1942, as the Red Army's enveloping pincers—along two primary axes, north and the south of Moscow, supported by airborne troops and partisans operating in the vast forested regions behind German lines—sought to close on the ancient little town of Viaz'ma, a major railroad junction far to the rear of Army Group Center's main line of resistance and more than 150 kilometers west/southwest of Moscow. Operations of both the Red Army and the German forces were severely hampered by the arctic cold and deep snow, with a mean temperature in January 1942 in the area northwest of Moscow of -32° Fahrenheit. On 26 January 1942, this same area experienced the lowest recorded temperature of the entire Russian cam-

paign: -63° Fahrenheit. Meanwhile, on 15 January 1942, due to increasing Soviet pressure, Hitler had finally acceded to the repeated pleas of his General Staff and Field Marshal von Kluge and given permission for the army group to withdraw its Fourth Army, along with Third and Fourth Panzer Armies (on 1 January 1942, 3rd and 4th Panzer Groups were designated as panzer armies), to positions east of Iukhnov, Gzhatsk, and Zubtsov and north of Rzhev, 150 kilometers and more west of Moscow. The new line was to be held at all costs. Moreover, as a condition for withdrawal to this winter line, Hitler insisted that the dangerous gap that had opened west of Rzhev be sealed off—a move that, if successful, would slice off the northern pincer of the massive Soviet envelopment aimed at Viaz'ma. Peter G. Tsouras (ed.), *Fighting in Hell: The German Ordeal on the Eastern Front*, 172; Magenheimer, *Moskau 1941. Entscheidungsschlacht im Osten*, 219; Klink, "*The Conduct of Operations*," in *GSWW*, Vol. IV: 726–29.

241. Hitler's decision to replace Strauss with General Model was a decisive one, as Model's deft moves in the weeks ahead would save German forces facing encirclement and annihilation in the embattled Rzhev salient. About the future field marshal and defensive specialist, David M. Glantz writes, "Model was not a philosopher, he was a fighter. . . . With a solid reputation as an energetic commander and brilliant tactician and the self-assured demeanor of a traditional (and monocled) old school Prussian officer, Model radiated confidence. . . . [In] the dark days of winter 1942, when German fortunes outside Moscow were at their lowest ebb . . . his quick and decisive action had confounded victorious Russian forces as they advanced from Rzhev deep into the German rear toward [Viaz'ma]. . . . While many German commanders had urged withdrawal from the snowy treacherous salient in the face of the fierce Russian attacks, Hitler had refused and, instead, had appointed Model to deal with the looming threat. Within a month his audacious counteractions had converted German defeat into victory, and the Russians had gone from being encirclers into being the encircled." David M. Glantz, *Zhukov's Greatest Defeat: The Red Army's Epic Disaster in Operation Mars, 1942*, 31, 227.

242. By 18 January, combat in the sector of 6 ID had ebbed significantly—the action now focused on the regions west and south of Rzhev, where Soviet forces had made a dangerous breakthrough. Total losses of 6 ID—as chronicled in the divisional war diary—amounted to less than one hundred men from 18 to 31 January. However, the number of frostbite cases from 11 to 20 January 1942 came to 158 men.

243. Dr. Haape's diary entry for 26 January 1942—his final entry of the month—was rather more fatalistic: "At our command post spirits are running high. We've all taken notice of the many gift parcels that have arrived from Bielefeld. We've already downed a drink or two. *Hauptmann* Noack suggests that he and I address each other with the informal 'Du.' The effect of the alcohol on *Oberstabsarzt* Gründig is not good. He foresees a second collapse of Germany and talks about the retreat of 1918. His remarks are not without some merit. We've practically come to terms with the fact that we've never going to get out of this mess. Yet still we seize the moment with fervor and joy."

244. Of course, Dr. Haape's overarching concern in caring for Russian civilians was to control the spread of disease, particularly the dreaded spotted fever. However, Dr. Haape's drawings and sketches— several of which are included in this edition of his memoirs—betray a genuine sympathy and respect for the Russian people.

245. The strain of so many months of battle under the dreadful conditions on the Eastern Front—of helplessly witnessing the death of so many beloved comrades—had clearly taken its toll on Dr. Haape. An official medical report prepared more than a year later (February 1943) noted that, in January 1942, he had not only suffered from influenza and a high fever but also experienced heart problems (angina). *Bericht, Dr. Pfeffer, Oberstabsarzt, Feldlazarett (mot.) 6 dem Div.-Arzt 6. Division*, 18.2.1943 (document in the Haape Family Archives).

246. For excellent works addressing the savage fighting in the Rzhev-Viaz'ma sector, see Svetlana Gerasimova, *The Rzhev Slaughterhouse: The Red Army's Forgotten 15-Month Campaign against Army Group Center 1942–1943* (Solihull, England: 2013); Oleg A. Kondratjew, *Die Schlacht von Rshew. Ein halbes Jahrhundert Schweigen* (Munich: 2001). For an older, yet firsthand, account by a former commander of 6th Infantry Division, see Horst Grossmann, *Rshew. Eckpfeiler der Ostfront* (Bad Nauheim: 1962).

247. In fact, by early February, Model's brilliant counterstrokes had sealed the dangerous gap in his Ninth Army's front, in the process trapping *both* the 29th and the 39th Russian Armies behind German lines. In the days ahead, despite furious Russian relief attempts, the 29th Russian Army would be broken apart and

annihilated, while the encirclement and destruction of 39th Russian Army—in the end stranded northwest of Viaz'ma—was not completed until July 1942.

248. Throughout the Russo-German War, the Red Army would, again and again, prove itself a master of improvisation, which helped to compensate—at least during the initial phases of the war—for its lack of tactical and operational acumen. One former German officer recalled a rather extreme—even humorous—example of the Russians' uncanny ability to improvise: "Once, while marching with my company along a narrow, but otherwise open piece of terrain far away from combat, we were suddenly fired upon, although nobody was to be seen. We wondered what had happened. Finally we realized that a Soviet soldier had hidden his loaded Sten gun in a tree and tied the trigger by a long cord to the foot of a cow. When the cow moved the gun fired. We asked ourselves: Had he read Karl May [a famous German author with a big imagination]?" Colonel Dr. Alfred Durrwanger (ret.), "28th Infantry Division Operations," in *The Initial Period of War on the Eastern Front, 22 June–August 1941*, David M. Glantz (ed.), 439.

249. One of the truly fatal errors of German occupation policy in Soviet Russia was the decision not to abolish the despised collective farms and return the land to the Russian peasantry. "The dearest hope of these peasants," averred historian Catherine Merridale, "was for an end to Soviet power. In September 1941, though, they learned that the Germans had ordered that the collective farms should stay. Like the prewar Soviet authorities, the conquerors cared only for the ease with which the peasants' grain could be collected and shipped off. It was an irreversible mistake." See Catherine Merridale, *Ivan's War: Life and Death in the Red Army, 1939–1945*, 133–34.

250. Nina is referring here to the Soviet secret police—the NKVD, or "People's Commissariat for Internal Affairs."

251. The war diary of Infantry Regiment 18 on 6 February 1942 notes the "increased enemy espionage activity [*Spionagetätigkeit*] behind the front of the division" and that strict measures need to be taken to address it. KTB I.R. 18: "*Winterfeldzug*."

252. Soviet partisan groups were made up in the main of local inhabitants, Red Army soldiers cut off in the great encirclement battles, and specialists flown in from Moscow. Thousands of Soviet soldiers had evaded capture in October 1941, during the encirclement battles of Viaz'ma-Briansk, and taken refuge in the vast belts of forest west and southwest of Moscow; many of these men had joined the burgeoning groups of "bandits," as the Germans derisively called them, which were making their presence increasingly felt by the fall and winter of 1941–1942. The Germans responded to Soviet partisan actions with sublime savagery, which was returned in kind by partisan groups. The "bandit" problem faced by the Germans at this time, however, was more of a nuisance than the existential threat it would become in 1943–1944.

253. The city of Rzhev was situated on the upper reaches of the Volga River, some 220 kilometers northwest of Moscow. "Rzhev was Army Group Center's northern cornerpost. Lying ... at the junction of a north-south and east-west railroad, it gave the army group left flank something to hang on to in what was otherwise a wilderness of forest and swamp in all directions for many miles" (Earl F. Ziemke and Magna E. Bauer, *Moscow to Stalingrad. Decision in the East*, 130). In January 1942, the city was swamped with three thousand German wounded—another reason it needed to be held at all costs as the army group's northern "cornerpost" (*Eckpfeiler*). Magenheimer, *Moskau 1941. Entscheidungsschlacht im Osten*, 216.

254. All told, the Russians would commit more than one million men to their Rzhev-Viaz'ma Operation from January to April 1942, sustaining nearly 275,000 casualties. Evan Mawdsley, *Thunder in the East: The Nazi Soviet War, 1941–1945*, 119.

255. *Oberst* Becker was correct in his analysis. As desperate as the situation seemed to *Hauptmann* Noack and Dr. Haape, Model's Ninth Army—and the *Ostheer* as a whole—had, by the second week of February 1942, largely mastered the terrible crisis that had begun just ten weeks before. On 12 February 1942, with the Eastern Front beginning to stabilize, the German Army High Command (OKH) issued a major directive addressing the conduct of operations after the winter, in which it acknowledged that "thanks to the incomparable achievements and toughness of the troops" the worst of the crisis was over—the Red Army had been stopped (*zum Stehen gebracht*). Indeed, despite pushing back German forces some 150–400 kilometers to the west, as well as liberating sixty cities and hundreds of towns and villages, Stalin's counteroffensive had failed to achieve any of its primary objectives. Contributing decisively to the defensive victory of *Ostheer* were: (a) the

handful of surviving low-ranking officers and NCOs, whose toughness, experience, combat skill, and, when required, ruthlessness in the face of human weakness, held the remnants of their exhausted units together and made them fight; (b) the remaining heavy weapons—artillery, flak, tanks, assault guns—deployed at pivotal sectors of the front and exercising an influence on tactical events well beyond their all-too-modest numbers. Jacobsen (ed.), *KTB des OKW*, Bd. I: 1093; A. S. Knjaz'kov, "Die sowjetische Strategie im Jahre 1942," in *Stalingrad. Ereignis—Wirkung—Symbol*, Jürgen Förster (ed.), 39.

256. As recorded in the war diary of I.R. 18 in mid-February 1942, the regiment was combing out rear area supply units to supplement—even marginally—its thin line of men along the main line of resistance (HKL). Yet even through the front was relatively quiet at this time, the regiment continued to incur sometimes painful losses from Russian harassing fire (*Störungsfeuer*) from artillery, heavy mortars, AT guns, and other weaponry. KTB I.R. 18: "*Winterfeldzug.*"

257. Heinrich Sutermeister's opera *Romeo und Julia* had its world premiere in Dresden in April 1940, under the direction of Karl Böhm. As Martha recalled in her unpublished memoirs, the premiere of the opera in Duisburg was in the fall of 1940 (just as Heinz had received his orders to report to 6th Infantry Division), her performance as "Julia" being hailed a great success.

258. As Martha explained in her memoirs, she and her artistic partner, Dr. Fabry, had been invited to the Frankfurt radio station to make recordings from Sutermeister's *Romeo und Julia* and *Der Sturm* (The Tempest), also based on a play by William Shakespeare. From Dr. Haape's account, it appears the recordings were made during a live broadcast on 3 March.

259. With the exception of isolated Russian attacks and sporadic Soviet artillery and mortar fire, the month of February 1942 had been a relatively quiet one for 6th Infantry Division, as the desperate struggle for Rzhev and the survival of Model's Ninth Army played out behind the division's front. According to its war diary, the division sustained just 139 casualties (including twenty-eight fatal losses) for the entire month. Taking advantage of the relative calm, the shrunken battalions of 6 ID propped up their positions (added dugouts and shelters, reinforced protective snow walls and wire entanglements, etc.), cleared roads of the inevitable snow drifts, probed the Russian lines with patrols (while contesting those of the enemy), shelled Russian positions, and prepared for the spring thaw, expected for late March. On 19 February, the first urgently anticipated reinforcements from Germany reached the regiment. Yet the unforgiving demands of the front—such as the lack of sleep resulting from long hours of guard duty during the arctic winter nights—coupled with inadequate rations, had caused a general decline in the soldiers' health and an increase in men reporting sick. Rhein, *Das Rheinisch-Westfälische Infanterie-/Grenadier-Regiment 18 1921–1945*, 161–62.

260. Dr. Josef Knust, the "young and well-liked" *Oberarzt* of Infantry Regiment 18's 2nd Battalion, was killed on 4 March 1942, attempting to rescue a horse from a building that had gone up in flames after being struck by Russian shell fire. Rhein, *Das Rheinisch-Westfälische Infanterie-/Grenadier-Regiment 18 1921–1945*, 162.

261. A special report prepared by I.R. 18 following the winter fighting noted that the "loss of horses during the winter campaign was catastrophic. The regiment alone lost, as a result of enemy action [*Feindeinwirkung*] and exhaustion, 480 horses." KTB I.R. 18: "*Winterfeldzug.*"

262. The lull in the fighting continued throughout March 1942. Total losses for the division amounted to only sixty-six men, with twelve KIA. The 6 ID war diary noted that hundreds of civilians and Soviet POWs were pressed into service to help clear the roads and make them passable for vehicles.

263. As early as mid-February 1942, 6 ID had received a shipment of skis, most of them via donations from the civilian population of Bielefeld; as a result, the division ordered I.R. 18 to set up a special ski hunter detachment (*Ski-Jagdkommando*). In response, the regiment put together a special training course in Malakovo, run by *Oberleutnant* Boehmer. The men assigned to the training found it a most delightful diversion from the monotonous work on field fortifications or the long hours of guard duty in the frigid cold. By early March, the new detachment had become a permanent fixture (*ständige Einrichtung*) in the regiment. KTB I.R. 18: "*Winterfeldzug.*"

264. Behind the lines of Army Group Center in the winter of 1941–1942, Soviet partisan groups derailed 224 trains, destroyed some 650 bridges, and 1,850 German vehicles; during Soviet offensive opera-

tions on the central front (December 1941–April 1942), sabotage by partisans delayed German rail traffic for a total of 180 days. As impressive as these figures seem, they pale in comparison to the havoc the partisans would cause in the years that followed. Leonid D. Grenkevich, *The Soviet Partisan Movement, 1941–1944: A Critical Historiographical Analysis*, 185.

265. Official rationing of certain foodstuffs and consumer goods had actually begun several days before Germany attacked Poland on 1 September 1939. For example, in Duisburg, the first ration cards (*Lebensmittelkarten*) were distributed on 28 August 1939. As the war progressed—and particularly after the war turned against Germany—the rationing would become ever more onerous. Reinhold Lengkeit et al., *Duisburger im Dritten Reich. Augenzeugen Berichten*, 95.

266. Only weeks later, on 30/31 May 1942, Cologne would be struck by the first RAF 1000 bomber raid of the war. All told, 1,047 British bombers would drop 1,455 tons of bombs on the city, killing 460 people and leaving 45,000 people homeless. Andreas Hillgruber (ed.), *KTB des OKW*, Bd. II: 1412.

267. One of Dr. Haape's favorite sayings—in good times or bad—was "Life has spoiled me infinitely" (*Das Leben hat mich grenzenlos verwöhnt*).

268. Dr. Haape began the long journey back to his 3rd Battalion at the start of May 1942, finally reaching the front on 11 May.

269. By late March 1942, the spring thaw had begun, gradually melting the mountains of snow—including the soldiers' defensive snow walls—and altering the landscape into a sea of mud and muck, not unlike what the Germans had encountered outside Moscow in October 1941. Dugouts and trenches filled with water and had to be drained and reinforced with stones or wooden beams, or new positions sought out on higher ground. Roadways again disintegrated, severely limiting movement of vehicles of all kinds and creating supply and transportation problems. Cross-country movement became virtually impossible. The corpses of thousands of men and animal cadavers—along with garbage and human waste—that had remained frozen throughout the arctic winter—the coldest in memory—now began to thaw, raising the specter of epidemic. With both German and Russian adversely affected by the spring thaw, major operations on most sectors of the front came to a halt for several weeks.

270. After anchoring the *Königsberg* Line northeast of Rzhev for more than six months, 6th Infantry Division was relieved by the 14th Infantry Division (mot.) and sent to the rear for replenishment; yet, as Dr. Haape makes clear, 6 ID was soon back in the thick of the fighting for Rzhev.

271. Operation *Blau*, the *Ostheer*'s summer offensive in southern Russia, aimed at the coveted oil fields of the Caucasus, began on 28 June 1942; it would end along the Volga, at Stalingrad, with encirclement and annihilation of Field Marshal Friedrich Paulus's Sixth Army (and elements of Fourth Panzer Army), whose entombed remnants had all surrendered to the Russians by 2 February 1943. For the German people, the cataclysmic defeat was the psychological turning point of the war.

272. Dr. Haape was awarded this highly coveted decoration in mid-November 1942. For a picture of the official award document, see the first photospread.

273. For the best account of the Red Army's third unsuccessful attempt to pinch off and destroy the Rzhev salient, in the fall of 1942, see Glantz, *Zhukov's Greatest Defeat: The Red Army's Epic Disaster in Operation Mars, 1942* (Lawrence: 1999).

274. In Operation "Buffalo" (*Büffelbewegung*), the German Ninth and Fourth Armies evacuated the great salient in the Rzhev-Viaz'ma sector, pulling back in deliberate fashion over a period of several weeks to significantly shorter lines, releasing some twenty divisions for new purposes. The evacuation also removed these armies from areas in which partisan activity had been particularly robust. The city of Rzhev had been so laid to waste during fifteen months of fighting that, when reoccupied by the Red Army, only four hundred of its original fifty-eight thousand inhabitants remained. Email, Christoph Rass to C. Luther, 2 October 2003.

275. On 22 June 1944, the Russians launched Operation "Bagration"—an enormous offensive aimed at the destruction of Army Group Center. In the weeks that followed, some twenty-eight of the army group's forty divisions—hopelessly overmatched by the Red Army in every category—would be smashed with a loss of 350,000 men. By mid-August 1944, the German front had been pushed back to the Vistula River in Poland and the frontiers of East Prussia.

276. Carl ("Corle") Becker would command the 253rd Infantry Division from early 1943 through the war's end. Captured by the Russians, he was tried and convicted of crimes against the civilian population of Rzhev. He was released from Soviet captivity in October 1955. Email, Christoph Rass to C. Luther, 2 October 2003; www.lexikon-der-wehrmacht.de.

277. Luther, *Barbarossa Unleashed*, 670.

278. Because almost all Dr. Haape's official *Wehrmacht* personnel papers (i.e., his service record book and other key documents) were most likely lost or destroyed during the war, this record of his military service has been gleaned largely from other sources (among them his letters to his fiancée and later wife); thus, minor errors may exist in this chronology.

279. In a letter to Martha on 11 March, Haape writes, "The night has fallen and the sky turned red. The villages are burning; war cannot be conducted in a more radical fashion. We are moving back through forsaken forested regions where a dreadful war rages with the partisans!!! These brigands attack isolated vehicles or small groups of our men without warning and butcher them. The Russians pursue us with their masses, but every assault collapses in the fire of our weapons."

280. Official papers reveal that Dr. Haape spent most of his captivity at an American military hospital for German POWs—designated 8277 General Hospital (Provisional). For several months at least he was assigned to the surgical department of the hospital. *Deutsche Dienststelle* (WASt).

281. In a letter to Martha on 4 February 1946, Dr. Haape refers to the facility in Wiesloch as an *Irrenhaus*, or mental hospital; the day before he told her, "I can no longer bear being in captivity." On 11 February, he writes, "I'm still in Wiesloch near Heidelberg. We've handed in our release papers and now we wait and wait. It seems to take forever."

282. Upon returning to his wife in Stuttgart, Dr. Haape explained how he and another imprisoned German doctor had feigned a war or prison psychosis, whereby the mere sight of barbed wire would transport them into a fury. In her memoirs, Martha recalls that her husband had simulated a *Stacheldrahtkoller*—literally, a "barbed wire frenzy." She writes, "They must have feigned their attacks so convincingly—while also insisting that both their wives were nurses, which for doctors was nothing unusual—that they were sent home to the care of their wives." Martha Haape, *Memoiren*, 129.

283. On 22 December 1947, in an affidavit for "Headquarters [U.S.] European Command, Office of the Provost Marshal, Prisoner of War Information Bureau," Dr. Haape stated that he was released from American captivity on 16 February 1946. *Deutsche Dienststelle* (WASt).

284. BA-MA RH 26-6/2, *Anlage zum Ia KTB 6. Inf.-Div.*

285. BA-MA RH 26-6/90, *Anlage zum Ib KTB 6. Inf.-Div.* This 6 ID strength report reveals that losses of both men and materiel—compared to most of the infantry divisions of Army Group Center—had been tolerable more than five months into the Russia campaign; that said, some of the division's rifle companies were down to an average combat strength of fifty men by mid-November. The division had received more than one thousand replacements in late September and on 1 October 1941; yet most of these men—from a replacement battalion that had marched on foot from Vilnius—had arrived exhausted at the front. And as a 6 ID report observed, "As reported throughout the division, [these] replacements, in terms of their training and moral fiber [*innere Einstellung*] are not as good as earlier replacements received by the division." *Tätigkeitsbericht der Abteilung IIa 6. Inf.-Div.*, cited in *Traditionsverband Inf.-Rgt. 37, Rundbrief Nr. 51*, December 1994, 12.

286. BA-MA RH 26-6/90, *Anlage zum Ib KTB 6. Inf.-Div.* These figures illustrate the dramatic plunge in 6 ID's personnel strength since 1 December 1941. The division had also lost more than half of its horses and sustained serious losses in artillery, mortars, and other categories of weapons. However, the division had received a battery of 21cm heavy howitzers (*Mörser*) that, as Dr. Haape notes in Chapter 24 ("A Veteran's Tears"), was in position near Malakovo in early January 1942.

287. Figures for "combat strength" exclude rear area services, medical personnel, and personnel belonging to the divisional baggage trains.

288. Civilian officials of the German armed forces (*Wehrmachtbeamte*) had nominal rank and wore uniforms; they were classified as combatants.

289. NCOs are *Unteroffiziere* and sergeants.

290. Enlisted personnel (*Mannschaften*) typically refer to those up to and including the rank of *Obergefreiter* (Corporal).

291. Figures for "ration strength" include all *Wehrmacht* personnel and horses provisioned by the 6 ID; the division's strength reports were prepared on or about the 1st, 10th, and 20th of each month, as was customary throughout the German Army.

292. The categories "light anti-aircraft gun" and "medium anti-aircraft gun" are most likely army anti-aircraft weapons of the caliber 20mm and 37mm, respectively.

293. *Völkischer Beobachter*, 24.6.41, 2. Cited in Roger Moorhouse, *Berlin at War*, 71.

294. Moorhouse, *Berlin at War*, 71.

295. Martha Haape, *Memoiren*, 86C-86D.

296. The events described here by Dr. Haape took place in early July 1941.

297. The war diary of Infantry Regiment 18 includes the following entry for 4 July 1941: "To monitor and screen the civilian population [in Oszmiana] the 3rd Battalion conducts an extensive roundup, which results in 66 Communists and 33 men suspected of being partisans taken into custody.... According to statements by inhabitants, the Russians, prior to their withdrawal, shot a large number of the town's residents." KTB I.R. 18: *"Der russische Sommerfeldzug mit dem I.R. 18"* (Staats- und Personenstandsarchiv Detmold. Bestell-Nr.: D 107/56 Nr. 10).

298. BA-MA RH 26-6/90, *Anlage zum Ib KTB 6. Inf.-Div.*

299. This document gleaned from the personal papers of Dr. Heinrich Haape.

300. This document gleaned from the personal papers of Dr. Heinrich Haape.

301. For 22 June 1941, the war diary of Dr. Haape's Infantry Regiment 18 recorded a total loss of thirty-one KIA (two officers and twenty-nine NCOs and men) and fifty-four wounded.

302. Interestingly, at the start of Chapter 9, Dr. Haape does not mention the minor injury to his nose; rather, he notes "a severe cut on my left forefinger."

303. Martha's reactions to the newsreel were not unusual. Many German women—millions of whom had sons, fiancées, or husbands fighting in the East—were deeply disturbed by what they witnessed in the *Wochenschauen*, even though these newsreels were highly sanitized depictions of events.

304. Martha had many "pet names" for Heinz, but *Heinzlmann* was perhaps her most common.

305. This is one of the few letters Dr. Haape wrote directly to his siblings during this period, as he normally relied on Martha to keep them informed.

306. There appears to be a break in Dr. Haape's letters from about late November 1941 until mid-January 1942. Like most German soldiers, he would have found little time to write during the struggle for naked existence on the retreat from Moscow. On 29 December, Martha had received a telegram and a letter from her future husband informing her that his leave—scheduled to begin midmonth—had been abruptly canceled; the next day, she responded in a letter of her own: "I downright wept as I read your letter. The shock of having your leave canceled, and just before you were to depart—that must have been simply awful. And so a marvelous dream comes to a sudden end before it has even begun. My dear, dear Heinz." See Chapter 18 for Dr. Haape's account of his leave cancellation.

307. All temperatures are Centigrade.

308. Dr. Haape and Martha Arazym had become engaged on 28 December 1941.

309. Dr. Haape had been on home leave from mid-April to early May 1942.

310. The ancient city of Smolensk, some 360 kilometers from Moscow, was the headquarters of Army Group Center.

311. Soviet losses included 272,320 fatalities. Col.-Gen. G. F. Krivosheev (ed.), *Soviet Casualties and Combat Losses in the Twentieth Century*, 122–23.

312. Grossmann, *Geschichte der 6. Infanterie-Division*, 309.

313. Precise figures for both German and Russian losses defy tabulation; however, given the normal casualty "exchange rate" on the Eastern Front—the fact that the Germans consistently inflicted significantly higher casualties on their adversary than they themselves sustained—Red Army losses were, no doubt, much higher than those of the *Ostheer*.

314. During his visit to the town of Rzhev as a guest of the *Kuratorium* in May 2005, Dr. Luther saw for himself the remains of German soldiers in makeshift graves that had been disturbed and vandalized by Russian grave robbers, looking for "dog tags" and other items of potential value. For photographs, see Luther, *Barbarossa Unleashed.*

315. According to Russian author Svetlana Gerasimova, the Red Army may well have sustained more than two million casualties during the fifteen months of combat in the Rzhev bridgehead (January 1942–March 1943). Gerasimova, *The Rzhev Slaughterhouse: The Red Army's Forgotten 15-Month Campaign against Army Group Center, 1942–1943*, 157–58.

316. In 1939, the civilian population of Rzhev was about fifty-four thousand; according to Russian sources, some nine thousand civilians died of hunger or disease in the city during the German occupation, while untold others were killed in the fighting or succumbed to disease or epidemics. Of the city's 5,443 houses, only 300 were still intact when the Germans withdrew in early March 1943; by that time, all but several hundred of the surviving civilians had fled or been evacuated from the city. Norbert Ellermann, *Vom "Eckpfeiler der Ostfront" zum Friedenspark Rshew. Eine Würdigung der Geschichte und der Arbeit des Kuratoriums Rshew*, 11–13 (hereafter cited as Ellermann, *Vom "Eckpfeiler der Ostfront" zum Friedenspark Rshew*); see also *Kuratorium* website at https://www.droste-haus.de.

317. See Glantz, *Zhukov's Greatest Defeat: The Red Army's Epic Disaster in Operation Mars, 1942*; see also the revised and expanded version of Glantz's *When Titans Clashed: How the Red Army Stopped Hitler* (Lawrence, KS: 2015).

318. "1.4: *Das Kuratorium Rshew*," in *Findbuch Inf.-Rgt. 18* (*Signatur*: D 107/56). *Landesarchiv NRW, Staats- und Personenstandsarchiv Detmold.*

319. Ellermann, *Vom "Eckpfeiler der Ostfront" zum Friedenspark Rshew*, 42; see also "1.4: *Das Kuratorium Rshew*," in *Findbuch Inf.-Rgt. 18* (*Signatur*: D 107/56). *Landesarchiv NRW, Staats-und Personenstandsarchiv Detmold.*

320. Ellermann, *Vom "Eckpfeiler der Ostfront" zum Friedenspark Rshew*, 18–20, 48, 50. Rhein would serve as chairman of the *Kuratorium* until 1 January 2003; however, he would continue to serve the group as its honorary chairman (*Ehrenvorsitzender*). On 30 January 2001, he was awarded the Cross of Merit of the Order of Merit (*Verdienstkreuz des Verdienstordens*) by the German government. Ellermann, *Vom "Eckpfeiler der Ostfront" zum Friedenspark Rshew*, 21.

321. As of 2016, contributions for humanitarian purposes exceeded 500,000 Euro. *Kuratorium* website at https://www.droste-haus.de. See also Ellermann, *Vom "Eckpfeiler der Ostfront" zum Friedenspark Rshew*, 109–12.

322. The words are those of Ernst-Martin Rhein from February 2005.

323. The exhibition in Rzhev took place from 30 May to 12 June 1997, embracing some fifty of Langer's sketches and paintings. After Langer's death in 1981, his children—purely by chance—discovered their father's Rzhev-themed artwork in his studio, along with his personal war diaries and thousands of pages of correspondence from the Second World War. Apparently, he had hidden it all away and never said a word about any of it. "1.4: *Das Kuratorium Rshew*," in *Findbuch Inf.-Rgt. 18* (*Signatur*: D 107/56). *Landesarchiv NRW, Staats-und Personenstandsarchiv Detmold*; Ellermann, *Vom "Eckpfeiler der Ostfront" zum Friedenspark Rshew*, 61.

324. Established in the immediate aftermath of World War I, in December 1919, the German War Graves Commission (as of 2018) maintains the graves of some 2,700,000 German soldiers in more than eight hundred military cemeteries in forty-six countries. A primary task of the commission is locating the remains of German soldiers across the battlefields of the former Soviet Union and providing them with proper burials. Without its full support, the Peace Park in Rzhev (with the German military cemetery) would not have come to pass—a fact readily acknowledged by the *Kuratorium* itself. For more on the commission and its activities, see its website at https://www.volksbund.de/ en/volksbund.html.

325. "1.4: *Das Kuratorium Rshew*," in *Findbuch Inf.-Rgt. 18* (*Signatur*: D 107/56). *Landesarchiv NRW, Staats- und Personenstandsarchiv Detmold.*

326. Ellermann, *Vom "Eckpfeiler der Ostfront" zum Friedenspark Rshew* (cited in "*Grusswort*" of the mayor of Gütersloh, no page number).

327. During their occupation of Rzhev from October 1941 to March 1943, the Germans had established numerous cemeteries for their fallen comrades in and around the city, the largest of which embraced some two thousand German dead. Following the withdrawal of German forces from Rzhev, these cemeteries, with their thickets of birch crosses, were razed to the ground on orders of Stalin himself. Ellermann, *Vom "Eckpfeiler der Ostfront" zum Friedenspark Rshew*, 66.

328. Asserting that to do so would constitute an "act of barbarism," the government of President Vladimir Putin, in December 2002, finally put an end to the plans of those "reactionary forces" that wanted to move the German military cemetery—and the soldiers' remains already interred there—to a location outside the city of Rzhev. Ellermann, *Vom "Eckpfeiler der Ostfront" zum Friedenspark Rshew*, 77–78. (For a detailed account of local Russian resistance to the goals of the *Kuratorium Rzhew* [and its German and Russian supporters], see Ellermann, *Vom "Eckpfeiler der Ostfront" zum Friedenspark Rshew*, 69–80.)

329. "1.4: *Das Kuratorium Rshew*," in *Findbuch Inf.-Rgt. 18 (Signatur: D 107/56). Landesarchiv NRW, Staats- und Personenstandsarchiv Detmold.*

330. Ellermann, *Vom "Eckpfeiler der Ostfront" zum Friedenspark Rshew*, 32.

331. Ellermann, *Vom "Eckpfeiler der Ostfront" zum Friedenspark Rshew*, 48.

Select Bibliography

This bibliography includes a selection of published sources (both primary and secondary) that will be useful to scholars and history "buffs" alike who want to delve deeper into Adolf Hitler's Operation Barbarossa in the summer and fall of 1941 and the winter battles that followed into early 1942. Most of these sources were used for the preparation of the introduction and the detailed historical commentary.

Other materials consulted include personnel records of the *Deutsche Dienstelle* (WASt) in Berlin; the war diary (KTB) of Dr. Haape's Infantry Regiment 18 (*Staats-und Personenstandsarchiv Detmold*, D 107/56 Nr. 10); and records of the 6th Infantry Division and Army Group Center, gleaned from the German Federal Military Archives (*Bundesarchiv-Militärarchiv*, or BA-MA) in Freiburg, Germany. Among the BA-MA files:

BA-MA RH 26-6/8, *Ia KTB 6. Inf.-Div.*, 22.6.–30.9.1941

BA-MA RH 26-6/15, *Ia KTB 6. Inf.-Div.*, 1.10.41–31.3.42

BA-MA RH 19 II/120, *KTB H.Gr.Mitte* (Okt. 41)

BA-MA RH 19 II/121, *KTB H.Gr.Mitte* (Nov. 41)

BA-MA RH 19 II/122, *KTB H.Gr.Mitte* (Dez. 41)

Dr. Luther also made use of his own extensive archive of official German documents, soldiers' letters, personal diaries, and photographs. Another vital source was the indispensable Haape Family Archives, which embraced Dr. Haape's personal papers (among them key official military documents) and the voluminous correspondence between Dr. Haape and his future bride, Martha Arazym. Finally, special mention should be made of the internet site *Lexikon der Wehrmacht* (www.lexikon-der-wehrmacht.de), a wonderful resource for any scholar or history "buff" researching the German armed forces in World War II.

LIST OF SOURCES (PRIMARY AND SECONDARY)

Barkhoff, Günther. *Ostfront 1941–1945. Ein Soldatenleben.* Unpublished memoir.

Bergström, Christer, and Andrey Mikhailov. *Black Cross Red Star: The Air War over the Eastern Front.* Vol. 2: *Resurgence: January–June 1942.* Pacifica, CA: 2001.

Blumentritt, Günther. "Moscow." In *The Fatal Decisions*, eds. William Richardson and Seymour Freidin. London: 1956.

Boeselager, Philipp *Freiherr* von. *Valkyrie: The Story of the Plot to Kill Hitler, by Its Last Member.* New York: 2009.

Boog, Horst, et al. *Das Deutsche Reich und der Zweite Weltkrieg*, Bd. 4: *Der Angriff auf die Sowjetunion.* Stuttgart: 1983.

———. *Germany and the Second World War*, Vol. IV: *The Attack on the Soviet Union.* Oxford: 1998.

Brown, Captain Eric. *Wings of the Luftwaffe: Flying German Aircraft of the Second World War*. Eds. William Green and Gordon Swanborough. London: 1977.

Bunke, Dr. Erich. *Der Osten blieb unser Schicksal 1939–1944. Panzerjäger im 2. Weltkrieg*. Self-published: 1991.

Burdick, Charles, and Hans-Adolf Jacobsen (eds.). *The Halder Diary, 1939–1942*. Novato, CA: 1988.

Carell, Paul. *Unternehmen Barbarossa. Der Marsch nach Russland*. Berlin: 1963.

———. *Hitler Moves East, 1941–1943*. Boston: 1964.

Creveld, Martin van. *Supplying War: Logistics from Wallenstein to Patton*. Cambridge: 1977.

Dear, I. C. B. (ed.). *The Oxford Guide to World War II*. Oxford: 1995.

——— (ed.). *The Oxford Companion to World War II*. Oxford: 2001.

De Vries, Louis. *German-English Medical Dictionary*. New York: 1952.

de Zayas, Alfred M. *The Wehrmacht War Crimes Bureau, 1939–1945*. Lincoln, NE: 1989.

DiNardo, Richard L. *Mechanized Juggernaut or Military Anachronism? Horses and the German Army of World War II*. New York: 1991.

Dismer, Hans-Joachim. *Artillerie-Offizier im II. Weltkrieg. Vom Beobachter bis zur Kriegsakademie*. Self-published: 1992.

Domarus, Max. *Hitler. Reden und Proklamationen 1932–1945*, Bd. II: *Untergang (1939–1945)*. Würzburg, Germany: 1963.

Duesel, Dr. Hans H. (ed.). *Gefallen! . . . und umsonst—Erlebnisberichte deutscher Soldaten im Russlandkrieg, 1941–1945*. Bad Aibling, Germany: 1993.

Dunn, Walter S., Jr. *Stalin's Keys to Victory: The Rebirth of the Red Army*. Westport, CT: 2006.

Durrwanger, Colonel Dr. Alfred. "28th Infantry Division Operations." In *The Initial Period of War on the Eastern Front, 22 June–August 1941*. Proceedings of the Fourth *Art of War Symposium*, Garmisch, October 1987. Colonel David M. Glantz (ed.). London: 1993.

Effects of Climate on Combat in European Russia. Center for Military History (CHM) Publication 104–6, 1986.

Ellermann, Norbert. *Vom "Eckpfeiler der Ostfront" zum Friedenspark Rshew. Eine Würdigung der Geschichte und der Arbeit des Kuratoriums Rshew*. Verl, Germany: 2012.

Ferguson, Niall. *The War of the World: Twentieth-Century Conflict and the Descent of the West*. New York: 2006.

Förster, Jürgen (ed.). *Stalingrad. Ereignis—Wirkung—Symbol*. Munich: 1992.

———. "The German Military's Image of Russia." In *Russia: War, Peace and Diplomacy. In Honour of John Erickson*, eds. Ljubica and Mark Erickson. London: 2005.

Forty, George. *German Infantryman at War, 1939–1945*. Hersham, England: 2002.

Freitag, August. *Aufzeichnungen aus Krieg und Gefangenschaft (1941–1949)*. Edited and annotated by Karl Sattler. Bochum, Germany: 1997.

Fuchs Richardson, Horst (ed. and trans.). *Your Loyal and Loving Son: The Letters of Tank Gunner Karl Fuchs, 1937–41*. Washington, D.C.: 1987, 2003. Historical commentary by Dennis E. Showalter, 1987, 2003.

Gerasimova, Svetlana. *The Rzhev Slaughterhouse: The Red Army's Forgotten 15-Month Campaign against Army Group Center, 1942–1943*. Solihull, England: 2013.

Gerbet, Klaus (ed.). *Generalfeldmarschall Fedor von Bock: The War Diary, 1939–1945*. Atglen, PA: 1996.

German Military Dictionary (German-English / English-German). Mt. Ida, AR. Originally published by the War Department, 1944.

Glantz, David M. *Zhukov's Greatest Defeat: The Red Army's Epic Disaster in Operation Mars, 1942*. Lawrence, KS: 1999.

———. *Barbarossa: Hitler's Invasion of Russia 1941*. Charleston, SC: 2001.

———. *Barbarossa Derailed: The Battle for Smolensk, 10 July–10 September 1941*, Vol. I: *The German Advance to Smolensk, the Encirclement Battle, and the First and Second Soviet Counteroffensives, 10 July–24 August 1941*. Solihull, England: 2010.

Glantz, David M., and Jonathan House. *When Titans Clashed: How the Red Army Stopped Hitler*. Lawrence, KS: 2015.

Grenkevich, Leonid D. *The Soviet Partisan Movement, 1941–1944: A Critical Historiographical Analysis*. London: 1999.

Grossmann, Horst. *Die Geschichte der rheinisch-westfälischen 6. Infanterie-Division 1939–1945.* Dörfler Zeit-geschichte n.d.; first published, 1958.

Guderian, Heinz. *Erinnerungen eines Soldaten.* Heidelberg, Germany: 1951.

———. *Panzer Leader.* New York: 1952.

Handbook on German Military Forces. Baton Rouge, LA: 1990. Originally published by U.S. War Department as TM-E 30-451 (March 1945).

Hart, Dr. S., and Dr. R. Hart and Dr. M. Hughes. *The German Soldier in World War II.* Osceola, FL: 2000.

Hart, Russell A. *Guderian: Panzer Pioneer or Myth Maker?* Washington, DC: 2006.

Hillgruber, Andreas. *Der Zweite Weltkrieg, 1939–1945. Kriegsziele und Strategie der grossen Mächte.* Stuttgart: 1982.

Hillgruber, Andreas (ed.). *KTB des OKW (WFSt.)*, Bd. II: *1. Januar 1942–31. Dezember 1942.* Munich: 1982.

Hofmann, Rudolf. "Die Schlacht von Moskau 1941." In *Entscheidungsschlachten des zweiten Weltkrieges*, eds. Hans-Adolf Jacobsen and Jürgen Rohwer. Frankfurt: 1960.

Hossbach, Friedrich. *Infanterie im Ostfeldzug, 1941/42.* Osterode, Germany: 1951.

Hoth, Hermann. *Panzer-Operationen. Die Panzergruppe 3 und der operative Gedanke der deutschen Führung Sommer 1941.* Heidelberg, Germany: 1956.

Hubatsch, Walther. *Hitlers Weisungen für die Kriegsführung, 1939–1945.* Frankfurt: 1962.

———. *Deutschland im Weltkrieg, 1914–1918.* Frankfurt: 1966.

Irving, David. *Hitler's War.* New York: 1977.

Jacobsen, Hans-Adolf (ed.). *1939–1945: Der Zweite Weltkrieg in Chronik und Dokumenten.* Darmstadt, Germany: 1959.

——— (ed.). *KTB des OKW (WFSt.)*, Bd. I: *1. August 1940–31. December 1941.* Munich: 1982.

Jentz, Thomas L. (ed.). *Panzertruppen: The Complete Guide to the Creation & Combat Employment of Germany's Tank Force, 1933–1942.* Atglen, PA: 1996.

Keegan, John. *The Second World War.* New York: 1989.

Kershaw, Ian. *Hitler 1936–1945: Nemesis.* New York: 2000.

Kershaw, Robert J. *War Without Garlands: Operation Barbarossa, 1941/42.* New York: 2000.

Killian, Hans. *Cold and Frost Injuries: Rewarming Damages, Biological, Angiological and Clinical Aspects.* Berlin: 1981.

Knappe, Siegfried (with Ted Brusaw). *Soldat: Reflections of a German Soldier, 1936–1949.* New York: 1992.

Krivosheev, Col.-Gen. G. F. (ed.). *Soviet Casualties and Combat Losses in the Twentieth Century.* London: 1997.

Lengkeit, Reinhold, Gisela Meyer, and Hartmut Pietsch. *Duisburger im Dritten Reich. Augenzeugen Berichten.* Duisburg, Germany: 1983.

Luck, Hans von. *Panzer Commander: The Memoirs of Colonel Hans von Luck.* New York: 1989.

Luther, Craig W. H. *Barbarossa Unleashed: The German Blitzkrieg through Central Russia to the Gates of Moscow, June–December 1941.* Atglen, PA: 2013.

Magenheimer, Heinz. *Moskau 1941. Entscheidungsschlacht im Osten.* Selent, Germany: 2009.

Mawdsley, Evan. *Thunder in the East: The Nazi-Soviet War, 1941–1945.* London: 2005.

Mehner, Kurt (ed.). *Die Geheimen Tagesberichte der Deutschen Wehrmachtführung im Zweiten Weltkrieg, 1939–1945*, Bd. 3: *1. März 1941–31. Oktober 1941.* Osnabrück, Germany: 1992.

Merridale, Catherine. *Ivan's War: Life and Death in the Red Army, 1939–1945.* New York: 2006.

Moorhouse, Roger. *Berlin at War.* New York: 2010.

Mueller-Hillebrand, Burkhart. *Das Heer, 1933–1945*, Bd. II: *Die Blitzfeldzüge 1939–1941. Das Heer im Kriege bis zum Beginn des Feldzuges gegen die Sowjetunion im Juni 1941.* Frankfurt: 1956.

———. *Das Heer, 1933–1945*, Bd. III: *Der Zweifrontenkrieg. Das Heer vom Beginn des Feldzuges gegen die Sowjetunion bis zum Kriegsende.* Frankfurt: 1969.

Musial, Bogdan. *Kampfplatz Deutschland. Stalins Kriegspläne gegen den Westen.* Berlin: 2008.

Nafziger, George F. *The German Order of Battle: Infantry in World War II.* London: 2000.

Overmans, Rüdiger. *Deutsche militärische Verluste im Zweiten Weltkrieg.* Munich: 2004.

Pabst, Helmut. *The Outermost Frontier.* London: 1958.

Pandolf, Kent B., and Robert E. Burr (eds.). *Medical Aspects of Harsh Environments*, Vol 1, Office of the Surgeon General, U.S. Army. Washington, DC: 2001.

Philippi, Alfred, and Ferdinand Heim. *Der Feldzug gegen Sowjetrussland 1941 bis 1945. Ein operativer Überblick.* Stuttgart: 1962.

Pleshakov, Constantine. *Stalin's Folly: The Tragic First Ten Days of World War II on the Eastern Front.* Boston: 2005.

Raus, Erhard. *Panzer Operations: The Eastern Front Memoir of General Raus, 1941–1945.* Compiled and translated by Steven H. Newton. Cambridge, MA: 2003.

Rehfeldt, Dr. Hans Heinz. *Mit dem Eliteverband des Heeres "Grossdeutschland" tief in den Weiten Russlands. Erinnerungen eines Angehörigen des Granatwerferzuges 8./Infanterieregiment (mot.) "Grossdeutschland" 1941–1943.* Würzburg, Germany: 2008.

Reinhardt, Klaus. *Die Wende vor Moskau. Das Scheitern der Strategie Hitlers im Winter 1941/42.* Stuttgart: 1972.

———. *Moscow—The Turning Point: The Failure of Hitler's Strategy in the Winter of 1941–42.* Oxford: 1992.

Reuth, Ralf Georg (ed.). *Joseph Goebbels. Tagebücher 1924–1945*, Bd. 4: *1940–1942.* Munich: 1992.

Rhein, Ernst-Martin. *Das Rheinisch-Westfälische Infanterie-/Grenadier-Regiment 18 1921–1945.* Self-published: 1993.

Sáiz, Agustín. *Deutsche Soldaten: Uniforms, Equipment & Personal Items of the German Soldier 1939–45.* Philadelphia: 2008.

Schneider-Janessen, Karlheinz. *Arzt im Krieg. Wie deutsche und russische Ärzte den Zweiten Weltkrieg erlebten.* Frankfurt: 1993, 2001.

Seaton, Albert. *The Russo-German War, 1941–1945.* London: 1971.

———. *The Battle for Moscow, 1941–1942.* New York: 1983.

Shay, Jonathan. *Achilles in Vietnam: Combat Trauma and the Undoing of Character.* New York: 1994.

Stahel, David. *Operation Barbarossa and Germany's Defeat in the East.* Cambridge: 2011.

———. *The Battle for Moscow.* Cambridge: 2015.

Stein, Marcel. *Generalfeldmarschall Walter Model. Legende und Wirklichkeit.* Bissendorf, Germany: 2001.

Stolfi, Russell H. S. "Chance in History: The Russian Winter of 1941–1942." *History* 65, no. 214: June 1980.

Thies, Klaus-Jürgen. *Der Zweite Weltkrieg im Kartenbild*, Bd. 5: Teil 1.1: *Der Ostfeldzug Heeresgruppe Mitte 21.6.1941–6.12.1941. Ein Lageatlas der Operationsabteilung des Generalstabes des Heeres.* Bissendorf, Germany: 2001.

Trevor-Roper, H. R. *Hitler's War Directives, 1939–1945.* London: 1964.

Tsouras, Peter G. (ed.). *Fighting in Hell: The German Ordeal on the Eastern Front.* New York: 1995.

Verton, Hendrik C. *In the Fire of the Eastern Front: The Experiences of a Dutch Waffen-SS Volunteer on the Eastern Front, 1941–45.* Solihull, England: 2007.

Weinberg, Gerhard L. *A World at Arms: A Global History of World War II.* Cambridge: 1994.

Werth, Alexander. *Russia at War, 1941–1945.* New York: 1964.

Winchester, Charles D. *Hitler's War on Russia.* Oxford: 2007.

Wray, Major Timothy A. *Standing Fast: German Defensive Doctrine on the Russian Front during World War II. Prewar to March 1943.* Fort Leavenworth, KS: 1986.

Ziemke, Earl F., and Magna E. Bauer. *Moscow to Stalingrad: Decision in the East.* New York: 1988.

Index

Gridino, 220; on Hitler, 79; on *Königsberg* Line, 221, 223; on Nazis, 79; respect and decorations for, 66, 269; Romanian Army taught by, 274

Böhmen (*Oberleutnant*), 180

Bolsheviks, 6, 81–82, 97, 134, 140, 142

Bolski (*Leutnant*): to 11th Company, 154; in 12th Company, 34; argument with, 126–27; death of, 163, 165–66; on Hitler, 40; Iron Cross 2nd Class for, 54, 57; von Kageneck, F., on, 40; spurs won at Gomely by, 49; Stolze complaint by, 53–54

Bonn, 285

von Brauchitsch, Walther (Field Marshal), 113, 186

Brest-Litovsk, 36, 282

Briansk, 103–4

Brownshirts, 139, 255, 290

Bukovo, 97, 101

Bulganin (Marshal), 180

burials, 80, 216, 273

Cardiazol injections, 74, 81, 82, 116, 234

cavalry squadron, 20, 62, 67, 75, 212, 269

Christmas, 26–27, 181–82, 184, 263

clothing: dead Russians and winter, 165, 168, 189, 192; Haape and winter, 157–58; newspaper insulation for, 132–33; not enough winter, 132, 138–39, 273; Russian soldiers with winter, 159

commissars: to be executed, 19–20; guerilla tactics by, 6, 139–40; old men and women shields by, 237; Russian soldiers and, 6, 20, 51, 237; as Soviet fanatics, 6, 102–3; Sychevka and wounded, 102–3, 281

Cossacks, 65–67, 70–72, 75, 77, 105

Dalezkye ford, 43, 49–51

defensive positions: by Appelbaum, 223, 225, 238; by Army Group Center, 61, 75; Cossacks overrunning, 66–67; at Dorogobuzh, 290; at Gorki, 169; at Gridino, 223; Hillemanns on, 65; *Königsberg* Line as winter, 172; Moscow as, 42; Moscow distance and, 59; by Red Army, 77; Russian reserve divisions for, 115; Stalin Line as, 42; Staritsa Line as, 187; Todt Organization for, 115; on Upper Dnepr, 101; for winter snows, 61

Dehorn (orderly), 122: Arazym heard by, 63–64; Christmas presents taken by, 26; death of, 69, 70; grave flowers for, 80; home town connection with, 24; Iron Cross 2nd Class

for, 57–58, 64; medical team including, 3; and shell explosion, 67; widow of, 284

Divisional Medical Adjutant promotion for Haape, 289–90

"Doctor's 50 Russians," 93–94

Doppelkopf (card game), 25, 65, 75, 234–35, 238

Dorogobuzh, 290

dressing station: advice on, 144; anti-tank shells hitting, 237; at Gomely, 46, 49; Gorki and closed, 171; in Gridino, 223, 225; at Height 215, 85, 89–90; von Kageneck, F., on, 204; at Kalinin, 116, 118–21, 156, 159–60, 162–63; at Knyaseva, 114; as makeshift, 177; medical practices at, 14–17, 64–65; at Memel River, 31; Müller returning to, 273; Neuhoff on selection and, 64; reassurances for, 203; at Schitinkovo, 190, 192, 201–7; self-defense by, 205–7; at Sychevka, 102; at Vassilevskoye, 106, 112, 177, 184

Düsseldorf, 137

dysentery: von Boeselager with, 78; Kramer with, 143; Neuhoff with, 166, 167, 173; soldier problems and, 31, 33, 40, 173, 224–25

England, 22, 24, 26, 29, 37, 78

executions: of Barbarovna, 288; officers on, 19–21; of Petrovna, 209; of spies, 141

"Fat Lina," 44, 45, 46

field howitzers, 45, 66, 104–5

Fischer (orderly): as driver, 77, 81, 90, 129, 135, 147, 151, 152, 155, 156, 180; wounding of, 181

Frankfurt-a.d.-Oder, 282–83

Freese (*Unterarzt*): to Divisional Headquarters, 173; at Gorki, 163, 171; as medical assistant, 142, 144–45, 155, 156; serious cases evacuated to, 163–64; sick bay charge to, 144–45, 160

frostbite: deep snow increasing, 132, 177; heavy toll of, 132, 150; as murderous, 162; percent cases of, 152; Red Army with, 164; treatment of, 132, 163

Furbach (*Oberst*), 288

"General Winter," 104, 117–18

German air force, 6, 110, 237. *See also Luftwaffe*

German Army: deserter invitation by, 141–42; Napoleon footsteps and problems for, 39–40; Neuhoff on, 36; Orel battle for, 290; Red Army attacking, 79, 180, 243; Red Army matching, 85; Russian civilians on, 255; Russian soldiers bypassed by, 33–34; Rzhev

T-34 Russian tank: anti-aircraft gun resisting, 111, 131; anti-tank guns overrun by, 111, 115; description of, 116; Haape attacking two, 289; Panzer IV countering, 111; T-mine hand grenades countering, 111, 114, 115–16; as weapon, 117–18
Taschadovo, 189
Terpilovo: defense and road to, 200; as evacuated, 212; Medical Company at, 188; Müller and, 183, 190; Volga crossed at, 215; walking wounded, Petrovna to, 207–8
Tietjen (*Oberleutnant*), 20, 28, 46, 49, 154
"Tietjen's Group," 140, 252, 261
"Tired Duck," 181, 278–79
T-mine hand grenades, 111, 114, 115–16
Todt Organization, 115
Torzhok, 104, 110–11
trains: German soldiers and, 226; Kalinin and, 149–50; Panino and, 220; Ruhr to Berlin and, 78, 283; to Rzhev, 280–81
Tula, 101
Tulpin (*Unteroffizier*): on attacks and panje wagons, 122–23; fighting by, 201, 202, 204; and horses, 118; Iron Cross recommendation for, 123; lice and, 99, 107, 108, 109; medical assistance from, 89, 90, 93, 99, 118, 122–23, 130, 162, 177–78, 181, 184, 206–7, 223; missing, 120, 121; as morphia addict, 142, 178–80, 192–93; with spotted fever, 251, 258–59; Wegener replaced by, 77–78; withdrawal by, 181–82

United States. *See* America
Unterarzt rank for Haape, 25, 28
Upper Dnepr River, 40, 101, 102
Uschakovo, 189

Vassilevskoye: dressing station at, 106, 112, 177, 184; Red Army at, 185, 189, 192; Russian girl students hanged in, 141; travel to, 153, 173, 278
vehicles. *See* motorized units
Viaz'ma, 103; 86th Infantry and railway from, 243; Army Group Center and, 103–4; Rzhev railway from, 242, 243, 251; to Smolensk railway, 280–81; Upper Dnepr to, 102
Vienna, 284–85
Vilna, 36
Vitebsk, 42, 56
Vitebsk-Smolensk, 55

Volga River, 103, 215
Volhynian fever, 130–31
Volpius (*Oberstabsarzt*): on 1914 war, 248; as fatalistic, 162; Germany transfer for, 257; as punished, 142; as returned, 172, 240; snoring of, 241, 242; Stalingrad death of, 292

weapons. *See* armaments
Wegener (medical NCO): head wound for, 49; impressiveness sought by, 24; medical team including, 3; Müller replacing, 56; sent to rear, 50; Tulpin replacing, 77–78
Wehrmacht (German armed forces): assigned to, 22–23; best for shock troops and, 35; coded signs of, 151; decorated doctor of, 289–90; defection permit from, 141–42; fighting methods of, 274; Hitler commanding, 186; invasion of England, 24; Moscow attack not mentioned by, 154; success of, 57, 139
von Weichs, Maximilian (General), 103
Westphalian Grenadiers (6th Division), 41
winter: approach of, 95; Barbarossa delay and, 132; clothes of dead Russian and, 165, 168, 189, 192; clothing problems and, 132, 138–39, 273; defensive positions for, 61; digging in for, 114–15; end in sight and, 272; front line cities of, 139; frostbite from, 132, 177; German civilians donating for, 273–74, 284; German horses unsuitable for, 38; Haape, clothes for, 157–58; horse riding versus walking in, 157; icy blast arrival as, 131–32; at *Königsberg* Line, 172, 213, 219, 221; *Kopfschützers* for, 132; lice and cold of, 238; Malakovo and blizzards of, 243; Moscow protected by, 152, 153; newspaper insulation for, 132–33; rain and cold before, 101–2, 103–4; retreat and death in, 171, 186; Russian home preparations for, 133; Russian soldiers dressed for, 159; sanity and madness from, 185; snow of, 117–18, 139, 177, 180; spurred by cold and, 215; vehicles sinking in, 102; warning on, 35, 98
women spies, 140–41. *See also* Petrovna, Natasha

Zellstoff (cellulose), 8
Zhukov (Marshal), 171, 172; night attacks order to, 190; seven Russian armies with, 243; Siberian troops given to, 180
Zubtsov, 97, 103